Interdisciplinary perspectives on modern history

Editors
Robert Fogel and Stephan Thernstrom

Out of work

Out of work

The first century of unemployment in Massachusetts

ALEXANDER KEYSSAR

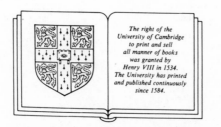

The right of the
University of Cambridge
to print and sell
all manner of books
was granted by
Henry VIII in 1534.
The University has printed
and published continuously
since 1584.

CAMBRIDGE UNIVERSITY PRESS

Cambridge
London   New York   New Rochelle
Melbourne   Sydney

Published by the Press Syndicate of the University of Cambridge
The Pitt Building, Trumpington Street, Cambridge CB2 1RP
32 East 57th Street, New York, NY 10022, USA
10 Stamford Road, Oakleigh, Melbourne 3166, Australia

First published 1986

Printed in the United States of America

Library of Congress Cataloging in Publication Data
Keyssar, Alexander.
Out of work.
(Interdisciplinary perspectives on modern history)
Includes bibliographical references and index.
1. Unemployment – Massachusetts – History – 19th
century. 2. Unemployment – Massachusetts – History –
20th century. 3. Massachusetts – Social conditions.
I. Title. II. Series.
HD5725.M4K49 1986   331.13'79744   85-19536

British Library Cataloguing in Publication Data
Keyssar, Alexander
Out of work : the first century of unemployment
in Massachusetts. – (Interdisciplinary perspectives
on modern history)
1. Unemployment – Massachusetts – History
I. Title II. Series
331.13'79744   HD5725.M4

ISBN 0 521 23016 0 hard covers
ISBN 0 521 29767 2 paperback

To the memory of
Zipa Reisa Keyssar,
my grandmother

Contents

Illustrations and tables

Preface

The inquiry that led to this book began by accident. Some years ago, while engaged in research on another topic, I found myself combing through parts of the old and richly detailed card catalog in the State Library in Boston. Among the thousands of cards that I glanced at was one that caught my eye and my attention: it referred to an 1887 Massachusetts government publication entitled "The Unemployed." Although I counted myself a labor historian – or at least an apprentice labor historian – I realized that I knew little, if anything, about unemployment in the United States before the 1930s. I could not even recall the titles of any books that I ought to have read on the subject.

The issue was sufficiently intriguing that I soon began to delve into the literature on unemployment. Within a short time, I learned that my ignorance was not altogether a personal failing. The library shelves contained numerous volumes dealing with unemployment and the unemployed in the 1930s. But the scholarly cupboard was nearly bare when it came to unemployment before the crash of the stock market in 1929. Although unemployment was widely, if not universally, recognized as a social problem of great importance, its history before the Great Depression was, for the most part, unexamined.

This gap in the historical literature was all the more notable – and surprising – because the subject was of obvious theoretical interest and because the very few studies that had been conducted suggested that unemployment was hardly a trivial, or inconsequential, phenomenon in the nineteenth and early twentieth centuries. My first months with the documentary record, moreover, rapidly convinced me that the subject ill deserved the neglect that had been its fate. Not only did the available statistics indicate that there was a great deal of unemployment long before 1930, but almost all firsthand accounts of working-class life were riddled with references to the unsteadiness of work and the social consequences of joblessness. The history of unemployment in the United States may have been an untold story, but it appeared nonetheless to be a significant one.

This book is an attempt to tell part of that story, to chronicle the history of unemployment in the Commonwealth of Massachusetts from the early decades of the nineteenth century to the 1930s. It is a study of the emergence of unemployment as an important phenomenon in American society, an examination of its significance and impact during the first century of industrialization in the United States. It is also an account of the changes in American life that gradually, if haltingly, thrust unemployment to the top of the nation's list of social problems.

In researching and writing this study, I have tried to recapture as fully as possible the history of unemployment in one part of the United States, to explore the economic, social, and political dimensions of the problem of joblessness. Accordingly, the patterns of economic behavior and business practice that produced unemployment are delineated in some detail. And I have also attempted to trace the evolution of unemployment policy, paying particular attention to the manner in which pre–New Deal reformers, businessmen, and public officials paved the way for the institutional programs that were adopted in the 1930s.

But, at heart, this book is a social history of unemployment. The spotlight, more often than not, is focused upon the unemployed themselves, and much of the story is told and analyzed from their point of view – rather than from the perspective of the reformers and policy makers who figure so prominently in most histories of social problems. The core of this study is, indeed, an effort to understand the role that unemployment played in the lives of the men and women – primarily blue-collar workers – who were most directly and most often affected by the problem. Central chapters offer an investigation of the incidence and distribution of unemployment among different groups of working people; a portrait of the experience of joblessness and the strategies that men and women developed to cope with it; an examination of the ways in which workers tried, individually and collectively, to enhance their personal security and to cure the social "evil" of joblessness. Unemployment was – and is – a characteristic problem of working-class life, and this book is largely an essay in working-class history.

The temporal and spatial boundaries that circumscribe this study invite a few words of explanation. First: I confess to using the word "century" rather loosely and to deliberately omitting the conventional pair of dates from the subtitle of this book. But the history of a phenomenon like unemployment is, of course, not bounded by very precise dates. The study begins with the advent of industrialization in Massachusetts in the early nineteenth century, a turning point in economic and social history that led to the rise to prominence of the problem of unemployment. The bulk of the book, however, deals with the years between the 1870s and the early 1920s, a period framed by the panic of 1873 and the sharp depression of the early 1920s – the last depression before the Great Depression. I have brought the story to a close with a brief account of the Great Depression itself and the institutional reforms of the 1930s. This end point was chosen, in part, because the 1930s ushered in a new era in the history of joblessness and, in part, because the problem of unemployment since 1930 has already been the subject of extensive scholarly research. In the penultimate chapter, I have tried to suggest some of the ways in which the history of unemployment can help to illumine the meaning of the changes wrought by the Great Depression. But the major events of that decade, as well as the subsequent history of the problem of joblessness, are too well known to warrant a detailed retelling here.

The geographic limits of this study were influenced by more practical concerns. Given the range of questions that I wished to address and the research strategies necessary to answer such questions, a national study was simply not feasible – not if I hoped to complete this book in my lifetime. Nevertheless, it became clear to me, while this project was still in its early stages, that the conventional unit of social historical study, the single community, was an inappropriate one for this inquiry. Unemployment levels seemed to vary enormously from one city or town to the next, and much of the political history of joblessness unfolded in state legislatures and statewide labor organizations rather than within individual communities. Focusing upon a state, therefore, loomed as a happy and useful compromise: a small enough arena to permit intensive research yet large enough to encompass both the politics of unemployment and the experiences of men and women who lived and worked in a wide array of industries and communities.

The selection of Massachusetts as the particular state to be studied was triggered by the availability of an unusually rich (and probably unparalleled) assembly of documentary records. The 1887 publication that had provoked the inquiry proved to be the tip of a surprisingly large iceberg of evidence bearing on the history of unemployment. As it turned out (although I did not know this when I settled on Massachusetts), the commonwealth also played a pioneering and influential role in the evolution of unemployment policy in the United States. Just how typical the history of joblessness in Massachusetts may have been is an issue addressed in the final chapter of this book; suffice it to say here that the implications of the Massachusetts experience seem to reach well beyond the borders of the Bay State.

Finally, a word about writing, reading, and arithmetic. Although most of the research presented in this study is drawn from "old-fashioned" literary sources (newspapers, labor journals, government investigations, charity reports, etc.), this book does contain several dozen tables. And a few chapters rely heavily upon quantitative evidence of a type that has driven some reviewers and historians to plead for a return to narrative history. Even worse, historical statistics of unemployment raise a raft of methodological issues that must be discussed explicitly by any scholar who attempts to use them. In an effort to overcome these obstacles to fluid and pleasing prose, I have consigned all discussions of method and statistical procedure to the notes and the appendixes. I have also tried to analyze the quantitative evidence as succinctly and crisply as I could (placing the more exegetical commentaries on the tables in the notes) and to leaven the quantitative sections of the text with at least an occasional lively quotation. It is my hope that, in doing so, I have helped to ease the passage of readers who are not particularly concerned with either the intricacies of the numbers or problems of method but who are interested in the history of men and women who were out of work.

In the years that this book has been in preparation, I have received a great deal of support – financial, logistical, intellectual, and moral – from many different quarters. And it is no small pleasure to take this opportunity to formally express my thanks to those who made this study possible.

Funding from several institutions facilitated the research for this project and gave me the time to think and write about it. While I was a graduate student, fellowships from the Mrs. Giles Whiting Foundation and the Joint Center for Urban Studies of Harvard University and the Massachusetts Institute of Technology permitted me to devote my energies full-time to the dissertation that became the first of many drafts of this book. Subsequent grants from the American Council of Learned Societies and the National Endowment for the Humanities enabled me to do new and much-needed research. A fellowship from the Russell Sage Foundation provided me with a year in which to finish the manuscript, superb working conditions, and that all-too-rare setting in the academic world, an invigorating community of scholars.

For their invaluable assistance and cooperation, I would like to thank the staffs of the following libraries and archives: the Widener, Littauer, and Baker libraries of Harvard University; the Schlesinger Library of Radcliffe College; the Archives of the Commonwealth of Massachusetts; the State Library of Massachusetts; the public libraries of Boston, Brockton, Lynn, and Springfield; the Social Welfare History Archives of the University of Minnesota; the Newberry Library of Chicago; and the library of the U.S. Department of Labor in Washington. The Family Service Association of Greater Boston, the Massachusetts State Labor Council, AFL-CIO, and the U.S. Census Bureau were also extremely helpful in locating and permitting me to use documents that were in their custody. For their efforts above and beyond the call of duty, I am particularly grateful to R. Nicholas Olsberg, Robert W. Lovett, Eartha Dengler, Pauline Rothstein, Eva Moseley, and Paula Schneider.

A small, yet dedicated, army of research assistants helped me to cast my research net as widely as possible, to code and computerize much of the quantitative data, to double-check the calculations and citations, and to perform many other – often tedious – tasks. Over the years, this army included: Elise Bloustein, Stuart Widowski, Margaret Sullivan, Lawrence Stone, T. Duk, Stephen Rabinowitz, Steve Waldman, and Elyana Sutin; Andrew Davis deserves special mention for his years of energetic and capable service. Thanks are also owed to Ina Malaguti, who typed most of the tables, and to Eliza McClennen of Boston University, who drew the map. Vivian Kaufman typed several versions of the text and notes with extraordinary accuracy, speed, and good cheer; her generous efforts greatly facilitated the process of getting the manuscript off to press. Transforming the manuscript into a book was accomplished through the highly professional and very patient collaboration of Frank Smith and Edith Feinstein, at Cambridge University Press, and of copy editor, Alfred Imhoff.

This study has benefited immeasurably from the ideas, suggestions, and criticisms offered by numerous friends and colleagues, all of whom took time from their own labors to assist me in mine. I would like, first, to thank Stephan Thernstrom, who has been involved with this project for longer than he intended or believed possible: his support and encouragement for the study never flagged, and his critical advice, offered at several stages, made this a better book. Bernard Bailyn taught me much about the writing of history before I launched into this project, and, as a reader of my dissertation, he raised challenging questions that helped me to make sense of the story that I was unearthing. Thoughtful comments on an early version of this study were also offered by David H. Fischer, Morton Keller, Michael Piore, Ellen Winner, Steve Fraser (then my editor at Cambridge), and two anonymous readers for the Press (one of whom was Eric Foner). David Montgomery more than lived up to his reputation as a scholar of unusual generosity to the young: his detailed and penetrating criticism saved me from various pitfalls and challenged me to contend with several tough and important issues.

For their insightful comments on portions of the manuscript, I am grateful to James Lazerow, Theodore Rosengarten, Joan Scott, and John Womack, Jr. Joel Perlmann shared his statistical expertise with me in numerous conversations and phone calls. Lou Ferleger's criticism of the text, tables, and appendixes – informed by his rare combination of skills in economics, history, and statistics – helped me to avoid errors, clarify arguments, and rethink some key questions. He also committed the ultimate act of colleagueship by reading and criticizing the notes.

John Demos applied his red pen and fine eye for literary detail to successive drafts of the manuscript, enriching the text while simultaneously encouraging its author. Jonathan Prude provided me with astute, hardheaded criticism from a close and trusted friend: unstinting in his support, he has twice read every word in this book and wrote at least a few of them. Last, but certainly not least, I would like to thank Robert K. Merton, whom I had the good fortune to meet just as this undertaking was entering its final stages. His editorial wizardry vastly improved the prose, while his interest in the project inspired me both to persevere and to finish.

My debt to my wife, Elizabeth Rapaport, is of a different order. She has been living with this book as long as she has been living with me, and she has always – sometimes at odd hours – been the first reader of any pages that emerged from my typewriter. Her good judgment and critical acumen contributed to every chapter. More importantly, she made certain that the necessarily solitary task of writing was never a lonely one.

This book is dedicated to the memory of a woman who was born in the 1870s and who died just as I was beginning to work on this project. She came to the United States only after the first century of unemployment had come to a close, and, as far as I know, she never set foot in Massachusetts. But her recollections of the past served to spark my interest in history. And the values that she upheld so tenaciously – through five migrations and several wars – had no small influence upon the concerns that prompted, and inform, this study.

Somerville, Massachusetts   A. K.
April 1985

1   *Introduction*

"Out of Work" is a simple phrase
  But one oft used before,
It hath a meaning all its own
  Familiar to the poor;
"Unemployed – the shop is closed;
  Supply exceeds demand,"
And men who've spent years at the bench
  Now with the idle stand.

From *The Carpenter*, 1914[1]

In June of 1878, the Massachusetts Bureau of Statistics of Labor launched a survey to determine the number of workers who were unemployed in the Bay State. The long depression precipitated by the financial panic of 1873 had given rise to widely publicized, and politically volatile, estimates that there were 3 million jobless wage earners in the United States, a quarter of a million in Massachusetts alone. But officials at the bureau (the first such agency in the country) were skeptical of these "reckless" estimates and took it upon themselves to develop more accurate figures. Their effort was unprecedented. As the bureau proudly noted, its survey was "the first attempt officially, or in any other way, to ascertain the facts." Before 1878, no state in the nation had ever tried to measure the incidence of "involuntary idleness" among wage earners.[2]

To "ascertain the facts," Carroll D. Wright, the chief of the Massachusetts Bureau (and later the first head of the U.S. Bureau of Labor Statistics) wrote to the police or the assessors in every community in the commonwealth. He asked these officials to investigate local conditions and to prepare "careful" estimates of the number of "able-bodied" workmen, skilled and unskilled, who were "unemployed." Wright and his colleagues were more than a little pleased by the figures reported to the bureau. In all of Massachusetts, only 22,000 men were unemployed; had women been included in the survey, the bureau estimated, the figure would still have been below 30,000. The claim that the state contained more than 200,000 jobless workers had proven to be a "wild guess," lacking even the "slightest foundation." "We have given the croaker the benefit of every doubt," Wright declared, but an "intelligent canvas" had established that less than 5 percent of the labor force was "out of employment."[3]

There were, however, several notable wrinkles in the procedure that produced those "gratifying" statistics. One was that Wright had asked the police and assessors to count as unemployed not *all* able-bodied, jobless workers but only those who were "over eighteen years of age." Omitted from the official tally were the thousands of children and young teenagers who normally labored in the commonwealth's industries. More importantly, Wright had also instructed local officials that the survey was to "comprehend those only who really want employment." Jobless men who appeared insufficiently eager to find work were not to be counted as unemployed. That this instruction affected the statistics was readily acknowledged by the bureau. "The testimony in very many cases was that a large percentage of those out of employment would not work if they could, or would not work for less than the wages of five years ago." The official total, then, included only those jobless men who, in the eyes of the police and assessors, possessed the proper attitude toward work. A "large percentage" of the able-bodied adult males who were "out of employment" were not counted as unemployed.[4]

The restrictions affixed to this pioneering survey certainly suggest that the "croaker" was not, after all, given the "benefit of every doubt" in the summer of 1878. From their inception, unemployment statistics were embedded in controversy, and Carroll Wright's desire to obtain modest and reassuring figures was barely disguised. But the detailed instructions issued to local authorities were not prompted by instrumental, or political, concerns alone. Something more fundamental, and more revealing, was involved as well. Wright and the bureau were attaching a different meaning to the word "unemployed" than they had in the past. In the letter that the bureau sent to city and town officials, the word was used to refer to workers who were experiencing "forced idleness," who were unable to find jobs because of the condition of the economy. The "unemployed," Wright explained in his official report on the survey, were individuals who were "out of work" and "who were seeking or were in want of employment."[5]

This definition contrasted sharply with one that the bureau had used just a few years earlier. In the state census of 1875, the word "unemployed" had been applied to individuals who were engaged in "no occupation," who "take no part in the work of life." According to the published results of that census, there were nearly 350,000 "unemployed" residents of the commonwealth in 1875 – most of whom were children who lived at home and were under the age of ten! In 1878, thus, the bureau was turning its own definition of "unemployed" on its head: the word was a label not for those "having no occupation" but rather for those who had occupations but did not have jobs. Given this radical shift in usage and meaning, it is hardly surprising that the bureau took pains to instruct local officials to count, as unemployed, only able-bodied adults "who really want employment."[6]

The ambiguity surrounding the word "unemployed" in the 1870s was not confined to the chambers of Massachusetts Bureau of Statistics of Labor. The word had long been a part of the English and American vocabularies, but it possessed two different – and, to some degree, contradictory – meanings. The definition that Carroll Wright gave to the term in 1878 ("out of work and seeking it") had appeared in print as early as the seventeenth century. But in the United States at least, this usage was very rare before 1850. Most often, men and women who had lost their jobs and wanted to work were described as "out of employment," "out of work," "idled," "involuntarily idle," or, under some circumstances, "loafing." No particular or formal label designated their condition. Only in the 1850s did references to such workers as "unemployed" become at all common, and not until the depression of the 1870s did this usage become widespread.[7]

The word's second meaning was older, more broad-gauged, and more literal. "Unemployed" men and women were those who were simply "not employed," who were idle or not working. Utilized in this way, the term could encompass young children, and, when applied to adults, it sometimes had connotations of sloth and willful idleness. As the state census of Massachusetts clearly reveals, this definition remained current, if not predominant, as late as 1875. It was for precisely this reason that the *Vindicator*, a labor newspaper in Lynn, urged its readers in January 1877 to refer to workers who were involuntarily idle as "dis-employed" rather than "unemployed."

> We have used the term dis-employed as more expressive and true
> . . . than the ordinary, and more general term un-employed –
> which includes not only this class but all who are voluntarily or
> involuntarily without employment; the sick and incompetent, the
> thriftless, the lazy and vicious, the willing paupers and the profes-
> sional beggars – all belong to the comprehensive and motley crowd
> of the un-employed; and we protest against the injustice of asso-
> ciating – even in idea – the honest, industrious workers – who are
> idle from no fault of their own – with that same motley crowd.[8]

The *Vindicator*'s protest notwithstanding, the "ordinary" term "unemployed" was used with increasing frequency, in the late 1870s, to describe men and women who were "idle from no fault of their own."

Indeed, between 1875 and 1885, the word was sloughing off its once primary and potentially pejorative meaning, while acquiring the status of a recognized and official label for "honest, industrious workers" who were "involuntarily without employment." In March 1878, the *Vindicator* itself tacitly withdrew its linguistic objection, publishing a poem entitled "The Unemployed Workingman's Soliloquy." Three months later, the Massachusetts Bureau tried to gauge the impact of the depression by counting the number of "unemployed" workers in the commonwealth.[9]

This shift in the usage and meaning of "unemployed" was followed, within a few years, by the appearance of the noun "unemployment." That term – which referred both to the condition of being unemployed and to the social problem that existed when workers were unable to find jobs – made its American debut on the printed page in 1887, in the *Eighteenth Annual Report* of the Massachusetts Bureau of Statistics of Labor. The subject of the report was the bureau's second (and more successful) effort to measure "the extent of unemployment" in Massachusetts.[10]

These unheralded events of the 1870s and 1880s marked a watershed in American social history. Their occurrence did not mean that the phenomenon of "forced idleness" suddenly appeared in the nation or in the state of Massachusetts during the depression of the 1870s; like most such events, they announced changes that had been under way for decades. But the shifts in language and efforts at measurement did reflect a new public awareness of the phenomenon, an unprecedented recognition of its potential significance as a social problem. Both the Massachusetts Bureau and the *Vindicator* were giving voice to a societal need for language that would clearly identify this problem, language that would capture the distinction between idleness that was personal in its origins and idleness that resulted from the structure and behavior of the economy. That distinction – which lay at the heart of the concept of unemployment – figured more prominently in the public discourse of the 1870s than it ever had in the past. So too did the question of numbers. Workers who were "not employed" through no fault of their own were a disturbing presence in a nation that celebrated opportunity, and it had become a matter of "great value and importance" (as Carroll Wright put it) for the public to know how many such workers there were. For the first time in American history, the phenomenon of "involuntary idleness" had become sufficiently widespread or important or visible to need its own name and to be measured.[11]

Those needs only intensified after the 1880s, and the name preferred by the Massachusetts Bureau proved, of course, to be a durable one. During the final decades of the nineteenth century, the adjective (and sometimes noun) "unemployed" relinquished all traces of the ambiguity that had been present in the 1870s: by 1900, both in the United States and in England, men and women who were jobless and in need of work were routinely described as unemployed. The more abstract noun "unemployment" caught on less rapidly, but by the beginning of the twentieth century it had become the standard label for the social problem of involuntary idleness. And in the course of the twentieth century, both of these terms became household words, permanently welded to the definitions articulated in the 1870s and 1880s. More than a century after the panic of 1873, the word "unemployed" still referred – officially as well as in common parlance – to men and women who were "out of work and seeking it."[12]

Similarly, the "intelligent canvas" that Carroll Wright had initiated in 1878 constituted the beginning of a long series of efforts to count the unemployed. Every federal census conducted between 1880 and 1910 contained questions about the regularity of work; the same was true of every Massachusetts census from 1885 to 1905. Early in the twentieth century, several states, including Massachusetts, began to collect quarterly or annual unemployment statistics. Later, in the wake of the Great Depression, the national government instituted a monthly survey of more than 20,000 American households. After the 1870s, in fact, not a decade passed without formal efforts being made, somewhere in the nation, to count the unemployed. For more than a century, the incidence of unemployment has been something that American society has wanted to know about itself.[13]

With good reason. As reformers, scholars, and government officials have discovered in the course of the past century, unemployment is a social problem of almost unmatched significance. For most adult Americans, work is an economic necessity, a fundamental task and obligation; for many, it is also a basis of their identity, a source of self-esteem. The consequences of being out of work are accordingly profound and far-reaching. Unemployed men and women are subject to material hardship, social dislocation, and psychological stress. The scars left by layoffs often endure for years. The road to poverty in the United States has frequently been punctuated by prolonged or recurrent spells of unemployment.

Moreover, as William H. Beveridge pointed out early in the twentieth century, in his pathbreaking study of unemployment in England, "the problem of unemployment lies, in a very special sense, at the root of most other social problems." Inadequate housing and medical care, unhealthy living environments, the malnutrition and undereducation of children – all these problems can be traced, in part, to the poverty and insecurity bred by involuntary idleness. Unemployment has been linked to the incidence of crime and alcoholism, to the instability of families, and to a host of other sources and symptoms of social disorder. Itself a malady, unemployment creates conditions in which other diseases fester and spread.[14]

The social problem of unemployment also carries uniquely heavy political freight. Since the 1930s, of course, the federal government has assumed responsibility for controlling unemployment levels – or, at the very least, for preventing mass joblessness of the sort that occurred during the Great Depression. Consequently, the incidence of unemployment has been an important issue in national electoral politics. Policies that would raise or lower joblessness levels have been the subject of widespread public debate. Unemployment rates themselves have been a key determinant of the longevity of national administrations and the popularity of political parties.

But the political significance of unemployment reaches well beyond the domain of partisan politics. The problem poses, and has long posed, a fundamental challenge to values and institutions that are central to the American political and economic order. This challenge stems from the fact that American society obliges able-bodied adults to be self-supporting, yet it does not, either by law or through its institutions, guarantee jobs to those who are expected to support themselves. "Man is vested with the right to work but vested with the right to no job," observed the *Shoe Workers' Journal* in 1905. Market forces govern the allocation of labor, while individuals who own productive property (a small minority in modern America) possess an unqualified right to lay off workers whose services are no longer needed. To the extent that these institutions and principles fail to provide full employment – and thus prevent men and women from fulfilling an obligation that society imposes upon them – their legitimacy can be, and sometimes has been, called into question. The success or failure of American capitalism has long been measured, in part, by its capacity to create jobs for American citizens. "If our moral and economic system is to survive," declared Secretary of Commerce Herbert Hoover in 1921, a "solution" to the problem of unemployment must be found. "Without it, our whole system is open to serious charges of failure."[15]

Yet despite its unmistakable importance, the phenomenon of unemployment has been the subject of very little historical inquiry. Although the study of joblessness has itself become a minor industry since the Great Depression – providing work for numerous economists and sociologists – scant attention has been paid to the presence of unemployment in American society prior to the stock market crash of 1929. An aggregate national statistical series has been developed, and the evolution of unemployment policy has been sketched in some detail, but the problem has otherwise been ignored by students and scholars of the American past. In the written histories of the nation, unemployment appears – if it appears at all – as a marginal phenomenon, as the occasional consequence of an occasional economic panic, as a problem well removed from the mainstream of American life.[16]

Indeed, the notion that unemployment had a significant history before 1929 stands as a challenge, almost an affront, to long-cherished images and conceptions of the American past. The United States, according to most popular and scholarly accounts, offered opportunities rather than obstacles, plenty rather than scarcity, to men and women who were willing and able to work. For much of its history, the American nation contained vast expanses of uninhabited, yet fertile, land; beginning in the nineteenth century, its manufacturing industries grew with astonishing speed; millions of immigrants fled from Europe and Asia to seek their fortunes in the Promised Land. It was presumably labor, not work, that was scarce in the United States. Class boundaries of the type that kept individuals poor and jobless in the Old World were diluted by the rich solvent of American democracy. The busy tempo of national life in the United States was set not by idleness or "slack times" but by a Protestant work ethic and excessive toil.

These images are compelling ones and not entirely without foundation. Nonetheless, unemployment did have a long and important history before the Great Depression of the 1930s. Many of the well-known developments of that decade were, in fact, profoundly influenced by events that had occurred and structures that had evolved during the first century of unemployment in the United States. It was during those years – stretching roughly from the third decade of the nineteenth century to the early 1920s – that unemployment emerged as a major social problem, threatening the well-being of workers throughout the nation. In the course of that century – and particularly the half-century that followed the panic of 1873 – unemployment molded working-class living patterns and institutions, protests of the jobless erupted periodically in American cities, and public officials devised what proved to be enduring strategies for contending with the issue. Unemployment was a significant presence in American life long before the federal government formally recognized the problem.

The history of unemployment during this period is one in which economic activity, social patterns, and politics are tightly intertwined.

It is a history of long, sweeping changes and sharp, cyclical movements, of the quotidian and the dramatic, of institutions and individual families, of private behavior and public policies. It is a history of both language and numbers, of progress and failures, the story of one critical thread in the fabric of working-class experience. Part of that history unfolded in Massachusetts.

2   *The social origins of unemployment*

For workers, the problem came before the word. Long before public officials had agreed on the terminology – indeed, long before there was a Bureau of Statistics of Labor in Massachusetts or anywhere else in the nation – men and women in the Bay State knew what it was to be jobless and in need of work. The rhythms of the business cycle were felt throughout the antebellum era, and sharp downturns in economic activity, such as those that began in 1819, 1837, and 1857, severed many working people from their jobs. Involuntary idleness was also produced by local or regional economic slowdowns, by seasonal shifts in the demand for labor, and by frozen rivers, fires, bankruptcies, and a host of other episodic events. Even during the unambiguously preindustrial colonial period, men and women were occasionally out of work and seeking it. No statistics were ever collected, but there were certainly unemployed people in Massachusetts well before anyone chose to count them.[1]

Still, the problem of unemployment did not disembark from the Mayflower and forever after remain a constant in American economic and social life. Throughout the colonial era and into the early nineteenth century, the phenomenon of involuntary idleness was largely invisible; it did occur but not on a sufficient scale to become a prominent or noticeable feature of the economic landscape. Even after Massachusetts and the United States began to industrialize, the problem of unemployment came to widespread public notice only gradually. The writings and proclamations of early trade unions and workingmen's associations were replete with lists of grievances, but they rarely complained of a shortage of jobs; similarly, antebellum reformers did not consider unemployment to be among the social problems that the state or the nation had to confront. Only after the middle of the nineteenth century did unemployment seem to become a persistent and palpable presence in the Commonwealth of Massachusetts.[2]

In fact, the modern phenomenon of unemployment was born and grew to maturity between the second war with Britain and the financial panic of 1873. During those years, Massachusetts ceased to be a predominantly rural, agricultural, and commercial state and became

9

an industrial and, to a lesser extent, an urban one. Interwoven with this well-known yet dramatic transformation – which was replicated sooner or later throughout most of the United States – were changes in the susceptibility of working people to both of the experiences that came to constitute the definition of unemployment: being altogether jobless and being in need of work. The emergence of the formal concept of unemployment after the Civil War was both a consequence and a public acknowledgment of a half-century of revolutionary change in the relationship between men, and women, and their work.

Early shelters

Work in early-nineteeenth-century Massachusetts was anything but steady. Inhabitants of the commonwealth, like their parents and grandparents before them, labored according to rhythms set by the natural environment and by the culture in which they lived. Farm families performed different tasks in different seasons, and during some periods, winter most notably, the pace of work slowed considerably. Less predictably, spells of rain, snow, and extreme cold often made productive labor difficult or impossible for days or weeks at a time; unusually severe conditions, such as the abnormally frigid year of 1816, destroyed crops and disrupted the entire annual cycle. Artisanal trades too had seasonal pulses, and many artisans were wedded to irregular working habits of the sort that a disciplined entrepreneur like Benjamin Franklin could only deplore. Indeed, commercial activity in general tended to be uneven in its rhythms and, by modern standards, leisurely in its pace. Roads were often impassable during some months of the year; sailing vessels could not be counted on to adhere to very exact schedules; cargo was loaded and unloaded whenever ships arrived; men who labored in ports and other depots performed their work when there was work to be done. Throughout the economy, work was discontinuous, and patches of slack work or leisure were common, though often unforeseen.[3]

Why, then, was there virtually no public mention of unemployment in early-nineteenth-century Massachusetts? Why, given the irregularity of work, was there no word for the phenomenon, perhaps no concept, and certainly no pattern of references to a shortage of jobs? To frame such a question is, of course, to ask why the dog did not bark in the night. But the dog did not bark, despite the apparent presence of prowlers – so the question must be posed. How could economic activity have been so unsteady without giving rise to a widely recognized and precisely identified social problem?

The answer to this question, in brief, is that several prominent features of Massachusetts society served to prevent the irregularities of economic life from spawning widespread unemployment. Perhaps the most important was the prevalence of self-employment: although precise and reliable figures are unavailable, it appears that a majority of adults in early-nineteenth-century Massachusetts worked either for themselves or as parts of property-owning family units. In 1820, nearly 60 percent of the labor force was engaged in agriculture, and most farmers were self-employed. In addition, a significant proportion of artisans and tradesmen also owned productive property with which they could earn a living. And self-employment meant that work was organized by those who performed it: individuals who worked for themselves wielded considerable control over their own working time and the pace of their labors. Farmers could anticipate the harsh New England winters and plan their work accordingly; indoor tasks and repairs could be set aside for months when outdoor work was impossible. Both artisans and farmers could adjust the pace of their labors to match the tasks before them and the time available. Work could be stretched out and interspersed with leisure during slow days or weeks; it could also be performed rapidly in order to free time for other activities. Men and women who were self-employed continuously made decisions about the allocation of their working and nonworking time. As a result, the complete and involuntary cessation of economic activity was unlikely to occur.[4]

When work stoppages did take place, moreover, their consequences were shaped and limited by the predominance of agriculture in the commonwealth. Whatever the vicissitudes of the weather and the economy, Massachusetts farm families could almost always count on being able to feed, clothe, and shelter themselves: even during slow seasons or bad years, the necessities could be obtained. In the early nineteenth century, Massachusetts agriculture was a mix of subsistence and market farming, but even those farmers who were most closely tied to the market (those who lived along the coast or near large towns) did not become either destitute or dependent when their cash incomes disappeared. Although poverty existed in rural Massachusetts, it was, as traveler Timothy Dwight so insistently noted, the poverty of families with homes and access to land. When these families were idled, they did not experience an immediate or acute need for employment. Farmers, in Massachusetts as elsewhere, were commonly underemployed, but rarely were they altogether idle and in need of work.[5]

Farm families were further protected against "involuntary idleness" by the fact that adverse market conditions did not generally lead to a reduction in economic activity. Agricultural prices fluctuated frequently during the late eighteenth and early nineteenth centuries, but a drop in prices did not cause farmers to restrict output and cut back on their labors. Although their incomes were diminished, they maintained or even increased the volume of their production. Trade depressions, moreover, commonly had the effect of stimulating or reviving household manufactures: when agricultural prices fell or the cost of imports rose, many farming households responded by producing more goods for their own consumption. The consequence was heightened activity rather than idleness.[6]

The most powerful buttress against unemployment was, however, not the mere existence of a large agricultural sector but rather the integration, the meshing, of agriculture and manufacturing. Long before the emergence of factories, the people of Massachusetts were producing sizable quantities of manufactured goods. But a large majority of the men and women who participated in this production retained significant ties to the world of agriculture. This meshing of activities took several different forms. The most common, perhaps, was the manufacture within the farm household of goods to be consumed by the farm family itself. As Alexander Hamilton noted in 1791, there existed throughout the nation a "vast scene of household manufacturing" that was distinct from "regular trades" and critical to the economic life of many communities. Farm families commonly produced their own clothing, bread, soap, candles, cheese, skins, and a variety of other goods.[7]

In addition, many farmers were also craftsmen who sold their wares or services in local and regional markets. Foreign observers in the late eighteenth and early nineteenth centuries frequently noted that Americans often combined farming with other trades, and the farmers of the Bay State were no exception. In the town of North Brookfield, for example, there were farmers at the turn of the century who were also gunsmiths, wheelwrights, carpenters, coopers, cobblers, and tailors. In Middleboro and numerous other towns, members of farm households spent their winters making nails and tacks, while along the coast fishing was a common accompaniment to farming. Still other households fused agriculture with manufactures through participation in the "putting-out" system that existed in some industries: manufacturers of shoes and textiles, among others, often "put out" raw materials to farm families who supplemented their incomes by turning these materials into semifinished or even finished goods. Many Essex County farmers were engaged in shoe manufacturing when they were not working on their farms, and some participants in this putting-out system devoted more of their

time to manufactures than to farming. Indeed, the meshing of agriculture and manufacturing encompassed a sizable number of persons
whose primary occupations were nonagricultural but who owned
land or belonged to households that were still actively engaged in
farming. The commonwealth contained craftsmen-farmers as well as
farmer-craftsmen.[8]

This integration of different economic activities helped to immu-
nize the society against unemployment. Because many people could
engage in more than one occupation, the disruption of a particular
line of work did not yield idleness or complete inactivity: things may
have been slow on the farm in winter, but farmers could turn their
attention to household manufactures or to the production of nails
and tacks. Conversely, when craftsmen were confronted with a slackened demand for their wares, they could devote more time to farming. Men and women who had more than one occupation were, in
effect, poor candidates for idleness. At the same time, the tight linkage between manufacturing and agriculture meant that many producers of manufactured goods did not require cash incomes simply
to survive or sustain themselves. As consumers, these families possessed some independence of the market, and the agricultural world
in which they lived virtually guaranteed their ability to weather fluctuations in trade. Men and women who lived on farms and made
shoes that had been put out could still feed, shelter, and clothe themselves even when the shoe industry was stagnant.[9]

There were, of course, people in Massachusetts who were neither
members of farm families nor self-employed artisans: men and
women who worked outside of agriculture, who were employed by
others, and who did not possess any productive property of their
own. But even these individuals – or many of them, at least – possessed some shelter against unemployment by virtue of the social
and communal relationships that enveloped economic activity. Workplaces were small, and employers and employees were often neighbors, friends, even relatives. Although hierarchical lines of authority
did exist, they were tempered by other ties, and the distribution of
work had to take account of personal bonds. In slack times, the master of a shop had good reason not to lay off a neighbor's son or a
journeyman who had worked alongside him for years.[10]

One final – and more celebrated – reason for the low incidence and
visibility of unemployment also warrants mention: the existence of
the frontier. Throughout the late eighteenth and early nineteenth
centuries, vacant, arable land was available in the Ohio and Mississippi valleys, and farmers from the eastern seaboard migrated west-
ward in large numbers. This migration relieved the pressures that a

growing population placed on the farming resources of states like Massachusetts, and, in doing so, it neutralized one potential source of a labor surplus.[11]

In concert with one another, these happy features of Massachusetts society sheltered the population against unemployment well into the early nineteenth century. To be sure, some involuntary idleness did occur: idle wage earners who were looking for jobs were certainly not unknown to the residents of the colony or state of Massachusetts. But unemployment remained a marginal phenomenon, incidental to the lives of the vast majority of citizens. The organization of society mitigated against both idleness and overt need; the poor relief system of Massachusetts operated fairly smoothly on the assumption that all able-bodied adults who wanted to work could earn a living. The dog failed to bark in the night because there was no real danger: the structure of the economy and the society prevented the irregularities of economic activity from taking the form of unemployment.[12]

During the first decades of the nineteenth century, these shelters against unemployment did begin to erode, to show some cracks. Nonagricultural occupations were becoming more common, household manufacturing was beginning to decline, and the population's dependence on the market was growing.[13] Some jobs were becoming more specialized, and large-scale manufacturing ventures began to appear in towns like Waltham and Dudley. Massachusetts society was far from static, and the commonwealth was probably less well immunized against unemployment in 1800 than it had been a half-century earlier. But even by 1810 or 1820, these trends had not advanced very far, and the changes that had occurred were dwarfed by those that were to follow.

The great transformation

Between the War of 1812 and the Civil War – the dates are more convenient than exact – Massachusetts became one of the most heavily industrialized territories on the face of the earth. Often self-consciously, sometimes proudly, in many instances reluctantly, the people of the Bay State lived at the cutting edge of the industrial revolution in the United States. They participated in a process that elevated manufacturing to a position of dominance in the state's economy, and they watched or joined an unprecedented flow of the populace toward the commonwealth's urban centers. Immigrants from abroad, most notably from Ireland, streamed into Massachusetts, contributing to a rise in the state's population from a half-million to a million and a half. These and other developments, the

Table 2.1. *The distribution of the labor force, Massachusetts, 1875*

	Males		Females	
	Number	Percentage	Number	Percentage
Government and pro- fessional service	19,061	3.8	10,669	6.5
Domestic and per- sonal service	11,292	2.2	66,976	40.6
Trade and transportation	101,413	20.2	3,522	2.1
Agriculture and fisheries	81,119	16.2	37	0.0
Manufactures and mechanical industries	233,252	46.5	83,207	50.4
Apprentices, laborers, and unspecified	55,967	11.1	715	0.4
Total	502,104	100.0	165,126	100.0

Source: *Census of Massachusetts: 1875*, I (Boston, 1876–7), pp. 610–11.

massive yet intricate set of shifts that accompanied the rise of industrial capitalism, overturned, indeed overwhelmed, the economic and social order that had prevailed in the early nineteenth century. One consequence of this transformation was the emergence of unemployment as a common occurrence in the lives of the Bay State's working people.[14]

The most basic of the changes, the shift from farming to manufacturing, led to a pronounced decline in the control that many people wielded over the distribution of their own working and nonworking time. The scale of the movement toward industry and away from agriculture was dramatic. Between 1820 and 1870, the proportion of the labor force engaged in farming plummeted from nearly 60 percent to roughly 13 percent, while the number of persons with primary occupations in manufactures rose from 33,000 in 1820 to 166,000 at midcentury and to more than 300,000 by 1875. As Table 2.1 reveals, more than half the state's working women in 1875 held jobs in manufacturing, and three-quarters of the men worked in industry, trade, or transportation. Although tens of thousands of families still owned and worked on farms, by the middle of the nineteenth century they were more representative of the commonwealth's past than its present. Competition from more productive agricultural regions in the

West had stalled the agriculture of the Bay State, leaving the characteristic work rhythms of the landowning farmer as the province of only a small minority of the state's residents.[15]

But the fact that people were producing shoes and textiles rather than growing grain did not by itself undermine their autonomy, their ability to determine the pace of work. From the viewpoint of the potentially unemployed working person, the real significance of industrialization was that it turned a majority of the labor force into employees, into wage earners who did not own productive property and had to depend on others for employment. By 1875, more than 85 percent of the people who worked in "manufactures and mechanical industries" were employees. In the labor force as a whole, at least 70 percent of all males and nearly all working females were wage or salary earners. During the half-century that followed the second war with Britain, self-employment became the exception rather than the rule: the era of the independent artisan came to a close, and even in agriculture the ratio of laborers to owners increased. The industrial development of Massachusetts meant that most working people came to labor in shops that they did not own or control, at a pace that was often determined by others. They could also, in slack times, be laid off or "thrown out of employment."[16]

The process of industrialization undercut the capacity of workers to ward off spells of idleness in other ways as well. Household manufacturing virtually disappeared from the commonwealth by 1860, while opportunities for working people to wear more than one occupational hat narrowed considerably. By the middle of the nineteenth century, there were far fewer craftsmen engaged in farming than there had been in 1800, and gradually the putting-out system gave way to factories in which employees worked full time. As occupations became more specialized, dull periods in any trade or industry tended increasingly to leave workers altogether without productive labor to perform.[17]

For some working people, the impact of this social division of labor was intensified by the loss of skills that accompanied the detailed specialization of tasks. As a resident of the town of Southbridge observed early in the 1870s, "Subdivision is a grand thing for the employer, but a curse to the employed. A man goes into a shop and goes to making screws that hold two parts of some machine together, and never makes anything else but screws. The minute that business is dull, he has not learned the use of tools enough to adapt himself easily to some other business."[18] He might have added that a man whose skills were confined to the production of screws to hold two parts of a machine together could easily be replaced by his employer and had very little power in the labor market. Skill dilution undercut the market position of individual workmen, while, simultaneously, the growth of large enterprises hastened the spread of market values by vitiating the personal bonds that had existed between employers and employees. Although most workplaces remained fairly modest in size, many workers found themselves being laid off by employers whom they barely knew and perhaps had not even met.[19]

In addition to heightening the chances of a worker becoming altogether idle, the process of capitalist industrialization in Massachusetts also reshaped the needs that a jobless worker was likely to experience. The key to this transformation was the severing of the links between agriculture and manufactures, between wage earners and the land. The bonds between the two sectors were snapped, between 1830 and 1860, by the pressure of several related and convergent forces.

The first steps in the process involved the detachment of the native-born industrial labor force from the agricultural sector of the economy. This arose, in part, because of the decline of both household manufacturing and the putting-out system, two developments that made it increasingly difficult for men and women to participate in manufactures while remaining on the farm. Between 1830 and 1860, there was also a critical shift in the locales from which full-time industrial workers were recruited. As the "workingmen of Charlestown" proclaimed in 1840, "Hitherto the great mass of our laboring population had been bred in the agricultural districts, and consequently could easily shift from the city or the factory village to the farm. But this will not continue to be the case for another generation."[20] And it wasn't. The rapid growth of industry, coupled with the stagnation of agriculture, produced a steady drop in the proportion of industrial workers who were recruited from the countryside and who could return to their native districts when manufacturing jobs were scarce. The shuttle between farm and factory became less common with each succeeding generation of industrial workers, and by the 1850s jobless men and women commonly found themselves stranded in industrial communities.[21]

The links between working people and the land were further attenuated by the rapid urbanization of the commonwealth. The population of Boston grew from 43,000 in 1820 to 160,000 in 1855 and to more than 300,000 by 1875. By 1855, 35 percent of the people in Massachusetts lived in the commonwealth's fourteen cities; twenty years later, a majority of the population lived in the state's nineteen cities.

By 1875, Massachusetts was the most densely populated state in the nation, with ten communities having populations greater than 25,000.[22]

The urban image ought not be exaggerated. Many people still lived in towns of varying sizes, and the typical industrial worker still inhabited a quasi-rural world even in 1870. But the growth of the commonwealth's cities did mean that an increasing proportion of working people lacked access to the basic income supplements that a rural environment could offer. In the late 1820s, for example, the employees of the Plymouth Cordage Company had been able to contribute to the support of their families by cutting their own wood for fuel, by fishing, by growing potatoes, by hunting ducks and partridge, and by keeping vegetable gardens. In Lynn, some shoemakers weathered the depression of the late 1830s thanks to their livestock, their gardens, and the availability of clams, eels, and fish. "There was a great deal of gardening done in Lynn in the summer of 1837," noted one of the town's citizens. But as cities grew larger and more densely inhabited, less gardening could be done, fewer families could raise chickens and pigs, and nature's bounty became less accessible. Urban life required a cash income to pay rent and to purchase food; an idle day laborer in Boston could not feed his family by cultivating his own garden.[23]

The death blow to the social order in which agriculture and manufactures were meshed was delivered by the massive wave of Irish immigration that hit the Bay State during the fifteen years before the Civil War. These men and women had no ties to the farming communities of New England, and, unlike some other immigrant groups, they came to the United States with the firm, even desperate, intention of remaining permanently. Most of them also lacked the ability or inclination to return even temporarily to the agricultural regions of their native country. And beginning in the 1840s, the Irish came to Massachusetts in very large numbers. While roughly 17,000 ocean passengers had entered Boston between 1836 and 1840, approximately 113,000 arrived between 1846 and 1850. By 1855, there were 181,000 Irish-born residents of Massachusetts; by 1875, after a temporary decline in immigration during the Civil War, there were 235,000. This dramatic population transfer produced a sudden and very sizable increase in the number of Massachusetts residents who were entirely dependent on wages to meet all their economic needs. The Irish clustered in the cities and usually worked in manufacturing and construction. And when these migrants from Ireland were jobless, they were unemployed.[24]

Indeed, the midcentury increase in immigration levels significantly accelerated the emergence of an unemployment problem in Massachusetts. The native-born population had already witnessed a heightening of its own vulnerability to involuntary idleness, and the arrival of the Irish (as well as other, smaller groups) meant the rapid addition of tens of thousands of workers who were vulnerable to unemployment the moment they stepped off the boat. The immigration of the Irish also swelled the size of the industrial labor force in Massachusetts, thereby contributing to the declining market power of labor as a whole. There may, at times, have been an authentic shortage of workers in Massachusetts during the first half of the nineteenth century, but neither unskilled nor semiskilled labor was ever scarce in the Boston area in the 1850s. The social processes that were transforming the sons and daughters of New England into a wage-earning population were climaxed, intensified, and, to some degree, overshadowed by the arrival of an Irish proletariat.[25]

The combination of immigration, urban growth, the demise of household manufactures, and the specialization of occupational skills also led industrial workers, as consumers, toward an increasing dependence on the marketplace. This shift was recorded accurately, if not very sympathetically, by one observer of working-class life in the 1870s:

> I have been in scores of the homes of unemployed workingmen, in different parts of our country, during the last five years, where the chairs, tables, and bedsteads were all worn out and breaking down, so that in many instances there was not a safe or comfortable seat in the house. Yet the furniture had all been bought of dealers at high prices, if we consider its quality and its capacity for use . . . and these workingmen were not able to sit while eating their food. They had been at work in shops, mills, or factories, and when these closed had so little power of self-help that months of idleness passed without anything being done to make their homes more comfortable. In such cases, everything that comes into the house, or that is used about it, must be bought, and requires money for its purchase.[26]

The declining "power of self-help" exhibited by these unemployed workers almost certainly stemmed less from a loss of will than from a loss of capability. Industrial employees, living in cities, engaged since childhood in the performance of routine tasks requiring few skills, had become largely unable to produce goods for their own consumption. But whatever the cause, a key consequence of this shift was that workers were more dependent on their wages and more overtly needy when they were "thrown out of employment." The necessities could be obtained only with cash, and layoffs did not present workers with the opportunity to perform productive, if unpaid, work.

Accompanying all these concrete, visible, even quantifiable shifts was another change, more elusive yet just as important: people began to expect to work more steadily, to work full-time, to work year round. As market relationships increasingly dominated the organization of work and consumption, time became money. Idle time meant a loss of profits to an employer, of wages to an employee. As workers came to rely on their cash incomes more and more heavily, as opportunities for doing something productive other than working for a cash income narrowed, men and women came to feel in need of steady work and entitled to it. Spells of inactivity were perceived less as interludes between tasks and more as irretrievable losses of income. And this perception of need was not rigidly tied to prevailing wage levels and the cost of living. A man did not have to be on the brink of starvation to "need" a job.[27]

This change in attitudes and expectations made it possible for one Massachusetts worker in the 1870s to state that "I earn three hundred dollars less than I ought to for the reason that I only have employment about two-thirds of the time . . . I consider I am underpaid because I am unemployed."[28] Time had become money for this anonymous American, and it even had a precise dollar equivalent. Recurrent as slack times may have been in his occupation, he felt entitled to a full year's earnings and to steady work. Such perceptions and attitudes would have seemed foreign to the working people of the Bay State earlier in the nineteenth century. In 1835, the carpenters, masons, and stonecutters of Boston, who were fighting vigorously for a shorter workday, accepted, as a given, that each winter "hundreds of us remain idle for want of work, for three or four months." These Jacksonian-era craftsmen viewed slack times as part of the natural economic order; they often considered themselves to be underpaid, but not because they failed to work for twelve months in the year.[29]

Ironically, the often frustrated yet growing expectation of steady work was probably fueled by those achievements of industrialization and urbanization that made uninterrupted labor more feasible. Increasingly efficient networks of transportation and communication, more reliable sources of power, greater protection against the weather – these developments did tend to produce more routine schedules and working rhythms for some of the Bay State's citizens. They did not, on the whole, make work any more steady – since there were many offsetting trends as well – but they did make steady work more imaginable, more plausible an expectation. In doing so, of course, they contributed to the perception that idle time was not a natural event but rather a socially imposed obstacle to maximizing one's earnings.[30]

While workers were coming to expect their jobs to be more regular, employers were finding it to be easier to lay off their employees as a means of coping with market fluctuations. During the first decades of industrialization, manufacturers had sometimes been reluctant to release their workers for two reasons. The first was economic: procuring an adequate labor force was a problem for some employers, and laying workers off entailed the risk of confronting a labor shortage when business improved. Skilled workers had to be recruited from Europe in many industries, and even semiskilled operatives often had to be enticed to the new mills, shops, and factories, particularly if they were located in the countryside. Consequently, employers sometimes responded to business slowdowns by putting all workers on part-time, by creating work on capital improvements, by suspending rental payments for company housing, by lowering prices in order to heighten demand, or by producing goods for inventory rather than for immediate sale. In some instances, particularly in small firms, employers were also motivated by compassion for employees whom they knew and with whom they worked. One machine shop in Lowell chose to respond to depressions not by laying off workers but by producing for inventory, a course advocated by the superintendent of the shop, a machinist who had come up through the ranks.[31]

The impulse to avoid or minimize layoffs never dominated the personnel practices of manufacturers, even in the early nineteenth century, but it did become noticeably weaker as the century progressed. In many industries, the proportion of skilled workers (the most difficult to replace) declined, leaving employers with less incentive to keep men on the job. And as Irish immigrants poured into the commonwealth, while the native labor force became increasingly dependent upon jobs in industry, unskilled and semiskilled labor became considerably more abundant. By the 1850s, urban employers, at least, did not have to worry about finding suitable replacements for workers they had laid off. "When an employer finds his business begins to slacken," noted one observer of the hat trade, "he immediately discharges a number of his men." In the 1860s, the Lawrence Manufacturing Company terminated its policy of allowing unemployed operatives to live rent-free in company housing: the policy was no longer necessary for the firm to maintain a cohesive labor force.[32]

Simultaneously, the growing physical and social distance between

employees and the men who shaped business policy served to remove noneconomic considerations from personnel decisions. In
Holyoke, during the late 1860s, the only cotton mill that ran steadily
was the one locally owned and locally managed firm in the city. Elsewhere in Holyoke and in much of the state, employers based their
strategies on the purely economic calculation that operatives could
be found when they were needed, that labor was abundant and available. On the whole, they were right. By 1870 – and earlier in some
locales – the economic and social transformation that had swept the
commonwealth had rendered year-round workers more plentiful
than year-round jobs, and men and women who were jobless were
likely to be in need of work.[33]

Different paths

The social changes that gave rise to unemployment did not, of
course, arrive in the same package in every community and industry
in Massachusetts. These shifts occurred in widely varied combina-
tions, with similar processes unfolding in different places at different
times. Industrial capitalism did not steamroll the early-nineteenth-
century economic order; its advance, however, triumphant, was
more scattershot, uneven, localized. The Bay State was home to a
diverse assortment of industries, which expanded at different rates
and had varied technologies, working rhythms, and labor force requirements. Over time, the structures that governed employment in
different locales and occupations began to converge, but there was
no single path that led to the creation of a work force vulnerable to
unemployment. The two largest manufacturing industries, textiles
and boots and shoes, had dissimilar antebellum histories. Yet by the
1870s workers in both industries found themselves laboring in factories, dependent on their wages, and in need of full-time jobs that
were not always available.

The textile industry of Massachusetts played a leading role in es-
tablishing the viability of manufacturing in the United States.
Prompted by the cutoff of British imports, Bay State entrepreneurs
began to construct textile mills during the second decade of the nineteenth century, and after a shaky start the industry grew rapidly and
dramatically. The output of cloth from Massachusetts mills rose from
23 million yards in 1826 to more than 400 million in 1860. The city of
Lowell became the leading center of textile production in the nation,
while large quantities of cotton, woolen, worsted, and flannel goods
were also produced in Fall River, Lawrence, Chicopee, and many
smaller communities. The industry was the first to utilize the factory

system, and throughout the antebellum era a high proportion of the nation's largest, most heavily capitalized manufacturing firms produced textiles. By 1875 the industry employed more than 70,000 persons in Massachusetts, most of whom labored in factories that housed more than 100 employees.[34]

This extraordinary growth was accompanied by profound changes in the organization of work and the composition of the labor force. The factory system itself, of course, constituted a major break with past methods of producing cloth, and it contributed to the ongoing decline of household manufacturing, a decline that had begun in the eighteenth century owing to the availability of British factory-made imports. Yet even after the factory system had been "borrowed" from Britain and installed in Massachusetts, the organization of production continued to change: the fledgling mills of 1815 were a far cry from their successors two generations later.[35]

Many of the earliest American mills, in fact, performed only part of the process of manufacturing cloth. Other steps were accomplished by putting out raw or semifinished materials to men and women who lived in the agricultural communities surrounding the mills. Well into the 1820s, for example, a majority of Samuel Slater's Worcester County employees were "outworkers"; not until 1828 were handloom weavers, who worked in their homes, replaced by factory hands who operated power looms inside the mills. Work in these enterprises was organized to take advantage of the pools of part-time labor that existed in the countryside. This meshing of new industrial methods with traditional household patterns was, however, shortlived. By 1830 – and earlier in some firms – technological advances, coupled with the need for a more reliable and disciplined labor force, had put an end to outwork in the textile industry. Production processes were integrated, and all employees worked full-time within the mills.[36]

Still, the employment of full-time operatives did not immediately sever the connections between the labor force and the agricultural life of the commonwealth. Lacking a ready-made factory labor force and confronted with periodic labor shortages, the Bay State's entrepreneurs were obliged to recruit operatives from the farming communities of New England. The most celebrated system of recruitment involved the hiring of young, unmarried women from farming families in northern New England. This system (known as the "Waltham system" and developed most fully in the city of Lowell) was originally designed both to satisfy the textile industry's need for labor and to prevent the appearance of a permanent wage-earning population that seemed inimical to widely held social values. The women who worked in the mills of Lowell served relatively short stints in the textile industry. Few of them intended to become, or in fact became, lifelong textile operatives. Of equal importance, most of these women did not seek positions in the mills because of strict economic necessity – neither they nor their families were in dire financial straits – and if they lost their positions as operatives, they were able to return to the farms from which they had come. The Waltham system meant that, for tens of thousands of female mill operatives, layoffs produced a sojourn at home rather than a search for work, a resumption of traditional tasks rather than unemployment.[37]

To a lesser extent, this was true also for workers who labored in mills that relied on entire families to produce cotton and woolen cloth. The Slater Mills in Dudley and Oxford, as well as many other factories scattered across the Massachusetts countryside, hired men, women, and children from the same family to perform different tasks in the production of cloth. During the first decades that these mills were in operation, the family units employed often came from the agricultural districts of New England. For these families, the needs induced by layoffs were probably more severe and immediate than they were for the women working in Lowell, but at least some of them could retreat to the world of farming when industrial jobs were scarce. Many of these families also possessed some of the advantages of rural life (e.g., gardens and livestock) even while they worked in the mills. Moreover, employers, who were fearful of labor shortages, sometimes shielded large family units from discharges during slack times.[38]

By the 1850s, however, the fragile interlacing of the textile industry with New England agriculture had come undone. The flow of young women from the countryside to the mills of Lowell had slowed considerably; the percentage of men in the textile labor force was on the increase. A rising proportion of mill operatives consisted of the children of industrial workers rather than the children of farmers, and throughout the industry both men and women were remaining at their jobs for lengthier periods. More and more, work in the textile mills was acquiring the cast of an occupation rather than an experiment, a long-term rather than temporary activity.[39]

But the coup de grace was administered to the early labor system by the availability of Irish immigrants, beginning in the 1840s. Textile manufacturers, still challenged by the task of finding sufficient labor to meet the needs of a rapidly growing industry, turned to the Irish and to other immigrants, and within a short period foreign-born operatives came to dominate the mills. In 1845 only 8 percent of the employees of the Hamilton Company in Lowell were foreign-born; within five years one-third of the operatives were immigrants, with the proportion reaching 60 percent by 1860. At the Dwight Mills in Chicopee, a labor force that had been 2 percent Irish in 1841 was predominantly Irish seventeen years later; similarly, by 1860, three-quarters of the operatives at the Slater Mills in Webster were either foreign-born or members of households headed by immigrants. The shift was rapid and dramatic, affecting mills that had relied on female labor as well as mills that had employed entire families. The well-springs of the textile labor force had moved from the rural townships of New England to the docks of Boston.[40]

These new textile workers were motivated by economic needs of the starkest kind. For both men and women, the wages earned in the factories of Lowell or Fall River or Chicopee were essential to the sustenance of the families to which they belonged. Many of the Irish women and children who entered the mills did so because the earnings of their husbands and fathers (who often worked sporadically as day laborers) simply could not support their families. Immigrants were looking for permanent jobs, and, not surprisingly, they tended to remain attached to individual firms for longer stints than their native-born colleagues. The textile industry had solved the problem of labor shortages – although manufacturers did occasionally find it necessary to recruit skilled workers from Europe – and, in so doing, it had promoted the formation of a permanent wage-earning population. Beginning in the 1850s, the vast majority of textile mill operatives were men and women who labored in large factories, lived in urban or quasi-urban settings, and were utterly dependent upon their industrial earnings in order to survive.[41]

Clearly, these changes in the organization of work and the sources of labor rendered midcentury producers of cloth far more vulnerable to unemployment than their predecessors had been. But more often than not, that vulnerability remained abstract and unrealized because the industry, in fact, tended to provide relatively steady jobs. Textile manufacturing was not seasonal, and both production and marketing were structured so that routine fluctuations in trade tended to be reflected in prices, wages, and inventories rather than in levels of output and employment.[42] Indeed, many workers were attracted to the industry, despite its low wages, precisely because jobs tended to be fairly steady. (Surviving payroll records reveal that, throughout the antebellum era, the number of operatives employed by individual firms tended to vary little within the course of a year and, usually, to rise from one year to the next.) Although bankruptcies, frozen rivers, fires, and equipment failures occasionally shut mills down for periods of varying lengths, jobs in textile factories were, as a rule, regular and secure.[43]

There was, however, one important exception to this pattern of steadiness: major downturns in business activity often produced swift and simultaneous layoffs for large numbers of operatives. At least once each decade between 1810 and 1870, trade became so slow that many mills either closed altogether or sharply curtailed their schedules, releasing large numbers of employees. The phenomenon was cyclical, but its impact was not: each time the mills shut down or cut back, more jobs were at stake and more jobs were lost. With every succeeding slump in trade, workers who were laid off were more prone to hardship, less able to cope easily with their loss of income. Numerous textile firms shut down or sharply curtailed production with the return of British imports in 1815, but the textile labor force included many outworkers who turned their energies back to farming. The depression of the late 1830s and early 1840s brought some branches of textile manufacturing to a standstill, yet the female operatives of Lowell and elsewhere were able to return to the rural towns from which they had come. By 1857, however, the closing of a mill meant unemployment for most of its workers: Yankees and immigrants alike were full-time and permanent members of the industrial order. Textile operatives had become hostages to the business cycle. They expected year-round employment, they needed year-round employment (given the low wages in the industry), and most often they had year-round employment. But they were acutely vulnerable to crises, and crises could and did occur.[44]

Workers in the boot and shoe industry had a different range of experiences between 1800 and the 1870s. The industry itself grew from localized eighteenth-century origins to include more than 75,000 employees in 1855. By the 1830s, there were more than thirty communities in Massachusetts that produced 100,000 or more pairs of boots and shoes each year, and by the 1870s nearly 60 million pairs of shoes were being manufactured annually in the Bay State. The industry was as important to the economy of Massachusetts as was the production of textiles, but its evolution followed very different lines. The technology of shoe manufacturing changed little during the first half of the nineteenth century, and integrated factories were not constructed until the late 1850s. The labor force remained dominated by natives, workplaces tended to be small – even after factories were introduced, thirty or forty workers per shop was about average – and firms with little capital entered and disappeared from the business at a high rate. Most importantly, the industry was a highly seasonal one, a characteristic that helped to shape both the evolving organization of work and the changes in the composition of the labor force.[45]

In the late eighteenth century, boot- and shoemaking was an artisanal trade, practiced by individuals and households in towns throughout the commonwealth. In some communities, shoemakers plied their trade exclusively for local markets, often producing shoes only after they had been ordered by individual customers. In others, most notably in Lynn, production was larger and geared toward more distant markets: by the end of the eighteenth century, the people of Lynn – which led the transformation of Essex County from an agricultural region into the shoe capital of the world – were producing as many as 400,000 pairs of boots and shoes in the course of a year. But even in Lynn, the technology of shoemaking remained simple and the division of labor rudimentary. Different tasks were often performed by men, women, children, and apprentices who belonged to the same household, but the shoemaking household itself sold finished products to the merchants who controlled the marketing networks. The makers of shoes were people who exercised considerable control over their working time and owned the homes and shops in which they worked. Many had more than one occupation, most probably owned some livestock and vegetable gardens, and shoemakers who were also farmers were hardly a rarity.[46]

The enormous expansion of the industry during the first half of the nineteenth century served to undermine these artisanal patterns. Enlarged and distant markets demanded more coordinated production, increased specialization of product, and more attention to different and changing styles; marketing pressures also yielded the seasonal rhythms that were to become a hallmark of the industry. These changes, in turn, led to a reorganization of work. Entrepreneurs who marketed boots and shoes – and who, during the early decades, were often former shoemakers themselves – purchased the raw materials themselves and hired men to cut the leather stock in central shops. Once cut, the leather was parceled out to local journeymen who actually made up the shoes – some working alone or with their families, others working in small shops with fellow journeymen. Gradually, tasks became more specialized, and the process of making shoes came to be carried out by workers who did not know how to make finished products and who were hired by journeymen to perform very specific operations. There was, simultaneously, an enormous expansion of outwork. Since local labor supplies were often inadequate during peak seasons, shoe manufacturers everywhere routinely put out piecework to be performed by rural families who lived dozens, even hundreds, of miles from the central shops. The Batcheller brothers in Brookfield, for example, supplied cut stock to families throughout Worcester County. And the city of Lynn became the center of a vast network of outworkers stretching across northern Massachusetts and into southern New Hampshire.[47]

This reorganization of boot and shoe production had varied consequences for the tens of thousands of working people who came to participate in the industry. For those who lived in or moved to shoe centers like Lynn, the changes meant that they became employees rather than independent artisans. Both the highly skilled cutters and the industry's journeymen were hired (and laid off) by the owners and managers of firms that controlled the raw materials and marketing. While their status was being transformed, these men were also becoming more dependent upon the wages they were paid for producing shoes. In Lynn, by the 1830s, most boot- and shoemakers had neither other occupations nor farms: they were full-time employees in the shoe industry, and their welfare depended entirely on the briskness of trade in boots and shoes. By the 1850s, this dependence was commonplace throughout the state.[48]

At the same time, the putting-out system brought into the industry a large number of working people who did have other occupations and retained roots in the agricultural sector of the economy. From Nantucket to New Hampshire to Hampden County in the west, there were farm families who took in piecework as a way of supplementing their incomes during slack seasons. In certain respects, these rural outworkers of the 1830s and 1840s recapitulated some of the experiences of Lynn's shoemakers during the late eighteenth century. In so doing, they provided the industry with a large reserve of part-time labor that could respond easily and rather painlessly to the seasonal demand for workers; their availability, in turn, served to perpetuate the seasonal rhythms of production. By the 1850s, the system had beome less painless – since many outworkers had moved to satellite towns around the shoe centers and were more reliant on their industrial earnings – but the outwork system still helped to cushion the impact of irregular production. Even in 1857, one New Hampshire farmer-shoemaker could record in his diary "Ben loafing – out of work and happy as a clam."[49]

Tidy as this system was, it did not endure. Shoe manufacturers, faced with growing competition and remote markets, desired more control over production than an outwork system could provide. And in the 1850s the development of new technology made it feasible to perform all the processes of shoemaking under a single roof. The factory system came to the industry late in that decade, and within twenty years both the putting-out networks and the small "ten-footers," the shops in which journeymen had plied their trade, had become artifacts of the past. The division of labor became more pronounced, obliging a large majority of boot- and shoemakers, in Lynn, Haverhill, Danvers, Brookfield, Brockton, and countless other communities, to assume new roles as machine operatives. These operatives were employees with single occupations, residents of communities that were increasingly urban. And personal bonds between employers and employees – which had been strong when the two were co-workers and had already been strained by the outwork system – were irretrievably broken.[50]

While these shifts in the organization of work rendered nearly all boot- and shoemakers fully vulnerable to the experience of unemployment, the introduction of factories did not make jobs any more regular than they had been under the outwork system. Each year there were two active seasons and two slack seasons, and, according to some contemporaries, "every year the busy seasons are becoming shorter, and the dull seasons longer."[51] New technology permitted more shoes to be produced in less time, and the incessant fluctuations in the demand for labor generated annual spells of joblessness for many makers of boots and shoes. In towns like Lynn and Danvers, seasonal rhythms also gave rise to a floating population of shoe factory workers who drifted into town when business was prosperous and who were released from their jobs as soon as the slack season began. The factory system transformed the reserve of labor from a network of outworkers into a stream of floaters.[52]

Indeed, labor markets in the shoe industry were chaotic and unpredictable from the 1830s through the 1870s. The demand for boots and shoes varied not only seasonally but from year to year, with employment and income levels fluctuating accordingly. The problem was compounded by the fact that every wave of prosperity in the industry was greeted by the establishment of many new firms and the arrival in the shoe centers of hundreds of workers seeking employment. The industry developed a serious problem of excess capacity, with each slump in trade producing the failure of numerous businesses and joblessness for their employees. Most of the firms that were operating in Lynn in 1836, for example, went bankrupt during the subsequent depression. By the 1850s, the rhythms of production had become even more frenetic (serious downturns in the shoe trade were occurring every two or three years), and the Civil War provided only a temporary halt to the irregularities that plagued the industry. For the working people who made boots and shoes, the vast majority of whom were native-born, erratic employment had become a recurrent and familiar experience. Busy seasons alternated with slack seasons, booms with depressions, the sprouting of new firms with epidemics of bankruptcy. As the organization of the industry changed, moreover, the import of a spell of idleness also changed – and an experience that had once been "loafing" gradually hardened into unemployment.[53]

Although they traveled different paths, the boot- and shoemakers and the textile operatives of Massachusetts eventually arrived at the same destination. By the 1870s, virtually all workers in both industries – totaling more than 100,000 persons – were factory employees structurally exposed to unemployment. However diverse their lives may have been in other respects, they shared this critical hallmark of their class position. And if misery did indeed want company, then the shoe and textile workers of the Bay State had ample reason to feel satisfied: the structural changes that had affected their own occupations altered the jobs and lives of hundreds of thousands of other workers as well. Many artisanal trades, like printing and tailoring, witnessed a decline in self-employment, the development of new production processes, and a loss of individual control over the pace of work. Other seasonal occupations, such as the building trades, grew rapidly, drawing more and more workers into jobs where idleness had long been endemic and was becoming increasingly harsh in its consequences. New industries, such as papermaking, developed factory production techniques and employed thousands of semi-skilled machine tenders. Throughout the economy, individuals witnessed and lived through their own private portions of an overwhelming social transformation.[54]

There were, as always, exceptions. Self-employed artisans and storekeepers, as well as professionals and businessmen, continued to live and labor in the commonwealth. And some industrial workers, particularly those who were highly skilled and employed by small firms in quasi-rural areas, remained nestled in a social order where both security and autonomy could be taken for granted.[55] Such niches were not rare in the 1850s or even the 1870s. But they were relics of the past. In 1865, one witness told the Massachusetts Commission on the Hours of Labor that

> there is a man in Ware Village that is nearly sixty years of age. He has worked in a machine shop all his life since he was of age except a small interruption. He owns a farm – but still works in the machine shop. When his hours are through he goes onto the farm and works. He is contented with his place and with the wages he receives and prefers to work on in the avocation he has pursued for so many years. . . . It is optional with him to work on the farm

or in the machine shop. He works in the shop because he thinks it
pays him better.[56]
The tone of the testimony was appropriately wistful. The man from
Ware Village did indeed possess an important immunity against the
problems that had come to afflict labor in Massachusetts. But he was
nearly sixty years old, and he had the good fortune both to own a
farm and to have a skilled trade. And by 1865 Ware Village had long
since ceased to be typical of the communities of the commonwealth.

A lengthening shadow

The cumulative effect of the step-by-step changes in the economic
and social structure of the Bay State was a gradual growth in the
significance of unemployment for the people of the commonwealth
as a whole. As one industry after another expanded and reorganized
production, as farms were abandoned in different townships and
counties, as migrants and immigrants trekked into Boston and other
cities, the problem of involuntary idleness deepened its imprint upon
Massachusetts society. For workers, the sting of joblessness became
sharper and more penetrating. For middle-class critics, observers,
and reformers, the phenomenon became more visible. Slowly, but
steadily, the proportion of the population vulnerable to unemployment increased, and periodically that vulnerability was exposed and
activated by downturns in the business cycle. Depressions, whether
local or national, generated the most widespread unemployment of
the antebellum era, and they also provided stroboscopic glimpses
into the structural changes that were taking place. Some features of
the new economic machinery became palpable and recognizable only
when the machinery came grinding to a halt.

For the first three-and-a-half decades of the nineteenth century, unemployment remained nearly as invisible as it had been during the
colonial era. Men and women were sometimes out of work and in
need of work – "I have tryed all the Country from New York to this
port . . . without being able to meet with employ," wrote one man
from Boston to Samuel Slater – but this did not happen with great
frequency. The society was sufficiently porous and agrarian to absorb, cushion, and disguise much of the idleness that did occur.[57]
Many of Lynn's shoemakers lost their jobs in 1827, and hundreds of
textile mill operatives were laid off in 1829. But these were scattered
episodes, brief and localized in their impact. Even during the depression of 1819–22, when many new manufacturing firms went bankrupt, only a small proportion of the labor force was altogether idle,
and the need for public relief was minimal. Seasonal slowdowns, of

course, were endemic in many trades, but, on the whole, carpenters, shipwrights, and other "mechanics" of the Bay State did not regard themselves as unemployed during predictable spells of slack work. As self-employed craftsmen, they anticipated slow seasons and usually had incomes sufficient to carry them through the year.[58]

The first signs of any persistent overcrowding of the labor markets came from Boston in the mid-1830s. Craftsmen complained of increasing difficulty obtaining employment, and the newly founded Boston Society for the Prevention of Pauperism set itself the task of finding suitable jobs for the poor. That the city of Boston regularly contained men and women who were out of work and in need of work was also suggested by the appearance of private employment or "intelligence" offices. One of these offices, operated by a "petty broker" named Aaron Dow, became renowned for fleecing job seekers out of a dollar and then sending them "to tramp the city o'er" in search of work.[59]

These hints from the metropolis were soon eclipsed by the severe depression that began in 1837 and lasted until 1842: it was during these years that the problem of unemployment first entered the lives and consciousness of many of the Bay State's citizens. Throughout the manufacturing and commercial centers of the commonwealth, workers lost their jobs and found it difficult to locate new ones. Predictable seasonal slowdowns stretched into slack periods of unprecedented length, while bankruptcies simply obliterated the jobs of many employees. Hundreds, perhaps thousands of Lynn's journeymen were simultaneously idled; the failure of a carriage factory in Amherst turned the area into a "deserted village." "We go about almost begging for labor," complained one group of workers to the readers of a Boston newspaper in 1838. Even in 1842, as the depression was coming to an end, more than a third of the woolen machinery in New England stood at a standstill. Public officials and middle-class citizens alike recognized that idleness during those years was not necessarily a sign of sloth, and special relief measures were adopted in more than a few communities.[60]

Still, given both the severity and the duration of the downturn, the distress generated by the depression was remarkably limited. Urban workers seemed to experience the most acute need, for both jobs and aid. Yet even in Boston, protest was muted and charitable activity restricted in scale. A great many working people were able to shift for themselves, to weather the prolonged slump by retreating into niches of the economy that were relatively unaffected by the market decline. Young female textile workers migrated back to the farms run by their families, while outworkers who made shoes and other goods devoted their energies to different pursuits. In Lynn, one contemporary even claimed that idled shoemakers could "bid defiance to financial tempests" because they had access to land and to the sea. This portrait of self-reliance may well have been exaggerated, but the "jours" (or journeymen) of Lynn did muddle through the slack times with a minimum of public aid. Although the pinch of hard times was widely felt, the number of idled workers who needed to be employed simply to maintain themselves and their families was held in check by the vestiges of a preindustrial and precapitalist social order. The characteristic consequence of the depression that began in 1837 was underemployment rather than unemployment.[61]

Nonetheless, the long economic downturn left scars in its wake, and, even after the state's industries had recovered, the social trends that were giving rise to unemployment continued to advance. As a result, the problem of involuntary idleness attracted some attention – as never before in prosperous times – during the 1840s. In contrast to earlier associations of Massachusetts workingmen, who had not listed unemployment among their grievances, the New England Protective Union declared it to be an "imperative duty" of the labor movement in the mid-1840s to procure "sure, steady, and profitable employment" for all workers. In 1847 the *Voice of Industry,* a labor newspaper, claimed that it was impossible for laborers with families to "lay up" anything for the winter months when expenses were high, wages low, and jobs scarce. In 1849 the Protective Union underscored the need for cooperatives by pointing a finger at "the lone streets and garrets of all our large cities, filled with the anxious, careworn, yet unsuccessful seekers of employment." During these same years, the newly formed Boston Employment Society maintained lists of women and men who needed jobs, and some reformers began to insist that, despite popular preconceptions, not everyone who sought employment could find it. The validity of such claims was confirmed by the relief rolls of towns like Danvers, where the proportion of able-bodied relief recipients continued to rise.[62]

In the major industrial centers of Massachusetts and in Boston most distinctly, a new plateau in the history of unemployment was reached in the 1850s. The event was announced at midcentury by the commonwealth's first legislative notice of the problem of involuntary idleness. "The necessities of a portion of the laboring classes are such, that they are dependent upon their daily toil for their support," concluded a committee investigating the hours of labor, "and in Massachusetts, there is always a surplus of labor unemployed." The urban labor markets of the state had indeed come to appear chronically, unmanageably, even dangerously overstocked. Thousands of Irish laborers wandered the streets of Boston, Cambridge, Newburyport, and other cities, looking for jobs that paid little and lasted only briefly. At the same time, Yankee men and women streamed into the cities in the hope of finding the more remunerative and prestigious jobs for which they were eligible.[63] "Does it never strike these young people that in coming to a city in pursuit of employment they have committed an error?" mused the Boston *Herald* in 1854.[64]

Perhaps it did, but they continued coming. In January 1855, a printer wrote to the *Herald* that he had been out of employment for twelve weeks, had exhausted his savings, and was unable to find a job in either Boston or Cambridge. "What shall I do?" he asked the editor. "I am young and willing to do almost anything . . . what would you advise me to do?" The *Herald* had little concrete advice to offer:

> Out of employment is the lot, at the present time, of hundreds, if not thousands, of smart, athletic, willing, anxious, suffering men. Yet there are those, particularly your closet teachers and pulpit expounders, who will write most earnestly, and preach most eloquently, upon the absolute ability of every man in "this highly favored land" to obtain employment if he is willing to work. If they would add the important information, how and where the work can be obtained, they would perform an important service to the labor people – But, unfortunately, they stop far short of that.[65]

The Boston Society for the Prevention of Pauperism seconded this bleak assessment, comparing conditions in the 1850s with those that had prevailed only two decades earlier. In the 1830s, according to the BSPP, there had been pauperism, but "the community, in general, was prosperous. Labor was in demand, remunerative and abundant; and none that sought it – the able-bodied, sober, and industrious – were left to sue for it in vain." But the intervening years had witnessed "a vast influx of foreign pauperism," "the redundancy of labor, especially of the unskilled and ruder sort . . . compared with the wants of our city," "fluctuations of trade and commerce," and "derangements in business operations."[66] One symptom of these "derangements" was that the Society received thousands of applications for work every year. And conditions in Boston were replicated, on a smaller scale, in cities throughout the commonwealth.[67]

All of which preceded the very sharp depression that began in 1857, a depression that starkly revealed how dependent the Bay State's populace had become upon steady employment in manufactures and in trade. Although the depression lasted only a year, its impact was unprecedented. Thousands of textile operatives and shoemakers were thrown out of work. In Taunton, skilled whitesmiths were jobless for months – hundreds of men were reduced to digging stumps on local pinelands for fuel – and in Newburyport, unemployed workers had regular leaning places along a wall in the center of town. Virtually everywhere, there was a sudden, drastic shortage of jobs, and virtually everywhere there were cries for public relief for the unemployed. In communities as diverse as Fall River, Lynn, Newton, Springfield, Lawrence, and Boston, relief programs had to be adopted, often at the insistence of local workers. Unlike the local trade depressions that occurred so often during these years, the general slump of 1857–8 did not permit workers to cure their unemployment simply by leaving town. And in contrast to conditions that had prevailed during previous national depressions, few of the Bay State's workers could disguise their idleness as rural underemployment. Although the rapidity of recovery, coupled with the onrush of the Civil War, tended to obscure the significance of the event, a threshold had been crossed and revealed. The people of Massachusetts were far more vulnerable to fluctuations of the national business cycle than they had ever been in the past.[68]

That vulnerability was not to be exposed again, on a large scale, for another fifteen years. Although the Civil War and the adjustments that followed the war produced significant dislocations in the economy, downturns in employment were either brief or confined to specific industries. The opening of the war precipitated a slowdown in business, and many cotton mills remained closed as long as the conflict endured, but the war years in general were prosperous ones for the Massachusetts economy. Woolen manufacturing thrived, the shoe industry was inundated by orders from the army, and the arsenal in Springfield set the pace for economic growth in the Connecticut River valley. At the same time, the labor supply was diminished by the entry of 160,000 Massachusetts men into the Union army. "In looking at the subject of labor," noted the rechristened Industrial Aid Society for the Prevention of Pauperism in 1867, "we find that it never was in such demand as during the war; never were such prices paid for labor." After the war ended, slackened economic activity, coupled with the return of soldiers, did produce crowded labor markets in many areas of the state, but some industries remained prosperous, and by the late 1860s the entire economy had rebounded. Many operatives and laborers sampled the experience of unemployment between 1865 and 1868, but the "life and death" struggle for jobs that some had feared did not materialize.[69]

While the unusual political and economic climate of the Civil War and Reconstruction diverted attention from the issue of unemployment, it did little to halt or slow the structural trends that had been nourishing the growth of the phenomenon. Although the rate of immigration temporarily declined during the war, the industrial sector of the economy continued to grow, more people became employed wage earners, cities expanded at the expense of the countryside, and the dependence of workers on continuous cash incomes did not subside. The problem of unemployment had reached a certain maturity in the 1850s, and there was no reversing the trend. More and more people were vulnerable to layoffs, and more and more people were sporadically laid off. "Operatives are . . . subjected at times, to the evils of excessive labor, and at other times, to the no less evil of being altogether unemployed," a legislative committee had concluded in 1850. For workers, involuntary idleness had become a nagging, chronic problem; for the society as a whole, it had become a potentially dramatic and explosive one. In the 1870s, the Lynn *Vindicator* referred to "disemployed labor" as "this vast evil that has for years past been gradually casting its portensious [*sic*] shadow over the nation." That shadow had been little noticed until the late 1830s, and its outlines became distinct only in the decade preceding the Civil War. Thereafter, the shadow would only lengthen and deepen, adding a dimension of uncertainty to working-class life and, on occasion, threatening the social order of the commonwealth. The problem of unemployment had arrived.[70]

Daily earnings and daily wants

In 1871, in one of its first annual reports, the Massachusetts Bureau of Statistics of Labor observed that the "mass of the people are people of small means, the result of daily earnings which supply each daily returning want, and are contingent upon continuous health and continuous work. But with the exception of some few in-door employments, continuous work is the exception and not the rule."[71] Much had changed during the previous half-century. The "mass of the people" of Massachusetts had long been "people of small means," but they had not always been dependent on daily or weekly earnings. Continuous work had never been the rule, but working people had increasingly come to need continuous work while, at the same time, they had lost control over its continuity. Residents of the Bay State in 1871 may not have worked any fewer days in the year, on average, than their predecessors had in 1800, but their needs had changed, and they had less power to choose which days they worked. The loose continuum that had once connected work and idleness had given way to the stark contrast between employment and unemployment.

Stated somewhat differently, the rise of industrial capitalism in Massachusetts promoted the formation of a labor reserve. It brought into existence a collection of men, women, and children who rarely had as much work as they needed or wanted and who consequently were available when the employers of the Bay State had need of them. There had, in a sense, always been a reserve of labor in the commonwealth, but by the second half of the nineteenth century, that reserve had become active rather than latent: it consisted not of underemployed members of farm households or people who simply had the time to perform additional labor but rather of men and women who needed jobs and were actively seeking work. Yankee farm girls had been supplanted by Irish immigrants; outworkers had been replaced by factory operatives who traveled from one town to the next in search of employment. The presence of such reserves enhanced the freedom with which employers could, without risk or penalty, dismiss their workers when faced with adverse market conditions; the repeated exercise of that freedom, in turn, perpetuated the existence of the reserve.[72]

The development of an active labor reserve was not a simple or straightforward consequence of an increase in the supply of labor. The appearance of an unemployment problem in Massachusetts cannot be traced directly to a Malthusian population dynamic, or to the potato famine in Ireland, or even to the decline of New England agriculture. To be sure, industrialization was possible only because labor was available, and the immigration of the Irish sounded the death knell for labor scarcity in New England. But the phenomenon of unemployment became a visible and important one as a result of complex and intricate changes in the structure of the economy and the society.[73] The people of Massachusetts began to search for a new and clearly understood label for the phenomenon of involuntary idleness because profound shifts had taken place in the organization of work, in power relationships, and in the felt needs of working people. Unemployment was one expression of the power of ownership and the dependence of employees in a market economy. For workers, joblessness was a symptom, a badge, a result, of their class position, and the emergence of unemployment was a key element in the making of the working class in America.

Even as late as 1870, however, the problem of unemployment attracted little public notice. The lack of a formal name for the phenomenon was a fitting emblem of its place in the official galaxy of economic, social, and political issues. Political energies were focused on other matters, and the state's reformers had just begun to turn their attention away from slavery and toward "the labor question." Like most problems that afflicted the working class, unemployment was, in fact, discovered by the middle-class public long after it had first arrived and only when it became acute. The depression of 1857 had briefly cast a spotlight on the problem, but the economy had recovered quickly and the severity of the downturn seemed to have been an aberration. And during nondepression years, the problem of unemployment was too scattered, too fragmented, to create the kind of disturbance or destitution that would attract public attention: laborers were idled in January and shoemakers in April, textile mill operatives in one year and paper factory employees the next. The problem was simply not explosive enough to make its way onto center stage – not, at least, for a few more years.

But in the tenements of Boston and the company housing of Lowell and Lawrence, in the working-class neighborhoods of a dozen small cities and in the industrial villages sprinkled across the commonwealth, unemployment was already a known and familiar phenomenon. By 1870, Massachusetts had a large and diverse working class, and involuntary idleness had become a common feature of working-class life. Yankee mechanics and Irish day laborers could be laid off on short notice; men and women, the respectably paid and the poorly paid, were all vulnerable to spells of joblessness. The builders of labor unions had twice faced the difficulties of maintaining an organization in the teeth of a depression, and craftsmen in various trades had already watched their jobs vanish as the result of technological change. Throughout the commonwealth, there were people who wanted and needed steadier jobs than they had, people who knew that unemployment – by whatever name – was something that happened to their neighbors, to their relatives, and to them. By 1870, the economic and social order that had given rise to unemployment was solidly in place.

3   *The era of uncertainty*

> In our trade we can't depend on steady employment more than
> nine months in a year. Our average earnings are about $460 per
> annum. A family can subsist on that, but can't live very comfort-
> ably. When wages were reduced there was no promise of steady
> employment. Work is no more regular under the low than under
> high wages. A knitter, 1871

> In my opinion there are too many men employed in these large
> shops. At any rate, in the one where I am employed, there are at
> least one hundred men out of employment now, or will be in the
> course of a month. Now this has happened several times within a
> few years. A pistol maker, 1879

> In last year's inaugural, Mayor O'Brien said that the paving de-
> partment could and should be run on full time. He has not kept
> his word. I and lots of others were loafing nearly all winter, and it
> looks as if we were to do the same this winter.
> Boston Paving Department employee, 1887

> Some people are getting almost crazy for the want of work.
> Daniel J. Sullivan, machinist, Boston, 1894

> Keeping so close to the demands of the market the Lynn manu-
> facturers have seasons of rush work, and when they change from
> the summer styles to the winter wear there is a dull season when
> the operatives have to loaf or go on part time.
> Boston *Evening Transcript*, 1910

> If there is one thing that I have learned on my labor travels, it is
> that the "job's the thing." Wages are interesting, but the job is the
> axis on which the whole world turns for the working man.
> Whiting Williams, *What's on the Worker's Mind*, 1921[1]

During the half-century that followed the Civil War, the United States
became the foremost economic power in the world. The nation's agricultural base continued to expand, its manufacturing industries
grew dramatically, and the pace of commerce was accelerated by new

networks of transportation and communication. Technological advances, coupled with growing markets and entrepreneurial skill, fostered the expansion of old and new industries, while steamships transported millions of immigrants from Europe to the workplaces of the New World. It was during these years – stretching roughly from Reconstruction to the beginning of the Roaring Twenties – that American society became predominantly industrial rather than industrializing, urban rather than urbanizing. The values of a vigorous and triumphant industrial capitalism came to dominate the nation's social and political institutions, and the dialogue of national politics focused increasingly upon the consequences of industrial growth.

During this same period, the problem of unemployment acquired an unprecedented prominence, particularly (but not exclusively) in the more urban, industrial states of the Northeast and Midwest. The depression of the 1870s opened an era in which the involuntary idleness of wage earners began to receive serious and sustained attention in the United States. As noted in Chapter 1, the words "unemployed" and "unemployment" became permanent additions to the American vocabulary during these years, and the unemployed were counted by both state agencies and the national government. With each passing decade, the visibility of the issue mounted until, by the end of the Progressive era, unemployment had become a major item on the nation's list of social problems.[2]

This crescendo of public concern reflected the material conditions of working-class life during a period when the American working class was becoming significantly larger every year. In Massachusetts and elsewhere in the nation, rapid economic growth generated dislocations as well as progress, insecurity as well as wealth, unemployment as well as jobs. In a developed, industrial society, working people had to be employed to earn a living, and the inability of workers to find and keep steady jobs proved to be one of the thorns that accompanied the flowering of industry in the United States.

Growth and dependence

Between the 1870s and the early 1920s, Massachusetts maintained its position as one of the leading industrial regions of the United States. Rapidly developing in directions charted prior to the Civil War, the Bay State relinquished most traces of its preindustrial past, and its society assumed an unmistakably modern tone. The commonwealth acquired thousands of manufacturing firms, buildings with elevators, regulatory commissions, a subway, extensive urban slums, telephones, new colleges and universities, and a decidedly ethnic political culture. It also possessed a social structure in which class boundaries were increasingly visible and salient and in which the industrial working class strengthened its numerical predominance.

One sign of the Bay State's development was the swift increase in its population. The number of inhabitants of Massachusetts rose from 1.5 million in 1875 to 3.5 million in 1915. Much of this increase resulted from immigration: migratory streams that originated in Canada, Ireland, Italy, Poland, and a variety of other nations brought as many as 100,000 new arrivals annually to the shores of the commonwealth. By 1915, there were more than a million persons of foreign birth living in Massachusetts, and a majority of the population consisted of immigrants and their children.[3]

These new immigrants, as well as their Irish predecessors and native Yankee hosts, tended increasingly to inhabit densely populated urban environments. The established cities grew rapidly, new cities emerged where there had once been towns, and the number of persons living in communities with fewer than five thousand residents actually declined between 1875 and 1915. Boston continued to dwarf the state's other cities (by 1915, the Hub had 745,439 inhabitants and most of the amenities of modern urban life, including a mayor named James Michael Curley), but urbanization was not restricted to the capital. At the beginning of World War I six other cities (Worcester, Fall River, New Bedford, Cambridge, Lowell, and Springfield) had populations greater than 100,000, and approximately half the commonwealth's inhabitants lived in communities of at least 50,000 persons. The typical Massachusetts resident had become a city dweller.[4]

These changes in the size, sources, and location of the state's population depended upon and fueled the growth of its economy. Although agriculture, on balance, remained stagnant, the economy expanded vigorously in all other sectors. Between 1875 and 1915, the size of the labor force more than doubled (an addition of nearly a million men and women), and the quantity of goods produced and capital invested rose even more rapidly. Boston continued to be one of the leading financial and commercial centers of the nation, the coastal fisheries remained prosperous, and the pace of trade quickened throughout the state. But the key to this economic growth was the ongoing expansion of manufacturing. By 1915, nearly 800,000 men, women, and children worked in manufactures (an increase of 250% in 40 years), and 12,000 manufacturing firms were producing goods valued at more than 1.6 billion dollars. Between 1915 and 1919, the rate of growth accelerated as a result of the economic exigencies and opportunities presented by World War I.[5]

Both new and old industries shared in this expansion. Well into the twentieth century, the Bay State led the nation in the production of shoes and some lines of textiles; even after competition from other regions had begun to undercut the commonwealth's supremacy, both industries continued to thrive. Output doubled between the 1870s and 1915 (with further increases occurring during the war), and at the end of the Progressive era these two industries together employed nearly a quarter of a million workers. And Massachusetts was not a two-industry state. The paper industry was preeminent in western counties; Worcester County contained numerous plants that produced wire and other metal goods; Attleboro had a prosperous jewelry industry; watches continued to be made in Waltham; and industrial machinery, foundry products, and leather goods were manufactured in a number of locales. After 1880, the Bay State also acquired the largest shipbuilding plant in the northeastern United States, an enormous center for the production of electrical goods in Lynn, and the second-largest rubber industry in the United States. A few key industries remained at the center of its economy, but by the end of the Progressive era the industrial base of Massachusetts was far more diverse – as well as much larger – than it had been a half-century earlier.[6]

Growth in the economy as a whole was matched by the expansion of individual firms. Although the major industries of the commonwealth were relatively resistant to the forces that produced monopolies and mammoth, integrated firms elsewhere in the nation, the trend toward corporate concentration did leave its mark upon the businesses of the Bay State. The number of manufacturing firms increased far less rapidly than did the number of workers (or the amount of capital invested), mergers were common in transportation, and both wholesale and retail trade were conducted by increasingly large enterprises. By the end of World War I, more than 70 percent of the goods manufactured in Massachusetts were being produced by less than 7 percent of its firms.[7]

Accompanying this trend, of course, was an increase in the number of employees attached to each company or workplace. By 1916 the average cotton mill had nearly 700 operatives, roughly 200 men and women worked in each shoe factory and paper mill, and the commonwealth also housed a number of workplaces – such as the General Electric plant in Lynn – where thousands of employees performed their labors simultaneously. Small shops, to be sure, were still plentiful, but in 1914 – even before the wartime expansion and inflation – roughly half of all manufacturing workers were engaged by firms that produced at least 1 million dollars worth of goods. In these larger enterprises, shop discipline was becoming more rigorous, while management simultaneously became more impersonal, more bureaucratic, more hierarchical. Personnel policies were increasingly formalized, tiers of supervisors separated most employees from the men who actually controlled businesses, and – particularly toward the end of the period – decisions over hiring and firing began to be removed from the shop floor (the foreman) and entrusted to specialized bureaus.[8]

This assembly of economic and social changes certainly enhanced the productive power and wealth of the Bay State and its inhabitants. But these same developments also deepened the imprint and extended the reach of the trends that had given birth to the problem of unemployment earlier in the nineteenth century. The dependence of workers upon cash wages and industrial employment was, for example, heightened by the combination of rapid urban growth, massive immigration, and the decline in the relative importance of agriculture. (Cf. Tables 2.1 and 3.1.) Indeed, these changes severed virtually all the remaining links between industrial workers and the land: by 1915 or 1920, few factory operatives or craftsmen had access to the nonmonetary income supplements common in rural settings, and even fewer were able to retreat to a familiar agricultural world when industrial jobs were scarce. Recent immigrants to urban Massachusetts, as well as second- or third-generation industrial workers, had to rely exclusively on their cash wages to obtain the food, shelter, clothing, and fuel that they needed.[9]

The proportion of the labor force that experienced this dependence also mounted steadily, and the absolute numbers rose dramatically. As Table 3.1 indicates, by 1915 more than 1.1 million men and women (roughly two-thirds of the labor force) worked in trade, transportation, and "manufacturing and mechanical industries." The vast majority of these people were employees. On the eve of World War I, there were sixty wage earners for every proprietor of a manufacturing firm, and at least 80 percent of the entire labor force consisted of employees. The industrial sector had become the primary source of income for a growing percentage of families, and the number of employees in the commonwealth had nearly tripled (from a half-million to 1.4 million) in forty years.[10]

Most of these employees were blue-collar workers. Despite the significant increase in clerical (and other white-collar) employment, more than 80 percent of all male employees and more than half of all females performed manual, blue-collar work in 1915. Factory operatives, day laborers, and domestic servants remained far more typical of the wage-earning population than clerks or secretaries. Furthermore, the blue-collar jobs that were available tended increasingly to

Table 3.1. *The distribution of the labor force, Massachusetts, 1915*

	Males[a]		Females[a]	
	Number	Percentage	Number	Percentage
Agriculture, forestry, and animal husbandry	78,781	6.7	604	0.2
Extraction of minerals	2,087	0.2	0	0
Manufacturing and mechanical industries	597,707	50.5	193,800	42.3
Transportation	110,048	9.3	7,407	1.6
Trade	172,644	14.6	28,454	6.2
Public service	40,150	3.4	307	0.1
Professional service	46,123	3.9	48,979	10.7
Domestic and personal service	64,588	5.5	115,666	25.3
Clerical (not classified elsewhere)	71,003	6.0	62,542	13.7
Total	1,183,131	100.0	457,759	100.0

[a]Age fourteen and older.
Source: Census of Massachusetts: 1915 (Boston, 1918), pp. 490–1.

be semiskilled: in many industries, changes in technology and the organization of work were diluting traditional skills and creating employment opportunities only for machine operatives. Knowledge of production processes was often gathered into the hands (or minds) of professional managers and college-trained engineers, while workers were hired only to execute specific tasks with the aid of power-driven machinery. As a result, manual workers in a variety of trades experienced a gradual stripping away of the skills that had once given them some control over the pace of production and a modicum of power in the labor market.[11]

In the final reckoning, of course (as well as in the annual reckonings of hundreds of thousands of households), the dependence of working people upon steady jobs was determined not only by these structural shifts but also by the wages that they received when they were employed. A semiskilled employee who earned enough in a week to permit his family to live comfortably for a month would certainly have enjoyed considerable independence of the employers in his trade. But such amply rewarded workers simply did not exist in

Massachusetts – although wage levels varied considerably within its working class. In the late nineteenth century, the most skilled workmen (such as masons, stationary engineers, plumbers, and marble cutters) were paid between fifteen and twenty dollars a week, and some other tradesmen (carpenters, blacksmiths, cabinetmakers, printers, machinists) earned only slightly less. Factory operatives, however, brought home much thinner pay envelopes: half of all male shoe workers earned less than twelve dollars a week, while paper mill operatives, leather workers, and rubber factory employees received even smaller wages. Near the bottom of the scale were textile operatives, who typically earned about nine dollars for a week's work, and laborers, hod carriers, and teamsters, who were commonly paid $1.50 per day. Wages for women also varied from one occupation to another, but ordinarily they were located near the lower end of the earnings spectrum.[12]

What such dollar figures meant was that the material texture of working-class life ranged from simple decency and modest comfort to outright poverty, with most working-class families living somewhere between these two poles. "It takes about all that we earn to live," observed a carpenter, William B. Adams, in the 1890s. "None of us save any amount of money to speak of."[13] A survey of household budgets in the Bay State in 1885 revealed that, among families that earned between $600 and $700 per year (which was well above the mean), 94 percent of all income was expended for food, clothing, rent, and fuel. The best-paid workers (if they were employed steadily) could certainly maintain their families respectably, but most workingmen did little more than keep themselves afloat, and many were not paid enough to support a family at all. A sizable number of working-class families did, to be sure, have more than one wage earner, but the labor force participation of children and married women (which violated the prevailing social norm of the household supported by an adult, male breadwinner) was a sign of material scarcity rather than a source of monetary abundance. The small yet critical sums brought home by women and children to households headed by factory operatives or day laborers rarely lifted working-class families much above self-sufficiency.[14]

Working-class incomes did increase between the 1870s and 1920. Real earnings for industrial workers rose throughout the deflationary years of the late nineteenth century, and after 1897 both prices and wages climbed upward, culminating in the inflationary boom of World War I. Progress was uneven and unsteady (the cost of living sometimes moved upward more rapidly and downward more slowly than did wages), but workers in most occupations had higher real

incomes at the end of World War I than they had had at the end of
the Civil War. Nonetheless, few working-class families moved into
income brackets that permitted luxuries, careless expenditures, or
much time off from work. Budgetary surveys conducted in 1901 and
1902 revealed that almost all working-class income was expended on
necessities. Similarly, a 1908 U.S. Bureau of Labor Statistics investigation of Fall River concluded that the maintenance of a "fair" standard of living required an annual income of $700, which was more
than most manufacturing workers earned. And even this fair standard of living would not have permitted a household head to save
any money, to provide for old age, or to allow his children to attend
high school.[15]

Diverse as working-class life was, thus, virtually all industrial
workers, throughout this period, shared the need for steady employment and regular incomes. The world of the manual worker included
families that resided in "trim, comfortable cottages" that "betoken a
state of modest comfort" and families that inhabited squalid, over-
crowded tenements. It encompassed both the households of textile
operatives where everyone over the age of ten had to enter the mills
and households headed by skilled machinists or masons who could
ordinarily support their wives and children with their own labor.[16]
Living standards varied, but, in order to maintain or improve upon
their own particular circumstances, workers had to maximize the
number of days and weeks that they were remuneratively employed.[17] The economic growth that had transformed most of the
state's residents into seekers of employment did not provide pecuni-
ary rewards abundant enough to lessen their dependence on having
steady jobs. For most workers there was precious little margin between weekly earnings and necessary weekly expenditures – which
was why, as Whiting Williams pointed out, "the job" was the "axis
on which the whole world turned" for working people.

The economic changes that occurred between the 1870s and the
1920s did, of course, bring substantial wealth to some residents of the
commonwealth and enhanced material comfort to many. Thousands
of individuals rode the waves of economic expansion to positions of
success and security, to membership in a growing middle class. But
for a majority of the state's inhabitants, dependence lurked in the
shadow of opportunity. The structure of economic development enlarged the size of the working class while simultaneously restricting
the ability of workers to provide for themselves by any means other
than selling their labor. The Commonwealth of Massachusetts moved
into the twentieth century with an increasingly complex, industrial
economy and with a working population that was utterly reliant

upon the prosperity of industry for its own advancement and well-being.

Panics and depressions

Unfortunately for working people, prosperity was not something that could be counted on between 1870 and 1920. At least once in the course of each decade, there occurred a wave of bank and business failures, the engines of progress coughed and sputtered, wages dropped, and some men and women were "thrown out of work." In the nineteenth century (until 1908, in fact) such episodes were referred to as "panics" or "crises," and they were commonly viewed as extraordinary, if disturbing, departures from the prosperous norm. But gradually the recurrence of these aberrations gave birth to the recognition that there was a cyclical component to the behavior of capitalist economies: surges in business activity were inexorably followed by slowdowns, booms by recessions, spells of new investment by spells of entrepreneurial caution. By the 1920s the undulations themselves had come to be viewed as normal, and the concept of the business cycle had supplanted the more dramatic image of the panic. This shift in understanding was ultimately to have a profound influence upon economic policy in the United States and elsewhere in the Western world. But it was little consolation to the men and women who rode the economic roller coaster of the late nineteenth and early twentieth centuries.[18]

Indeed, a man who was seventy years old in 1921 had experienced six major cyclical downturns in the course of his adult life. The first of these was the prolonged depression that began in 1873 and lingered until 1879; the second, which was less severe, lasted from 1882 until 1885. A decade later, the nation faced the sharp double-dipped depression that began in the summer of 1893, eased in late 1894 and 1895, and then resumed its downward course until June 1897. In 1907, levels of economic activity once again plummeted rapidly, if briefly (the downturn was over by the end of 1908), and 1913 witnessed the beginning of yet another sharp decline in business. World War I contributed to a great expansion in business activity, but the wartime boom was followed by a deep postwar depression that began in 1920 and bottomed out in the summer of 1921. These "major" cyclical downturns were accompanied by a comparable number of "minor," less pronounced declines in the economy. In all, the business cycle rose and fell thirteen times between 1870 and 1921; roughly two out of every five years contained periods of recession or depression.[19]

No two of these downturns – even the major downturns – were exactly alike. The contractions of the 1890s and 1920s were the most severe, while those of the 1870s and 1880s were the longest in duration. And some business downturns had a proportionately greater impact upon prices than they had upon output and employment. Nonetheless, each depression was characterized by a general slackening of business activity, by a decline in production, prices, wages, and employment. Not all industries were affected equally (makers of producers' goods, for example, tended to be harder hit than makers of perishable consumer products, like food and cigars), but the pinch of hard times was widely felt. The collapse of one bank or firm often led to the collapse of others; stagnation, for a time at least, bred more stagnation. As Thomas Murphy of the Horse Shoers' Union of Roxbury observed in 1894, "If business isn't good, horses stay in the stables and consequently don't wear out their shoes."[20]

For employers, managers, and entrepreneurs, these incessant fluctuations in economic conditions were both a challenge and a scourge. "We have been through all stages of trials since 1849," noted an official of the Emerson Piano Company in 1914. In most industries, business was fiercely competitive, and the vicissitudes of the business cycle demanded a steady stream of important managerial decisions. Depressions, by reducing the demand for a company's goods or services, threatened profits and even the existence of individual firms. Some businessmen responded to this threat by cutting prices in the hope of stimulating demand; others, in manufacturing at least, tried to produce for inventory – if style changes were not an issue and if fluctuations in the cost of credit and raw materials permitted the gamble. But most businesses (even those that also tried price cutting and producing for inventory) eventually responded to cyclical downturns by reducing their labor costs. Exactly how an individual entrepreneur reacted to a particular depression depended, of course, upon a great many different factors, but labor costs were almost always a flexible element in the economic calculus, and "cutting back" was a prudent method of weathering depressions and even salvaging a profit.[21]

Each employer or manager had a choice of several different, but not mutually exclusive, strategies for reducing the cost of labor. One was simply to lower wages, and depressions invariably launched an epidemic of wage cuts. But there were limits to the strategic value of wage reductions and the price cuts that normally accompanied them. One such limit was that workers were sometimes troublesomely reluctant to accept lower wages. In 1886, for example, the employees of Francis Breed's shoe manufacturing firm in Lynn were told that "if you are willing to take less, you can have steady work. If not you can get. We got." And even if their workers were more malleable than Breed's employees, many businessmen tended to fear the long-term implications of price wars, while others were unable to peddle their wares in the teeth of a depression no matter how cheaply they were produced.[22]

Employers, therefore, often turned to a second method of reducing costs: running their enterprises on "short time," which meant reducing output and limiting the number of hours or days that each employee worked. (The meaning of the phrase "short time" appears to have shifted during this period: in the 1880s, it referred to plants that shut down at some point during the year, but by 1910 the phrase was commonly used in reference to employees who were working fewer days or hours per week than normal, while their plants were running.) During depressions factories often operated three or four days a week, with everyone working a few days less than usual. One virtue of short time (a virtue particularly compelling to employers located in rural areas or dependent upon workers with unusual skills) was that it served to guarantee the availability of labor when business rebounded. A second was that it helped prevent hardship by providing everyone with some income, a value not unimportant to many businessmen. "Down in our factory, we divided up the work so that all could get something to do," claimed one shoe manufacturer in the 1890s. Employees of firms such as Reed and Barton in Taunton or the Whitin Machine Works in Whitinsville customarily worked part-time during depressions.[23]

But many managers and owners found short time to be unwieldy, unprofitable, or simply unnecessary. They restricted their output and cut their costs by discharging employees or by closing their shops altogether for a period of weeks or months. "Owing to the general depression in business," reported an officer of the Plymouth Cordage Company to his superior in 1921, "we have found it necessary to curtail our output. This has been done to the extent of . . . discharging a portion of our night force, we have also made some reduction in our day force." The matter-of-fact tone reflected the conventional nature of the decision: "reducing force" or laying off workers was a routine step in the conduct of business in a depressed economy.[24]

Layoff decisions made by individual firms did not, of course, necessarily result in unemployment: as William Beveridge aptly observed early in the twentieth century, "The cause of a man's being unemployed is not that which led him to lose his last job but that which prevents him from getting another job." But under depression conditions, when hundreds, even thousands, of firms were simultaneously cutting their payrolls, being laid off often was tantamount to being involuntarily idled. Most men and women were prevented from getting new jobs by the same forces that had severed them from their old jobs: the condition of the economy itself and the widespread readiness of employers to respond to economic downturns by producing less and hiring fewer people. That readiness, indeed, was rooted in the assumption that workers who were laid off would not easily find jobs and would consequently be available when their services were needed – an assumption that proved to be very well founded, as working people repeatedly discovered.[25]

During each of the six major downturns that occurred between 1870 and 1922, a substantial portion of the commonwealth's labor force was, in fact, unemployed. Despite Carroll Wright's pioneering efforts, no reliable unemployment statistics were collected in the 1870s, but the Massachusetts state censuses of 1885 and 1895 did register the incidence of joblessness during the last two depressions of the nineteenth century. Although neither of these statistical snapshots captured the worst economic conditions of the era, they reveal that unemployment levels were high even when the business cycle was not at its absolute nadir. As Table 3.2 indicates, roughly 240,000 men and women experienced some unemployment during the census year that ended May 1, 1885. The toll was similar in 1895 when the period covered by the census survey happened to overlap with the brief upswing in business conditions that bridged the two troughs of that decade's depression.[26]

In both 1885 and 1895, the annual unemployment *rate* (indicating the average proportion of the labor force that was idled at any one time) was in the vicinity of 8 to 10 percent. But the *frequency* of unemployment (the percentage of labor force members who were unemployed at some point during the year) was close to 30 percent. And from the viewpoint of workers, it was the frequency that was the more meaningful statistic – since it revealed the likelihood of their becoming unemployed. Nearly one out of every three members of the labor force was laid off during the census years of 1885 and 1895. Of equal importance, for workers, was the mean duration of unemployment. In 1885, the average jobless worker remained idle for four months; ten years later, the figure was slightly greater than three months.[27]

These statistics, coupled with both impressionistic evidence and other (less direct or less extensive) quantitative indicators, suggest that upwards of 40 percent of all Massachusetts workers were unemployed in the course of the most depressed years of the late nineteenth century. An 1875 survey of the economic welfare of 50,000 Bay

Table 3.2. Unemployment levels in Massachusetts, 1885–1900

Year ending[a]	Number unemployed	Unemployment frequency(%)	Mean duration (mo.)	Annual unemployment rate (%)	Percentage of unemployed who were jobless for:[b]		
					1–3 mo.	4–6 mo.	7–12 mo.
May 1, 1885							
Males	178,628	29.6	4.2	10.4	42.5	47.0	10.5
Females	62,961	29.6	3.9	9.6	53.0	35.7	11.3
May 31, 1890							
Males	136,374	19.0	3.3[c]	5.2	57.1	32.8	10.1
Females	43,088	16.4	3.3	4.5	60.0	28.2	11.8
April 30, 1895							
Males } Females	260,795	28.2	3.3	7.8	—	—	—
May 31, 1900							
Males	175,777	20.0	3.8[c]	6.3	48.3	35.7	16.1
Females	65,389	19.9	3.8	6.3	51.2	31.1	17.6

[a]See Appendix B regarding the census surveys and changes that occurred in methods of counting the unemployed.
[b]Dashes indicate that no data are available.
[c]Estimated mean from census data. See Appendix B.

Sources: Massachusetts Bureau of Statistics of Labor [hereafter MBSL], *Eighteenth Annual Report* [hereafter in the form *18 AR*] (Boston, 1887), pp. 156, 216, 218; *Eleventh U.S. Census, Population*, part II (Washington, 1897), pp. 568–9; *Census of Massachusetts: 1895*, VII (Boston, 1900), pp. 90–1, 102–3; *Twelfth U.S. Census, Occupations* (Washington, 1904), pp. 300-7.

State wage earners suggested that the unemployment *rate* in the middle of that depression exceeded 15 percent; in 1878, two-thirds of the 230 respondents to an official questionnaire reported that they had been jobless during the previous year, for an average of 100 days per person. Informed estimates for the worst years of the 1890s suggest that the national unemployment rate (for nonagricultural workers) surpassed 15 percent, and contemporary reports from Massachusetts manufacturers reveal that layoffs were much more common in 1893 and 1896 than during the census year of 1895. Precise figures cannot be extracted from such data, but it seems likely that, during the depths of the depressions of the 1870s and 1890s, the frequency of unemployment was well above 30 percent. And the average jobless worker was probably idle for more than four months.[28]

After the turn of the century, major downturns in the business cycle tended to be shorter but comparably severe in impact. Unfortunately for historians, both state and federal officials ceased compiling unemployment statistics from the census after 1900. But in 1908 the Massachusetts Bureau of Statistics of Labor, once again spurred into action by a depression, began to calculate quarterly unemployment rates from data provided by trade unionists. These statistics did not accurately reflect the extent of unemployment in the labor force as a whole, but they do offer a reasonable gauge of idleness levels among workers in "manufacturing and mechanical industries."[29] And, as Table 3.3 indicates, a third or more of these workers were unemployed during the depressions of 1908, 1914, and 1920–22. Only the postwar downturn, when the annual unemployment frequency exceeded 50 percent, seems to have matched the stagnation of the worst years of the 1870s and 1890s. But even during the more mild crises of 1908 and 1914, a hefty proportion of all trade unionists found it impossible to find a full year's work. The growth of the labor force, moreover, meant that the number of workers represented by such percentages rose considerably between the 1870s and the 1920s. A conservative extrapolation of the trade union statistics would suggest that roughly 450,000 Massachusetts residents experienced some unemployment in 1914.[30]

The workers who joined the ranks of the unemployed during these depressions were drawn from many industries and occupations. In 1885, the year for which the most detailed data are available, male workers in seventy-five occupations had to contend with unemployment frequencies greater than 30 percent; in fifty of those occupations more than 40 percent of all men were involuntarily idled. (The patterns for women were in many respects the same, but since women – who constituted roughly one-quarter of the paid labor force

Table 3.3. *Unemployment among trade union members in Massachusetts,
1908–22*

Year	Average no. of members reporting	Annual unemployment rate (%)[a]		Estimated unemployment frequency(%)[b]
		"All causes"	"Lack of work"	
1908	81,673	14.2	12.1	36.8
1909	108,039	8.0	5.6	22.3
1910	120,083	7.5	5.5	20.6
1911	129,057	8.1	5.4	21.9
1912	154,449	8.3	4.5	17.1
1913	174,691	8.7	5.8	22.3
1914	172,277	13.0	9.9	32.0
1915	169,547	10.7	7.0	26.7
1916	176,012	5.7	2.5	11.0
1917	189,113	7.2	3.4	15.1
1918	222,334	6.1	2.6	11.0
1919	259,027	7.5	5.1	18.5
1920	270,228	19.7	15.6	43.5
1921	231,734	26.5	21.0	57.9
1922	220,879	18.0	10.8	34.5

[a]Average of 4 quarterly figures. The meaning of the 2 different rates (and the
difference between them) is discussed in Appendix B.
[b]Estimates based on the conversion (of rate into frequency) formula presented in Appendix B. The rate utilized includes all unemployment due to
"lack of work" and "unfavorable weather" and one-half of the unemployment resulting from "other causes." See Appendix B.
Sources: MBSL, *49 AR* (Boston, 1919), part IV, pp. 28–30; MBSL, *Labor Bulletin
of the Commonwealth of Massachusetts no. 135* [hereafter in the form *Bulletin 135*]
(Boston, 1921), pp. 33–5; MBSL, *Bulletin 140* (Boston, 1923), pp. 18–21.

– tended to have different work histories and potentially different expectations regarding continuous employment, the occupational distribution of unemployment for women is treated separately in Chapter 4.) Similarly, in 1895, Boston's building tradesmen, Fall River's
cotton mill operatives, and shoe workers in Lynn, Brockton, and
Haverhill all experienced unemployment frequencies above 35 percent. And each of the three twentieth-century depressions produced
double-digit unemployment rates (and thus frequencies of 30%, 40%,
and even 50%) for unionists in dozens of occupations.[31] (See Appendix A, Tables A.1, A.3, A.5.)

That unemployment levels were high in many trades did not mean,
however, that the burden of involuntary idleness was evenly shared
among all members of the labor force. In 1885, the odds of a shoemaker becoming unemployed – to cite an extreme case – were

roughly ten times greater than the odds of a salesman becoming jobless.[32] Indeed, throughout this period, blue-collar workers as a whole were far more likely to be idled than were men who held white-collar jobs, even white-collar jobs of the least exalted kind. Every one of the occupations that had above-average unemployment frequencies in 1885 involved the performance of manual labor, while virtually all white-collar jobs seemed to promise steady employment. (See Appendix A, Table A.1.) White-collar workers who did have the misfortune of being laid off tended to remain idle for relatively long spells, but working with a pencil rather than a wrench was an unmistakable emblem of job security.[33]

Among blue-collar workers also, there were significant differences in unemployment levels during each depression. In 1894, a carpenter from West Newton reported that 500 of the 600 carpenters in his area had been "out of employment for one month to four," while a representative of the newspaper stereotypers' union noted that in his trade there were few idle workmen and that "employment is about as steady one year as another."[34] The statistical record amply, if colorlessly, confirms the thrust of this verbal testimony. Overall, there was considerably more unemployment in manufacturing and construction than there was in transportation or trade, but, as Tables A.1, A.3, and A.5 indicate, much depended upon the specific occupation to which a man belonged.[35] The workers most frequently unemployed during depressions were those in the building trades, in the shoe, clothing, rubber, and textile industries, and day laborers and longshoremen. Machinists, metal workers, teamsters, and paper mill operatives were somewhat less vulnerable to cyclical downturns, while printers, cigarmakers, and employees in the food and railway industries worked fairly steadily during bad years as well as good ones. Men who belonged to different trades also tended to remain jobless for varying lengths of time. Differences in the mean duration of unemployment were relatively small in magnitude, but even slight contrasts were surely of some moment to many individuals. In 1885 longshoremen and day laborers might well have envied the shoe factory operatives who averaged "only" 3.9 (rather than 4.7 or 4.8) months of involuntary idleness.[36]

There was, however, surprisingly little relationship between the degree of skill demanded by a man's job and the odds of his ending up out of work. In certain plants, to be sure, the most skilled workers (machinists, loom-fixers, engineers, foremen) were less likely to be laid off than were operatives; similarly, in the building trades, laborers and helpers were sometimes let go while more skilled tradesmen were still drawing their pay. But, on the whole, depressions had little respect for the boundaries that separated skilled from unskilled workers.[37] The organization of production in most industries was such that slowdowns had a proportional impact on all departments and branches, and few manual workers possessed skills so rare or valuable that employers felt obliged to keep them on the payroll when business was slack. As George H. Wrenn, the president of Springfield's Central Labor Union observed in 1915, "The reason a greater number of unskilled than skilled laborers are out of work is because the proportion of unskilled to skilled is greater. It does not mean that employers are discharging the unskilled and keeping the skilled." Tables A.1, A.3, and A.5 support Wrenn's observation: during each major cyclical downturn there were some skilled, semi-skilled, and unskilled workers who had to contend with relatively high unemployment frequencies while others – who fit the same descriptions – were far more likely to work steadily. The most unskilled workmen in the commonwealth probably did have the most difficult time securing jobs, but they did not pound the pavements by themselves. In Springfield in 1915 they were joined by "a great many machinists, competent workers who are going around begging for work."[38]

Coexisting with these patterns in the distribution of unemployment were countless unpredictable events, seemingly random developments, variations in the experiences of men who worked for different employers or in different branches of an industry. The incidence of joblessness during depressions was always checkered, erratic, variegated. "What is a loafing period in one factory is not in another," observed Michael Moran, a shoe worker from Brockton, in 1894. Textile mill operatives from Lawrence and Fall River would certainly have agreed with Moran – since more than 80 percent of the operatives in Lawrence labored steadily in 1894–5, while a comparable percentage were laid off in Fall River. Economic stagnation tended to filter through rather than blanket the state, and the currents of depression never followed a straight and narrow course.[39]

They also never followed exactly the same path twice. Since no iron laws governed the behavior of depressions, each crisis left its own particular imprint on the labor force. Compared to other factory workers, paper mill operatives were employed rather steadily in 1885 and 1895, but they did not fare nearly as well in 1908 or 1920. Carpenters confronted much higher unemployment rates in 1914 than they had in 1908, while masons had precisely the opposite experience. Uncertainty and unpredictability were as characteristic of depressions as were business failures and unemployment.[40]

Cyclical downturns in the economy, thus, had an uneven yet extremely widespread impact upon working men – and, as is discussed in detail in Chapter 4, upon working women as well. The burden of unemployment was shouldered largely by employees who performed manual labor, and the vast majority of blue-collar workers belonged to occupations in which the incidence of joblessness during depressions was far from negligible. Each decade, panics and crises produced spells of unemployment for more than a third of all employees and an even higher proportion of industrial workers. In all likelihood, those depressions that persisted for two years or more generated prolonged stints of idleness for half the workers in the state.[41] Although most working people were not laid off during each and every depression, the consequences of business stagnation were sufficiently far-reaching to threaten the well-being of the entire working class.[42]

Workers, of course, were not alone in suffering losses during downturns in the business cycle. The effects of major depressions were felt by storekeepers and peddlers, by professionals, managers, and entrepreneurs; many businesses had reduced earnings, and some went bankrupt altogether. Still, it was not unusual for firms, particularly large firms, to continue paying substantial dividends to their stockholders while they reduced wages, output, and employment. The depression-era strategies adopted by businesses were commonly designed to preserve profits rather than, and sometimes at the expense of, jobs. Moreover, those firms that did experience temporary reverses during panics were often able to recoup their losses with the return of prosperity. As the U.S. Commission on Industrial Relations pointed out in 1915, business calculated a "fair return" on its investment by the year rather than by the week, and "capital," unlike labor, could "offset the fat years against the lean" without suffering hardship or deterioration. During "fat years," indeed, firms in Massachusetts and elsewhere commonly sought to maximize their profits by investing in new facilities and enlarging their productive capacity, a strategy that both brought in additional revenues and increased the likelihood of having to lay workers off when the tempo of trade slackened. Faced with unpredictable fluctuations in demand, fierce competition, and rapidly expanding markets, businessmen navigated among the crests and troughs of the business cycle with maneuvers that maintained the buoyancy of their own enterprises and translated the uncertainties of industrial capitalism into unsteady work for the men and women that they employed.[43]

As the final decades of the nineteenth century gave way to the first decades of the twentieth, the visible signs of depression became grimly familiar to the people of Massachusetts. Downturns in the economy were social and public occurrences, and, during the half-century that began in 1870, the public features of economic stagnation became more recognizable with each passing decade. Noisy plants grew silent for days, weeks, or months at a time. Adult men congregated on streets where adult men had been seen only on Sundays and after dusk. Newspapers carried small notices about the decline of trade, while charity organizations recorded a brisk upturn in activity. Strangers moved into town, neighbors moved out, and rumors of available jobs brought hundreds of workers to the gates of individual factories. During the final decades of the nineteenth century, the recurrence of such scenes was for many Americans a source of anxiety and apocalyptic visions. The utopian novels of Edward Bellamy and William Dean Howells, as well as the political rhetoric of Ignatius Donnelly and Terence Powderly, struck a resonant chord in men and women who feared that the economy was both uncontrolled and uncontrollable and that the succession of crises was a sign of impending disaster.

After the turn of the century, these fears seemed to subside a bit. The very familiarity of depressions rendered them less frightening: experience had demonstrated that business would, sooner or later, revive. But even for the pragmatic citizens of the twentieth century, depressions were benchmarks in their own careers, boundaries in the passage of time. Memories of severe downturns were vivid, and each depression brought forth a host of references – from workers, businessmen, public officials, and charitable agencies – to the depressions that had preceded it. Time was measured by the season and by the year and also by the movements of the business cycle.[44]

Idleness in good times

Difficult as depressions were, many workers would have considered themselves blessed with good fortune had their spells of unemployment been confined to major economic downturns. Although the spotlight of public attention was focused on the problem of unemployment only during serious slumps in business, a significant proportion of the state's working people had to contend with the problem year in and year out. One of the key findings of the investigations of unemployment prompted by the depressions of the late nineteenth century was that involuntary idleness was not exclusively a depression phenomenon. Efforts to count the unemployed were invariably precipitated by depressions, but they generally continued into prosperous years, revealing that workers often had great difficulty locating steady jobs even during "a normal period of activity, that is when business is good."[45]

As Table 3.2 indicates, roughly 20 percent of the Massachusetts labor force experienced some unemployment during the census years of 1890 and 1900; in each of these relatively prosperous years the average unemployed person was idle for three to four months. Similar difficulties confronted the trade unionists whose unemployment was measured after 1907. The rather conservative estimates presented in Table 3.3 reveal that, except in wartime, approximately one-fifth of all union members were unemployed during every non-depression year between 1908 and 1922.[46] Although such figures were startling to some contemporaries, their validity was confirmed by a host of other sources. "More than one-quarter of the persons engaged in productive industry in the Commonwealth" were "irregularly employed," acknowledged the Massachusetts Bureau of Statistics of Labor early in the twentieth century.[47] Even when the clouds of business stagnation were not hovering over the commonwealth, hundreds of thousands of working people were unable to find a full year's work.[48]

In good years, as in depressions, those men who were unemployed were drawn from a wide range of blue-collar trades.[49] In 1900, for example, men who belonged to nearly forty working-class occupations encountered unemployment frequencies that exceeded the statewide average of 20 percent. White-collar joblessness was a rarity when the economy was purring smoothly, but there were numerous blue-collar trades in which the incidence of unemployment was consistently greater than 30 or even 40 percent.[50] (See Tables A.2, A.4, A.5, A.6.) This was true for shoe factory operatives, laborers, stonecutters, rubber factory workers, fishermen, and many building tradesmen and garment workers. An additional group of workers, including textile and paper mill operatives, iron- and steelworkers, and cabinetmakers, confronted idleness levels that were more moderate yet still considerable: roughly 20 percent of these men were laid off during prosperous years. And those who were idled lost an average of three months' work.[51] To be sure, steady work did accompany prosperity for many men, including some blue-collar workers: in 1900, a happy third of all males faced unemployment frequencies, in their occupations, of less than 10 percent.[52] But a majority of the working class (encompassing skilled, semiskilled, and unskilled workers) found that the threat of unemployment remained palpable even when business was good.[53]

The uncertainty generated by this chronic unemployment was heightened by the changes continuously occurring within individual occupations. Even when economic conditions remained relatively stable, unemployment frequencies in many trades bobbed up and down with stunning irregularity. Between 1909 and 1912, the annual unemployment rate for boilermakers twice fell and rose quite sharply; in 1911, unemployment rates rose for building tradesmen, while they fell for machinists, shoemakers, and garment workers. (See Table A.5.) Every occupation tended to have a characteristic prosperity-era range of unemployment levels, but shifts within this range were commonplace, and there were occasional moments when jobs became uncharacteristically scarce or abundant. Even when the economy was not being rocked by a panic, few workers could confidently expect that the employment patterns of one year would be replicated the next.[54]

What all these statistics registered was a harsh, yet immensely significant, truth about working-class life between the 1870s and the early 1920s: employment was chronically unsteady, and every year hundreds of thousands of workers went two, three, or four months without working and without being paid. Unemployment frequency statistics reveal a dimension of labor history obscured by more conventional unemployment "rates." During prosperous years the proportion of working people who were simultaneously unemployed may well have averaged only about 6 percent, but one-fifth of the labor force (and an even higher proportion of the working class) experienced some unemployment. And those men who were jobless when the economy was expanding were not marginal members of marginal occupations. A group portrait of the unemployed in 1900 would have closely resembled a thinned-out, scaled-down portrait of the unemployed during the worst years of the 1890s. For many workers, insecure and irregular employment was as much a part of daily life as low wages and overcrowded housing. "Evidence is too clear," concluded the pathbreaking Massachusetts Board to Investigate the Subject of the Unemployed in 1895, "that even in so-called normal times there is an amount of non-employment which occasions suffering."[55]

The sources of this chronic "non-employment" were diverse and often overlapping. Some involuntary idleness stemmed from uncontrollable or unpredictable acts of nature. Fires were not uncommon events, and major factories (or even manufacturing districts) were destroyed by fire in Boston in 1872 and 1893, Haverhill in 1882, Lynn in 1889, Brockton in 1887 and 1905, and Salem in 1914 – the last of which left 4,500 operatives idle in the midst of a depression. Similarly, the collapse of a dam near Northampton in 1874 wiped out numerous workplaces, and droughts, floods, and frozen rivers periodically closed mills and factories throughout the state. In addition to these episodic calamities, the annual rhythms of the New England climate recurrently disrupted work and employment in some occupations. Agricultural labor could be performed only in certain seasons, outdoor work in several of the building trades was close to impossible in winter, and there was simply no ice to be chopped on the rivers and reservoirs in July and August.[56]

But most of the unemployment that afflicted the workers of Massachusetts was rooted in economic rather than natural developments, in the organization of production rather than the demands of the climate. Businesses failed in good years as well as in depressions, and each time that a firm failed, some workers were idled for a spell before they found new jobs. The collapse of several bicycle manufacturing firms in Chicopee at the turn of the century left many employees jobless; the failure of the Boston Piano Company in 1900 produced long-term unemployment for a number of skilled craftsmen.[57] Other workers lost their jobs when firms relocated their plants (e.g., the departure of *Good Housekeeping* magazine from Springfield) or when the introduction of new machinery permitted an employer to carry on his business with fewer employees. In the 1880s, the use of a new machine to cut rags idled 200 employees in Holyoke's paper industry, while the development of a new process of putting Roman numerals on watch dials threw "out of employment a large number of skilled workmen" in Waltham. Economic changes that reflected either the success or failure of individual firms were capable of dislocating workers and creating involuntary idleness.[58]

Most commonly, however, unemployment resulted not from "events" like bankruptcies or relocations but from business practices designed to cope with fluctuations in the demand for specific goods and services. Virtually all firms occasionally confronted a drooping demand for their products, and the markets for many of the goods manufactured in Massachusetts were highly seasonal. The demand for coal deliveries and candy tended to peak during the winter, while the heat of summer increased the consumption of beer and soap ("for obvious reasons," according to an official of Lever Brothers). Sales of shoes and clothing had sharply seasonal rhythms, which became more pronounced as annual style changes came to dominate consumption patterns and to discourage advance purchasing. Fluctuations in demand also affected the manufacture of some producers' goods. Firms that manufactured materials for the construction industry, ranging from bricks to elevators, had busy and slack seasons, and the same was true for companies that were linked to the shoe, garment, or brewing industries. The demand for leather and rubber, to cite two examples of prominent Massachusetts industries, came largely from shoe manufacturers.[59]

But fluctuations in demand did not necessarily – or by themselves – have to generate irregular rhythms of production and employment. With the exception of some outdoor trades and the manufacture of perishable goods, there were no absolute, environmental obstacles to steady production or to the buildup of inventories during seasons when sales were slack.[60] But there were important business considerations involved in the pacing of economic activity, and many manufacturers, faced with competitive and fluid market conditions, found it to be more profitable to produce "close to the market" than to "run steady." By the final decades of the nineteenth century firms in many industries had ceased producing for inventory and insisted on having orders in hand before commencing production. In the 1890s shoe workers complained bitterly that "manufacturers no longer made a steady quantity from week to week, against a probable demand." Twenty years later, a report commissioned by the Boston Chamber of Commerce concluded that the "irregularity" of economic activity was heightened by the "tendency in practically all lines of business to produce much closer to the market."[61] Whenever possible, firms (particularly in competitive industries) sought to avoid the risk of misjudging the market and the cost of accumulating inventories by producing only at the last minute, by allowing the rhythms of demand to set the rhythms of production. Their ability to do so was enhanced by technological advances. Although in some instances the introduction of new equipment encouraged steadier production, in others the presence of faster, more efficient machinery made it easier for employers to respond to rush orders, to produce sizable quantities of goods in a short span of time. This latter trend was epitomized in shoe manufacturing, where firms did not tie up their capital in the purchase of machinery but rather paid a royalty on each pair of shoes that they produced. Employers consequently had little incentive to run their machinery steadily rather than producing "close to the market."[62]

Whatever their financial circumstances and technological capabilities, employers were able to maintain irregular rhythms of production and to lay workers off during slow times only because they knew, or believed, that even in prosperous years labor would be available when it was needed. Had manufacturers been constrained by any real or perceived scarcity of labor, by the fear that workers would be in short supply when the busy season came around, they would have been obliged to develop different strategies for coping with fluctuating markets. Some companies, particularly in rural areas, did try to run steadily for just this reason, and others, as noted earlier in this chapter, kept their workers on short time when demand was slack. But on the whole the behavior of Bay State employers reflected the assumption that labor would be available whatever the condition of the economy. Early in the twentieth century, one manufacturer reported to the Boston Chamber of Commerce that he regarded all his employees as "permanent," although he reduced his payroll from 800 to 500 workers in the course of each year. Similarly, when the superintendent of streets in Brockton was asked the size of his permanent work force in the 1890s, he replied, "We hire men when we want them. We have no permanent force." There was nothing problematic about laying off employees or about finding new workers when they were needed. The availability of labor influenced the nature of the demand for labor which, in turn, affected the supply. The relationship between supply and demand was both dynamic and dialectical, and the perception that labor was abundant was a source, as well as a reflection, of the chronic unemployment in the commonwealth.[63]

For workers, the diversity in the sources of involuntary idleness meant that there was also considerable diversity in the cadences with which unemployment interrupted their wage earning. At least four distinctive cadences, in addition to the movements of the business cycle, can be discerned. The first was episodic: some spells of unemployment began suddenly, with little or no forewarning, but were unlikely to be repeated. When a fire occurred or a firm went bankrupt, employees were unexpectedly tossed out of their jobs and often spent weeks or even months looking for work. But their idleness was a one-shot occurrence – unless, of course, they had the misfortune of joining another firm that moved, burned, or went under. At the opposite end of the spectrum were the experiences of men whose jobs were "casual," who were always employed temporarily and for relatively brief stints. Day laborers and longshoremen, as well as some building tradesmen, rarely worked very long at any one job or for any single employer, and they were often idle between engagements. On the docks of East Boston or at construction sites throughout the commonwealth, intermittent unemployment was a way of life.[64]

Most of the unemployment that occurred in nondepression years had a seasonal cadence. In the labor force as a whole, there was always more idleness in winter than in the spring, summer, or autumn. Unemployment levels rose sharply during the winter for many building tradesmen, as well as for stonecutters, quarrymen, agricultural laborers, and fishermen. However, upholsterers, theater employees, carriage makers, and rubber factory operatives were most commonly idled in summer; paper mill employees had to contend with a slack season early in the fall; and workers in the shoe industry faced very pronounced slow seasons in the spring and, in some branches of the trade, again in the autumn. Garment workers also had two slack seasons and two busy seasons. "We generally reckon six months steady work and six months what we can get," explained a tailor in the 1890s. Seasonal employment rhythms were themselves diverse, but virtually all occupations that had chronically high levels of unemployment had at least one slow season at some point during the year.[65]

For the men (and women) who belonged to these seasonal trades, the working year was commonly composed of alternating spells of hectic activity and idleness or underemployment. Months when all members of a trade labored for sixty hours a week were followed by months when jobs were scarce. T. T. Pomeroy, a shoemaker, described the annual rhythm of work in Haverhill in the 1880s and 1890s:

> I have been in Haverhill seven years . . . Haverhill is what is called a low cut town, that is we make low cut women's shoes. They are only worn in the summer, and we make them in the winter for summer wear. Now our business will commence here, that is the bulk of our business, the first of November. That is the manufacturers will commence picking out their crews, and it will gradually pick up until in December we will get a fairly comfortable living. January, February, March and April we are rushed to death, and do a good deal more work than we ought to; then it begins to slack up again and about the 1st of July it is very flat. We have considerable McKay work, a man's slipper, that we make here in town that sort of keeps us alive in the meantime; but the bulk of the work is done in the latter part of the winter and spring, and the rest of the time there is any quantity loafing all the time, even in a prosperous year . . .[66]

Since Haverhill was a "low cut town," it had its own peculiar seasonal cadence, but there was nothing at all peculiar about either the existence of a slow season or about Pomeroy's complaint that employees were overworked in some months and idle in others.[67] In several seasonal trades, in fact, the demand for labor during busy months was so great that thousands of temporary migrants were drawn into the labor markets of Massachusetts. These "floaters," as they were called – carpenters from Nova Scotia, quarrymen from Maine, operatives from French Canada – traveled to the Bay State each year, spent a number of months working in its industries, and returned home when business began to slacken. Seasonal industries sometimes needed more, and sometimes less, labor than was permanently available in the cities and towns of the Bay State.[68]

The regularity with which seasonal slowdowns occurred had its compensations, as contemporary analysts, and less contemporary economists, delighted to point out. In contrast to idleness rooted in business depressions or episodic events, seasonal unemployment was relatively predictable, and workers could lessen the sting of joblessness by preparing for it, financially and psychologically. Daily and weekly wages, moreover, tended to be higher in seasonal industries than they were in branches of the economy that ran more steadily. Workers with roughly the same degree of skill earned more per week in a seasonal than in a nonseasonal industry: shoe factory operatives were better paid than textile workers. The cloud of recurrent unemployment had a silver lining.[69]

There was, however, much more cloud than lining – or, to be more precise, the lining was thin. For most workers who belonged to seasonal trades, spells of unemployment were not really all that predictable. Although workers knew that jobs would be relatively scarce during certain months, they could not foresee from one year to the next just how scarce jobs would be or how long the slow season would last. Table 3.4 provides abundant evidence of this unpredictability. Painters, for example, knew that the winter months were relatively slow, but their ability to foresee spells of winter idleness was certainly limited – since, between 1908 and 1916, the unemployment rate for painters on March 1 ranged from 5 percent to more than 40 percent. Similarly, shoe workers tended to work steadily in December, but their unemployment rate during that month was 2 percent in one year and nearly 15 percent in another. In virtually all occupations, seasonal cadences were simply tendencies easily (and commonly) overwhelmed by cyclical forces or by conditions peculiar to the industry. For workers, this meant that there was no way to gauge with any precision the odds of being laid off during a particular slack season. There was also no way for a worker to predict how long he would remain jobless if he were let go by his employer. "I expect to be out of work soon now," stated a shoemaker in 1879, "and how long I may be out is a conundrum – perhaps two months, and perhaps four."[70]

This conundrum was deeply felt since neither shoemakers nor most other seasonal workers earned enough money when they were working to render them indifferent to the loss of two, three, or four months' wages. Members of seasonal trades may have been paid more than their counterparts in nonseasonal industries, and some

Table 3.4. *The range in seasonal unemployment rates for Massachusetts trade union members, 1908–16*

| | Highest and lowest unemployment rate (%) reported on last day of: | | | | | | | |
| | March | | June | | September | | December | |
Occupation	High	Low	High	Low	High	Low	High	Low
Boot and shoe workers[a]								
Total	22.4	5.1	18.2	3.4	17.1	4.5	14.7	2.2
Mixed unions	25.1	2.3	10.8	1.8	41.9	2.5	13.1	1.1
Cutters	35.7	9.8	19.9	1.3	17.2	4.8	17.0	0.8
Edgemakers	11.7	2.1	11.4	5.0	6.6	3.5	18.6	3.3
Lasters	33.7	2.2	36.9	5.5	27.6	2.9	33.6	1.0
Stitchers	26.9	1.1	13.5	1.9	8.0	1.9	23.6	1.4
Treers, dressers, and packers	14.3	1.3	13.2	5.8	17.1	2.5	10.0	1.6
Others	15.3	3.3	14.2	4.8	12.1	3.4	11.4	0.2
Textile operatives[a]								
Total	43.0	4.3	21.3	2.4	15.5	2.2	21.2	3.5
Loomfixers	9.2	1.6	40.8	1.3	8.0	1.5	7.1	0.8
Mule spinners	23.6	3.8	22.9	0.7	18.9	1.6	24.7	1.2
Weavers	2.9	0.9	4.7	0.4	12.9	1.3	26.2	0.6
Others	20.6	1.8	36.4	3.0	22.7	1.9	27.8	3.0
Building trades and related occupations								
Bricklayers, masons, and plasterers	62.8	19.8	41.2	4.6	24.2	3.8	50.6	1.9
Carpenters	24.3	6.5	12.3	2.4	14.9	1.9	32.7	8.8
Hod carriers and building laborers	42.3	4.6	43.2	4.4	20.2	1.5	49.8	11.0
Painters, decorators, and paperhangers	44.0	4.9	23.3	3.9	15.0	2.6	48.0	16.7
Plumbers, gas fitters, and steamfitters	27.3	8.2	13.0	1.1	14.8	0.8	18.0	3.2
Engineers (hoisting and portable)	24.3	5.0	14.3	3.1	15.0	0.4	25.2	7.1
Quarry workers	55.3	1.6	40.3	1.2	23.0	1.0	78.1	9.2
Granite cutters and polishers	74.8[b]	3.6	17.2	1.1	19.1	1.2	42.8	13.9
Electrical workers	16.6	1.8	16.4	0.8	10.7	0.1	10.2	1.6

Table 3.4. *(cont.)*

Occupation	Highest and lowest unemployment rate (%) reported on last day of:							
	March		June		September		December	
	High	Low	High	Low	High	Low	High	Low
Iron and steel, metal workers, machinists								
Boilermakers and helpers	21.0	3.0	40.1	1.6	29.5	1.3	35.6	0.5
Machinists	11.1	2.9	13.6	1.6	20.0	1.0	15.0	2.0
Metal polishers, buffers, platers	18.4	1.2	21.8	0.4	18.5	1.9	27.9	0.8
Molders and coremakers (iron, brass)	31.2	4.3	23.9	3.6	18.4	3.3	38.2	3.0
Blacksmiths and horseshoers	12.0	0.3	6.5	0.6	6.5	1.6	11.0	2.5
Sheet metal workers	19.6	2.8	36.7	0.8	22.5	0.2	.2	3.3
Printing and related industries								
Bookbinders	40.0	0.8	23.9	3.1	64.0	2.8	62.0	1.4
Compositors	13.7	3.9	11.9	2.1	11.4	4.1	16.3	2.5
Printing pressmen	6.9	1.7	12.6	2.0	6.4	1.7	5.8	2.5
Stereotypers and electrotypers	1.7	0.3	5.2	0	4.6	0.5	4.7	0.7
Transportation								
Railway clerks	1.5	0.5	7.9	0.2	0.9	0	2.0	0
Railway conductors	4.0	2.9	4.3	1.0	4.8	1.0	6.4	1.2
Engineers (locomotive)	10.5	1.8	10.0	0	10.8	2.8	10.3	2.8
Firemen (locomotive)	14.9	0	18.3	1.0	12.3	0.1	11.2	1.1
Station agents and employees	10.0	0.1	2.1	0.4	6.4	0	14.7	0.3
Street and electric railway employees	9.1	0.1	3.3	1.2	4.9	1.4	4.8	1.6
Railroad telegraphers	1.9	0.2	1.1	0.2	1.6	0.2	2.0	0.5
Railroad trainmen	6.1	2.2	4.0	1.4	3.5	1.4	5.7	2.2
Teamsters, chauffeurs, drivers, etc.	21.2	1.0	14.0	1.0	9.4	0.4	11.5	1.5
Railroad workers	10.5	0.7	13.0	1.3	9.2	0.6	15.9	0.5

Table 3.4. *(cont.)*

| | Highest and lowest unemployment rate (%) reported on last day of: | | | | | | | |
| | March | | June | | September | | December | |
Occupation	High	Low	High	Low	High	Low	High	Low
Food, tobacco, and related industries								
Bakers and confectioners	17.6	2.3	30.9	2.1	10.7	2.1	15.5	6.0
Bartenders	13.3	4.2	20.7	3.6	13.6	4.1	16.2	3.6
Bottlers and drivers	19.2	3.7	5.3	1.1	14.6	2.4	33.3	2.2
Brewery workmen	11.5	3.2	14.1	4.3	9.8	3.9	11.8	4.0
Cigarmakers	15.7	4.9	12.2	0.8	10.4	1.9	40.6	1.5
Cooks and waiters	15.0	2.5	26.2	0.9	9.5	1.0	14.3	0.8
Other								
Barbers	6.0	1.7	3.6	0.7	4.9	1.2	4.2	1.3
Clerks (retail and wholesale)	6.5	1.7	7.4	1.5	2.6	1.6	5.8	1.4
Firemen (stationary)	4.7	2.4	6.9	1.1	6.1	1.1	10.3	1.2
Garment workers	55.3	2.8	50.2	0.1	38.5	0	56.7	4.7
Municipal employees	77.6	6.6	15.6	0.9	15.1	1.5	28.6	3.9
Paper and pulp makers	28.2	0	34.2	0	87.8	0.1	30.0	0
Telephone operators	5.6	1.4	3.8	1.3	1.1	0.8	8.8	3.3
Theatrical stage employees	20.5	4.4	69.1	19.7	16.6	2.6	22.2	3.6
Freight handlers and clerks	16.2	3.5	22.1	2.3	11.8	1.2	14.3	0.9
Engineers (stationary)	40.5	1.2	3.5	0.8	3.6	1.3	5.8	0.5

[a]Figures for all reporting dates not available for all occupational categories.
[b]Percentage inflated due to strikes. See Appendix B.
Sources: See Appendix A, Table A.5 source note.

skilled workmen, such as masons, were probably able to maintain a decent living standard even if they worked for only nine months. But on the whole seasonal workers – like all blue-collar employees – needed and wanted all the income they could get. Their wages were simply too low for these men and women to regard layoffs of three or four months as vacations financed by the pay differential accorded to seasonal employees. *Most* members of seasonal occupations did, in fact, work year-round, and virtually everyone tried to work as continuously as possible, which was why seasonal unemployment levels dropped significantly when business was booming. Given the wages that they earned and the duration of most layoffs, spells of unemployment were a serious matter for the men and women who belonged to seasonal trades. The uneven and erratic rhythms of production transformed each year into something of a lottery and a contest, in which the prize for winning was regular work and a regular income.[71]

Many workers, in both seasonal and nonseasonal trades, also had to contend with the distinctive and extended cadence of unemployment rooted in technological change. Although some shifts in technology and work organization did produce a sudden, rapid loss of jobs and the permanent severance of workers from an industry, this was not a typical pattern. A more common consequence of technological innovation was the prolonged and gradual erosion of opportunities for steady employment. Skills were rarely rendered obsolete overnight, but a gradual diminution in the demand for skilled labor affected a great many trades during the half-century that followed the Civil War. New machinery tended both to restrict the opportunities for tradesmen to practice their traditional crafts and to increase the labor supply by permitting semiskilled workers to produce goods that had once demanded the attention of experienced craftsmen. The result, often, was an increasingly sporadic rhythm of work. In the late nineteenth century shoe lasters, as well as some leather and garment workers, complained that new technology was shortening their busy seasons and stretching out their annual spells of unemployment. At the same time, carpenters were contending with a scarcity of "indoor" jobs because of the technological changes in woodworking that permitted certain goods to be mass-produced in mills. "It took a man half a day to make a bath-tub and make it properly," lamented F. H. Jordan, a carpenter from Newton, "but now they can make it in fifteen minutes."[72] In each of these trades, and numerous others, technological unemployment took the form of a lengthy process, lasting a decade or more, in which steady work became harder to find with each passing year. Over time, the rise in unemployment levels was checked or even reversed, as some members of a trade changed occupations or industries or locales. But the new equilibrium was generally attained only after thousands of workers had been buffeted by the long wake of technological change.[73]

Unemployment, clearly, came in different packages, during prosperous years as well as depressions. Its economic sources were multiple and often intertwined with one another; the unemployed themselves were not a discrete group but rather a fluid, and somewhat skewed, cross section of working people; unemployment experiences were immensely varied in duration, predictability, and the sharpness of their bite. But more important than this diversity was the simple fact that joblessness afflicted hundreds of thousands of manual workers even when the economy was running smoothly. Between 1870 and 1920, "good" economic years greatly outnumbered "bad" ones, and the economy of Massachusetts grew by leaps and bounds, but neither growth nor prosperity could provide steady work for all wage earners. As public officials and reformers gradually learned, unemployment was not a disease that appeared exclusively in the form of epidemics. "Not only is practically every wage earner in constant dread of unemployment," concluded the U.S. Commission on Industrial Relations in 1915, "but there are few who do not suffer bitterly many times in their career because they are unable to get work." The commission was confirming something that wage earners had known for at least half a century: that for workers to be unemployed was "normal."[74]

The reserve army of the unemployed

Between the 1870s and the early 1920s, there was little long-term or "secular" change in the incidence of unemployment in Massachusetts. Idleness levels bobbed up and down incessantly, but the available statistics contain few signs of long-run change in the proportion of working people unemployed during either prosperity or depressions.[75] There may, perhaps, have been a slight overall increase in the regularity of work during upturns in the business cycle, and there was probably a slight diminution in both the mean duration of unemployment and the likelihood of a worker remaining idle for lengthy spells of four months or more. But such shifts, if they occurred, were small in scale and limited in impact. On the whole, the chances of a worker becoming unemployed, and losing a few months' work in the course of a year, neither improved nor deteriorated. Steady jobs were as hard to find during the first quarter of the twentieth century as they had been during the last quarter of the nineteenth.[76]

Within most occupations, unemployment levels also appear to have maintained a rough consistency over the long run. Table 3.5 presents annual unemployment rates for all occupations included in both the census and trade union surveys; relatively few secular shifts can be discerned amid the ubiquitous hills and valleys carved out by

Table 3.5. *Annual unemployment rates (%) in selected occupations, Massachusetts, 1885–1922*

Occupation[a]	1885[b]	1890[b]	1895[b,c]	1900[b]	1908–10[d]	1911–13[d]	1914–16[d]	1917–19[d]	1920–22[d]
Boot- and shoemakers	21.9	12.1	16.1	15.3	9.2	7.5	9.4	6.9	28.2
Masons and plasterers	24.5	13.0	19.8	18.1	26.2	19.0	26.7	28.0	26.6
Marble cutters, stonecutters and quarrymen	13.1	9.5	—	11.6	9.3	15.5	22.6	—	39.7
Laborers	24.1	11.4	—	14.3	21.2	18.1	17.9	10.5	33.9
Painters	19.4	9.2	17.9	13.0	18.0	16.0	23.4	12.7	20.0
Carpenters	15.3	7.8	13.7	11.9	8.4	9.3	15.2	8.5	16.6
Plumbers and fitters	8.6	4.1	9.1	7.8	8.2	5.7	12.5	9.0	16.9
Textile operatives	12.3	3.8	21.4[e] / 8.5	4.3	14.0	12.2	6.9	5.6	27.0
Iron- and steelworkers	16.2	5.0	—	5.7	13.6	14.8	12.2	7.3	24.9
Paper mill operatives	4.8	3.1	10.0	4.9	8.4	2.1	14.5	18.5	38.0
Teamsters	5.1	3.3	—	4.8	9.6	4.4	6.7	3.4	9.6
Cigarmakers	6.5	—	—	4.8	10.0	4.0	7.4	5.7	12.7
Blacksmiths	6.5	3.3	—	5.0	5.0	3.2	4.8	4.9	41.0
Machinists	9.3	2.9	—	3.9	6.1	4.3	8.3	7.1	22.6
Printing trades	3.5	2.8	—	4.1	5.0	4.5	6.6	4.1	10.1
Bakers	4.8	2.6	—	4.0	7.3	7.7	10.5	5.8	7.7
Engineers and firemen (not locomotive)	5.6	2.8	—	3.5	4.9	3.1	3.5	2.3	9.0
Street railway employees	3.9	2.4	—	3.1	2.4	2.4	3.5	4.0	6.6
Barbers	2.4	1.4	—	2.5	2.6	2.0	3.2	1.9	1.7
Clerks	3.0	1.5	—	2.5	2.9	1.9	3.3	3.5	2.3
Brewery workers	—	—	—	4.5	7.8	8.3	6.4	13.8	32.4
Railroad employees	4.4	2.7	—	3.0	2.1	2.1	3.4	2.1	7.2

[a] See note 77 regarding the occupational labels and groupings.
[b] Figures for 1885–1900 are for males only.
[c] Figures for 1895 are based upon a limited number of communities: see Table A.3.
[d] Average annual rate for years specified.
[e] Rate was 21.4% for cotton mill operatives and 8.5% for woolen mill operatives.
Sources: Tables A.1–A.5.

the movements of the business cycle. Idleness levels seemed to decline for boot and shoe workers and to rise for masons, textile operatives, brewery workers, and paper workers. But in most listed occupations, the range of unemployment rates, from prosperity to depression, was relatively stable from the 1880s until the aftermath of World War I.[77]

In a number of trades, however, there were changes of a different type, changes not necessarily in the total volume of unemployment but rather in the distribution of idle time among members of an occupation. While the lenses of official statistics only partially captured (or even obscured) such shifts, fragments of evidence suggest that they did occur and did alter the rhythms of work in some industries. Among rubber factory operatives and fishermen, for example, the frequency of unemployment seemed to decline at the end of the nineteenth century while the mean duration increased. Fewer people were laid off, but those who were idled tended to remain jobless for longer periods. Woolen mill operatives and some building tradesmen had the same experience: work did not become any steadier in the occupation as a whole, but more members of the occupation were able to labor year-round.[78] In other industries, the reverse occurred. Layoffs became less common, but more workers found themselves on short time or being paid by the piece rather than by the day or week. Idle time, in these trades, was shared among workers in a form that reduced (or masked an increase in) the formal unemployment level. The apparent decline in unemployment rates for shoe workers resulted in part from the more widespread use of both short time and piece rates, and machinists in Worcester in 1911 grumbled loudly that they had begun "working on short time owing to the adoption of the so-called Taylor System of scientific efficiency."[79] Whether such distributive shifts occurred in an industry and whether they proved to be durable depended upon a variety of factors, including policy decisions made by both management and trade unions. But the scattered signs of their existence suggest that there were more undercurrents of change in the incidence of unemployment than the official statistical record reveals.[80]

Nonetheless, in the commonwealth as a whole – and for workers as a class – things did not change much during these years. Few occupations seemed to undergo significant long-run increases or declines in the steadiness of work, and the shifts that did occur tended to offset one another. Unemployment rose a bit in one trade and fell a bit in another; short time became more prevalent in some industries while layoffs became more common or lengthier in others. So too, the major structural changes in the labor force had countervailing effects on unemployment: the proportion of employees in the work force increased steadily, but those occupations that grew most rapidly (which were clerical and white-collar) had comparatively low rates of unemployment. The upshot of all these changes – of the many twisting eddies and crosscurrents – was to leave intact the essential shape and size of the pool of the unemployed. Or, to be more precise, the size of the pool remained constant in proportion to the size of the commonwealth's population and labor force. The most visible long-term change in unemployment during this period was that it affected many more people in 1920 than it had in 1870.[81]

The durability and persistence of the problem of unemployment led the Massachusetts Bureau of Statistics of Labor to conclude in 1911 that "however prosperous conditions may be, there is always a 'reserve army' of the unemployed." The bureau's language was apt and revealing, despite its peculiar echoes for late twentieth-century Americans who associate the idea of a reserve army with Karl Marx rather than with bureaucrats at state agencies. The use of this resonant phrase (variants of which were common in labor and reform circles between 1875 and 1920) did not necessarily mean that officials of the bureau had read and accepted the analyses offered by Marx in the first volume of *Capital*. But it did mean that after decades of first-hand investigation these officials had come to share, with Marx and others, certain observations and insights (that were both descriptive and explanatory) regarding the problem of unemployment. The concept of a reserve army implied both that there were always involuntarily idled workers in the commonwealth and that such idleness was produced (and demanded) by the normal functioning, rather than the malfunctioning, of the economy. Unemployment was viewed as systemic rather than accidental in its origins, and at least some involuntary idleness was perceived to be essential to the performance of the industrial, capitalist economy that had evolved in Massachusetts.[82]

That a reserve of labor existed in the Bay State, that there were always more workers than jobs available, seems beyond dispute. All the existing statistics, assembled in a variety of ways over a period of four decades, testify to the presence of such a reserve, and the recorded utterances of working people eloquently, if painfully, confirm the stark, quantitative indicators. The experience of the commonwealth during World War I, moreover, vividly illuminated the presence of a chronic labor surplus. The abnormal conditions of wartime produced the lowest unemployment levels recorded between the 1870s and 1922. Even before the United States officially entered the war, the conflict in Europe generated a great surge in activity in the Bay State's economy. The shoe industry received orders from the Russian and Italian governments, plants that produced metal goods ran on extra shifts, and one munitions firm in Lowell increased its payroll from 350 to nearly 9,000 workers in 1916. As a result, the incidence of unemployment dropped to unprecedented levels in most occupations, while some industries, probably for the first time since the Civil War, confronted an actual scarcity of workers. Building contractors complained that unskilled laborers were in short supply, in part because immigration had ceased and some Italian workmen had returned home. And during the winter of 1916 ice harvesters could not be found despite the offer of unusually high wages.[83] For trade unionists as a whole, the war produced unemployment rates between 1916 and 1918 that were roughly half those that had prevailed during the most prosperous peacetime years. World War I thus made plain the difference between "normal" conditions and full employment. In so doing, it also revealed that the reserve army of labor consisted largely of the unemployed rather than the unemployable. When jobs were available, people did go to work. The vast majority of men and women who were idled in peacetime were neither lazy nor lame: they were willing and able to work, and they deserted from the ranks of the reserve army when they had somewhere else to go.[84]

In operation, of course, there was not a single, unified (or homogenized) reserve of labor in Massachusetts but rather an assortment of different brigades or reserves that were clustered around each of the state's industries and blue-collar occupations and that were more or less distinct from one another.[85] Every major trade or industry, or even firm, had its own labor surplus, its own pool of men and women who could not be guaranteed steady employment but who were sometimes needed and who retained some attachment to a particular employer or type of work. These reserves were structured in various ways: there were men and women who were idle during slow seasons, employees who worked on short time, floaters who migrated from one place to another, casual laborers, and substitute spinners and printers who were called up only when regular workers were absent or when the demand for labor was unusually great. The different brigades had diverse principles of organization, but virtually all blue-collar occupations claimed more members than could possibly work steadily year in and year out. The dilution of skills during these years made it easier for workers to change trades or industries, and, as a result, the boundaries separating different pools of workers became more permeable. But each industry, nonetheless, continued to maintain its own labor reserve – which was why, as some critics pointed out, unemployment levels were persistently high in a host of different occupations.[86]

That these reserves of labor were both widespread and enduring lends considerable support to the notion that unemployment was systemic in its origin and its function. Accidents rarely last for forty years, and exceptions are unlikely to occur simultaneously in dozens of different industries. There can, indeed, be little doubt that most of the unemployment that occurred in Massachusetts was produced by economic behavior and activities that were intrinsic to the working of the economic system. As one state agency noted in 1913, "seasonal industries, the introduction of machinery and new processes, decaying trades, casual labor, commercial failures, and the regularly recurring periods of trade depression keep constantly in involuntary idleness great numbers of our working population." Each of these listed sources of involuntary idleness was a prominent feature of economic life in the commonwealth. As long as the economy functioned as it did – as long as there were seasonal industries, business cycles, and changes in technology, and as long as the majority of the population consisted of men and women who were not guaranteed jobs and who were dependent upon employers for their livelihoods – there was bound to be some unemployment.[87]

A certain quantity of unemployment (but not necessarily all of the unemployment that occurred) also seems to have been required for the economy to operate during these years. The Massachusetts Bureau acknowledged this fact, late in the Progressive era, when it quoted approvingly from a New York State report that a reserve of labor "must be ever present to allow for the extension of industrial enterprises and for new undertakings, to meet the demand of the busiest months in the seasonal industries, and to supply the demand for casual workers, who are needed not steadily, but off and on, for a day, a week, or a month or two."[88] Many different types of economic behavior were possible only because workers were continuously available, and some of these activities (such as the expansion of plants during cyclical upswings) were entirely central to the functioning of the economy.[89]

Businessmen were well aware of this dependence. As Don Lescohier, an astute analyst of American labor markets, pointed out early in the twentieth century, American employers had grown accustomed to finding a crowd of idle workers at the factory gates each morning, and they generally believed that a labor surplus was necessary for businesses to run properly and effectively. It was for precisely this reason that businessmen sought to maintain their own reserves of labor and vigorously opposed governmental policies, such as immigration restriction, that might reduce the labor supply. In effect, both the customary behavior and the beliefs of the business community reflected a reliance on chronic unemployment. Whether or not capitalism per se required the existence of a reserve army of the unemployed is an issue that the Massachusetts experience alone cannot resolve. But industrial capitalism as it developed in the Bay State certainly did depend upon and create a palpable reserve army.[90]

By virtue of both its origins and its incidence, then, unemployment was a central phenomenon in Massachusetts society from the end of the Civil War until the early 1920s. While the state's social landscape acquired decidedly modern features, while the growth of the economy and the population gave birth to an overwhelmingly industrial and urban world, involuntary idleness was a persistent and pervasive feature of working-class life. Despite the traditional and hallowed image of the United States as a vast, thinly populated continent eagerly welcoming the brawn of millions of immigrants, the nation – or the Bay State at least – was not a labor-scarce society during these years, not if the concept of labor scarcity implies that jobs were plentiful and easy to keep. Steady jobs were more the exception than the rule. "The labor market," lamented a Boston baker in the 1890s, "is over done." His metaphorically apt words were echoed by working people throughout the commonwealth from the 1870s until well into the twentieth century.[91]

Chronic vulnerability to spells of unemployment, moreover, was something that distinguished working-class life from life in the upper echelons of the social structure. Members of the middle classes were not totally insulated against all hardships or reversals of fortune, but the state's employers, managers, professionals, and salaried employees did enjoy a level of job security that few blue-collar workers could hope to attain. Among middle-class citizens, unemployment was an uncommon rather than routine event, a violation of expectations rather than an endemic problem.[92] In 1888, a labor newspaper pointed to this contrast between middle-class and working-class experiences, noting that the city of Boston provided only "partial employment for the men in its departments, turning them out in cold weather to live as best they may. The salaried officials," claimed the paper's editor, "would not like that kind of a racket."[93] Indeed, the salaried officials of Boston or anywhere else would certainly not have liked the "racket" of being unemployed for a few months each year. But one of the prime benefits of an ascent into the middle class was that it greatly increased one's chances of working and being paid year-round.

For those men and women who were not graced with membership in the middle classes, who received wages rather than salaries, who lived in the blue-collar towns and neighborhoods of Massachusetts, the insecurity bred by unsteady work was one of the hallmarks of this entire, long period in American history. Altogether dependent upon employers in order to earn a living, and lacking institutional support if they were idled, these manual workers inhabited a world that not only seemed, but was, fast-changing, unpredictable, over-crowded, and chaotic. Their incomes could, and often did, disappear at a moment's notice; their daily routines and workplace friendships could suddenly be interrupted for any one of a dozen possible rea-sons; their plans could be altered and hopes dashed by decisions over which they had no control, made by men whom they had never met. The attainment of some economic stability was by no means impos-sible, but footholds were precarious, and the threat of loss or disaster was omnipresent. "There is scarcely a workman, whatever the pres-ent comfort of his life," intoned an article in the *Labor Leader* in 1893, "who is not oppressed by the horrible nightmare of a possible loss of his situation. No faithfulness, no skill, no experience can protect him against the danger of being cast adrift with his family at the next shift of the market. He is part of the grist in the great mill of demand and supply, and when his time comes it remorselessly crushes him between its iron rollers."[94] The *Leader's* rhetoric was, perhaps, a bit extravagant, but the apprehension that it voiced was authentic and solidly grounded in economic reality. The uncertainty that was a by-product of "the great mill of demand and supply" was one of the dominant features of the era.

4   *Sharing the burden*

That a reserve army of labor existed in Massachusetts, that there were functioning reserves in virtually all working-class occupations – these important facts tell only part of the tale. The impact of unemployment upon Bay State society was shaped not only by the incidence of joblessness but also by its distribution among different groups of workers. Throughout the "era of uncertainty," the state's labor force contained a mix of young men and older men, men of native birth and foreign birth, "old" Irish immigrants and "new" immigrants from eastern and southern Europe. It also included hundreds of thousands of women who were themselves of different ages and ethnic backgrounds. Just how the heavy volume of unemployment was parceled out among these groups was a key determinant of the problem's significance and social consequences. Indeed, the historical record, despite its frustrating imperfections, suggests that one of the distinctive features of economic life in this period was the breadth of the threat of unemployment. Not everyone was equally insecure – and the variations themselves were extremely revealing – but the burden of joblessness was widely shared among the working people of the commonwealth.

Immigrants and natives (males)

> Anton Dumel, a Russian Pole, about thirty-five years of age. He can speak but two words of English, and those are "No work," and we can find no one to interpret for him. The rooms of the Society are his refuge; and when a job is finished, whether in the city or out of it, he does not attempt to obtain work for himself, but comes back and says "No work." We have now sent him to a 162tant town. He is willing to work, and is steady and industrious. We hope he may learn English enough not to come us again.
>
> Case report, Industrial Aid Society, 1873

> Q. Do you think there has been any reason aside from the general depression which makes it more difficult for a weaver to get employment than five years ago?

A. It is a matter of concern to an American how long he can work
in these mills, because immigration will drive him out.

Q. In what way?

A. In numerous ways. We couldn't put up with the amount of
work that is put upon him, and the immigrant can. I wouldn't
like to name any class in particular. I am an immigrant myself.

Testimony of Thomas E. Sherry, a weaver in
Lowell, 1895[1]

After the Civil War, and particularly after the long depression of the
1870s, immigrants poured into Massachusetts in unprecedented
numbers. Each year witnessed the arrival of thousands, and sometimes scores of thousands, of foreign-born men and women who
sought to earn their livings, permanently or temporarily, in the industries of the Bay State. This flood of immigrants enlarged the commonwealth's working class and transformed the social landscape of
its industrial centers. By the second decade of the twentieth century,
less than a third of the men who labored in Massachusetts were the
native-born children of native-born parents, and immigrants themselves constituted more than one-quarter of the population of almost
every city. The sources of this immigration were more diverse than
they had been earlier in the nineteenth century, and consequently
society became more heterogeneous, ethnically and linguistically.
Irish, English, and German immigrants were joined, after 1880, by
large contingents of Italians, eastern European Jews, French Canadians, and Portuguese, as well as by smaller delegations from more
than a dozen other nations. Ethnic neighborhoods sprouted in urban
areas; industrial workplaces were often peopled by clusters of men
and women who shared a common language, religion, and ethnic
heritage. By the beginning of World War I, when the parade began to
thin out, the combined forces of social change abroad and economic
growth in the United States had brought more than a million immigrants to the shores of the Bay State.[2]

In one respect, at least, these immigrants did, in and of themselves, provide a reserve of labor for the industries of Massachusetts.
The rhythms of immigration were influenced by business conditions
in the commonwealth, and the supply of immigrant labor tended to
adjust itself, albeit imperfectly, to the demand. When the economy
was buoyant, the pace of immigration quickened, while slumps in
business led to a reduction in the number of new arrivals. Depressions also produced an exodus of migrants from Massachusetts.
When their labor was no longer needed, both discouraged immigrants and temporary sojourners (who had never intended to settle
permanently) returned to their native countries in large numbers.

There was, in addition, a seasonal dimension to the rhythms of migration. Many industries and trades attracted "birds of passage," foreign-born men (particularly Canadians) who came to the United States during the busy season of each year and returned home when work was slack. Nova Scotian carpenters, according to one contemporary, "come in the spring, and just as soon as the woodcock takes his flight, they take theirs backward." Workers in Europe and Canada constituted a reservoir of labor that was tapped when needed and that reabsorbed jobless workmen when business was slow in Massachusetts.[3]

Many foreign-born workmen, moreover, were particularly susceptible to bouts of irregular employment because of the handicaps that they brought with them into the competitive labor markets of Massachusetts. The predicament of Anton Dumel may have been a bit extreme (since he arrived in the vanguard of eastern European immigration, he had to search for work without the aid of kin or a sympathetic ethnic community), but his lack of surefootedness was not uncommon. Most immigrants entered the strange and unfamiliar world of Massachusetts without any readily marketable skills, and many of them had English vocabularies not much larger than Dumel's. Their willingness to work long hours, at menial jobs, for low wages certainly enhanced their attractiveness to employers, but immigrants were too numerous, too inexperienced, and too desperate for jobs to have had much power in the labor markets. One recurrent sign of their powerlessness was the abuse and exploitation that foreign-born workers suffered at the hands of unscrupulous foremen and employment agencies. Early in the twentieth century, to cite one example, the Lithuanian employees of a rubber factory were obliged to pay a portion of their weekly wages to their foreman in order to keep their jobs. When nineteen of these men eventually protested to the president of the company, they were all fired. Other immigrants found themselves paying fees to employment agencies that shuttled them off to nonexistent jobs in distant towns or to factories where, after a few weeks, they were laid off to make room for a new gang of fee-paying immigrants. Many foreign-born workers, to be sure, had more benign introductions to job seeking, but the existence of such practices offered vivid testimony to the particular difficulties that immigrants encountered in the labor markets of the promised land.[4]

Nonetheless, foreign-born workers had no monopoly on the experience of unemployment; nor did they, by themselves, comprise the reserves of labor that were so widespread in Massachusetts. During the final decades of the nineteenth century, immigrants were unemployed more often than were men born in the United States, but the experiences of the two groups were not qualitatively different from one another. In the course of the depressed census year of 1884–5 (the only year for which statistics for the entire male labor force can be developed), approximately one-third of all immigrant workmen were laid off at least once. Yet more than one-quarter of all natives were unemployed during the same period. (See Table 4.4.) And in prosperous years, if national census data from 1890 and 1900 can serve as a guide to conditions in Massachusetts, the gap between natives and immigrants appears to have narrowed.[5] Immigrants shouldered more than their share of the burden of involuntary idleness, but steady work was not a birthright of the native sons of Massachusetts. As one governmental commission concluded, with appropriate ambiguity, "The native-born were found to be rather more continuously employed than the foreign-born."[6]

The gap between immigrant and native unemployment levels was largely the result of the types of jobs that immigrants held. Or, to be more precise, it was largely the result of the types of jobs that immigrants did not hold: middle-class or white-collar positions in which the threat of joblessness was negligible. As the "concentration index" figures in Table 4.1 reveal, immigrants in 1885 tended to be overrepresented in many blue-collar occupations in which unemployment was commonplace, while they were notably underrepresented in sales and clerical (not to mention professional and managerial) positions. Similarly, in 1900 only 19 percent of all immigrants worked in occupations in which the odds of being laid off were less than 1 in 10. (See Table 4.2, part A.) But those same occupations (most of which were white-collar) employed roughly 40 percent of all natives and nearly half of all natives whose parents had also been born in the United States. Native-born men were less likely to be jobless than were immigrants primarily because natives were less heavily concentrated in the working class – a fact that helps to account for the apparent cyclical fluctuation in the gap between native and immigrant unemployment frequencies.[7]

But native-born men who remained in the working class did not fare much better than immigrants. In almost all blue-collar trades, unemployment levels for immigrants and natives were similar, and they were often nearly identical. Table 4.1 presents unemployment frequencies, for the census year of 1885, among foreign-born and native-born men who labored in forty-one occupations: in twenty-five of these occupations the unemployment frequencies were within 5 percentage points of one another.[8] In most of the listed trades, natives enjoyed a slight advantage over their foreign-born colleagues, but there were no occupations in which immigrant workers were laid

Table 4.1. *Unemployment among native-born and foreign-born males, by occupation, Massachusetts, 1885*

Occupation[a]	Unemployment frequency (%)		Immigrant concentration index[b]	Number unemployed (total)
	Native-born	Foreign-born		
Longshoremen	74.4	84.8	2.3	1,504
Straw workers	82.4	74.5	0.4	1,108
Nail and tack makers	71.6	63.2	0.6	1,153
Masons	59.6	77.6	1.5	5,789
Boot- and shoemakers	67.1	67.9	0.7	32,374
Jewelry makers	62.9	72.0	0.8	2,039
Brickmakers	60.4	61.9	2.5	1,205
Laborers	58.2	63.2	1.9	20,346
Cutlery makers	53.5	58.4	1.6	680
Painters	55.9	54.2	0.8	5,176
Quarrymen	51.1	51.1	2.0	584
Ironworkers	46.3	53.5	1.4	2,864
Rubber factory operatives	49.7	45.0	1.5	1,276
Carpenters	46.2	48.8	1.1	10,747
Glass works employees	46.5	46.5	1.3	420
Gardeners and assistants	41.2	46.6	1.9	1,330
Fishermen	59.2	28.0	1.4	3,452
Wire workers	36.7	45.9	1.9	1,122
Hosiery mill operatives	34.6	44.2	1.5	380
Woolen mill operatives	40.8	38.2	1.6	5,332
Cotton mill operatives	36.0	40.8	1.9	10,414
Print works, dye works, and bleachery operatives	40.9	37.4	1.5	1,236
Worsted mill operatives	35.6	36.1	2.0	400
Stoneworkers, marble workers, and granite workers	35.4	33.4	1.7	1,510
Mariners and master mariners	34.3	24.5	0.8	1,140
Watchmakers	28.5	39.0	0.7	588
Machinists and machine shop employees	28.9	34.4	0.9	3,816
Farm laborers	28.2	35.2	0.8	10,759

Table 4.1. *(cont.)*

Occupation[a]	Unemployment frequency (%)		Immigrant concentration index[b]	Number unemployed (total)
	Native-born	Foreign-born		
Piano and organ makers	27.3	26.2	0.9	716
Carpet factory operatives	22.7	22.2	1.7	266
Apprentices	20.3	23.8	0.6	1,102
Blacksmiths and helpers	15.9	19.7	1.4	1,040
Tailors	10.1	21.4	1.8	673
Stationary engineers and assistants	16.8	15.5	1.0	577
Teamsters	15.0	15.9	1.0	2,144
Paper mill operatives	13.6	16.7	1.4	670
Steam railroad employees	5.9	21.4	1.0	1,733
Bookkeepers and clerks	7.3	7.5	0.3	2,020
Salesmen	6.8	8.3	0.4	1,041
Farmers	6.8	7.6	0.4	2,504
Merchants and dealers	4.2	4.0	0.9	1,367

[a]Occupations ranked by unemployment frequency, in descending order. See note 8.
[b]Ratio of the percentage of occupation members who were foreign-born to the percentage of the male labor force that was foreign-born (35.1%).
Sources: MBSL, *18 AR* (Boston, 1887), pp. 254–60. *Census of Massachusetts: 1885*, I, part 2 (Boston, 1888), pp. 612–21.

off wholesale while native men remained on the job.[9] The same pattern obtained among shoe workers in Brockton in 1900, who were studied through a sample drawn from the census manuscripts. As Table 4.3 indicates, there was only a small (and statistically insignificant) difference between the unemployment frequencies of natives and immigrants.[10] As always, there were exceptions: in 1885, foreign-born masons worked less steadily than did their native counterparts, and in 1900 immigrant laborers in Boston (particularly those who had recently arrived in the United States) also seem to have been at a serious disadvantage in the competition for steady work.[11] But on the whole the joblessness that occurred in any particular trade or industry was fairly evenly distributed among men who were born in the United States and men who were born abroad.[12]

As importantly, native-born manual workers were nearly as likely

Table 4.2. *The distribution of native-born and foreign-born males in occupations with different unemployment frequencies, Massachusetts, 1900*

	Percentage of males in occupations with unemployment frequencies (%) of:							Total (no.)
	0–9.9	10.0–19.9	20.0–29.9	30.0–39.9	40.0–49.9	50.0–59.9	
A. All occupations								
Native white:								
Native parents	48.8	21.4	9.1	6.1	7.0	7.6		302,811
Foreign parents	30.3	34.6	11.4	5.4	9.9	8.4		189,760
Foreign white	19.0	36.6	10.8	9.0	18.8	5.7		339,620
Total (no.)	269,564	254,936	85,932	59,397	103,758	58,604		
B. Blue-collar occupations only[a]								
Native white:								
Native parents	12.7	36.6	14.4	10.7	12.3	13.4		172,664
Foreign parents	9.1	45.1	14.4	7.2	13.0	11.1		143,830
Foreign white	6.9	42.0	12.3	10.4	21.7	6.6		293,650
Total (no.)	55,178	251,444	81,763	59,397	103,758	58,604		

[a]See note 7.
Source: *Twelfth U.S. Census, Occupations* (Washington, 1904), pp. 300–7.

Table 4.3. *Unemployment among native-born and foreign-born males: shoe industry personnel in Brockton and laborers in Boston, 1900*

	Unemployment frequency (%)		Mean duration (months)		Number in sample	
	Native-born	Foreign-born	Native-born	Foreign-born	Native born	Foreign-born
Brockton (all shoe industry personnel)	66.9	64.0	3.4	3.2	293	111
Brockton (blue-collar shoe workers)	72.7	66.0	3.4	3.2	264	106
Boston (laborers)	29.2	42.3	4.3	4.9	48	175

Source: Manuscript schedules, Twelfth U. S. Census, 1900. See notes 10 and 11.

to be engaged in high-unemployment occupations as were immigrant members of the working class. Natives, to be sure, often had better-paying jobs than did foreigners, and several of the most unstable jobs in the economy (e.g., longshoring and day laboring) were largely consigned to immigrants. But there were sizable reserves of labor in many of the best-paid blue-collar trades, and there was no systematic link between the incidence of unemployment and the proportion of immigrants in an occupation.[13] In 1885, in fact, natives were overrepresented in four of the six occupations that had the highest unemployment frequencies in the commonwealth. (See Table 4.1.) And in 1900, as Table 4.2, part B, reveals, native and immigrant *workers* had roughly equal chances of belonging to occupations that had either above- or below-average levels of joblessness. Those blue-collar trades that promised relatively steady employment were not controlled by natives; nor were immigrants boxed into positions with unusually high rates of joblessness. Where a man was born appears to have had a significant effect on his chances of becoming a clerk or a salesman or a banker, but it had little influence upon his ability to locate a secure job within the industrial labor force. There was a gap between immigrant and native unemployment levels because many natives had ascended into the middle class. The gap was relatively small because, among workers, unemployment was a threat to natives and immigrants alike.[14]

Unemployment did not, however, pose the same threat to each of

Table 4.4. *The distribution of unemployment among males by specific place of birth, Massachusetts, 1885*

Place of birth	% of male labor force	% of all males in manufac-turing	% of male unemployed	Unemploy-ment frequency (%)
Total native-born	64.9	59.2	57.4	26.1
Massachusetts	46.9	41.9	44.0	27.7
Other New England states	13.6	13.3	10.0	21.8
Other states	4.5	4.0	3.4	22.3
Total foreign-born	35.1	40.8	42.6	35.9
Canada (French)	4.4	6.5	6.4	43.2
Ireland	15.7	15.6	21.5	40.6
Portugal	0.5	0.3	0.7	38.5
England	4.1	6.0	4.6	33.1
Sweden	0.7	1.0	0.8	32.3
Prince Edward Island	0.4	0.5	0.4	30.4
New Brunswick	0.9	1.1	0.9	30.1
Nova Scotia	2.5	2.5	2.5	29.8
Canada (English)	1.0	1.1	0.9	27.8
Scotland	1.1	1.6	1.0	25.8
Other foreign countries	2.0	1.9	1.8	25.5
Germany	1.8	2.7	1.3	20.0

Sources: MBSL, *18 AR* (Boston, 1887), pp. 254–60; *Census of Massachusetts: 1885*, I, part 2 (Boston, 1888), pp. 612–21.

the different immigrant groups that came to Massachusetts. In 1885, the only year for which extensive, direct data are available, most groups of immigrants had unemployment frequencies that were within a few percentage points of the statewide average. But there were several important exceptions to this pattern of uniformity. German immigrants, as Table 4.4 indicates, encountered unusually low levels of involuntary idleness; they worked more steadily than did natives. At the other end of the spectrum were the two largest immigrant groups in the state, the Irish and the French Canadians, both of whom had unemployment frequencies of roughly 40 percent. That these groups had such disparate experiences was the result of two separate, yet probably related, dynamics. The first was a process of selection or discrimination within individual occupations. In most trades, as Table A.7 in Appendix A reveals, men born in Ireland and in French Canada were jobless more often than were their co-workers who had migrated from Germany or Scotland. The Irish indeed had higher unemployment frequencies than Germans in every one of the twenty occupations listed in Table A.7. Whether this pattern was the consequence of the ethnic biases of employers or the relative skills of workers from different nations is unclear. But when business was slack, in many of the state's workplaces, Irish and French Canadian workers were among the first to be let go.[15]

Irish and French Canadian men were also likely to be found in some of the most unstable working-class occupations in the common-wealth. Throughout the late nineteenth century, men from different ethnic groups tended to cluster in particular occupations or types of occupations, and this clustering had a significant impact on the distribution of unemployment. As a result of their own skills and preferences, as well as the ethnic networks that they relied upon to find jobs and the discriminatory hiring policies that they may have encountered, members of some immigrant groups were much more likely than others to end up in unsteady trades. In 1885, more than 15 percent of all Irish immigrants were day laborers, and roughly 85 percent of all foreign-born laborers were either Irish or French Canadian. Similarly, more than a third of all masons were Irish, a great many French Canadians worked in the building trades, and more than 20 percent of all Portuguese immigrants were engaged in fishing. Men from Germany and Scotland, however, rarely took jobs as laborers, and there were more German immigrants working in the quite steady metal goods industry than there were in construction.[16] Table 4.5 confirms the significance of this phenomenon with summary statistics for 1900, roughly the midpoint in the era of uncertainty. In that year, less than one-quarter of all men from German immigrant families were attached to occupations with above-average (20%) unemployment frequencies. Simultaneously, the figure for French Canadians was 37 percent, for the Irish it was 40 percent, and among Italian immigrants it was nearly 60 percent.[17] The ethnic clustering of the industrial labor force was sufficiently pronounced that it probably diluted the significance of the boundary separating immigrants from natives. In all likelihood, native-born sons of Irish parents had more trouble obtaining steady jobs than did German immigrants.

For the years between 1900 and 1922, there are, unfortunately, no data that illumine directly the comparative unemployment experiences of natives and immigrants. But the basic patterns that prevailed in the late nineteenth century seem to have endured. Immigrants remained more concentrated in the working class than natives, and

Table 4.5. *The concentration of different immigrant groups in occupations with high unemployment frequencies, Massachusetts, 1900 and 1915*

Country of origin	1900 Percentage of males, of foreign-born parentage, engaged in occupations with unemployment frequencies greater than 20%[a]
Italy	59.0
Ireland	40.0
Scandinavia	40.0
Poland	39.1
Canada (English)	38.7
Canada (French)	36.8
Russia	37.6
Great Britain	26.0
Germany	24.2
	1915 Percentage of foreign-born males engaged in occupations in which the 1900 unemployment frequency was greater than 20%[a]
Italy	47.4
Poland	41.4
Russia	37.5
Portugal	34.5
Scandinavia	30.3
Canada	30.3
Ireland	23.6
Great Britain	21.4
Germany	21.4

[a]See note 17.
Sources: Twelfth U.S. Census, Occupations (Washington, 1904), pp. 300–7; *Census of Massachusetts: 1915* (Boston, 1918), pp. 536–631.

consequently they were more exposed to unemployment. Yet workers who were born in the United States continued to play an important role in some of the commonwealth's least steady industries, and trade unionists, many of whom were natives, encountered high unemployment levels throughout this period. In all likelihood, then, there was no dramatic shift in the relationship between immigrant and native unemployment rates after the turn of the century.[18] Similarly, different ethnic groups continued to cluster in different occupations and industries, and, as a result, some immigrants were probably jobless far more often than others. In 1915, as Table 4.5 reveals,

German-born men still led the way in finding work in the more stable niches of the economy. The most irregular jobs, however, appear to have changed hands. By the end of the Progressive era, the groups that were most heavily concentrated in high-unemployment trades were the "new" immigrants from southern and eastern Europe rather than the Irish and French Canadians. (See Table 4.5.) The massive wave of immigration that reached the shores of Massachusetts between the 1890s and World War I appears to have lifted earlier immigrant groups into more secure strata of the industrial labor force, replacing them with Italians, Jews, and Poles. Ethnic variations persisted, but there were new players at the bottom of the roster.[19]

Finally, a word about blacks, who have shouldered such a disproportionate share of the burden of unemployment in recent American history. During the years between the Civil War and the 1920s, black men constituted a very small proportion (1.2%) of the male labor force in Massachusetts. Although their numbers gradually increased, in 1920 there were only sixteen thousand black males at work in the commonwealth. These men encountered unusual difficulties in the state's labor markets: they were denied access to many occupations, and they were obliged to earn their livings in some of the worst-paid, most menial jobs that the economy had to offer.[20]

But black men did not suffer from abnormally high unemployment levels, and they may well have been idled less often than white workers. Although unemployment rates (or frequencies) for blacks cannot be developed from existing data, it is clear that black men tended to be concentrated in service occupations that offered relatively steady employment. To be sure, many blacks did hold "casual" jobs as day laborers or agricultural workers, but there were more blacks working as servants than there were in any other single occupation until 1910, and even in 1920 there were three times as many black janitors as shoemakers. Racial discrimination kept blacks out of manufacturing (there were three black male woolen mill operatives in Massachusetts in 1900) and obliged them to take jobs that were menial, yet as a rule, more stable. "Probably owing to the fact that a large proportion of our families are colored, and are therefore not employed upon factory or shop work," reported a ward committee of the Associated Charities of Boston in the 1890s, "there was, as compared with some of the other wards, a smaller number who actually lost their work on account of the business depression." When blacks did lose their jobs, they often found it difficult to locate new ones in the handful of occupations that were open to them, but, on the whole, they probably experienced less unemployment than did white immigrants from Europe. Only during the second decade of the twentieth century did this picture begin to change. Wartime labor shortages led some employers to hire blacks – by 1920 there were roughly three thousand black male textile operatives – and, as a result, black unemployment rates probably reached or surpassed the statewide average during the postwar depression.[21]

Throughout the years between 1870 and 1920, thus, the problem of unemployment traversed boundaries of nativity, ethnicity, and race. Immigrants may have been idled more often than natives, but working-class children, born in the United States, had no guarantee of steady employment. Newly arrived immigrants and members of some recently arrived ethnic groups were particularly disadvantaged in the search for jobs, but the problem of involuntary idleness was not a problem of transitions. Low wages probably rendered foreign-born men particularly vulnerable to hardship when they were unemployed, but native workers also suffered when their incomes were shut off. (In 1893, half the applicants for relief at the YMCA in Boston were native-born; when the first state-run Free Employment Office opened in the winter of 1906–7, two-thirds of the men who came hunting for jobs were natives.[22]) The commonwealth's labor markets were, in certain respects, ethnically stratified, but the presence of labor reserves in nearly all blue-collar occupations meant that joblessness was not confined to any single stratum of the industrial labor force. Unemployment was a class phenomenon, not an ethnic or a racial one.[23]

Still, many people who lived and worked in Massachusetts during these years believed that immigration was a major cause, if not *the* cause, of unemployment. That belief was itself an important social consequence of immigration, and its origins were hardly obscure: jobs always seemed to be scarce, yet new workers were continuously streaming into the state. The supply of labor, visibly augmented by immigration, appeared to exceed the demand. In its simplest and most straightforward forms, however, the notion that immigration caused unemployment did not accord with the facts. Immigration did not generate unemployment by bringing to the shores of the Bay State a massive population of surplus labor that remained idle or only sporadically employed. Nor did immigrants create unemployment by systematically displacing native-born workers who were unwilling to work as hard or as cheaply as they would. Incidents of displacement certainly occurred, and the flow of migrants kept a lid on wages. But natives were idled less often than immigrants, and – as defenders of unrestricted immigration pointed out – unemployment levels in manufacturing were as high in regions of the United States that received few immigrants as they were in the Northeast. Unemployment was not the consequence of a simple numerical imbalance between the demand for labor in Massachusetts and a labor supply artificially swollen by refugees from abroad.[24]

There was, nonetheless, a causal link between immigration and unemployment. The massive movement of immigrants and migrants into Massachusetts helped to produce a labor supply sufficiently large to permit the demand for labor to fluctuate widely and often. The presence of hundreds of thousands of foreign-born workers enhanced the ability of employers to run their businesses unsteadily or "close to the market," to lay workers off without fearing that labor would be scarce when it was needed. Each year, new arrivals from abroad replenished the ranks of a labor reserve that enabled businessmen – despite a growing demand for labor – to regard all workers as potential members of the reserve. Immigration contributed to economic growth and the creation of new jobs, yet the jobs created through economic expansion were themselves neither secure nor stable. Immigration, in sum, fueled and lubricated the machinery of an economic system that idled hundreds of thousands of workers in the course of every year.[25]

Boys and men

For immigrants and natives alike, much depended upon the relationship between age and unemployment. Working-class males commonly entered the labor force in their teens and remained there as long as they were physically able. At any one time, roughly half the male labor force was between the ages of 25 and 45, and the other half was composed of equal proportions of younger and older men.[26] Did a man's age affect the odds of his being able to work year-round? At what point or points in a man's life was he most vulnerable to layoffs? Did workers acquire job security as they aged? The questions are critical ones. An unemployment frequency of 30 percent, in the labor force as a whole or in any particular occupation, could have meant either that every man stood a 1-in-3 chance of losing his job or that some men were virtually certain to be laid off while others were essentially secure. Unemployment, to cite one obvious possibility, could have been primarily a threat to the young, an experience associated with the opening stages of a man's career. In the United States in 1974, the unemployment rate for males between the ages of 16 and 21 was nearly 14 percent while the figure for men aged 35 to 64 was less than 3 percent. New entrants to the labor force, in 1974, were far more exposed to unemployment than were experienced workmen.[27]

But the patterns that prevailed in the late nineteenth century differed from those recorded in 1974. Between 1880 and 1900, men who performed manual labor in Massachusetts suffered spells of joblessness throughout their careers, and the limited data available suggest that a man's age had relatively little bearing on the odds of his becoming or remaining unemployed. In 1885, the only year for which age breakdowns for the entire labor force can be developed, males in almost all age groups had to contend with unemployment frequencies between 27 and 30 percent, while mean durations were uniformly in the 4-to-5 month range. (See Table 4.6.) As Table A.8 in Appendix A indicates, this consistency prevailed in cities and towns with widely varied industrial structures.[28] In the shoe manufacturing center of Lynn, for example, all men between the ages of 20 and 59 confronted unemployment frequencies between 39 and 43 percent, while their compatriots in the textile city of New Bedford all lived with idleness levels in the vicinity of 20 to 25 percent. Similarly, during the prosperous year of 1900, unemployment was evenly distributed among shoe workers of different ages in Brockton, as well as among laborers in Boston who were between the ages of 20 and 50. (See Tables 4.7 and 4.8.) The precise contours of the pattern varied from trade to trade, but a worker's susceptibility to unemployment appears to have changed little in the course of his lifetime.[29]

There were, however, two notable departures from this general pattern: both the youngest and the oldest workers were at something of a disadvantage in the competition for steady work. In 1885, teenagers between the ages of 14 and 19 had to contend with the highest unemployment frequency in the state (37%) and they were also idled for relatively long stints (an average of 4.5 months).[30] In communities throughout the commonwealth, the depression of the mid-1880s had a disproportionately severe impact on teenagers, and in 1900 youthful shoe workers and laborers also seem to have worked more sporadically than did men who were ten or twenty years older. Mature workmen sometimes grumbled that their places were being taken by youths who would work for less than a man's wages, but young men, in fact, were idled more often and for longer than their elders. Youthful workers were neither confined to nor particularly concentrated in high-risk occupations, but they were apparently regarded, by many employers, as relatively dispensable and relatively impervious to the suffering that could accompany layoffs.[31] "We have used every care to cause as little hardship as possible," reported one plant manager in 1921. "About all that have been discharged are married women, boys, and single men."[32]

The plight of older workers was different and, to many contemporaries, more distressing. Men in their fifties, sixties, and even seven-

Table 4.6. Unemployment among males of different ages, Massachusetts, 1885

Age	Unemployment frequency (%)	Mean duration (months)	Annual unemployment rate (%)	Number unemployed	Percentage of unemployed males
10–13	17.9	4.8	7.2	341	0.2
14–19	37.2	4.5	14.0	26,216	14.7
20–9	30.1	3.9	9.8	51,051	28.6
30–9	27.1	3.9	8.8	36,626	20.5
40–9	28.4	4.1	9.7	29,337	16.4
50–9	28.9	4.4	10.6	20,028	11.2
60–79	27.7	5.0	11.5	14,650	8.2
80–	22.0	5.9	10.8	361	0.2

Sources: MBSL, 18 AR (Boston, 1887), pp. 152–7; Census of Massachusetts: 1885, I, part 2 (Boston, 1888), pp. 612–21.

Table 4.7. *Unemployment among males of different ages in the shoe industry, Brockton, 1900*

Age	All shoe industry personnel[a]			Blue-collar employees only[b]		
	Unemployment frequency (%)	Mean duration (mo.)	Number unemployed	Unemployment frequency (%)	Mean duration (mo.)	Number unemployed
≤20	76.0[c]	4.3	38	75.5	4.2	37
21–30	67.3	3.0	72	67.6	3.1	71
31–40	65.0	2.9	76	71.2	3.0	74
41–50	64.3	3.5	54	71.6	3.6	53
≥51	59.6	3.8	28	71.8	3.8	28
Entire sample	66.2	3.3	268	70.9	3.4	263

[a]Sample, *n* = 405.   [b]Sample, *n* = 371.   [c]See note 31.
Source: Manuscript schedules, Twelfth U.S. Census, 1900. See note 10.

Table 4.8. *Unemployment among males of different ages, laborers in Boston, 1900[a]*

Age	Unemployment frequency (%)	Mean duration (months)	Number unemployed
≤20	45.5[b]	4.4	5
21–30	35.3	3.8	18
31–40	31.3	4.9	21
41–50	33.3	4.7	15
51–60	61.8[c]	4.9	21
≥61	53.3	6.8	8
Entire sample	39.5	4.8	88

[a]Sample, n = 223.   [b]See note 31.   [c]See note 33.
Source: Manuscript schedules, Twelfth U.S. Census, 1900. See note 11.

ties were not necessarily unemployed more often than their younger colleagues (although this did occur in some occupations, e.g., day laboring), but once laid off they had great difficulty locating new jobs. In 1885, the mean duration of unemployment began to increase once a man had reached his forties, and in 1900 both shoe workers and day laborers who had passed the age of fifty were idled for longer stints than were men in their twenties.[33] "A man in the paper mills can get work until he is fifty or sixty if he has steady work," observed a Holyoke resident in the 1890s, "but if he gets out of work when he is forty-five he is not likely to get work again."[34] This prognosis may have been excessively dire, but industrial workers who had passed the prime of life (in contrast to professionals, white-collar employees, and men who remained in agriculture) did have particularly powerful reasons to fear layoffs.[35] Both semiskilled and unskilled workers found that the experience that accompanied advancing age counted for less, in the eyes of their employers, than did the strength and agility possessed by younger men. Older skilled workmen were also particularly hard hit by technological changes because they had limited opportunity and little incentive to learn new trades. For many older men, indeed, a spell of unemployment carried the implicit threat of forced retirement and a permanent loss of income. Since pensions of any sort were rarities during this period, middle-aged unemployed men often found themselves, as Samuel Gompers put it, "living 'twixt hope and fear, searching for work," while their "days of enforced idleness . . . stretched into weeks, the weeks into months."[36]

There were, however, some older workers who had more positive experiences: men who lived in small towns seem to have acquired protection against unemployment as they aged. In 1885, in communities with only a few thousand inhabitants (some of which are listed in Table A.8), men in their fifties and sixties commonly constituted a relatively large, and steadily employed, proportion of the labor force. In the town of Shirley, for example, more than a third of all productive males were over the age of fifty (the proportion was closer to 15% in the state's major cities), and these men were idled far less often than their younger neighbors. By 1885 towns like Shirley were, of course, vestiges of an earlier social order – in which farming and skilled crafts persisted and relationships between employers and employees were still personalized – but that social order seems to have provided older workmen with a level of job security that was unequaled in the state's industrial centers. It was also purchased at a price, paid for by the young. Teenagers in Shirley and Southborough and Leverett and Wilbraham encountered idleness frequencies that were far higher than the norm in their communities, and many young men who grew up in these towns appear to have responded to their joblessness by migrating to the cities. During the depression of the 1880s, at least, there was a trade-off between the security of older men and opportunities for the young.[37]

But the experiences of small-town residents – revealing as they may be – were sideshows to the main event. In the major population centers of the commonwealth, men of all ages were vulnerable, and more or less equally vulnerable, to spells of involuntary idleness. In the labor force as a whole and within most occupations, a man's age had little impact on his fate during slack times. Although some blue-collar workers, particularly among the native born, eventually escaped the threat of unemployment by graduating into fairly secure white-collar or quasi-managerial positions, most manual employees, native and immigrant alike, did not climb that far up the occupational ladder.[38] The reserve army of labor, during good years and bad, contained recruits of all ages. Mature men who headed households and were expected to be primary breadwinners always constituted a majority of the unemployed.[39]

What this meant, of course, was that most working men in Massachusetts did not acquire job security as they aged. Exceptional employers may have protected the positions of faithful employees who had given them years of service, but there was no widespread prin-

ciple of seniority that governed the distribution of layoffs.[40] Young
workers found that their ability to procure steady employment
tended to improve as they reached their twenties or early thirties, but
the improvement was neither dramatic nor ongoing. And once these
no-longer-young workers had reached the age of fifty, the prospect
of long-term joblessness began to loom larger on the horizon. During
the final decades of the nineteenth century – and there is no reason
to believe that things changed decisively between 1900 and 1922 –
men with thirty years' experience in the labor force were about as
vulnerable to unemployment as they had been when they were just
starting to raise families. Little wonder, then, that the sense of uncertainty ran so deep, that anxiety about job loss was so pervasive.
Working-class men knew, from their own experience and from the
experiences of their fathers, uncles, and co-workers, that the problem
of unemployment was theirs for life.[41]

Women without work

> When we are told that girls earn six dollars, ten dollars, or even
> fifteen dollars a week, it has a comfortable sound, if unconnected
> with its accompanying fact that it is from sixteen to thirty-four
> weeks of the year only that they earn these wages, very few earn-
> ing fifteen dollars. There is a great disproportion between the
> yearly earnings and the weekly wages.
> Massachusetts Bureau of Statistics of Labor, 1871

> One of the evils existing in this city is the gradual extinction of
> the male operative. The female operative has the preference . . .
> as quickly as it can be done, women are given men's work to do
> . . . Within a radius of two squares in which I am living, I know
> of a score of young men who are supported by their sisters and
> their mothers, because there is no work in the mills for them.
> A weaver in Lawrence, 1882

> We shut down for two weeks in January for stock taking and gen-
> eral repairs. Only women and boys are laid off.
> Carter's Ink Company, 1914[42]

Women played a variety of roles in the economic life of the commonwealth. Throughout the years between 1870 and 1920, teenage and
adult women performed vitally important, if unpaid, domestic labor;
they often contributed to their households by taking in, and caring
for, boarders; and many women were also full-time members of the
paid labor force. Roughly one-quarter of all "gainful workers" were
female (the percentage rose very gradually during these decades),

and the number of women who worked for wages or salaries increased from approximately 130,000 in 1870 to half a million in 1920. Most of these women were drawn from working-class families; nearly all were employees. There were few female professionals or entrepreneurs in Massachusetts, but there were a great many female factory operatives and service workers. Working women, like working-class men, were dependent upon employers and vulnerable to cyclical, seasonal, technological, and episodic shifts in the demand for labor.[43]

Yet the economic roles and work experiences of women were, in some respects, distinctive. Unlike men, the majority of adult women did not work for pay, and, in general, women, even working-class women, neither expected to become, nor in fact became, permanently or continuously attached to the paid labor force. Most women – and virtually all working-class women – were "gainfully" employed when they were young and single, but marriage typically ended or interrupted a woman's career outside of the home. In 1915, less than 10 percent of the married women in Boston belonged to "gainful occupations"; even in the mill city of Fall River, where wages for men were low and employment opportunities for women abundant, the figure was only 25 percent. The female labor force, thus, was always dominated by women who were single, widowed, or divorced, while married women – in fact as well as in ideology – devoted their energies to raising children and to the performance of unpaid, domestic labor within the home. Women in most households were regarded as supplementary wage earners, and often the relatively meager wages they could earn were less essential than other tasks that they were expected to perform.[44]

Female work experiences were also distinctive in that men and women tended to work in different occupations or in different branches of industry. Although employment opportunities for women expanded considerably between 1870 and 1920, most jobs remained sex-typed, and most females belonged to occupations (or subspecies of occupations) that were dominated by women. In 1900, more than a fifth of all working women in Massachusetts held jobs as domestic servants, and tens of thousands of others worked as nurses, midwives, laundresses, seamstresses, teachers, housekeepers, stenographers, typists, and saleswomen in stores. Similarly, in the state's large manufacturing industries, the detailed division of labor was often accompanied by the sex-typing of specific tasks. In the shoe industry, men were lasters and women were stitchers; in textiles, men were backtenders and women were spoolers. The sources of this sex-typing were varied, but most jobs assigned to women tended to be semiskilled or unskilled, tedious, indoors, and poorly paid. Many men, to be sure, held jobs that possessed these same virtues (except that male wages were usually higher), but the distinction between "men's work" and "women's work" was sufficiently pronounced and extensive that males and females were not simply interchangeable units in one vast labor market – or labor reserve.[45]

Working women, then, had to contend with the same economic conditions and class relationships as did men, although they did so from slightly different social and occupational vantage points. But were these women unemployed when they were not at work? Were all women who had gainful occupations "involuntarily idle" when they were jobless? Such questions are both historical and methodological – since the census surveys of the late nineteenth century did collect unemployment statistics for women, but the meaning of such statistics is open to question. Female workers were, without doubt, subject to spells of idleness, but it has sometimes been suggested that women (or many women, at least) were (and are) able to move in and out of the labor force much as farmer-shoemakers, or Lowell mill girls, did during the first stages of industrialization – without really suffering from unemployment when not working for pay. This suggestion stems from the notion that most women, in the industrial era, have neither needed nor wanted year-round paid employment – because they have commonly belonged to households in which they were not the primary breadwinner and because society has not expected them to work full-time. It could also be argued that female workers have not been altogether idle or unproductive when jobless – because they have often performed useful, if unpaid, domestic labor. Women, therefore, can be, and have been, viewed as a latent reserve of labor that does not become unemployed when its productive energies are released from the harness of capitalist enterprise.[46]

This image of female employment patterns clearly does not apply to many of the women who worked in Massachusetts between 1870 and 1920 – widows who headed households and single women who lived in boardinghouses, for example – but it does possess some empirical foundation. The majority of working women, throughout these years, did belong to households that also contained male breadwinners whose earnings were generally larger than those of females. And some of the most predictably unsteady occupations in the state (e.g., seamstresses and straw workers) had a disproportionately large number of married female members. This last fact, in particular, suggests that irregular jobs may sometimes have been filled by women who perceived themselves to be part-time, supplementary wage earners.[47] Moreover, detailed study of a sample of working women in Brockton in 1900 (Table 4.9) reveals that those women whose fa-

Table 4.9. *Unemployment among women in Brockton, 1900*

Occupation	No. in sample	Unem-ployment frequency (%)	Mean duration (mo.)	% single	% married	%widowed and divorced	% native-born
All shoe workers	257	63.8	3.1	68.5	21.0	10.5	79.0
Shoe stitchers	137	63.5	2.8	57.7	29.2	13.1	81.0
All other occupations[a]	302	23.8	4.5	70.9	15.2	13.9	66.9
White-collar employees	80	28.7	4.7	77.5	11.3	11.3	85.0
Garment industry	55	38.2	5.7	50.9	32.7	16.4	81.8
Domestic service	105	6.7	3.0	77.1	5.7	17.1	43.8
Other blue-collar	35	54.3	3.3	71.4	22.9	5.7	80.0
Professional	6	0	0	66.7	16.7	16.7	50.0
Other	21	9.5	5.0	66.7	19.0	14.3	57.1

[a]All occupations outside of the shoe industry.
Source: Manuscript schedules, Twelfth U.S. Census, 1900. See note 48.

milial situations were least likely to engender a need for year-round work were most likely to be found in relatively unsteady trades. The wives and daughters of resident male household heads were notably more concentrated in high-unemployment occupations than were women who were boarders or who were themselves heads of households.[48] Such evidence is not conclusive, but there apparently were women in the labor force who did not view themselves as year-round workers and for whom idleness may not have been altogether involuntary.

But such women were not typical of female workers in Massachusetts during these years. Although there may well have been a transitional period, in the middle decades of the nineteenth century, when women welcomed the expansion of part-time employment opportunities in highly seasonal industries, most working women, by the 1880s or 1890s, preferred to have year-round jobs.[49] A large majority of the women who declared themselves to be "gainful workers" did labor year-round between 1880 and 1900, and the proportion that did so fluctuated with the business cycle – which strongly suggests that opportunities rather than inclinations determined the rhythms of employment. Female workers throughout the state also complained loudly when their jobs were unsteady: although most working women were not entirely self-supporting as individuals, they contributed to a family wage and a family income, and a spell of idleness for a female worker diminished her family's income just as surely as – if less markedly than – a spell of idleness for her father or brother. The material and psychological needs that led women to seek employment may have been somewhat different, and less pressing, than those that propelled men, but only a small fraction of the female labor force seems to have been so indifferent to layoffs that they can properly be excluded from the ranks of the "unemployed." (Indeed, there is some evidence to suggest that women who wanted to work only part-time did not report themselves to be "gainful workers" and therefore were not counted as unemployed.)[50] Unemployment statistics for females need to be handled with some extra care, but it appears likely that working women who were idle and who reported themselves to be unemployed knew what they were talking about.[51]

In fact, the available statistical evidence reveals that, in many respects, female unemployment patterns closely resembled those that obtained for men. As noted in Chapter 3, women and men encountered virtually identical statewide unemployment frequencies (and mean durations) in both 1885 and 1900, while in 1890 women were slightly more likely to work steadily. In all three years, men and

women also had similar experiences in each of the state's major urban, industrial centers. During the depressed year of 1884–5, the difference between male and female unemployment frequencies exceeded 7 percent in only one of the state's ten largest cities (Fall
River); in 1900 the figures were almost uniformly within 2 percent of
one another. Throughout the commonwealth, unemployment levels
for women fluctuated with the business cycle, and, during good
years and bad, similar proportions of men and women lost their jobs
for comparably long stretches of time.[52]

For women, as for men, unemployment levels also varied considerably from one occupation or industry to the next. In 1885, women
who belonged to twenty-two occupations faced idleness frequencies
that were greater than 50 percent, while members of twenty-one
other occupations had a less than 1-in-4 chance of losing their jobs.
(See Appendix A, Tables A.9–A.12.) Through this period, women
who held white-collar or professional positions were rarely out of
work, and women in service occupations and trade also tended to be
steadily employed. But women who worked in manufacturing – particularly those who made shoes, clothing, straw goods, and jewelry
– were frequently jobless during depressions and during prosperous
years. The broad contours of the sectoral distribution of unemployment were the same for women as they were for men: the odds of a
woman becoming unemployed depended less on her sex than on the
industry in which she worked.[53]

Men and women who worked in the same occupation or industry,
moreover, usually encountered similar levels of involuntary idleness.
As Tables A.9 through A.12 reveal, there were numerous exceptions
to this pattern, particularly in 1885, but, on the whole, occupations
that were unsteady for women were also unsteady for men, and low-
risk trades were comparably consistent.[54] In the textile and shoe industries, for example, statewide unemployment frequencies (and
mean durations) for males and females were very close to one another in every census year from 1885 to 1900. And the figures for
individual communities confirm that the practice of laying off equal
proportions of men and women was a common, although not universal, one.[55] That this was so, that there was little sex discrimination
in the allocation of unemployment, was, in good part, a consequence
of the sex-typing of jobs in both industries. When shoe production
was cut back, similar proportions of female stitchers and male lasters
had to be laid off. Yet even among men and women who performed
exactly the same tasks, unemployment levels also tended to be uniform. When James Whitehead, a weaver, was asked in 1895 whether
male or female weavers were let go first during depressions, he re-

plied simply that "it would affect both."[56] His succinct statement was confirmed by the unusually detailed statistics that were collected during that year. (See Table A.11.) Not all industries, to be sure, were quite as egalitarian as textiles and shoes, but, as a rule, men and women who worked in the same industry or occupation faced similar odds of losing their jobs.[57]

Women who belonged to the paid labor force thus encountered the same general uncertainties of employment as did men. But there were, nonetheless, some significant and revealing differences between male and female unemployment patterns, differences that stemmed from the sexual division of labor in the workplace and in the household. The sex-typing of jobs and the distinctive domestic role of women, coupled with the attitudes and expectations that accompanied women into the labor force, produced some notable twists in the distribution of unemployment among working women. Males and females both belonged to the reserve army of labor, but their experiences did not always run parallel to one another.

One important twist was that several of the largest, feminized occupations in Massachusetts offered unusually steady employment. Throughout this period, the single largest, and perhaps least exalted, female occupation was domestic service, and servants were rarely unemployed. The percentage of working women who were domestic servants declined considerably between 1870 and 1920 (from more than 30% to roughly 10%), but even in the latter year there were more than 45,000 domestics whose jobs were little affected by either seasonal or cyclical fluctuations in the economy. And the declining importance of domestic jobs was counterbalanced by the extremely rapid growth and feminization of clerical work, particularly after 1900. Clerical jobs, too, were uncommonly steady, and by 1920 one out of every five working women held a clerical position of one sort or another. In effect, the sex-typing of domestic labor and office work (as well as some sales occupations) created a large number of essentially stable jobs that were open to women – and, in the case of domestics, open to women who lacked both schooling and industrial skills. None of these jobs paid particularly well, but their prominence in the economy meant that a sizable proportion of the female labor force (and a sizable number of working-class women) had some assurance of continuous employment.[58]

Such assurance must have been highly valued because many other sex-typed jobs offered women both low wages and sharply seasonal rhythms of employment. Some manufacturing occupations, in fact, seem to have become "women's work" precisely because they yielded annual incomes that could only have been adequate for workers who were (and were viewed as) supplementary wage earners. One of the very first reports of the Massachusetts Bureau of Statistics of Labor noted that "many employments in which women are engaged last but half, or less than half the year." Similarly, Carroll Wright's well-known study of the "working girls of Boston" in the 1880s discovered that three-quarters of these "girls" (his sample did not include domestics) were unable to find year-round jobs.[59] Women constituted the bulk of the labor force in the manufacture of several seasonal products, including chocolates and straw goods. (The state's baseball makers were all female, and baseball makers in 1885 had the highest recorded unemployment frequency of the late nineteenth century.) They also dominated many of the most poorly paid branches of the garment and shoe industries. The proportion of working women who belonged to these low-wage, sex-typed, and chronically irregular occupations probably declined between 1870 and the close of the century, but the economy of Massachusetts always contained some industries that relied on women to fill positions in which a living wage could not be earned, even in prosperous years.[60] Although some of the women who held such positions were, no doubt, choosing to work for only part of the year, there were certainly thousands of others who would have preferred to work year-round.[61] "It is the constant occurrence of waiting spells," concluded Carroll Wright, "which makes the lives of the working girls so hard."[62]

The belief that women were (and certainly ought to be) supplementary wage earners who did not depend on their incomes for self-support – a belief that was particularly prevalent in the middle class – also led employers who hired workers of both sexes to discriminate against women during slack times. As noted earlier in this section, the gaps between male and female idleness levels within occupations and industries were rarely large, but they were strikingly consistent in their direction: women were unemployed more often than men. During each of the three years for which statewide data are available (1885, 1890, and 1900), unemployment frequencies were higher for women than they were for men in more than 75 percent of the occupations that claimed members of both sexes. (See Tables A.9, A.10, and A.12.) And the patterns within individual communities were similar.[63] Apparently, employers and foremen did, at the margins at least, distinguish between men and women – either in selecting workers for layoffs or in assigning workers to particularly dispensable tasks.

The extent of this discrimination may, perhaps, have diminished during the final decades of the nineteenth century (the available data are inconclusive), but in 1900 there remained a significant number of employers who felt even fewer compunctions about laying off women than they did about laying off men.[64] The rationale for such practices appears to have been ideological rather than economic – since women, as a rule, were paid less than their male counterparts. Indeed, the practice of giving preferential treatment to adult men was sometimes cited by management as evidence of a firm's interest in the welfare of its employees. Women did not "need" to work as badly as men did, and, as a result, they could be laid off more easily.[65] Given prevailing wage structures and the sex-typing of jobs, women were rarely the "last hired and first fired." But in many trades they did constitute something of a "reserve within the reserve," a decentralized and relatively immobile supply of labor that was called upon to absorb an extra share of the irregularity that was endemic to the economy.

Female employment patterns were distinctive in one other respect as well: women served not only as a reserve of labor for industry but also as a reserve source of income for the households to which they belonged. Adult women who customarily remained at home were still potential, and often experienced, wage earners who could enter or reenter the labor force when male unemployment levels were unusually high. Systematic data revealing this dynamic are scanty, but a unique assembly of monthly statistics, collected during the depression of the 1890s, indicates that it did indeed occur in locales offering diversified employment opportunities. In Boston, Cambridge, and Somerville, during the census year 1894–5, the number of women in the labor force rose and fell each month in tandem with the male unemployment rate. In communities dominated by single manufacturing industries (like Fall River, Lowell, or Brockton), no such phenomenon occurred.[66] Women did not displace or replace male workers, but, when necessary (and possible), they obtained jobs in niches of the economy that were open to women and relatively unaffected by the business cycle. Thanks to the sexual division of labor in the household and the sex-typing of some stable jobs in the service sector, there were adult women in Massachusetts who probably had the incongruous experience of being paid wage earners only during depressions.[67]

Finally, it should be noted that the distribution of unemployment among women of different ages and nationalities differed, in several ways, from the patterns that prevailed for men. Somewhat surprisingly, women, unlike men, did tend to work more steadily as they grew older. As Tables 4.10 and 4.11 indicate, not only did women in their thirties experience fewer layoffs than did "girls" in their teens and early twenties (something that was also true for men), but

Table 4.10. *Unemployment among women of different ages, Massachusetts, 1885*

Age	Unemployment frequency (%)	Mean duration (mo.)	Annual unemployment rate (%)	Number unemployed
10–13	19.4	4.8	7.8	219
14–19	38.0	4.2	13.3	18,689
20–9	28.9	3.7	8.9	27,533
30–9	27.0	3.8	8.6	9,052
40–9	23.2	4.1	7.9	4,388
50–9	21.8	4.4	8.0	2,091
60–79	18.2	4.9	7.4	960
80–	0.5	5.6	0.2	27

Sources: MBSL, *18 AR* (Boston, 1887), pp. 152–7; *Census of Massachusetts: 1885,* I, part 2 (Boston, 1888), pp. 540–41, 612–22, 628.

women in their forties and fifties witnessed a further improvement in their ability to work year-round. Exactly why this occurred is unclear. In part, no doubt, it was the result of job selection. The fairly small number of older women who were gainfully employed (most of whom were widowed, divorced, or single) were often primary, rather than supplementary, wage earners. They may consequently have placed a higher value on job security than did the young: older women, and particularly widowed and divorced women, did tend to congregate in relatively steady jobs.[68] But the data from Brockton suggest that job selection was not the only factor – since even among shoe workers, older women seem to have been laid off less often than their younger colleagues. Perhaps these women were more skilled or more hardworking; or, perhaps, employers and foremen gave these older workers preferential treatment because they recognized that women in their forties and fifties who labored as shoe stitchers were very much in need of maximizing their incomes.[69] If so, then older female workers, ironically, acquired some job security precisely because they were not expected to be members of the paid labor force.

The incidence of unemployment among women born in different nations contrasted even more sharply with the male pattern – at least during the final decades of the nineteenth century. Immigrant women, from 1885 to 1900, were jobless less often than were native-born female workers. In 1885, 23 percent of all foreign-born women in the commonwealth were unemployed, compared to 34 percent for natives; fifteen years later, among Brockton women who worked out-

Table 4.11. *Unemployment among women of different ages, Brockton, 1900*

Age	All shoe workers[a]			Shoe stitchers[b]			All other occupations[c]		
	Unemployment frequency (%)	Mean duration (mo.)	% of sample	Unemployment frequency (%)	Mean duration (mo.)	% of sample	Unemployment frequency (%)	Mean duration (mo.)	% of sample
≤17	64.3	4.0	5.4	66.7	3.5	4.4	50.0	4.8	5.9
18–20	72.7	3.4	17.2	92.9	2.8	10.2	28.6	4.4	16.2
21–5	72.7	3.4	21.4	80.0	3.4	14.6	23.3	3.9	19.9
26–30	64.6	2.6	18.6	69.0	2.4	21.2	19.6	4.5	16.9
31–5	51.4	2.6	13.7	50.0	2.6	20.4	20.0	3.9	11.6
36–40	58.3	2.7	9.3	60.0	2.7	10.9	27.6	4.5	9.6
41–50[d]	55.6	3.7	10.5	41.2	3.1	12.4	15.6	5.8	10.6
51–65	50.0	2.2	3.9	50.0	2.0	5.8	17.4	5.8	7.6
66–	—	—	0	—	—	0	20.0	2.0	1.7
Entire sample	63.8	3.1	100.0	63.5	2.8	100.0	23.8	4.5	100.0

[a]Sample, *n* = 257.   [b]Sample, *n* = 137.
[c]All occupations outside the shoe industry. Sample, *n* = 302.   [d]See note 68.
Source: Manuscript schedules, Twelfth U.S. Census, 1900. See note 48.

side the shoe industry, native-born workers were more than twice as likely to have been laid off as their immigrant counterparts. The source of this pattern was hardly obscure: immigrant women worked in domestic service, while native white women, as a rule, did not. Domestic jobs may have been steady, but their shortcomings – in pay, hours, and status – rendered them unacceptable to many natives. Consequently, immigrants dominated the occupation, and a sizable proportion of all foreign-born female workers were servants.[70] For much the same reason, women from different immigrant and ethnic groups faced widely disparate odds of becoming unemployed. Irish, Scandinavian, German, and English Canadian immigrants, all of whom were heavily concentrated in domestic service, were far less likely to have been unemployed than were women from England and French Canada, who tended to work in manufacturing.[71] Similarly, black women were probably unemployed less often than native-born white women because black women, like black men, were obliged to find jobs in the service sector of the economy.[72]

During the first decades of the twentieth century, however, changes in the occupational structure turned the tables on immigrant women. The declining importance of domestic service, coupled with the rapid expansion of clerical work, shifted the majority of steady, feminized jobs from immigrant to native terrain. The daughters of immigrants did have access to clerical positions, but immigrants themselves did not: in 1920, fewer than 10 percent of all female clerical workers were foreign-born. It is likely, then, that by the end of World War I native-born women were working more steadily than were immigrants. Although Irish-born women probably continued to enjoy considerable job security, since they remained in domestic service, "new immigrant" women, from eastern and southern Europe, commonly took jobs in manufacturing, often in seasonal industries. (See Figure 4.1.) In 1915, roughly 10 percent of all Italian-born working women in Massachusetts were employed in candy factories alone; nearly 16 percent of all Russian women were sewing machine operators. The lines of stratification within the female labor force were being redrawn, and job security increasingly became a perquisite of native birth. As domestic service gradually lost its preeminent position among female occupations, joblessness became a more widespread problem for immigrants, and unemployment patterns among women came to resemble more closely the patterns that obtained for men.[73]

In sum, there were a number of characteristic (and gender-related) patterns to the distribution of unemployment among women. Yet the role of women in the history of unemployment was not nearly as

Figure 4.1. Unemployed women, from Lithuanian and Syrian families, who were participating in an "out-of-work" class conducted by the International Institute for Young Women (a branch of the YWCA) in Lawrence, 1914. (Courtesy Immigrant City Archives, Lawrence, Massachusetts.)

distinctive or as simple as certain models might suggest. Working women were not blessed with a structural immunity to unemployment when they were jobless; nor did women, in and of themselves, constitute a reserve of labor that absorbed the impact of economic fluctuations while men worked steadily year in and year out. Adult women who normally did not work for pay did function as a reserve source of labor – since they could be drawn into the work force by extreme conditions of familial or societal need, such as depressions or wars – but membership in the reserve army was not a sex-linked condition.[74] Men were unemployed as often as women, and the sex-typing of occupations meant that most reserves of labor were also sex segregated. Employers of both men and women sought to maintain pools of workers who would be available when they were needed; the social composition of individual labor reserves reflected and reinforced the sexual division of labor in society.[75]

The existence of reserves – rather than *a* reserve – also meant that
men and women, as a rule, were not directly competing with one
another for jobs or displacing one another from occupations. Episodes of competition and displacement did, of course, arise. In the
1880s and 1890s, male printers (who, not surprisingly, had excellent
access to the press) complained bitterly and loudly that their skills
were being diluted and their jobs taken by half-trained "girls." Simultaneously, female garment workers were complaining, with equal
vehemence, that Christian women were losing their jobs to Jewish
men who were favored by Jewish employers. Although both complaints had some merit, they were significant not because males were
entirely pushed out of the printing industry or females out of the
garment trades (neither, in fact, occurred) but rather because they
expressed fears and anxieties that were widespread among men and
women. In fact, relatively few trades witnessed the wholesale displacement of workers of one sex by workers of the other, but employees in most occupations were acutely sensitive to the threat of competition, to the possible constriction or disappearance of employment
opportunities. Members of the opposite sex were potential rivals as
well as partners, and the insecurity bred by years of chronic unemployment was a condition – and an emotion – that men and women
shared.[76]

Segmented competition

There was something both random and egalitarian about the distribution of unemployment during the era of uncertainty. Layoffs affected young Irish laborers, female shoe stitchers in their forties, Yankee machinists in midlife, and newly arrived Lithuanian rubber
factory operatives. Some social groups fared better than others and
enough better to be the legitimate objects of envy and anger. But few
members of the working class could realistically regard unemployment as somebody else's problem: the ranks of the unemployed always included men and women of all ages and nationalities. The con-
tinental divide that separated the secure from the insecure ran along
fault lines of class rather than age, sex, race, or ethnicity.

This democratic sharing of misfortune was, in part, a reflection of
the plurality of labor reserves and the segmentation of the labor market. Since reserves existed in nearly all blue-collar occupations and
since many trades tended to be either sex segregated or dominated
by employees from particular ethnic groups, workers with very diverse social characteristics inescapably came to belong to the "reserve

army." But another factor was involved as well: the absence of formal internal structures within most individual labor reserves. In most occupations or industries, there were few rules – or even widespread prejudices – that governed either the allocation of layoffs or access to stable jobs. Employers and foremen, in general, could hire and fire whomever they wanted. The labor markets of Massachusetts were, in effect, less rationalized and more purely competitive than they were eventually to become. It was the absence of systematic privilege that made insecurity such a pervasive presence. Indeed, the development, in the twentieth century, of new principles and formal policies for allocating the insecurities endemic to capitalism (e.g., seniority systems) can only be understood as a response to the intolerably widespread uncertainty that dominated working-class life between the Civil War and the 1920s. But those developments – of policy and politics – constitute a later chapter in the story.[77]

5   *From place to place*

Although predominantly industrial and – by American standards – unprepossessing in size, the Commonwealth of Massachusetts housed more than three hundred communities with widely varied economic and social structures. Boston, of course, was the largest city in the state, and its densely populated metropolitan area served, throughout this period, as the commercial and financial capital of New England and as a manufacturing center in its own right. The populous eastern counties of Massachusetts also contained the well-known textile cities of Lowell, Lawrence, Fall River, and New Bedford, major shoe manufacturing centers like Lynn, Brockton, and Haverhill, and fishing towns that lined the coast from Gloucester on the north shore down to Cape Cod and the islands of Martha's Vineyard and Nantucket. West of Boston was the city of Worcester, which specialized in wire manufacturing and metalworking; still further west was the steadily growing city of Springfield, as well as a row of Connecticut River valley mill towns, including Holyoke and Chicopee. Sprinkled throughout the state were dozens of medium-sized towns and small (yet hopeful) cities that contained sizable, and often specialized, manufacturing interests. And in scores of small communities, farming remained the mainstay of economic life.

Where, amid all this diversity, were the unemployed? Scattered allusions in preceding pages certainly suggest that involuntary idleness was not a weed that flourished only in a few peculiar local soils, but the issue demands more direct and systematic treatment. Did the community in which workers lived have a significant impact on their chances of becoming jobless? Did unemployment statistics for the state as a whole reflect the overcrowding of Boston's labor markets, while men and women elsewhere tended to work steadily? Or was unemployment, perhaps, more common in semirural backwaters than in the dynamic cities? The answers to such questions are essential to an understanding of both the evolution of unemployment and the experiences of the unemployed. As it turns out, they also shed a great deal of light on the restless, and seemingly rootless, mobility of Americans that was so common during these years.

111

Cities and towns

By the time unemployment was first reliably measured in Massachusetts, it had become a statewide phenomenon and a statewide problem. In 1885, the annual frequency of unemployment, for men and women, exceeded 20 percent in eleven of the state's fourteen counties; the mean duration, in each of these counties, was at least 3.8 months. Unemployment levels were not everywhere the same, but working people throughout the state – from Berkshire and Hampshire counties in the west to Essex County in the northeast to Bristol County in the southeast – were vulnerable to spells of "enforced idleness." (See Figure 5.1.) Ten years later, the pattern was similar: in twelve counties, more than one-fifth of all workers were jobless at some point during the census year. Had unemployment statistics been collected in the 1840s or 1850s, they might well have looked different, but by the final decades of the nineteenth century the problem of unemployment had taken root in most, if not all, regions of the state.[1]

By the 1880s, unemployment levels were also remarkably consistent in communities of different sizes. As Table 5.1 demonstrates, joblessness was a serious threat to wage earners, during the last two depressions of the nineteenth century, in small towns, medium-sized towns, and cities with thirty thousand or more inhabitants.[2] The only marked exception to this consistency was Boston, where unemployment levels were below average (often well below average) throughout the era of uncertainty.[3] This exception was an important one (and is discussed further later in this chapter), but outside the Hub the size of the community in which workers lived had little bearing on the odds of their becoming, or remaining, unemployed.[4] Capitalism flourished in the countryside as well as in the cities, and market forces took their toll wherever there were employers and employees.[5]

Similarly, the experience of joblessness was a common one in communities that were growing rapidly and in communities that were stagnant. In the 1880s and 1890s, as Table 5.2 indicates, a community's decadal rate of population growth had fairly little to do with the unemployment levels encountered by its residents during depressions. Not surprisingly, relatively few of the fastest-growing communities suffered extremely high (more than 40%) unemployment frequencies in either 1885 or 1895. And the figures for the 1890s, when the unemployment survey was restricted to employees, suggest that stagnant communities were particularly likely to have witnessed abnormally high joblessness levels among wage earners.[6] Yet what is most striking about the breakdowns in Table 5.2 is not the

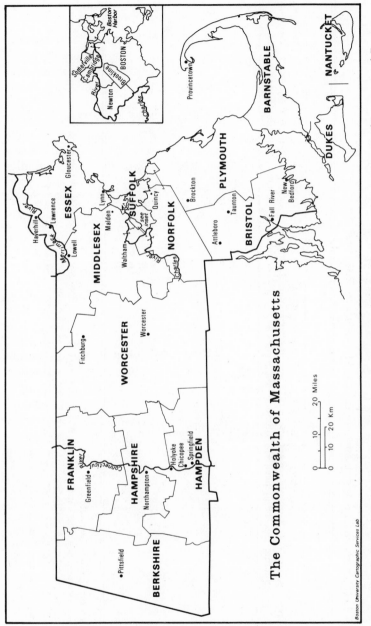

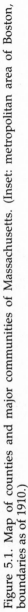

Figure 5.1. Map of counties and major communities of Massachusetts. (Inset: metropolitan area of Boston, boundaries as of 1910.)

Table 5.1. *Unemployment levels by community size, Massachusetts, 1885 and 1895*

Population (thousands)	1885[a]				1895[b]			
	Number of communities	Average[c] unemployment frequency (%)	Average mean duration (mo.)	Average annual unemployment rate (%)	Number of communities	Average unemployment frequency (%)	Average mean duration (mo.)	Average annual unemployment rate (%)
>100	1	19.4	4.4	7.1	1	18.3	3.4	5.2
70–100	0	—	—	—	4	32.9	3.3	9.0
50–70	4	36.2	4.1	12.4	5	27.6	3.2	7.4
30–50	4	31.2	4.7	12.2	5	29.7	3.5	8.7
20–30	8	29.3	4.2	10.3	8	24.7	3.5	7.2
15–20	3	25.6	3.5	7.5	5	21.0	3.3	5.8
10–15	11	36.8	4.1	12.6	11	26.0	3.3	7.2
5–10	32	32.4	4.1	11.1	46	29.8	3.2	7.9
3–5	53	37.0	4.4	13.6	46	31.3	2.8	7.3
2–3	54	32.7	4.3	11.7	41	33.2	2.9	8.0
<2	178	22.4	4.5	8.4	181	33.8	2.5	7.0

[a]Figures for males only. See note 2.

[b]Males and females. See note 2 and Appendix B regarding the differences between the 1885 and 1895 unemployment surveys.

[c]The term "average," used in this table to avoid confusion, refers to the mean.

Sources: MBSL, *18 AR* (Boston, 1887), pp. 5–151; *Census of Massachusetts: 1885*, I, part 1 (Boston, 1888), pp. xxv ff.; *Census of Massachusetts: 1895*, VII (Boston, 1900), pp. v–xv, 5–103.

Table 5.2. *Unemployment and population growth in Massachusetts communities, 1880–1900*

Communities with 1880–90 population growth of:	Percentage of communities with 1885 unemployment frequency of:[a]			
	0–19.9 (%)	20.0–39.9 (%)	≥40.0 (%)	Number[b]
<5%	42.9	33.1	24.0	175
5–25%	31.8	32.9	35.3	85
>25%	41.4	42.9	15.7	70
All communities	39.7	35.2	25.2	330

Communities with 1890–1900 population growth of:	Percentage of communities with 1895 unemployment frequency of:[a]			
	0–19.9 (%)	20.0–39.9 (%)	≥40.0 (%)	Number[b]
<5%	25.6	39.4	35.0	160
5–25%	21.6	51.0	27.5	102
>25%	21.3	58.7	20.0	75
All communities	23.4	47.2	29.4	337

[a]Males and females.
[b]Excludes communities in which boundary changes affected growth rate.
Sources: MBSL, *18 AR* (Boston, 1887), pp. 267–9; MBSL, *21 AR* (Boston, 1891), pp. 118–35; *Census of Massachusetts: 1895*, VII (Boston, 1900), pp. 90–103; MBSL, *31 AR* (Boston, 1901), pp. 8–18.

presence but the absence of clear-cut trends, the apparent weakness of the relationship between population growth and unemployment.[7] Some cities and towns that were hit hard by the depressions of the 1880s and 1890s were growing very rapidly; others were not growing at all. Some communities in which unemployment levels were well below average were luring migrants in large numbers; others were stagnant. The short-run link between unemployment and population growth was doubtless much stronger, but both Table 5.2 and more limited collections of data for the first decades of the twentieth century reveal that a community's growth record, over a period of five to ten years, offered few clues to its vulnerability to unemployment.[8] Reserves of labor existed in dying rural backwaters, in small cities that had lost their vitality, and in dynamic communities that were attracting thousands of newcomers.

There were, however, dramatic and widespread differences in unemployment levels among the individual towns and cities of the Bay State. The incidence of joblessness was quite consistent in different regions and among communities of different sizes and with different growth rates. But during any given year the incidence of unemployment varied greatly from one community to the next. In both 1885 and 1895, less than half the communities in the commonwealth had unemployment frequencies that were within 10 percentage points of the statewide average. (See Table 5.2.) In the latter year, more than seventy cities and towns had unemployment frequencies below 20 percent, while a comparable number had frequencies that exceeded 40 percent. There were dozens of communities in which more than half the labor force was unemployed and more than a score in which the incidence of joblessness was below 10 percent.[9]

These contrasts were most extreme among the smaller towns of the commonwealth – in 1895 a resident of Foxborough was seven times more likely to be unemployed than an inhabitant of Orange – but unemployment levels in the major cities were also highly varied.[10] During the census year of 1895, for example, the incidence of joblessness in Fall River and New Bedford was more than twice as great as it was in Lawrence, Springfield, and Somerville; workers in Worcester tended to remain jobless for five weeks longer than their counterparts in Lowell.[11] Similarly, twentieth-century trade unionists who lived in different cities often faced radically different odds of being able to work year-round. Even during prosperous years, when the range in unemployment frequencies narrowed considerably, workers in some cities were idled far more often than were others.[12] (See Table 5.3.)

As importantly, the landscape of unemployment was constantly being rearranged. Major swings in the business cycle affected virtually all communities, but, since they did not hit every city and town with the same force, comparative conditions often changed substantially between prosperous years and depressions. In 1890 and 1900, when the economy was thriving, workers in Fall River labored as steadily, or more steadily, than workers in Lynn and Cambridge. But when the economy was depressed, it was much harder to find a job in Fall River.[13] (See Table 5.3.) And the conditions that prevailed during any one depression did not necessarily recur during the next drop in business activity. Although the small town of Upton did earn the dubious distinction of having the highest idleness frequency in the state in both 1885 and 1895, Upton's persistent ill fortune was unusual: only a third of the sixty communities that had the highest

Table 5.3. *Unemployment levels in ten cities, 1885–1922*[a]

	1885, males		1885, females		1890, males		1890, females		1895, males and females		1900, males		1900, females		Trade unionists[d]	
	UF[b]	MD[c]	UF	MD	UF	MD	UF	MD	UF	MD	UF	MD	UF	MD	1908–16	1917–22
Fall River	51.5	3.7	65.1	3.2	17.5	3.3	15.8	2.7	63.0	2.8	15.6	4.0	14.0	3.9	26.1	39.7
Lynn	42.4	3.9	44.9	3.8	32.1	3.3	30.0	3.4	32.0	4.1	25.0	3.7	25.3	3.7	21.5	53.0
Lawrence	34.5	5.2	39.4	4.4	—	—	—	—	19.9	2.6	19.4	3.3	19.8	3.1	36.0	56.1
Worcester	34.1	4.1	27.9	4.2	13.7	3.3	14.1	3.4	24.6	4.0	15.8	3.9	18.2	3.7	20.1	33.6
Lowell	32.9	3.9	34.5	3.2	11.9	3.6	11.3	3.3	26.0	2.7	16.1	3.7	15.3	3.6	30.7	33.6
Cambridge	27.1	4.5	24.8	4.9	15.9	3.6	13.0	3.7	21.6	3.7	21.3	4.2	18.5	4.0	11.9	—
New Bedford	23.4	5.0	19.7	4.9	—	—	—	—	48.0	2.9	13.1	4.5	11.0	4.1	34.3	42.5
Springfield	20.6	4.7	19.1	4.1	—	—	—	—	22.9	3.1	15.7	4.2	17.8	4.0	13.5	32.0
Boston	19.4	4.4	16.0	4.3	14.1	3.7	11.2	3.4	19.5	3.9	17.7	3.9	15.9	3.9	22.8	29.6
Somerville	13.3	4.7	15.1	5.1	—	—	—	—	20.0	3.5	14.1	4.3	16.1	4.4	—	—

[a]The ten largest cities in the state in 1900.

[b]Unemployment frequency (%).

[c]Mean duration (mo.).

[d]Estimated mean annual frequencies (%) for the years indicated. Estimates based upon adjusted "all causes" quarterly unemployment rates. See Appendix B.

Sources: MBSL, 18 AR (Boston, 1887), pp. 166–215; *Eleventh U.S. Census, Population* (Washington, 1897), part II, pp. 638–9, 644–5, 668–9, 686–9, 742–3; *Census of Massachusetts: 1895*, VII (Boston, 1900), pp. 5–103; *Twelfth U.S. Census, Occupations* (Washington, 1904), pp. 494–9, 506–11, 560–3, 588–91, 598–603, 625–7, 732–9, 760–3. For the sources of the 1908–22 figures, see note 12.

unemployment frequencies in 1885 achieved the same ranking ten years later.[14] Similarly, the trade union statistics suggest that the cities that were hardest hit by the depressions of 1908, 1914, and 1921 were not those that had suffered the worst unemployment of the late nineteenth century.[15]

Indeed, even during spells of prosperity, unemployment levels in different communities bobbed up and down like horses on a merry-go-round. In October 1899, reports from manufacturers revealed that unemployment was increasing in ten cities and declining in four others; ten months later, employment conditions were improving in eight cities and deteriorating in six. "Local conditions so affect the state of employment," concluded the Massachusetts Bureau of Statistics of Labor during the Progressive era, "that there is no uniform correspondence between the percentages of idleness in the respective cities with the corresponding percentages for the State as a whole."[16]

These variations and fluctuations were not random in their occurrence: the experiences of individual communities were, to some extent, predictable reflections of their economic structures. Among the smaller towns of the commonwealth, those that had little industry and remained primarily agricultural (and consequently had a relatively large proportion of self-employed adults) tended to have the lowest and most stable unemployment frequencies.[17] Towns that were devoted to fishing or to manufacturing had more erratic rhythms of work, and the highest unemployment levels invariably occurred in those small or medium-sized manufacturing towns that were dominated by a single industry or firm.[18] As the Reverend Jesse H. Jones of North Abington observed during the depression of the 1890s, "Anyone who will look over the village could see . . . in a day that the very constitution of a manufacturing village, shoe or otherwise, is such that when the business of the village is stopped, there isn't and can't be anything else that they can go into."[19]

Large cities that were dominated by single industries also tended to have high or volatile unemployment rates. In Lynn, Brockton, and other cities where the dominant industry was sharply seasonal, joblessness levels were chronically above average. In contrast, the major centers of textile and paper manufacturing generally witnessed relatively little unemployment in prosperous years but often had extremely high levels of joblessness during cyclical downturns. During depressions, the most severe urban unemployment problems were almost always to be found in Lowell, Lawrence, Fall River, or New Bedford.[20]

Conversely, unemployment rates tended to be comparatively low and stable in those cities that offered diverse employment opportu-

nities to their inhabitants. Workers in Boston labored relatively steadily because manufacturing in the Hub was highly diversified and because the commercial sector, where jobs were reasonably secure, was
large. Indeed, Boston was one of two cities in 1900 (Somerville was
the other) where there were more jobs for men in trade and transportation than in manufacturing. The benefits of this diversity extended to residents of nearby communities – Cambridge, Somerville,
Chelsea, and Malden all had relatively low unemployment frequencies in both 1885 and 1895 – and they were replicated in Worcester
and Springfield. Neither of these cities had a single, dominant industry, and both tended to have below-average unemployment frequencies throughout the period.[21]

But these structural characteristics did not account for all the variety in local unemployment levels. Far from it. The experiences of
different communities were too disparate, too changeable, and too
unsynchronized to be attributed to a few clear-cut and foreseeable
factors that distinguished economic life in one city or town from economic life in another. Many of the shifts and contrasts that occurred
had little to do with any discernible statewide patterns, and there
were numerous exceptions to the patterns themselves. Communities
dominated by the same industry, for example, sometimes had radically different unemployment frequencies. In 1895, conditions were
far worse in Fall River than they were in Lowell or Lawrence; in 1921,
the unemployment rate in the shoe city of Haverhill was nearly triple
the rate that prevailed in Brockton.[22]

This was so because local unemployment levels were determined
not only by the health of the national economy and the characteristics
of particular industries but also by circumstances, conditions, and
decisions that were themselves local. Floods, fires, bankruptcies, and
plant shutdowns occurred not in "Massachusetts" but in individual
locales. Cities and towns often specialized not merely in the production of textiles or shoes but rather in the production of particular
kinds of textiles or shoes: Brockton made men's shoes, while Lynn
made women's shoes, and the demand for each had its own
rhythm.[23] In every industry, moreover, some firms had better market
positions than others, some were better managed or luckier than others, and not all companies pursued identical strategies for coping
with market fluctuations. Economic competition yielded variety, and
growth produced flux. In 1895, workers who lived in North Adams
worked much more steadily than did residents of most textile manufacturing centers because the Arnold Mills happened to be making
a new and (despite the depression) successful line of "toy stuffed"
dogs and cats.[24]

Table 5.4. *Unemployment frequencies (%) in selected occupations in major cities, 1885, 1890, and 1900*

City (ranked by aggregate male unemployment frequency in each year)	Laborers	Masons	Carpenters	Machinists	Boot- and shoemakers		Cotton mill operatives[a]		Servants (female)	Seam-stresses[b]	Laun-dresses
					Male	Female	Male	Female			
1885											
Fall River	85.5	87.8	65.9	44.2	—	—	69.8	75.5	—	—	47.4
Lynn	75.2	63.3	62.0	16.8	64.2	74.2	—	46.9	7.5	28.2	23.1
Lawrence	72.2	79.6	43.2	26.5	—	—	39.6	55.7	4.3	25.0	34.2
Worcester	70.7	76.2	43.8	42.9	68.4	56.6	—	39.6	8.7	37.3	15.2
Lowell	67.5	75.3	50.2	37.5	21.5	—	35.5	—	8.7	18.3	25.7
Cambridge	64.6	67.6	52.3	34.8	27.1	—	14.8	15.7	15.8	33.8	78.2
New Bedford	56.2	65.2	56.4	—	47.2	52.2	79.4	76.6	8.7	—	—
Springfield	62.4	67.1	34.8	17.8	—	—	—	—	6.0	19.0	19.1
Boston	54.4	68.7	39.1	16.5	21.0	29.7	—	—	8.6	25.4	—
Somerville	48.2	49.5	43.7	11.0	—	—	—	—	11.1	30.4	—

1890											
Lynn	57.5	45.2	33.9	14.8	55.5	54.5	—	51.6	6.5	23.4	21.3
Fall River	44.7	53.6	34.5	7.7	14.0	25.0	15.5	18.3	4.6	12.8	12.5
Cambridge	27.9	42.1	29.9	8.9	14.7	—	—	14.6	7.7	14.9	21.9
Boston	32.9	38.5	29.7	9.9	13.9	20.2	—	21.6	6.0	17.8	13.6
Worcester	23.4	46.1	21.5	8.9	32.1	31.9	15.4	14.2	7.2	17.5	7.0
Lowell	27.2	38.0	19.9	8.1	7.8	11.5	10.7	12.8	3.6	9.7	10.9
1900											
Lynn	45.0	52.9	46.2	11.8	43.4	42.9	—	—	9.0	34.9	16.5
Cambridge	41.1	63.6	49.2	13.3	31.3	—	—	—	12.5	34.4	25.5
Lawrence	39.4	60.2	35.8	12.5	33.3	39.0	20.0	20.4	9.9	17.1	20.5
Boston	40.6	54.3	39.2	13.7	23.4	28.2	—	14.9	10.5	28.3	21.2
Lowell	31.1	52.0	29.8	8.1	21.6	16.7	16.8	14.6	17.5	16.3	18.3
Worcester	38.2	49.9	29.2	11.1	36.8	32.4	—	25.4	10.2	27.0	18.4
Springfield	45.3	56.9	29.8	13.0	16.0	—	—	15.2	10.9	21.7	15.1
Fall River	44.0	59.2	37.7	8.9	9.8	—	12.3	14.7	9.0	13.5	19.4
Somerville	38.2	51.4	32.3	7.6	—	—	—	—	10.7	28.9	16.9
New Bedford	33.7	51.2	37.1	9.2	27.8	53.3	6.2	8.4	6.6	17.2	11.9

[a] In 1890, census category included cotton and other mill operatives.

[b] In 1890, census category included dressmakers and milliners.

Sources: MBSL, *18 AR* (Boston, 1887), pp. 166–215; *Eleventh U.S. Census, Population,* part II (Washington, 1897), pp. 638–9, 644–5, 668–9, 686–9, 742–3; *Twelfth U.S. Census, Occupations* (Washington, 1904), pp. 494–9, 506–11, 560–3, 588–91, 598–603, 625–7, 732–9, 760–3.

One key consequence – and sign – of the importance of local conditions was that workers who belonged to the same occupation but lived in different communities often faced significantly different odds of being able to work year-round. In 1885, the only year for which data for all communities are available, unemployment frequencies in many trades ranged from less than 30 percent in some cities and towns to more than 90 percent in others.[25] Even during the prosperous years of 1890 and 1900, unemployment levels in most occupations varied from one major city to the next: laborers and seamstresses in Lynn, for example, were idled much more often than were laborers and seamstresses in the nearby city of Lowell.[26] (See Table 5.4.) Most occupations did have a typical spectrum of unemployment frequencies and mean durations, but the spectrum was often broad, departures from the norm were common, and the relative ease or difficulty with which individuals found work in their trades, in their communities, was always liable to change.[27] A person's occupation remained the single most important factor in determining his or her chances of being able to work steadily, but the odds were always subject to local modification. It was precisely for this reason that some labor organizations, like the United Brotherhood of Carpenters and Joiners, published continuously updated lists of communities to be avoided by members in search of work.[28]

Unemployment, in sum, was a problem for working people throughout Massachusetts: from Cape Cod to the Berkshires, from the metropolis of Boston to the hamlet of Hinsdale, residents of all communities were vulnerable to spells of joblessness. Statistics for the commonwealth as a whole do not distort or conceal the story. Unemployment was neither confined to, nor particularly concentrated in, any single region or type of community; from the 1870s to the 1920s, joblessness was a statewide phenomenon.

But statistics for the entire state do mask the unevenness and the fluidity of unemployment levels in different communities. During any particular year or month, some cities and towns were in much better shape than others; over time, the map of unemployment was continuously being redrawn. Between 1870 and 1920, rates of joblessness in individual communities may have become slightly more uniform (as the economy became more integrated and as transportation and communication networks improved), but sharply contrasting, rapidly shifting idleness rates remained common.[29] The shifts and contrasts, moreover, were too kaleidoscopic, too complex or obscure in their origins, to have been consistently foreseen by working people. The erratic and uneven geographic distribution of unemployment added one more dimension to the uncertainties of economic life. Staying employed meant having the right job at the right time in the right place.

Unemployment and mobility

> The impossibility of getting work has been felt in every employment and in every state of the Union. The result has been the influx into the cities of people who could obtain no work in the country, and many of whom found none in the cities.
>
> Boston Provident Association, 1877

> Q. Don't lasters get a longer period of work than intimated . . . by moving to other towns? By going to other towns, don't they get where the season is on, so to speak, so in that way they are enabled to get a steady job?
>
> A. The majority of the people who have jobs dare not leave them for their life. There is a class of help that do move about in that way, but they are as a general thing the least prosperous.
>
> Q. What is the character of that shifting population, who are they, – are they married or are they single?
>
> A. Oh lots of them are married. Lots of them are steady industrious men.
>
> Testimony of H. M. Easton, shoe laster, Lynn, 1895[30]

The people of Massachusetts moved around at an almost astonishing rate during these years. Immigrants poured into the commonwealth, emigrants flowed out of it, and mobility within the state's borders was continuous and commonplace. The visible shift in population from rural to urban areas was merely one net consequence of the many different migratory currents that carried the Bay State's inhabitants from town to town, from town to city, and from one city to the next. Only 60 percent of the men who lived in either Boston or Waltham in 1880 were still living in those cities a decade later; the number of families that resided in Boston at some point between 1880 and 1890 was three times greater than the number that ever lived in the city simultaneously. Twenty years later, Boston's "persistence" rate dropped to roughly 40 percent, and the state's immigration commission noted that "everywhere in Massachusetts" there was a "restless movement of the immigrant from place to place and from mill to mill." No comprehensive data are available, but it seems likely, indeed certain, that a large majority of the commonwealth's residents inhabited more than one community in the course of their working lives.[31]

These high rates of residential mobility have proven to be easier for scholars to detect than to explain.[32] Yet they appear less puzzling when located against the backdrop of unemployment. Each year, more than one hundred thousand male workers were unemployed, for weeks or months at a time, and many, if not most, of these men were obliged to hunt for new jobs. Since existing transportation facilities were too limited and too costly for working people to live far from their place of employment, changing jobs often entailed a change of residence as well. As importantly, the uneven geographic distribution of unemployment meant that it was realistic for jobless men and women to expect that moving would heighten their chances of finding work. And the constant flux in idleness levels meant that no single migration was likely to provide a permanent haven against unemployment. A family that improved its fortunes by moving from Fall River to Lowell in the 1880s might well have found it necessary to retrace its steps at some point during the following decade. The structure of employment opportunities in the commonwealth put a premium on a worker's ability, and willingness, to move. It seems more than coincidental that the men who were most likely to be mobile in Massachusetts were also those whose jobs were most unsteady: blue-collar workers, both skilled and unskilled.[33]

Sharp reductions in the demand for labor, in the economy as a whole or in individual industries, were, in fact, a common wellspring of the migratory currents that crisscrossed the state. Although major depressions seem to have inhibited movement for some working people (who preferred to remain in familiar surroundings when times were bad), they sent other workers into motion. Half the members of the Lasters' Protective Union in Haverhill left town during the depression of the 1890s. A large proportion of the families that had received aid from the Citizens' Relief Committee of Boston during the winter of 1894 could not be located anywhere in the city eight months later. And every depression of the late nineteenth and early twentieth centuries was accompanied (as discussed in the next section of this chapter) by an increase in the number of homeless men who roamed the commonwealth in search of work.[34]

Seasonal declines in employment sometimes had a similar effect. Building tradesmen, particularly carpenters, often led a peripatetic existence as they finished jobs in one community and moved on to new construction sites; upholsterers from the city went to the countryside to ply their trade during the summer; shoe lasters sometimes tried to catch the busy seasons in several different communities; female garment workers went "away to the beach doing domestic work" during the summer slack season in Boston; and cranberry pickers on Cape Cod moved to New Bedford and Fall River when they were no longer needed in the cranberry bogs. Each winter, large numbers of working people migrated from rural areas to the cities, while each spring the flow was reversed. To be sure, much of this seasonal migration was of short duration and may not have led to a permanent change of residence. But people clearly did move when they lost their jobs and had some reason to believe that they could find work in another community.[35]

A more precise – or at least more quantitative – grasp of the links between unemployment and residential mobility can be derived from Tables 5.5, 5.6, and 5.7. These tables present the persistence rates that prevailed among the sample of men (introduced in Chapter 4) who worked in the shoe industry in Brockton in 1900. The unemployment experiences of these men, in 1900, were recorded in the federal census, and the 1901 city directory of Brockton indicated whether members of the sample still resided in the city a year later. This measuring gauge is roughly hewn, and the arena itself is not one in which dramatic differences between the employed and the unemployed were likely to appear – since seasonal layoffs in the shoe industry tended to have fairly predictable endpoints in prosperous years like 1900. But the results of the inquiry, nonetheless, are revealing. Although working people did not automatically pack their bags and leave town when they were laid off, spells of joblessness did make a difference, particularly to some groups of workingmen.[36]

In the sample as a whole, men who were unemployed during the census year of 1900 were significantly less persistent (i.e., less likely to remain in Brockton) than were those who worked steadily. (See Table 5.5.) This contrast stemmed, in part, from the inclusion in the sample of white-collar and managerial personnel who, like their counterparts in other communities, tended to display high rates of persistence and to encounter low levels of unemployment. But among factory operatives too, men who had been jobless were more likely to have been mobile than were men who worked year-round, although the contrast was less distinct and did not attain the same level of statistical significance.[37] Not everyone who left Brockton had been unemployed, and only one-quarter of the unemployed failed to appear in the 1901 city directory, but being laid off did affect the odds of a shoe worker remaining in town.

Operatives who were at certain stages of their careers appear to have been little affected by spells of joblessness, while, for others, the ties between unemployment and residential mobility were much stronger than the aggregate figures suggest. As Table 5.6 reveals, youthful factory workers were highly mobile whether they were unemployed or not, and men in their fifties and sixties tended to be

Table 5.5. *Persistence rates in Brockton, 1900–1*

Males	All shoe industry personnel		Blue-collar operatives	
	No. in sample	% persistent[a]	No. in sample	% persistent[a]
Employed year-round in 1900	119	84.9[b]	91	81.3
Unemployed in 1900	239	74.9	234	74.8
Jobless 1–2 mo.	110	77.3	106	76.4
Jobless 3–4 mo.	77	70.1	77	70.1
Jobless 5–12 mo.	52	76.9	51	76.5
Total	358	78.2	325	76.6

[a]Listed in the Brockton city directory in 1901. See note 36.
[b]Significantly different from the unemployed. See note 37.
Sources: Manuscript schedules, Twelfth U.S. Census, 1900. *The Brockton Directory,* compiled by A. W. Greenough and Co. (Boston, 1901).

Table 5.6. *Persistence rates among blue-collar operatives, by age, Brockton, 1900–1*

Age (males)	Employed year-round		Unemployed in 1900		Total	
	No.	% persistent	No.	% persistent	No.	% persistent
≤20	10	40.0	35	51.4	45	48.9
21–30	28	82.1	64	71.9	92	75.0
31–40	25	88.0	66	81.8	91	83.5
41–50	18	94.4	46	78.3	64	82.8
>50	10	80.0	23	91.3	33	87.9
All males, 21–50	71	87.3[a]	176	77.3	247	80.2

[a]Significantly different from the unemployed. See notes 36 and 37.
Sources: See Table 5.5.

Table 5.7. *Persistence rates among blue-collar operatives, by place of birth and household status, Brockton, 1900–1*

Males	Employed year-round		Unemployed in 1900		Total	
	No.	% persistent	No.	% persistent	No.	% persistent
Native-born:						
Total	60	88.3[a]	174	74.7	234	78.2
Household heads	37	100.0[a]	91	80.2	128	85.9
Foreign-born:						
Total	31	67.7	58	74.1	89	71.9
Household heads	22	72.7	33	78.8	55	76.4
All household heads[b]	59	89.8	125	80.0	184	83.2
All others[b]	32	65.6	109	68.8	141	68.1

[a]Significantly different from the unemployed. See notes 36, 37, and 38.
[b]Total (n) varies slightly in different groupings because not all data were available for all sample members.
Sources: See Table 5.5.

relatively persistent regardless of the steadiness with which they worked. But for men who were between the ages of twenty-one and fifty – and these men constituted the bulk of the male labor force – layoffs did matter: those who worked year-round were significantly more persistent than were operatives who had been unemployed. Similarly, men who headed households were more likely to leave town if they had been idle than if they had worked steadily, while operatives who had lesser responsibilities were highly transient in either case. (See Table 5.7.)[38]

Comparable differences existed between immigrants and native-born workers. Shoe factory operatives who had been born abroad were relatively mobile, whether or not they were unemployed. In contrast, native-born men (who were predominant in the shoe industry) tended to be settled residents of the community unless they were laid off.[39] (See Table 5.7.) All native-born household heads who worked year-round in 1900 were still living in Brockton a year later, while 20 percent of their unemployed colleagues had left town. (The contrast was almost as sharp for natives who were over the age of 30, regardless of their household status.)[40] Or, to state the matter a bit differently, all the native-born household heads who left Brockton had been unemployed during the census year of 1900. These mature, and presumably experienced, operatives were stable citizens who tended to remain in one place as long as they had steady work.

Unemployment, thus, was an important precipitant of geographic mobility even among workers in a highly seasonal industry, where most layoffs were not freighted with the threat of permanent or indefinite job.loss. Relocation decisions obviously were influenced by many different factors, but spells of unemployment do seem to have triggered the departures of a number of men who might otherwise have remained in Brockton. Although seasonal slowdowns did not launch a massive flood of migration, they did generate a migratory stream that over time could easily have carried a substantial proportion of Brockton's population to other cities and towns. If layoffs were directly responsible for the annual departure of even 5 to 10 percent of Brockton's shoe workers, then layoffs were directly responsible, in the course of a decade, for a population turnover rate of 50 to 100 percent – thousands of families in all.[41] And if Brockton was in any way representative of the state's shoe manufacturing centers, then layoffs in the shoe industry accounted for the mobility of tens of thousands of families during every decade from the 1870s to the 1920s.

What the toll may have been elsewhere, or when business conditions were less favorable, remains a matter of conjecture. But it is likely that the links between unemployment and geographic mobility were sometimes much tighter than they were in Brockton in 1900. Joblessness that was produced by business failures, plant closings, long-term cutbacks in production, the introduction of new technology, or other relatively unpredictable economic events probably had a greater impact upon residential stability than did seasonal slowdowns of the type afflicting turn-of-the-century Brockton.[42] There is no way to calculate with precision the proportion of all residential mobility directly attributable to unemployment, but the assembled evidence – circumstantial, impressionistic, and statistical – suggests that unemployment was a major source, and perhaps *the* major source, of the low persistence rates that were so widespread in Massachusetts. Geographic mobility was such a common feature of working-class life because jobs were chronically unsteady and because unemployment levels varied considerably among the hundreds of cities and towns within the commonwealth's borders. It was the threat of joblessness that prompted contemporary commentators to suggest that prudent working men ought not purchase homes in the communities in which they lived.[43]

Viewed from a certain perspective, of course, there was nothing either unexpected or problematic about this transience – or about transience as the consequence of unemployment. "Modern industry demands mobility in its force," noted two early twentieth-century observers of life in Boston's poorer neighborhoods, and both critics and defenders of capitalism have generally agreed that a free enterprise economy depends upon the existence of a geographically mobile labor force. Migration was a logical and straightforward mechanism for balancing the supply of labor and the demand for labor in a rapidly changing and growing economy. Men and women moved from towns to cities in part because jobs were more abundant in the cities; they moved, in large numbers, to the Boston area because (among other reasons) unemployment levels were relatively low in the state's capital. They moved from city to city because there was always flux in the demand for labor. Low rates of persistence were a sign that employment opportunities did exist somewhere, and the freedom with which working people circulated lessened the need for individual communities to contend with severe unemployment problems for long stretches of time.[44]

But for the blue-collar workers who were themselves transient, migration had a less rosy coloration. The market was successful in allocating the supply of labor only because the felt needs of working people were strong enough to propel them into motion. Much of the mobility that was so rampant in Massachusetts was an expression of need rather than opportunity, a response not to the lure of a better job but to the condition of joblessness. "Push" and "pull" factors, of course, were usually present simultaneously, but the "pull" represented by the possibility of employment as a factory operative or day laborer would, in most cases, have meant little in the absence of the "push" provided by unemployment. Residential mobility was a strategy for coping with joblessness: it was a way of making ends meet in a world where jobs were chronically unsteady, where the demand for labor differed from one community to the next, and where there were few institutional incentives (such as seniority systems) for a worker to remain stationary. The men who kept disappearing from the census records and city directories were, by and large, neither drifting aimlessly nor seizing opportunities for occupational advancement. They were responding purposively, if not always successfully, to an oft-repeated condition of need.[45]

All of which is not to say that reports of wanderlust in the American temperament are completely unfounded or that the high rates of mobility so characteristic of American life have always been occasioned by unemployment. The available evidence, in fact, suggests that residents of Massachusetts and other states were extremely mobile not only after the Civil War but also during the first half of the nineteenth century, when unemployment was not a particularly pressing or widespread concern. But the phenomenon of mobility may well have had different sources and motivations during different periods in the nation's history. In 1810 or 1840, the migratory impulse was, perhaps, rooted in a spirit of restlessness, a desire to acquire more land, or, as has recently been suggested, an individualized resistance to the imposition of "industrial order."[46] "Pull" rather than "push" factors may have predominated. But between 1870 and 1920, when most people had only their labor to sell and when the demand for that commodity was erratic and uncertain, unemployment appears to have been the key to the peripatetic careers of so many Americans. People had to work in order to live, and to work, they often had to move.

A brief epilogue: the presence of a strong link between unemployment and geographic mobility helps to explain the increase in working-class persistence rates that occurred sometime after 1920. Not that there was a permanent or dramatic decline in unemployment after the first quarter of the twentieth century, but there were significant institutional changes that weakened the migratory pressures on the unemployed. Twentieth-century improvements in transportation enhanced the ability of working people to find new employers without changing their place of residence; the development of seniority provisions served both to protect workers who had roots in a community and to encourage idled workmen to remain in town; and the emergence of unemployment insurance made it easier for jobless men and women to simply wait out spells of idleness wherever they happened to be living. By the middle of the twentieth century, unemployed workers had better reasons and better resources for being "persistent" than their predecessors had had at any point during the era of uncertainty.[47]

Tramps

> "What does that long procession mean,
> Who are the people there?
> From whence they come, and whither bound,
> Their destiny is where?
> I've watched them since the early morn,
> Upon the public way.
> A fearful line of haggard men
> Thronging the street, today."

"It's just a long procession, sir,
As anyone may see,
Of hungry men out on the road:
Sullen as men can be.
They come from homes where sorrow is,
And haunt each public street,
That they may chance for wife and child
To get a crust to eat."

From "A Procession" by Henry White,
written for the *Labor Leader*, December 30, 1893

Q. You say that this year more than former years you have had
   men you thought were genuinely unemployed, that is honest
   mechanics?
A. That is what I thought, and old officers who have been here
   for years in the station express the same opinion.
Q. As a rule, have you noticed that the majority of tramps were
   unskilled labor?
A. The majority of them call themselves laborers.
Q. Does it ever happen that you meet a mechanic that comes
   along with a kit of tools?
A. Oh yes, a good many of the shoe-makers carry their kit or
   part of their kit with them.
Q. Where do they go to from here going north?
A. We don't know where they go to; we only know where they
   come from. They probably tramp from here to Newburyport;
   if north, they go to Exeter or stop at some of the smaller
   towns. We have a good many that come from Lawrence;
   sometimes they come from Exeter.

Testimony of George H. Dole, city marshal,
Haverhill, 1894

Finally I told the selectmen that I could drive tramps out of the
town if they would like to have me go ahead, which they agreed
to. In the early part of December, I began to take tramps over to
Stoughton, and during that month put fifteen out of eighteen
through for vagrancy. . . . There are no more than three or four
honest men out of a hundred of them. The three that got off, in
my opinion, were not honest men more than those that were convicted though they had their dues paid up in a trade union. This,
I am very certain of, is merely a means of getting an easier living
off the public, because it ensures them against conviction for vagrancy. Another trick is to have a kit of tools, which would seem

to be evidence that the owner is in search of work. He really uses it simply as a blind to obtain money and food under false pretences.

Testimony of E. M. Nixson, tramp officer, Sharon, 1895[48]

No discussion of the links between unemployment and geographic mobility can ignore the subject of tramps. The word "tramp," as a label for homeless, unemployed, traveling men, came into common usage in the United States during the 1870s, and the "tramp evil" was periodically a touchstone of public anxiety until after the turn of the century. Between the Civil War and World War I, tramps appeared in all Massachusetts cities, as well as in towns that lined the major highways and railroads. Particularly during depressions, idle men, anchored neither to jobs nor families nor communities, roamed from place to place, with no visible means of support, dependent for their survival upon strangers and public institutions. Their widespread presence taxed those agencies that had traditionally offered aid to the poor, and proved troubling, even frightening, to many of the state's more respectable citizens. Tramps were mobile Americans – hardly a new breed – but these mobile Americans evoked an unusually intense – and hostile – public reaction.[49]

Vivid as the image of the tramp may have been in late nineteenth-century America, the word itself was ambiguous in its meaning and ambivalent in its connotations. More often than not, after 1870, the term "tramp" was loaded with a heavy judgmental freight. A tramp was a ne'er-do-well, a willful vagrant, a shirker or a vagabond who preferred life on the road to life on the job. But the word had another meaning as well: it was often used simply as a descriptive, rather than pejorative, label for poor, unemployed workingmen who were traveling outside their home communities and who needed free or inexpensive lodgings. Many contemporaries, to be sure, believed that there was no meaningful difference between these two definitions, because only shirkers ended up jobless, homeless, and penniless, but the ambiguity latent in the term eventually generated efforts to refine the language. In the 1890s, Horace Wadlin, then chief of the Massachusetts Bureau of Statistics of Labor, carefully distinguished between "tramps proper," who were itinerant freeloaders, and "worthy" workingmen, who were "earnestly" searching for jobs. At roughly the same time, a detective who claimed to be a specialist in tramp problems offered a colorful set of labels for the three different "grades of tramps on the road." "Shovel bums," declared the detective, were laborers who would work for three or four months and then travel to another construction site, while "town bums" tramped a circuit from Boston to western Massachusetts and back again, living off of public largesse. Most vile of all were the "hobos" who never worked and who defended their sloth as a matter of principle. Hobos, according to the detective, believed "that the country owes the President of the United States a living, and they have as good a right to get a living out of the country as the President has."[50]

Beneath these lexical complexities were serious issues of understanding, ethics, and policy. Everyone in Massachusetts seemed to agree that there were more homeless, jobless migrants between the 1870s and World War I than there had been prior to the Civil War, but there was little shared understanding of the sources or meaning of the increase. Were there more shiftless men in Massachusetts? Was the moral obligation to work losing its force? Or were there simply more unemployed workers who had to travel from place to place in order to find jobs? Such questions loomed large in late-nineteenth-century America because communities had to respond, one way or another, to the impoverished strangers who walked their streets and sometimes asked for aid. If tramps, or even most tramps, were unemployed workmen who were out of cash but who were honestly striving to support themselves, then they merited compassion and support from the public and from public officials. But if, in fact, the typical tramp was a shiftless vagrant who had left the labor force and was unwilling to work, then harsher and more discouraging policies were needed. The issue was difficult to skirt: cities and towns throughout the commonwealth were confronted with either a problem of poor relief or a problem of social discipline, or both.

Facts that helped to illuminate the problem were not long in coming. According to figures collected by public officials, the number of tramps tended to increase dramatically during depressions and to diminish rapidly when jobs were more plentiful. The number of occasions when vagrants were given relief in Massachusetts more than tripled (to an annual total of nearly 150,000) between 1873 and 1876. In the city of Lynn, the number of lodgings paid for by the Poor Department increased more than fivefold between 1881 and 1886 and then plunged as soon as business conditions improved. And during the depression of the 1890s, cities and towns everywhere were called upon to aid unprecedented numbers of homeless men. The town of Melrose, for example, lodged 6 tramps in January 1892 and 256 in January 1894.[51] There is no way to determine exactly how many tramps there were in Massachusetts, despite the remarkable fact that the commonwealth conducted formal tramp censuses in both 1895 and 1905. But it seems likely that the number ranged from roughly a thousand during prosperous years to as many as three or four thousand during the troughs of depressions.[52]

Two key conclusions emerge from these figures. The first is that the phenomenon of tramping was obviously linked to the incidence of unemployment. The state of Massachusetts did, in all likelihood, contain some vagrants who were unwilling to work, unemployable, or downright criminal, but most tramps seem to have stopped tramping as soon as business picked up and jobs were available. "Tramps proper," to use Horace Wadlin's memorable phrase, seem to have been far less numerous than were "wayfarers" who were searching for work. What is less obvious but not necessarily less important is that tramping was not an altogether rare or uncommon experience. If, as seems likely, there was substantial "turnover" in the tramp population, if most men tramped for months and few were tramps for years on end, then the total number of men who were tramps in Massachusetts sometime between 1870 and 1920 was probably in excess of fifty thousand.[53] Tramps – in the descriptive, rather than moralistic sense of the term – were not typical workingmen or even typical unemployed workingmen. But neither were they a numerically trivial group. By 1920, there were certainly more men who had had the experience of tramping in Massachusetts than there were who had been state legislators, mayors, or company presidents.

And the experience of tramping was a harsh and dispiriting one, far too harsh and dispiriting to buttress the claim that men typically became tramps by choice rather than by necessity. Tramps were disconnected from the conventional routines of working-class life, and they were engaged in a struggle both to endure each day and, in most cases, to find some way to cease being tramps. They traveled from town to town by riding the rails illegally or by walking along highways and railroad tracks; they often spent the morning hours standing in front of factory gates or construction sites; and they commonly traipsed from street to street, neighborhood to neighborhood, inquiring about work. Tramps fed themselves by begging for meals at private houses or at charitable agencies, by performing odd jobs, or by panhandling to collect the five cents needed to obtain a schooner of beer and its accompanying free lunch at a saloon.[54] At night, when the weather was too cold for sleeping out of doors – which, in Massachusetts, was most of the time – they sought shelter in the "evil-smelling" tramp rooms of police stations, in fifteen-cent lodging houses that catered to wayfarers, in shanties like "Bughouse Mary's" near Boston's South End, or in municipal institutions like the Wayfarers' Lodges of Springfield and Boston. The latter abode, which was also known as the Hawkins Street Woodyard, offered tramps the rare luxury of cots (50 to a room) rather than bare boards to sleep on. (See Figure 5.2.) The rules of the house also demanded that men bathe in the evening, while their clothes were being fumigated, and chop wood for two hours in the morning before leaving.[55]

Yet neither the visibly grim details of tramp life nor the reams of statistics linking tramping to the business cycle gave rise to a coherent and consistent set of policies toward tramps. During the final decades of the nineteenth century, the mounting evidence that there were many "worthy" tramps on the road made it seem increasingly sensible – in both humanitarian and economic terms – for the public to offer some assistance to these itinerant, unemployed men. But many communities were deeply reluctant to expend their meager resources on men who had no local ties, and some officials argued that assistance should be withheld because tramps, when numerous, constituted a threat to public order.[56] As importantly, many middle-class citizens remained convinced that most tramps were malingerers. This conviction gradually succumbed to the evidence, but throughout the late nineteenth century and even during the Progressive era, attitudes toward tramps were powerfully influenced by the fear of encouraging indolence and the nightmare of attracting the indolent to Massachusetts. (See Figure 5.3.) Faced with these competing images and impulses, public authorities, particularly after 1893, tried to devise policies that would discriminate between legitimate wayfarers who deserved help and shirkers who deserved to be punished. In practice, however, it proved to be exceedingly difficult to cast a net that would ensnare "tramps proper" while permitting wayfarers to continue their travels in search of work.[57]

The more fearful and punitive strains in public opinion were embodied in laws that actually made tramping illegal in Massachusetts. In the 1870s, men who traveled in the commonwealth without "visible means of support" or "lawful employment" could be charged with vagrancy, and in 1880 the state legislature reacted to the newly swollen ranks of the itinerant by passing an "act for the protection of the people of the commonwealth against tramps." This act defined tramps as "all persons who rove about from place to place, begging or living without labor or visible means of support," and it specified that "any act of begging or vagrancy by any person having no known residence" in Massachusetts constituted "prima facie evidence" that the person was a tramp. (Exemptions were granted to women, the blind, boys under the age of 17, and men seeking charity within their own communities.) The penalty for tramping was a sentence of six months to two years in a house of correction or in the state workhouse at Bridgewater. Other pieces of legislation made it illegal for

Figure 5.2. "Tramps sawing wood for their lodging and breakfast" at the Lodge for Wayfarers on Hawkins Street in Boston, 1879. *Frank Leslie's Illustrated Newspaper*, August 2, 1879. (Courtesy Immigrant City Archives, Lawrence, Massachusetts.)

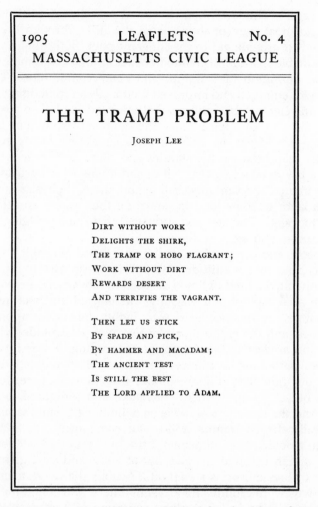

Figure 5.3. Cover page of leaflet published by the Massachusetts Civic League, 1905.

traveling men to ride in freight cars or to walk on railroad tracks. In 1896 the tramp act was amended and toughened to eliminate the exemption for women and to extend the "prima facie evidence" clause to all persons who lacked a legal residence in the community in which they begged or solicited alms.[58]

State law, then, made it a crime for a poor, unemployed man who lacked the resources to pay for his own food and lodging to travel in search of work. But the relationship between tramps and public authorities was far more complex and ambiguous than the statutes alone suggest. The laws themselves were rarely enforced with any vigor, and most municipalities, from the 1870s through the 1920s, continued to provide aid to the itinerant poor. Both public and private charitable institutions offered shelter and meals to men who fit the legal definition of a tramp, and some communities, such as Springfield, enlarged and improved their facilities for lodging impoverished travelers. Public policies that tolerated, and even sustained, tramps did not disappear from the commonwealth just because tramping was illegal. In 1905 the state legislature tacitly acknowledged the gap between the statutes and common practices when it passed a law demanding that "cities and towns which provide lodgings for tramps and vagrants shall require them, if physically able, to perform labor of some kind in return for the lodging and food furnished to them." The law also stipulated that public lodging houses for tramps – who technically ought to have been arrested – had to meet specifications prescribed by the state board of health.[59]

This curious mix of attitudes and policies meant that tramps themselves inhabited a kind of limbo, a social terrain where the boundary between acceptability and illegality was blurred and shifting. Men who tramped in Massachusetts were highly dependent upon public authorities, and the enduring ambivalence of policy added elements of risk and anxiety to the enterprise of traveling in search of work. The laws pertaining to tramps were more often ignored than enforced, but homeless migrants were, from time to time, arrested, thrown out of town, or tried, convicted, and sentenced to Bridgewater. And the looseness of the legal definitions meant that even the most well-behaved tramps could, and sometimes did, find themselves in trouble. "As I understand the law," reported one local official, "if a man is found sleeping out of doors and can't give a good account of himself, he is a vagrant." Actions that were tolerated in some towns were grounds for arrest in others, and communities that were known to be lenient in their treatment of tramps periodically engaged in crackdowns to rid themselves of beggars, vagrants, and other undesirables. Some cities and towns gave free lodgings to the homeless for weeks at a time, while others arrested men who asked for shelter three nights in a row. The city marshall of Springfield testified in the 1890s that his office did not charge men with vagrancy "very often, unless we want to get rid of them."[60]

Tramps, indeed, lived at the mercy of local public officials, and one danger of tramping in Massachusetts was that there were numerous municipal officials who did not think that mercy was what tramps deserved. When the deputy sheriff of Springfield discovered, to his chagrin, that he could not arrest men for sleeping in freight cars, he began to prosecute them for having walked on the railroad tracks.[61] And E. M. Nixson, the tramp officer of Sharon, who was so deeply suspicious of men who carried either union cards or tools, devised his own ingenious method of convicting tramps for vagrancy:

> The way I worked the conviction was, as soon as the tramps were locked up at night, I would tell them that a number of thefts and robberies had been committed recently, and that they were suspected of being guilty parties, and that they must give a good account of themselves as to where they had been for the previous three weeks. Almost invariably then, they would pull out a little book and show me just where they had lodged for, perhaps, three weeks' time. These lodgings would usually be a list of police stations and poorhouses in as many different towns. I would copy this down and the next day I would turn it in as evidence that the fellows were tramps. Naturally they could not say anything in refutation of this statement, and conviction was certain.[62]

The threat of arrest was not the only obstacle that Bay State officials placed in the path of men who tramped from town to town. Policies that were designed to discourage malingerers while sustaining worthy, unemployed workingmen had a compelling theoretical rationale, but, in practice, it was nearly impossible to distinguish one group from the other or to deter the lazy and vicious without hindering the efforts of the honest unemployed. Many communities, for example, tried to prevent tramps from lingering around town by refusing to give lodgings to homeless men for more than two or three days in a row. This policy may well have diminished vagrancy, but it also made it difficult for migrants to familiarize themselves with local labor markets and to establish the personal contacts that might lead to employment. Similarly, many lodging houses – and all lodging houses after 1905 – demanded that men who received a night's shelter perform several hours of physical labor the following morning. The aim of this work requirement was to prevent the shiftless from receiving free shelter; one of its consequences was that the industrious were unable to get an early start in the search for work.[63]

Something of what it was like to be caught in the web of these contradictory policies, to be able to move freely yet to risk arrest for doing so, to be utterly vulnerable to the arbitrary exercise of power by local officials, was conveyed in a rare firsthand account of tramp life in Massachusetts, written early in the twentieth century. The account appeared in a letter, dated January 24, 1910, received by Edwin Brown, a writer and reformer who championed the cause of the homeless unemployed. The author of the letter was an English immigrant who had come to the United States as a child and had worked in the textile mills of Woonsocket, Rhode Island. Tiring of life in the mills, he left Woonsocket and went to Boston,

> where one night finding myself stranded I went to the Municipal lodgings, and got a poor bed and some soup. God only knows what it was made of and the next morning I was out and hustling . . . and I found out a man could always pick up a piece of change running horses up and down the streets and taking them down to depot, and getting warmed up one day and having no other clothes I caught cold which turned into pneumonia and I went to the city hospital. The treatment there was fine and I never will forget the face of my nurse.

But then his luck turned for the worse.

> When I came out I was weak and scaled about 90. Having no money that night I had to go to the Municipal lodging, and I told the officer in charge about coming out of the hospital that morning and he asked me to show him my discharge papers and I handed them out to him and he looked at them and tore them up right in front of my face, and said you —— your working the hospitals are you, and then he kicked me all the way down to the bath room and said he'd see that I sawed enough of wood in the morning, and he was there and after working a while I fell from weakness and the brute kicked me while I lay helpless. . . . he told me to get out and never show my face again, which I never have.[64]

Brown's correspondent may have been a rather unruly character – he ended up spending thirteen months in the reformatory at Concord before heading on to New York – but his adventures in Boston nonetheless revealed the mix of attitudes that tramps could and did encounter. Tramps were quasi-outcasts in Massachusetts society, aided and disciplined by the public authorities that had jurisdiction over their fate. A poor, jobless man who set out on the road could receive free shelter or be arrested for seeking shelter; police stations offered both sanctuary and the threat of a jail term; the homeless unemployed could be greeted with kindness one day and with contempt the next; the face of the nurse who treated Brown's correspondent was accompanied by the image of the "brute" who kicked him down the stairs. The daily drama of a tramp's life was structured not only by poverty and dislocation but also by the ambiguity of his station in society. Indeed, it was precisely that ambiguity that distinguished tramps from the jobless migrants who traveled the commonwealth during other epochs.

Tramps roamed through the cities and towns of Massachusetts throughout the years from 1870 to 1920, but public apprehension about tramps (and thus the tramp "problem") peaked during the depression of the 1890s and then gradually began to subside. During the first decades of the twentieth century, the word "tramp" appeared in print far less often than it had earlier, and local officials seemed to lose their zest for capturing and imprisoning the homeless unemployed. Tramps still had to contend with deeply erratic and ambivalent public policies, but the edge of antagonism so prominent in the late nineteenth century softened considerably during the Progressive era. By 1913, the Boston Provident Association, in conjunction with the Associated Charities of Boston, was maintaining a "department for homeless men," and the state legislature, which had once seemed single-mindedly bent upon punishing tramps for their transgressions, was calling for an investigation of the possibility of creating "industrial homes for vagrants, outcasts, and others." Although the treatment that tramps received did not change dramatically during this period, the cloud of suspicion that had hovered over the homeless unemployed and shaped their experiences did begin to lift.[65]

This shift in attitudes may have had some immediate, material basis: depressions were relatively brief during the first decades of the twentieth century, and the number of tramps on the road may have declined accordingly. But the softening of attitudes toward tramps seems to have been primarily a reflection of changing middle-class understandings of the "problem." Gradually, the evidence spawned by depressions did sink in, and the belief that tramps were just "wily imposters" who refused to work became less tenable. The fear of malingerers persisted, but it was checked by the increasingly widespread recognition that unemployment did exist in Massachusetts and that most tramps were merely jobless migrants. And jobless migrants appeared far less threatening to the moral and social order than "shirkers" who were escaping the rigors of industrial discipline. It was both ironic and telling that tramps received less public attention once it became apparent that they were victims rather than villains, that they were obeying rather than flouting the dictates of the economy.[66]

Both the phenomenon of tramping and the powerful reactions that tramps evoked were signs of the strain that unemployment placed upon the social fabric of nineteenth-century Massachusetts. It was no coincidence that the word "tramp" and the word "unemployed" became current during the same decade. The unprecedented levels of involuntary idleness in the 1870s created new pressures for geographic mobility, and the poorest of the mobile unemployed became "tramps." Tramps were the flotsam of the new industrial order, a grim parody of the geographically mobile labor force that industrial capitalism demanded, encouraged, and even celebrated. That the state initially responded to this mobility by trying to outlaw tramping, by making it illegal for a poor man to travel in search of work, was an expression of its unfamiliarity with the problem of mass unemployment, an emblem of the confusions that accompanied the changing social meaning of idleness. That the state failed to effectively prevent tramping, that it could not, in practice, enforce the stern letter of its laws, revealed the limits and the irrationality of governmental efforts to prohibit behavior that the economy required. As public authorities gradually discovered, tramping could not be eradicated, and the polity of Massachusetts had to accommodate itself to an economic environment in which unemployment, poverty, and mobility were inextricably intertwined.[67]

6   Coping

> For a family of three to save one hundred dollars a year, the head
> of the family must earn twelve dollars each week the whole year
> round . . . Suppose a man is idle a couple of months, or sick:
> what is going to become of his family?
>
> A furniture polisher, 1879

> We do all kinds of inside work, such as setting up the dy-
> namo, etc. . . . This last year seventy percent were loafing
> from the middle of October until the first of June, and then the
> building trades starting up kind of started them again, but
> now they are as bad off as ever. Seventy percent represents
> three hundred and fifty men.
> Q. How could they live during all these months?
> A. That is a mystery.
>
> Testimony of T. E. McCarthy, inside electrician,
Boston, 1894

> How people subsist when out of work is a question which is ex-
> ceedingly difficult for the outsider to understand.
>
> Robert A. Woods, 1902[1]

How did workers and their families cope with unemployment between 1870 and the early 1920s? The question looms large, thrust
toward the center of the historical stage by the statistics that registered the incidence of involuntary idleness in the commonwealth.
Long before there were any governmental insurance benefits for the
unemployed, workers had to make ends meet without their regular
weekly wages; families with limited resources were repeatedly
obliged to live for twelve months on earnings derived from ten or
eight or even six months' labor. Whether they moved from place to
place or not, jobless workers somehow had to obtain, food, shelter,
heat, and clothing. They also had to contend with the disruption of
familiar routines and the psychological stress that commonly accompanied spells of idleness. How did the unemployed approach these
tasks? What resources did they tap, what strategies did they devise
for adjusting to their loss of employment? What were the effects of

143

unemployment upon workers themselves and upon members of their households?

Unfortunately, the historical record is largely mute on such questions. Workers rarely left written accounts of their efforts to cope with joblessness, and few systematic (or, for that matter, unsystematic) sociological investigations of the unemployed were conducted prior to the 1930s.[2] The descriptive evidence that has survived from the period between 1870 and 1922 tends, moreover, to focus primarily on the experiences of a special group of unemployed workers: those who were idled during depressions and became so impoverished that they sought aid from public or quasi-public agencies. The documentary record is indeed so incomplete and partial that answers to certain questions – particularly questions concerning changes that may have occurred during these years – remain elusive.

Nonetheless, the bits and pieces of evidence that have survived, the terse case records transcribed by charity officials, the occasional stories that made their way into newspapers, do permit some understanding of the lives of the unemployed, the hardships they endured, the range of coping strategies available to them. These sources also suggest that, in fact, there was little change in the experience of unemployment, that workers who were idled in 1921 tended to encounter the same problems and resort to the same solutions as their predecessors had in 1875.[3] And scanty as the evidence may be, it does provide some unusual glimpses of the material and psychological texture of working-class life throughout the period.

A spectrum of needs

On February 24, 1894, at roughly eight o'clock in the evening, George A. Smith of Charlestown entered a local police station and asked for help in finding work. Smith was twenty-seven years old, married, and the father of two young sons; according to his neighbors and acquaintances, he was a "steady, industrious man." Smith had worked for the Boston and Maine and Fitchburg railroads until the middle of November 1893, when he was laid off because of the "dull times." In the months that followed, Smith managed to obtain two weeks' work with a railroad and three days' work with the street department of Charlestown. His small savings soon exhausted, by mid-February Smith and his wife had no money left to buy yeast to bake bread, and their six-month-old son continued to suffer from a skin disease on his face because they could not afford to pay a doctor. Smith also owed his landlord three months' rent, for an apartment that had no heat except for the kitchen stove. The landlord was threatening to evict the family if they did not pay the rent by March 1.[4]

While George Smith was entering the Charlestown police station, another former railway employee in Boston – a man known to posterity only as "number six" – was nearing the end of a five-month stint of unemployment. Number six had worked for sixteen years in a railroad shop as a mixer of paints and dispenser of supplies. He lost his job in 1893 when the railway changed owners, remaining idle until March of 1894 when he obtained a position in the wholesale furniture house of Jordan Marsh and Company. His good fortune, however, was short-lived. After several months, all "new hands" were discharged from Jordan Marsh, and number six was unemployed once again. He was married and had two children, an eleven-year-old boy and a daughter who had been working for five years as a bookkeeper. When number six approached the Citizens' Relief Committee of Boston for aid, an investigator who was sent to his home reported that "there was no evidence of poverty anywhere." The family lived in a "most pleasant flat" for which they paid fifteen dollars a month, and the rooms were "comfortably, even luxuriously furnished." They even had a piano. Number six appeared to have had considerable savings from his sixteen years of uninterrupted work in the railroad shops. Like a handful of other men who had applied to the relief committee, he apparently did so less out of pressing need than from a desire to "earn something" by performing relief work.[5]

Another applicant for charitable aid in Boston, during the depression of the 1890s, was a forty-year-old Irish-born widow, whose husband had been dead for nine years. She worked as a dressmaker and a tailoress, earning five dollars a week when she could find employment. In December 1893, her employer closed his business because of the depression, and she was "thrown out of work." Later in the winter, her rent paid up, but owing bills for groceries and provisions, she sought work relief from the Wells Memorial Institute. She received nine shifts of work at Wells Memorial, during which time the institute also gave her shoes and some clothing. When the workrooms were shut down in the spring of 1894, she tried to find work at her trade, but she was employed only occasionally during the summer, sewing for one dollar a day. In the fall of 1894, a relief worker noted that "her prospects were very bad for the winter."[6]

Finally, there was F. P. Hatch of Whitman, a small manufacturing town near Brockton. "I am myself a shoemaker, and I have not had any work since September 6, 1893," reported Hatch during the winter of 1894–5. "I have a farm, and consequently I can employ myself under the circumstances. I haven't taken but little pains to look for employment, for the reason that if I seek employment I will only step into some other man's place and push him out."[7]

These four accounts from the depression of the 1890s tell one key part of the story: men and women who were unemployed in Massachusetts had extremely diverse experiences. Theirs was not a homogeneous lot. From 1870 to 1922, during both good years and bad, some of the unemployed fared far better than others; some suffered much more acutely than others. Even among workers who were jobless at virtually the same time and for similar reasons – like George Smith, number six, the Irish widow, and F. P. Hatch – spells of idleness had different colorations. The unemployed, by definition, were men and women who needed (or wanted) to work, but the urgency of their needs (and sometimes the strength of their desires) varied considerably from one person to the next.

This variety had two principal sources. The first was that some men and women remained idle much longer than did others. As Table 6.1 indicates, more than a quarter of all unemployed workers were jobless for two months or less in 1885, while a third lost at least five months' work in the course of the year. In 1895, one-fifth of Lawrence's unemployed textile operatives returned to work after two months, while one-third were jobless for more than six months.[8] The exact figures varied from year to year and from trade to trade, but the reserve army of labor always contained men and women who had been drafted into service for radically different periods of time. This meant, of course, that some of the unemployed lost only a small part of their yearly wages, while others had to do without a third or even half of their potential annual incomes.[9]

As importantly, workers began their stints of unemployment in diverse economic circumstances – a diversity that reflected both the range of incomes earned by members of different occupations and the changes that typically occurred in the life cycle of individuals and households. Skilled tradesmen tended to live more comfortably and to possess more ample financial resources than did day laborers or factory operatives; cutters in a shoe factory were better off than spinners in a textile mill; middle-aged men with grown children had fewer expenses and more potential sources of revenue than did young couples with young children. A worker's capacity to weather a layoff of any given length depended upon a host of different factors, including his or her age, occupation, household status, wages, the number of dependents and wage earners in the household, the size of any existing savings accounts, the local cost of living, and the recency of previous bouts of unemployment or illness. George Smith ended up in desperate straits after being jobless for only three

Table 6.1. *The distribution of unemployment durations, 1885–1900*

	Percentage of the unemployed who were jobless for:				Number unemployed
	1–2 mo.	3–4 mo.	5–6 mo.	7–12 mo.	
1885:					
All occupations (Mass.)					
Male	25.6	38.0	25.9	10.5	178,628
Female	34.4	33.9	20.4	11.3	62,961
1895:					
Boot- and shoemakers					
Lynn					
Male	15.5	30.7	27.0	26.8	2,554
Female	19.7	29.7	28.4	22.2	1,061
Brockton					
Male	37.6	30.9	18.4	13.1	2,234
Female	35.3	34.1	16.0	14.5	580
Cotton mill operatives					
Fall River					
Male	44.3	44.9	6.1	4.7	9,526
Female	43.2	44.7	7.0	5.1	10,174
Woolen and worsted mill operatives					
Lawrence					
Male	19.0	24.5	22.1	34.5	612
Female	28.3	24.9	15.1	31.7	417
Paper and paper goods					
Holyoke					
Male	15.7	24.8	27.0	32.5	363
Female	19.0	29.7	24.7	26.7	300
Building trades					
Boston (male)	13.7	42.2	27.7	16.3	5,364
1900[a]					
Laborers					
Boston (male)	23.9	36.4	18.2	21.5	88
Boot- and shoemakers					
Brockton					
Male	46.1	32.3	11.9	9.7	269
Female	53.7	27.5	10.3	8.4	164
Brockton females outside the shoe industry	31.9	26.4	23.6	18.1	72

[a]Figures for 1900 are based on samples. See Chapter 4, notes 10, 11, and 48.
Sources: MBSL, 18 AR (Boston, 1887), p. 156; MBSL, *Bulletin 13*, pp. 16–24; *Bulletin 14,*, pp. 54–67; *Bulletin 17*, pp. 14–15 (Boston, 1900–1); Manuscript schedules, Twelfth U.S. Census, 1900. See notes 8 and 9.

months because he was a young, urban employee with a dependent family and no other wage earners in his household. The Irish-born widow had few expenses but even fewer opportunities to save money. Number six was blessed with a working daughter and the advantage of having labored steadily for sixteen years before the panic of 1893.[10]

For these reasons (and others as well), the material consequences of unemployment were immensely varied, and so too were the financial needs that prompted jobless men and women to search for work. At one end of the spectrum were the happy few who were barely fazed by their idleness: young men and women who were supplementary wage earners in relatively prosperous households; some semiskilled operatives who were jobless for only a month in the course of a year; well-paid craftsmen in highly seasonal industries who could afford to wait out predictably short "slack times" in their trade. Such benign encounters with unemployment were never very numerous, but there were always jobless men and women who felt, for a brief period at least, that returning to work was a choice rather than a necessity. Indeed, continued working-class use of the term "loafing" suggested (despite its increasingly ironic tinges) that unemployment could be, and sometimes was, experienced as a partially welcome release from the obligation to labor.[11]

At the other end of the spectrum were men and women who were rendered destitute by unemployment. The poorest workers in the state suffered even during short stints of idleness, while long-term joblessness was capable of producing severe hardship for most working-class households. These unfortunate, or unlucky, men and women occasionally ended up homeless and often ended up living in dank, crowded rooms or unheated tenements. They commonly went hungry; their children were sometimes malnourished; they wore patched and threadbare clothing; and sometimes they suffered overly long from illnesses because they lacked the funds to see a doctor. Only during depressions did the destitute unemployed become so numerous that they attracted widespread attention. Yet every year, particularly in winter, there were thousands, sometimes tens of thousands, of working people in Massachusetts who could "barely . . . keep body and soul together" while they were unemployed.[12]

Most encounters with unemployment fell somewhere between these two extremes. The majority of workers who were idled each year did not end up teetering on the brink of starvation, but unemployment did put noticeable dents in their household budgets and savings accounts, which were generally none too ample to begin with. Most spells of joblessness made it difficult for workers to maintain their living standards – whether that meant paying the rent on a cheap tenement or paying off the mortgage on a small house, keeping enough food on the table or keeping teenage children in school, buying a long-desired piece of furniture or meeting the payments on a burial insurance policy. Men and women who were laid off suddenly and without warning ("you get all the way from three to ten minutes' notice," reported one Brockton resident) had to alter their standards of living soon after they lost their jobs. Employees in seasonal industries were obliged both to limit their expenditures year-round and to improvise if "slack times" lasted longer than was customary. Although the details varied from trade to trade and from household to household, diminished living standards, sacrifices, hard choices, and stress were common hallmarks of spells of unemployment. For most jobless workers, wages were too low and stints of idleness too prolonged to permit them to feel unhurried about returning to work.[13]

Despite the changes that occurred in economic and social life during this period, the range of unemployment experiences, the spectrum of needs felt by the unemployed, did not shift much between the 1870s and the 1920s. The changes that took place in the material dimensions of working-class life were limited in magnitude and offered mixed results to the unemployed. Real wages, as noted in Chapter 3, did increase considerably during this period: most industrial workers lived better and had more money to spend in 1920 than they had had in 1875 or 1900. But working-class expectations (and standards of acceptable living conditions) also rose, and blue-collar employees continued to devote a high proportion of their earnings to payments for food, shelter, fuel, and other necessities. The quality of these necessities may well have improved, but shoe workers, carpenters, and day laborers did not end up in the lap of luxury or acquire great wads of disposable cash. Working-class living standards remained modest at best, and losses of income were just as unwanted in the 1920s as they had been in the 1870s.[14]

Nor did rising real wages lead to a decline in the proportion of unemployed workers subject to severe hardship. Indeed, if scattered and impressionistic evidence can be trusted, this period probably witnessed a slight overall increase in the incidence of serious deprivation among the unemployed. "Never in the eighty years since this society began to labor in behalf of those out of work," reported the Industrial Aid Society of Boston in 1915, "were the demands for assistance of all kinds so insistent." The source of this increase was the ongoing urbanization of working-class life. Workers were moving to the cities, and the cities themselves were becoming more densely populated. As a result, there was a steady decline in the proportion of working people who had access to nonmonetary income supplements (like vegetable gardens and livestock) that could help them weather spells of joblessness. The significance of this trend was recognized by agencies like the Industrial Aid Society which tried to help the unemployed by giving them garden plots and by encouraging them to move to rural areas.[15]

Few workers, however, left Boston or Fall River to move to the countryside, and the provision of vegetable gardens to several hundred of the unemployed could not turn the clock back on urbanization. Men and women who worked in industry were increasingly dependent on their cash earnings to satisfy all their basic needs: jobless workers who could ward off hardship by growing their own food or returning to the land were becoming a rare and endangered species. F. P. Hatch, the shoe factory operative who also owned a farm, was an anachronism in 1894. And by the 1920s, there were precious few industrial workers who could match the claim of one Plymouth Cordage Company employee that his family could make ends meet because he owned a garden and a pig.[16]

Unemployed workers, in sum, shared a common predicament but not a common fate. The fundamental economic problems posed by unemployment were the same for virtually all working people. But the very fact that unemployment was so widespread – that it afflicted men and women from so many occupations, at such different stages in their careers – meant that the difficulties created by spells of idleness always varied in magnitude and intensity. Many, if not most, workers had some firsthand acquaintance with this variety, with the uneven and shifting impact of layoffs. In the course of their careers they were themselves jobless for periods ranging from one to five months, when they were single and when they were married, when they had young mouths to feed and when their children were grown. They knew well that layoffs were costly, and they also knew that the exact price to be paid for a spell of unemployment was – like so much else in working-class life – beyond anyone's power to predict.

Institutional relief

> One of the overseers of the poor told me of a man who came to
> him and sat around and talked as chipper as could be until finally
> he said, there is no use in talking, I might as well tell you what I
> am here for. There are five little children at our house. My wife
> and I could get along, but we can't see those little children starve,
> and he broke right down and cried. The overseer of the poor gave

him money, and covered it up in some way so that it wouldn't
get out.

The Reverend Jesse H. Jones, North Abington, 1894

It is only when idleness has been long continued that the normal
workingmen's families begin to come to the acquaintance of the
organized channels of charity.

Associated Charities of Boston, 1908[17]

There were many agencies and institutions that provided aid to unemployed men and women in Massachusetts. According to one unusually detailed survey conducted in the 1890s, hundreds of organizations, scattered throughout the commonwealth, were engaged in
the task of unemployment relief during the harsh, depressed winter
of 1893–4. Spottier evidence suggests that, at one time or another
between 1890 and 1922, hundreds of thousands of jobless workers
received some material support from either public or private agencies. Yet despite these impressive-sounding figures, formal institutions played only a marginal, and in key respects insignificant, role
in helping the unemployed to cope with the consequences of being
out of work.[18]

The only institutions that offered aid to men and women expressly
because they were jobless were trade union locals that maintained
"out-of-work" benefits. The Knights of Saint Crispin, a union of shoe
workers, allowed its unemployed members to draw $6 a week from
union funds as early as the 1870s, and, in subsequent decades, cigarmakers, iron molders, weavers, and a smattering of other trade
unionists also participated in benefit plans sponsored by their local
unions. But these plans, important as they may have been in estab-
lishing precedents for public policy, did little to relieve the distress of
the unemployed. Most workers did not belong to unions, and relatively few unions were ever able to institute benefit or insurance
schemes. As late as 1908, only 76 out of 937 Massachusetts locals
reported that they provided out-of-work benefits to their members.
And the insurance programs that did exist typically delivered very
small amounts of aid to individual unionists. Between July 1, 1893,
and July 1, 1894, the weavers' union in Fall River paid a total of $5,642
to 1,900 unemployed weavers; over roughly the same time period,
nearly 2,000 jobless cigar makers shared $8,000 in benefits. Even dur-
ing the relatively prosperous year of 1909, when unions were larger
and union treasuries more flush, idleness benefits in the state as a
whole averaged less than $10 per recipient annually. Trade union
benefit plans made up for only a tiny fraction of the wages that
unionists lost as a result of unemployment.[19]

There were, of course, numerous other institutions to which jobless workers could apply for aid. Every community had its Overseers of the Poor, and during depressions, particularly after 1890, most cities and many towns created emergency relief committees or launched work relief programs. Workers could also seek support from private charitable organizations, like the Boston Provident Association and the Associated Charities, or from churches and church-sponsored charities, such as the Society of Saint Vincent de Paul. Ethnic organizations constituted yet another source of aid for the jobless, as did a panoply of small, local agencies that served specific constituencies, such as the homeless or single, working women. From this assembly of institutions, unemployed workers could – and did – obtain food, shelter, hot meals, coal, clothing, medical care, and even cash.[20]

Yet these institutions, whether public or private, were not designed to support the unemployed per se; their aim, rather, was to provide aid to the most poverty-stricken residents of the commonwealth. Charitable organizations, as well as public agencies such as the Overseers of the Poor, were dedicated primarily to the task of helping the unemployable: the aged, the infirm, and children. Unemployed workers entered their purview only if, and when, they neared the brink of destitution. Between 1870 and the early 1920s, there were many changes in the format and administration of relief to the unemployed, but this one key fact remained constant: men and women received help not when they lost their jobs but when they became "cases of extreme need from loss of work." It was for this reason that so much of the available aid came in the form of goods and services rather than cash. Relief was intended not to compensate for lost wages but to alleviate distress.[21]

The limits of institutional aid were quantitative as well as conceptual. Although the total amount of money expended by charity organizations and relief committees was sometimes considerable, the sums parceled out to individuals and their families were almost invariably minuscule. During the winter of 1893–4, the emergency work relief program in Boston provided an average total of $9 in aid (roughly the equivalent of a week's wages) to each relief recipient. In Lawrence, the figure was similar, while in Holyoke it was $24 and in Cambridge $28. "In actual dollars and cents the relief was hardly more than insignificant," concluded an investigating commission. "Especially is this felt after one learns that the men reported that they had been out of employment, on the average, more than three months." Despite an overall expansion in the scale of relief programs, the story did not change much after the turn of the century. In 1914–15, a work relief project in Springfield distributed $5,000 among 500 applicants for aid; in 1921–2, the Boston Provident Association expended roughly $4,000 in support of more than 1,000 jobless men. There were exceptions to this spareness – the town of Gardner, for example, launched a very substantial public works program for its unemployed residents in the early 1920s – but they were exceptions and were few and far between.[22]

The terms on which aid was offered, moreover, were often unattractive: jobless men and women who sought institutional support commonly had to subject themselves to semipublic scrutiny and to a kind of moral policing. Relief for the unemployed was widely regarded as charity, and charity was dispensed only to families that were demonstrably poor and certifiably worthy. Applicants for aid, particularly from public agencies or from large charity organizations, had to be prepared to offer detailed descriptions of their plight and to have their stories investigated and verified. In the 1890s, the Citizens' Labor Bureau of Lynn provided three dollars a week in work relief to "actual citizens of Lynn in extreme need, and having no other friends or resources, – these facts ascertained by thorough domiciliary investigation in every case." Similarly, investigators for the Wells Memorial Institute in Boston went to great lengths to confirm that the women participating in their work relief program were genuinely poor, virtuous, and sober. Not all agencies were equally stringent or thorough, and some officials were certainly sensitive to the feelings of embarrassment and discomfort that often accompanied applications for relief. But institutional policies made clear that the able-bodied unemployed could not expect help unless they were morally worthy and in unmistakably dire straits.[23]

Not surprisingly, working people themselves either shared or respected those expectations. Most applicants for institutional aid were drawn from the poorest strata of the working class, many of them having suffered other misfortunes (such as illness) in addition to their unemployment. For virtually all the unemployed, institutional relief was a last resort: only when their material needs became urgent did jobless workers turn to their churches, to the Overseers of the Poor, to charity organizations, or to the emergency committees formed during depressions. "People are coming now who wear comparatively good clothes and who have waited until their last crust and hod of coal were gone," reported the head of Chelsea's relief committee in 1894. "The families often did not come . . . until every other source of help had failed," noted the Associated Charities of Boston more than twenty years later.[24]

There was, to be sure, one additional way in which public and private institutions could – and did – help the unemployed: by finding them jobs. Private charities routinely informed relief applicants of any permanent or temporary positions known to be available, while charity officials sometimes used their own personal contacts to place men and women whom they thought particularly deserving. As early as the 1870s, there was at least one organization, the Industrial Aid Society of Boston, that specialized in finding work for the involuntarily idle, and beginning in 1906 the state government maintained Free Employment Offices in several large cities. Every year, thousands of men and women obtained jobs through these institutional networks.[25]

But these agencies were never able to find work for more than a minute proportion of the unemployed. Relatively few employers notified charitable organizations, or even the Free Employment offices, when they were hiring workers, and the organizations themselves could do nothing to create jobs when business was slack. "The cry for work could but seldom be met," noted the East Boston branch of the Associated Charities in 1897. "We have always tried to find it; but it is sad to look back upon the cases in which employment would have worked a certain cure, and in which permanent work could not be obtained."[26] Although jobless men and women frequently turned to charity officials for help in finding jobs – because they preferred work to relief and because these officials were among their only contacts with the middle class – their hopes were more often frustrated than fulfilled. In October 1921, George Greener, the director of the North Bennet Street Industrial School in Boston, wrote to a young man, then living in Lawrence, to tell him that there might be jobs available at the soda fountains of two Boston drugstores. He received the following expression of disappointment, mixed with pleading and a trace of anger, in reply:

> Dear Mr. Greener
>   last wensday I recieved your letter about the job . . . I saw these two people just two hours after I recieved your letter and they did not have nothing to do for me so I spended three dollars for my train fare for nothing, Mr. Greener. So Mr. Greener if you would do me a favor of getting me a job in some stores or some hotels because I have been out of work for a long time and my father is not working to so if you think you can get me a job in some place I would be very much pleased because there is nothing for me to be doing in Lawrence. Mr. Greener if there is anything to please you I will do it. –
>
>   This is Yours Truly,
>   G.G.[27]

To be sure, for many workers and their families, the aid provided by relief and charitable organizations was, despite its limitations, timely and of no small value. Some men and women did obtain jobs through these institutions; for others, the receipt of ten or fifteen dollars in cash, at a critical juncture, meant that the rent could be paid, milk could be bought for children, valued possessions could be saved rather than sold. Soup kitchens and store orders for food were a godsend to the hungry, a half-ton of coal could heat an apartment during the coldest months of winter, and new shoes made it possible for adults to go on looking for work and for children to attend school. The most desperate and stricken of the jobless did have someplace to turn; the worst sufferings of the unemployed were often alleviated by institutional systems of support.

Still, these institutions played only a small part in the ongoing and recurrent drama of unemployment. Most jobless workers had no contact whatsoever with charitable or relief agencies, and, even among relief recipients, institutional aid accounted for only a small fraction of the resources necessary to weather spells of idleness. However important these institutional programs may have been in the evolution of social thought and public policy (a subject discussed in Chapter 9), they mattered little to the men and women who were unemployed during the era of uncertainty.[28]

Self-insurance, snowfalls, kin, and grocers

> No. 39. A German Jew, 19 years of age. Tailoress by trade, at $5 a week. She lived with father, mother, three brothers and three sisters. The father is a shoemaker, and earns $7 a week when working. One brother sells papers, and earns about $2.50. One sister is a tailoress at $6 a week, and one is in a glove factory at $3 a week. They had four rooms, and paid $13 a month rent. The shop was closed and she was thrown out of work in January, 1894. They had aid from the Overseers of the Poor in 1894, in January $2 worth of groceries, and in February groceries and one-quarter of a ton of coal. The wage-earners of the family were all out of work in the winter of 1894. One sister received work at Bedford Street, and this young woman received four shifts of work at Wells Memorial. She was discharged when the father had work at his own trade found for him through Wells Memorial at $14 a week. She worked through June, September and October as a machine stitcher, at from $3 to $5 a week, but was idle two months in the summer. Her prospects are good, as others in the family are working.

No. 12. His work is bronzing. This requires no special training.
This work is never steady, and there was no particular depression
in it during 1894. It is never carried on during the winter, but
commences about April 1. The wife also worked, – obtained three
days' tickets for sewing at Bedford Street. Family consisted of self
and wife; now have young babe. Two rooms. Did not ask credit of
landlord, but did get credit at grocers, etc. Lived upon some
funds laid by, and had some assistance from friends. After April,
had work four days in the week. Has not been able to lay up anything, as the wife has been severely ill, requiring operation. Obtained this work through his own personal effort. Has no work
now except one day in the week, when he assists in unloading a
fruit steamer at $2.50.[29]

Coping with unemployment was essentially a private affair, a challenge confronted by families, a burden shared with kin, friends, and
neighbors. Men and women who were out of work were, by and
large, left to their own devices, and they devised a richly varied array
of methods for adjusting to unemployment. Workers tailored their
coping strategies to match the severity of their material needs and
the resources at their command; they also improvised, continuously
and ingeniously, in response to happenstance and luck. Yet beneath
the variety and ingenuity were common and fundamental patterns:
relatively few different types of strategies were, in fact, available to
jobless workers, and the improvisations of the unemployed were
similar during each and every year from the 1870s to the 1920s. The
options open to the jobless were defined and circumscribed by the
underlying, and compelling, logic of scarcity and poverty. For some
workers, indeed, the task of coping with unemployment was finally
inseparable – and indistinguishable – from the larger and more permanent task of coping with being poor.[30]

In February 1894, *Lend a Hand*, the semiofficial magazine of Boston's
organized charities, noted, with considerable satisfaction, that despite the depression the winter months had witnessed less suffering
among the unemployed than "the most sanguine dared to hope."
This happy turn of events, according to the journal, demonstrated
that "workingmen and women understand their own business exceedingly well, – better than some of the philanthropists. They have
taken care of themselves; when the tempest struck, they were ready."
Lend a Hand's pronouncement was overly sanguine and more than a
little exculpatory (Boston's charities had come in for criticism during
the early months of the depression), but it contained some truth
nonetheless. Workers in the 1890s, like their counterparts during
other decades, did cope with unemployment, in part, by preparing

for it in advance, by insuring themselves, by organizing their economic lives so as to prevent or minimize hardship in the event that they were unemployed.[31]

The most obvious way in which they did so was through savings. Although precise figures are unavailable, most workers probably did possess small savings accounts that served to cushion the impact of layoffs. Seasonal workers, such as construction tradesmen and shoemakers, habitually put aside small sums when they were working to help cover their expenses during slack seasons. Cyclical rhythms were similar: working people saved during prosperous years and expended their savings during depressions. Between 1890 and 1909, withdrawals exceeded deposits in the savings banks of Massachusetts only in 1893, 1896, 1898, 1907, and 1908.[32]

Savings accounts, however, provided a thin cushion against layoffs that were as frequent and prolonged as those that occurred in numerous working-class occupations. Studies conducted in the 1890s and the early 1920s revealed that many workers had no savings at all when they began their stints of unemployment, and even those who had put some money aside were generally able to cover only a small portion of their living expenses with their savings. "It is impossible for a man to save money enough, when he is at work, to carry him through his term of idleness," claimed a shoemaker in the 1870s. "Italians rank with the most frugal people of the world," noted a North End charity association in 1909, "but even their economy cannot make up for the loss of four or five months' wages."[33]

Workers' savings accounts also tended to be so modest and precious that jobless men and women called upon them only sparingly and reluctantly. Workers who were forced to deplete their savings withdrew funds from banks in excruciatingly small amounts. "They seem to be taking out only just enough for simple living expenses," reported a bank treasurer in 1893. "Many of them tell us that they hate to take out a cent, but they have been out of work for two or three months and have to withdraw some dollars for food or coal." "A man having a small amount of money in the bank," observed another bank official, "is very careful and hates to touch it for fear he may need it worse some other time than he does now. It is only when he is in need of food or clothing for his family that he comes to the bank and then the smallest adequate amount is taken." Savings accounts were a key line of defense against hardship, but few workers could count on their savings for anything more than partial support during a short stint of idleness.[34]

A less obvious, but perhaps more significant, method of self-insurance was the maintenance of multiple sources of income in working-class households. Many, if not most, wage earners belonged to households in which they were not the sole source of revenue. Even in nuclear families, the earnings of adult male household heads, particularly among the unskilled and semiskilled, were commonly supplemented by income from boarders and lodgers, by the earnings of married women, or by the wages brought home by children. In 1900, less than half the male shoe workers in Brockton were the sole wage earners in their families; more than one-quarter of all households headed by male shoe workers had at least two resident wage earners, and more than 10 percent had boarders. Although the figures varied from trade to trade and from ethnic group to ethnic group, the typical working-class household probably had more than one income, at least during certain stages in its own developmental cycle.[35]

There were, to be sure, numerous reasons for working-class families to multiply their sources of revenue. But in many households the critical goal was not maximizing earnings so much as preventing the cessation of all income during periods when the primary wage earner was unemployed. It was not just the small size but the irregularity of working-class incomes that often led parents to take their children out of school and send them into the labor force. In Boston's North End, according to a study conducted by the North Bennet Street Industrial School, the instability of employment created "a tendency to fall back on the childrens' earnings." "'There's nobody working in the family,'" was the most common reason given for the "impatient waiting for the fourteenth birthday." Boarders and lodgers served a similar purpose. "The keeping of lodgers . . . provides a source of income in times of little or no work." In families headed by day laborers who were chronically unemployed, "the woman takes into her three room apartment lodgers and more lodgers."[36]

This strategy of coping with unemployment by maintaining several ongoing sources of income was often effective. In 1914, Dominic Ferri was a fifty-year-old "pick and shovel" man, with eight children, who earned $13.50 a week when he was working. Although he was frequently unemployed, especially in winter, his family was able to make ends meet because his son sent some money home from Lynn each week and because his two teenaged daughters had left school when they were fourteen to work in a candy factory. The Ferri family was far from unique. Charity and relief officials repeatedly noted that in many households "the number of bread-winners" was "a safeguard" against suffering, that families often weathered spells of unemployment by relying on the earnings of one member who remained at work. Indeed, one key reason that depressions produced such dramatic increases in applications for charitable aid was that

business downturns greatly increased the likelihood that a household would lose all its sources of revenue simultaneously. Relief applicants commonly reported that they had been able to manage on
their own until unemployment struck two or three household members at the same time. Similarly, the impact of depressions in immigrant neighborhoods was sharpened by the return to Europe of
single men who had been boarding with families that were already
suffering from joblessness.[37]

These strategies of anticipation and self-insurance provided an important buffer against hardship for working people. Only occasionally, however, were such strategies successful enough to relieve unemployed men and women entirely of the need to improvise and
adapt after they lost their jobs. Most savings accounts were small,
many wage earners did support themselves and their families with
only one income, and there were few households that could subsist
for long on the earnings of a fifteen-year-old child. Spells of unemployment, particularly if they lasted for more than a few weeks, demanded adjustments and improvisations, changes and sacrifices. To
state the matter starkly, jobless workers had to come up with either
new sources of cash or ways to cut their expenditures. Or both.[38]

Perhaps the most common method of obtaining small doses of cash
was the performance of "odd jobs." Some seasonally unemployed
workers were able to contribute to their household budgets by finding temporary, part-time work outside their usual trades. (This practice was frowned upon in mid-nineteenth-century working-class
circles because it meant that members of one trade were "taking
bread from the mouths" of other workers. But the frowns seem to
have receded by the 1890s.[39]) During depressions too, jobless men
and women could often pick up a dollar or two, here and there, by
laboring for a day or an afternoon. Men loaded coal and unloaded
freight; women did occasional domestic work; both men and women
could earn a dollar a day by posing as artists' models. In the spring,
gangs of men were sometimes hired to do ardent, if brief, battle with
the gypsy moth, while in winter there was ice cutting to be done on
the commonwealth's rivers and lakes. The harsh New England climate was, in fact, responsible for the most widespread and important
odd job in the state: snow shoveling. Snowstorms were a blessing for
the unemployed because the task of clearing streets, highways, and
railroad tracks generated jobs for hundreds, often thousands, of men
during a season when work tended to be scarce. A bright spot in the
harsh, depressed winter of 1893–4 was a very severe snowstorm that
hit Massachusetts in February: several hundred men were employed
to clear tracks by the West End Railroad Company alone. Fourteen

years later, in the winter of 1907–8, the "financial stringency" was "aggravated" by abnormally warm weather, "the usual opportunities for the employment of common labor in the removal of snow and in the ice cutting and wood chopping industries being lacking."[40]

Another strategy for generating funds to replace lost earnings was the entrance into the labor force of women and children who had not been working for pay. This was far from a preferred strategy, for it meant disrupting established household routines or short circuiting the education of children. But preferred or not, it was sometimes a necessary step, particularly when a principal wage earner was idled for a lengthy stretch of time. If some women and children entered the labor force as an anticipatory safeguard against unemployment, others did so as an emergency measure, as an improvised response to financial strains.

Perhaps the most common of these improvisations was for married women to earn a few needed dollars by taking in washing, ironing, and boarders – or more boarders. Less often, the wives of jobless workmen obtained full-time jobs outside their homes.[41] During the depression of the 1890s (as noted in Chapter 4) the number of women in the labor force, in economically diverse communities, tended to increase as male unemployment levels rose. Twenty years later, a study of 1,100 female job seekers in Boston discovered that nearly 200 of these women were "not ordinarily bread winners" but were "trying to save the day for their husbands who were themselves hunting for work." In prosperous years too, as Table 6.2 suggests, women sometimes entered the labor force in response to the unemployment of their husbands. In turn-of-the-century Brockton, married women who were working for pay were significantly more likely to have had jobless husbands than were women who stayed at home.[42]

The role played by teenage children appears to have been slightly different. Although teenagers were often called upon to perform odd jobs, there is little evidence that depressions prompted working-class families to withdraw their children from school and send them into the labor force full-time – probably because it was extremely difficult for the young to find jobs during depressions.[43] But households that were hard-hit by unemployment when the economy was more buoyant did, when necessary, mobilize the labor power of young children who might otherwise have remained in school. In Brockton male shoemakers who were unemployed for three months or longer in 1900 were much more likely to have had children in the labor force than were their colleagues who labored more steadily. Fragmentary numerical evidence from other cities suggests that similar trends pre-

Table 6.2. *Adult male unemployment and the employment status of women and children, Brockton, 1900*

	Percentage with unemployed husband	No. in sample	Excluding husbands/fathers in white-collar occupations	
			Percentage with unemployed husband	No. in sample
Married women				
In paid labor force	58.2[a]	55	63.8[a]	47
At home	36.8	76	43.5	62
	Percentage with unemployed father	No. in sample	Percentage with unemployed father	No. in sample
Girls, aged 14–16				
In paid labor force	63.4[b]	14	69.2[b]	13
In school	25.4	67	30.2	53
Boys, aged 14–16				
In paid labor force	45.0	20	47.4	19
In school	36.0	50	41.5	41

[a]Significantly different from "married women at home." See note 42.
[b]Significantly different from "girls in school." See note 45.
Source: Manuscript schedules, Twelfth U.S. Census, 1900. See notes 42 and 45.

vailed in families headed by laborers, carpenters, mule spinners, and iron molders.[44] And Table 6.2 indicates that girls in Brockton who entered the labor force between the ages of fourteen and sixteen were far more likely than schoolgirls of the same age to have had unemployed fathers.[45] Permitting a child who could legally work to remain in school was a luxury that some of the unemployed could not afford.[46]

These strategies for obtaining cash were almost always accompanied by cutbacks in expenditures, cutbacks that proceeded in monotonously predictable sequences as spells of unemployment dragged on and financial needs deepened. The first items to go were incidentals, recreation, and the small extravagances that graced some working-class budgets: books, newspapers, church donations, tobacco, music lessons for children. Then unemployed workers and their families began economizing on the essentials. Clothing was patched rather than replaced, insurance policies were dropped, sick children were treated with home remedies. Fuel expenses were reduced by keeping rooms unheated, by scavenging the streets for coal and wood, and by switching from electric to kerosene lamps or from lamps to candles. (In 1915, investigators for the Central Labor Union of Boston found an unemployed woman who had sold her stove and was trying to "use candle light to warm herself and her baby.") Food budgets, which always consumed a hefty proportion of working-class incomes, were cut steadily and inexorably. Meat and fresh vegetables made increasingly rare appearances at the dinner table, while milk was purchased only sparingly. For those in dire straits, meals ended up having little nutritional value or were sometimes skipped altogether. During the depression of the 1890s, one family lived for "two weeks upon bread and molasses"; others purchased, for a few cents, the leavings from restaurants.[47]

Unemployed workers also economized by moving to cheaper apartments, tenements, and boarding houses. "I'll give you one instance out of a hundred how workingmen manage to live these hard times," exclaimed a worker in the 1870s. "A man moved eighteen times in two years without paying his rent." Most jobless workers were not quite that peripatetic (or wily), but they were often obliged to move to smaller and less expensive quarters. A study of relief applicants in Springfield in 1922 determined that one-third had changed addresses during the year. Similarly, 10 percent of all unemployed household heads in Brockton moved from one address to another, within the city, between 1900 and 1901.[48] The recorded experiences of Brockton's shoe workers also reveal some of the interplay that existed between residential mobility and other strategies for coping with unemployment. Changes of residence within the city appear to have been more common among households with only one (unemployed) wage earner than among households with two or more active members of the labor force. At the same time, families that had boarders seem to have been unusually likely to depart from Brockton altogether – which suggests that taking in a boarder was often a stopgap, a prelude to more drastic methods of contending with the loss of work.[49]

Then there was debt. However resourceful the unemployed may have been, however frugally they lived, however diligently they looked for new ways to earn a living, they often ended up owing money "in all directions" by the time they returned to work. Men and women in seasonal trades commonly had to devote a portion of each year's earnings to the repayment of debts incurred during the previous slack season. And workers who were idled for unusually long spells almost invariably needed extensive credit just to get by.

Families "got shift of the rent" for months on end from "lenient" and "trusting" landlords; homeowners were obliged to "eat up their houses" by taking out second mortgages; furniture and, in extreme circumstances, tools were also "mortgaged." By the 1920s, jobless workers, occasionally at least, were borrowing cash from local credit agencies.[50]

Above all, the unemployed went into debt to their local grocers and shopkeepers. Most grocery store owners extended credit to known customers, usually within limits set by neighborhood conventions. (The figure was a fairly generous $75 in one district of Boston in 1908.) And grocers were an invaluable source of support for the unemployed, much more important than charity and relief organizations. Most men and women who applied for relief did so only after they had already piled up considerable debts; in Springfield in 1922 the credit extended by grocers was, for most families, far more substantial than any relief that they received.[51]

Just how heavy the burden of debt could become was revealed by the experience of one Italian immigrant family in the early 1920s. The father of the family was a laborer who had been in the United States for ten years and was "eager to get ahead." He supported his wife and four young children with his own earnings. In 1919 he purchased an old and dilapidated house on which he planned to make repairs himself, but in October of 1920 he lost his job and remained unemployed for fourteen months. At the same time, his wife became ill, needing an operation, and his brother died, leaving funeral expenses to be paid. The family drastically cut down on its living expenses: the children's clothing became "torn, thin, and much patched," while meals consisted entirely of bread, coffee, and either spaghetti or beans. Still the debts mounted up. Since the family was known in the neighborhood, it was able to get credit, and by the end of 1921 they were nearly $1,200 in debt. They owed $400 for groceries, $140 in overdue payments on their house, more than $100 to a doctor, and another $150 for a cash loan that they had received. Both of the adults in the household were reported to be "nearly frantic with worry." The father figured that it would take him ten years to get out of debt, if he worked steadily.[52]

The debts incurred by the unemployed testified both to the financial needs of jobless workers and to the presence of informal networks of assistance that were of critical importance to working people during periods of adversity. Many of the loans and much of the credit that the unemployed received were something other than purely commercial transactions; they were expressions of social bonds and conventions, of a culture that valued mutual aid and mutual obligations. Inhabitants of working-class neighborhoods knew well that economic life was precarious and insecure. Almost as a matter of course, they offered help to one another during hard times. To be sure, some grocers and merchants would have done precious little business during depressions had they been unwilling to offer credit. But shopkeepers were motivated also by ties of friendship and sympathy, by the fact that their customers were their neighbors, by the widespread expectation that they should give credit to regular customers down on their luck. The same may also have been true of many of the state's "lenient" landlords. And most of the cash loans that workers received came not from lending institutions but from relatives and friends.[53]

Relatives, indeed, constituted the inner ring of these support networks. Unemployed workers who could not make ends meet by themselves usually turned first to their kin, and kin, when able, either gave or lent cash, clothing, and food to the unemployed. "Doubling up" with relatives was a frequent practice for families that could no longer afford to pay rent, while sending young children off to live with grandparents or cousins was not unknown. Kin networks also played a vital role in helping the unemployed to find jobs and in providing a sanctuary for men and women who were leaving town, leaving the state, or leaving the country. The exodus of immigrants during the depressions of the 1890s, 1907–8, and 1913–14 was, in part, a flight to kinfolk who could be counted on to provide food and shelter.[54]

Friends and neighbors also helped, in many of the same ways. They lent money, paid medical bills, bought food, and sometimes offered (or created) odd jobs that could be performed for pay. "I know of shoemakers that carried other shoemakers along last winter," noted a resident of Lynn in 1895. Boston's municipal employees, who tended to work steadily, were a common source of loans to friends who had the misfortune of being employed in the more volatile private sector. Men who were drinking companions in saloons and bars routinely helped one another when they were idle; young men's clubs in Boston usually contained a contingent of unemployed members who were supported by their colleagues and known as the "day club."[55]

This culture of reciprocity and mutuality also led working people to aid jobless men and women who were neither kin nor close personal friends. Ethnic and community ties gave rise to informal, ad hoc offers of help to the needy, while labor unions that lacked out-of-work benefits sometimes assessed their working members to provide funds for the unemployed. Workers also participated in voluntary institutional programs designed to help the victims of depressions. In Lynn in the early 1920s, 75 percent of the employees at the General Electric Company contributed 1 percent of their wages, for twenty-three weeks, to a relief fund for workers who had been laid off.[56]

The most desperate of the unemployed also found that help was most forthcoming from industrial workers who themselves lived fairly close to the margins of poverty. In the 1890s, Barley E. Bradley, a town official in Williamstown, observed that tramps were more likely to be fed "on the factory ground" than "up on Main Street," while a Springfield official insisted that "the most successful begging is among the poorest classes in the poorest streets." "The kind that always helps you," pointed out a tramp who traveled briefly with Walter Wyckoff, is "the kind that's in hard luck themselves, and knows what it is." Their familiarity with hard luck also led working people to contribute generously to public relief programs. "The working classes . . . have set a splendid example," concluded the Boston *Globe* in a discussion of the city's emergency relief fund in 1894, but "there is a large body of citizens of ample means who have not yet been heard from."[57]

The willingness of working-class families to share their limited resources with unemployed relatives, friends, neighbors, and even strangers ought not and need not be romanticized. It was a virtue born of necessity. The economic climate was always unpredictable and sometimes harsh, and the institutional shelters provided for the unemployed were flimsy and inadequate. Living in such an environment, working people had little choice but to depend heavily upon one another. Empathy and self-interest went hand in hand in promoting a culture that prized loyalty, reciprocity, and solidarity. Workers, witnessing the hardships of the unemployed at close range, were well aware of their own susceptibility to the same fate: a friend or relative who was given help during one depression might have to be asked for help a few years down the road. "Does it seem strange to you," a poor woman was asked by William Dean Howells's fictional traveler from Altruria, "that people should found a civilization on the idea of living for one another, instead of each for himself?" "No, indeed," she answered. "Poor people have always had to live that way, or they could not have lived at all."[58]

In sum, the strategies that workers developed for coping with unemployment amounted to a set of endlessly detailed variations on a few simple themes. Jobless women and men expended the remnants of their past earnings and mortgaged a portion of their future incomes; they relied on the wages of other household members; they picked up any part-time employment that was available; they cut their expenses back, often to the bare bones; and they were helped by their friends. By utilizing one or more of these methods, workers in 1920, like their predecessors in 1875, managed to stay afloat without their regular wages. In most cases, they managed also to avoid the most extreme material deprivations while refraining from asking for public relief or charity. That "outsiders," as settlement house resident Robert A. Woods observed, found it difficult to understand "how people subsist when out of work" was hardly surprising. The process of coping with unemployment unfolded within the confines of working-class neighborhoods, with the most critical steps often taken in kitchens, grocery stores, bars, or conversations on the street. Adjusting to unemployment was an undramatic and informal process, tedious, grinding, and usually uneventful. The efforts of the unemployed were relatively invisible to outsiders because they were deeply embedded in the fabric of everyday life.[59]

Indeed, many routine features of working-class social life were themselves shaped by the need to cope with unemployment. It was not merely poverty but insecurity, not only low incomes but the absence of incomes, that led workers to send their children into the labor force, to take in boarders, to move from one place to another, to hoard their small savings while living in substandard conditions. It was not only sentiment but the need for mutual support that led working people to maintain close ties with their relatives and to cluster in ethnic communities. The structures of life in the working class were molded by the recurrent task of adjusting to unemployment as well as by the ongoing challenge of being prepared to adjust to unemployment. To understand how workers coped with joblessness is, in part, to understand how they lived.

Anxiety and despair

Unemployment left a mark upon the spirit as well as the flesh. Spells of idleness were an obvious source of financial anxiety for many workers; the inability to obtain a job was demoralizing; and personal relationships, at the workplace and within households, were sometimes disrupted and strained by layoffs themselves and by the steps taken to cope with layoffs. Joblessness, thus, often compelled workers and their families to contend with emotional stress as well as material scarcity. Acute as this stress may have been, however, it left only the faintest and most sporadic imprint upon the written historical record. The emotional and psychological consequences of unemployment were neither described in detail nor studied in any depth until the depression of the 1930s. But the scraps of evidence

that do exist certainly indicate that unemployment was a psychologically trying experience long before psychologists and sociologists began interviewing the unemployed. They suggest, in fact, that many
of the patterns observed during and since the 1930s prevailed in earlier years as well.[60]

Some unemployment experiences were, to be sure, relatively free
of emotional strain. Short stints of idleness were taken in stride by
most workers; seasonal layoffs, if not unusually prolonged, probably
produced more boredom than anxiety. Longshoremen spent their
idle days in barrooms near the docks, waiting to be called back to
work, while building laborers in Boston customarily spent their winter afternoons playing cards. For many workers, short and seasonal
layoffs were so familiar and so predictable as not to be a source of
worry or fear, despite their material consequences. Nor is there reason to believe (as some observers have suggested) that American
workers, steeped as they were in a culture that celebrated the abundance of opportunities, were invariably burdened by a sense of personal failure when they were unemployed. Although workers may
well have shared in the faith that the United States was the land of
opportunity, unemployment was far too common an occurrence to
have automatically induced feelings of guilt, self-blame, or individual
inadequacy. Brockton's seasonally unemployed shoe factory operatives may or may not have wondered why they did not belong to the
happy third of the labor force that worked year-round, but surely
they knew that two-thirds of their colleagues were also out of work.[61]

The psychological toll of unemployment began to mount when
stretches of idleness grew longer and their endpoints became less
predictable. As layoffs lengthened in duration, jobless workers and
their families were increasingly beset with financial worries, with
anxiety about the loss of savings, the accumulation of debts, the welfare of their children, and uncertainty about the future. "In the end,
we've always had food," noted one woman whose husband was repeatedly unemployed, "but worse than hunger is the worry and
strain of wondering from where the next meal is coming. Often on
Saturday night at eleven o'clock there was no Sunday dinner." These
bouts of anxiety were frequently accompanied, or followed, by dejec-
tion, pessimism, and resignation. William H. Douglas, who applied
for relief from the Industrial Aid Society in the 1870s, was described
as "a worthy man, but depressed in mind for want of work." In 1879,
a Bay State carpenter offered the revealing observation "that a man
would do more work at home when he is at work than when unemployed; for he is down-hearted and does not feel like working at
home."[62]

Figure 6.1. "Out of Work." From *Harper's Weekly*, September 2, 1893. (Drawing by J. Macdonald.)

Depression, indeed, was probably the characteristic mood of workers who had been unemployed for four or five months or longer. (See Figure 6.1.) Not only were their finances strained, but these men and women were also subjected to the repeated, demoralizing experience of failing to find work. Each day brought a new series of rejections that nibbled away at their confidence and self-respect; each morning they assembled at factory gates or construction sites, only to witness the selection of luckier or more able workers for the few positions available. Each time they ventured outside their homes, they were confronted with the spectacle of other men and women who were either at work or on their way to and from work. For the long-term unemployed, these repeated rejections often bred despondency and inertia. They halted their daily efforts at job seeking and remained at home, listless and isolated. It was among these men, perhaps, that a gnawing sense of personal failure did begin to take root. Being laid off was one thing, but remaining jobless for a comparatively long period of time – longer than other men in the neighborhood, longer than other members of one's trade – could easily be counted as a reflection of a man's ability and worth.[63]

Feelings of demoralization and anxiety, guilt and fear, were often compounded by domestic tensions that arose when a household member (particularly a male household head) was unemployed for a substantial period. Both daily routines and the emotional tones of daily life were disrupted by the presence at home of a bored, discouraged, and sometimes irritable man who had customarily been away at work for ten hours a day, six days a week. Adult men sometimes felt that their authority within the household was undermined by their inability to earn a living; if their wives were obliged to enter the labor force, they were subject to the added discomforts of being financially dependent and of having to perform "women's" domestic chores. In the 1920s, John Daly, an unemployed laborer in Jamaica Plain, was praised by local settlement house workers for his unusual capacity to adjust to his own joblessness and to dependence on his wife's wages. "He has shown great courage and has taken on all the heavy household work such as scrubbing and even washing the clothes, though he refuses to hang them out!" Women who went out to work when their husbands were unemployed were sometimes deeply concerned about neglecting their young children, and teenagers who were sent into the labor force were not always pleased at having to interrupt their schooling to help support their families. Dora Sciarro, a teenager who lived in Cambridge, was "resentful towards her" unemployed father because she wanted to complete her training for a secretarial career and disliked working in a factory.[64]

The consequences of these emotional and psychological strains varied from one individual or family to the next: much depended not only on "external" factors (such as wage levels or the duration of spells of unemployment) but also on personal characteristics that elude a historian's retrospective probings. In some households, men, women, and children banded together in the face of adversity, supporting and comforting one another, while in others resentment and recriminations tore at the fabric of family life and even broke families apart. Some men remained cheerful, or at least stoical, no matter how long they were idle; others began drinking heavily, venting their anger at anyone who came into view. Some jobless workers withdrew into the secure confines of their families, while others abandoned their families, temporarily or permanently, and went out on the road.[65]

Two unusually detailed family histories, compiled by settlement house workers in the 1920s, illustrate the range.[66] The Taber family of Roxbury had to cope with recurrent unemployment for a period of roughly fifteen years. Shortly after he was married, toward the end of the Progressive era, Mr. Taber passed the civil service examination to become a letter carrier. Since he was initially appointed only a substitute, he was obliged to supplement his unsteady wages by working (when he could find work) as a porter, clerk, teamster, and snow shoveler. After six years of irregular employment, he finally joined the Boston police force, only to lose his job during the police strike of 1920. He then spent another seven years working sporadically until his permanent appointment as a letter carrier came through. His wife also worked, but even with their combined earnings it was difficult for the Tabers to support themselves, their seven young children, and an aunt who lived with them. Their home was "dingy looking," they had no savings, and the children showed signs of being undernourished.

Yet morale in the family remained high. "There is a happy atmosphere in the house," reported settlement workers who knew the family well. "The parents exercise good control, and command the love, respect and cooperation of the children." Mr. Taber was apparently known to his neighbors as "a wonder" for his efforts to be a responsible provider and father, and Mrs. Taber displayed "great patience and fortitude." "The struggle against obstacles which seemed at times insurmountable has increased the affection, love, and patience of both parents." Mr. and Mrs. Taber agreed that faith and prayer had been essential to their success in coping with years of unemployment.

The Murphy family was a different story. Thomas Murphy, the father of six children, was forty-one years old in the mid-1920s when he lost his job as a freight handler for the Boston and Maine Railroad, a job that had paid twenty-five dollars a week. The family lived in a five-room tenement that was kept "spotlessly clean" by his wife Mary, who also worked as the janitress of their building in return for a ten-dollar-a-month reduction in their rent. Mr. Murphy remained unemployed for eighteen months, occasionally getting work for a day or two at his old job, but never earning more than six dollars a week. His young children sold newspapers illegally on the streets, one son left school early to go to work, and the family took in a boarder. The Murphy children seemed to be undernourished. They were frequently sick, "stunted in growth," and their teeth were neglected.

The material difficulties that the Murphy family had to confront were exacerbated by a "lack of spirit" that prevailed within the household. Thomas Murphy had been "a silent, industrious person, kindly to his children" before losing his job, but he showed little initiative in trying to find work, and, as the months wore on, he became discouraged and stopped going out to look for work at all. Instead, he remained at home and began drinking heavily. When his wife and children became critical of his behavior, Murphy – feeling both "unhappy and helpless" – responded with cruelty and anger. For the first time in his life, he began to hit his children, and, during one of his drunken outbursts, his oldest son (who was 15 at the time) summoned the police to have his father arrested. The entire family, which had been "quiet" and "self-respecting," was acutely "embarrassed by their family affairs being cause for public comment."

And finally: there were some men and women who fared worse than the Murphys, men and women who, in the end, were not able to cope with the financial and psychological strains engendered by unemployment. Mental hospital admissions tended to increase during business downturns, and newspapers occasionally carried stories reporting the suicide of an unemployed man or woman. "He must have brooded over the affair," noted the Boston *Globe* in 1894 when it reported that Peter A. Masterson of South Framingham had shot himself after being laid off by the Fitchburg Railroad. "Have you noticed how many people have committed suicide of late in a fit of despondency over the loss of their jobs?" queried the *Labor News* of Worcester in February 1921. There were never, of course, "many" people who were driven to take their own lives because of unemployment or whose suicides were even triggered by layoffs. But such tragedies did occur. Jobless workers were, from time to time, so overcome by despair that they abandoned the struggle to survive, so filled with helpless rage that they brought a violent end to their spells of idleness.[67] Those who did so had their final acts duly noted by the state medical examiner.

C.W., 45   Suicide by bullet
Boston   Death May 21, 1895

Out of work and poor, left home a.m. May 21, to collect some old bills. About noon, went to shop of one P. and demanded $5 on account of an old trade. Payment was refused. After some words, W. drew a revolver and fired at P.'s head, without effect; a second shot made a scalp wound and P. fell. W. then turned the weapon on himself and fired into his right temple, making a wound from which he died at once.

K.R., 29   Suicide by drowning
Boston   October 2, 1896

Out of work and despondent for a long while. Body found floating in the Charles.

F.S., 29   Suicide by arsenic
Boston   January 1, 1896

Much depressed for several weeks. Loss of employment. At 7:50 a.m. Jan 1, she called her father and told him she had taken poison and wished to die.

L.M., 38   Hanging suicide
E. Boston   October 15, 1895

Had been out of work for several weeks and was very despondent. Wife went to market at about 11 a.m. and upon returning at about 12 p.m. found him hanging from bedroom door . . . Slipped noose about his neck and falling forward upon it.

J.L., 54   Suicide, gas
S. Boston   April 13, 1896

Out of work for some time and despondent. On the 11th he registered under an assumed name at the Falmouth House. On the 12th owing to odor of gas the room was forced and L. was found dead – he left a note telling his reasons for self-slaughter.

R.N., 23   Suicide by bullet wound of brain
Boston   June 22, 1896

Out of work. Mentally depressed. About 3 p.m. June 21 shot himself in right temple, in an outbuilding in Jamaica Plain. Left a letter explaining that he killed himself to save others the trouble of caring for him.[68]

Aftereffects

Despite the stresses, material and psychological, virtually all the unemployed did succeed in coping with their stints of idleness. No one really had to "starve or freeze," as the governor of Massachusetts rather cavalierly put it in 1908. Deaths were exceedingly rare: jobless men and women did, on the whole, manage to keep body and soul together without their regular wages. They also – with relatively few exceptions, most of them elderly – returned to work, either at their old jobs or in new positions. The resumption of paid employment, however, did not necessarily put closure on the experience of involuntary idleness. For many workers, the effects of unemployment continued to be felt long after they had rejoined the ranks of the state's active and productive citizenry.[69]

Working-class living standards were commonly diminished for many months, or even years, as a result of layoffs that had themselves been of far shorter duration. Some workers lost their homes because they had failed to meet mortgage payments; others found themselves living in tenements that were smaller, darker, and less well-located than those they had inhabited before their layoffs. Working people had to do without insurance policies that had been lost and without furniture and personal possessions that had been sold or pawned. Savings accounts – with their promise of a better future – had often disappeared or dwindled to disturbingly low levels. And workers, once rehired, had to begin repaying the debts incurred in previous months, debts to the grocer and the butcher, debts to the landlord, debts to friends and relatives. For numerous men and women, the resumption of paid labor signaled not the end of their financial difficulties but rather the beginning of a slow and sometimes extended process of recouping the losses suffered while unemployed.[70]

For a small, but probably not trivial, proportion of the jobless, the long-term consequences were even more severe. These were men and women who did not immediately (or ever) regain jobs that were as satisfying or as remunerative as those they had held before being laid off. This was certainly the fate of some skilled employees whose trades were transformed by technological change. It was also the fate of many workers whose careers were built on loyalty to an individual firm that went into decline, went bankrupt, or moved: men and women who were highly valued by particular employers, precisely because they had been working in one place for years and knew the essential, unwritten details of an individual firm's operations, often had difficulty obtaining the same wages or working conditions elsewhere. In addition, some workers chose or were obliged to terminate their spells of unemployment by accepting jobs that offered lower pay and less status than they had once received, while others found that their efficiency was impaired by lengthy spells of idleness – which for pieceworkers, in particular, meant that their earnings were reduced. For all such men and women, unemployment marked the beginning of a prolonged, or even permanent, decline in income or occupational standing.[71]

In some households, the long-term impact of a spell of idleness was transmitted from one generation to the next. Children who left school early in order to enter the labor force and help their families often paid a considerable price for doing so. They generally began their careers in unskilled, poorly paid, dead-end jobs, often drifting from one position to another during their first years in the labor force. More importantly, their lack of schooling and training sometimes crippled their careers for decades to come. T. T. Pomeroy, a shoemaker who lived in Haverhill in the 1890s, was painfully aware that his chronic inability to find year-round work was going to dash his and his wife's hopes for the occupational mobility of their children:

> My oldest girl is fourteen and my boy twelve, and my wife was telling at the breakfast table this morning what she was going to

do with them. The girl is going through the high school, and she is going to teach school. The boy is going through high school and is then going to the school of technology. I was just thinking how hard it was that I couldn't do this for them. I have got to take my children out of school next year and hand them over to the task master.[72]

Long-term plans and hopes were also dashed, or, at the very least, deferred, for many immigrants. Among the thousands of foreign-born workers who left Massachusetts (and the United States) each year, there were always some who were reluctant to leave, who would have stayed had they been able to obtain steady work. For these men (and, less often, women), unemployment meant abandoning the prospect of settling permanently in the United States or surrendering the hope that they could save enough money in the New World to be able to buy a farm or start a business in their country of origin. Indeed, for migrants who intended to return to their families in Europe after accumulating enough cash in the United States, spells of unemployment presented a particularly agonizing dilemma. They could either wait out their stints of idleness, thereby prolonging their absence from home and family, or they could put a premature end to their sojourn in the United States. Either way, the cost was considerable. "Nothing job, nothing job, I return to Italy" – a line from a song popular early in the twentieth century – was a statement of failure as well as intent, a lyric expression of the decisive blow that joblessness could deliver to the aspirations of the foreign-born.[73]

Within Massachusetts too, the geographic mobility prompted by unemployment sometimes had durable and far-reaching consequences. The bonds of friendship and community so often of great value to jobless workers were weakened or severed by the mobility that the labor market seemed to demand. Men and women who moved from towns to cities sometimes found themselves sorely missing the familiar faces who might have helped them when they were in need; a worker who had only recently settled in a neighborhood was relatively unlikely to get credit from the local grocer; families that moved from one place to another to obtain jobs not infrequently left their closest friends and relatives a hundred miles behind. The mobility needed to end a particular spell of unemployment, thus, often had the consequence of leaving workers more isolated and more vulnerable to hardship if they lost their jobs once again. The workers who qualified for aid from the Citizens' Labor Bureau of Lynn in the 1890s – workers who could prove that they had no nearby friends or relatives – were presumably recent migrants to the city.

The emotional toll of unemployment also lingered on after the jobless had returned to work. Depressed spirits may have lifted fairly quickly once idled men and women were able to resume their workaday routines, but financial worries persisted, particularly in households that were heavily in debt. The strains and tensions that emerged within families also left wounds that took time to heal. Families like the Murphys had to contend for months, perhaps years, with the guilt and resentment stirred up during periods of unemployment, with the scars left by angry, alcoholic outbursts, with altered patterns of authority and respect within the household. In some families, the emotional equilibrium existing before a prolonged layoff was – for better or worse – never restored; in others, family units themselves were split apart and never restored. And almost everyone who had to endure a long or difficult spell of joblessness carried some anxiety and fear away from the experience. "The fear of being turned off," observed one worker, "is the worst thing in a workingman's life, and more or less acutely it is almost always . . . present to his mind."[74]

These aftereffects of joblessness testified, of course, to the significance of unemployment in the lives of working people. "Involuntary idleness" was not only a frequent and recurrent experience; it was also an experience that mattered, often deeply. Unemployment helped to shape the material and psychological quality of working-class life both because episodes of joblessness were difficult and painful and because they frequently left harsh and durable legacies. People's lives and plans were altered by unemployment, often for long stretches of time, and in some instances, irretrievably. The slate was not wiped clean the instant that men and women returned to work.

Despite the commonwealth's economic growth and despite deepening public concern about the problem of unemployment, the impact of joblessness upon the well-being, emotions, and plans of working people did not diminish between the 1870s and the 1920s. Indeed, if there were any changes at all, they ran in the opposite direction: jobless men and women may well have felt their losses more keenly in 1920 than they had in 1875. As workers became more fully dependent upon their cash wages, interruptions in the flow of income may have become more threatening to their living standards, more jarring to their hopes and expectations. As the anonymity of urban society extended its sway over the commonwealth and as workers continued to move from place to place, informal, community-based networks of support probably became less cohesive and less available. It is possible, then, that spells of unemployment gradually became more penetrating in their consequences and more difficult to weather. And it is certain that, with each passing decade, there was a sizable increase in the number of workers who were compelled to cope with unemployment.[75]

7   *Organizing labor*

> Now you ask what shall be done with these poor shoe makers
> who have been out of work and will need help this winter. Of
> course the state can build factories – some people suggest this,
> but that would be socialism, and it would be impossible, in my
> judgment, for the state to go into that. Of course that would be
> ideal. Although I am not a socialist. I would like to see a national
> condition of things brought about, so that no man would need to
> be out of work.
>
> Michael Moran, secretary, Central Labor Union
of Brockton, 1894

> It is simply this theory with me: I believe the working men them-
> selves will have to take action. I believe those men that are em-
> ployed will have to look out for the unemployed that work at the
> same business as they do.
>
> George H. Wrenn, cigarmaker, Springfield, 1894

> If two men compete for the same position when there is a place
> only for one, unavoidably one must be unemployed, whereas the
> other will work for just a little more than nothing.
>
> J. F. Carey, heel maker, Haverhill, 1895[1]

Unemployment was a political problem as well as a personal one, a
source of social conflict as well as individual anguish. Beginning in
the 1870s, the unsteadiness of employment was a critical social issue
for working people, a major item on any list of working-class grievances. The problem of unemployment cut deep, and workers wanted
it solved or, at the very least, contained. They desired steady jobs
and predictable incomes; they also wanted to stop footing the bill for
panics and depressions that occurred through no fault of their own.

    In Massachusetts and elsewhere in the nation, working-class ef-
forts to reduce or "abolish" unemployment were spearheaded by labor unions. The years between the Civil War and World War I witnessed the emergence of large and, in some cases, durable unions
that gave voice and muscle to the demand for steady work. Labor
unions tried to obtain enough power in the labor markets to be able
to dictate, or at least influence, the conditions and terms of employ-

ment; they also developed a host of strategies designed to stabilize the rhythms of work and limit the damage wrought by joblessness. In doing so, they often found themselves squaring off against employers and employers' associations. The regularity of work was an issue that touched the raw nerve of class interest, and labor's efforts to eradicate or minimize unemployment sparked enduring antagonism and recurrent conflict.

Class conflict, however, constituted only one axis of the struggle. Workers and unions also had to contend with another opponent: the competitive pressures spawned by the scarcity of jobs. Chronic unemployment meant that the labor markets of Massachusetts were highly competitive. Faced with this competition, with scarcity and deprivation, it was no simple task for working people or for unions to maintain their solidarity with one another. Individuals were all too familiar with the temptation to undercut a fellow worker in order to keep or get a job, and unions were subject to equally powerful pressures to protect their own members at the expense of "outsiders." Involuntary idleness was such a widespread problem that it provided a basis for – and demanded – collective action; at the same time, unemployment was a condition, and a threat, that fostered rivalry and distrust. Indeed, the interplay between solidarity and competition, between class conflict and internecine warfare, played a critical role in determining the policies and the structure of the labor movement throughout its formative decades.

The collective problem

The decade of the 1870s was a bleak one for organized labor in Massachusetts. The widespread and successful upsurge in organizing that had followed the Civil War was first checked, then reversed, during the long cyclical downturn that began in 1873. Trade union membership plummeted in every major industry, and the Knights of Saint Crispin, who had proudly claimed ten thousand Bay State shoe workers as members in 1870, had all but disappeared ten years later. Although the commonwealth had been something of a union stronghold at the beginning of the decade, by 1878 the Iron Molders' *Journal* was complaining that "so far as trade or *bona fide* labor unions are concerned, there is not a state . . . so devoid of organization as Massachusetts." A retrospective study, conducted by the Bureau of Statistics of Labor in the 1890s, issued the same verdict. "Trade unionism . . . at the close of the year 1879," concluded the bureau, "was without force in Massachusetts."[2]

The debacle of the 1870s was not the first time that abnormally high levels of unemployment had decimated the ranks of organized labor. Between 1830 and 1860, dozens, perhaps hundreds, of local labor unions and workingmen's associations had sprouted into existence, only to falter or collapse under the pressure of adverse trade conditions. Long before the 1870s, depressions had led some jobless workers to drop out of labor organizations, while their employed colleagues became increasingly reluctant to take steps that might cost them their jobs, such as joining a union or insisting on a union pay scale. Nor did the depression of the 1870s mark the first time that employers had taken advantage of economic conditions by attempting, with some success, to break unions that had formed among their employees. Unemployment had long been a weed that choked off the flowering of trade unionism.[3]

But an important change took place after the 1870s: although unemployment continued to hinder the development of labor organizations, workers were able to form unions that could and did survive depressions. Tens of thousands of Massachusetts workers rushed to join unions in the course of the 1880s, and more than one hundred of the locals founded during that decade lasted into the twentieth century. The largest, most well-known organization of the 1880s, the Knights of Labor, did not, of course, turn out to be a very hardy specimen. But some of its affiliated locals remained in business for decades, and the overall decline of the Knights was accompanied by the growth of national trade unions and the fledgling American Federation of Labor. The Massachusetts state branch of the AFL was founded in August 1887 at a meeting, attended by Samuel Gompers, that was held in Boston's Pythian Hall. The state AFL was committed to sponsoring craft unions of a type that seemed well-suited to the task of weathering the vicissitudes of the business cycle.[4]

In Massachusetts and in other states, national trade unions proved their mettle during the depression of the 1890s: they were badly shaken by that depression, losing thousands of members, but they did endure. And once the depression had ended, unions began to grow at a very rapid rate. By 1908, there were more than 1,300 locals in the commonwealth, with a combined membership of more than 160,000. By 1915, the figure had climbed to a quarter of a million, or roughly 15 percent of the labor force; in 1919, after a wartime boom in organizing, there were 368,000 union members in the state. Between two-thirds and three-quarters of these unionists (the figure varied from year to year) belonged to organizations affiliated with the American Federation of Labor.[5]

By the second decade of the twentieth century, then, the labor movement had demonstrated its capacity to survive during economic downturns and to grow despite chronic unemployment. In Massachusetts, there were active unions in more than one hundred communities and more than sixty occupations. Skilled craftsmen in the building trades, in the metal and machinery industries, and in transportation were heavily organized. Shoe workers had regrouped after the demise of the Crispins and built two of the three largest unions in the state. By 1920 there were even 35,000 organized textile workers in the commonwealth. Between 1880 and World War I, labor unions had become a permanent and significant feature of the Bay State's institutional landscape.[6]

Nonetheless, unemployment remained a threat to the strength and even the existence of unions. The brief cyclical downturns of 1907–8 and 1913–14 both produced modest declines in union membership, and the postwar depression had sharper consequences. During the first year of that depression alone, organized labor lost more than twenty thousand members, with very sizable losses occurring in the shoe and textile industries. The majority of unskilled and semiskilled workers, moreover, remained unorganized. These were the men and women who were most vulnerable to the fear and threat of unemployment (because they could easily be replaced by virtually any jobless worker), and, with a few exceptions, they had been thwarted in their efforts to build strong and durable unions. As a result, less than one-quarter of the commonwealth's labor force was organized, even during the peak year of 1919.[7]

The size of the labor movement was not the only issue. Throughout the years between 1870 and the early 1920s, the presence of unemployed workers served to limit the achievements, as well as the strength, of organized labor. Workers who joined unions hoped to increase their wages, reduce the hours of labor, and improve their working conditions. The attainment of all these goals, and others, was hindered by the irregularity of employment.

This occurred, in part, because unemployment put a damper on the militance of the working class. "The market is glutted and we have seasons of dullness," noted a leather currier in 1879. "Our tasks are increased, and, if we remonstrate, we are told our places can be filled." Workers, in fact, often decided not to "remonstrate" during dull seasons or cyclical downturns, although it was precisely during these periods that employers generally tried to reduce wages, increase the workload, and get rid of troublesome organizations and individuals. Depressions usually led to a decline in the number of strikes. Slow seasons had the same effect: strikes were much more common in the busy months of the late spring and early summer than they were in the fall and winter. And unskilled workers were chronically wary of strikes because, as the Massachusetts Bureau of Statistics of Labor observed in 1909, the supply of unskilled labor was "frequently so great that a strike would be sure to meet defeat."[8]

Year in and year out – but most visibly during depressions – workers found themselves sizing up the condition of the labor market and concluding that they had little choice but to forgo hoped-for gains or to acquiesce to the demands of their employers. In Lowell in 1894, the executive committee of the woolen spinners' union "met and decided that it would be better to accept the reduced wages than to be out of employment altogether, which was the only alternative." In 1898, Brockton's shoe factory operatives "made concessions owing to the large number of shoemakers out of employment." In Worcester in 1920 workers accepted significant wage cuts after first witnessing a large round of layoffs. "If a man can afford it, I believe in his standing up for his rights," proclaimed O. D. Cummings, a carpenter in Springfield in the 1890s. "But I don't believe in a man's jumping out of the frying pan into the fire."[9]

The caution that workers displayed was rooted in experience: the size of the commonwealth's labor reserves diminished the bargaining power of working people sufficiently that they frequently ended up on the losing side of workplace conflicts. Between 1881 and 1900, roughly one out of every six strikers in Massachusetts lost his or her job to a new employee. During the first quarter of 1902 (a prosperous year), one out of every eight strikes came to an end when new workers were hired "almost immediately," and a rash of strikes in the building trades in 1908 met the same fate. Indeed, it appears (from vastly imperfect statistics) that at least half the strikes that took place in Massachusetts between 1870 and 1922 ended in defeat for the strikers, a track record attributable, in part, to the ease with which workers could be replaced from the ranks of the unemployed. As one might expect, labor leaders, particularly during the final decades of the nineteenth century, were ambivalent about the utility of strikes in general and adamant in urging (or ordering) local unions not to strike during depressions or seasonal slack times.[10]

There were, of course, more upbeat sides to the story. Unions did occasionally manage to win strikes despite gluts in the labor market, while long or recurrent layoffs sometimes infused workers with an angry and determined militance – which was one reason why strikes were very likely to occur when business conditions were just beginning to improve. Throughout these years, moreover, some workers were able to recoup the losses suffered during slowdowns by taking collective action during periods (such as the early summer or World

War I) when favorable labor market conditions prevailed. But the very rhythms of victory and defeat, of action and inaction, of achievements and losses, testified to the significance of unemployment. And without question the net impact of involuntary idleness upon the progress of the labor movement was a negative one. Organized labor's efforts to obtain better pay, shorter hours, improved working conditions, union recognition, and more control over the workplace were all – to some extent – checked by the presence of reserves of labor in the commonwealth.[11]

Unemployment, in sum, was a critical, multipronged issue for the labor movement. It harmed workers as individuals, while offering a compelling challenge to unions as organizations. Itself a source of discontent and hardship, joblessness also impeded efforts to remedy other sources of discontent and hardship, such as low wages and poor working conditions. Both the strength and the agenda of organized labor were limited and threatened by cyclical downturns, by seasonal fluctuations, by the chronic presence of jobless workers. From the disaster of the 1870s to the depression of the early 1920s, unemployment was a problem that the labor movement could not ignore.

It was also a difficult problem for the labor movement to solve or even alleviate. Unions could not create jobs, and they never possessed the financial resources necessary to provide funds to the hundreds of thousands of workers who were idled each year. Efforts to limit the incidence of unemployment were further hampered by the apparent complexity of the phenomenon and the diversity of its sources. Late-nineteenth-century unionists agreed that the most severe outbreaks of joblessness stemmed from the "unnatural" panics that occurred from time to time. Yet panics were not the only problem. Seasonal rhythms of production also created widespread idleness; labor-saving machinery was being deployed in a host of different industries; immigrants, by the tens of thousands, were pouring into the commonwealth and hunting for work. Not surprisingly, many unionists felt buffaloed by the issue. "We are talking all the time . . . trying to figure out some plan to keep work all the time," confessed C. W. Seager of Springfield in 1894, "but we can't do it."[12]

Labor's difficulties were compounded by the fact that the issue could not be addressed directly through conventional trade union methods: confronting and making demands upon an employer was a strategy peculiarly ill-suited to the problem of unemployment. Jobless men and women had no leverage or bargaining power (they obviously could not threaten to strike), and what the unemployed wanted – and felt entitled to – was *work*, rather than specific jobs in specific enterprises. Workers also recognized that, during depressions and seasonal slowdowns, employers were laying people off in response to market forces. It seemed pointless, therefore, to try to compel companies to hire more labor, only to produce goods that could not be sold. From time to time, unions did voice the suspicion that layoffs were unnecessary, that firms were releasing workers merely as a strategic prelude to wage cuts. But organized labor never claimed that such machinations were a prime source of unemployment. Employers, after all, extracted profits from the labor of working people when they were working, not when they were idle.[13]

Unions, thus, were in a tactical quandary when it came to the problem of joblessness. Carpenters could not band together to insist that contractors hire them even if no buildings were being erected; it made little sense for a shoe workers' local to demand that factories run year-round to manufacture more shoes than could possibly be sold. Although employers and employees frequently skirmished over issues linked to the question of job security, organized labor did not expect that it could actually cure the malady of unemployment by demanding jobs from individual employers. The problem seemed to be rooted more in the behavior of the economy than in the practices of particular firms or industries.

Labor's search for solutions – a search that was seriously launched during the final decades of the nineteenth century – was limited in two other respects as well. The first was that governmental authorities played only a small role in the drama. Organized labor did sometimes turn to public officials for help in contending with unemployment (a subject discussed later in this chapter), but governmental responsibilities for managing the economy were sharply circumscribed. The problem of joblessness was not placed squarely on the doorstep of government until well into the twentieth century. The second limit was less political than intellectual. Most unionists, like most of their contemporaries, understood the workings of the economy in terms that were essentially rigid: they believed, among other things, that there was a fixed ceiling on the amount of work that needed to be performed in any society at any particular time. "There can be only about so much work to do any way, and when that is done, business has got to stop," observed a shoemaker in 1879. His views were echoed in labor circles throughout the late nineteenth and early twentieth centuries. Although economic thinking was in a state of considerable flux during these years, the "lump of labor" notion persisted, and most unionists consequently did not believe, or could not imagine, that unemployment could be remedied through short-run, expansionist economic policies. What this meant, of course, was that strategies for combating unemployment that were to become commonplace during the middle decades of the twentieth century – Keynesian strategies of government intervention to stimulate the economy – were politically and intellectually unavailable to labor during much of this period.[14]

For many workers, both within and outside the labor movement, the conceptual and strategic difficulties posed by the problem of unemployment were convincing evidence of the need to radically transform the nation's economic and social structure. Unemployment was an evil built into the "wage system" or capitalism, an evil that could be eradicated only by replacing capitalism with some system of cooperative enterprise. In the eyes of these men and women, the experience of unemployment exposed and underscored the significance of class power: a small minority of the population had the ability to decide when and whether the majority would work. The existence of widespread joblessness and recurrent panics also testified to the inability of private enterprise to run the economy smoothly and justly. Not surprisingly, cooperative production became an explicit goal of large segments of the labor movement in the 1870s and 1880s. In Massachusetts small groups of workmen, many of them unemployed, tried to end their dependence on employers and the wage system by creating producers' cooperatives. Between 1867 and 1885, at least thirty cooperative ventures were launched in the commonwealth, most of them in industries sorely afflicted by unemployment.[15]

A decade or two later, the same reasoning led many working people to conclude that socialism constituted the only definitive solution to the problem of joblessness. Socialism would give workers power over their jobs and control over their working time; a planned socialist economy could also avoid the crises and fluctuations that plagued the lives of workers under capitalism. "There is only one remedy" for unemployment, observed William B. Adams, a carpenter from West Quincy in the 1890s, "and that is, government control of all means of production and transportation." F. P. Quinn, a compositor from Boston, stated the matter more colloquially. "Give the working man the full product of his labor, and every obstacle will be removed, and there will be no kicking at all," he told a government commission.[16]

This socialist critique never became a predominant one in Massachusetts, but men like Quinn and Adams were hardly exotic creatures on the late-nineteenth-century political spectrum. During the decade that followed the panic of 1893, socialist political parties won a number of victories, gaining particular strength in the centers of boot and shoe manufacturing. Brockton and Haverhill elected socialist mayors; Holyoke, Amesbury, Newburyport, Chicopee, and Georgetown had socialist town officials; the legislature had two socialist representatives; and in the state elections of 1902 the Socialist Party received more votes than any third party since the Know-Nothings. Although socialist strength in Massachusetts declined after 1902, it did not disappear. Throughout the Progressive era and into the 1920s there were thousands of workers and active trade unionists who believed that unemployment would be "abolished" only when capitalism gave way to socialism.[17]

Coherent as the socialist and cooperative diagnosis may have been, it did little to alter the immediate challenge facing the labor movement. Producers' cooperatives tended to have short lifespans, and few union members or leaders believed that the cooperative commonwealth or the socialist revolution was about to appear in Massachusetts. As a result, even unionists committed to the long-term goal of restructuring society had to devise methods of combating unemployment within the framework of the "wage system" – both to respond to working-class needs and to enhance the strength of working-class organizations. Throughout this period, moreover, much of the labor movement was less interested in long-run visions of social change than in immediate, concrete objectives. Particularly after the turn of the century, when the increasingly conservative AFL was ascendant, "bread and butter" unionism was the predominant strain in the Massachusetts labor movement. And bread and butter unionists viewed unemployment as a problem to be cured or alleviated within the context of American capitalism, difficult as the task might be.[18]

In 1880 as in 1920, that context offered organized labor four logically possible approaches to the problem. The first was to redistribute existing jobs, to share the work available as a means of correcting the chronic imbalance between overwork and idleness. The second was to somehow stimulate an increase in the demand for labor – a desirable goal, but one difficult to attain in light of the political and intellectual constraints discussed earlier. The third was to restrict the labor supply, to reduce the number of men and women who were competing for jobs. The fourth – which involved alleviating the misery rather than curing the problem – was to provide financial support to men and women who were out of work. Each of these approaches had its adherents within the ranks of organized labor; each had its own political and institutional logic; each gave birth to a number of programs, strategies, and experiments. And with varying degrees of energy and enthusiasm, unions explored all these approaches throughout the era of uncertainty.[19]

Helping one's own

The most basic task that unions had to face in contending with unemployment was that of aiding their own members who were out of
work. Union activists were well acquainted with the suffering that
unemployment could induce, and they were acutely aware, particularly after the depression of the 1870s, that unions, to survive and
grow, had to demonstrate their capacity to help working people during hard times. Pressured by their own poverty as well as by employers, jobless workers had to be offered reasons or incentives to retain
their union membership and adhere to union standards. Both "brotherly feelings" and the imperatives of organization obliged trade
unions to develop strategies for aiding their unemployed members.
Almost inescapably, this obligation led unions to adopt policies and
programs that required members to share their resources with one
another; somewhat less inescapably, it also led some unions to devise
strategies that were profoundly egalitarian in their approach to the
problem of scarcity.[20]

The easiest, most straightforward, least costly way in which unions
could help their unemployed members was by providing them with
information about available jobs. Workers' organizations had traditionally served as information exchanges, and by the end of the nineteenth century virtually all local unions had developed some formal
mechanism for monitoring labor market conditions and informing
jobless members of places where they might find work. Unions
everywhere kept "out-of-work" lists, while in the building trades,
among others, matching men with jobs was one of the principal du-
ties of local union officials. "Our union is our employment agency,"
declared the secretary of the carpenters' union in Waltham. In Haverhill, the Boot and Shoe Workers' Union operated a registration bureau where idled members could apply for jobs. In Holyoke every
meeting of the bricklayers and masons' union opened with two questions: "1. Are any of the members out of work? 2. Does any member
know where work can be procured?" Similarly, national trade unions,
through their newspapers and journals, tried to keep workers informed about communities where jobs could be found and locales
where the labor market was glutted. Worcester in February 1912 was
"a good place for traveling carpenters to avoid," reported *The Carpenter*. None of these mechanisms had much impact upon the incidence
of unemployment, but the information they provided was often of
considerable value to jobless individuals. Perhaps more importantly,
the very existence of out-of-work lists and employment bureaus offered workers a signal that unions were willing to assume some col-

lective responsibility for the problem of unemployment. Finding work, by the late nineteenth century, had become a task for the union as well as for the union member.[21]

The notion that the burden of unemployment had to be shared also lay at the heart of trade union efforts to provide out-of-work benefits to members. In the aftermath of the depression of the 1870s, unions began to take a serious interest in the development of systematic benefit plans. Some prominent labor leaders, including AFL president Samuel Gompers, spent decades urging unions to increase their dues to generate funds to pay an out-of-work benefit. The argument in favor of such benefits was a powerful one. Not only would they mitigate the sufferings of the unemployed, but they would also fortify the union and protect members who were working steadily. Jobless workers who were receiving an unemployment benefit would be less likely to leave the union, to scab, or to work for reduced wages. Employed unionists consequently would have a better chance of winning strikes, maintaining wage rates, and resisting "the demands of employers in times of depression." Since the fortunes of the employed and the unemployed were inextricably linked, subsidizing or insuring the jobless was a way of protecting the interests of all workers.[22]

Scores of local unions in Massachusetts accepted this argument and paid out-of-work benefits to their members. But most of the state's labor organizations were either unable or unwilling to create durable, systematic, benefit programs. The reasons for this failure had more to do with finances than with principles or politics. Funding out-of-work benefits required substantial (and unpopular) increases in union dues, and the programs themselves had a disheartening tendency to collapse financially just when they were needed most: during severe depressions. The high rates of geographic mobility that prevailed among workers may also have heightened their reluctance to contribute to benefit plans that were customarily run by local, rather than national, organizations.[23]

Despite this institutional failure, the idea that unions should help to underwrite the cost of joblessness remained popular, and many unions tried to compensate for the absence of formal benefit programs by adopting other, more modest methods of subsidizing their unemployed members. Some unions allowed members to forgo dues payments as long as they were jobless; many locals had loan funds for the unemployed or traveling loan funds for workers who wanted to try their fortunes in other locales. In addition, during depressions labor organizations often demanded extra dues from members who were still working in order to relieve the hardships of the unemployed and protect the union. In January 1895, for example, the garment workers' union of Boston voted to assess all employed members twenty-five cents a week in addition to their regular dues. The purpose of the assessment was "to enable the union to sustain the unemployed and successfully resist the efforts of contractors to reduce wages and increase the hours of labor."[24]

These same goals were pursued by arranging, formally and informally, to have union members share whatever work was available during slack seasons or cyclical downturns. Work-sharing schemes were particularly attractive to employees in seasonal industries who had to contend with layoffs once or twice each year. And during depressions unions in numerous trades tried to combat unemployment by spreading the work among as many people as possible. "We have no established trades-union 'out of work' benefit," noted John Griffin of the Newspaper Mailers' Union of Boston in 1894, "excepting that members lay off for a few days to allow those out of work to take their places for a while."[25]

The simplest, and most limited, form of work sharing was the prohibition of overtime during periods when jobs were scarce. Between 1880 and 1900, a number of unions adopted rules that prohibited members from working extra hours as long as other members were jobless. In several instances, labor organizations also mounted public protests "against the working of overtime . . . while there are . . . competent operatives out of employment." During the early decades of the twentieth century, overtime restrictions were embedded in the constitutional bylaws of some national unions. As the practice of signing written contracts between unions and employers grew more widespread (which it did between 1880 and 1920), the distribution of overtime to the unemployed became, in certain industries, a contractual obligation.[26]

Many unions extended the principle of work sharing well beyond the rather easy issue of overtime. At considerable cost to those union members who would otherwise have labored steadily, regular jobs were divided up or shared in order to limit the number of workers who were altogether idle. In 1894, for example, members of the carpenters' union in Lynn voted to reduce their own hours "in order to furnish employment for the . . . idle." According to the AFL's national journal, the *American Federationist*, the size of the "army of the unemployed" in the 1890s was, in fact, held in check by the willingness of craftsmen throughout the nation to share their jobs with one another. After 1890, it was also commonplace for unions faced with cutbacks in production to demand that employers put everyone on "short time" instead of laying off a portion of the labor force. Some employers were more receptive to this notion than others, and many unionists themselves were less than enamored with the idea. But the demand for an egalitarian distribution of work (and unemployment) was frequently voiced and sometimes achieved.[27]

Between 1893 and the early 1920s, unions and employers in several industries even signed contracts that provided for the rotation of layoffs among all union members. As one might expect, these contractual arrangements appeared primarily in industries that were sharply seasonal and that had unions with strong socialist contingents. The brewery workers seem to have pioneered the movement to regulate layoffs through rotation: by 1904 the Boston local of the United Brewery Workmen had a written agreement with employers that "in case of slack business, as many men as necessary may be laid off alternatively not longer than one week at a time, all men taking their turn as far as possible without interfering with the business." Similar arrangements were forged by the hat and cap makers of Boston as well as the cutting die makers of Lynn. The Boston Protocol, which governed labor relations in the garment industry at the end of the Progressive era, also stipulated that work was to be distributed equally among all union members. And by the early 1920s, the shoe workers' unions too had concluded that the best way of coping with the chronic unemployment of their members was to compel manufacturers to retain "all help during a period of temporary reduction of . . . factory production." But shoe workers, unlike some of their colleagues in other trades, met with only temporary and scattered success in their efforts to systematically spread the work.[28]

One final method of work sharing warrants mention: restricting output. This was certainly the most controversial and probably the most widespread technique that workers utilized to avoid unemployment and to allocate whatever work was available. Throughout the years between 1870 and 1922, organized and unorganized workers alike responded to the threat of joblessness – particularly seasonal joblessness – by reducing their output, by slowing down the rate at which they worked, by "pace setting" or "soldiering." By the first decade of the twentieth century, unions of printers, bricklayers, and machinists, among others, had adopted formal work rules that effectively limited the productivity of members. In a few celebrated cases, they did not even attempt to disguise their restrictive intentions: the plumbers' union, for example, prohibited members from riding bicycles between jobs because the bicycle was too efficient a means of transportation. Moreover, even in unions that lacked formal restrictions there were widely shared understandings of the pace at which work was to be performed and the amount of work that constituted

a fair day's labor – the standard varying with business conditions. For
men and women who were paid by the day or by the hour, restricting
output was a means of increasing both the demand for labor and
annual wages; for those who were paid by the piece or by the job, it
served to steady the rhythms of work and to promote a relatively
even distribution of employment and wages. In either case, output
restriction was a method of sharing the "lump of labor" in an essentially egalitarian fashion.[29]

Whether fully egalitarian or not, all these strategies were designed
to respond to the scarcity of employment in ways that would promote
working-class solidarity. Rooted both in the institutional needs of labor organizations and in the mutualistic ethos so deeply embedded
in working-class culture, these programs emphasized the desirability
of collective, rather than competitive, approaches to the problem of
joblessness. They aimed at fostering alliances between the employed
and the unemployed; they encouraged, even demanded, sacrifice in
the name of unity. In dealing with their own members at least, trade
unions typically treated security and solidarity as inseparable goals.

There were, however, serious limits to what these strategies could
accomplish. Trade union efforts to offer direct aid to unemployed
members had little or no effect upon the regularity of work: they were
defensive measures, palliatives designed to relieve symptoms rather
than to cure the malady. Union-sponsored employment bureaus
could do nothing more than lubricate the machinery of the labor market, while sharing the work was, in the end, the same thing as sharing the misery. (This was true also of out-of-work benefits, which
simply redistributed funds among members of a trade.) At best, organized labor's self-help programs could ease some of the most extreme hardship that resulted from unemployment; at best, they could
slightly strengthen the hands of unions in their dealings with employers.

Even these modest objectives were not so easy to attain. Employers
like the master brewers, who were reluctant to surrender absolute
control over hiring and firing, sometimes fought "tooth and nail" to
prohibit or undermine work-sharing schemes. In many industries
employers also refused to list available jobs with union officials or
employment bureaus. Within unions too there was often resistance,
both to work-sharing plans and to expensive benefit programs. Some
workers, who were particularly favored or efficient, believed that
they personally would fare better if market forces were allowed to
operate. And during severe economic downturns, benefit programs
tended to fold, while work-sharing devices often became impractica-

ble because there was too little work to be usefully shared among all
union members. Even as palliatives, self-help measures had their
shortcomings.[30]

Nonetheless, these strategies endured, appearing and reappear-
ing, in one union after another, in one form or another, for at least a
half-century after the depression of the 1870s. Organized labor had
few options, and, imperfect as they may have been, these self-help
measures did provide some aid to thousands of workers each year.
In all likelihood, they also contributed to the growth and survival of
many local unions. That these programs did not "cure" the problem
of joblessness was no surprise to trade unionists: neither in 1880 nor
in 1920 did anyone expect that organized labor could eradicate the
evil of unemployment by maintaining out-of-work lists, by offering
cash benefits to the unemployed, by rotating layoffs, or by restricting
output. Such arrangements were always viewed as stopgaps, as in-
terim measures, as partial solutions at most. Unionists understood
that they also had to find a way to prevent unemployment from occurring. But that battle was to be fought on other fronts.

Shorter hours

There was no shortage of ideas or proposals for solving the problem
of unemployment in the late nineteenth century. Political and social
reformers of many different stripes – ranging from silverites to free
traders to single-taxers to Bellamyite nationalists – were convinced
that their particular schemes would stabilize the economy and put an
end to involuntary idleness. From labor circles too came a long list of
suggestions and programs. Some workers stressed the need for cooperatives, while others favored the immediate creation of state-run
farms or factories for the unemployed. The Cotton Spinners' Union
of Fall River advocated the colonization of vacant lands by the jobless,
and A. J. Nason, a Haverhill shoemaker who held particularly strong
views about the Goodyear stitching machine, believed that the problem would be solved by requiring that all patents "be owned by the
people." Out of this intellectual ferment there emerged one idea,
rooted in the daily experience of the working class, that captured the
imagination of the labor movement and became the focus of organizing drives for decades: the idea of shortening the hours of labor.[31]

Movements to reduce the length of the working day (and the working week) had, of course, appeared in Massachusetts long before the
final quarter of the nineteenth century. Prior to the Civil War, orga-

nized labor had devoted much of its energy to campaigns for the ten-hour day, and in the late 1860s and early 1870s the demand for shorter hours (and specifically for the 8-hour day) was a major item on the agenda of the resurgent labor movement. But it was only toward the end of the 1870s, and more emphatically in the 1880s and 1890s, that workers began to link the issue of shorter hours to the problem of unemployment. Before the depression of the 1870s, the reasons most frequently given for reducing the hours of labor were that such reductions would increase wage rates, minimize the harmful effects of arduous labor, and offer working people leisure and the opportunity to become informed, educated citizens. Unemployment was rarely, if ever, mentioned. But during the final decades of the nineteenth century these traditional arguments were first buttressed and then over-shadowed by the claim that a reduction in the length of the working day would cure the evil of involuntary idleness. During this same period, it became increasingly common for workers to view shorter hours as *the* most logical and feasible solution to the problem of unemployment.[32]

The link between unemployment and the length of the working day stemmed from a straightforward and obvious perception: some workers were compelled to labor more hours per week than they wanted to, while others were involuntarily idle. Similarly, employees in many trades were obliged to work "beyond their strength" during busy seasons and then forced to "loaf" during slack times. "There is not enough work to last the year round, and work over eight hours a day, or forty-eight hours a week," concluded a shoemaker in 1879. "We have too much work to do in a short season," noted one of his colleagues. "If we could have the same amount of work which we have to do in four months now lengthened out to six months, we should all be better off."[33]

This perception, coupled with the notion of the "lump of labor" so prevalent in working-class circles, gave rise to a simple, clear-cut argument: shorter hours would spread the work. Whether achieved by legislation or by direct trade union action, a reduction in the length of the working day would redistribute the work available and create jobs for the unemployed. "If there was an eight-hour law, things would be more even," claimed a shoe worker late in the 1870s. "If the mechanics and laborers of these times could be required to do less time labor per day, it would extend over a greater length of time," observed a carpenter in 1879. "I shall certainly look for the remedy for enforced idleness in this direction."[34]

The idea that shorter hours could and would solve the problem of unemployment caught hold in the labor movement in the 1880s and

1890s, even acquiring some arithmetic precision. "A reduction of one hour a day in a shop employing 100 men will place eleven more men at work daily, which will thus remove the surplus help from the market," claimed an article in the *Labor Leader* in 1887. (The *Leader*, published weekly in Lynn, was the most prominent labor newspaper in late-nineteenth-century Massachusetts.) A correspondent to the *Leader*, two years later, based his projections on a shift from the ten-hour to the eight-hour day:

> Suppose that on a small island there is a total population of six men, one being an employer (and "owning" the land), four being in his employ, and one able and willing to work, but unable to get it. And suppose that the four employed men each work ten hours a day: then – 4 × 10 equals 40. Now let the hours of labor be reduced to eight a day, and the fifth man be employed; then – 5 × 8 equals 40.

Calculations of this type were not confined to fringe elements in the labor movement; they were widely discussed and widely endorsed. P. J. McGuire, the national head of the United Brotherhood of Carpenters and Joiners, used such figures repeatedly. In 1894 George McNeill, one of the leaders of the eight-hour movement (and the labor movement) in Massachusetts, wrote a letter to the Boston *Globe* in which he argued that the eight-hour day would unquestionably eradicate unemployment in the commonwealth. His logic was identical to that of the "small island" letter writer, and he defended his claim with calculations derived from the 1885 census of Massachusetts.[35]

There was, however, a problem with this argument, with the notion that shorter hours would redistribute the available work and consequently reduce or eliminate unemployment. Reductions in the hours of labor would, more or less automatically, succeed in spreading the work only if operatives and craftsmen were willing to accept wage cuts proportional to the decline in their working time. But that was not what most trade unions had in mind. Throughout these years, in fact, unionists also argued that they could perform as much work in eight hours as they could in ten and that wages, therefore, should be held constant while hours were cut back. The contradiction between the two arguments was too flagrant to escape notice. "We had a witness who favored eight hours as a means of giving employment to those out of employment, and then he said that men could do as much work in eight hours as in ten," commented a member of the Massachusetts Board to Investigate the Subject of the Unemployed in the 1890s. "If this is true," he asked one witness after another, "how is it going to benefit anybody?"[36]

Labor leaders and spokesmen were indeed guilty of offering ostensibly contradictory arguments in favor of the shorter workday. This resulted, in part, from labor's desire to persuade, or appeal to, different audiences. The assertion that workers would be just as productive in eight or nine hours as they were in ten was a potentially valuable one when unions were dealing with employers and insisting on maintaining wage rates. But when they were rallying workers or appealing to the public for support, the argument that the shorter workday would cure the problem of unemployment was more powerful and compelling. Unionists themselves were well aware of the tension between these two arguments. "Speaking truthfully, I certainly don't believe we can accomplish as much in eight hours as in ten," acknowledged J. P. Rivetts of Springfield to the dubious member of the Massachusetts Board. "But it may be good policy to say that we will accomplish as much in order to gain our end."[37]

The issue was, in fact, more complicated than it appeared to be on the surface. Organized labor was not simply engaging in an instrumental use of rhetoric and argument: by 1890, trade unionists and labor intellectuals had developed several formal and intricate economic arguments to defend the proposition that shorter hours could cure the problem of unemployment without necessitating a reduction in wages. The simplest of these arguments was one that tried to split the difference. Men whose hours were reduced from ten to eight would not, it was conceded, do as much work as they had done previously, but they would do better work and more work per hour. Wage cuts, then, were not warranted, yet the demand for labor would be increased, with roughly half the unemployed being put back to work. A different argument was one suggesting that shorter hours could effectively enlarge the "lump of labor": if workers did manage to perform as much work in eight hours as they had been doing in ten, their newfound leisure would lead them to consume more – which would stimulate the economy and provide jobs for the idle.[38]

Other thinkers on the subject urged workers and unions to accept wage reductions in order to obtain shorter hours – because they would quickly gain back everything that they gave up and then some. According to this argument, reducing the hours of labor, with proportional wage cuts, would have the short-run effect of spreading the work and creating jobs for the unemployed. Then, with "the army of discontent, the unemployed" removed from the scene, wages would begin to rise, and "before long," they "would be higher for eight hours than they are now for ten." This argument was also used to urge pieceworkers to join the eight-hour movement. "The logic of shorter hours is as plain as a pike staff," wrote one correspondent to the *Labor Leader* in 1890. "If those crafts doing piecework will reduce their labor to eight hours . . . and refuse to work overtime, is it not clear . . . that the unemployed surplus of that avocation will be largely reduced and that eventually the wage scale will go up?"[39]

Some writers and theorists, including George Gunton (a friend of both George McNeill and Ira Steward), fused these and other arguments into a single overarching rationale for the eight-hour day. In a tract written in 1889 and published by the American Federation of Labor, Gunton declared that "the immediate effect of the general adoption of an eight-hour work day" would be to eliminate "enforced idleness." He went on to claim that "since enforced idleness is the most powerful obstruction to a rise of wages," the earnings of workers would gradually increase. The absorption of the unemployed into the labor force would also "increase the number of consumers" in the society and "thereby enlarge the market for commodities" – which would further "tend to increase wages." Finally, Gunton argued, the leisure time that workers would acquire by laboring for fewer hours each day would lead them to develop new desires and needs. They would consequently demand a higher standard of living, and since "wages are governed by the standard of living," "a general rise of real wages" would be "inevitable." The eight-hour day, in sum, would both eradicate unemployment and produce a tremendous advance in wage levels.[40]

Trade unionists who sought to defend the goals of the eight-hour movement could, thus, fall back on any of a number of theories that were far more elaborate, and less static, than either the simple "spread the work" notion or the proposition that workers would perform as much labor in eight hours as they could in ten. There were ideas available that both permitted and encouraged workers to believe that shorter hours could solve the problem of unemployment without reducing the earnings of working people. Advocates of a shorter workday did sometimes make claims that appeared to be contradictory, but there were plausible (and potentially persuasive) ways of resolving the contradictions.

Yet the complex and formal versions of the argument played only a limited role in the thinking of workers and labor activists. The detailed economic theories offered by Gunton and others may well have been adopted in their entirety by some workers, and many, no doubt, felt reassured by the existence of such theories. But for most people unemployment was not linked to the length of the working day by an elaborate chain of economic arguments. The intricacies of the theory mattered no more to unionists than the details of *Coin's Financial School* did to silver advocates or Henry George's exhaustive treatment of land economics did to single taxers.

What most trade union members embraced was the commonsensical logic of the simple version of the "eight-hour philosophy." If men worked fewer hours during busy seasons, then slack times would be shorter. If everyone reduced his or her working time by 20 percent, then there would be jobs available for the unemployed. In all likelihood, relatively few workers believed that they would actually perform as much labor in eight hours as they had been doing in ten; it was intuitively evident then that shortening the length of the working day would create jobs for the jobless. Whether or not short-run wage reductions would have to be accepted was a thorny issue, but a tactical one, a question to be answered in the heat of battle. The critical fact was that the irrational coexistence of overwork and idleness would be corrected by shortening the hours of labor. The eight-hour day would go a long way toward solving the dread problem of unemployment, and, in so doing, it would dramatically transform the fortunes of the working class. Not only would work be steady and leisure more ample, but, with the "army of the unemployed" dispersed, it would be far easier to build unions and to wrest concessions from employers.[41]

It was this commonsensical logic, a logic that emerged less from theory than from the material conditions of working-class life, that prompted workers in the 1880s and 1890s both to advocate shorter hours as the most straightforward solution to the problem of joblessness and to justify the traditional demand for a shorter workday with the claim that it would eliminate unemployment. Throughout the commonwealth and throughout the labor movement, the voices of organized labor expressed similar convictions and identical demands. "While there are men and women who seek employment and cannot obtain it, the hours of labor are too long," proclaimed Charles Rawbone, the president of the Massachusetts State Branch of the American Federation of Labor in 1888. "The eight hour work day has become a necessity, in order to give labor to the vast army of unemployed," announced Gloucester's carpenters a year later. "The eight hour law is the only solution of the problem of employing the unemployed," testified Garrett Donker of Brockton in 1895. Four years later, the North Adams Central Labor Union also determined that "lessening the hours of labor" was "the only rational solution of this vital economic question." "I think the shortening of hours is one of the just demands of labor organizations," concluded R. R. Clarke, a carpenter from Haverhill, in the mid-1890s. "It is right in every sense of the word, morally, physically, economically right."[42]

These beliefs inspired a massive wave of organizing activity between 1885 and the turn of the century. One goal of this activity was to secure the passage of legislation placing the government on record as being in favor of shorter hours. Trade unions sponsored bills that would make the eight-hour (or nine-hour) day mandatory for state and municipal employees; they also supported legislation that would declare eight hours to be the length of the "legal workday." In 1895, some unionists even endorsed a bill, introduced in the state legislature by a representative from Haverhill, that would have made the eight-hour day "compulsory" in all the industries in the commonwealth. (Most unions did not endorse the "compulsory" bill because it violated their freedom to make contracts and involved the state too closely in the affairs of labor.) Organized labor had sufficient strength and support to get several of these bills passed in the state House of Representatives, but they were invariably killed in the more conservative state Senate. "That useless portion of our legislative machinery, known as the senate, is liable to fall afoul of the bill and murder it," editorialized the *Labor Leader* in 1893 after the House had approved one piece of legislation. "The Honorable Verdant Green of Belchertown will probably twang his strident bazoo in opposition to the bill."[43]

Most of labor's efforts were aimed not at legislators but at employers. The core of labor's strategy was to take direct action to compel employers to recognize eight hours (or, in some cases, nine hours) as the standard workday. In 1886 and again in 1890, Massachusetts workers joined in national campaigns designed to achieve the shorter workday through widespread collective action. These campaigns were sponsored by the new national trade unions affiliated with the AFL (the Knights of Labor also backed the 1886 drive, albeit reluctantly) and spearheaded by workers from the building trades – who, not coincidentally, suffered from chronic unemployment. Between 1888 and 1890, the state AFL devoted most of its energies to the campaign for the eight-hour day: throughout the commonwealth, unions held meetings, demonstrated, conferred with employers, and went on strike to shorten their hours of labor. But despite this activity, neither of these campaigns came anywhere close to achieving the goal of a universal eight-hour day, although the 1890 drive was slightly more successful than its predecessor.[44]

After 1890, organizing efforts became more local in their focus, but unions continued to pour their resources and energies into the crusade for a shorter working day. Month after month, year after year, local unions in many occupations, in scores of communities, agitated, demonstrated, and struck in order to "persuade" employers to reduce the hours of labor. Some of these efforts met with success; others were complete failures; still others resulted in partial or temporary victories. The campaign went on throughout the early 1890s, seeming to mount in intensity with each passing year. "The demand for shorter hours is stronger today than ever before," noted the *Labor Leader* in April 1893.[45]

The sharp depression that began in the summer of 1893 placed a major obstacle in the path of these local efforts. In October of that year, the master builders of Boston reneged on an earlier agreement to grant carpenters the eight-hour day. In numerous other trades, victories that had been won in the early 1890s were reversed in the aftermath of the "panic," while in several industries unions were wiped out altogether. But even the depression did not bring the campaign to a halt. To many unionists, it simply underscored the urgency of the issue. In December 1895, the granite cutters of Quincy, the bakers of Fall River, and the building tradesmen of Boston all took steps to reduce their hours of labor, and the Central Labor Union of Boston debated a resolution calling for "a general strike throughout the United States to enforce an eight-hour day." In August 1897, as the depression was drawing to a close, the annual convention of the Massachusetts AFL reaffirmed its determination to do "everything possible . . . to establish the eight-hour working-day in this State."[46]

The agitation for shorter hours continued after the turn of the century. Throughout the Progressive era, organized labor in Massachusetts sponsored or promoted legislation that favored the eight-hour day, while individual unions repeated their efforts to wrest the shorter workday (or week) directly from employers. During World War I, the AFL endorsed yet another national campaign for the eight-hour day and the forty-eight-hour week; after the war, the organizing was buttressed by the patriotic claim that shorter hours were necessary for America's soldiers to be absorbed back into the economy.[47]

These twentieth-century efforts were far more successful than their nineteenth-century predecessors had been. By 1902, more than forty cities and towns had adopted the eight-hour day on public works, and in 1906 an eight-hour bill for public employees, although watered down and much amended, managed to pass through both houses of the legislature and escape a gubernatorial veto. In 1911, the legislature passed a law mandating a fifty-four-hour week for women workers – which effectively created a fifty-four-hour week in the textile industry; eight years later, the limit was further reduced to forty-eight hours. Between 1900 and 1915, unions also succeeded in whittling down the hours of labor through direct confrontations with employers. During World War I, when their bargaining power was at its peak, many workers were finally victorious in their demand for a working day of eight hours. Although the eight-hour day was neither universal nor entirely secure, most employees, by the early 1920s, were working fewer hours each day and each week than had been the norm in 1900 or in 1880.[48]

Yet something important had changed in the movement for shorter hours during the first decades of the twentieth century. Despite the continuity of activity, the goals of the movement had slowly shifted, and the drive for the eight-hour day had gradually surrendered the aura of a crusade to solve the problem of joblessness. By the end of the Progressive era, the labor press was routinely running articles that endorsed the eight-hour day without mentioning unemployment. In 1916, when Samuel Gompers announced the AFL's commitment to an eight-hour drive, he stressed that its goals were higher wages and the stimulation of workers' "intellectual desires and cravings." Neither Gompers nor any other national officer of the AFL made reference to joblessness or to sharing the work.[49]

The argument that a shorter workday would create jobs for the idle did not, to be sure, entirely disappear. Members of the building trades, in particular, continued to support the idea in the early 1920s, and it resurfaced, from time to time, during and after the Great Depression. But by the second decade of the twentieth century the argument, when offered, tended to be voiced in tones that carried less conviction, urgency, and precision than had once been the case. "We favor a further reduction of the hours of labor to minimize unemployment in any industry where a surplus of idle labor may exist," noted the editor of the *Carpenter* in 1919. "If present conditions cause more unemployment, the argument advanced that the shorter workweek will afford opportunities for work for more men is one that should meet with favor on the part of all fair-minded employers," editorialized the *Labor News* of Worcester in 1920. The drive for shorter hours never came to a halt between the depression of the 1890s and the early 1920s, but after 1900 there was a discernible shift both in its rationale and in the source of its motive energy. The great upsurge in eight-hour organizing that took place during World War I was propelled not by the hope of stabilizing the rhythms of employment but rather by the desire for better wages and working conditions. By the time that workers achieved the eight-hour day, most of them had ceased believing that it was a solution to the problem of unemployment.[50]

There were, no doubt, numerous reasons for this loss of faith. But certainly prominent among them was the fact that it had become increasingly evident to workers that shortening the hours of labor had no appreciable impact upon unemployment levels. Although nineteenth-century unionists had occasionally claimed that reductions in the length of the working day had actually "put the idle to work," by 1910 or 1920 the long-term record was becoming disturbingly clear. The hours of labor, particularly in some trades, had been significantly reduced without a corresponding drop in the incidence of unemployment. Carpenters and plasters worked an eight-hour day, yet they continued to suffer from high levels of seasonal idleness. Despite shortened working hours in most occupations, depressions still produced massive layoffs. Some true believers argued that the persistence of high unemployment rates did not undermine the "eight-hour philosophy," that the problem of joblessness would have grown worse had hours not been reduced. Others maintained that only the "real short day" of six or five or four hours would eliminate unemployment. But these claims were too hypothetical to prevent the ebbing of faith. The theory appeared to be – and was – deeply flawed: most glaringly, it failed to take into account the increase in the labor supply that resulted from immigration and migration, an increase that permitted hours to be shortened without producing the sellers' market for labor or the steady rhythms of work that Gunton and other advocates had envisioned. By the second decade of the twentieth century, the shortcomings of the eight-hour argument had manifested themselves both in statistics and in lived experiences. Most union members had begun to conclude, however reluctantly, that they would have to look elsewhere for a cure for unemployment.[51]

In retrospect, it is the appeal of the eight-hour philosophy that commands attention. The drive for shorter hours did not rid the commonwealth of joblessness, but for a time scores of thousands of working people were convinced that it would. Particularly during the final decades of the nineteenth century, union leaders and members alike viewed the eight-hour movement as a vehicle that would transport the working class into a world where jobs were plentiful and idleness was never involuntary. That they did so reflected the power of an idea that possessed numerous attractions in addition to its internal, commonsensical logic. The first of these was that the eight-hour remedy offered unions a way to slice the Gordian knot presented by a complex problem that had multiple causes and widely varied manifestations. Seasonal, cyclical, and technological unemployment could all be eliminated in one fell swoop. In addition, the eight-hour philosophy gave unions a way out of the strategic impasse that unemployment seemed to present: if shorter hours could stabilize the rhythms of work, then unions could actively fight joblessness by making demands directly upon employers. Employed union members could take advantage of their bargaining power to press for changes that would enhance their own security while simultaneously creating new positions for the jobless.

Like many late-nineteenth-century reform movements, the drive for shorter hours also promised that the attainment of a tangible and specific goal would precipitate a far-reaching transformation of the society. Workers could set their sights on the eight-hour day, a concrete and realistic objective, and the eight-hour day, once achieved, would unlock the doors to a future in which unemployment would be unknown, wages would increase steadily, leisure would be abundant, and unions would be strong enough to remedy all other working-class grievances. In the structure of its promise, thus, the shorter workday bore a close resemblance to the unlimited coinage of silver and the single tax on land: its popularity stemmed, in part, from the widespread late-nineteenth-century craving for a single device or mechanism that would eradicate the manifold evils associated with industrialization. Concurrently, the mix of pragmatic and utopian elements in the eight-hour philosophy permitted it to capture the energies and the allegiance of different tendencies in the labor movement. Briefly fusing the business unionism of the AFL with the more visionary ideology of the Knights of Labor, the eight-hour movement, in the 1880s and 1890s, offered direct, incremental action as a means of achieving profound and dramatic change.[52]

The eight-hour remedy for unemployment possessed two other virtues as well, virtues important to many trade unionists. It was egalitarian in spirit, and, as a strategy, it promoted working-class solidarity. Shorter hours promised to solve the problem of joblessness not merely for a particular group of workers but for all members of a trade and, eventually, for all working people. The drive for shorter hours offered a common goal to men and women who labored in different occupations, while forging a bond of unity between the employed and the unemployed. This was work sharing on a grand scale, and no one had to take a permanent pay cut. Unions could obtain job security for their members with strategies that were equitable in principle and unifying in practice. The energy and resources that workers poured into the drive for shorter hours were testimony to the desire – and the commitment – of organized labor to solve the problem of unemployment in a way that would preserve the values of mutuality and solidarity. That the eight-hour movement failed to fulfill its promise, that this generous vision ended up leading unions down a blind alley, proved to have important repercussions for the subsequent history of labor.

Protecting turf

> Humanity forbids that obstacles should be flung in the way of those who seek to escape from the harder conditions of the old world, but what is to become of our American wage-workers under this terrible competition?
>
> *Labor Leader*, May 21, 1887

> Self-preservation is the first law of nature.
>
> *Shoe Workers' Journal*, December 1915

Some of labor's efforts to combat unemployment were far less magnanimous in spirit than the drive for the eight-hour day. Despite their authentic attachment to the value of working-class solidarity, unions often responded to the scarcity of jobs with competitive as well as cooperative strategies, with measures designed to protect their own members at the expense of other working people. Since reserves of labor existed in most trades and since employers routinely tried to find the least expensive labor available, workers and unions were frequently forced to compete with one another for jobs. And in virtually all occupations, throughout the years between 1870 and 1920, workers believed that the labor market was glutted. "The country" will "soon be overrun with unemployed barbers," lamented a Boston barber in 1906. Unions reacted to these conditions self-protectively, devising a variety of strategies to help their own members emerge victorious in the competitive struggle. They attempted to control access to jobs and to restrict the labor supply both in individual trades and in the society as a whole. During the final decades of the nineteenth century, these competitive strategies developed alongside more cooperative and egalitarian ones. After 1900, after the trade unions of the AFL had established themselves, and after some of the faith and steam had gone out of the eight-hour movement, restrictive and exclusionist measures became increasingly prominent features of organized labor's defense against unemployment.[53]

The most broad-gauged method of limiting the supply of labor was, of course, to restrict immigration into the United States, and the labor movement gradually – but only gradually – came to endorse immigration restriction as a means of reducing joblessness. In the 1870s and 1880s, trade unions were adamantly opposed to "the importation of foreign labor under contract," but there was little sentiment in favor of restricting "voluntary" immigration (at least for nonorientals). However, the depression of the 1890s, coming as it did after more than a decade of massive immigration, provoked a wide-spread chorus of complaints against foreign-born workers. Building tradesmen blamed migrants (particularly Nova Scotians) for flooding the labor market during busy seasons; Worcester's trade unionists claimed that Armenians were displacing natives in that city's wire mills; J. F. Willand, a paper hanger, asserted categorically that "the real primary and actual cause" of unemployment in Fall River was the number of immigrants, "destitute of honor as of knowledge," who had "flocked" into the city in the late 1880s and early 1890s. The scarcity of steady jobs seemed to be irrefutable evidence of an over-supply of labor, and the most obvious source of this surfeit was the stream of foreigners that kept pouring into the state.[54]

Nonetheless, organized labor remained deeply ambivalent about immigration restriction through the 1890s. Some trade unionists, many of whom were foreign-born themselves, simply dismissed the idea that immigration was a cause of unemployment. Others, like Frank K. Foster, the editor of the *Labor Leader,* believed that it would be unprincipled and impolitic for unions to compensate for the short-comings of American capitalism by denying sanctuary and opportu-nities to European workers. "I freely confess that the immigration question is a hard one for me," wrote Foster. "In its consideration heart and head are more often pulling against each other than in harmony." More than a few Bay State labor activists did come out in favor of immigration restriction during the depression, and in 1897 the national AFL began to advocate a literacy test for immigrants. But the dominant voices in organized labor refused to support legisla-tion, backed by Boston's Brahmins among others, that would have sharply curtailed the flow of immigrants into the United States.[55]

After the turn of the century, restrictionist pressures continued to mount. Immigration rates rose to unprecedented levels, while the problem of unemployment remained unsolved: the compunctions ex-pressed by men like Foster were overridden by the increasingly wide-spread conviction that unrestricted immigration was depressing wage levels and depriving workers of their jobs. "There is no im-ported article we need so much protection against as the immigrant," declared the *Shoe Workers' Journal* in 1903. Three years later, the AFL demanded that the national government pass a general law restrict-ing immigration into the United States, and between 1906 and World War I organized labor lobbied vigorously on behalf of such legisla-tion. "The salvation of the labor movement rests on this question," proclaimed Joseph J. Hunt, president of the Massachusetts state branch of the AFL in 1916.[56]

The pace of activity quickened after the war. Fearful that a new wave of immigration would follow the cessation of hostilities, aroused by employers' claims that there was a shortage of labor, and shaken by the severity of the postwar depression, the trade union movement, in Massachusetts and elsewhere, conducted a strident publicity campaign to promote the passage of restrictive legislation. The AFL called for a complete moratorium on all immigration for four years. Unions in the Bay State charged that opponents of restriction were "cheap labor advocates" who were inviting a "vast horde of undesirable immigrants" into a region that already had a serious unemployment problem. "NO MORE IMMIGRATION" headlined an editorial in the *Labor News* of Worcester in 1923. "There is one sound American policy to be followed in regard to immigration," announced the *Shoe Workers' Journal* less than a year later. "That is the policy of rigid exclusion – and the more complete the exclusion the better."[57]

This 180-degree shift in labor's stance was significant in at least two respects. The first was that it contributed to the formation of national policy. The immigration restriction laws enacted in the early 1920s did not solve (or much affect) the problem of unemployment, but they did constitute a landmark in American history, as well as a turning point in the history of the American labor supply. Of equal importance, labor's embrace of immigration restriction displayed the growing willingness of trade unions to respond to competitive pressures by trying to reduce the number of competitors in the field – which meant treating fellow workers as rivals rather than as allies or "brothers." Many unionists who endorsed immigration restriction felt that they had no choice in the matter (and they may well have been right), but the campaign to keep foreigners from Amercian shores nonetheless represented a narrowing, if not a tarnishing, of the ideal of working-class solidarity.[58]

Trade unions in Massachusetts attempted to limit the size of the labor force in other ways as well. During the final decades of the nineteenth century, they focused their attention on two groups of workers who allegedly did not belong in the labor force in the first place: children and convicts. Unions lobbied repeatedly, and with some success, to raise the minimum working age for children. This demand was justified on a variety of grounds, among them that the employment of children in factories "flings the parent oftentimes out of work." The case of convicts was more complex. It was the custom in Massachusetts (and other states) to have convicts underwrite the cost of their incarceration by producing manufactured goods, including shoes and clothing. Unions protested bitterly that this system was intolerable because it deprived honest workmen of their jobs in industries where work was already scarce. Many manufacturers in the shoe and clothing industries, despite their desire to limit the cost of maintaining prisons, agreed that there was no justice in compelling free wage earners to compete with convicts for work. "A case in point," noted the head of the Georgetown Boot and Shoe Company:

> A good workman, but a drunkard, barely maintained his family. Went to jail and as he had to work steadily, had work sent him from the town where he lived. Which was taken from a steady man but a rougher mechanic. Result. Steady man lost his work in a dull time and his little house and garden. Was taxed to support the convict's family in the poor house. Convict came back after serving his time, fat, in a new suit, money in his pocket, and in two weeks was on another spree.[59]

Much more controversially, trade unions also aimed their exclusionist fire at working women. Particularly after the depression of the 1890s, the male leadership of the AFL frequently gave voice to the view that women did not belong in the industrial labor force. The argument that woman's place was at home, rather than in a factory, was buttressed by the claim that working women displaced men, that every woman who obtained a job deprived a man of employment. The craft unions of the AFL did not, of course, succeed in driving women out of the labor force, but their policies did contribute to keeping the vast majority of working women outside the ranks of organized labor. Early-twentieth-century unions made few efforts to recruit female members, and often they actively discouraged women from joining or forming labor organizations.[60]

Women, moreover, were not the only members of the labor force who were sometimes barred from trade unions. Although unions, by themselves, could do little to limit the aggregate labor supply, they could and did, through their own internal policies, restrict access to individual occupations and to the benefits of union membership. The most straightforward way of doing so was to limit the number of apprentices allowed into a trade, usually by fixing a maximum permissible ratio of apprentices to journeymen in any union local. Union rules limiting the number of apprentices appeared long before the 1870s, but it was only toward the end of the nineteenth century that such rules came to be regarded as a necessary antidote to unemployment. "Labor organizations would not oppose the learning of apprentices were there plenty of work to do after they learned their trade," concluded an editorial in the *Labor Leader* in 1888. "But it is plain to see that there would not be by the present industrial arrangements." In the 1890s, weavers in Lawrence voted not to teach anyone to weave as long as the depression persisted; a decade later, a barber in Boston claimed that apprenticeship limitations were needed to keep "tradesmen clothed with years of experience" from having "to walk the streets of our cities and towns in idleness." When unemployment rates increased in an occupation, unions typically reacted by trying to lower the ratio of apprentices to journeymen; in trades dominated by foreign-born workers, stringent apprenticeship ratios were widely viewed as a politically palatable alternative to immigration restriction. Although many employers and several charity organizations argued that apprenticeship ratios served only to protect mature workmen by penalizing the young, few union members were swayed by the argument. During the first decades of the twentieth century, building tradesmen, cigarmakers, printers, molders, machinists, and even shoemakers all maintained (or attempted to maintain) a ceiling on the number of youths allowed into their occupations.[61]

Other restrictive mechanisms and policies also appeared, particularly in unions that had established themselves, signed contracts with employers, and gained control over jobs. Difficult qualifying examinations, high initiation fees, and high dues payments were common devices for limiting membership in skilled trades. Although such devices were justified on the grounds that they helped to maintain craft standards and insure the financial health of unions, they served another purpose as well. "As a general proposition with us, we appear to think that a new applicant means another person to apply for the various jobs," observed the editor of one labor journal in 1908. Unions of semiskilled workers were not necessarily more inviting. "It was the general feeling that it would not be best to take in new members while we may have men unemployed who can fill the place of applicants," concluded a meeting of Local 357 of the Boot and Shoe Workers' Union in Bridgewater in 1912. This same rationale, of course, could be, and was, mobilized to keep "undesirable" groups of "new" immigrants outside the house of labor.[62]

Some local unions were even reluctant to admit new members when business was booming and jobs were relatively plentiful – because they feared that the next seasonal or cyclical downturn would leave the labor market overstocked with workers who had full-fledged union credentials. When the demand for labor became unusually great, these locals (in the building trades and the shoe industry) issued temporary permits to nonmembers, allowing those workers to hold union-controlled jobs without giving them any long-term claim to employment or the benefits of membership. To the chagrin of national officials, the permit system was used by some locals in lieu of notifying the national organization that jobs were available.

This spirit of "home guardism" had additional manifestations as well. Some locals were suspiciously consistent in reporting to national trade journals that the labor market was glutted in their communities. Others illegally charged entrance fees to workers who already belonged to the national union. In 1894, the painters of Springfield admitted to using "a mild course of intimidation" to create "a scarcity of labor in our trade in the city."[63]

The sense of scarcity that spawned these efforts also led local unions into active conflicts with one another. When workers found themselves competing with fellow tradesmen in different communities, they sometimes responded by vigorously protecting their own interests at the expense of their union "brothers." Between 1890 and 1915, both the granite cutters and the garment workers of Boston complained repeatedly that they were suffering from high levels of unemployment because work that "ought" to have been performed in Boston (or had once been performed in Boston) was being shipped to other cities and towns. Local unions in both industries mounted public protests over the issue, enlisting the support of the Central Labor Union of Boston and the state branch of the AFL. The granite cutters, like many building tradesmen, sought to pressure city governments to agree to have all municipally sponsored work performed exclusively by local workmen. The garment workers, after first trying other tactics, wanted articles of clothing to carry labels indicating the city and state in which they had been manufactured – so the union could urge local residents to restrict their purchases to clothing that had been made in Massachusetts.[64]

Both the granite cutters and the garment workers were aware that their strategies for maximizing employment in Boston would, if successful, create unemployment elsewhere. And on at least two occasions, these unions offered revealingly defensive rationales for their competitive conduct toward fellow trade unionists. In April 1894, the granite cutters' union justified its claim to municipal stonecutting work by pointing out that the cutting was then being performed in "Sullivan, Maine, where the men own their own farms and do not need the work as much as we do here in Boston." In 1903 the garment workers argued that it was preferable to have clothing manufactured in Boston, rather than in New York, both because the "sanitary condition of . . . New York City workshops" was inadequate and because the "unfortunate, persecuted people" who labored in the sweatshops of Manhattan were being exploited. Sensitive to the value of working-class solidarity and uncomfortable with the prospect of appearing greedy, both locals felt some obligation to offer a principled justification for their actions. Sensitive and uncomfortable as they may have been, however, these unions (and others as well) did everything in their power to protect their own jobs.[65]

Perhaps more important than these geographical conflicts were the jurisdictional disputes that emerged among national trade unions. In a number of trades, particularly those in which technological change had erased or blurred traditional craft boundaries, two or more unions claimed the exclusive right to perform certain types of labor and to organize workers who performed such labor. Jurisdictional conflicts, to be sure, had numerous sources, but the ferocity with which unions pressed their jurisdictional claims often stemmed from the need to maximize the amount of work available to their frequently unemployed members. One of the most celebrated jurisdictional disputes of the period pitted the United Brotherhood of Carpenters and Joiners against the Amalgamated Wood Workers' Union. At the core of the struggle (which was played out in Boston, among other places) was the shortage of steady jobs for members of both unions. Faced with this shortage, the carpenters were determined to control all jobs that had ever been a part of their craft. "The boys in Boston believe in going ahead at all times," announced H. M. Taylor, president of the Roxbury local of the carpenters' union in 1905. "'Hold what we have and get all we can' is our motto." Jurisdictional disputes were commonplace in the building trades after the depression of the 1890s; they also occurred among iron molders, shoe workers, and machinists. By 1902, jurisdictional conflicts were so widespread that President Gompers declared them to be the single most serious threat to the survival of the American Federation of Labor. Under the pressure of scarcity, collaboration gave way to rivalry, and unionists fought vigorously to protect or enlarge their own turf.[66]

One other – very important – trade union strategy for contending with unemployment warrants inclusion, although not full membership, in this list: the regulation of layoffs by seniority. Formal seniority arrangements first appeared, toward the close of the nineteenth century, among printers and railway workers: by 1912 a number of Massachusetts locals in each of these industries had signed contracts that contained explicit seniority provisions. The typographers and master printers of Brockton, for example, agreed that "when, through the exigencies of business, it becomes necessary to decrease force, the last member employed shall be the first discharged." Similarly, the contract signed by the Boston and Maine Railroad with its conductors and trainmen specified that during periods of slack business "the forces shall be reduced from the division roster in the inverse order to which they were promoted or entered the service." Contractual commitments of this type were never widespread during the first quarter of the twentieth century, but informal seniority arrangements existed in many shops, and the idea of allocating layoffs on a "last hired, first fired" basis was becoming increasingly popular. In the 1920s, according to one national survey, most union contracts that regulated layoffs at all did so according to seniority.[67]

Seniority arrangements, of course, were not purely restrictive or exclusionist in their thrust. The underlying principle of seniority – that workers could acquire job security through years of service – was arguably a fair one, and institutionalized seniority agreements served to rationalize the operation of the labor market and enhance its predictability. The existence of rules governing layoffs also put a check on the arbitrary exercise of power by management: workers who belonged to unions with seniority provisions in their contracts could not be let go simply because they incurred the disfavor of a foreman or manager. Nonetheless, seniority was a double-edged sword. It was, at heart, a defensive strategy that gave some workers security of employment while virtually guaranteeing that others would lose their jobs. The principle of seniority created a divergence of interest between newly employed (or young) union members and members with years of service. And, in operation, seniority plans were often a source of discord within unions. (The rather straightforward idea that the "last hired" would be the "first fired" lost much of its clarity when applied to firms that had several plants, numerous departments, and scores of job categories.) Whatever their virtues, seniority systems were at least potentially divisive because they enhanced the job security of some workers at the expense of others who labored in the same shop or belonged to the same union.[68]

Between 1880 and 1920, virtually all Massachusetts trade unions (in contrast to the Knights of Labor and, later, the Industrial Workers of the World) adopted one or more of these competitive and restrictive strategies for coping with unemployment. Precisely which approach a union developed or emphasized depended largely upon the structure of the labor market in its trade and the ethnic composition of its membership. Apprenticeship restriction tended to be emphasized in skilled trades like plumbing, where restriction could have some effect. Seniority systems emerged first in industries in which workers expected to remain with one employer for a lengthy stretch of time. Jurisdictional fights were most likely to appear when unions could actually control jobs in a trade. And the energy with which labor organizations campaigned for immigration restriction depended, of course, upon the gravity of the threat posed by immigrants and upon the ethnic backgrounds of union members. Not surprisingly, immigration restriction was viewed as the key to survival by the shoe workers' union, which was dominated by easily displaced, native-born, semiskilled employees.

Almost all these unions, it must be stressed, adopted exclusionist strategies while also implementing, or attempting to implement, more collaborative and universalistic approaches to the problem of unemployment. Turn-of-the-century building tradesmen were just as adamant about the eight-hour day as they were about the jurisdictional boundaries of their craft. Rhetorically, at least, the carpenters' union in the 1890s was as committed to abolishing the wage system as it was to ridding the commonwealth of Nova Scotians. Some locals experimented with both out-of-work benefits and seniority arrangements; the shoe workers, after World War I, agreed to an egalitarian distribution of layoffs while they were clamoring for an end to immigration. That unions could simultaneously embrace strategies embodying such different, even contradictory, principles can be attributed only in part to their willingness to treat outsiders less generously than they treated their own members. The mix of elements and values in the trade union response to unemployment was also a sign of confusion and uncertainty. Unions were groping, experimenting with several strategies at once, reacting to demands made by members with different interests and political beliefs, responding to changes that occurred from decade to decade. Labor organizations were trying to treat symptoms as well as develop a cure, and it was not always evident that any single set of strategies or principles could achieve both objectives. From the 1870s through the 1920s, unions were beleaguered, stumbling, first trying one approach and then another.

Yet there was a trend. Between 1880 and the early 1920s, mainstream labor organizations in Massachusetts became increasingly reliant upon restrictive, rather than cooperative, methods of combating unemployment. Particularly after the turn of the century, unions began to place less emphasis on finding a social solution to the problem of joblessness and more emphasis on enhancing the job security of their own members. They focused less on the demand for labor and more on the labor supply. That this occurred was the result of several separate, yet related, developments: the failure of the eight-hour remedy, the relentless pressures generated by large-scale immigration, the triumph of business unionism within the AFL, and the ever more apparent resilience of the "wage system" itself. Unions turned their attention to the supply of labor because it was one element in the equation that they had some chance of controlling and because their own organizational strength was always jeopardized by the presence of a labor surplus. One significant, if deeply ironic, consequence of chronic unemployment was that it encouraged internecine warfare as a vehicle for the expression of class conflict.

Voluntarism and involuntary idleness

At no point between 1870 and 1922 did organized labor expect public authorities to rid the commonwealth of unemployment. During the final decades of the nineteenth century, most unionists, like most of their contemporaries, believed that government bore little responsibility for the existence of joblessness; few union members believed that government either could or would devise a solution to the problem. These beliefs began to change during the first quarter of the twentieth century as the national government, in particular, assumed more responsibility for the workings of the economy. But this change was, to a considerable degree, offset by the increasingly strong commitment of the AFL to the doctrine of "voluntarism," to the notion that labor's problems were best solved through direct trade union action, with only minimal intervention by the state. Still, both before and after 1900, unions did try to influence public policy, to prod municipal, state, and federal authorities into taking steps that would limit the incidence and the impact of unemployment. Although organized labor never spoke with a single unified voice regarding the appropriate limits of government intervention, unions frequently did unite to demand action on a limited and piecemeal basis.

Indeed, a number of the ideas that labor advanced to solve the problem of unemployment required changes in public policy. Immigration restriction could be achieved only through national legislation; increasing the minimum working age for children was a matter for the state government; the abolition of the "contract system" for public works was an issue for municipal officials; and advocates of a shorter workday tried to achieve their goal not only through direct action but also through legislation. During the Progressive era, Massachusetts unionists also urged the state government to create two sets of institutions designed expressly to aid the unemployed: public labor exchanges, which would help men and women find jobs, and "homesteads" in rural areas where workers could grow their own food and weather spells of idleness more easily than they could in cities. In campaigning for these demands, labor never claimed that government held the key to solving the entire problem, but it did insist that public authorities, at all levels, adopt policies that would lessen joblessness – and avoid making things worse.[69]

Labor also demanded that government offer direct aid to the unemployed by launching public works programs during depressions.

This demand appeared in some communities (including Boston, Lynn, and Holyoke) as early as the 1870s, and it reappeared during every subsequent depression. During the downturn of the 1890s, Massachusetts unionists were virtually unanimous in urging local and state officials to build and repair roads, bridges, and reservoirs; at the same time, the national executive council of the AFL sent a memorial to the president and to Congress asking that there be "liberal appropriations for Government public works, and for the improvement of rivers and harbors." Similar demands were voiced in 1907–8, 1913–14, and, most vociferously, after World War I. A government that could muster the resources to fight a war in Europe could certainly mount a public works program, proclaimed labor's spokesmen. And a nation that sent men into battle had a moral and political obligation to make sure that they had jobs when they returned home.[70]

Although the demand for public works was a recurrent one, the rationale for the demand gradually shifted between 1870 and the early 1920s. In the nineteenth century, labor tended to portray public works programs as an extension of traditional, community-based systems of poor relief. While radical unionists claimed they had a "right to work" that the state was obliged to honor, the more common argument was that the creation of jobs on public projects was a rational and humane method of helping the able-bodied poor during periods of economic crisis. Frank Foster, in 1894, justified the call for governmental action by pointing out that "of course in the ordinary courtesies of daily life it will not do to grasp anybody by the hair of the head. But if they are drowning, common humanity demands that they be got out of the water the quickest way you can reach them." Unionists stressed that public works programs were preferable to simple poor relief in three respects: they paid workers a living wage rather than a pittance; they permitted jobless men and women to avoid the demoralizing consequences of accepting charity; and they performed a useful public service. Putting the unemployed to work on the reservoirs, one Boston resident claimed in the 1890s, would reduce the number of "snakes, eels, and frogs that find their way into our supply pipes and through our faucets, and not infrequently down our throats."[71]

By the second decade of the twentieth century, labor had taken several giant steps away from these nineteenth-century notions of poor relief and – as it turned out – toward the New Deal. Unions began to insist that government had an obligation to compensate for the swings of the business cycle by acting as a countercyclical employer: public works projects were called for not simply to relieve the poor but because it was the duty of government to create jobs whenever private enterprise was floundering. Labor further argued that government ought to stop treating each depression as a new emergency and begin planning in advance for cyclical downturns. Both in 1913–14 and after World War I, unions called not only for immediate public works programs but also for a long-term governmental commitment to act as a countercyclical employer. The 1920 convention of the Massachusetts state branch of the AFL passed a resolution urging "the enactment of laws directing all appropriate branches of the state and federal governments to plan their public undertakings so as to push them ahead when necessary to provide work for the unemployed in times of depression in private industry." In 1923, the *Labor News* of Worcester editorialized that public construction ought to serve "as a balance wheel for business."[72]

This shift in the rationale for public works projects was accompanied by another change: unions increasingly directed their appeals to state and federal as well as to municipal authorities. During the depression of the 1870s, all demands for public works programs were aimed at local governments; in the 1890s, the spotlight was on both municipal and state authorities; by 1921, labor was addressing many of its appeals to the national government. This shift occurred largely because local, and then state, officials claimed that they lacked the financial resources and credit necessary to mount adequate public works programs. The buck was passed from one level of government to another, stopping in Washington. Although city and state authorities may have been genuinely strapped, the federal government (according to labor at least) could not claim that it lacked the funds to act as a countercyclical employer. "The credit of the United States is excellent," noted Samuel Gompers in 1921.[73]

Still, trade unionists never believed that public works projects would solve the problem of unemployment. Public construction programs could reduce unemployment rates, particularly in the building trades, but even if municipal, state, and federal authorities all acted as countercyclical employers, work would remain chronically irregular for hundreds of thousands of workers in Massachusetts alone. And despite the fervor with which unions demanded public works, they remained deeply wary of – and more than a little cynical about – government involvement in the problem of unemployment. "The Commission on the Unemployed has got a lot of nice new stationery and an office," the *Labor Leader* had observed in 1894. "Telling Congress there are 6,000,000 idle men and women in this nation," declared the *Carpenter* in 1921, "made about the same impression upon its membership as though they had been told that there are 6,000,000,000,000,000 gallons of water in the ocean."[74]

Nowhere was labor's wariness more evident than in its ambivalent stance toward unemployment insurance. As is discussed in detail in Chapter 9, the idea of creating a government-sponsored benefit system for the unemployed began to receive serious consideration in Massachusetts near the end of the Progressive era. In 1916 and again in 1922, unemployment insurance bills were introduced into the state legislature by reformers who had concluded that joblessness could not be altogether eradicated in a capitalist economy and that aiding the unemployed was a societal responsibility. Labor's position on these proposals was mixed, but at least initially the majority of Bay State unionists seemed to favor the idea. Expressions of positive interest in an insurance program were voiced by Local 97 of the Cigarmakers' Union, by the Central Labor Union of Worcester, and by the Shoe Workers' Union. In 1915, the annual convention of the state branch of the AFL passed a resolution that was unequivocal in its support of insurance:

> WHEREAS: The extent of unemployment is in good years and bad, winter after winter, a very serious social affliction, which causes semi-starvation and sickness to unnumbered families and discouragement and loss of earning power to the workers, and
>
> WHEREAS: Even assuming that many suggested remedies were put into successful operation, there will still be an irreducible minimum of unemployment which must be compensated for, therefore be it
>
> RESOLVED: That we desire to put ourselves on record as heartily in favor of State Unemployment Insurance, and we do earnestly hope that legislation along similar lines may be speedily submitted in this country and in this state.[75]

After 1916, however, organized labor retreated from this hearty endorsement of "State Unemployment Insurance." The more staunchly voluntarist (and antisocialist) factions in the national AFL mounted a vigorous and successful attack on the idea of government-sponsored insurance benefits for the jobless. The issue indeed became a litmus test of an individual's adherence to the voluntarist principle that unions, rather than the state, could best protect the interests of workers. While most left-wing unionists continued to insist that it was the responsibility of government to subsidize men and women who were idle through no fault of their own, the dominant voluntarist wing claimed that such subsidies were neither desirable nor necessary.

"The fundamental objection," declared President Gompers in 1921, was that unemployment insurance would place "working people . . . under the guardianship of the government of the country," a guardianship that would limit the ability of trade unionists "to organize . . . and to live our own lives." "Working people themselves" could bring about "insurance against unemployment of an effective character" within their trade unions, whereas a government program would lead to "outside" interference "with the business of wage earners." Opponents of insurance also maintained that the goal of organized labor was the abolition of unemployment rather than "compensation for lack of employment." American workers wanted jobs, not a "dole," and the existence of insurance would undermine efforts to prevent joblessness from occurring. Whether trade unionists in Massachusetts were persuaded by these arguments or simply knuckled under to pressure remains unclear. But the leadership of the state AFL did not join the fight for insurance during the postwar depression. In 1921, only two ideas for combating unemployment were discussed at the annual convention of the state federation: public works programs and support for worker-owned cooperatives. In 1922, few spokesmen for organized labor endorsed the insurance bill that was before the legislature. In 1923, at the annual convention, the subject of unemployment was never mentioned.[76]

Neither in Massachusetts nor elsewhere did organized labor's opposition to unemployment insurance signal a rejection of all forms of government involvement with the problem of joblessness. Voluntarism was never a particularly pure, or even coherent, doctrine, and trade unions in the 1920s continued to press public authorities to take action (such as restricting immigration and launching public works projects) to enhance the steadiness of work. Yet in drawing the line at unemployment insurance, the AFL was implicitly relieving the state of full responsibility for the unemployed. At the same time, it was asserting that trade unions themselves could effectively solve the problem. Unfortunately, there was very little in the historical record – or in the AFL's published pronouncements – to warrant or justify that assertion. The federation's antagonism to insurance was far more deeply rooted in ideology than in a careful assessment of either the economic realities of unemployment or the capacities of trade unions. It is hardly surprising, then, that during the next major downturn in business, the downturn that became known as the Great Depression, the leadership of organized labor shed its voluntarist principles and actively supported legislation to create a state-run insurance program for the unemployed.[77]

The fruits of their labor

> Well, what can be done for our unemployed? Alas! it is, in the
> end, one of the deepest questions confronting our Government,
> our civilization, our social system.
>
> > John Mitchell, second vice-president of the AFL, in the
> > *Labor News*, 1913

> Labor organizations have endeavored to protect primarily their
> own members and incidentally all workers.
>
> > Editorial in the *American Federationist*, 1914[78]

Organized labor's prolonged and richly varied efforts to combat unemployment did yield some victories. During the half-century that
followed the depression of the 1870s, unions were able not only to
survive and grow but also to offer their members various forms of
protection against the burden of joblessness: out-of-work benefits,
loans for traveling, employment offices, short time instead of idle
time, contracts that provided for a rotation of layoffs, contracts that
contained seniority provisions. The minimum working age for children was increased, year-round workers replaced "contract" laborers
in many municipalities, and public works projects were far more
abundant during the depressions of the twentieth century than they
had been in the nineteenth. Some workers also encountered less
competition in the labor markets because their unions had successfully gained control of jobs while maintaining a ceiling on the number
of union members who could compete for those jobs. In addition,
labor achieved a shorter workday and contributed to the passage of
immigration restriction laws, two important developments even if, in
the end, they failed to have much impact on unemployment.

   The labor movement was able, thus, to cushion the hardships experienced by a portion of the unemployed and to enhance the job
security of some union members. Although no reliable statistical data
are available, the strategies developed by trade unions probably did
lead to steadier rhythms of employment for thousands of unionists.
At the very least, these efforts appear to have lessened the unpredictability of employment, to have brought some order out of the
chaos of late-nineteenth-century labor markets. Although shoe and
garment workers continued to be plagued by seasonal joblessness,
by the early 1920s there were rules that governed the distribution of
layoffs. Building tradesmen rarely worked continuously, but they had
agreements among themselves to control the pace at which they
worked and agreements with some employers to give all available
jobs to union members. The labor markets were being rationalized

(the process was still in its early stages in 1920), and workers who belonged to unions were acquiring a modicum of control over the economic environment.[79]

Yet these were small and partial victories. Unemployment levels in most occupations did not change much between the 1880s and the 1920s: as the statistics presented in Chapter 3 indicate, unionists themselves were often unemployed during the first quarter of the twentieth century. There is, in fact, no evidence, either quantitative or impressionistic, to suggest that any trade union during this period succeeded in producing a sizable and sustained diminution in unemployment for its own members. In 1914, after decades of strategizing, organizing, and demonstrating, a Bay State cigarmakers' local claimed that unemployment was still "the greatest evil that confronts organized labor." Almost simultaneously, an official of the typographers' union observed that joblessness remained "the most difficult to handle" of all problems facing trade unions. "The biggest job facing us is to find jobs for the jobless," echoed the *Shoe Workers' Journal* in 1921. Organized labor's strategies had not produced job security for trade unionists. Nor, needless to say, had they helped the 75 percent of the Massachusetts labor force that remained unorganized: in fact, to the extent that trade unionists were working more steadily, unorganized workers may have been less secure – since they were excluded from those relatively steady positions that some unions had come to control.[80]

Labor's efforts to contend with unemployment had, for the most part, failed. A half-century of organizing and experimentation, a half-century marked by confusion, hope, and faith, by militance, dedication, and frustration, had neither solved the problem of unemployment nor even given rise to an agreed-upon strategy for pursuing a solution. Trade unions had posted a few small gains for their own members, but, in dealing with unemployment as a social problem and as a class issue, organized labor was as far from a remedy in 1920 as it had been in 1870.

Indeed, the problem of unemployment almost certainly had a more profound impact upon the labor movement than the labor movement had upon unemployment. Not only did joblessness restrict the size and growth of unions; it also left a deep imprint upon their structure, their breadth, their policies, and their politics. The unions that developed and endured during this period were unions constructed to withstand depressions, unions led by a cohort of men who had been deeply affected by the devastation of the labor movement in the 1870s. These labor leaders, as well as members of the rank and file, were convinced that unions of skilled workers, organized on craft lines, would have the best possible chance of surviving cyclical and seasonal slowdowns. The emergence of national trade unions (rather than industrial unions or local and regional assemblies of the type advocated by the Knights of Labor) was a response not only to the nationalization of markets but also to the recurrent threat of unemployment.[81]

Chronic insecurity of employment also contributed heavily to the AFL's twentieth-century reluctance to expand the scope of its organizing, to recruit semiskilled and unskilled workers into the ranks of organized labor. Skilled unionists who had some leverage in the labor market were fearful of allying themselves with workers who were less advantaged, with men who were a strategic liability because they could all too easily be replaced from the vast, interchangeable reserves of semiskilled and unskilled labor. Craft unionists who were certain that the labor market was overcrowded similarly saw little advantage in welcoming women and "new" immigrants into the labor force or into their unions. The narrow social base of the AFL was, in part, a defensive – if shortsighted – response to job scarcity.

The climate created by the irregularity of work stifled the growth of unified working-class institutions in another way as well: by exacerbating the tensions that existed within the state's heterogeneous working class. Under the pressure of chronic unemployment, fissures emerged where boundaries were latent. In a world where jobs were scarce, it was all too easy for antagonisms to develop between native-born workers and their European counterparts, between the Irish and the French Canadians, between men who already belonged to a trade and men who sought to enter one, between skilled craftsmen and semiskilled machine tenders, carpenters and woodworkers, men and women, residents of Boston and residents of Sullivan, Maine. The bonds of solidarity that the labor movement sought to strengthen were strained by competition and often severed by the strategies that unionists adopted to protect themselves against competition. Class consciousness was diluted by group consciousness in an environment that pitted workers against one another in an almost unceasing search for jobs.[82]

In some trades, unemployment also played a key, if indirect role, in nurturing the growth of conservative, bureaucratic forces within unions. Chronically irregular employment led many unions both to increase their dues and to hire full-time paid officials to monitor local labor markets and maximize the volume of work that went to union members. Almost inescapably, these business agents or shop collectors came to acquire a narrowly self-interested outlook on labor's problems and labor's goals. Their job was to protect the interests of their own members and only "incidentally" (in the words of the *American Federationist*) to further the interests of the working class. To retain their own positions, they had to deliver jobs to local unionists, even if that meant taking work away from the unorganized or from members of other unions. Like bureaucrats everywhere, they were more interested in maintaining stability than in grand schemes for long-range reform. It was no accident that the drift away from socialism in both the carpenters' and shoe workers' unions coincided with the accession to political power of paid business agents. The enduring political strength of these officials stemmed, moreover, from their ability to control and dispense jobs: in occupations with chronically high unemployment levels (like the building trades or shoemaking), a worker's livelihood often depended upon his being in the good graces of his business agent.[83]

In certain respects, the emergence of seniority systems further reinforced the conservative tendencies existing within the labor movement. Formal seniority arrangements effectively vested mature workers with a proprietary interest in their jobs, and the existence of such an interest made workers understandably reluctant to engage in actions (such as strikes) that could place their seniority rights at risk. At the same time, seniority systems tended to depersonalize the threat of unemployment for experienced workers; in so doing, they deprived these men (who were sometimes highly valued by employers and politically influential within unions) of a personal incentive for seeking social solutions to the problem of joblessness.[84]

Unemployment, to be sure, did not single-handedly account for the shape of the Massachusetts (or American) labor movement between 1870 and 1920. A host of factors contributed to the dominance of craft organization, to the conservatism of the AFL's leadership, to policies that sometimes gave unions the air of a self-protective elite rather than the cutting edge of a working-class movement. But the scarcity of steady work was a critical element in the environment that gave rise to these institutions and policies, an important influence upon the perceptions and decisions that governed organized labor's development during its formative decades. To indulge in a brief counterfactual fantasy: had the Bay State's labor movement emerged from a "full employment" economy, it would have been a radically different labor movement. Had job security not been an urgent issue, trade unions could have devoted their energies to other matters. They could more easily have avoided defensive strategies and divisive measures; they would likely have been more flexible in their membership requirements, more inviting to women and immigrants; they might well have been able to overcome, rather than accentuate, the social divisions that existed within the working class. Selig Perlman was correct when he observed, in the 1920s, that "business" or "job conscious" unionism had its roots in the "scarcity consciousness" of workers who knew from experience that "the number of jobs available" was "almost always fewer than the number of job seekers."[85]

If unemployment helped to shape the changes that took place in the labor movement from 1870 to 1920, those changes, in turn, had a significant impact upon labor's approach to the problem of joblessness. As the preceding pages have suggested, there were two important, and related, trends in the evolution of organized labor's efforts to combat unemployment. The first was that unions increasingly devoted their energies to the task of protecting their own members rather than enhancing the job security of all workers. The second was that organized labor, despite its rhetoric, gradually surrendered the goal of abolishing unemployment, focusing instead on finding ways of accommodating itself to the irregularity of work. Both these trends reflected not only the intractability of the problem but also the rise of unions that increasingly served as custodians of the interests of an advantaged minority of the working class.

By the second decade of the twentieth century, the labor movement that unemployment had helped to create was, in fact, learning to live with unemployment. Trade unions had discovered that they could survive during cyclical depressions and that they could offer some aid and shelter to their members without altering the rhythms of industry. Putting an end to unemployment loomed as a less urgent issue in 1920 than it had in 1880. Although the AFL's leadership declared in 1922 that unemployment was "a social crime of the highest order," that "to deny the opportunity to work is to enforce death," the federation's program for combating joblessness was not worthy of its rhetoric. That program called for public works projects during depressions and for the "regularization" of industry. Yet the AFL acknowledged that public works would treat only one symptom of the malady, and it offered only the most skeletal suggestions for "regularizing" industrial production. Organized labor's most insistent demand, moreover, was that wages not be reduced during cyclical downturns. Although this demand was justified by an underconsumptionist analysis of business cycles, it was evident that the primary beneficiaries of a floor on wages would be men with relatively secure jobs rather than the unemployed. At the same time, of course, the federation refused to endorse state-run insurance programs that would have benefited all workers, organized and unorganized alike. This was hardly a blueprint for solving a life-and-death problem. In comparison with the eight-hour movement, it offered a less compelling vision of the future as well as a less concrete strategy for eradicating a "social crime" that affected all working people.[86]

Whether by design or not, the mainstream of the labor movement, in the early 1920s, was participating in the formation of a new political economy of unemployment. This political economy was partially grounded in organized labor's acceptance of capitalism and its (usually unspoken) recognition that the problem of joblessness was not about to be "abolished" in capitalist societies. Building on these fundamental premises, the unions of the AFL were opting for strategies that would offer some protection to organized workers, while deepening the existing stratification of the labor force. Strong, if narrowly based, craft unions would seek to control jobs for their own members, thereby shifting more of the burden of unemployment to nonmembers. Unions would resist wage cuts during slowdowns, underwrite spells of idleness with wage increases won during prosperous times, and enhance the predictability of work by implementing formal methods of regulating or allocating layoffs. And despite Samuel Gompers's abhorrence of unemployment insurance, unionists were also looking increasingly to the state as the ultimate source of relief for the hardships inescapably caused by joblessness. It would take the Great Depression to fuse these responses into a durable set of national policies and institutions, but by the early 1920s organized labor had already demonstrated that it was willing to settle for something less than a job for every worker.[87]

8   *From the Common to the State House*

Only occasionally did unemployed workers join together to protest against the shortage of jobs. While trade unions were engaged in an ongoing effort to combat unemployment, collective expressions of discontent, on the part of the jobless themselves, were few and far between. During most years between 1870 and the early 1920s, the Commonwealth of Massachusetts did not witness any protests or demonstrations by unemployed workers. The protest movements that did arise, moreover, generally captured the support and allegiance of only a small proportion of the unemployed.

At first glance, the sporadic and limited incidence of protest seems surprising. More than a hundred thousand workers were laid off each year, most of whom did not belong to labor organizations through which they could voice their desire for steady work. Many of these men and women were exposed to serious hardship, and almost all were convinced that involuntary idleness was an injustice, a societal wrong that needed to be set right.

Yet formidable obstacles stood in the way of collective action by jobless workers. Perhaps the most significant was the turnover that continuously occurred in the unemployed population of communities and, to a lesser extent, individual trades. Tens of thousands of workers were jobless in the city of Boston each year, but they were not all idled at once. Building tradesmen everywhere tended to be unemployed in winter, but some were jobless in December, while others were "loafing" in February. Even during depressions, the annual turnover rate in the reserve army of labor was close to 300 percent. Relatively few workers who were laid off during the early phases of a cyclical downturn were still jobless eight months later; less than half of all workers who lost their jobs during a depression were idled at the same time. "The unemployed" were neither permanent outcasts from the mainstream of the labor force nor a stagnant group of economically disenfranchised workers.[1]

Furthermore, those men and women who were unemployed simultaneously often had little in common with one another. They lived in different communities, were attached to scores of different trades, and encountered widely varying levels of stress and hardship while they were idle. At any particular moment, the unemployed population of a city or town consisted of skilled workmen who had been earning good wages and unskilled laborers who always had difficulty making ends meet. During any given week, there were workers who had just been laid off, workers who had been idle for two months, and workers who had been jobless for six months or more. Consequently, only a small fraction of the unemployed ever arrived in the same straits, with the same expectations, grievances, and sentiments, at even roughly the same time. As Bohan Zawadski and Paul Lazarsfeld observed in the 1930s, the unemployed were "a mass only numerically, not socially." And numerical masses have never been very likely to protest together or to form social movements.[2]

The social diversity of the unemployed also made it difficult for anyone to develop a program or strategy that could provide a plausible and promising basis for collective action. The strategic difficulties encountered by trade unions (discussed in Chapter 7) were compounded for the unemployed themselves. If jobless workers were to join forces to remedy their condition, what precisely could they do or demand? Although they could certainly ask for relief, what most of the unemployed wanted was not relief, with its attendant social stigma, but work. And what plan could the jobless offer that would create work for tailors, shoe factory operatives, carpenters, seamstresses, and day laborers? What program could promise to meet the urgent, short-term needs of such a disparate assembly of people? To whom should appeals or protests be addressed in a society that contained thousands of employers and that did not entrust the state with much responsibility for or power over the economy? The answers to such questions were far from self-evident. In their absence, most jobless workers, understandably enough, believed that they had little choice but to pursue private and individualized terminations to their spells of unemployment.[3]

The psychological consequences of joblessness also served to impede collective action. Layoffs, as discussed in Chapter 6, left many workers feeling downhearted and vulnerable. The long-term unemployed, in particular, seem to have been characteristically depressed rather than angry, inert rather than active. Acutely aware that they constituted only a small minority of the labor force, workers who had been idle for five months or longer, and who might otherwise have been prime candidates for protest movements, tended to withdraw from, rather than to seek out, social relationships and involvements. To be sure, these psychological reactions may have resulted, in part, from the very absence of channels for collective activity, from an ideological and institutional context that deepened workers' sense of isolation and despair. But whatever the source of these emotions, workers who felt listless and powerless, who retreated to the privacy of their homes after months of futile pavement pounding, could not easily be mobilized into public and political action.[4]

Despite these obstacles, however, demonstrations by unemployed workers did take place during this period. In the 1870s, groups of jobless citizens in Springfield, Holyoke, Lynn, Boston, and other cities held meetings, marched, and submitted petitions demanding work relief and public works programs. During subsequent depressions too, there were periodic displays of "anger and sorrow" by idled workers in most of the commonwealth's medium-sized cities. In general, the goal of these actions was to prod municipal officials into launching public works projects.[5]

The most significant demonstrations of the unemployed were those that took place in Boston between 1890 and the early 1920s. Although the Hub had been the scene of scattered protests by jobless workers during the depression of the 1870s, it was in the 1890s that these activities first erupted into dramatic and important public events. And during every depression after the 1890s, there was at least one major, and militant, demonstration by workers who were involuntarily idled. Some of the most powerful, gripping, and colorful political protests of the era were, in fact, protests mounted by and on behalf of the unemployed.[6]

In retrospect, it was predictable that the most notable collective displays of despair and determination by jobless workers took place during depressions and in the city of Boston. Unemployment may have been a chronic presence in working-class life, but it was during downturns in the business cycle that workers were most likely to become utterly desperate due to the scarcity of jobs. It was in the 1890s, and again in 1907–8, 1913–4, and 1920–1, that the commonwealth did indeed house a large number of persons who, at roughly the same moment, had exhausted their resources and lost faith in their private strategies for finding work. And Boston was the logical arena for public protests both because the Hub contained the largest number of jobless workers and because it was the site of the state government. What was far less predictable was the character of the demonstrations that occurred, the demands that were put forward, the tactics utilized. Nor was it predictable that the leadership of these protests would come from two eccentric and charismatic men who seemed to appear out of nowhere to ignite the simmering discontents of Boston's unemployed.

Morrison I. Swift: Capitalists Are the Cause of the Unemployed[7]

> There is probably no parallel in the history of Massachusetts for the scene which was presented within the state house yesterday afternoon.
>
> Boston *Daily Globe*, February 21, 1894

Every major demonstration of the unemployed that took place in Boston between 1894 and 1914 was led by Morrison Isaac Swift. Little in Swift's personal background prefigured this destiny. Born to a middle-class family in Ravenna, Ohio, in 1856, he was raised in Ashtabula and attended Western Reserve College in Cleveland for two years. He came to Massachusetts in 1877 to complete his education at Williams College, where he belonged to a fraternity, edited the college newspaper, and graduated with honors. In 1879, Swift began graduate studies at Johns Hopkins. He wrote a dissertation entitled "The Ethics of Idealism, as Represented by Hegel and Aristotle," receiving a Ph.D. in 1885. He spent the following year studying at universities in Germany.[8]

Swift never took up the scholarly career for which he had been trained. When he returned to the United States, he settled in a tenement district of Philadelphia and spent the late 1880s and early 1890s in Philadelphia, New York, and Boston, trying to organize a "social university" that would educate and serve the interests of the urban poor and the industrial working class. At the same time, he began writing political pamphlets, as well as a utopian novel, which contained his own peculiar mix of antimonopolist, socialist, and anarchist ideas. In 1891 Swift underscored his personal rejection of American institutions by trying, without success, to return his Ph.D. to Johns Hopkins and to have his name "erased from the list of graduates of the university." In 1893, he returned to Boston to work with two small reform organizations, the Equity Union and the Social Reform Educational Institution in the South End.[9]

Swift's efforts to organize the unemployed began in the winter of 1893–4. Accompanied by Herbert Casson, who was rumored to have been a defrocked priest, and aided by representatives of the Socialist Labor Party, Swift initiated a series of meetings of jobless workers on the Boston Common. At these meetings, he urged the unemployed to band together to demand immediate relief from governmental authorities as well as far-reaching reforms of the nation's economy. He drew up petitions spelling out these demands in detail and led marches of the unemployed through the streets of Boston and to the offices of state officials. His words and actions struck a resonant chord among at least some of Boston's idled workers. On February 6, 1894, only weeks after he had launched his campaign, more than a thousand unemployed men attended one of Swift's meetings on the Common. The crowd then marched down Washington Street carrying placards proclaiming that "ours is the right to work and we demand that it be recognized." The marchers also demanded shorter hours of labor, state ownership of the railroads, and the creation of "municipal factories where the unemployed can work for themselves." A week later, Swift led a march to the State House to deliver a petition demanding government programs to aid the unemployed.[10]

This series of protests reached its dramatic peak on February 20, 1894. In the early afternoon of that day, a crowd of several thousand working people (some estimates ran as high as 10,000) assembled on the Common to hear speeches by Swift and other activists. After the speeches, the crowd marched across the street to the State House to "interview" and present a petition to Governor Frederick T. Greenhalge. Upon arriving at the State House, Swift and Casson entered the governor's office and handed him the petition, which, in polite and almost deferential language, called for state farms and factories, a public works program (building the Cape Cod Canal), and the formation of a commission to study the problems of the unemployed.[11]

To the surprise of nearly everyone in attendance, Governor Greenhalge accepted the petition and walked out to the front steps of the building to address the crowd. But his speech displayed little sympathy for the demonstrators. He began by questioning whether many of the protestors were, in fact, his "fellow citizens," and he proceeded to nervously lecture the crowd on the functions of state government and the difficulty of creating public works programs. He also reminded the unruly throng that "obedience to the law is the first duty of the citizens of this commonwealth." Greenhalge's one gesture of support for the unemployed was tentative and conditional. "If, under the constitution and the laws, either by public or private means, industry can be started or employment can be given, I pledge you my word that my best endeavors shall be given to that end."[12]

The protestors were not placated by Greenhalge's address. After the governor had retreated back to his office, they mounted the State House stairs and poured into the building, "until Doric hall, the stairs leading to the legislature, and every nook in the lower portion of this state house was occupied with a surging crowd." Once inside, Swift declared that if the demands of the demonstrators were not met, they would "clean out" the entire State House – by electoral means, he hastened to add. Swift's speech was greeted by "frantic yells" of support from the crowd and by the arrival of the police, who began forcibly evicting the demonstrators. Swift, Casson, and several hundred others managed to remain in the building long enough to hand a state representative a petition addressed to the legislature from "the unemployed on the Boston Common." This petition reiterated the demands that had been placed before the governor; it also asked the legislature "to take steps to amend the constitution of Massachusetts, so that it shall affirm the right of every one to have work." The legislature immediately suspended its rules to accept the petition, which was referred to a committee for investigation.[13]

The crowd then reassembled on the Common, where Swift triumphantly reported the legislature's action. "We may be reasonably satisfied with what we did today," Swift declared. "We have come to a point where we are influential because we have stuck together." He denounced the governor for calling the police and then asked the crowd whether it favored taking all "property from the wealthy." The answer that came back was a resounding "yes."[14]

The "invasion of the State House," as the Boston *Globe* called it, served as a springboard for protests that continued throughout the winter and into the spring. (See Figure 8.1.) On February 27, after being denied a permit to hold a meeting on the Common, Swift led an "orderly crowd" of five thousand jobless workers to Faneuil Hall, where he proclaimed that the principle "for which we shall stand to the end" was "that men have a right to work." Responding to personal attacks that had appeared in the press, he explained that he was a socialist and not an anarchist: "the word is always flung at everybody who desires to have things a little better than they really are." He also read to the crowd a letter that he had received from President Eliot of Harvard, who took a dim view both of Swift himself and of the idea of creating public employment for the unemployed. President Eliot's disapprobation notwithstanding, Swift led weekly processions and rallies of the unemployed throughout the month of March. Attendance at these events gradually began to flag, but there were always at least five hundred demonstrators lending full support to Swift's agenda.[15]

Although this series of protests did not produce any immediate relief for jobless workers, it did succeed in focusing governmental attention upon the problem of unemployment. On February 27, when the legislative committee that had been created during the "invasion of the State House" began to hold hearings, the first person

INVASION OF THE STATE HOUSE.

Gov Greenhalge Addressed and Police Ejected the "Army of the Unemployed."

Headed by Swift and Casson They Petitioned Executive and Legislature for State Farms and Factories, or for Other Immediate Means of Relief---House Committee of Seven Appointed.

SCENE IN FRONT OF THE STATE HOUSE; CROWD WAITING FOR THE GOVERNOR.

Figure 8.1. Front page of the Boston *Globe*, February 21, 1894

called to testify was Morrison Swift. In measured tones, Swift described the plight of the unemployed and carefully argued the case for state farms and factories. "New problems require new solutions," he noted. The "question is one of conscience." He insisted that the state, at the very least, create a commission to carefully and systematically investigate the problem. The legislature rejected Swift's argument for state farms and factories, but late in March, after holding weeks of hearings, it endorsed a public works program while also appointing a Board to Investigate the Subject of the Unemployed. That board spent more than a year conducting what proved to be nineteenth-century America's most extensive and thorough investigation of the problem of unemployment.[16]

These demonstrations also shook organized labor out of the silent and self-protective torpor into which it had fallen after the panic of 1893. Although M. J. Bishop, the head of the Knights of Labor in Massachusetts, wrote a letter to Governor Greenhalge denouncing the "exhibition of European hoodlumism" that had occurred at the State House, unions affiliated with the AFL were more supportive. A few days after the "invasion," the *Labor Leader* published an editorial defending the motives of Swift and Casson. In early March the Central Labor Union of Boston and the Boston Building Trades Council called for a mass meeting of the unemployed to be held at Faneuil Hall on March 20. At that meeting, attended by thousands of trade unionists, Swift shared the platform with local labor leaders and with AFL president Samuel Gompers. Harry Lloyd of the CLU opened the meeting by acknowledging that many people had questioned "the wisdom of organized labor remaining silent through the winter while our members were on the verge of starvation." He also announced that the time had come for unions to demand action from the state. Gompers, recognizing the catalytic role that Swift had played, proclaimed that "if you are true to Mr. Swift, you will be true to the labor movement."[17]

Despite the newfound support of organized labor, Swift and his colleagues made little headway in convincing the state government to adopt their program for aiding the unemployed. As a result, they shifted the focus of their efforts and began to address their appeals to the federal government. In April, shortly after Jacob Coxey had announced his plan to send a "living petition" of the unemployed to Washington, Swift declared his intention to send a New England Industrial Delegation to the nation's capital. This delegation, Swift insisted, was not an army and certainly not a part of Coxey's army. "We are in sympathy with Coxey's movement," he explained, "but our petition includes a great deal that Coxey is not looking for at all." Indeed it did. The demands put forward by the New England Industrials were far more radical than those advanced by Coxey or by any of the other brigades in Coxey's loose-knit army. Swift's petition asked Congress to provide farms and factories for the unemployed, to begin a massive program of public works, and to "amend the constitution of the United States, so that it shall affirm the right of every one to have work." It also urged Congress to abolish interest-bearing bonds, to nationalize the railroads, the telegraph, and mines, and to "investigate the advisability of nationalizing the trusts."[18]

Although only sixty jobless men joined the New England Industrial Delegation, the group's departure from Boston produced one of the largest and most turbulent mass gatherings in the city's history.

EXCITING TIMES ON THE COMMON.

Turbulent Scenes Attending the Start of Boston's "Industrial Delegates" for Washington.

Figure 8.2. Scene on the Boston Common as the New England Industrials departed for Washington. Boston *Globe*, April 23, 1894.

(See Figure 8.2.) On Sunday, April 22, 1894, Swift and "field director" M. D. Fitzgerald began the march to Washington by leading their small band of recruits from the offices of the Equity Union to the Boston Common. There, carrying a banner with a quotation from Abraham Lincoln, they encountered a crowd of at least 25,000 men and women who had assembled to witness the departure of the New England Industrials. The size of the throng spoke to both the support and the hostility that Swift had sparked in his months of organizing. Although most of the crowd offered encouragement to the delegation, sizable elements were openly antagonistic to Swift and his followers. When the six policemen who had been present at the beginning of the gathering disappeared, "pandemonium" broke out. Swift and others were prevented from speaking, "fights were too numerous to count," scores of people were injured, the anticipated parade of the unemployed was canceled, and the delegation itself was hustled out of downtown Boston with no further public fanfare.[19]

Outside the city, the New England Industrials continued to attract far greater attention than their paltry numbers would seem to have warranted. In Hyde Park, their first stop, they were greeted with applause and the ringing of church bells; several thousand people poured into a public square to listen to an address by Swift. Two days later, the delegation's arrival in Providence reportedly "turned the city upside down," while its passage through Wakefield, Rhode Island, produced such paroxysms of fear that the marchers were driven out of town without breakfast. Terror, as well as sympathy, was evoked by the spectacle of an army of the unemployed marching on Washington to assert its right to work.[20]

As the delegation traveled southward, it moved out of the public spotlight. From Connecticut, the Industrials took a boat to Baltimore, proceeding on to Washington by foot. They arrived in the capital late in May, weeks after Coxey and his army had entered the city. Once in Washington, the New Englanders shared the dismal fate of the other "living petitions" to the federal government. Their demands were largely ignored by Congress, and they themselves were shunted from campsite to campsite in and around the capital. By the end of the summer, the New England Industrial Delegation, as well as America's first national protest movement of the unemployed, had fallen apart.[21]

There were no further protests of the jobless in Boston during the depression of the 1890s, and – not coincidentally, perhaps – Swift himself left Massachusetts in 1895. He moved to California, where he became the national organizer for the Brotherhood of the Cooperative Commonwealth (a post later held by Eugene Debs) and participated in an attempt to create a model socialist colony in the Santa Rosa Valley. Over the next decade, he published a steady stream of political articles and pamphlets, while also organizing workers in San Francisco, Los Angeles, Philadelphia, and the coalfields of Pennsylvania. He was arrested at least twice during this period: once while helping to organize a strike of coal miners in Hazleton, Pennsylvania, and a second time when he pasted a circular "criticizing the attitude of the wealthy" on the New York home of John D. Rockefeller.[22]

Swift came back to Massachusetts in 1907, and within a year he was again leading demonstrations of the unemployed on the Boston Common. (See Figure 8.3.) On January 8, 1908, a crowd of several hundred jobless men, led by Swift, assembled on the Common and passed a set of resolutions to be presented to the mayor of Boston, the state legislature, and the governor. These resolutions, which demanded state farms for the unemployed and a public commission to study the problem, echoed the petitions of the 1890s. But they were

Figure 8.3. Morrison Swift addressing a rally of the unemployed at the entrance to the State House, probably in 1908. (Photograph by G. Frank Radway; courtesy collection of Gino Agraz.)

more adamantly anticapitalist in tone and contained a more imaginative blend of concrete and very grand proposals for reform. "The present crisis exhibits anew the incapacity of the capitalists and financiers to carry on the nation's business without disaster," declared Swift and his followers. "As usual the chief burden of panic suffering is shifted upon the poorer and working classes, who deserve none of it." Maintaining that "the state and city are the agencies for rectifying these wrongs," the assembly on the Common asked public authorities to appropriate five hundred thousand dollars for a public works program, to reduce "the rents of the poorer classes" by 25 percent, and to enact a minimum wage law for all industries. The gathering further demanded that the legislature "immediately inaugurate a system of pensions for the unemployed":

While men are out of work, the State should provide for them with a certain per cent of what they customarily earn. Taxes falling on the community for this purpose would be just because unemployment is a social phenomenon due to mismanagement by the whole of society. Pensions are a right and contain no element of charity.

With the intention, perhaps, of making these reforms appear less radical, the assembly also urged the legislature to "wholly and finally" cure the problem of unemployment "by voting over the title of all great industries to united popular ownership."[23]

After passing these resolutions, the unemployed marched to City Hall, where Swift and two others met with Mayor George Hibbard and presented him a copy of the group's demands. A week later, after amending the resolutions (to underscore the need for "pensions" and to request an antisuicide bureau for the unemployed), Swift led a march of two hundred men to the State House to deliver the resolutions personally to Governor Curtis Guild, Jr. Although both the mayor and the governor promised to give serious consideration to the group's proposals, neither official ended up displaying much sympathy for the demonstrators or their ideas. On January 14, Hibbard issued a statement declaring that he had "no control" over most of the matters discussed in the resolutions; he also expressed his belief that the Salvation Army was doing an excellent job of aiding the needy unemployed. On January 22, the governor took a more forceful stand, delivering a lengthy blast at Swift himself and at the resolutions adopted by the unemployed. "The resolutions," Guild declared, "show . . . an almost complete ignorance of conditions and law in this Commonwealth." Unemployment levels were not unusually high, he claimed; there were many public and private agencies that were furnishing adequate relief to the poor; and the idea of increasing public expenditures while reducing rents was both "unconstitutional" and "impossible." Pensions for the unemployed, similarly, were "not only a constitutional impossibility, but a logical absurdity." The governor denounced Swift as an "agitator" who posed as an "advocate of socialism" but was really an anarchist interested only in "self-advertisement." Guild announced that he would have nothing more to do with a man who "openly and publicly reviles all religion, encourages unchastity in women, and advocates housebreaking and theft."[24]

Swift may indeed have reviled organized religion in his published polemics, but nonetheless the major success of his 1908 organizing campaign took place at Trinity Church in Copley Square. On the morning of Sunday, January 19, he led a solemn procession of four hundred jobless men from the Boston Common through the streets

of the Back Bay and into the decidedly upper-crust Trinity Church.
The men were escorted to empty seats by astonished, but polite, ush-
ers. "The assemblage," reported the *Globe*, "undoubtedly was the
strangest that ever passed the threshold of Trinity." During a brief
prayer session, "a hum of voices" speaking German, Polish, Greek,
and Yiddish could be heard, and "an odor like unto garlic" per-
meated the vestibule. The unexpected congregation was, however,
"peaceful and reverent." "There was not a tramp in the crowd," reported one Boston newspaper. "They were men out of work."
Through one of the sextons, Swift sent a message to the rector, Dr.
Alexander Mann, asking that the day's sermon focus on the problem
of unemployment and that the day's collection be earmarked for relief
of the unemployed.[25]

Dr. Mann rose to the occasion. He read Swift's message to the congregation and explained that he preferred not to depart from the
planned agenda for the day because it happened to be the one Sunday in the year when the church devoted its sermon and its collection
to the support of foreign missions. But he promised that on the following Sunday a collection would be taken up for the unemployed.
Mann also expressed his personal conviction that there was indeed a
serious unemployment problem in Boston and that the jobless were
deserving of aid. He was, he declared, moved and pleased that the
unemployed, "in their time of trouble," had turned "with true in-
stinct to the house of God." A week later, the congregation of Trinity
Church raised more than a thousand dollars for relief of the unemployed.[26]

Swift's tactical innovation – confronting the church rather than the
state, middle-class citizens rather than public officials – caused a considerable stir in and around Boston. And the response of Trinity's
congregation did constitute something of a victory for Swift and the
unemployed. Yet despite the publicity that this event received, the
movement of the jobless did not gain any further momentum during
the winter of 1908. For several weeks after their surprise attendance
at Trinity's services, Swift and a fairly small band of followers continued to rally on the Common and to march through the streets of
downtown Boston. But they were insistently harassed by the police,
arrested for minor infringements of the law, and, more importantly,
ignored by most public officials and the press. By the beginning of
spring, the protests had come to a halt. A few months later, the
depression itself was over.[27]

But Morrison Swift's career as an organizer of the unemployed had
not yet come to an end. Swift remained in Boston after 1908, lectur-
ing, writing political tracts as well as his second novel, and sending

numerous petitions to the state legislature for consideration. How he supported himself during these years (or any years, for that matter) remains unclear, but he continued to act as an independent and idiosyncratic spokesman for social reform and for left-wing political causes.[28]

During the brief, but sharp, depression of 1913–14, Swift appeared again at the head of protesting crowds of unemployed workers. His program for solving the problem contained a familiar mix of concrete proposals and scathing indictments of capitalism, and the demonstrations that he led displayed the same tactical imagination, the same mastery of political symbols, that had garnered so much attention during previous depressions. In this campaign Swift took direct aim at the business community itself. On March 12, 1914, he led one hundred and fifty jobless workers to the Chamber of Commerce building in Boston, where they asked that the building be used at night as a dormitory for the homeless unemployed. Their request was refused, and the entire group was evicted by the police. Nine days later, an assembly of eight hundred unemployed men and women passed a resolution calling upon clergymen "of all denominations to resign their pastorates and help the workless." The crowd then marched to the exclusive Algonquin Club in the Back Bay, where Swift unsuccessfully demanded entrance. Standing outside the club, Swift proclaimed to his followers that their movement ought to have two overarching aims: "to get what is coming of the good things of life, and to make the rich loafers work."[29]

These symbolic confrontations with the private wealth of Boston led the governor of the state to give a hearing to Swift and his fellow demonstrators. Two days after the march on the Algonquin Club, Governor David Walsh met for more than an hour with Swift, Caleb Howard, an organizer from the Industrial Workers of the World, and a handful of Boston's unemployed. While two hundred other jobless men waited outside the State House, Swift urged the governor both to provide immediate relief to the unemployed through a public works program and to seek a permanent solution to the problem by creating (once again) an investigative commission. John F. Malloy of South Boston, one of the unemployed men in the delegation, told Walsh that "our actions may become antagonistic because of the plight we are in and because of the views of society." The governor was receptive, but noncommittal. He congratulated the men for having come to the State House in a "peaceable, law-abiding manner" and promised to do what he could "to improve matters as soon as possible."[30]

Both the governor and the Boston Chamber of Commerce did, in fact, take steps to improve matters, as is discussed in Chapter 9. While they were doing so, several hundred jobless workers, led by Swift, continued to hold rallies on the Common and to stage marches around the city. The gradual return of prosperity, however, kept a ceiling on the number of demonstrators, making it less imperative for public officials to respond quickly and amply to their demands. Morrison Swift's last protest about unemployment – or, to be more precise, the last protest that made its way into the newspapers – occurred in early May 1914. The event was fittingly symbolic in its details. Swift led an assembly of two hundred jobless workers from the Common to the State House to offer testimony in support of a bill to create state farms for the unemployed, Swift's long-held and most deeply cherished idea for solving the problem of joblessness. On this occasion, the demonstrators got only as far as the front steps of the State House. There they were met by Representatives George Ellis and William Armstrong of the Committee on Social Welfare, who told the group that the proposal for state farms was not worthy of consideration because there was no work to do on farms during the winter and because there were already plenty of farm jobs available during the summer. Ellis expressed sympathy with the protestors, insisting that everyone "in this State House" had "the great problem of the unemployed at heart." "But," he noted, "nobody seems able to solve it."[31]

Although Morrison Swift retired from his role as tribune of the unemployed after 1914, he did not abandon the political arena altogether. In 1915, he participated in the formation of the Socialist Propaganda League; during World War I he was an ardent advocate of American military intervention to save democracy by defeating Germany. He settled in Newton in 1917, and well into the 1920s he continued writing political polemics and letters to newspapers, both of which became increasingly cranky and occasionally anti-Semitic. Swift, who was born just before the Civil War, lived until after World War II, long enough to see many of the proposals that he had championed implemented as policies of the national government of the United States. Although his more radical ideas were never adopted, Swift did witness the creation of massive public works programs for the jobless, the passage of minimum wage legislation, and, most importantly, the development of a nationwide system of "pensions" for the unemployed. Morrison Swift died in 1946, the same year that Congress passed an Employment Act making the federal government responsible for promoting "maximum employment" in the United States. Swift's last words, reportedly, were "Tell the people to unite or they will certainly be destroyed." A brief obituary in the Boston *Herald* made no mention of his activities on the Boston Common.[32]

Urbain J. Ledoux: "Lift Up Your Hearts"

> Shades of Garrison, Phillips, and Whittier, those noble abolition-
> ists of slavery days! How they must have turned in their graves
> yesterday noon, when "human flesh on the hoof" was sold at
> auction from the granite blocks of the Parkman Bandstand on
> Boston Common, under the shadow of the State House, that
> these slaves of unemployment might escape further terrible depri-
> vations and death by starvation.
>
> Boston *Globe,* September 9, 1921

In September 1921, the city of Boston was once again the scene of sensational, nationally publicized demonstrations by unemployed workers. These demonstrations were led by Urbain J. Ledoux, a man every bit as unusual as Morrison Swift and a good deal more charismatic. Ledoux was born into a working-class family in Quebec in 1875 and spent most of his childhood in Biddeford, Maine. When he was twenty-one, he entered the American consular service, and over the next dozen years he held posts in Three Rivers, Quebec, Bordeaux, and Prague, where he developed a new, and much-heralded, system for indexing government records. He then abruptly left the consular service and went into business. For a short while at least, he was an executive for a firm that produced denatured alcohol.[33]

Not long thereafter, Ledoux appears to have had a conversion experience, a spiritual vision that led him to embrace the cause of world peace and to preach "the universal brotherhood of man." When he was in his early forties, he began to devote all his energies to the pursuit of those goals. He attended a peace conference in the Hague, worked with the Ginn World Peace Foundation, and attracted considerable public notice when he jumped into New York harbor and attempted to swim after Henry Ford's peace ship. During World War I, he worked for the Government War Camp Community Service, distributing food and arranging shelter for transient soldiers. After the war, he dedicated himself to the cause of jobless ex-soldiers in New York, opening up an old bakery building on Broadway and offering free lodging and meals to unemployed veterans. It was at this juncture that he began to be called "Mr. Zero," a sobriquet that gave Ledoux an air of mystery and remained with him until he died.

> I was feeding the men in the park one day and some of the boys
> wanted to know my name. I told them it did not matter. "What do
> you care about my name?" I said. "I am just a man who is feeding

you. I am nothing. Don't think of me." The Irishman said: "I have your number. I know who you are. If you are nothing, your number is zero. You are Mr. Zero." That joke stuck and I became Mr. Zero.[34]

Ledoux's dedication to peace and social reform was rooted in spiritual rather than political values. A Bahaist, according to one account, and a mystic, according to all accounts, he insisted that his mission was not to transform American capitalism but to save the nation from "spiritual suffocation." "I have no 'isms,'" he declared. "I belong to no faction, nor have I any political affiliations. I am absolutely free. I am not a Bolshevist nor an agitator." For Ledoux, giving food and shelter to the poor was more a personal calling than a political statement, an expression of brotherhood rather than ideology. His interest in the unemployed, he claimed, began one night while he was staying in a hotel in New York. "As I lay awake suddenly I knew my duty. I got up at three o'clock and walked out in the street. I went to the Bowery. The wretched men there needed me." Ledoux defined his public role in similar terms. He was, he claimed again and again, simply "an alarm clock" whose job was "to awaken the slumbering conscience of the people."[35]

Ledoux came to Boston late in August 1921. He immediately rented a building at 31 Howard Street, and, with the help of some assistants who had come with him from New York, began equipping the facility with cots and gas ranges so that it could serve as a shelter for the homeless unemployed. While work on the building was under way, the "mysterious Mr. Zero" announced his arrival in Boston by distributing meal tickets to the hundreds of homeless, jobless men who were then sleeping on the Common. The tickets could be exchanged for food at a local restaurant; at the close of each day, Ledoux went to the restaurant and paid the bill. On August 28, he attempted to offer another service to the homeless by bringing a safety razor, mirror, shaving brush, and mug to the Common. But his "outdoor barber shop" was quickly shut down by the police.[36]

On Sunday, September 4, Ledoux formally opened his shelter. He went to the Common at six o'clock in the morning and invited the two hundred and fifty men sleeping there to join him for breakfast at 31 Howard Street. His invitation was accepted: the entire crowd – dominated by ex-servicemen but including men of all ages – trooped off to the building that was officially christened the "Church of the Unemployed" but soon became known as "Hotel Jobless." When the men arrived, they were given an ample breakfast (termed "physical Christianity" by Ledoux) and then given a chance to engage in a round of community singing ("mental Christianity"). Ledoux gave a brief talk to the men, indicating that he would try to help them find jobs. The new residents of Hotel Jobless then formally dedicated the building by raising an American flag and singing "The Star Spangled Banner." More than one hundred and fifty of the homeless slept at Howard Street that night.[37]

The next morning, the residents of Hotel Jobless held a meeting at which they decided to stage a demonstration at Boston's City Hall. They proceeded to march through the streets of Boston, led by ex-servicemen carrying a placard reading "we did our bit; now you do yours." When they arrived at City Hall, they asked to see Mayor Andrew Peters, who appeared almost immediately. A spokesman for the crowd thanked the mayor for having permitted the unemployed to sleep unmolested on the Common throughout the summer. They also asked him to take steps to provide shelter for the homeless during the coming cold months and to create jobs by starting public works projects. Peters announced that he would, within a matter of hours, call a conference of all municipal department heads to instruct them to start work on any job-creating projects as soon as possible. He also promised to meet with Ledoux later in the day to report any progress that had been achieved. The assembled crowd broke into cheers. The mayor responded by calling for "three cheers for the unemployed." The men then marched in columns back to 31 Howard Street.[38]

The friendly atmosphere spawned by this encounter with the mayor was soured, two days later, by a meeting that Ledoux held with Boston's Overseers of the Poor (or Overseers of Public Welfare, as they were officially called). The meeting had been arranged by Mayor Peters after Ledoux had criticized the way in which the municipal wayfarers' lodge on Hawkins Street was being run. Ledoux objected in particular to the practice of having men chop wood for three or four hours each morning, a practice that hampered their ability to find jobs. The overseers were emphatically uninterested in Ledoux's proposals and openly hostile to Ledoux himself. "I don't remember experiencing such an inquisition as that of this afternoon," reported Mr. Zero, after the meeting. "It appears that there are many Bostonians who can't or don't desire to believe that my only object in my work here is to aid the unemployed."[39]

Perhaps in response to this rebuff, Ledoux, on the very next day, September 8, launched a series of demonstrations that seized the attention of the entire city and made headlines in newspapers across the United States. Shortly after noon, he led seventy-five residents of 31 Howard Street in a march to the Parkman Bandstand on Boston Common to attend a previously announced meeting and rally of the unemployed. Hundreds of jobless men, as well as several thousand interested onlookers, stood on the Common awaiting the arrival of the "Shorn Lambs of Unemployment," as Ledoux's followers had begun to call themselves. While the "shorn lambs" sat down to eat box lunches provided by the Winchester Country Club ("a real communion," according to their leader), Ledoux addressed the growing crowd. He began his speech by lamenting that the "wonderful city of Boston" had "so neglected these noble boys, who have been so tortured by hunger and a terrible war for democracy for us all."[40]

Ledoux then announced, to the shock of the audience, that he would sell the unemployed, as "slaves," to the highest bidders in the crowd. Eight "brave men" had already volunteered to go "on the auction block," to sell their bodies and their labor for a week's time in return for food, shelter, and a small sum of cash. "It is a shame," Ledoux proclaimed, "that we have to come here today, in this home of culture, refinement, and wealth, to make this kind of appeal for ordinary comforts for . . . honest men."[41]

Ledoux began the auction by administering an oath to each of the eight volunteers. "I solemnly swear to give my brawn and brain, faithfully, honestly, and to the fullest of my ability to the highest bidder who buys my body, so help me God." One by one, the "slaves" then mounted the bandstand and explained why they were willing to let themselves be sold in public. "I have been without work for six months and have often gone along on two meals a week," one man stated. "I'm afraid," confessed eighteen-year-old Willie Davis, almost in tears. "I'm afraid I will be let to starve to death and I don't want to die that way." After speaking, each man stripped to the waist and at Ledoux's command performed exercises to display his physical strength. Ledoux then asked for bids for the man's services. When it came the turn of James Mitchell, a "burly, powerfully built" black man from the Virgin Islands, the already agitated crowd became hysterical. Men and women throughout the Common began to sob and scream. Mitchell himself stood trembling on the bandstand, naked from the waist up, wearing soleless sneakers and a Navy hat. He too began sobbing after several members of the audience offered him food, shelter, shoes, and enough money to live on for several weeks.[42]

Few of the unemployed "slaves" were actually sold on September 8, largely because the onlookers were too stunned to participate very readily in a performance that was both a plea for help and a reenactment of the nation's historic sin. But when Ledoux repeated his auctions on September 9 and 10, the crowds that assembled on the Common were much larger and more openly supportive. Several dozen

Figure 8.4. Young unemployed "slave" being "sold" at auction by Urbain Ledoux (right) on the Parkman Bandstand, Boston, September 1921. (Copyright 1978 by Dennis M. Brearly, Boston.)

jobless men went up on the auction block: most were between the ages of twenty and thirty, many were veterans, some had trades, and almost all told tales of suffering and long, futile searches for work. (See Figure 8.4.) The thousands of men and women who surrounded the bandstand reacted to the scene with a mixture of cheers and weeping. They also offered food, shelter, clothing, and money to the "slaves," without demanding any services in return. Some of the men who were auctioned off were taken into the homes of their "purchasers"; one family even announced that it intended to legally adopt its young "slave." Most of the "purchasers" themselves appear to have been middle-class residents of Boston and the nearby suburbs. Among them was Mrs. Mary Thatcher Hollis of Newton Centre, who had come into Boston to buy a new set of furs but decided instead to give money to dozens of the "shorn lambs of unemployment."[43]

On September 11, Ledoux announced that instead of an auction there would be a community "songfest and band concert" on the Common. At two o'clock in the afternoon, he led his "shorn lambs" to the Parkman Bandstand. There they found an assembled audience of more than ten thousand people, the core of a crowd that would grow larger as the afternoon wore on. Ledoux opened the session by mounting the bandstand, extending his arms to make a "sign of the cross," and offering several minutes of silent prayer. He then spoke to the hushed crowd. "Boston has lost its sense of God," he proclaimed. "That is the trouble with Boston. But Boston will regain its sense of God, and that will be its redemption." After he had finished speaking, Harry Barnhardt, a friend of Ledoux's from New York and the leader of community sings in Central Park, asked the crowd to join him in singing "America." Barnhardt then conducted a band concert and community sing that lasted for several hours: the program included "The Battle Hymn of the Republic," "Old Folks at Home," and Tchaikovsky's Symphony in F Minor. The service ended with Ledoux and Barnhardt standing together in a tearful "brotherly embrace" before a singing crowd of more than twenty thousand people. Later that evening, Ledoux announced that the slave auctions would be suspended for a week. "I am confident," he told reporters, "that the public conscience has been sufficiently aroused . . . and that means will be provided for the feeding and employment of these men."[44]

Boston's initial response to these four days of tumult seemed to justify Ledoux's optimism. The city may or may not have regained its sense of God, but donations and offers of help poured into the Church of the Unemployed. Small sums of cash were given daily; free food was delivered by restaurants and bakeries; an experienced cobbler set up shop to repair the shoes of the jobless; several women volunteered to sew and clean the bed linens; furniture was donated; a local dentist announced that he would take care of any toothaches that occurred among the unemployed; and tickets were sold for a benefit baseball game between the Dorchester All-Stars and the "shorn lambs." Just as important, scores, perhaps hundreds, of Ledoux's followers obtained jobs as a result of the auctions. During the second and third weeks of September, a steady stream of employers arrived at 31 Howard Street to offer positions to the shelter's residents. At the same time, unemployed men from throughout the metropolitan area flocked to the Hotel Jobless for shelter and help.[45]

The auctions also evoked some positive responses from public authorities. Within a few days of the first "slave sale," it was announced that the municipal lodging house on Hawkins Street would be expanded and renovated and that some of its regulations would be revamped. On September 16, Mayor Peters hosted a small conference at City Hall to discuss the city's unemployment problem. The conference was attended by the chairman of the Overseers of the Poor, representatives from Boston's leading charities, Ledoux, and W. K. Brice of New York, Ledoux's reputed financial "angel." Ledoux offered a number of proposals to his fellow conferees, stressing that the most critical step was to appoint a committee of "human engineers" to study the "unemployment situation" in detail. (A few days later, he mentioned that one "human engineer" who was ideally equipped to deal with the problem was Herbert Hoover.) Although the conference was not authorized to take formal action, both the mayor and the city's charity officials appeared receptive to Ledoux's suggestions. After the conference, Peters underscored his sympathy for Ledoux and the jobless by going to 31 Howard Street for supper. At that supper, the mayor expressed his appreciation for what Ledoux had done for the city and promised to do everything in his power to aid the unemployed.[46]

Not everyone in Boston reacted as positively as Mayor Peters. The city's clergy – unnerved, perhaps, by Ledoux's evocation of himself as the redeemer – remained aloof from the protest movement, and few churches offered to help the Church of the Unemployed. Most of the Overseers of the Poor continued to insist that Ledoux was thoughtless and ill-informed, while many Bostonians were suspicious of his motives and disapproving of his methods. Indeed, the shocking spectacle of the slave auctions was condemned in numerous circles, including the labor movement. On September 18, after a heated debate, the Central Labor Union of Boston issued a statement deploring the "slave auctions" and formally asking Mayor Peters to prevent any further auctions from being held.[47]

Despite these criticisms, Ledoux was convinced by the middle of September that he had succeeded in awakening the people of Boston. He announced that there would be no further slave auctions in the city and that he was entrusting the Church of the Unemployed to the care of his assistants. Mr. Zero then left Boston. For the next six weeks, his associates managed the Hotel Jobless, providing shelter and food to hundreds of unemployed workingmen.[48]

Ledoux himself went to New York, where he proclaimed his intention to hold a new round of slave auctions on the steps of the New York Public Library. The auctions were scheduled to begin after a parade down Broadway that Ledoux planned to lead while carrying an umbrella on which was printed his motto "Lift Up Your Hearts." But the reception that Ledoux received in New York was far more hostile than anything that he had encountered in Massachusetts. Fearful that Ledoux could spark even more disorder than he had in Boston, the commissioner of public welfare denounced him as an "exceedingly plausible but dangerous man." City officials denied him a permit to hold any auctions or rallies, and, when he attempted to distribute food to the jobless in Bryant Park, the police intervened and severely beat many of the intended recipients of his largesse. Nonetheless, the very threat of Ledoux's slave auctions prompted municipal authorities to take immediate steps to improve public and private programs for the homeless and the jobless. After witnessing these efforts and after several meetings with city and church officials, Ledoux declared himself to be satisfied, called off the scheduled auctions, and conducted a community sing with Harry Barnhardt in Central Park.[49]

On September 25, Ledoux announced that he was going to Washington to see President Warren G. Harding. He wanted both to discuss the unemployment problem with the president and to ask Harding to publish a list of "war profiteers." Ledoux proclaimed that he would, if necessary, "sit on the threshold" of the White House until Harding agreed to receive him. Ledoux left for Washington on the night of the twenty-fifth, and the very next day President Harding granted him an interview. The president "was most kind and courteous," according to Ledoux, although Harding declined to publish a list of persons who had profited excessively during the war.[50]

After his audience with the president, Ledoux remained in Washington to attend the President's Conference on Unemployment. (He tried to have himself appointed as the "direct representative" of the unemployed to the conference, but he settled for the status of official "observer.") Testifying at a formal hearing of the conference, Ledoux eloquently described the plight of the homeless unemployed, denounced private employment agencies as "parasites upon the backs of labor," and demanded that the federal government develop a network of offices to help workers find jobs. At the conference, Ledoux also had an impromptu run-in with Samuel Gompers. Encountering one another in the halls of the Commerce Department, Ledoux stopped Gompers and told him that organized labor was not doing enough for the immediate relief of the unemployed. Gompers denied the charge. Ledoux then expressed his hope that capital and labor were "getting together at the conference in a conciliatory spirit." Gompers, according to one newspaper account, replied that "he was not so sure, and related the story of the lion and the lamb in which the lamb found himself being devoured by the lion."[51]

A month later, Ledoux returned to Boston. There, to his dismay, he found the Church of the Unemployed (which had come to be called the Stepping Stone) desperately short of funds, its inhabitants suffering from lack of food and fuel. Angry and disappointed that "the public" had not "done its share," he immediately shut down the shelter at 31 Howard Street and placed across the front of the building a sign that read "closed until Boston regains its sense of God." Then, taking a page from the book of Morrison Swift, he led thirty-eight homeless men on a march from Howard Street to the luxurious Copley-Plaza Hotel. The men entered the lobby, and Ledoux went to the front desk to ask for accommodations. He explained who the men were and why the Stepping Stone had been shut down.

> But we are a Christian people, and this is a Christian hotel, and so we come to you and we ask that you give shelter to these men who are without work, through no fault of their own; without food and without a roof to shield them from the rain or walls to protect them from the cold. Between us we have $5.39 which we have placed in one fund. Aside from this our credentials are from the word of God.

Ledoux proceeded to cite sixteen relevant verses from the Gospel according to Saint Matthew. Although the desk clerk appeared moved, he nonetheless replied that there was not a vacant room in the house. The men received the same answer at the Hotel Touraine. When they asked if they could sleep on the "thick, soft, warm" carpets in the public parlors, they were told that it was "out of the question." The "shorn lambs" ended up spending the night at the Salvation Army. Disturbed by the treatment that his flock had received, Ledoux threatened to revive the slave auctions to bring Boston to its senses. But he changed his mind and, within a few days, abandoned the city altogether. Boston, in his eyes, remained unredeemed.[52]

With the closing of the Stepping Stone, the Massachusetts chapter in Ledoux's life came to an end. Later that same year, however, Ledoux again attracted the spotlight of national public attention. In December 1921, he appeared in Washington to picket an international conference on the limitation of armaments. Carrying his umbrella, a copy of the Bible, and a lighted lantern, Ledoux marched up and down in front of the Pan American Union building, claiming to be in search of an "honest man" or a "Christian delegate" to the conference. He was arrested for disorderly conduct, but the charges were dismissed. He then tried, unsuccessfully, to have the delegates to the conference arrested for "trafficking in stolen goods": the territories that the United States and the European powers "illegally" controlled. On December 27, Ledoux announced that he had finally found an honest man, and, in a Washington hotel room, he presented his lantern to the aging socialist leader, Eugene Victor Debs.[53]

A postscript: Quixotic as Urbain Ledoux undeniably was, his dedication to the unemployed and his concern for world peace were not simply passing fancies. Throughout the 1920s and into the 1930s, he devoted much of his energy to helping the poor and the unemployed on New York's Bowery. There, he established a home for the jobless and spent his winter holidays standing in the cold, doling out stew, soup, and coffee to anyone who was hungry. He ceased these efforts only when the public relief programs of the New Deal were able to provide comparable care for his constituents. In 1930, he married an actress whom he had met while conducting the slave auctions in Boston. Five years later, the two of them went to Latin America, where they made movies, in Spanish, to promote Ledoux's vision of universal peace and brotherhood. Mr. Zero died in 1941.[54]

Confrontation and redemption

The differences between the protests led by Morrison Swift and the demonstrations orchestrated by Urbain Ledoux stand out clearly in even the briefest of narratives. Swift's protest movements were secular and anticapitalist in their vision; Ledoux's Church of the Unemployed was Christian, communitarian, and patriotic. Swift's strategy for advancing the interests of the unemployed was, at heart, confrontational. Ledoux's slave auctions, in contrast, were an appeal to the middle-class conscience through the use of a dramatic and resonant historical metaphor. The men who marched to the State House under Swift's command were asserting their economic "rights," demanding immediate institutional reforms as well as sweeping structural changes to guarantee those rights. The "shorn lambs of labor" were pleading with Boston to be more generous in its treatment of the neediest residents of the city, many of whom were veterans of an overseas war.

Despite these pronounced differences, the protests led by Swift and Ledoux had several important, and revealing, elements in common. Among them was the fact that all the demonstrations – with the possible exception of the "invasion of the State House" – were essentially theatrical rather than coercive. They were displays of anger and despair rather than tests of strength. Even Swift's confrontations with public authorities were more symbolic than threatening. The theatrical nature of these protests meant, of course, that they were aimed at audiences rather than targets, and the audiences were invariably the same: public officials, middle-class citizens, and the press. That this was so was a direct reflection of the limited strategic options available to jobless workers. In sufficient numbers, they could be disruptive, but, as a group, the unemployed had no power in the marketplace and very little at the ballot box. Lacking such power, there was not much that the unemployed could do other than to dramatize their grievances and vocalize their discontents – on the Common, at the State House, in the Copley-Plaza, or in front of the Algonquin Club.

The two leaders of these demonstrations also shared certain characteristics: they were both men with strongly held convictions who stood far from the mainstream of American politics, were outsiders to Boston, and had no significant organizational affiliations or backing. How did it arise that two such men led all the major protests of the unemployed in Boston prior to the 1930s? The answer appears to reside, in part, in the very willingness of Swift and Ledoux to try to organize the jobless, a willingness that was not displayed by trade unions, the dominant political parties, or most social reformers. The patterns of protest activity in Boston between 1894 and 1921 strongly suggest that some unemployed workers stood ready to participate in public demonstrations if they were offered determined and vocal leadership. In the 1890s, thousands of men were marching with Morrison Swift within weeks of his first appearance on the Common. In 1921, Ledoux's slave auctions began only days after he had arrived in Boston. The unemployed may have been politically isolated and fragmented, but there were a fair number, during depressions at least, who could be mobilized into collective action by a forceful champion of their cause.

Both Swift and Ledoux, moreover, presented the unemployed with attractive and powerful rhetorical programs. They gave voice to the anger of jobless workers while simultaneously offering them the possibility of immediate relief and an inspiring vision of social change. The jobless men who gathered on the Common were told that they were victims but not helpless victims. They could, by acting in concert, improve their material circumstances and contribute to the emergence of a more just social order: the socialism of Swift or the universal brotherhood envisioned by Ledoux. The success of these two tribunes of the unemployed may also have stemmed from their ability to couch their programs, and even their indictments of American society, in language and symbols that stressed traditional American values and touched traditional taproots of working-class protest. Ledoux's slave auctions, of course, were an explicit evocation of a social injustice that American society had recognized and rectified; his appeal to Christian morality was also an appeal to the abolitionist heritage of which New Englanders were so proud. And even Swift's more radical agenda was usually – although not always – clothed in patriotic garb. The "right" to work, like other fundamental rights, was to be guaranteed by the Constitution. State farms for the unemployed – a latter-day version of homesteads in the West – would provide a semblance of the agrarian self-sufficiency that played such a large role in the nation's democratic self-image.[55]

One additional, if more speculative, factor may have further contributed to the ability of Swift and Ledoux to rally the unemployed. The men who responded to their calls for action may have identified with, or felt an affinity for, these leaders precisely because Swift and Ledoux themselves stood on the fringes of society. The experience of unemployment, particularly prolonged unemployment, was intrinsically an alienating one, and fragmentary evidence suggests that many of the workingmen who joined these protests were very much "outsiders." They were homeless men who slept on the Common because they had no kin and few friends in Boston; unskilled and semiskilled workers who did not belong to unions; new arrivals in town with no neighborhood connections; militant socialists who had little to do with mainstream political culture. These men were estranged from the dominant institutions of Massachusetts society, and their estrangement may, perhaps, have drawn them to leaders who stood apart from and had personally rejected those institutions.[56]

The protests of the unemployed that took place in Boston between 1894 and 1921 shared another feature as well: they resulted in few concrete gains for the protestors themselves or for other jobless workers. Demonstrations aimed directly at middle-class citizens often produced an immediate outpouring of donations, but, as Urbain Ledoux discovered, those outpourings slowed to a trickle once the initial tumult had subsided and the spotlight of public attention had dimmed. Similarly, protests directed at public officials commonly gave rise to earnest promises and lengthy investigations rather than funds or new programs for the unemployed. Politicians, on the whole, seem to have been far more interested in deflecting or defusing protest than they were in developing substantial methods of aiding the jobless. None of the major reforms advocated by either Swift or Ledoux were implemented prior to the 1930s.

Still, the energies of Swift, Ledoux, and the thousands of men who flocked to the Boston Common were not expended in vain. Their protests succeeded in producing better treatment for the homeless; they gave rise to pathbreaking studies of the problem of unemployment; they elicited contributions for relief at moments when cash was needed and in short supply. Swift's rallies in 1894 spurred the labor movement into action, and his demonstrations at the Chamber of Commerce and the Algonquin Club in 1914 helped to prod the business community into developing a program for reducing the incidence of joblessness. In the latter year, as well as in 1921, the protests that took place also contributed to the development of countercyclical public works projects.[57]

Most importantly, these demonstrations served to focus attention upon the issue of governmental responsibility for the unemployed. Long before social reformers had begun to seriously tackle the problem and long before organized labor had softened its adherence to voluntarism, the protesting unemployed were addressing their grievances to the state. The followers of Morrison Swift, and later Urbain Ledoux, loudly and publicly proclaimed that society as a whole, through state institutions, ought to take responsibility for the welfare of men and women who were involuntarily out of work. In advancing this view, the protestors were ahead of their time, but the demonstrations that they participated in were sufficiently large and militant that public officials had to take notice. It was a fact of no small significance that the governors of Massachusetts felt obliged to meet with Morrison Swift in 1894, 1908, and 1914 and that Mayor Peters (not to mention President Harding) met with Urbain Ledoux in 1921. These elected officials may not have endorsed the proposals that the protestors put forward, but they tacitly acknowledged that those proposals were worthy of consideration and that something had to be done to aid the jobless. Politically as well as literally, the men who rallied on the Boston Common succeeded in placing the problem of unemployment on the doorstep of government.

9 *"The greatest evil of our competitive industrial system"*

> Gentlemen of the committee, if you solve the question of the unemployed, that is, how to employ them to advantage, you will solve everything else; there will be absolutely no use for those two halls that we have in this building.
>
> Testimony of W. S. Isidor, at the State House, 1903

> Until recent years the problem of unemployment in the United States, except during comparatively brief and infrequent seasons of industrial inactivity, has received but scant and inadequate attention. Occasionally demonstrations by large numbers of the unemployed who have congregated in urban centers . . . have called brief public attention to this phase of industrial life. At such times, temporary and merely palliative remedies have been offered, only to be summarily dismissed from thought as soon as the disturbances have ceased.
>
> Massachusetts Bureau of Labor Statistics, 1915[1]

The evolution of unemployment policy had an unmistakably cyclical rhythm. Local and state officials paid little or no attention to the joblessness of workers during upswings in the economy, but every depression or "panic" gave rise to a frenetic, if brief, burst of concern and activity. Responding both to protests and to the visible suffering of thousands of people, public authorities, during depressions, typically launched both emergency relief programs and investigations of the problem of unemployment. Just as typically, the relief programs were cut back or dismantled as soon as the economy showed signs of recovering. And the results of the investigations – usually published only after the crisis had passed – were almost invariably ignored.

Despite this cyclical pattern, significant changes in the public responses to unemployment did occur during the half-century that followed the panic of 1873. Public authorities became increasingly willing to accept responsibility for the maintenance of the unemployed, while efforts to provide relief to jobless workers became more energetic. Understandings of the issue deepened, and a growing number of middle-class citizens – both in and out of government – came to

250

the conclusion that the state had to create permanent institutions to cope with the problem. In the 1870s and 1880s, the phenomenon of involuntary idleness was sufficiently unfamiliar to Massachusetts officials that they were obliged to coin a new word to describe it. By 1915, their successors, all too familiar with the problem and the word, were considering the merits of policies that were to have a profound impact upon American political and economic life for the remainder of the twentieth century.

Lag time: 1870–1907

Despite the insistent presence of unemployment in the lives and thought of working people, middle-class citizens and public officials displayed little interest in the problem during the final decades of the nineteenth century. Only during depressions did the leading newspapers and magazines in Massachusetts mention the subject, and even then coverage of the issue was skimpy and sporadic. Republican and Democratic politicians alike rarely alluded to the presence of jobless workers in the commonwealth; not until 1894 did the state legislature entertain a bill that referred explicitly to the "unemployed." Throughout this period, there were no permanent public agencies, other than the police and the Overseers of the Poor, to which unemployed men and women could turn for aid.[2]

This disinterest reflected the reluctance or inability of the middle class to believe that a new social problem had emerged in Massachusetts. Living as they did at a considerable social, and often geographic, distance from the working class, the state's more prosperous residents had little firsthand acquaintance with the burdens of joblessness. Moreover, their convictions and values – their trust in the efficacy of work, the justice of the marketplace, and the availability of economic opportunities – made it difficult for them to accept, or even register, the fact that jobs did not exist for all able-bodied and willing workers. No one doubted that business panics occasionally threw some men and women out of work, but it was widely believed that these were transient episodes, affecting a small number of workers, who found new jobs in short order. If a worker was idled repeatedly or for a prolonged period of time, it was almost certainly his own choice or his own fault. In 1878, after five years of economic depression, as enlightened a figure as Carroll Wright, the chief of the Bureau of Statistics of Labor, was convinced that only a portion of the idled were workers who "really want employment." A few years later, the Associated Charities of Boston, a far from benighted organization, declared emphatically that "there is work for all somewhere."[3]

These convictions were buttressed by the most prominent economic theories of the era. Classical economists, both in Europe and the United States, treated unemployment as a transitory and essentially insignificant phenomenon. They recognized that employers did sometimes lay workers off, because of slack demand for their goods and because of changing methods of production, but they emphasized that these were temporary dislocations that would be cured automatically, and rapidly, by the play of market forces. If the demand for labor declined, then wages would fall, and employers would soon find it to be profitable to hire additional workers. If new machinery reduced the need for labor in one industry, workers would shift their allegiances to other industries. Any jobs that were chronically unsteady had to offer relatively high wage rates, or they could not attract workers at all. The implication of such reasoning was that unemployment could become a serious problem only if – and when – workers themselves refused to obey the dictates of the market. Men and women willing to accept wage cuts, to transfer from one industry to another, to leave town and move elsewhere, would never be out of work for long. The responsibility for sustained idleness, therefore, rested largely on the shoulders of the working class itself.[4]

The public inattention that greeted the problem of unemployment also stemmed from prevailing beliefs regarding the appropriate role of the state in economic affairs. Although economic issues figured prominently in the politics of the era, as the battles over the currency and the tariff clearly attest, the years between 1870 and 1900 nonetheless constituted the heyday of laissez-faire, of the conviction that government could best promote prosperity by not interfering with the conduct of private business. The national government was not expected to tamper with the rhythms of economic life; relations between employers and employees were shielded against local, state, and federal intervention by law as well as by popular ideology. Similarly, public authorities in Massachusetts were asked to play only a minimal role in aiding the poor. Municipalities (and residually, the state) had traditionally assumed responsibility for the maintenance of the helpless poor (the infirm, the insane, orphans, and some of the elderly), but little historical precedent existed for public aid to the able-bodied. Indeed, most "respectable" citizens agreed that public support for the able-bodied poor could only weaken the social fabric by undercutting the self-reliance of working people. According to one charity organization, "outdoor" relief (given to men and women who were not placed in custodial institutions) "creates a dependent feeling – a sort of moral dry rot – which leads the recipient . . . to look upon it as something due, as a reward for destitution." Such

ideas, embraced by Republicans and Democrats alike, served to keep
the subject of unemployment outside the realm of political discourse.
Even if the problem did exist, there was, by common agreement, little
that government could do about it.[5]

This constellation of beliefs and understandings led public authorities to respond to depressions – when the problem of unemployment
became acute and unavoidable – in ways that were hesitant, con-
fused, and ambivalent. Deeply ingrained preconceptions collided
with a changing social reality. The result was an assortment of policies that pulled in two directions simultaneously. Faced with unmistakable suffering among their citizens, cities and towns sought to fulfill their traditional responsibilities to the poor by extending aid to
the "new" poor: men and women who were able-bodied but jobless.
At the same time, communities everywhere tried strenuously to limit
their obligations and to discourage applications for relief.[6]

This ambivalence was highly visible during the long economic
downturn of the 1870s. In response to the hardships experienced by
the unemployed, local officials dispensed food, fuel, clothing, and
shelter to able-bodied men and women who were out of work. The
number of persons receiving "outdoor" relief from the Overseers of
the Poor increased dramatically; in a few cities, including Boston,
small public works projects were launched as well. The depression
also tapped the humanitarian impulses of private citizens. Charitable
organizations expanded their activities significantly during these
years, and the state witnessed the formation of several large private
agencies (including the Associated Charities of Boston and the Union
Relief Association of Springfield) that aimed to provide for men and
women who could not be adequately helped by the Overseers of the
Poor.[7]

Yet there was also a harsher, more disciplinary, side to the treatment of the unemployed in the 1870s and in the 1880s. Both because
funds were scarce and to insure that workers could not live as well
on relief as they could on their wages, aid was meted out to the jobless in extremely small quantities. In addition, most of the unemployed were compelled to demonstrate their worthiness by performing a "work test" (such as shoveling gravel) in order to obtain any
help at all. "Happily, we have the woodyard to which to send men in
case of extreme need from loss of work," announced the Associated
Charities of Boston in 1883. (See Figure 5.2.) Similarly, the state government's primary response to the unemployed was the passage of
anti-tramp legislation that served not to help the jobless but rather to
discipline "shirkers." (See Chapter 5.) The actions of both public authorities and private charities were shaped by the fear of giving aid

to the unworthy and by the conviction that relief, if given too freely, would transform industrious workers into permanently dependent paupers.[8]

This mixture of compassion and fear, of charity and suspicion, persisted into the 1890s. On the one hand, the severe depression that began in 1893 led to relief efforts that were unprecedented in scale. In communities throughout the commonwealth, from the fall of 1893 until late in the decade, local officials and a growing number of charitable agencies offered aid to jobless men and women who had exhausted their own resources. Several cities also created emergency committees to raise funds and administer the delivery of relief. In Boston, the Citizens' Relief Committee appointed by the mayor raised, and spent, more than one hundred thousand dollars during the winter of 1893-4 alone. Special relief programs were designed for women in some communities, and in 1895 the Industrial Aid Society, borrowing an idea from the city of Detroit, offered garden plots to the jobless so they could grow their own food. At the same time, many cities and towns either accelerated or created municipal construction projects to generate jobs. In 1894 the state government itself took a gingerly step toward aiding the unemployed when the governor recommended that the Metropolitan Parks Commission begin work, ahead of schedule, on a series of improvements to the boulevards and parks around Boston.[9]

On the other hand, the relief efforts of the 1890s retained a very sharp disciplinary edge. Able-bodied applicants for aid were viewed with suspicion, and relief programs accordingly were crafted to insure that the slothful and the "unworthy" did not enjoy the benefits of charity. Relief continued to be given in tiny amounts, usually in the form of goods rather than cash; residency requirements were invoked to avoid helping transients; and many agencies insisted on investigating the backgrounds of all applicants for support. In Boston, the emergency relief program was even accompanied by a widespread publicity campaign cautioning private citizens not "to give money or food to persons who ask it in the street, at the door, or in the business office." "Hard times increase also the number of unworthy persons who ask aid," warned a circular signed by seventeen charitable organizations in the metropolitan area. "The unworthy poor were more clamorous than ever," reported the Associated Charities of Boston in 1895. "The police have proved of the greatest service."[10]

Whenever possible, both government authorities and charitable organizations also demanded that relief applicants do some work in return for any aid they received. (See Figure 9.1.) In theory, these work requirements were to serve several purposes simultaneously:

Figure 9.1. The Bedford Street workroom for unemployed women, *Harper's Weekly*, March 3, 1894. (Drawing by Henry Sandham.)

they would weed out the "lazy," harness the energies of the unemployed in the production of socially useful goods, and preserve the self-respect of workers who would otherwise feel pauperized by outright donations of food, fuel, and clothing. But, in practice, as the dispensers of relief quickly discovered, it was exceedingly difficult to create productive jobs that did not compete either with ongoing municipal projects or with private enterprise. Consequently, applicants for relief usually found themselves performing tasks that served no purpose other than to demonstrate their own desperate need and their willingness to work. Chopping wood and crushing stone were common work tests throughout the state, while in Boston men who were too old or too weak to perform arduous physical labor were given the job of making rag carpets. The selection of this particular activity was explained by Charles S. Miller, a member of the Citizens' Relief Committee:

> We had to employ them in some work that was from an economical sense useless. We could not employ them in making things that would interfere with other people, and that is why we adopted the absurd alternative in one respect of making rag carpets because nobody wants rag carpets and therefore we could make them without interfering with anybody's industry.

As might be expected, the requirement that men and women perform useless and humiliating labor did succeed admirably in keeping a ceiling on the number of applicants for relief – a fact that officials reported with considerable satisfaction.[11]

Despite such practices, the depression of the 1890s did witness something of a breakthrough in middle-class thinking about the problem of involuntary idleness. The severity of the depression convinced many well-to-do citizens that honest, industrious workers were sometimes jobless through no fault of their own. And the scale of the relief programs constituted a formal, if tacit, public acknowledgment that unemployment was, in part, a social problem rather than an expression of individual failure. The experience of mounting large-scale relief efforts under emergency conditions also led some public officials, reformers, and charity activists to conclude that existing institutions could not adequately respond to the legitimate needs of the unemployed.

This shift in thought was promoted and recorded by the Board to Investigate the Subject of the Unemployed, the commission formed by the state legislature in the wake of Morrison Swift's "invasion of the State House" in 1894. The three-man commission, headed by economist Davis R. Dewey, held hearings in cities and towns throughout Massachusetts, collecting thousands of pages of testimony and evidence from ministers, public officials, businessmen, officers of charitable societies, trade unionists, rank-and-file workers, and spokesmen for a host of political viewpoints. The board's final report, published in 1895, was a massive, detailed examination of the causes of unemployment and the types of relief available to working people. Both the appointment of the commission and its final report were small milestones in the history of public policy toward unemployment.[12]

Two substantive features of the board's written report (and the hearings that preceded it) are noteworthy. First, the board seriously explored the proposition that local governments ought to respond to panics and depressions with large-scale public works programs. This idea, advocated by organized labor among others, flew in the face of prevailing conceptions of the appropriate role of government. Nonetheless, its virtues became increasingly apparent as the commission gathered information on the administration of relief during the winter of 1893–4. If public agencies were going to aid the unemployed during depressions, and if, as was argued, jobless men and women ought to perform some labor in return for such aid, then it seemed far more sensible to build roads or canals than to oblige the unemployed to chop wood or make rag carpets. In the end, the board did not embrace the idea of public works, largely because most municipal officials felt that they were inefficient and prohibitively expensive.

But the notion that public payrolls could be increased to compensate for declines in private employment had entered the arena of mainstream debate.[13]

Second, the board recommended that public authorities enact "permanent measures" to reduce unemployment levels in Massachusetts. It endorsed six specific steps: eliminating competition from convict labor; reducing the daily hours of work; restricting immigration; improving or replacing the private employment agencies that existed in most cities; extending industrial education programs; and removing city residents to the country. None of these proposals was particularly new or radical: the first four had been discussed in labor circles since the mid-1880s. But coming as it did from a formal government commission, the board's list of "permanent measures" was nothing less than pathbreaking. It implied both that the problem of unemployment was permanent and that public authorities were obliged to assume some responsibility for combating it.[14]

The breadth of this shift in thought ought not be exaggerated. Regardless of the conclusions reached by the board, many citizens, particularly in the business community, remained convinced that few jobless workers were genuinely in need of aid merely because of the economic downturn. "I don't think there was very much suffering last winter," claimed D. B. Wesson, of Smith and Wesson in Springfield, in the spring of 1894. "There are a great many men who have earned large wages that haven't saved a dollar," observed Preston Keith, the owner of the second largest factory in Brockton. "The thrifty, intelligent man ought to be able . . . to make enough savings in a year to carry him through a bad year," echoed Rodney Wallace, the treasurer of the Fitchburg Paper Mill. A sizable segment of the business community also adamantly opposed the use of public funds to support the jobless poor. "I don't believe in people getting the idea that the city or state is going to take care of them," insisted James Ramage, a paper manufacturer from Holyoke. Henry Faxon, a businessman from Quincy, advised state officials to "keep the people sober that ask for relief, and you will have no relief asked for."[15]

Accompanying this skepticism (and hostility) was massive public indifference to the plight of the unemployed. Members of the Citizens' Relief Committee of Boston may have been deeply disturbed by the presence of thousands of jobless workers in the city, but a large majority of Boston's most prosperous residents declined to contribute any money at all to help the unemployed. Late in the winter of 1894, when the relief committee was desperately short of funds, it issued an urgent appeal for donations to the people of Boston. The appeal was largely ignored while, at precisely the same time, residents of the city were expending $75,000 in nine days to hear two entertainers at the Music Hall. Newspapers throughout Massachusetts also seemed to be only marginally interested in the issue: although the Boston *Globe* provided ample coverage of the exploits of Morrison Swift, in the spring of 1894, after the tumult had subsided, it devoted far less space to the grinding poverty of the unemployed than it did to a breach-of-promise suit brought by Madeline Pollard against Colonel Breckenridge.[16]

This indifference was further manifested in institutional and political inertia. Although local officials did what they could to cope with emergency conditions, they displayed little interest in setting up permanent machinery to help the unemployed. Neither state nor county authorities succeeded in creating work for the jobless at any point during the depression, and no action was taken by the state government on the recommendations put forward by the legislature's much-heralded special commission. Aside from several minor modifications of the anti-tramp laws, the only unemployment bill to emerge from the state legislature between 1893 and 1898 was the bill that created the Board to Investigate the Subject of the Unemployed.[17]

With the return of prosperity, the problem of unemployment virtually disappeared from public view for nearly a decade. In the absence of either a severe economic crisis or active protest movements, neither local officials nor private citizens paid much attention to the demands of organized labor, to the reams of statistics published in the 1895 census reports, or to the policy suggestions that had been put forward by the board. Newspapers and magazines made few references to the problem of unemployment between 1897 and 1907. Perhaps most telling, the Bureau of Statistics of Labor, hoping perhaps that unemployment would turn out to have been a nineteenth-century phenomenon, decided not to tabulate the unemployment statistics that had been collected as a part of the 1905 state census.[18]

The state's lawmakers too acted as though there were few lessons to be learned from the depression of the 1890s. The state government was dominated by the Republican Party, which unabashedly represented the business interests of the commonwealth and saw little need for innovative legislation that might aid the unemployed. Led by Murray Crane and Henry Cabot Lodge, the Republicans insisted, as they had for decades, that the welfare of wage earners depended primarily upon the maintenance of a gold-backed currency and a sound tariff policy. Although the legislature did contain representatives more sympathetic to the views of labor (some Democrats, a handful of Republicans from factory districts, and a few socialists), the working class was too weak and politically divided to control or even seriously influence any branch of the state government. The working-class vote tended to split along ethnic lines, with the Irish voting Democratic while "new" immigrants and older-stock Protestants generally voted Republican. And many immigrant workers, either recently arrived or intending to return home, were not citizens and did not vote at all. Consequently, labor's allies on Beacon Hill were always far too few in number to secure the passage of legislation that challenged the interests and beliefs of the governing elite. During the mild economic downturn of 1903–4, George Schofield, a Democrat from Ipswich, sponsored a bill that would have permitted cities and towns to establish reserve funds to be used for public works projects "in times of business depression." The bill was soundly defeated in the house, as were two more radical public works measures introduced by socialists. Similarly, bills that aimed to reduce the hours of labor were routinely stalled in the state Senate or vetoed by whatever (usually Republican) governor happened to be in office.[19]

The sole exception to this pattern of inactivity was the enactment of a law in 1906 that authorized the Bureau of Statistics of Labor to create Free Employment Offices in selected cities around the state. For more than a decade, trade unionists and reformers had urged the passage of such a law, claiming that publicly run free employment offices would serve two worthwhile purposes. They would help working people escape from the clutches of private, fee-charging "intelligence offices" that were notorious for their unscrupulous treatment of needy job applicants – "leeches engaged in sucking the life blood from the poor," one critic called them. It was also argued that free employment offices would reduce unemployment levels by efficiently placing jobless workers in contact with employers who had positions available. The first Free Employment Office opened in Boston in December 1906; branches were established in Springfield and Fall River during the following year. (See Figure 9.2.) These offices were modest enterprises that could, at best, expedite the process of job hunting for idled workers in a few locales. Nevertheless, they constituted the state government's first effort to erect permanent institutions to serve the unemployed.[20]

The creation of State Free Employment Offices was a step forward in the emergence of an unemployment policy in Massachusetts. But it was a small, cautious, and indirect step, coming after decades of inaction. Halfway through the Progressive era, public authorities remained altogether passive and reactive in their approach to unemployment: they dealt with the issue only when it was forced upon them. Although workers were preoccupied with the problem, as they

Figure 9.2. Scene in front of the State Free Employment Office on Kneeland Street, Boston, 1915. (From Dennison House papers; courtesy Schlesinger Library, Radcliffe College.)

had been since the 1870s, neither their interests nor their sense of urgency were shared by the state's more powerful and affluent residents. Outside labor circles, the issue was rarely debated or even discussed. Some things, to be sure, had changed since the 1870s: the problem had an agreed-upon name; certain traditional assumptions had eroded; new ideas had been placed into circulation; the state government had broken its silence and begun to respond to an issue that had earlier been treated as a purely local matter. But, on the whole, the fact that hundreds of thousands of workers were unemployed each year seemed – from the written record of middle-class responses – to have been one of the best-kept secrets in Massachusetts.

There was, however, an important subplot to this tale of passivity and neglect. Several cities in the commonwealth did contain political figures who were acutely aware of the needs of the unemployed and responsive to them. These were the Democratic machine politicians, the ward heelers, the urban bosses, who flourished in Boston, Lawrence, Fall River, and a few other communities in the late nineteenth and early twentieth centuries. From working-class, and usually Irish, backgrounds themselves, these men were entirely familiar with the chronic irregularity of work in the cities of Massachusetts. Martin Lomasney, the "mahatma" of Boston's West End, did not have to pore through the census reports to learn that 40 percent of all Irish men were unemployed each year. Turn-of-the-century readers of the *Globe* and *Transcript* may not have known that joblessness was a pressing issue in prosperous times, but the young James Michael Curley held individual meetings, at least twice a week, with unemployed men from his council district.[21]

Democratic bosses like Lomasney, Curley, and John Breen of Lawrence did lend a helping hand to jobless workers. Political machines were built upon highly personalized constituent service, and one of the key services that machine politicians provided was aid to the unemployed. Ward bosses dispensed cash, food, and credit to families that were in need due to loss of work. Of equal or greater importance, they obtained city jobs for their unemployed, or irregularly employed, constituents. Municipal payrolls were growing rapidly during this period, and positions with the city were desirable not just because they were jobs but also because they were unusually steady and secure jobs. The best position that an unskilled Irish laborer could hope to obtain was a job as a city laborer. Even skilled workers sometimes abandoned their seasonal trades in favor of the security of the police or fire departments. Such jobs were controlled by politicians and constituted the currency in which political machines transacted much of their business. At one point, members of Lomasney's Hendricks Club accounted for $80,000 of the city payroll of Boston; even before Curley became mayor, he was obtaining five hundred jobs a year for residents of his district. Early in his career, in fact, Curley went to jail for ninety days because he was caught taking a civil service examination for a constituent who wanted a job in the post office. Although the event scandalized political reformers in Boston, it greatly increased Curley's popularity in his own ward.[22]

The machine politicians who controlled working-class wards in Boston and other cities did not possess or offer a solution to the social problem of unemployment. But they were far more alert and responsive to the issue than were the Republicans who sat on Beacon Hill. That these politicians themselves benefited from aiding the unemployed was both undeniable and undisguised. Jobs were handed out as rewards for political loyalty, and a jobholder was expected to work actively for the politician who had arranged his berth. "According to the ethics of the district," noted a settlement house resident in Boston, "a man who receives a job is under the most sacred obligations to the politician who bestowed it." Political power gave the machine politician the ability to control and dispense jobs, and that ability was itself a critical source of power in a society with chronically high levels of unemployment. Urban political machines emerged and flourished in a world where jobs were scarce and where the threat of layoffs was omnipresent. The strength of those machines was part of the price that respectable Massachusetts had to pay for ignoring the problem of unemployment.[23]

Reformers and businessmen

> The literature on the subject of unemployment has reached a volume unapproached in any year, at least during the present decade . . . More significant . . . is the change in character of the discussion of the problem itself . . . During the past two years much has been written in an endeavor to bring to public attention constructive plans for the ultimate solution of the problem through the adoption of permanent measures not confined to any single locality or industry.
>
> Massachusetts Bureau of Statistics of Labor, 1915

> It seems to me that the happy contented employment of the people is a desirable thing on the part of the commonwealth and that everything that the state can do to contribute to such a condition of affairs, it ought to do and it is a legitimate function of the state to do.
>
> Charles J. Gettemy, commissioner of labor statistics, 1916

> Every manufacturer is beginning to recognize that regular and steady business throughout the year is of vital importance to his success.
>
> Boston Chamber of Commerce, November 25, 1914[24]

A sea change in middle-class thinking about unemployment took place between 1908 and the early 1920s. It was during this period that the chronic dimension of the problem came to be widely recognized, that the recurrence of depressions became an acknowledged fact of economic life, that the links between joblessness and poverty began to attract sustained attention. After 1907, the state of Massachusetts collected unemployment statistics every three months, the number of books and magazine articles published on the subject rose dramat- ically, and debates regarding unemployment policy were heard in the State House even in the absence of Morrison Swift. In striking con- trast to the climate of opinion that prevailed in 1880 or 1900, the com- monwealth, by the end of the Progressive era, contained a good many social critics, reformers, and public officials who were con- vinced that unemployment was neither an episodic occurrence nor a sign of personal failure but rather "the greatest evil of our competi- tive industrial system."[25]

The immediate precipitant of this shift was the panic of 1907–8. That brief, yet severe, business downturn produced widespread and visible suffering, renewed protests from the unemployed, and sharp outcries from a labor movement that was institutionally and politi- cally stronger than it had been during any previous depression. These developments delivered a jolt to the early-twentieth-century optimism of many of the Bay State's more affluent residents. Coming as it did after ten years of more or less uninterrupted prosperity, the panic of 1907 seemed to shatter an unspoken hope that depressions were a thing of the past, that the economic and political tumult of the 1890s would not be replayed in the twentieth century. The panic came as a psychological shock and served as a warning. The problem of unemployment was not going to disappear, and someone was going to have to do something about it.

The panic of 1907 also exposed the fact that joblessness was becom- ing a more serious social problem. Although unemployment rates did not rise during the first two decades of the twentieth century, the *number* of workers who were unemployed each year, and during each depression, did increase. In all likelihood, the commonwealth housed many more jobless workers during the winter of 1907–8 than it had during the grim winter of 1893–4. There were probably twice as many unemployed men and women in Massachusetts during the downturn of 1913–14 as there had been during any year of the 1870s. Moreover, the visible poverty induced by joblessness may have been growing even more rapidly than the number of unemployed workers – since, as noted in Chapter 6, unemployment was gradually becom- ing a more harsh and difficult experience. The heightened public awareness of the issue did, then, have a material basis. The unem- ployment problem that confronted officials and charitable organiza- tions was increasing in size, and, at some point early in the twentieth century, it seems to have attained a critical mass that made it impos- sible to ignore.[26]

Other, less tangible, factors played a role as well. One was a pronounced shift in formal understandings of the economic sources of unemployment. Between 1908 and 1920, empirical research led some economists to conclude (and to argue persuasively) that fluctuations in business were inherent to capitalism, that rather than being aberrant events depressions were phases in an ongoing cyclical process of expansion and contraction. Wesley Mitchell's famous *Business Cycles* was published in 1913, and the concept of the "business cycle" soon supplanted the more episodic notion of "panics." This new understanding implied, of course, that severe outbreaks of unemployment would recur periodically and were intrinsic to the workings of the economy. At roughly the same time, the influential writings of William Beveridge in England were illuminating the systemic sources of chronic unemployment. In *Unemployment: A Problem of Industry*, first published in 1909, Beveridge argued that the maintenance of labor "reserves" in individual industries produced unsteady employment for a large proportion of the working class even during prosperous years. Although some of this joblessness, he argued, was unavoidable and necessary, much of it was a wasteful consequence of poorly organized labor markets. Beveridge's ideas crossed the Atlantic quickly, prompting studies of seasonal unemployment and labor reserves in the United States. These studies, like those conducted on the behavior of business cycles, lifted the responsibility for joblessness from the shoulders of the working class. Unemployment became a recognized and important phenomenon in formal economic thought, a "problem of industry" and institutions, a characteristic – yet, to some degree, preventable – feature of capitalist economies.[27]

The growth of sustained public interest in unemployment was also nurtured by the broad-gauged impulse for social reform traditionally associated with the Progressive era. Casting aside the nineteenth-century faith in natural laws and laissez-faire, Progressive reformers (as well as many of their less activist contemporaries) adopted a pragmatic, optimistic, and interventionist outlook on social problems. "Evils," such as prostitution, slum housing, industrial accidents, and even poverty itself could be examined, understood, publicized, and remedied. Piecemeal reforms, guided by human intelligence and good will, were both necessary and desirable; the state was, or ought to be, an instrument for actively promoting social change and justice. This new outlook helped pave the way for the polity of Massachusetts to address the issue of unemployment. If the state was responsible for remedying or alleviating the social ills that accompanied industrialization, then joblessness belonged on the agenda for public action.[28]

Both in Massachusetts and elsewhere, the shift in middle-class thinking about unemployment was, in fact, led and promoted by a small group of Progressive reformers. Nationally, the campaign to place the problem of unemployment directly in the public spotlight was spearheaded by the American Association for Labor Legislation. Founded in 1906, intellectually guided by John R. Commons, and supported by a sizable network of politically engaged intellectuals, settlement house workers, and trade union officials, the AALL devoted much of its energy to the development of policies to combat unemployment. Well into the 1920s, its journal, *The American Labor Legislation Review,* was the nation's principal literary arena for the discussion of unemployment policy. In 1914, the AALL sponsored the first two national unemployment conferences to be held in the United States. That same year its members helped to form the American section of the International Association on Unemployment and several affiliated state committees. The Massachusetts Committee on Unemployment was chaired by Robert G. Valentine, a reformer and "industrial counselor." Among its members were Louis Brandeis, Felix Frankfurter, settlement house residents Helena Dudley and Robert Woods, and labor leader Henry Abrahams.[29]

These reformers offered three reasons for their concern with the problem and for their insistence that the state assume responsibility for aiding the unemployed. The first was humanitarian and moral. Year in and year out, unemployment produced suffering and misery for working people: men, women, and children were hungry, cold, ill, and poorly housed because jobs were scarce. Reformers argued that much of the poverty that was being "discovered" in cities like Boston, Lawrence, Brockton, and Fall River was produced less by low weekly wages than by the unsteadiness of work. Armed with reams of data and an increasingly lengthy historical record, men like Commons, John B. Andrews, and William Ewing of Boston also maintained that the vast majority of the jobless were out of work through no fault of their own. "The classes who most suffer by industrial depression are least responsible for it," noted an article in *The Survey* in 1915. "They are unjustly left to bear the brunt of the burden." Solving or alleviating the problem of unemployment was, therefore, a moral obligation that ought to be assumed by the society as a whole.[30]

The call for action did not rest on humanitarian grounds alone: reformers also argued that unemployment was costly to the entire society, that it produced "evil consequences not limited to the individual, but attacking the social structure of which he is a part." Joblessness, they claimed, was directly responsible for a great deal of intemperance, gambling, divorce, and crime. Between 1908 and 1915, reformers noted, there was a close correspondence between unemployment levels and the incidence of crimes against property in Massachusetts. In addition, by contributing to a high rate of poverty, joblessness accelerated the spread of contagious diseases such as tuberculosis. "There is no doubt about it," testified Courtenay Crocker of the Massachusetts Committee on Unemployment in 1916. "Unemployment is the cause of sickness and drunkenness and a great many other evils, for which every year we spend millions of dollars here in the state . . . Simply as insurance against the evils of pauperism and drunkenness and crime it would be well within our duty to put out a large amount of money in trying to prevent the evils of unemployment." Other reformers, most notably Robert Woods, stressed the deleterious impact of unemployment upon the political culture of the commonwealth. "The lack of employment . . . is one of the most important factors working in the interest of the boss and boss rule," Woods warned as early as 1898, a warning that he repeated during the Progressive era. The implication of such arguments, of course, was that solving the problem would benefit the middle class as well as working people.[31]

A third reason that reformers put forward for actively combating unemployment was expressly political: joblessness was producing labor unrest and leading workers to espouse socialism and other radical doctrines. "More good men have been turned into embittered advocates of social revolution by unemployment than by any other single cause," proclaimed Henry R. Seager, the president of the AALL in 1914. Robert Valentine stated the issue more abstractly (and turgidly) in 1915:

> Either we must advance rapidly toward a statewide socialistic control of the bulk of individual action, or else we must make our present freedom of individual action socially legitimate by thoroughgoing organization of social responsibilities; of which the most significant feature would deal with the evils of unemployment.

The fear of socialism was, in fact, a vivid one during this period. The national electoral strength of the Socialist Party was on the increase; the success of the Industrial Workers of the World in Lawrence in 1912 raised the specter of radical uprisings; and the wave of strikes sweeping Massachusetts that same year suggested that the textile operatives of Lawrence were not alone in their discontent. These fears were reinvigorated later in the decade by the Bolshevik Revolution, the Boston police strike, and the publicity surrounding the postwar "Red scare." The notion that capitalism had to be reformed if it was going to be preserved was not a mere rhetorical flourish in the political climate that prevailed between 1912 and 1922.[32]

To preserve American capitalism, enhance the well-being of workers, and restore the health of the social and political order, the men and women who belonged to the AALL and the Massachusetts Committee on Unemployment advocated a multipronged approach to the problem of joblessness. They urged both that steps be taken to prevent unemployment from occurring and that the state assume responsibility for aiding and subsidizing those workers who did lose their jobs. John B. Andrews's *Practical Program for the Prevention of Unemployment in America*, an extremely influential manifesto first published in 1914, called for public employment exchanges, the expansion of public works projects during depressions, alterations in the productive rhythms of seasonal industries, and state-sponsored unemployment insurance. Andrews's *Practical Program*, which was the intellectual starting point for reform agitation in Massachusetts and elsewhere, also advocated a reduction in the hours of labor, an immigration policy sensitive to the dangers of an oversupply of labor, the stimulation of an agricultural revival in the United States, the development of industrial training programs, and the prohibition of industrial employment for boys and girls under the age of sixteen. By acting on most or all of these fronts, reformers believed that state and federal authorities could dramatically reduce the incidence and impact of unemployment.[33]

Progressive social reformers were not alone in their newfound concern with the issue of joblessness. During the second decade of the twentieth century, interest in the problem also began to develop within the state's business community. The businessman most widely known for his efforts to reduce unemployment was Henry S. Dennison, president of the Dennison Manufacturing Company in Framingham. Dennison, a founding member of the Massachusetts Committee on Unemployment, was a pioneer in developing managerial practices to limit the incidence and cushion the impact of joblessness. By 1921, his firm, which manufactured paper boxes, had refined its production and marketing methods to reduce seasonal fluctuations in employment. Much more boldly, it had also established an "unemployment fund" that paid workers a portion of their wages if they had to be laid off. Dennison claimed that such reforms were valuable for two reasons. The first, echoing the concerns of the AALL, was that joblessness was "the greatest cause of social unrest" in American society. The second was that "irregular employment" was inefficient and costly to manufacturers themselves. Dennison argued that the practice of running plants unsteadily, of dismissing workers when trade slackened only to hire new workers when trade picked up again, was not the most profitable way to run a business.[34]

Dennison's concern with the economic cost of unsteady production and the ceaseless "hiring and firing" of workers was widely shared. Throughout the commonwealth, as throughout the country, employers began to display a keen interest in these issues in the years just before World War I. The reasons for this sudden burst of concern are not altogether clear, but "labor turnover" became a much-discussed problem, rather than an obscure phrase, between 1910 and 1915. And during the war years, when turnover rates increased dramatically, the instability of the labor force was perceived by management as a significant threat to the smooth functioning of American industry. Studies of the phenomenon indicated that annual turnover rates in many plants exceeded 200 or sometimes 400 percent even before the war, while a widely cited analysis by Magnus Alexander of the General Electric Company in Lynn suggested that the cost of hiring and training each new employee ranged from $39 to $150. Managers also voiced their dismay about the cost of leaving capital unused during slow seasons and about the losses they suffered because workers habitually restricted output when layoffs were impending. The business practices that were producing high levels of unemployment appeared to be reducing the productivity and profitability of business.[35]

These concerns were publicized, investigated, and translated into policy proposals by a new breed of management experts who specialized in personnel matters and acted as advisers to individual businesses. One such expert was Meyer Bloomfield, a former member of the board of directors of the Industrial Aid Society, who, by 1912, was the publisher of *Bloomfield's Labor Digest* and the director of the Vocation Bureau of Boston. Bloomfield urged managers to steady their rhythms of employment in order to increase the efficiency of their plants. "Reasonable security of employment is the first step in any genuine industrial relations program," Bloomfield wrote. "It is the mother of industrial morale. Joblessness is next to godlessness." Similarly, Robert Valentine's firm (Valentine, Tead, and Gregg) counseled its clients to create personnel departments to control all hiring and firing, a task traditionally entrusted to foremen. A key goal of such departments was to "maintain a steady" work force, to monitor and minimize rates of turnover and layoff. Personnel directors who worked full-time for individual firms also stressed the economic value of a stable labor force. In 1922, C. P. Marshall, who had been hired by the Plymouth Cordage Company to revamp its personnel practices, wrote a lengthy memo to the treasurer of the firm urging that steps be taken to enhance the job security of employees. "The thing that weighs heaviest on the workman is unemployment," he noted.

> This may seem like sentiment but could he feel secure, sure of a job and old age it would mean dollars in dividends. Lighten the laborer's load and he will go faster. Management is handicapped in making improvements many times by the lack of cooperation on the part of the worker not only because of his ignorance but because many times he knows what management is after and fears the loss of a job.[36]

These economic considerations, as well as the "labor unrest" that erupted periodically, also led the Boston Chamber of Commerce to investigate the problem of "irregular employment" in the Boston area. In 1914, the chamber's Committee on Industrial Relations was instructed to study the issue of seasonal employment. The committee wrote for advice to John B. Andrews of the AALL, sent out questionnaires to scores of firms, and hired an investigator to prepare a report on the subject. The questionnaires returned to the committee amply confirmed the chamber's suspicion that the problem warranted attention. Manufacturers in many industries indicated that market forces obliged them to run their plants unsteadily, and they complained vociferously that such practices increased their labor costs. "After a layoff we invariably find their 'hands out,'" noted one cigar manufacturer. The "quick employment of inexperienced help" made it much more expensive to run a factory, observed another employer. Several manufacturers who claimed that their own businesses did run steadily also complained that the prevalence of seasonal employment patterns in their industries drove up daily and weekly wage rates. The committee's report concluded that inefficient managerial practices and the "disorganization of the labor market" were "responsible for much unemployment."[37]

In 1915, the chamber broadened the scope of its inquiry by appointing a Committee on Irregular Employment to suggest "remedies for this condition and for the economic waste involved." The committee was chaired by Magnus Alexander and, for a year at least, counted Robert Valentine as one of its members. Its report, delivered to the chamber in 1916, concluded that two key factors contributed to the irregularity of employment. The first was the nature of the market for manufactured goods, over which businessmen had little control. The second, more susceptible to reform, was "the organization and utilization of the labor market." The committee recommended the creation of a new institution, the labor exchange: a "highly efficient and centrally located organization which will have as its chief purpose not merely to bring some man to some job . . . but to bring together the right job and the right man." In addition, the committee concluded that "greater thought and foresight on the part of individual employers" would "eliminate much of the existing irregularity . . . and also reduce some of the economic waste involved in unscientific 'hiring and firing.'"[38]

This flurry of activity within the business community was significant in several respects. First, it constituted a public acknowledgment, by at least some employers and influential business organizations, that unemployment was a serious problem and that management was partially responsible for its existence. Second, it introduced into managerial circles the notion that certain dimensions of the phenomenon of unemployment were costly to capital as well as to workers. Just as reformers had pointed to the hidden social costs of unemployment, men like Henry Dennison, Magnus Alexander, and Meyer Bloomfield were arguing that businesses too paid a price for incessant fluctuations in the number of men and women that they employed. Although the presence of labor reserves made it possible for firms to function and grow without paying much attention to their hiring and firing policies, high rates of turnover and "unscientific" personnel practices were nonetheless wasteful and needlessly expensive. Steadying the rhythms of employment could produce higher profits as well as a more contented labor force.[39]

Management's concern with unemployment was also political in origin and cooptative in its thrust. Progressive business figures like Bloomfield and Dennison were convinced that private enterprise would not endure if the grievances of the working class were ignored. The "awakened employer" (the phrase was Robert Valentine's) agreed with reformers that capitalists had to offer workers some job security for capitalism itself to survive. Among less awakened, or progressive, members of the business community, socialism was not the only perceived threat. To be sure, it was no coincidence that the Chamber of Commerce began its investigation of seasonal employment in the immediate wake of Morrison Swift's demonstration at the chamber's headquarters. But the leaders of the chamber were also trying to head off policy initiatives much more mild than anything that Swift or the Socialist Party had in mind. The chamber carefully monitored the activities of the AALL and tried, in several ways, to promote close ties between its Committee on Irregular Employment and the Massachusetts Committee on Unemployment. By conducting and publicizing its own studies, moreover, the chamber was signaling the business community's willingness to address, and help cure, the "social evil" of joblessness. It was also trying to shape the terms of public debate. By emphasizing the centrality of unemployment prevention – rather than relief or insurance – the chamber was defining the problem as one that could best be solved by the business community itself. If more efficient labor markets and managerial techniques could substantially lower the volume of unemployment, then there was little need for intrusive public policies. In assuming some responsibility for the unsteady rhythms of work, business was attempting to channel the rising tide of reform sentiment. For businessmen, as for the voluntarist leaders of the AFL, the unchallengeably desirable goal of unemployment prevention constituted, at least in part, a rhetorical shield against unpalatable state intervention.[40]

Cooptative or not, the actions of the business community revealed the breadth of the changes that had taken place in the span of a single decade. By 1915, unemployment had ceased to be an exclusively working-class preoccupation: it had become, more or less suddenly, a source of widespread concern among intellectuals, reformers, social critics, management experts, and manufacturers. The middle class had discovered the problem of unemployment, and respectable, well-to-do citizens were forming committees dedicated to reducing idleness levels and aiding the unemployed.

Alongside this shift in understanding and attitudes was a change in the political climate of Massachusetts, a change that made the state government more receptive to demands for a public unemployment policy. Although the Republican Party retained the upper hand in electoral politics throughout the years between 1908 and 1922, there were periodic stirrings of reform sentiment within the Grand Old Party. After 1908, an increasing proportion of Republican legislators supported bills that were "prolabor," and the failed 1910 reelection bid of Governor Eben Draper (a wealthy, conservative manufacturer who had earned the enmity of trade unions) drove home the party's need to make itself more attractive to working-class voters. The party's traditional conservatism was also challenged by the departure of some Republicans to the Progressive Party in 1912. This revolt was a small and tepid one by national standards, but the breach was healed only in 1915 when the Republican platform endorsed several reforms that had first been put forward by Progressives.[41]

Meanwhile, the Democratic Party threatened to outgrow its role as a permanent minority. Not only did Eugene Foss (himself a wealthy manufacturer and an ex-Republican) defeat Eben Draper in 1910, but in 1913 and again the following year, Democrat David Walsh was elected to the state's highest office. Walsh was the first Irish Catholic to become governor of Massachusetts. He was also a progressive Democrat, an admirer of William Jennings Bryan, a friend of Louis

Brandeis and Edward Filene, and a lawyer who had spent much of his early career representing workers in workmen's compensation cases. Walsh's success was accompanied by Democratic gains in the state legislature, particularly in the House of Representatives. There, the combined efforts of Democrats and progressive Republicans – reflecting the formation of political alliances among the Irish, "new" immigrants, and reform-minded Yankees – were often successful in securing the passage of legislation that aimed to democratize political life or to aid the less advantaged citizens of the commonwealth. After 1920, the conservative, probusiness wing of the Republican Party reestablished its dominance in state politics – as the nation returned to "normalcy" and the Democratic Party collapsed under the joint strains of Wilsonian internationalism and Irish nationalism – but, for a time at least, the currents of reform were flowing freely through the body politic of Massachusetts.[42]

By the second decade of the twentieth century, thus, the commonwealth stood ready to address, and publicly debate, the issue of unemployment. The working class had acquired sufficient organizational and political strength that its grievances could not easily be ignored; a voluble and influential segment of the middle class was pressing for action; the intellectual rationales for ignoring the problem had eroded; and public officials had become more sympathetic to the notion that the state ought to serve as the guardian of the poor and the powerless. Joblessness may or may not have been "next to godlessness" in the eyes of most citizens, but it had become a recognized "social evil." Translating that recognition into policy, however, proved to be a complex and conflict-ridden task.

Two steps forward, one step back

One expression of the shift in middle-class attitudes was a change in the spirit with which unemployment relief was delivered during depressions. The need for relief was greater during the downturn of 1913–15 than it had been at any time since the 1890s, and relief applicants were greeted with more sympathy and less suspicion than their predecessors had been during earlier depressions. Private charities, which remained responsible for most of the direct aid to the jobless, tended to treat unemployed workers more as victims than as suppliants or potential imposters. Humiliating "work tests" were relatively uncommon; work relief programs were designed to welcome, rather than deter, applications from the impoverished unemployed. In Boston several work relief projects allowed men and women to choose jobs that matched their own skills. In Springfield numbered tickets were distributed to jobless men so that they did not have to spend hours waiting in line for the chance to claim a work relief position. Private citizens in Springfield also created a loan fund for jobless men and women who needed money but did not want to ask for "charity."[43]

Public officials and charity workers also placed a new emphasis upon the desirability of creating full-time jobs, at decent wages, for the unemployed. The mayors of several cities significantly expanded municipal payrolls in 1914 (Boston's newly elected Mayor Curley was, for many reasons, exemplary in this regard), and they also urged private firms to hire or retain as many workers as possible. The construction industry was urged to "Build Now," while private citizens were encouraged to think of any work that they would need done in the next few years and to have it done immediately. The Massachusetts Committee on Unemployment created a work relief program that paid union-scale wages in unionized occupations. The Worcester Chamber of Commerce, at its own expense, established an employment bureau for residents of the city.[44]

As importantly, for the first time in the commonwealth's history, the state government assumed a leadership role in the fight against unemployment. In the winter of 1914–15, Governor Walsh appointed a Committee on Unemployment, which immediately (and tellingly) changed its name to the "Committee to Promote Work." The committee was chaired by Henry Dennison and included several representatives of organized labor, including C. F. Howard of the Industrial Workers of the World. On January 8, 1915, in his second inaugural address, Walsh also asked for an appropriation of state funds for public works projects that would "properly afford" relief to the unemployed. The legislature granted Walsh's request, allocating $200,000 for public works programs to furnish jobs to victims of the depression.[45]

Innovative as these measures may have been, they did not, in anyone's eyes, constitute a solution to the problem. The funds available for relief were minuscule when matched against the needs of the unemployed; jobs were created for only a tiny fraction of all idled workers. For reformers and progressive politicians, not to mention working people, the depression of 1913–15 simply underscored the need for more systematic and comprehensive policies. "We shall be entirely dissatisfied with our efforts," wrote William C. Ewing of the Massachusetts Committee on Unemployment to James A. McKibben of the Boston Chamber of Commerce in May 1915, "if we do not follow up the emergency work with some constructive measures which will have the double effect of relieving future unemployment more adequately, and . . . preventing the situation from again becoming so serious as it has been this winter." A few months later, the Republican Party of Massachusetts declared itself to be in favor of the "development of such industrial organizations as will tend to minimize unemployment." Early in 1916 Governor Walsh's progressive Republican successor, Samuel W. McCall, acknowledged that the commonwealth was not dealing with the "problem methodically and effectively" and issued a call for new policies.[46]

Two different, but not mutually exclusive, approaches to the problem were put forward and debated. The first was prevention – the lowering of unemployment levels – which everyone agreed was the ideal solution. By 1915, members of the Committee on Unemployment, leaders of the Chamber of Commerce, and most trade unionists also agreed that a great deal of the joblessness occurring in the commonwealth could be eradicated.[47]

There was, however, far less agreement regarding specific proposals; nor was there a consensus view of the appropriate role of the state in the task of unemployment prevention. The business community, of course, advocated completely voluntary measures: managerial reforms to steady the rhythms of work as well as labor exchanges to facilitate contacts between employers and jobless workers. Organized labor placed little faith in these proposals and pressed instead for immigration restriction and – with less conviction – a shorter working day. Reformers welcomed (and endorsed) all these ideas, but they were most enthusiastic about a proposal of their own. As the centerpiece of its prevention program, the Committee on Unemployment urged that the Free Employment Offices be expanded and transformed into a statewide (and eventually national) network of exchanges through which all employers would be required, by law, to do their hiring. Spokesmen for business were hostile to this proposal and labor was suspicious at best, but reformers argued that a mandatory system of exchanges was necessary to rationalize the labor market and increase the steadiness of employment.[48]

This menu of proposals strongly suggested that, in fact, there was little that the state government, or local governments, could realistically hope to accomplish in the way of unemployment prevention. The business community's prescription offered no role whatsoever to public authorities, while the foremost item on labor's agenda, immigration restriction, could be addressed only in Washington. The idea of creating compulsory labor exchanges was politically doomed from the outset, and it was not at all clear that a network of voluntary exchanges – which the state could have created – would have much impact on unemployment levels. "The subject of employment . . . is undoubtedly one of our greatest social problems," testified Charles Gettemy, the commissioner of labor statistics, in 1916, "and it is not going to be solved simply by opening up free employment offices and hanging out a sign, and inviting the unemployed to come in and register for work."[49] From the viewpoint of state-level policy makers at least, the goal of unemployment prevention appeared as elusive as it was desirable.

The second approach to the problem was to insure the unemployed, to create a state-run program that would automatically provide funds for workers who were idled through no fault of their own. This idea was strongly backed by reformers, many of whom were convinced that some unemployment was unavoidable and unpreventable in a capitalist economy. The rationale for insurance was straightforward. Since unemployment was the responsibility not of workers alone but of the entire society, the financial cost of joblessness ought to be borne by the state. A system of insurance benefits would effectively replace the haphazard, emergency relief efforts launched during every downturn of the business cycle; it would offer workers psychological, as well as financial, security; and it would provide aid that did not carry the stigma of charity. Supporters of the idea argued further that a carefully crafted insurance plan would help to reduce the incidence of joblessness by offering financial incentives to employers who ran their businesses steadily. Revolutionary as the concept may have sounded to many American ears (Morrison Swift had been denounced as a crackpot for demanding "pensions" for the unemployed as recently as 1908), the notion that the state should insure workers against joblessness was hardly a new or untried one in 1915. Social insurance plans had been operating in Germany and Belgium for decades, and Great Britain had established a nationwide insurance system in 1911.[50]

Beginning in 1915, the Committee on Unemployment devoted much of its energy to a campaign to establish a statewide unemployment insurance program. Members of the committee spoke and wrote widely on the subject; many citizens, disturbed and frustrated by the second serious depression in less than a decade, were receptive to the idea. The principle of unemployment insurance was endorsed by the state AFL, numerous individual trade unions, and the Associated Charities of Boston. Progressive business figures such as Meyer Bloomfield, Henry Dennison, and Ordway Tead energetically supported the campaign, while the chambers of commerce of both Boston and Worcester acknowledged that the subject ought to be explored. By the fall of 1915, the Republican Party of Massachusetts was on record as being in favor of "an investigation for the purpose of devising a form of social insurance to protect the worker against the vicissitudes of sickness, unemployment, and old age." In his inaugural address in 1916, Governor McCall quoted Bismarck approvingly and urged the legislature to "inaugurate" an investigation of social insurance "with a view to the passage of suitable laws."[51]

In January 1916, this campaign took a major step forward when an unemployment insurance bill, written and sponsored by the Committee on Unemployment, was officially introduced into the state legislature. The event was a notable one: it marked the first time in American history that any such bill had formally entered the legislative arena. The bill itself (House Bill 825) was far more than a statement of principles or a general call for action: modeled on the British act of 1911, it was an intricately detailed piece of legislation that tried to carefully thread its way through the political and administrative minefields that awaited any effort to develop pathbreaking social policy.[52]

The bill proposed an insurance system that would cover adult workers in all the major manufacturing industries in the commonwealth. Funded by contributions from workers, employers, and the state government, the program was to provide benefits to all eligible men and women who had been jobless for at least one week – up to a maximum of ten weeks. Benefit levels would vary, depending upon a worker's normal wages, always constituting less than two-thirds of regular weekly earnings. Trade unions that had their own unemployment benefit programs would receive subsidies from the state insurance commission, and employers were promised a refund of one-half their annual contribution for any worker who was employed for at least forty-eight weeks. The bill permitted insurance funds to be used for railway fares by jobless workers who were leaving the state. They could also be converted into old-age pensions by workers who had passed the age of sixty and had paid more into the insurance fund than they had received in benefits.[53]

The legislature responded to House Bill 825 – and to other proposals linked to the problem of unemployment – by appointing a Special Commission on Social Insurance. That commission was handed the task of studying "the effects of sickness, unemployment, and old age in Massachusetts," collecting "facts as to actual experience with . . . insurance," and recommending "practical and expedient" legislation to protect the "wage earners of the commonwealth." Composed of two members of the state Senate, four members of the House of Representatives, and three private citizens, the commission collected its facts and held hearings for more than six months. Its final report was delivered to the legislature in 1917.[54]

That report endorsed virtually the entire reform program of the Massachusetts Committee on Unemployment. It declared that joblessness constituted "a serious injury to the entire community" and that the "cost of relieving unemployment is not a net expense." While urging employers to do everything in their power to steady the rhythms of work, the Commission on Social Insurance recommended that the state play an active role in dealing with the problem. It advocated an increase in the number of Free Employment Offices as a "first step in organizing the labor market on a scientific basis." It also encouraged the state government to act as a countercyclical employer by delaying public construction projects until periods when private enterprise was faltering and by accumulating an "unemployment reserve fund" during prosperous years to finance public works during depressions. To coordinate these efforts, the legislature was urged to create a permanent board of employment. Perhaps most striking, the commission cautiously approved the idea of unemployment insurance. After hearing testimony from both advocates and bitter opponents of House Bill 825 (the opponents were drawn from the less "awakened" segments of the business community), a majority of the commission concluded that the "principle of insurance" was "desirable" but that the time was not yet "ripe" for an insurance program to be established in the Bay State.[55]

The *Report of the Special Commission on Social Insurance* was another milestone in the fitful evolution of unemployment policy. Speaking on behalf of the state government, the commission concluded both that unemployment was an utterly fundamental problem and that the responsibility for solving it rested largely with public authorities. Although businessmen were encouraged to pursue private strategies for unemployment prevention, the commission insisted that it was an obligation of the state to protect working people against joblessness. Fulfilling that obligation, it implied, would require new, permanent, and potentially expensive programs.

This call for reform, this pathbreaking application of "progressive" principles to the problem of unemployment, fell, however, on deaf or distracted ears. Indeed, the *Report of the Special Commission* may well have been the last gasp of social progressivism in Massachusetts. The report was written late in 1916 and issued only in 1917. By then, unemployment, in the words of Courtenay Crocker, was "more or less of a dead issue." Public attention was riveted on international events, while unemployment levels, thanks to the war, were lower than they had been in decades. The sense of crisis and urgency that had been so palpable in 1915 had vanished, and the state government felt little pressure to embark on a series of innovative, costly, and controversial reforms. The recommendations of the special commission were altogether ignored, and by 1918 the reformers' Committee on Unemployment had itself disbanded.[56]

But the problem of unemployment did not remain out of the public spotlight for long. The depression that began after World War I was far more severe than its predecessor: by the winter of 1920–1 there were almost certainly more unemployed workers in Massachusetts than there had been at any other time in the state's history. The demand for relief placed a severe strain upon public and private institutions. And sympathy for the jobless was heightened by the fact that many of the unemployed were ex-servicemen recently returned from the battlefields of Europe.

Relief policies during the postwar depression were indeed affected by the patriotic notion that American society ought to find work for men who had risked their lives in an overseas war. While private charitable agencies handled the traditional task of dispensing goods to the neediest of the unemployed, public authorities attempted, even more vigorously than they had in 1914, to find or create jobs for the jobless. In 1919, Governor Calvin Coolidge, scarcely a progressive or a spendthrift, asked the state legislature to appropriate more than 2 million dollars for public works projects. Similarly, the mayors of all the major cities made widely publicized efforts to speed up or begin municipal construction. In 1921, Coolidge's conservative successor, Channing Cox, created a statewide Committee to Promote Work, and Mayor Peters of Boston (prodded by the exploits of Urbain Ledoux) announced the formation of a thirty-two-member Committee on Unemployment. In the end, these efforts proved to be more rhetorical than substantive: they had little impact on the extremely high unemployment rates that prevailed in 1920 and 1921. But the rhetoric itself was revealing: the creation of jobs was implicitly recognized as a legitimate goal of public policy during depressions. In 1921, Governor Cox even suggested that all departments of the state government try to anticipate their expenditures five or ten years in advance to permit the state to act more effectively as a countercyclical employer.[57]

The postwar depression also gave rise to renewed demands for long-range solutions to the problem of unemployment. Although no new policy ideas appeared, trade unionists once again clamored for immigration restriction, while reformers reintroduced the unemployment program of the AALL. In the early 1920s, however, advocates of reform were swimming against the prevailing political tides. The Democratic Party was in disarray, the political and ethnic coalitions that had secured the passage of reform legislation in the Progressive era had fallen apart, and organized labor itself was becoming more voluntarist in its ideology and increasingly defensive in its strategic posture.[58]

Between 1919 and 1925, in fact, all branches of the state government were controlled by the Republican Party, and the Grand Old Party had lost interest in social reform. "It is a time to conserve," announced Governor Coolidge in his inaugural address in 1920, "a time to retrench rather than reform, a time to stabilize the administration of the present laws rather than to seek new legislation." Two years later, Governor Cox successfully ran for reelection on a platform announcing that the state government had already assumed too many responsibilities. Although David Walsh was elected to the Senate and remained a prominent figure in Massachusetts politics, the State House was dominated by conservative Republicans who were convinced that public intervention in economic affairs was already excessive, that taxes and government expenditures had to be curtailed, and that the best way to contend with unemployment was to maintain a sensible tariff policy and (in a new twist, sparked by the wartime inflation) to lower wages.[59]

One result of this shift in the political climate was the inability of reformers to prod the state into creating labor exchanges of any type, although the institutional skeleton for a national system of exchanges had been established during the war. Responding to labor shortages that had developed in 1917, the federal government had created the U.S. Employment Service. After the war, reformers urged the government to maintain the service as a mechanism for reducing unemployment. Their efforts were fruitless. Under pressure from manufacturers, Congress refused to appropriate sufficient funds to keep the service active in peacetime. Similarly, in Massachusetts, despite the lobbying of reformers, the Free Employment Offices remained few in number and limited in operation.[60]

The conservatism of the early 1920s also determined the fate of the second unemployment insurance bill to be introduced into the Massachusetts legislature. In January 1922, Henry L. Shattuck, one of the few reform Republicans left in the state House of Representatives, filed a bill that would have required employers to obtain unemployment insurance policies, through private insurers, for all their employees. The premiums on these policies were to be paid by employers and would vary with the layoff rates of individual firms, thereby giving employers an incentive to keep workers on the payroll. Workers who were laid off would receive a benefit of $1.50 a day for a maximum of thirteen weeks. Shattuck argued that his insurance program would reduce idleness levels and protect workers against a "hazard" that was "in large part a product of the present industrial system."[61]

Shattuck's bill was (of course) referred to a committee, the Special Commission on Unemployment, Unemployment Compensation, and the Minimum Wage. In hearings before that commission, the bill received support from reformers like Henry Dennison as well as from several representatives of organized labor who were willing to contradict, in public, the well-known views of Samuel Gompers. But most trade unions either opposed the bill or remained silent, while the measure was strenuously attacked by businessmen and business organizations. "The bill puts a premium upon loafing and fraud," insisted one manufacturer. "It is the quintessence of Sovietism and is worse than the insurance of bank deposits."[62]

The commission itself seemed to agree: it unanimously condemned Shattuck's bill and the whole idea of unemployment insurance. Flatly rejecting the views expressed by the Commission on Social Insurance in 1916, the 1922 commission concluded that "the adoption of any form of State insurance against unemployment would neither be to the interest of Massachusetts industries nor to the permanent advantage of Massachusetts wage earners." Citing the expert testimony of Dr. Frederick Hoffman, an "eminent statistician" who worked for the Prudential Insurance Company, the commission claimed that Britain's unemployment insurance system had been a costly failure that had increased idleness levels. Shattuck's proposal would yield similar results, costing the industries of the commonwealth as much as 19 million dollars a year only to reward "the sluggard." "Just as health insurance has apparently encouraged malingering, unemployment insurance bids fair to encourage shiftlessness and improvidence." "Compulsory indemnification during unemployment," the commission declared, in what proved to be the obituary notice of the campaign for unemployment insurance in Massachusetts, "is not consistent with American principles."[63]

The American solution to the problem, the commission maintained, was one that the business community had been advocating for nearly a decade: prevention. "Unemployment is regarded as a social and economic evil, yet it is recognized as one which it is possible to reduce and eliminate to a great extent." And prevention was not a task for public authorities. Echoing the views of the Boston Chamber of Commerce, the commission insisted that sound business practices were the key to lower unemployment rates. The "regularization of industry," it concluded tautologically, was "one of the best means of reducing unemployment." To achieve this goal, the commission urged companies to resist the tendency to overexpand during economic upswings, to set aside "depression reserves" of cash to finance expansion during cyclical downturns, and to minimize seasonal fluctuations in production. It also recommended, rather lamely, that "the Massachusetts Chamber of Commerce and local boards of trade and Chambers of Commerce . . . give serious consideration to the matter." In keeping with the political temper of the time, the commission defined the role of the state largely as one of exhortation. Endorsing the prescriptive vision of business leaders, it insisted that there was no need for a systematic public policy. After years of agitation at the State House, the problem of unemployment had been entrusted to the voluntary efforts of the business community.[64]

The commission's enthusiastic embrace of unemployment prevention was, in good part, a thinly disguised rationalization for governmental inaction. Nevertheless, the businessmen of Massachusetts did make attempts to fulfill the mandate they had been given. Many manufacturers were sensitive to the political desirability of enhancing the security of workers, and, as management experts had pointed out, there were also profits to be made by stabilizing the rhythms of production. Consequently, firms did try to "regularize" their operations both before and after the depression of 1920–2. They developed new and more diverse product lines, they sought larger markets, and they altered their sales methods to increase the continuity of demand for their goods. Many businesses, heeding the advice of management specialists like Meyer Bloomfield and Robert Valentine, created personnel departments to hire and fire workers and to monitor turnover rates. They also installed corporate welfare plans that served to heighten the allegiance of workers to individual firms. According to several national studies, labor turnover rates did diminish between 1915 and the late 1920s, and at least a few firms succeeded in narrowing the range of seasonal fluctuations in employment. Several well-known companies, following the example of Dennison Manufacturing, even established private unemployment insurance systems for their workers.[65]

There were, however, stringent limits to what business could do and was willing to do to prevent unemployment from occurring. No individual firm could influence the vicissitudes of the business cycle, and there were often compelling reasons for companies to expand their productive capacities during prosperous years, even if expansion did lead to excess capacity and layoffs during downturns. Similarly, the demand for many products remained seasonal or uneven, and it was generally less risky for entrepreneurs to follow the market than to devise an innovative strategy for producing steadily year-round. Most managers, moreover, remained indifferent to the issue of "continuity of employment," to the concerns voiced so eloquently by politicians, personnel experts, and progressive businessmen. As long as their companies were turning a profit, they saw little reason to depart from long-established methods of conducting their operations.[66]

Of equal importance, those businessmen who *were* committed to lowering turnover rates and eliminating "waste" were discovering that they could achieve those goals without having to attack the problem of unemployment frontally. Farsighted managers were devising strategies for reducing turnover that involved rationalizing the distribution of layoffs rather than increasing the regularity of work. With the memory of wartime turnover rates still vivid, an unusually large number of firms responded to the depression of 1920–2 not with layoffs but by putting their workers on short time, a strategy geared to retaining the allegiance of their employees. More significantly, employers were also discovering that by offering relatively secure jobs to some (even a majority) of their employees, and by transferring the entire burden of unemployment to others who were less favored, they could sharply reduce turnover without necessarily steadying the overall rhythms of production and employment.[67]

One method of performing this feat was sketched out in 1922 by C. P. Marshall of the Plymouth Cordage Company in a series of memos to the treasurer of the firm:

> We could have two groups of workers. A permanent one of those who have proved their loyalty, faithfulness, and efficiency. A group in number of a size that we could always keep. If the plant works they work. If there isn't work enough for all on full time the plant will go on short time rather than have any of this group loaf. These are people who would get houses. They should also be assured of a pension . . .
>
> Second group of younger, temporary or floaters, or of those who have not been long enough to attain to first group . . . newcomers and youths. I should like to see this group divided into apprentices and hands. After a given time . . . if they proved worthy they could be promoted to the first group as vacancies occurred.
>
> I believe that could such an impression get abroad, the thought that a real Cordage man was secure in his job it would make for loyalty and work.

At about the same time, the Plimpton Press in Norwood "hit upon" an ingenious solution for dealing with its summer rush season without creating high rates of turnover: it began to hire high school and college students to work during the summer. Similarly, a personnel expert at Dartmouth College's Tuck School, which was something of a pioneer in personnel matters, observed that one effective way for firms to deal with "rush periods" was to hire "former women employees" for jobs that were of explicitly short duration. By creating what was, in effect, a two-tiered labor force – in which members of the "upper" tier were given relatively secure jobs while those in the "lower" tier were almost certain to be laid off – manufacturers could reduce turnover and discontent while leaving the total volume of unemployment unchanged.[68]

These same goals could also be attained by the installation of a seniority system. And, as noted in Chapter 7, it was precisely during this period that seniority provisions began to appear with some frequency in union contracts. The formalization of seniority rules (with or without union contracts) emerged not merely from the desire of workers to enhance the predictability of their jobs but also from management's desire to cut labor costs by limiting turnover. Workers who had acquired ten or fifteen years' seniority with a particular firm were relatively unlikely to leave to accept another job; if they had to be laid off, they were more likely to return to the firm once business picked up again. Companies that had seniority agreements with unions could still dismiss a sizable proportion of their employees during slowdowns, but, since the distribution of these layoffs was less random and arbitrary, they were less threatening to the stability of the labor force. The establishment of a seniority system, like the creation of a two-tiered work force, afforded management a technique of eliminating or reducing the "hidden" business costs of unemployment without actually preventing joblessness from taking place.[69]

In practice, then, the voluntary, free enterprise route to reduced unemployment was riddled with obstacles and unforeseen detours. Despite the confident assertions of personnel experts, progressive businessmen, and Republican politicians, the imperatives of efficiency and the desire to eliminate "waste" did not necessarily lead managers to steady the rhythms of employment. Throughout the 1910s and 1920s, many firms completely ignored the call for more scientific personnel practices. Others chose not to "regularize industry" but rather to rationalize the allocation of layoffs. "Prevention," even in the 1920s, was proving to be less promising an approach to the problem of joblessness than the Special Commission on Unemployment, Unemployment Compensation, and the Minimum Wage had claimed.

The sea change in middle-class thinking about unemployment, thus, produced far more talk than action between 1908 and 1922. The recognition that unemployment was a fundamental social problem spawned a significant policy debate but not a policy. Unemployment prevention came to be a widely accepted societal goal, but little was actually done to reduce the incidence of joblessness. Public officials assumed rhetorical responsibility for the well-being of idled workers, but conservative political forces, abetted by the voluntarist stance of organized labor, deflected and then defeated demands for concrete and permanent programs.

Interest in the issue, moreover, remained cyclical or, to be precise, countercyclical. Although the problem was acknowledged to be a chronic one, state and local authorities continued to notice the unemployed only during crises – when the suffering of the jobless became highly visible and when dramatic protests raised the specter of political turmoil. Between 1909 and 1913, and again between 1916 and 1919, public officials utterly ignored the problem. And the issue was shelved once more at the end of the depression of 1920–2. Indeed, with return of prosperity in 1923, the drive for unemployment reform in Massachusetts came to a decisive – if temporary – halt.

One additional feature of the policy response to unemployment in the early 1920s warrants mention: for the first time, the federal government attempted to offer some leadership in dealing with the issue. In September 1921, President Harding, at the urging of his secretary of commerce, Herbert Hoover, signaled the national government's concern by convening an unemployment conference in Washington. The stated aim of the conference, which was attended by more than fifty invited representatives of business and labor, was to devise relief and employment programs that would alleviate the consequences of the depression. The president himself opened the conference, declaring in one of his inimitable locutions that

> there has been vast unemployment before and will be again . . .
> But there is excessive unemployment today, and we are concerned
> not alone about its diminution, but we are frankly anxious under
> the involved conditions, lest it grow worse, with hardships of the
> winter season soon to be met.

Secretary Hoover was more impassioned, and considerably more precise, as he told the conference of its mandate:

> There is no economic failure so terrible in its import as that of a
> country possessing a surplus of every necessity of life in which
> numbers, willing and anxious to work, are deprived of these ne-
> cessities. It simply can not be if our moral and economic system is
> to survive. It is the duty of this Conference to find a definite and
> organized remedy for this emergency, and I hope also that you
> may be able to outline for public consideration such plans to miti-

gate its recurrence . . . We possess the intelligence to find a solution. Without it our whole system is open to serious charges of failure.[70]

Despite the stated gravity of the problem, the President's Conference failed to develop any new or pathbreaking ideas for coping with the emergency or for mitigating "its recurrence." After meeting on and off for several weeks, the assembled conferees ended up embracing a set of ideas and proposals that were already a part of mainstream thinking in Massachusetts and other states. The conference endorsed the notion that public construction was "better than charity" as a means of offering relief to the unemployed; it advocated the use of public employment offices to help "the right man" find "the right job"; it urged the government to lower taxes to improve the business climate; and it demanded that businessmen do everything in their power to "eliminate waste" and stabilize the rhythms of production. When formal sessions of the conference had come to a close, Secretary Hoover appointed several committees to conduct detailed studies of specific dimensions of the problem, including the nature of business cycles and the sources of seasonal fluctuations in the construction industry.[71]

More striking than the inability of the conference to devise new policies was its reluctance to assign much responsibility for the problem to the federal government itself. Despite his assertion that the survival of "our moral and economic system" depended upon curing the malady of unemployment, Secretary Hoover, in his opening address, had declared that sound solutions ought not involve either federal expenditures or national legislation. Most delegates to the conference seemed to agree: to help alleviate the near-desperate conditions created by the depression, federal authorities were urged only to "expedite" construction that was already "covered by existing appropriations." The conference also stressed that "meeting the emergency of unemployment is primarily a community problem" and that "the responsibility for leadership is with the mayor." The problem of unemployment had finally traveled to Washington, only to be rapidly dispatched back to the cities and towns of the nation.[72]

Toward a new political economy

Institutionally and legally, the status of the unemployed in Massachusetts changed little between the 1870s and the early 1920s. At the end of the first quarter of the twentieth century, the vast majority of the commonwealth's working people could still be "thrown out" of their jobs at a moment's notice.[73] Coping with unemployment remained largely a private matter, an individual rather than social responsibility. Aside from the happy (and largely male) few who obtained public works jobs, men and women who could not make ends meet by themselves still had to turn to the overseers of the poor, private charities, or makeshift emergency relief committees. Over the course of a half-century, the state government had enacted only a handful of laws pertaining directly to the problem of unemployment, and most of those served either to discipline tramps or to create commissions to study the matter further. Fifty years after Carroll Wright had undertaken his first investigation of the "involuntary idle," there was no unemployment policy in Massachusetts.

Nonetheless, significant changes had occurred during this period. By 1922 much of the groundwork had been laid for institutional reforms that would bring – and, in several respects, were already bringing – the era of uncertainty to a close. The nineteenth-century consensus that nothing could be done about unemployment had given way to a twentieth-century consensus that something had to be done about it. Sizable segments of the politically dominant middle class had come to view unemployment as a permanent, rather than transient, phenomenon; as an expression of systemic, rather than individual, failings; as a problem that, left untended, would have unacceptably high social and political costs. Labor's demand for steady work had not been answered, but it had, at least, been heard. By the early 1920s, the need for programs to combat joblessness was being articulated not only by trade unionists, socialists, and reformers but also by conservatives like Herbert Hoover and Channing Cox.

Not surprisingly, the growing awareness of the need for action was accompanied by an enhanced legitimacy for the notion that the state itself ought to assume responsibility for protecting working people against unemployment. Although the Massachusetts Committee on Unemployment had not garnered nearly enough support to secure the passage of its program, it had succeeded in injecting the issue into the mainstream of political discourse. Conservatives remained wary of governmental solutions to the problem of unemployment, yet even Calvin Coolidge had expressed his support for public works projects during depressions.

Indeed, by 1922 the specific ideas and programs that would constitute the core of unemployment policy in Massachusetts, and the United States, for much of the twentieth century had already emerged – as experiments, as innovations, as detailed pieces of legislation, as proposals backed by significant political constituencies. Although the official view of the state government was that business-sponsored prevention was the best method of contending with unemployment, other strategies were waiting in the wings. Support for the idea that the state should serve as a countercyclical employer had grown steadily since the 1890s, and by the early 1920s both state and local authorities had experimented with fairly sizable public works projects. During this same period, the idea of unemployment insurance had ceased to be the utopian fantasy of a handful of radicals and had become the subject of serious political debate. Legislation to create a mandatory insurance program had been drafted, and the principle of insurance had been endorsed by politically active reformers, some trade unionists, charity workers, and one government commission.

Two other developments also heralded the arrival of a new era in the history of unemployment. The first was President Harding's Conference on Unemployment. Despite the conference's pronouncement that joblessness was primarily a "community" matter, the very fact that the conference was held suggested that unemployment was a national issue and that men and women throughout the United States were looking to Washington for aid. For a variety of reasons – including the precedents established by other reforms, the difficulties that state governments had encountered in trying to "solve" the problem, the attention focused on the issue of immigration restriction, and the fact that many of the postwar jobless were veterans – it was also becoming increasingly difficult for the federal government to disclaim all responsibility for the plight of the unemployed. Almost in spite of itself, the President's Conference on Unemployment signaled the formal beginning of the nationalization of unemployment policy in the United States.

The second development had little to do with public policy but was certainly as important as anything that unfolded in the governmental arena. This was the emergence (described in Chapter 7 and earlier in this chapter) of formal mechanisms for allocating work and layoffs among members of a union or employees of a firm. Seniority provisions, work rotation agreements, closed-shop union contracts, the creation of two-tiered labor forces as was proposed at Plymouth Cordage: these arrangements, arising out of the collaborative efforts and convergent interests of business and trade unions, constituted a powerful tool for reducing the economic and political costs of unemployment. Such mechanisms permitted some workers to acquire a meaningful degree of job security. They also lowered turnover rates and localized the discontents engendered by insecurity of employment. These rationalizing devices were not widespread in 1922, but

their growing popularity sounded the death knell of the utterly chaotic labor markets that had dominated the Massachusetts economy in
the late nineteenth and early twentieth centuries.

These expressions and harbingers of change were all clearly visible
in the early 1920s. After the postwar depression, however, the problem of unemployment was placed on a back burner, where it remained for the rest of the decade. The 1920s witnessed few advances
in either the development or implementation of unemployment policy. To be sure, legislation permanently restricting immigration was
finally passed by Congress in 1924, and mechanisms for rationalizing
the distribution of joblessness were extended to new groups of workers. But most employees remained unprotected by seniority (or other
such) arrangements, and immigration restriction turned out to have
little or no impact upon the incidence of unemployment. With the
exception of a few ongoing studies sponsored by the President's Conference on Unemployment, the federal government retreated from its
momentary engagement with the issue. At the state level, there was
no serious campaign for unemployment reform, and no new legislation was passed.[74]

Nor was the decade of the 1920s one of unalloyed prosperity in
Massachusetts. Although the national economy was, on the whole,
buoyant, and some of the Bay State's industries continued to expand,
the number of manufacturing jobs in the commonwealth dropped
significantly between 1920 and 1929, with the two leading industries,
textiles and shoes, suffering serious and irreversible losses. Hard hit
by competition from Southern manufacturers, firms in both these industries cut production, slashed wages, and sometimes closed their
plants altogether. "Empty factory windows" became a common sight
in cities like Lynn, Brockton, Lowell, and New Bedford, leaving
workers, by the tens of thousands, exposed to the unfamiliar prospect of long-term unemployment in an era of national prosperity. Yet
neither this troubling erosion of the state's industrial base nor the
routine, annual joblessness of hundreds of thousands of workers
gave rise to any innovative or energetic efforts to reduce idleness levels or aid the unemployed. Republican politicians maintained that
changes in the tariff would cure the "sick" industries of Massachusetts. Manufacturers insisted that taxes and labor costs were already
too high, that the state could not bear the expense of new social programs. Trade unions, beleaguered and committed to voluntarism,
had little to say on the subject. And the distress experienced by shoe
and textile workers was too localized to spark a broad-gauged movement for reform. Average unemployment levels in the 1920s were
probably higher than they had been during any decade since the

1890s, but there was no crisis sufficiently grave to compel the polity of Massachusetts to adopt or formulate new policies.[75]

The crisis came, of course, in the 1930s. The depression precipitated by the stock market crash of 1929 was more severe than any previous downturn in the nation's history, and unemployment rates in Massachusetts rose to unprecedented levels. In January 1934, after the trough of the depression had passed, a special census revealed that one-quarter of the commonwealth's labor force was wholly unemployed; an additional 10 percent of all wage earners were working part-time. More importantly, idleness rates remained at critically high levels for an entire decade. Although no precise figures are available, in all likelihood the unemployment *rate* (not the frequency) never dropped much below 20 percent in Massachusetts between 1931 and 1939. Under these conditions, the forces of institutional inertia and Republican conservatism were overwhelmed, and ideas that had been in circulation for decades were finally embodied in programs and policies.[76]

Nonetheless, the initial public responses to the spread of joblessness were limited and retained a familiar ring. Particularly in 1930 and 1931, the people of Massachusetts, unaware that the depression they were living through was to become the Great Depression, reacted to rising unemployment levels much as they had in 1907, 1914, and 1921. The burden of relief giving was shouldered largely by private charitable organizations; in Boston, municipal relief efforts and work tests were administered at the Hawkins Street woodyard; severe snowstorms, which promised to create thousands of temporary snow-shoveling jobs, loomed once again as a godsend to the unemployed. State and local authorities, following precedents established in 1914–15 and 1921–2, did allocate funds for public works projects, and James Michael Curley, again the mayor of Boston, threatened to become the biggest builder and spender the commonwealth had ever known. Yet, as had been true during earlier depressions, only a very small proportion of the unemployed were able to obtain jobs on public works. Politicians from both parties were deeply reluctant to create budget deficits, while conservative organizations, such as the Boston Chamber of Commerce, adamantly opposed public spending on the scale envisioned by Curley. Meanwhile, the federal government kept the problem of unemployment at arm's length. Although President Herbert Hoover encouraged Congress to authorize funds for public construction, the administration's overall policy reflected the president's long-standing belief that the problem could best be handled by private enterprise and local authorities.[77]

As the depression deepened, these traditional approaches became increasingly inadequate. In 1932 and 1933, the number of jobless men and women in Massachusetts remained above a quarter of a million; in many blue-collar occupations, towns, and neighborhoods, more than a third of all workers were unemployed. By the beginning of 1934, roughly 40 percent of all Irish- and Italian-born men in Boston were jobless, while comparably high idleness rates afflicted black males throughout the state. Joblessness was also taking a toll among white-collar and middle-class citizens who had been spared the ravages of earlier depressions. Of equal, if not greater, significance, extremely prolonged spells of unemployment were becoming grimly common. By January 1934, more than 60 percent of the unemployed (roughly 200,000 men and women) had been idle for at least a year; 40 percent, or approximately 10 percent of the labor force, had been jobless for two years or more. What was distinctive about the Great Depression, in fact, was less the frequency of unemployment than the *extraordinary lengths of time* that most jobless men and women remained out of work.[78]

The demands for relief generated by these extreme conditions placed an impossible strain upon private charities and local governments. Late in 1931, several national charity organizations warned that they lacked the financial resources to continue providing even minimal aid to the unemployed; many Massachusetts agencies arrived in similar straits at roughly the same time. Every passing month witnessed an increase in the number of destitute men and women who applied for help, while charitable fund-raising became more difficult as the slump continued. Municipal and state officials faced a similar dilemma. Since public treasuries were being drained by the depression, the growing demand for relief and public works projects could be met only by increasing taxes or by borrowing. But tax increases were politically unpopular, as well as potentially harmful to the prospect of economic recovery. And many communities were either unwilling or unable to borrow funds to support their jobless citizens. The bankruptcy of Fall River in 1930 served as a sobering reminder of the danger of budget deficits: by 1932, any government, state or local, that seemed too tolerant of indebtedness was likely to lose its credit rating. Hemmed in by these constraints, many public officials, although sympathetic to the plight of the unemployed, found themselves unable to mount effective relief programs.[79]

The presence of tens of thousands of simultaneously unemployed, and increasingly desperate, men and women also led to the reappearance of collective protests by jobless workers. As was true in earlier depressions, most of the unemployed were eerily passive, avoiding public displays of discontent. But, from time to time, demonstrations did occur in Boston and in other cities. In both 1930 and 1931, the patch of public turf stretching from the Boston Common to the State House again became the scene of a series of unemployment protests, this time led not by Morrison Swift or Urbain Ledoux but by the Council of the Unemployed, an organization linked to the Communist Party. Attendance at these rallies sometimes reached into the thousands, with the protestors typically lambasting government officials for their inaction and demanding unemployment insurance as well as more ample public works programs. Almost as typically, these protests were broken up by the police – since Mayor Curley had little sympathy for either demonstrations or Communists. None of these protests reached the dramatic heights of Ledoux's "slave" auctions or Swift's invasion of the State House, but they were viewed nonetheless as a disturbing threat to political order. Much as earlier demonstrations had done, they also focused public attention on the issue of state responsibility for the welfare of the unemployed.[80]

The deterioration of local conditions in 1931 and 1932 produced widespread popular pressure for federal programs to aid the jobless. As the inadequacy of municipal relief efforts became more apparent, a growing number of Massachusetts residents were convinced that satisfactory support for the unemployed could be obtained only by mobilizing the financial resources of the federal government. In 1932, Mayor Curley, acting on behalf of a national committee of mayors, petitioned Congress and President Hoover to appropriate 500 million dollars for direct unemployment relief and to launch a 5 billion dollar public works program. Republicans in general and President Hoover specifically displayed little interest in implementing such proposals. But Republicans in general and President Hoover specifically were out of step with the electorate. Massachusetts in the early 1930s was fast becoming a solidly Democratic state (Mayor Curley was soon to become Governor Curley), and in the elections of 1932 the Democratic Party won a sweeping national victory, forcing Herbert Hoover into early retirement. The election of 1932, indeed, constituted a decisive popular rejection of the conservative shibboleths – localism, trust in the business community, and fear of anything that resembled a "dole" – that had dominated governmental responses to unemployment throughout the first third of the twentieth century.[81]

The New Deal that Franklin Roosevelt offered to the American people did, of course, include unemployment programs similar to those that Curley and his fellow mayors had advocated. Between 1933 and 1940, the federal government created and funded an array of different agencies and programs (the Federal Emergency Relief Administration and the Works Progress Administration, among others) that offered either direct relief or public works jobs to the unemployed. The New Deal's efforts did not put an end to the misery experienced by jobless workers; nor did they reach all the unemployed in Massachusetts or other states. But they did dramatically increase the public resources available to men and women who were out of work. By the beginning of 1934, 15 percent of Boston's unemployed were engaged in federal work relief projects; early in 1940, a third of the city's jobless were still being supported by the WPA; between November of 1933 and the end of 1938, more than 70 million dollars in federal funds were expended in Boston alone. The New Deal, in practice as well as in its rhetoric, embraced a proposition that Samuel Gompers had put forward at President Harding's Unemployment Conference in 1921: that it was the responsibility of the national government to serve as a countercyclical employer. The federal government, moreover, was willing – despite deep reluctance – to pay for such programs by borrowing. Although President Roosevelt never endorsed Keynesian deficit spending as a matter of principle or economic theory, his administration did incur substantial budget deficits to create work for the unemployed.[82]

The early years of the Great Depression also witnessed an upsurge of interest in, and support for, unemployment insurance. In Massachusetts, an insurance bill was introduced into the state legislature in 1931. That same year, the executive council of the state labor federation, under pressure from rank-and-file workers, abandoned its commitment to voluntarism and espoused the idea of state-sponsored compensation for men and women who were out of work. In 1932, the labor federation affirmed its support for unemployment insurance, the state Democratic Party did likewise, and the governor of the commonwealth, Democrat Joseph B. Ely, joined with the governors of six other industrial states in endorsing an interstate insurance plan. (This interstate initiative was aimed largely at defusing the objection that the competitive position of a state's industries would be damaged if the state installed an insurance program.) By 1933 and 1934, when socialists and reformers again brought insurance bills before the legislature, the tide of public opinion was running strongly in favor of unemployment insurance. Even the Boston Chamber of Commerce had substantially softened its once-adamant opposition. In August 1935, after a final year of protracted legislative maneuvering, Massachusetts became the fifth state in the nation to adopt an unemployment insurance program for its citizens.[83]

These developments in Massachusetts were closely paralleled by events in Washington and elsewhere in the nation. Final passage of the Massachusetts bill was, in fact, delayed while the state's lawmakers tracked the progress of national legislation pending before Congress. Early in the depression, New York's liberal Democratic senator, Robert Wagner, had resurrected the unemployment program of the American Association for Labor Legislation, while reformers, social workers, and charity officials had renewed their calls for a systematic insurance program. More importantly, the American Federation of Labor, after witnessing a series of defections from voluntarism on the part of state federations and individual unions, endorsed the idea of unemployment insurance at its national convention in 1932. In June 1934, President Roosevelt announced that the time had arrived for a nationwide social insurance program in the United States. He appointed a Committee on Economic Security, chaired by the secretary of labor, Frances Perkins, to draft legislation to achieve that end. The committee, after drawing on the expertise of reformers who had been advocating unemployment insurance for two decades, wrote a bill that provided for the creation of both an old-age pension system and an insurance program. To the dismay of many reformers, the bill was watered down, brokered, and amended as it made its way through the committee and then through the House and the Senate. But the much-amended bill was passed by Congress in the summer of 1935. In its final form, the legislation established an insurance system mandated and supervised by the federal government but permitting individual states to determine many details of their own programs – including levels of benefits and the use of "merit" ratings to offer employers an incentive to minimize layoffs. President Roosevelt signed the Social Security Act on August 14, 1935. Soon afterward, many – and, eventually, most – of the nation's workers became eligible for insurance payments when they were unemployed.[84]

One other significant development bearing directly on the problem of unemployment also unfolded in the 1930s. Particularly after 1935, there was a dramatic increase in the number of workers covered by union contracts that regulated layoffs. Despite the depression and thanks in part to the passage of the National Labor Relations Act, the ranks of organized labor swelled considerably in the 1930s. In Massachusetts, where the rate of increase was well below the national average, the number of trade unionists more than doubled between 1932 and 1940, reaching a total of some 300,000 during the latter year. Much of this increase was centered in the manufacturing industries organized by the Congress of Industrial Organizations. Not surprisingly, the semiskilled workers who labored in those industries regarded job security as a critical issue. Consequently, many of the contracts they negotiated contained provisions that governed and routinized the distribution of layoffs. Work-sharing arrangements were hammered out by unions in the garment industry and several other seasonal trades, while agreements to lay workers off according to seniority became commonplace in numerous industries, including rubber, steel, textiles, autos, railroads, printing, and electrical machinery. It was in the years between 1935 and 1945 that the principle of seniority became firmly embedded in the workplaces and personnel practices of American industry.[85]

This cluster of institutional changes marked a watershed in the history of unemployment. The ideas that shaped these changes were, to be sure, neither new nor particularly innovative. The programs of the New Deal had their roots in proposals that reformers and socialists had put forward between 1890 and 1916. And formalized seniority arrangements had first appeared in union contracts at the end of the nineteenth century. But the implementation of these ideas, and particularly their implementation on a national scale, did have a significant impact upon the experience, the distribution, and the politics of joblessness. The reforms of the 1930s completed the formation of a new political economy of unemployment and, at long last, brought the era of uncertainty to an end.

This new political economy had several distinctive features. The most visible, and perhaps the most consequential, was that the state – in this case, the federal government – assumed some direct responsibility for the welfare of jobless workers. The task of aiding the unemployed was transferred from private charities to government agencies; the hardships that resulted from joblessness were mitigated by the expenditure of substantial sums from the public treasury. The presence of an insurance program meant, moreover, that workers became eligible for public support not by virtue of their indigence but rather by virtue of their economic citizenship. Insurance benefits, as Morrison Swift had pointed out in 1908, were not a matter of charity but rather a right that men and women acquired by participating in the paid labor force. The insurance system created by the Social Security Act aimed not merely to relieve suffering but to guarantee that workers would receive a partial wage, for a short period of time at least, whenever they were idled through no fault of their own.

During and after the Great Depression, the state also assumed responsibility for unemployment prevention, for minimizing the incidence of joblessness. It attempted to do so both by adopting policies that would stimulate private enterprise and, more directly, by countercyclically expanding government expenditures and enlarging the public payroll. Although the precise strategies the federal government utilized to keep a lid on idleness levels were sometimes the subject of heated public debate, the national government's obligation to control the unemployment rate was rarely questioned. The existence of that obligation led officials in Washington to measure unemployment on a monthly basis. It also served to overtly politicize the problem of joblessness. After Herbert Hoover's fall from grace, political parties and candidates for national office were expected to have – and usually did have – a policy for contending with unemployment.

The growth of organized labor, coupled with the increasingly widespread adoption of seniority as the governing principle in allocating layoffs, added a key dimension to this new political economy. After the Great Depression, a sizable number of blue-collar workers either possessed or could reasonably hope to possess authentic job security. The signing of "closed shop" or "union shop" contracts gave many trade unionists the right to claim certain jobs as their own. Formal seniority or work-sharing arrangements buttressed and extended those job rights. Contracts that regulated layoffs limited the arbitrary power that employers wielded over their employees and lessened the uncertainty that had been such a pervasive feature of working-class experience. For a significant minority of the labor force, in Massachusetts and elsewhere, unemployment ceased to be an omnipresent and lifelong threat. An adult male worker who belonged to a union and had been employed by the same firm for fifteen or twenty years had little to fear from the routine vicissitudes of economic life.

The institutional reforms that emerged from the crucible of the Great Depression did, thus, have enduring, far-reaching, and undeniably salutary consequences. Some workers acquired a virtual immunity against layoffs. Many others found that their rhythms of employment had, at the least, become more predictable. Government programs cushioned the financial cost of joblessness while alleviating the suffering of the least advantaged of the unemployed. The private drama of unemployment became a matter of sustained public interest, local relief efforts were superseded by national policies, and the inability of men and women to find jobs became a recurrent issue in national politics.

Still, this new political economy had profound and important limits. The policies and reforms implemented in the 1930s did not solve the problem of unemployment – not if solving the problem meant finding a definitive cure of the type that had long been sought and demanded by workers, trade union leaders, and some reformers. The pace of production remained seasonal in many industries; business activity continued to expand and contract according to cyclical rhythms; employers retained an unfettered right to respond to market conditions by laying off as many workers as they thought necessary. Unemployment did not disappear after the Great Depression (except briefly, perhaps, during World War II), and the new policies of the federal government failed to produce any sustained or marked reduction in the incidence of joblessness. The ongoing flight of manufacturing industries from Massachusetts produced high idleness levels in the commonwealth in the late 1940s and early 1950s. Nationally, there was no long-term decline in the unemployment rate during the half-century that followed the first inauguration of President Franklin Roosevelt.[86]

The government programs initiated by the New Deal also failed to eliminate the stress and hardship that so often accompanied spells of involuntary idleness. Since insurance benefits compensated for only a portion of a worker's lost wages, jobless men and women were still obliged to lower their living standards, to deplete their savings, to go into debt, and to search for new jobs. Even workers on explicitly temporary layoffs who expected to be recalled to their old positions continued to feel the financial pinch of joblessness. Moreover, insurance benefits generally expired after a period of three to six months – which meant that the long-term unemployed easily could, and often did, find themselves in genuinely desperate straits. The American welfare state did not liberate workers either from the curse that God placed upon Adam or from the specter of deprivation that could follow from a failure to find employment.[87]

Of equal importance, the gains achieved through union contracts and through rationalized personnel practices were unevenly distributed within the industrial labor force. Some workers did acquire job security. But others did not, and certain groups of workers ended up shouldering a disproportionate share of the unemployment that the economy continued to generate. Even after the passage of the Wagner Act, the majority of American workers did not belong to unions. And despite the voluntary adherence of many nonunion firms to seniority principles, their employees did not possess the formal security that union contracts could provide. Furthermore, in many partially organized industries and trades, the most secure jobs available were reserved for unionists, while less steady positions were filled by workers who were not, and sometimes could not become, trade union members.[88]

Seniority systems, similarly, enhanced the security of experienced workers, while increasing the likelihood that newly hired employees would be laid off. Youthful entrants to the labor force, who had always been idled more frequently than their elders, became even more vulnerable to fluctuations in business conditions. Their plight was often shared by workers who changed jobs in midcareer and by women who did not participate continuously in the paid labor force. The combination of seniority systems and the restrictive membership policies of some unions also served to keep men and women from newly arrived ethnic and racial groups disproportionately concentrated in unsteady employment situations. After the passage of laws restricting European immigration, American industry was obliged to recruit labor from new sources, and these new recruits – most visibly blacks from the agricultural South – suffered from unusually high unemployment frequencies. The gap between black and white unemployment levels in the third quarter of the twentieth century was far greater than the native–immigrant differential of earlier decades. Not surprisingly, this highly uneven, yet often formalized, distribution of unemployment was an ongoing source of tension and conflict within the working class as well as within trade unions.[89]

Stated somewhat differently, the mid-twentieth-century political economy of unemployment did not terminate or diminish the reliance of American capitalism upon a reserve army of labor. What was distinctive about the post–New Deal era was that the reserves that continued to exist in most blue-collar occupations were subsidized by public funds and organized according to new rules and principles. The likelihood that a worker would be assigned to the labor reserve in his trade was determined less by the arbitrary exercise of an employer's power and more by objective, rationalized criteria, such as age, work experience, and union membership. And most men and women who were placed in the reserves did not have to bear the full cost of that experience by themselves. The state, tacitly recognizing the permanence of a reserve army, offered financial support to its members, taxing citizens who were employed in order to underwrite the expense of maintaining pools of surplus labor. Indeed, it was precisely the thrust and function of this political economy to perpetuate the existence of a labor reserve while minimizing the suffering, the anger, the anxiety, and the threats to political order that the presence of a reserve army inescapably engendered.

The era of uncertainty was succeeded, then, not by an era of steady work and stable incomes but rather by an era of managed unemployment. After 1940, insecurity of employment was a less widespread, less universal, feature of working-class life; the consequences of joblessness, for individuals and their families, were less harsh than they once had been; the discontent spawned by unemployment was circumscribed and redirected into bureaucratic or electoral channels.

The phenomenon of involuntary idleness was also routinized and institutionalized, absorbed into the familiar and accepted fabric of American life. The federal government signaled its mastery of the problem by announcing the unemployment rate each month, and, when viewed against the backdrop of the Great Depression, these figures suggested – until the early 1980s at least – that considerable progress had been achieved in the fight against joblessness. The concept of a reserve army was replaced by the more antiseptic notion that "full employment" existed when only 4, 5, or 6 percent of the labor force was jobless. For many Americans, the very word "unemployment" came to refer not to the condition of being out of work but rather to the benefits that they received from a government agency. The problem of joblessness had not been solved, but it had been contained – which was no small achievement in a society that continued to witness the unemployment of millions of its citizens in the course of each and every peacetime year.

10   Epilogue: the Bay State and the nation

There can be little doubt that the Commonwealth of Massachusetts played an unusually prominent and pioneering role in the history of unemployment in the United States. The first attempt to systematically count the unemployed took place in the Bay State in the 1870s; the earliest reliable unemployment statistics, for any part of the nation, were those collected in conjunction with the state census of 1885. The word "unemployment" first appeared in print in a publication of the Massachusetts Bureau of Statistics of Labor, and in the 1890s the Board to Investigate the Subject of the Unemployed conducted nineteenth-century America's most thoroughgoing examination of the problem of joblessness. Massachusetts, in 1916, was the first state to formally consider the passage of unemployment insurance legislation. In 1935 it became the fifth state in the nation to actually implement an insurance program.

Facts such as these buttress the reputation of Massachusetts as a stronghold of innovative and progressive responses to social problems. At the same time, they raise questions regarding the representativeness of the commonwealth's experience. Were the people of the Bay State especially alert to the issue because unemployment was a more severe problem than it was elsewhere in the nation? Did the state's industrial structure or its location as an arrival point for immigrants give rise to abnormally high levels of joblessness? Did workers everywhere in the United States, after the Civil War, suffer from much the same insecurity of employment, from recurrent layoffs and chronically unsteady work? Such questions are commonplace whenever the spotlight of historical research is focused on only one corner of a national stage. They are particularly inescapable here – both because public agencies in Massachusetts played a vanguard role in responding to the problem of joblessness and because the history of unemployment, as it unfolded in the commonwealth, stands at odds with traditional conceptions and images of the American past.

Unfortunately, detailed and definitive answers to these questions are not very readily available. The history of unemployment in other states, or even cities, during the century that preceded the Great Depression, remains to be studied. And the extant data for many locales may prove to be scanty in the extreme. Nevertheless, certain broad-gauged comparative conclusions can be drawn, more or less safely, from a preliminary survey of the national terrain.

First: it is clear that unemployment, as a distinctive phenomenon and an identifiable social problem, appeared in Massachusetts somewhat earlier than it did in many other parts of the United States. The Bay State was among the first to industrialize; it was also among the first to acquire a full-time, industrial labor force that was largely disconnected from local agriculture. The economic and social processes that gave birth to the modern phenomenon of unemployment, processes outlined in detail in Chapter 2, were set in motion relatively early in Massachusetts. In all likelihood, Rhode Island, New Jersey, and Connecticut, as well as parts of eastern Pennsylvania and New York, had parallel experiences between the 1830s and the 1850s: as industrializing, seaboard areas, they were exposed to the same cluster of social changes that brought unemployment to Massachusetts. But the states of the Midwest probably lagged a generation or two behind, while, in rural areas of the South and the West, unemployment (as distinct from underemployment) may have become widespread only in the twentieth century. That joblessness was first measured in Massachusetts rather than in New York was something of a historical accident. That this event occurred north of the Chesapeake and east of the Ohio River was a reflection of the regional development of industrial capitalism in the United States.[1]

After the Civil War, however, unemployment became a significant, and highly visible, phenomenon in states far removed from the eastern seaboard. The long economic downturn of the 1870s left wage earners jobless in cities and towns throughout the northern United States; the problem was sufficiently widespread that a question about unemployment was included in the 1880 federal census. And the next severe depression, that of the 1890s, sparked the first national protest movement of unemployed workers. Indeed, the census surveys of 1890 and 1900 indicate that involuntary idleness had become a chronic problem for industrial workers virtually everywhere in the United States. In the relatively prosperous year of 1890, the national unemployment frequency for men and women engaged in "manufacturing and mechanical industries" was 21 percent; ten years later, the figure was 27 percent. In only three states were fewer than one-fifth of all workers in manufacturing idled in the course of the 1900 census year.[2]

The unemployment levels recorded for the entire Massachusetts labor force in 1890 and 1900 were, in fact, quite similar to those reported for other industrial states and for the nation as a whole. (See

Tables 10.1 and 10.2.) In 1890, the commonwealth's aggregate unemployment frequency was slightly above the national average; in 1900, the reverse was true. In both years, the mean duration of joblessness in the Bay State was within one week of the national norm. To be sure, some predominantly rural states, like Vermont and North Dakota, continued to witness relatively little involuntary idleness. But joblessness was no more widespread in Massachusetts than it was in most of the industrial states of the Northeast and the Midwest or in mining areas such as West Virginia, Montana, and Nevada. By the end of the nineteenth century, most Americans were wage earners, whether they worked in manufactures, transportation, agriculture, or extractive industries. And unsteady employment had become the lot of wage earners throughout the nation. In 1900, the frequency of unemployment, in the labor force as a whole, exceeded 20 percent (the Massachusetts figure) in thirty-two of the forty-eight states and territories of the United States. The differences between the 1890 and 1900 figures suggest that, with respect to unemployment at least, other regions were in the final stages of catching up with older industrial centers like Massachusetts and Pennsylvania.[3]

The rhythms of work and joblessness in individual occupations in Massachusetts also appear to have been characteristic of national patterns. Trades that were chronically unsteady in the Bay State tended to be equally unsteady in locales as diverse as New York, Ohio, Minnesota, and California. Occupations that offered relatively secure employment in Boston and Worcester usually provided comparable job security in other parts of the country. In 1900, day laborers and painters had a 40 percent chance of becoming unemployed, whether or not they lived in Massachusetts; the figure for clerks, in the state and in the nation as a whole, was 7 percent. In 1890 and again in 1900, national unemployment frequencies in most occupations were within 5 percentage points of the frequencies registered in the commonwealth.[4]

After the turn of the century, unemployment levels in many areas continued to match or exceed those recorded in Massachusetts. Although no state-by-state statistics are available for the years between 1900 and 1930, the existing evidence makes clear that the incidence of joblessness in the Bay State was far from unusual. According to the 1910 census, the unemployment rate for all manufacturing workers in the United States was almost identical to the rate simultaneously reported by the commonwealth's trade unionists. A survey of fifteen eastern and midwestern cities, conducted in the spring of 1915, found that Boston's unemployment rate was the tenth highest, less than a percentage point below the median for all cities in the

Table 10.1. *Unemployment levels by state, 1890[a]*

State	Both sexes		Males		Females	
	UF (%)[b]	MD (mo.)[c]	UF (%)[b]	MD (mo.)[c]	UF (%)[b]	MD (mo.)[c]
Maine	18.4	3.6	18.6	3.5	17.8	3.7
New Hampshire	12.8	3.3	12.5	3.3	13.9	3.4
Vermont	13.5	3.6	13.2	3.5	15.4	3.8
Massachusetts	18.3	3.3	19.0	3.3	16.4	3.3
Rhode Island	15.2	3.5	15.6	3.5	14.3	3.5
Connecticut	12.5	3.3	12.3	3.3	13.0	3.1
New York	14.3	3.6	15.0	3.6	11.8	3.5
New Jersey	15.7	3.2	16.4	3.2	13.1	3.1
Pennsylvania	19.2	3.6	20.8	3.6	11.5	3.6
Delaware	15.4	3.0	16.2	3.0	11.0	3.4
Maryland	17.3	3.6	18.5	3.6	12.9	3.7
Dist. of Columbia	12.0	3.6	12.7	3.6	10.5	3.6
Virginia	12.9	3.4	12.9	3.3	13.0	3.7
West Virginia	22.6	3.1	23.7	3.0	11.7	4.0
North Carolina	14.2	3.1	13.3	2.9	17.7	3.4
South Carolina	12.4	3.0	10.7	2.8	16.5	3.3
Georgia	9.7	2.9	8.9	2.8	12.0	3.3
Florida	11.7	3.3	11.7	3.3	11.6	3.3
Ohio	17.3	3.7	18.3	3.7	11.4	3.7
Indiana	17.6	3.9	18.4	3.8	11.9	4.1
Illinois	13.7	3.5	14.5	3.5	9.1	3.7
Michigan	17.2	3.7	17.8	3.7	13.6	3.8
Wisconsin	14.9	3.7	15.4	3.7	12.1	3.9
Minnesota	14.0	3.8	14.4	3.8	11.5	3.9
Iowa	12.0	3.9	11.9	3.8	12.9	4.0
Missouri	13.4	3.6	13.8	3.5	10.8	3.8
North Dakota	10.7	4.0	10.4	4.0	12.6	4.1
South Dakota	11.9	3.8	11.7	3.8	13.4	4.2
Nebraska	10.6	3.6	10.6	3.5	10.6	3.8
Kansas	11.3	3.9	11.2	3.9	12.2	4.2
Kentucky	15.9	3.5	16.7	3.5	10.4	3.8
Tennessee	23.5	2.9	25.0	2.8	14.3	3.5
Alabama	13.6	2.6	13.2	2.6	15.1	2.8
Mississippi	16.1	2.8	14.8	2.7	19.7	3.0
Louisiana	16.4	3.1	15.9	3.1	17.9	3.2
Texas	10.6	3.1	10.7	3.0	10.3	3.5
Oklahoma	10.2	4.6	10.2	4.6	9.8	4.7
Arkansas	23.7	2.9	25.1	2.8	14.7	3.3
Montana	21.5	3.3	22.3	3.3	9.2	3.9
Wyoming	22.2	3.4	23.1	3.4	9.2	4.1
Colorado	15.6	3.4	16.4	3.4	8.0	3.7

Table 10.1. *(cont.)*

	Both sexes		Males		Females	
State	UF (%)^b	MD (mo.)^c	UF (%)^b	MD (mo.)^c	UF (%)^b	MD (mo.)^c
New Mexico	18.7	3.7	19.5	3.6	9.6	4.3
Arizona	13.2	4.0	13.1	4.0	14.5	4.4
Utah	21.0	3.7	22.3	3.7	10.6	4.1
Nevada	22.3	4.2	23.1	4.2	12.7	4.1
Idaho	20.8	3.8	21.3	3.8	12.7	4.2
Washington	20.4	3.3	21.1	3.2	11.4	4.1
Oregon	14.4	3.8	14.7	3.8	11.1	4.1
California	16.6	3.9	17.4	3.8	10.9	4.1
United States	15.5	3.4	16.0	3.4	13.0	3.5

^{a}Figures as reported in the original census publications. A decade later the national totals were revised slightly to adjust for an apparent undercount of working children; "corrected" figures, however, are available only for the nation as a whole, not for individual states. The corrections themselves are small in magnitude. See *Twelfth Census, Occupations*, pp. lxvi, ccxxvi–ccxxviii. See also note 3. ^{b}Unemployment frequency.
^{c}Estimated mean duration. See Appendix B.
Source: Eleventh U.S. Census, Population, part II (Washington, 1897), pp. 302, 448.

sample. A similar survey, initiated a few months later, suggested that there was slightly more joblessness in western cities than there was in either the East or the Midwest. Throughout these years, trade unionists in New York State were unemployed more often than their counterparts in Massachusetts, while in Pennsylvania, Kentucky, and West Virginia, coal miners suffered from chronically high levels of involuntary idleness. In both the Midwest and the West, hundreds of thousands of migrant agricultural laborers had great difficulty finding work each winter.[5]

The breadth of the problem was vividly illumined during the depression that followed World War I. Traditional methods of relieving the poor and the jobless were strained to the limit in communities as widely scattered as Augusta, Georgia; San Francisco; Seattle; Lincoln, Nebraska; Saint Paul; Phoenix; Grand Rapids; Toledo; Memphis; Manchester, New Hampshire; Chicago; Saint Louis; and Tacoma. There were doubtless many small towns and rural counties, particularly in the South, where unemployment remained an unfamiliar and barely visible phenomenon. But joblessness, during the

Table 10.2. *Unemployment levels by state, 1900*

State	Both sexes		Males		Females	
	UF (%)[a]	MD (mo.)[b]	UF (%)[a]	MD (mo.)[b]	UF (%)[a]	MD (mo.)[b]
Maine	22.4	3.8	21.7	3.7	25.4	4.2
New Hampshire	15.5	3.7	15.1	3.6	17.0	4.0
Vermont	15.9	3.9	14.4	3.7	23.3	4.2
Massachusetts	20.0	3.8	20.0	3.8	19.9	3.8
Rhode Island	17.0	3.9	16.7	3.9	17.5	3.8
Connecticut	17.1	3.7	16.9	4.1	17.5	3.5
New York	18.6	3.7	18.9	3.7	17.4	3.6
New Jersey	20.3	3.4	20.6	3.4	19.1	3.4
Pennsylvania	22.0	3.7	23.0	3.7	17.6	3.9
Delaware	20.0	3.3	20.4	3.3	18.5	3.7
Maryland	21.0	3.6	22.0	3.6	17.3	3.6
Dist. of Columbia	15.0	3.9	14.7	3.9	15.8	3.8
Virginia	20.9	3.7	20.5	3.6	23.0	4.0
West Virginia	26.9	3.7	27.3	3.5	22.2	4.4
North Carolina	27.0	3.1	25.1	3.0	33.4	3.4
South Carolina	26.1	3.1	21.5	2.9	36.0	3.3
Georgia	20.7	3.1	18.5	3.0	27.4	3.6
Florida	24.0	3.3	23.2	3.2	27.4	3.6
Ohio	22.3	3.8	22.7	3.8	19.9	4.0
Indiana	23.8	3.9	24.0	3.8	22.4	4.1
Illinois	23.8	3.7	24.4	3.6	20.5	3.9
Michigan	19.9	3.7	19.6	3.6	21.6	3.9
Wisconsin	17.5	3.7	16.9	3.7	20.8	4.1
Minnesota	18.4	3.9	17.8	3.8	21.7	4.1
Iowa	20.1	3.8	18.7	3.8	28.4	4.0
Missouri	25.3	3.5	25.9	3.5	21.4	4.1
North Dakota	15.3	3.8	14.7	3.8	19.7	4.1
South Dakota	16.4	4.2	15.1	4.2	27.1	4.1
Nebraska	16.3	3.9	15.2	3.8	24.0	4.1
Kansas	18.4	4.3	17.5	4.2	25.7	4.6
Kentucky	25.5	3.8	25.9	3.8	23.1	4.4
Tennessee	29.2	3.5	29.7	3.4	26.7	3.8
Alabama	30.4	2.9	28.3	2.7	36.2	3.2
Mississippi	27.4	3.2	24.5	3.1	35.1	3.4
Louisiana	24.1	3.2	22.6	3.1	28.7	3.5
Texas	25.5	3.4	24.2	3.2	28.3	4.0
Oklahoma	17.7	3.9	17.1	3.8	24.9	4.4
Arkansas	31.2	3.1	30.2	3.1	36.1	3.4
Montana	26.4	3.6	26.7	3.6	22.4	3.9
Wyoming	20.0	3.4	19.8	3.2	21.9	4.1
Colorado	21.4	3.8	21.4	3.7	21.6	4.1

Table 10.2. *(cont.)*

	Both sexes		Males		Females	
State	UF (%)^a	MD (mo.)^b	UF (%)^a	MD (mo.)^b	UF (%)^a	MD (mo.)^b
New Mexico	22.4	3.4	23.2	3.4	14.6	4.0
Arizona	20.8	4.1	21.5	4.0	16.1	4.8
Utah	24.9	4.1	24.7	4.0	26.2	4.6
Nevada	27.4	4.6	26.9	4.6	32.2	4.8
Idaho	24.9	4.1	24.9	4.1	25.0	4.6
Washington	24.8	3.4	24.6	3.3	26.5	4.4
Oregon	21.7	3.8	21.3	3.7	25.5	4.5
California	19.8	4.1	19.6	4.1	21.0	4.6
United States	22.3	3.6	22.0	3.6	23.3	3.8

^{a}Unemployment frequency. See note 3.
^{b}Estimated mean duration. See Appendix B.
Source: Twelfth U.S. Census, Occupations (Washington, 1904), pp. lxxxviii–xciii, 214.

first decades of the twentieth century, was unmistakably a national problem, a malady that could and did afflict large numbers of workers in all regions of the United States. "Sparsely settled states have just as acute problems of unemployment as the states with very large populations," concluded a report submitted to the U.S. Commission on Industrial Relations during the Progressive era. "Unemployment is a constant and inevitable risk for almost all working people."[6]

Other dimensions of the history of unemployment in Massachusetts also appear to have been replicated elsewhere. Reports from charity organizations suggest that workers throughout the nation resorted to the same assortment of familial strategies for coping with joblessness. High rates of geographic mobility were a characteristic of blue-collar life in most of the nation's cities. Tramping, during the late nineteenth century, posed a challenge to local officials from New York to California. Unemployment hampered, and shaped, efforts to build effective labor organizations in all the industrial states, and the strategies that Massachusetts unions adopted to combat joblessness were far from parochial. The movement for shorter hours was a national movement; the demand for immigration restriction was a national demand; seniority rules and work-sharing techniques appeared in plants across the country.[7]

Similarly, the evolution of public policy in Massachusetts was par-

alleled by developments in other locales. During the depressions of
the late nineteenth century, charity organizations and hastily appointed municipal committees delivered relief to the needy in cities
and towns throughout the nation. As they had done in Boston, Lynn,
and Holyoke, these agencies tailored their efforts to weed out "shirkers" and to discourage the "unworthy" poor. After the severe downturn of the 1890s, several states established public employment offices, while New York began to monitor unemployment rates by
collecting statistics from trade unions. The tide of reform sentiment
that swept through Massachusetts after 1908 also left a mark upon
attitudes and policies elsewhere. Special investigating commissions
were appointed in New York, Chicago, and Spokane; businesses in
scores of communities were urged to "regularize" their rhythms of
employment; by the early 1920s, free employment offices were operating in more than a dozen states, including California, North Caro-
lina, Illinois, Kansas, and North Dakota. In 1921, public works programs were under way in almost all the major cities of the Northeast
and Midwest as well as in Phoenix, Oakland, Fort Worth, Seattle,
Shreveport, and Jackson, Mississippi. That same year, the California
legislature passed a law requiring the state to plan public works projects years in advance in order to prepare for "periods of extraordinary unemployment." And by the mid-1920s, proposals for unemployment insurance had been drafted for the state legislatures of
Pennsylvania and Wisconsin.[8]

All of which is not to claim that the history of unemployment, after
1870, unfolded in precisely the same manner everywhere in the
United States. Nor does this brief foray outside the borders of Massachusetts warrant the conclusion that the Bay State's experience
was, in all important respects, typical. No state chronicle can fully
and satisfactorily capture a national past, and the history of unemployment was intrinsically a history of flux, local variety, and unpredictable episodes. As Tables 10.1 and 10.2 indicate, unemployment
levels were notably higher in some states than in others in both 1890
and 1900. These disparities almost certainly would have been larger
had the census surveys been conducted during depressions, and, in
all likelihood, they changed considerably from decade to decade.
Economic conditions were never utterly uniform throughout the
United States; unemployment rates always varied from place to
place.[9]

The social and political responses to the problem may also have
varied, in important ways, from region to region or from state to
state. The ideas, attitudes, and behavior of shoemakers in Brockton,
coal miners in Pennsylvania, agricultural laborers in the Mississippi

Valley, and longshoremen in San Francisco may have been more unlike than alike. Local policies for meeting the needs of the unemployed may prove, upon close inspection, to have been notably different in Seattle and Chicago than they were in Boston. But all this is
uncharted terrain: a great deal of exploring remains to be done before
a detailed historical map of unemployment can be drawn for the entire United States.

What *is* evident, even from this preliminary examination of the national record, is that the Massachusetts experience was not a unique
or aberrant one. The Bay State was not alone in witnessing the emergence of the phenomenon of unemployment during the middle decades of the nineteenth century; by 1890, if not earlier, workers in
most parts of the country were jobless roughly as often as they were
in Massachusetts. Signs that unemployment had a significant impact
upon social and political life can be spotted in New York and California, as well as many places in between. The Bay State's encounter
with the problem of unemployment probably had numerous distinctive features, but it was nonetheless, and without question, within
the mainstream of American history.[10]

This implies, of course, that the phenomenon of unemployment
itself was very much a part of the mainstream of nineteenth- and
twentieth-century American history. The problem of joblessness did
not suddenly lurch into view, or prominence, in the 1930s. Nor were
its earlier appearances confined to those well-known, yet brief, panics that serve as punctuation marks in the political and economic history of the United States. Long before the Great Depression, unemployment was a chronic and pervasive feature of working-class life.
It was also an unusually consequential phenomenon and social problem. The existence of poverty in a land of plenty, the incessant movement of workers from town to town, the division of labor within
households, the growth of craft unions, the presence of tensions (and
sometimes conflict) between ethnic and racial groups, the development of charity organizations, urban political machines, and government welfare programs – all these (and other) important elements of
the American past were influenced by the scarcity of steady and secure jobs. Indeed, if the history of Massachusetts can serve as a
guide, the first century of unemployment in the United States left a
deep, and perhaps indelible, imprint upon American society.

Appendix A

Supplementary tables

All tables are for the state of Massachusetts except where otherwise noted.

Table A.1. *Unemployment levels by occupation, males, 1885*

Occupation	Unemployment frequency (%)	Number unemployed	Mean duration (mo.)	Annual unemployment rate (%)
Market gardeners and assistants	88.2	127	4.5	33.1
Longshoremen	82.7	1,504	4.8	33.1
Straw workers	81.4	1,108	4.5	30.5
Cranberry growers and employees	79.4	189	3.5	23.2
Nail makers	73.5	657	3.9	23.9
Comb makers	71.7	182	3.5	20.9
Calkers	71.5	203	5.7	33.9
Lathers	69.2	243	4.1	23.6
Masons	69.2	5,789	4.3	24.8
Agricultural implement makers	69.1	237	4.1	23.6
Rattan furniture makers	67.8	297	2.8	15.8
Coal heavers (vessels)	67.4	209	4.5	25.3
Boot- and shoemakers	67.3	32,374	3.9	21.9
Rolling mill operatives	66.4	164	4.0	22.1
Tack makers	65.4	496	3.9	21.3
Jewelry makers	65.3	2,039	4.6	25.0
Plasterers	63.3	453	4.1	21.6
Building movers and employees	61.7	137	4.3	22.1
Slaters	61.7	161	4.3	22.1
Brickmakers	61.7	1,205	5.4	27.8
Laborers	61.5	20,346	4.7	24.1
Masons and plasterers	58.9	106	4.0	19.6
Linen mill operatives	58.1	194	2.9	14.0
Cutlery makers	56.3	680	3.9	18.3
Painters	55.4	5,176	4.2	19.4
Ship carpenters	54.7	464	5.3	24.2
Riggers	54.4	99	5.2	23.6

Table A.1. *(cont.)*

Occupation	Unem- ployment frequency (%)	Number unem- ployed	Mean dura- tion (mo.)	Annual unemploy- ment rate (%)
Hat makers	54.0	472	4.8	21.6
Carriage trimmers	53.3	233	3.5	15.5
Stovemakers	51.3	314	4.1	17.5
Quarrymen	51.1	584	4.4	18.7
Button makers	50.4	141	3.9	16.4
Morocco workers	50.2	904	3.5	14.6
Paperhangers	50.1	338	4.2	17.5
Iron workers	50.0	2,864	3.8	15.8
Loom makers	47.9	134	3.8	15.2
Rubber factory operatives	47.3	1,276	2.4	9.5
Carpenters	47.2	10,747	3.9	15.3
Glass works employees	46.5	420	2.9	11.2
Stone workers	46.4	1,244	4.1	15.9
Gardeners and assistants	44.9	1,330	4.8	18.0
Fishermen	44.0	3,452	4.9	18.0
Carriage blacksmiths	44.0	324	2.8	10.3
Painters and paperhangers	43.9	90	3.6	13.2
Print works operatives	43.6	896	4.4	16.0
Wire workers	42.8	1,122	3.8	13.6
Pail and tubmakers	42.2	149	3.4	12.0
Boat builders	41.9	98	4.3	15.0
Silk mill operatives	40.5	225	3.4	11.5
Dye works operatives (woolen mill)	40.5	217	4.0	13.5
Hosiery mill operatives	39.6	380	4.8	15.8
Woolen mill operatives	39.4	5,332	4.0	13.1
Boiler works employees	39.3	279	4.6	15.1
Cotton mill operatives	39.1	10,414	3.5	11.4
Miners	38.9	108	3.1	10.0
Sail makers	37.8	135	4.7	14.8
Eyeglass and spectacle makers	37.8	151	3.0	9.5
Carriage painters	37.2	583	4.0	12.4
Teachers	37.0	483	3.3	10.2
Worsted mill operatives	35.9	400	4.0	12.0
Wooden box makers	35.2	244	3.6	10.6
Mariners (sailing)	34.8	866	4.0	11.6
Tannery employees	34.5	2,135	3.8	10.9
Cemetery service	33.2	134	4.6	12.7
Organ and organ parts makers	33.1	258	4.4	12.1
Machine shop employees	33.1	439	4.2	11.6
Coopers	33.0	422	4.3	11.8
Copper workers	32.4	145	3.1	8.4

Table A.1. *(cont.)*

Occupation	Unem-ployment frequency (%)	Number unem-ployed	Mean dura-tion (mo.)	Annual unemploy-ment rate (%)
Basket makers	32.2	130	3.4	9.1
Dye works operatives	31.8	118	4.4	11.7
Cabinetmakers	31.1	585	3.8	9.8
Watchmakers	31.0	588	2.2	5.7
Saw mill employees	31.0	360	4.1	10.6
Machinists	30.3	3,377	3.7	9.3
Farm laborers	30.2	10,759	4.5	11.3
Bleachery operatives	30.0	222	3.1	7.8
Dye works operatives (cotton mills)	29.8	108	4.2	10.4
Artisans' tools makers	29.8	426	4.0	9.9
Shovel makers	29.3	116	4.9	12.0
Furniture makers	29.3	430	3.9	9.5
Lumberyard employees	29.1	155	3.9	9.5
Whip makers	29.1	95	4.2	10.2
Pistol makers	29.1	152	3.8	9.2
Box makers	27.8	189	4.0	9.3
Door, sash, and blind makers	27.6	135	2.9	6.7
Picture-frame makers	27.5	137	4.2	9.6
Paper box makers	27.3	94	4.1	9.3
Porters and helpers (in stores, etc.)	26.5	784	4.1	9.1
Master mariners (sailing)	24.9	274	3.8	7.9
Piano and piano parts makers	24.4	458	4.1	8.3
Plumbers	24.0	470	4.3	8.6
Boys in offices and stores	24.0	603	5.7	11.4
Bookbindery employees	23.2	217	3.9	7.5
Woodworkers	22.9	324	4.0	7.6
Wheelwrights and wheel makers	22.6	193	4.0	7.5
Carpet factory operatives	22.4	266	3.6	6.7
Steamboat employees	21.9	188	4.5	8.2
Marble workers	21.6	179	4.3	7.7
Upholsterers	21.4	265	4.3	7.7
Apprentices	21.1	1,102	5.2	9.1
Carriage makers	21.0	248	3.7	6.5
Brass workers	20.9	272	4.3	7.5
Drivers of delivery wagons	20.7	317	4.5	7.8
Arms makers	20.4	157	3.6	6.1
Cigarmakers	20.4	313	3.8	6.5
Cordage factory operatives	20.1	211	4.2	7.0
Chair makers	19.8	451	3.5	5.8
Musicians	19.5	167	4.4	7.2

Table A.1. *(cont.)*

Occupation	Unem-ployment frequency (%)	Number unem-ployed	Mean dura-tion (mo.)	Annual unemploy-ment rate (%)
Tin workers	18.9	353	4.2	6.6
Sugar refinery employees	18.2	101	3.8	5.8
Gasworks employees	18.1	164	4.0	6.0
Blacksmiths and helpers	17.8	1,040	4.4	6.5
Tailors	17.4	673	4.4	6.4
Stationary engineers and assistants	16.3	577	4.1	5.6
Model and pattern makers	16.2	127	4.1	5.5
Teamsters	15.3	2,144	4.1	5.2
Paper mill operatives	15.2	670	3.8	4.8
Boarding and livery stable employees	15.1	571	4.5	5.7
Harness makers	14.0	182	4.5	5.3
"Other" occupations	13.6	8,893	4.5	5.1
Restaurant employees	12.6	122	4.9	5.1
Slaughterhouse employees	12.4	121	4.6	4.8
Car makers	12.4	101	4.0	4.1
Bakers	12.1	294	4.8	4.8
Steam railroad employees	11.5	1,733	4.6	4.4
Servants (in families)	10.1	166	4.9	4.1
Hotel employees	10.0	273	4.7	3.9
Bartenders	10.0	186	5.1	4.3
Compositors and printers	9.9	450	4.2	3.5
Horse railroad employees	9.7	297	4.8	3.9
Granite workers	9.6	87	3.5	2.8
Watchmen	8.4	163	4.6	3.2
Coachmen	7.5	164	4.6	2.9
Bookkeepers and clerks	7.3	2,020	4.9	3.0
Salesmen	7.0	1,041	4.6	2.7
Farmers	6.9	2,504	4.7	2.7
Express company employees	6.8	181	4.6	2.6
City and town government service	6.6	359	4.2	2.3
National government service	6.2	163	4.7	2.4
Barbers and hairdressers	6.2	193	4.7	2.4
Agents	5.2	192	4.7	2.0
Merchants and dealers	4.1	1,367	4.8	1.6

Source: MBSL, *18 AR* (Boston, 1887), pp. 280–3.

Table A.2. *Unemployment levels by occupation, males, 1890*

Occupation	Unemployment frequency (%)	Number unemployed	Mean duration (mo.)[a]	Annual unemployment rate (%)
Boot- and shoemakers and repairers	48.4	25,341	3.0	12.1
Rubber factory operatives	47.7	1,803	2.1	8.3
Masons (brick and stone)	44.7	4,182	3.5	13.0
Brickmakers, potters, etc.	42.4	1,010	3.9	13.8
Gold and silver workers	40.6	1,441	2.3	7.8
Marble cutters and stonecutters	39.2	2,166	2.9	9.5
Fishermen and oystermen	38.9	3,595	2.7	8.8
Leather curriers, dressers, etc.	38.1	3,402	3.0	9.5
Laborers (not specified)	36.9	23,298	3.7	11.4
Painters, glaziers, and varnishers	33.5	5,329	3.3	9.2
Carpenters and joiners	30.1	9,844	3.1	7.8
Gardeners, florists, etc.	20.9	843	4.1	7.1
Agricultural laborers	20.2	5,538	3.7	6.2
Boatmen, canalmen, pilots, and sailors	19.8	872	3.5	5.8
Iron- and steelworkers (includes molders)	19.2	1,948	3.1	5.0
Cabinetmakers and upholsterers	17.9	808	3.1	4.6
Woodworkers (not otherwise specified)	17.6	1,213	2.9	4.3
Apprentices	17.3	813	4.1	5.9
Messengers, packers, and porters	14.9	998	4.2	5.2
Plumbers, gas fitters, and steamfitters	14.9	725	3.3	4.1
Cotton, woolen, and other textile mill operatives	14.6	7,826	3.1	3.8
Tailors	13.7	726	3.5	4.0
Blacksmiths and wheelwrights	12.4	1,138	3.2	3.3
Draymen, hackmen, teamsters, etc.	11.9	3,069	3.3	3.3
Paper mill operatives	11.4	512	3.3	3.1
Machinists	10.4	1,959	3.3	2.9
Engineers and firemen (not locomotive)	10.3	713	3.3	2.8
Livery stable keepers and hostlers	10.0	593	3.5	2.9

Table A.2. *(cont.)*

Occupation	Unemployment frequency (%)	Number unemployed	Mean duration (mo.)[a]	Annual unemployment rate (%)
Printers, engravers, and bookbinders	9.9	847	3.4	2.8
Piano and organ makers and tuners	9.7	301	2.3	1.9
Street railway employees	9.4	337	3.1	2.4
Servants	9.3	873	3.3	2.6
Steam railroad employees	9.1	1,272	3.5	2.7
Bakers	8.5	295	3.6	2.6
Butchers	7.9	192	3.7	2.4
Engineers (civil, mechanical, electrical, and mining) and surveyors	6.8	206	3.7	2.1
Salesmen	5.7	979	3.8	1.8
Bookkeepers, clerks, etc.	4.9	1,797	3.6	1.5
Barbers and hairdressers	4.7	205	3.5	1.4
Officials (government)	4.6	178	4.1	1.6
Commercial travelers	4.4	162	3.6	1.3
Watchmen, policemen, and detectives	4.0	202	3.5	1.2
Agents (claim, etc.) and collectors	4.0	324	3.7	1.2
Farmers, planters, and overseers	3.9	1,419	4.2	1.4
Merchants, dealers, and peddlers	3.7	1,479	3.7	1.1
Manufacturers, publishers, etc.	3.4	410	3.5	1.0
Bankers, brokers and officials of banks, etc.	2.2	80	4.1	0.8
Clergymen	2.0	57	4.2	0.7
Lawyers	0.9	23	4.0	0.3
Physicians and surgeons	0.9	29	3.6	0.3

[a]Estimated from census data indicating the number of persons unemployed for 1–3 months, 4–6 months, and 7–12 months. See Appendix B.
Source: Eleventh U. S. Census, Population, part II (Washington, 1897), pp. 568–9.

Table A.3. *Unemployment levels in selected occupations, males, 1895*

Occupation[a]	Unemployment frequency (%)	Number unemployed	Mean duration (mo.)	Annual unemployment rate (%)
Boot and shoe workers				
Lynn	38.7	2,554	5.1	16.4
Brockton	42.6	2,234	3.8	13.5
Haverhill	48.2	2,191	4.6	18.5
Cotton mill operatives				
Fall River	85.5	9,526	3.0	21.4
Woolen and worsted mill operatives				
Lawrence	17.6	612	5.6	8.2
Lowell	26.3	275	4.4	9.6
Paper workers				
Holyoke	21.0	363	5.7	10.0
Building trades				
Boston (total)	38.3	5,364	3.6	11.5
Carpenters	36.5	1,776	4.5	13.7
Masons (brick)	55.0	563	4.6	21.1
Masons (stone)	44.8	233	4.6	17.2
Painters (house)	45.6	814	4.7	17.9
Plumbers	21.9	298	5.0	9.1

[a]The only occupations for which 1895 data are available.
Sources: MBSL, *Bulletin 13*, pp. 16–24; *Bulletin 14*, pp. 54–67; *Bulletin 17*, pp. 14–15 (Boston, 1900–1).

Table A.4. *Unemployment levels by occupation, males, 1900*

Occupation	Unemployment frequency (%)	Number unemployed	Mean duration (mo.)[a]	Annual unemployment rate (%)
Boot- and shoemakers and repairers	55.6	27,049	3.3	15.3
Masons (brick and stone)	53.4	5,313	4.1	18.2
Straw workers	50.5	164	2.9	12.2
Plasterers	49.8	621	4.1	17.0
Hat and cap makers	44.1	437	3.4	12.5
Marble cutters and stonecutters	43.6	2,341	3.3	12.0

Table A.4. *(cont.)*

Occupation	Unemployment frequency (%)	Number unemployed	Mean duration (mo.)[a]	Annual unemployment rate (%)
Paperhangers	42.4	529	3.7	13.1
Laborers	41.8	31,834	4.1	14.3
Painters, glaziers, and varnishers	41.2	7,950	3.8	13.0
Brick- and tilemakers	41.0	668	4.3	14.7
Carpenters and joiners	38.5	12,701	3.7	11.9
Miners and quarrymen	36.7	683	3.4	10.4
Gold and silver workers	36.1	1,570	2.5	7.5
Leather curriers and tanners	36.1	2,579	3.8	11.4
Woodchoppers	36.1	228	3.7	11.2
Roofers and slaters	35.8	346	3.9	11.6
Rubber factory operatives	34.7	1,444	3.3	9.5
Stove, furnace, and grate makers	34.6	182	3.5	10.1
Fishermen and oystermen	31.3	1,986	3.3	8.6
Glass workers	30.5	209	3.8	9.6
Actors, professional showmen, etc.	29.5	373	4.0	9.8
Teachers and professors in colleges, etc.	29.2	867	3.1	7.5
Sail, awning, and tent makers	27.3	99	4.4	10.0
Tool and cutlery makers	26.6	807	2.9	6.4
Boatmen and sailors	25.8	868	4.3	9.2
Meat, fish, and fruit packers, etc.	24.8	170	3.8	7.9
Tailors	24.6	1,760	3.8	7.8
Plumbers, gas fitters, and steamfitters	24.5	2,512	3.8	7.8
Carpet factory operatives	23.2	240	3.5	6.8
Seamstresses	22.8	47	4.1	7.8
Linen mill operatives	22.3	78	3.5	6.5
Woolen mill operatives	22.1	3,171	3.4	6.3
Trunk and leather case makers	22.0	57	3.8	7.0

Table A.4. *(cont.)*

Occupation	Unemployment frequency (%)	Number unemployed	Mean duration (mo.)[a]	Annual unemployment rate (%)
Coopers	21.9	304	4.4	8.0
Box makers (paper)	21.5	95	3.1	5.6
Potters	21.4	41	3.8	6.7
Messengers and errand and office boys	21.2	919	5.0	8.8
Sawmill and planing mill employees	20.9	379	3.3	5.8
Upholsterers	20.6	435	3.9	6.8
Agricultural laborers	20.6	6,434	4.2	7.2
Electroplaters	20.3	109	4.0	6.7
Worsted mill operatives	20.1	216	3.3	5.5
Iron- and steel-workers	19.5	3,065	3.5	5.7
Nurses	19.5	189	4.5	7.3
Tin plate and tinware makers	19.1	415	4.0	6.3
Piano and organ makers	18.6	272	4.1	6.3
Cabinet makers	18.5	409	4.3	6.6
Paper and pulp mill operatives	18.3	875	3.2	4.9
Steam boiler makers	18.3	203	4.2	6.4
Bleachery and dye works operatives	18.2	599	3.3	5.0
Box makers (wood)	17.8	142	3.1	4.6
Tobacco and cigar factory operatives	17.5	389	3.3	4.8
Furniture manufactory employees	17.5	452	3.5	5.1
Print works operatives	16.8	289	3.2	4.5
Button makers	16.1	46	3.3	4.4
Textile mill operatives (not otherwise specified)	16.1	1,348	3.4	4.6
Brassworkers	15.9	294	3.8	5.0
Lumbermen and raftsmen	15.8	36	3.6	4.7
Candle, soap, and tallow makers	15.8	44	4.7	6.2
Gasworks employees	15.5	89	3.6	4.7
Bottlers and soda makers	15.4	118	4.9	6.3

Table A.4. *(cont.)*

Occupation	Unemployment frequency (%)	Number unemployed	Mean duration (mo.)[a]	Annual unemployment rate (%)
Shirt, collar, and cuff makers	15.3	32	2.5	3.2
Hosiery and knitting mill operatives	15.3	165	3.5	4.5
Silk mill operatives	15.2	127	3.1	3.9
Bootblacks	15.2	84	4.0	5.1
Copper workers	15.1	59	3.7	4.7
Hucksters and peddlers	15.1	875	4.1	3.2
Packers and shippers	15.0	750	3.6	4.5
Wireworkers	14.8	567	3.9	4.8
Draymen, hackmen, teamsters, etc.	14.7	5,515	3.9	4.8
Blacksmiths	14.2	1,234	4.2	5.0
Bookbinders	14.1	203	3.9	4.6
Gardeners, florists, nurserymen, etc.	14.0	396	4.7	5.4
Wheelwrights	13.9	122	4.9	5.7
Confectioners	13.9	170	4.0	4.6
Musicians and music teachers	13.8	355	3.7	4.3
Stewards	13.6	88	5.1	5.8
Servants and waiters	13.4	1,577	3.8	4.2
Model and pattern makers	13.0	150	3.8	4.1
Telegraph and telephone linemen	13.0	88	3.7	4.0
Printers, lithographers, and pressmen	12.8	1,147	3.8	4.1
Hostlers	12.8	664	4.2	4.5
Harness and saddle makers and repairers	12.4	187	4.4	4.5
Machinists	12.3	3,367	3.8	3.9
Janitors and sextons	12.3	605	3.8	3.9
Weighers, gaugers, and measurers	12.2	36	5.0	5.1
Bartenders	12.2	400	4.5	4.6
Porters and helpers	11.8	208	4.4	4.3
Bakers	11.8	581	4.1	4.0
Piano and organ tuners	11.8	59	4.0	3.9
Engravers	11.7	117	3.8	3.7

Table A.4. *(cont.)*

Occupation	Unem-ployment frequency (%)	Number unem-ployed	Mean duration (mo.)[a]	Annual unemploy-ment rate (%)
Broom and brush makers	11.2	52	4.8	4.5
Cotton mill operatives	11.1	4,313	3.6	3.3
Butchers	11.1	386	4.2	3.9
Engineers and firemen (not locomotive)	10.6	1,326	4.0	3.5
Rope and cordage factory operatives	10.6	124	4.4	3.9
Gunsmiths, locksmiths, and bellhangers	10.3	35	5.1	4.4
Electricians	10.2	393	3.6	3.1
Photographers	10.2	110	4.7	4.0
Electric light and power company employees	9.9	63	4.3	3.5
Street railway employees	9.7	686	3.8	3.1
Stenographers and typewriters	9.6	97	4.5	3.6
Steam railroad employees	9.3	1,629	3.9	3.0
Millers	9.2	28	5.2	4.0
Artists and art teachers	8.2	78	4.6	3.1
Engineers and surveyors	7.5	223	4.4	2.7
Salesmen	7.4	2,378	4.1	2.5
Barbers and hairdressers	7.2	459	4.2	2.5
Bookkeepers and accountants	7.2	792	4.8	2.9
Brewers and maltsters	7.0	52	4.7	2.7
Telegraph and telephone operators	6.8	92	4.4	2.5
Clerks and copyists	6.6	2,035	4.5	2.5
Clock makers and watchmakers and repairers	6.6	114	3.5	1.9
Chemical works employees	6.3	20	4.8	2.5
Architects, designers, draftsmen, etc.	6.3	169	4.3	2.3
Commercial travelers	6.0	333	4.1	2.1
Butter and cheese makers	6.0	13	5.5	2.7

Table A.4. *(cont.)*

Occupation	Unem-ployment frequency (%)	Number unem-ployed	Mean duration (mo.)[a]	Annual unemploy-ment rate (%)
Literary and scientific persons	5.8	52	5.1	2.4
Restaurant keepers	5.8	93	4.8	2.3
Agents	5.6	708	4.4	2.1
Officials (government)	5.6	213	4.2	1.9
Hotel keepers	5.1	62	5.3	2.3
Saloonkeepers	4.9	39	3.9	1.6
Manufacturers and officials, etc.	4.6	730	4.2	1.6
Clergymen	4.5	161	6.0	2.2
Watchmen, policemen, firemen, etc.	4.5	392	4.5	1.7
Journalists	3.8	58	5.5	1.8
Merchants and dealers (wholesale)	3.7	98	5.2	1.6
Foremen and overseers	3.4	71	4.0	1.1
Soldiers, sailors, and marines (U.S.)	3.2	60	4.5	1.2
Bankers and brokers	3.1	103	7.0	1.8
Launderers	3.1	123	3.9	1.0
Veterinary surgeons	3.1	10	5.3	1.3
Boarding and lodging house keepers	3.0	21	1.3	0.3
Farmers, planters, and overseers	3.0	894	4.9	1.2
Merchants and dealers (excluding wholesale)	2.9	1,109	5.1	1.2
Hemp and jute mill operatives	2.9	16	2.5	0.6
Dentists	2.9	43	5.3	1.3
Livery stable keepers	2.6	34	5.7	1.2
Undertakers	2.5	24	3.9	0.8
Officials of banks and companies	2.1	78	4.0	0.7
Physicians and surgeons	1.9	89	5.6	0.8
Lawyers	1.7	59	4.8	0.7

[a]Estimated from census data indicating the number of persons unemployed for 1–3 months, 4–6 months, and 7–12 months. See Appendix B.
Source: Twelfth U.S. Census, Occupations (Washington, 1904), pp. 300–7.

Table A.5. *Annual unemployment rates among trade union members, by occupation, 1908–22*

Occupation	Annual unemployment rate (%)[a]														
	1908	1909	1910	1911	1912	1913	1914	1915	1916	1917	1918	1919	1920	1921	1922
Boot and shoe workers															
Total	12.4	7.8	7.5	5.8	9.0	7.7	13.8	10.3	4.0	12.0	4.5	4.2	33.6	27.0	24.1
Mixed unions	24.9[b]	9.2	6.7	4.2	6.6	9.8	14.0	9.6	2.5	—	—	—	—	—	—
Cutters	10.9[c]	9.9	11.2	9.0	17.4	9.0	13.0	14.0	5.1	17.0	2.5	8.7	51.8	28.2	32.4
Edgemakers	11.1[b]	6.3	4.8	4.6	4.5	5.0	8.2	6.8	6.3	5.5	2.0	2.8	18.3	14.4	19.9
Lasters	12.7[c]	8.0	8.2	4.0	11.4	11.6	30.5	21.4	12.0	21.8	6.2	6.4	50.3	42.2	39.0
Stitchers	4.6[b]	5.2	7.3	7.9	4.5	3.6	13.0	9.4	2.4	11.9	4.0	1.9	21.5	16.0	23.1
Treers, dressers, and packers	—	9.0[b]	5.5	4.5	5.6	4.0	7.7	9.0	3.9	16.3	5.6	2.1	39.3	23.9	24.7
Others	8.9[c]	4.2	7.0	6.1	10.9	4.9	12.0	6.3[c]	5.5[c]	11.1	2.2	4.1	31.3	29.9	21.0
Textile operatives															
Total	23.5	7.9	10.7	12.6	12.4	11.6	11.1	6.2	3.3	3.9	5.5	7.4	29.1	24.0	27.8
Loomfixers	5.1[b]	2.0	6.0	13.0	3.4	3.7	4.2	5.7	3.0	3.8	2.4	6.7	24.6	20.7	21.3
Mule spinners	10.5[c]	19.6	17.2	19.4	8.4	15.0	16.0	7.3	1.8	2.5	5.9	6.4	25.6	27.0	14.4
Weavers	—	—	1.8	5.9[c]	2.1	2.6	7.6	2.4	0.9	1.4	4.7	7.3	9.6	21.7	14.3
Others	20.4[c]	2.8	6.4	7.0	14.5	22.0	15.1	10.5	6.4	6.2	7.4	7.9	34.1	23.5	34.8
Building trades and related occupations															
Bricklayers, masons, and plasterers	42.9	20.2	15.5	25.2	10.4	21.3	33.0	26.9	20.3	28.0	31.9	24.1	22.2	44.5	13.1
Carpenters	11.1	7.5	6.7	9.6	7.1	11.2	20.0	14.4	11.3	8.7	8.5	8.3	11.4	28.3	10.0
Hod carriers and building laborers	30.7	23.2	9.8	13.8	17.8	22.7	29.1	12.4	12.1	13.1	6.7	11.6	19.6	66.7	15.5

Painters, decorators, and paperhangers	24.6	17.8	11.5	14.2	15.9	17.9	32.5	22.9	14.7	16.6	13.6	7.8	12.6	29.9	17.5
Plumbers, gas fitters, and steamfitters	11.5	8.4	4.7	5.8	4.2	7.1	11.6	17.3	8.6	9.0	4.7	13.2	12.2	28.8	9.6
Engineers (hoisting and portable)	16.4[c]	7.2	6.4	10.5	6.0	10.8	18.6	14.7	8.4	3.1[b]	4.4	3.8	5.8	49.6[c]	16.9
Quarry workers	6.6	20.6	25.5	26.2	14.7	13.5	26.1	25.6	25.5	12.8	—	—	22.2	35.0	63.1
Granite cutters and polishers	9.9	6.6	5.6	20.4	12.7	11.7	14.9	12.7	38.1	14.4	—	15.8	18.8	41.8	58.2
Electrical workers	11.9	2.1	5.5	7.0	5.8	4.4	7.1	6.7	1.5	3.2	2.9	3.1	6.3	16.9	10.0
Iron- and steelworkers, metal workers, machinists															
Boilermakers and helpers	35.1[c]	17.2	6.9	12.3	8.3	2.5[c]	—	6.2[b]	3.5	4.9	4.0	8.3	11.3	50.9	41.3
Machinists	10.7	2.8	4.8	3.9	4.2	4.7	11.3	10.9	2.8	2.4	6.2	12.8	21.0	32.8	14.0
Metal polishers, buffers, platers	19.4[b]	10.4	2.6	6.4	2.9	5.2	19.6	8.5	6.9	4.0	5.6	0.8	12.4	33.2	12.2
Molders and coremakers (iron, brass)	21.7	10.1	11.0	15.5	17.9	18.5	20.8	11.5	4.7	4.0	7.5	13.0	12.7	44.0	22.1
Blacksmiths and horseshoers	6.4[c]	4.7	4.0[c]	3.4	3.5	2.7	4.2	5.1	5.2	5.3	5.6	3.8	13.3	68.0	41.8[b]
Sheet metal workers	15.3[b]	3.4	3.0	8.0	7.8	7.8	16.2	11.9	5.6	3.9	3.3	2.0	2.5	19.2	8.5

continued

Table A.5. (cont.)

Occupation	Annual unemployment rate (%)[a]														
	1908	1909	1910	1911	1912	1913	1914	1915	1916	1917	1918	1919	1920	1921	1922
Printing and related industries															
Bookbinders	47.3	20.4	4.6	4.0	—	—	—	3.8[b]	3.9[c]	1.1	6.1	0.3	0.6	39.2	26.2
Compositors	8.1	4.4	3.7	5.9	6.0	5.2	9.6	10.1	6.1	4.4	5.6	3.7	4.2	14.0	13.9
Printing pressmen	7.9	3.7	4.0	4.1	2.4	3.2	4.1	4.0	2.1	3.6	3.1	2.8	4.4	16.2	5.3
Stereotypers and electrotypers	3.6[c]	1.0	0.6	0.7	0.7	1.4	—	—	3.9[c]	2.8[c]	—	—	—	—	—
Transportation															
Railway clerks	2.8	0.5	0.8	0.8	0.4	0.9	1.0	1.1	0.5	1.1	2.0	1.1	3.5	12.1	4.1
Railway conductors	1.1[c]	1.9	1.9	2.1	2.5	3.2	3.7	4.7	4.1	4.0	4.3	5.1	6.0	6.9	7.8
Engineers (locomotive)	2.7[c]	2.6	4.8	5.4	8.7	9.4	9.8	9.3	9.6	9.0	8.3	9.4	9.0	12.5	10.2
Firemen (locomotive)	6.5[c]	1.3	1.3	1.9	1.5	2.4	9.0	9.8	3.4	3.5	5.2	8.1	4.9	18.5	10.6
Station agents and employees	0.4	0.4	0.6[c]	2.8	1.0	1.7	6.2	3.8	1.3	0.7	1.5	1.3	3.9	7.3	4.2
Street and electric railway employees	2.4	2.5	2.4	2.1	2.5	2.5	2.7	4.4	3.3	3.2	4.2	4.7	8.7	8.5	2.5
Railroad telegraphers	1.2	0.9	1.2	1.0	0.7	0.7	1.4	0.9	0.4	0.3	—	—	—	—	—
Railroad trainmen	2.6[c]	2.0	2.0	2.9	2.7	4.2	3.9	3.4	2.6	2.6	3.6	3.5	4.3	16.3	7.1

Teamsters, chauffeurs, drivers, etc.	11.5	6.6	10.6	2.7	4.0	6.4	11.2	7.8	1.1	1.5	2.1	6.7	7.1	13.5	8.3
Railroad workers	7.7[c]	2.6	1.4	1.6	1.0	2.9	5.9	4.4	5.2	1.3	—	2.0	3.5	7.8	14.6[b]
Food, tobacco, and related industries															
Bakers and confectioners	7.6[c]	8.4	5.9	12.9	5.0	5.2	9.7	13.3	8.5	6.1	5.6	5.6	6.4	7.7	8.9
Bartenders	13.5[c]	16.0	6.8	5.3	4.6	5.4	9.7	13.6	6.3	8.4	—	—	—	—	—
Bottlers and drivers	9.6[c]	8.9	15.2	11.9[c]	7.6	4.9	7.8	4.4	1.9[c]	3.9	—	—	—	—	—
Brewery workmen	8.5	9.5	5.4	7.8	8.1	9.0	7.4	6.3	5.5	5.3	5.2	30.9	38.7	44.1	14.5
Cigarmakers	17.9	6.7	5.3	4.8	3.7	3.5	7.7	10.0	4.6	5.9	6.6	4.6	19.4	10.7	8.1
Cooks and waiters	12.2[c]	3.0	6.7	5.9	4.6	4.9	8.4	8.3	3.0	4.6	—	—	—	—	—
Other															
Barbers	3.4	2.4	2.1	2.1	1.7	2.3	3.5	4.6	1.5	1.8	2.0	1.8	1.2	2.3	1.7
Clerks (retail and wholesale)	2.7	3.5	2.5	2.3	1.9	1.6	3.2	4.6	2.0	2.7	2.9	4.8	4.1	0.8	2.0
Firemen (stationary)	5.4	3.0	2.0	1.8	2.8	5.1	4.2	2.6	2.9	1.7	1.6	2.0	3.3	4.8	1.4
Garment workers	38.3	5.2	18.8	13.7	27.4	25.4	36.8	18.4	5.3	7.2	—	—	—	38.9	16.5
Municipal employees	26.2	9.9	8.8	18.6	5.6	7.9	16.4	15.8	5.4	7.7	12.3	5.0	7.0	11.7	14.2
Paper and pulp makers	22.3	1.5	1.5	4.9	0.5	0.8	13.0	23.8	6.8	11.3	10.0	34.2	24.3	63.3[c]	26.3[b]

continued

Table A.5. (*cont.*)

| | Annual unemployment rate (%)[a] | | | | | | | | | | | | | | |
Occupation	1908	1909	1910	1911	1912	1913	1914	1915	1916	1917	1918	1919	1920	1921	1922
Telephone operators	—	—	—	—	—	—	—	3.1	3.5	1.6	3.5	0.9	0.2	0.3	1.0
Theatrical stage employees	36.1[b]	20.8	16.3	10.8	17.6	19.5	23.8	24.6	17.2	11.6	19.4	8.7	10.3	25.3	12.7
Freight handlers and clerks	10.3	4.6	7.0	9.9	3.9	9.6	10.8	9.7	—	—	2.1[c]	20.2	13.3	54.2	34.2
Engineers (stationary)	12.2	2.3	2.4	2.0	1.7	2.9	3.9	2.4	1.2	1.3	1.2	2.5	4.8	3.6	1.7

[a] Average of 4 quarterly figures based on MBSL category of unemployment resulting from "all causes." See Appendix B.
[b] Data available for 2 quarters only.   [c] Data available for 3 quarters only.

Sources: The data regarding unemployment rates for trade unionists in different occupations were gathered from more than fifty tables published in various reports and bulletins of the Massachusetts Bureau of Statistics of Labor. Most of the quarterly figures collected by the bureau were presented in summary tables periodically published in the annual reports of the MBSL. See MBSL, *44 AR*, pp. 112–13; *47 AR*, pp. 56–7; *48 AR*, part IV, p. 53; *52 AR*, part III, pp. 41–2. However, not all quarterly figures for all occupations found their way into these summary tables. Consequently, the individual quarterly reports also had to be consulted. These appeared first in the MBSL, *Labor Bulletin*, numbers 61–4, 66, 69, 71, 72, 74, 77, 79, 80, 82, 85, and 89 (Boston, 1908–11). Thereafter, they were published in the MBSL's *Quarterly Report on the State of Employment*, numbers 17–36 (Boston, 1912–16). Beginning with number 23, the title of this publication was changed to the *Quarterly Report on Unemployment*; beginning with number 33, the title changed again to the *Quarterly Report on Employment*. All figures for 1917–20 were published in the annual reports cited above. Supplementary figures for the early 1920s were located in the quarterly reports published in MBSL, *Massachusetts Industrial Review*, nos. 5, 6, 7, 9, 10, and 11 (Boston, 1921–23).

Table A.6. *Estimated average annual unemployment frequencies, trade union members, by occupation, 1908–22*[a]

Occupation (or union)	Frequency (%)
Bricklayers, masons, and plasterers	75.4
Quarry workers	72.6
Garment workers	61.6
Hod carriers and building laborers	59.4
Granite cutters and polishers	58.8
Lasters (boot and shoe)	55.4
Theatrical stage employees	53.0
Painters, decorators, and paperhangers	52.0
Cutters (boot and shoe)	47.4
Paper- and pulp makers	46.5
Molders and coremakers	44.5
Boilermakers and helpers	43.0
Freight handlers and clerks	41.1
Textile operatives (other)	41.1
Brewery workmen	38.3
Bookbinders	36.4
Textile operatives (total)	36.4
Mule spinners	36.4
Boot and shoe workers (total)	33.5
Engineers (hoisting and portable)	33.3
Blacksmiths and horseshoers	32.1
Carpenters	31.5
Treers, dressers, and packers (boot and shoe)	31.2
Municipal employees	31.1
Boot and shoe workers (other)	29.6
Plumbers, gas fitters, and steamfitters	27.8
Metal polishers, buffers, and platers	26.3
Mixed unions (boot and shoe)	25.4
Machinists	25.3
Stitchers (boot and shoe)	23.4
Bartenders	23.0
Loomfixers	21.1
Engineers (locomotive)	20.1
Edgemakers (boot and shoe)	20.0
Cigarmakers	19.8
Sheet metal workers	19.6
Bakers and confectioners	19.2
Bottlers and drivers (food, tobacco, etc.)	18.7
Compositors	16.7
Teamsters, chauffeurs, and drivers	15.9
Weavers	14.5
Electrical workers	14.4
Cooks and waiters	14.0
Firemen (locomotive)	13.0
Printing pressmen	9.4
Railroad workers	8.2

Table A.6. *(cont.)*

Occupation (or union)	Frequency (%)
Street and electric railway employees	7.9
Railroad trainmen	7.9
Railway conductors	6.9
Firemen (stationary)	4.8
Clerks: retail, wholesale	4.5
Engineers (stationary)	4.1
Station agents and employees	4.0
Barbers	3.7
Railway clerks	3.5
Stereotypers and electrotypers	2.9
Telephone operators	2.8
Railway telegraphers	1.4

[a]These average (mean) frequencies were developed from the unemployment rates presented in Table A.5, using the formula for converting rates into frequencies discussed in Appendix B. The "all causes" rates were adjusted downward by 1.8 percentage points to adjust for the idleness that ought not to have been counted as unemployment. For occupations in which the average annual unemployment rate was less than 3.0%, the figure was divided in half, in lieu of subtracting 1.8. Regarding the procedures used to develop these estimates, see Appendix B.
Sources: Same as Table A.5.

Table A.7. *Unemployment frequencies in selected occupations by specific place of birth, males, 1885*

Occupation	Unemployment frequency (%) for males born in:[a]														
	Mass.	Other N.E. States	Other States	Ireland	Canada (Eng.)	Canada (Fr.)	England	Scotland	Nova Scotia	Prince Edward Island	New Brunswick	Germany	Sweden	Portugal	Other foreign
Bookkeepers and clerks	7.6	6.3	5.9	7.5	4.1	8.5	8.5	4.6	7.9	6.8	9.6	3.3	7.0	12.2	6.3
Teamsters	16.5	11.0	13.7	15.7	15.6	20.9	19.4	17.7	11.7	9.1	14.0	7.5	17.8	26.4	16.9
Farmers	7.0	6.0	5.1	8.1	6.6	8.8	7.2	2.4	7.9	27.6	16.1	5.1	8.3	3.4	6.5
Farm laborers	28.0	28.1	30.1	39.9	33.9	45.8	34.7	29.5	24.7	19.5	23.3	21.1	27.6	21.8	23.9
Fishermen	63.6	30.3	45.8	30.2	26.4	44.0	20.0	30.9	18.0	7.5	19.7	15.1	10.3	62.5	21.3
Boot- and shoemakers	68.4	60.7	68.8	73.7	60.8	76.1	51.8	54.9	59.7	42.5	55.9	22.4	65.5	19.2	50.2
Carpenters	48.3	42.5	45.8	54.0	43.3	54.6	46.9	47.6	46.5	49.1	46.3	36.0	44.7	24.6	44.1
Masons	62.4	54.3	65.3	79.3	60.1	77.5	66.3	66.9	68.5	100.0	100.0	65.9	67.2	37.3	72.0
Painters	57.2	51.7	54.6	57.8	52.5	69.5	48.8	59.4	59.1	41.2	52.1	31.5	55.4	37.7	42.9
Cotton mill operatives	40.2	27.2	33.7	39.9	31.4	40.5	51.0	33.0	43.1	46.9	31.3	12.0	15.1	35.3	29.5
Furniture makers	28.5	20.5	26.2	42.5	19.5	28.5	40.6	33.5	32.2	21.6	21.1	29.9	27.2	45.2	34.2
Machinists	31.2	23.2	27.0	39.5	26.8	32.5	36.2	32.7	25.9	18.0	14.3	27.6	24.9	40.4	22.1
Ironworkers	50.1	37.2	43.8	56.3	46.4	41.6	53.6	47.1	50.0	55.3	51.3	40.2	59.4	74.5	59.6
Jewelry makers	61.7	64.3	68.8	94.0	68.6	80.4	62.0	82.9	48.4	32.7	45.1	73.8	18.8	54.4	48.6
Woolen mill operatives	41.7	35.9	43.0	40.7	41.3	35.0	34.6	31.7	55.5	26.3	46.8	39.6	44.4	31.5	43.4
Laborers	60.1	53.9	49.2	64.4	60.4	71.8	63.8	45.2	55.7	43.1	50.1	44.9	46.9	40.8	56.2
Brickmakers	38.4	42.3	62.2	66.6	100.0	59.5	33.3	50.0	83.8	50.0	—	18.8	—	95.0	33.3
Carpet factory operatives	19.9	15.3	30.7	20.9	27.2	22.2	23.8	11.1	25.0	50.0	28.5	14.2	—	—	20.0
Paper mill operatives	13.5	9.1	11.9	17.7	15.3	16.9	17.8	12.0	10.0	33.0	—	6.1	16.6	—	12.5
Steam railroad employees	8.0	3.8	6.6	18.8	6.2	39.1	13.1	8.9	13.8	9.1	9.0	11.6	13.1	16.6	40.2

[a]See Chapter 4, note 15.

Sources: MBSL, *18 AR*, pp. 254–7. *Census of Massachusetts: 1885,* I, part 2 (Boston, 1888), pp. 532–664.

Table A.8. *The age distribution of unemployment in selected communities, males, 1885*

City/town	Unemployment frequencies (%) and mean durations (mo.) for males age[a]								Number of males[b]
	10–13	14–19	20–9	30–9	40–9	50–9	60–79	80–	
Boston	18.5	17.3	17.9	18.0	19.4	20.0	20.9	9.3	127,319
	5.7	5.0	4.4	4.1	4.3	4.7	5.0	5.9	23,584
Fall River	84.2	63.5	50.2	44.9	47.1	46.2	39.0	—	17,172
	3.3	3.5	3.5	3.7	3.9	4.4	4.9	—	8,675
Lynn	13.8	44.0	43.0	40.7	39.4	40.5	40.0	20.7	15,335
	5.6	4.3	3.6	3.5	3.9	4.1	4.7	7.3	6,342
Worcester	—	35.6	34.1	30.1	33.3	29.2	24.5	16.0	21,906
	—	4.6	3.9	3.9	3.9	4.3	5.1	4.5	6,989
Lawrence	33.3	42.2	32.3	28.2	33.5	33.9	34.8	11.1	11,749
	7.5	5.3	4.7	4.7	5.1	5.9	7.3	6.3	3,908
New Bedford	33.9	25.9	19.8	19.5	21.3	25.7	30.4	22.6	10,530
	4.8	5.1	4.6	4.9	4.8	5.2	5.7	6.6	2,377
Natick	32.5	66.5	66.8	63.1	66.4	66.0	58.3	21.6	2,759
	8.0	5.0	4.2	4.2	4.4	4.6	5.2	4.0	1,791
Hopkinton	65.5	77.5	72.9	66.6	69.1	62.3	39.6	16.4	1,334
	5.0	4.2	3.9	3.8	3.9	4.3	4.6	4.5	874
Chicopee	47.9	51.9	48.4	45.4	49.1	47.9	38.8	31.9	3,446
	11.0	4.5	4.1	3.6	4.2	4.1	5.0	9.0	1,651
Grafton	—	70.7	54.7	51.0	52.8	44.6	30.4	10.4	1,439
	—	3.7	3.0	2.8	2.9	3.1	3.8	2.0	751
Pittsfield	6.7	42.2	26.5	20.6	26.1	25.4	22.3	17.9	4,567
	5.0	4.5	4.1	4.1	4.5	4.6	4.8	5.0	1,225
Dedham	—	37.1	39.4	28.9	33.6	34.9	32.1	—	2,060
	—	3.9	3.4	3.6	3.2	3.8	3.8	—	709
Gloucester	21.3	31.7	16.7	17.3	19.4	27.9	38.1	21.3	8,381
	6.0	4.5	3.7	3.4	3.5	3.7	4.5	4.8	1,781

continued

Attleborough	10.2	55.9	55.5	51.2	48.9	43.8	38.8	16.9	4,364
	6.0	4.9	4.2	4.5	4.4	4.6	4.9	5.0	2,216
Malden	—	37.2	34.1	24.2	23.0	22.7	22.5	—	5,242
	—	3.6	2.4	2.5	2.9	3.6	4.6	—	1,454
Upton	—	79.3	79.4	69.0	70.7	60.0	57.5	44.4	652
	—	6.3	4.1	3.7	3.8	4.1	4.0	3.5	450
Methuen	—	48.7	51.1	44.1	38.9	33.6	32.1	—	1,381
	—	3.8	3.6	3.3	3.9	4.0	5.2	—	588
Chelsea	—	7.4	10.0	11.5	10.8	11.2	10.8	—	8,072
	—	5.0	4.1	3.9	4.5	4.5	4.5	—	841
Westborough	—	36.0	42.9	37.5	29.1	26.0	13.6	9.4	1,548
	—	3.7	3.4	3.3	3.5	3.5	4.2	4.0	507
Athol	—	58.6	48.2	44.1	38.4	41.4	32.9	—	1,572
	—	3.6	2.8	3.0	2.9	3.1	3.7	—	683
Fitchburg	—	16.1	14.6	15.3	14.9	19.3	14.7	15.5	5,063
	—	4.9	4.1	3.7	4.4	4.5	4.6	3.0	783
Falmouth	—	33.4	37.7	28.4	32.7	24.4	18.8	34.2	877
	—	5.1	4.8	4.3	4.5	4.0	5.3	5.0	260
Leverett	—	49.9	14.5	3.7	10.4	10.5	1.9	—	283
	—	5.3	5.7	6.0	6.4	5.3	6.0	—	33
Wilbraham	—	36.5	17.4	16.0	17.5	23.9	11.4	16.1	512
	—	5.2	4.8	4.8	5.6	5.7	6.2	6.0	99
Reading	—	16.7	16.5	8.4	17.1	16.3	25.9	16.1	1,069
	—	4.7	5.1	4.8	4.8	5.0	5.1	6.0	172
Harwich	—	22.2	22.7	14.7	13.1	14.9	8.7	—	988
	—	4.5	4.8	5.2	5.2	5.1	5.1	—	158
Southborough	—	54.3	39.0	27.7	30.5	24.4	17.2	—	714
	—	3.5	3.9	3.3	3.9	5.4	5.5	—	233
Yarmouth	—	57.1	54.5	56.7	58.7	64.2	60.0	50.0	557
	—	3.5	3.2	3.2	3.4	3.1	3.6	4.5	337
Egremont	—	4.0	11.3	12.5	8.8	15.8	6.5	—	286
	—	11.0	7.8	5.6	5.7	5.2	4.7	—	29

Table A.8. (cont.)

City/town	Unemployment frequencies (%) and mean durations (mo.) for males age:[a]								Number of males[b]
	10–13	14–19	20–9	30–9	40–9	50–9	60–79	80–	
Hancock	25.0	50.0	19.2	7.1	8.0	14.3	10.8	—	202
	7.0	5.7	4.8	4.3	4.7	5.0	4.8	—	30
Somerset	25.0	88.6	69.1	64.1	59.1	53.4	51.2	—	933
	5.0	4.1	3.6	4.0	4.2	4.0	4.4	—	611
Boxford	—	47.1	15.1	14.3	14.6	17.2	11.9	33.3	281
	—	3.8	3.8	5.4	4.8	5.0	4.6	3.5	52
Conway	—	40.9	22.8	24.4	20.5	18.0	20.3	50.0	507
	—	5.3	5.3	5.6	5.5	6.0	6.1	8.0	128
Longmeadow	—	18.9	51.3	48.7	31.5	24.1	8.2	—	636
	—	5.6	5.2	4.5	4.0	4.9	3.1	—	225
Montgomery	—	7.2	6.7	15.8	14.3	12.5	8.0	—	106
	—	4.0	2.0	5.7	4.0	5.5	7.5	—	11
Plainfield	—	44.4	11.1	4.8	23.3	36.4	18.4	—	172
	—	5.9	3.7	6.0	5.1	3.9	4.0	—	38
Shirley	—	57.5	42.1	36.8	49.3	34.5	29.7	16.7	381
	—	5.3	3.5	4.8	5.5	6.4	5.3	6.0	152
Millis	—	33.3	9.3	10.8	13.8	3.2	4.0	—	233
	—	4.8	2.8	3.8	5.2	3.0	2.0	—	23
Carver	—	51.4	53.0	43.8	31.7	41.1	32.5	20.0	382
	—	3.4	2.8	2.9	3.5	3.8	4.7	2.0	164
Northborough	—	54.2	54.4	37.0	32.9	32.5	27.0	—	646
	—	3.8	4.3	3.1	3.2	4.6	4.7	—	266

[a] For each community, the first row of numbers indicates the unemployment frequency and the second the mean duration.

[b] For each community, the first row indicates the number of males in the labor force; the second indicates the number of males who were unemployed. The labor force figures are drawn from the census volume listed below and differ slightly from the figures presented in the MBSL's report on unemployment.

Table A.9. *Unemployment levels by occupation, females, 1885*

Occupation	Number employed	Unemployment frequency (%)	Mean duration (mo.)	Difference between male and female:[a]	
				UF (%)	MD (mo.)
Baseball makers	58	94.8	5.1	—	—
Straw workers	3,289	93.7	5.0	− 12.3	− 0.5
Rattan furniture makers	127	92.9	3.3	− 25.1	− 0.5
Tassel makers	38	84.2	2.9	—	—
Jewelry makers	641	80.0	4.6	− 14.7	0
Chocolate makers	93	78.5	4.1	—	—
Cutlery makers	60	78.3	3.3	− 22.0	0.6
Metal burnishers	74	77.0	5.3	—	—
Tack makers	232	72.0	4.1	− 6.6	− 0.2
Boot- and shoemakers	14,420	71.1	3.8	− 3.8	0.1
Picture-frame makers	59	62.7	4.6	− 35.2	− 0.4
Linen mill operatives	468	60.9	2.6	− 2.8	0.3
Hat and cap makers	322	60.6	4.8	− 6.6	0
Glass works employees	81	60.5	2.6	− 14.0	0.3
Cartridge makers	129	58.1	3.6	—	—
Needle makers	63	57.1	3.7	—	—
Skirt makers	73	56.2	5.8	—	—
Rubber factory operatives	1,757	55.2	2.4	− 7.9	0
Corset makers	539	53.4	3.2	—	—
Silk mill operatives	1,419	53.1	3.2	− 12.6	0.2
Whip makers	147	51.0	3.7	− 21.9	0.5
Tobacco workers	135	50.4	4.2	—	—
Teachers	9,979	49.6	3.4	− 12.6	− 0.1
Envelope makers	149	49.0	3.6	—	—
Carpet sewers	71	47.9	4.6	—	—
Worsted mill operatives	1,720	46.6	3.4	− 10.7	0.6
Rubber gossamer makers	113	46.0	4.5	—	—
Print works operatives	333	46.0	4.3	− 2.4	0.1
Scrubbers and cleaners (in mills)	303	45.2	4.5	—	—
Woolen mill operatives	9,176	45.0	3.9	− 5.6	0.1
Suspender makers	442	43.9	3.2	—	—
Cotton mill operatives	31,741	43.6	3.4	− 4.5	0.1
Paper box makers	1,426	43.2	3.7	− 15.9	0.4
Hosiery mill operatives	2,320	40.6	4.1	− 1.0	0.7
Cordage factory operatives	646	40.3	3.5	− 20.2	0.7
Watchmakers	1,025	40.1	2.0	− 9.1	0.2
Brush makers	286	39.5	5.3	—	—

Table A.9. *(cont.)*

Occupation	Number employed	Unemployment frequency (%)	Mean duration (mo.)	Difference between male and female:[a]	
				UF (%)	MD (mo.)
Box makers, not specified	288	38.2	3.6	−10.4	0.4
Cigarmakers	427	37.9	3.6	−17.5	0.2
Cloak makers	304	37.8	4.3	—	—
Hoop-skirt makers	120	37.5	4.3	—	—
Apprentices	503	36.0	6.7	−14.9	−1.5
Button makers	598	34.8	4.3	15.6	−0.4
Bookbindery employees	1,108	33.9	4.1	−10.7	−0.2
Tailoresses	4,466	33.0	3.9	−15.6	0.5
Nail makers	123	32.5	5.8	41.0	−1.9
Necktie makers	164	32.4	3.8	—	—
Nurses	3,030	32.3	4.7	—	—
Wire workers	191	30.4	4.0	12.4	−0.2
Sewing machine operators	442	30.3	4.4	—	—
Rubber clothing makers	135	28.9	4.1	—	—
Girls in offices and stores	468	28.2	6.1	− 4.2	−0.4
Shirtmakers	461	27.6	4.5	—	—
Milliners	2,218	27.5	4.9	—	—
Button-hole makers	124	27.4	3.9	—	—
Seamstresses	3,733	27.1	4.6	—	—
Confectionery makers and packers	267	25.8	3.7	—	—
Laundry workers	4,862	24.0	5.2	—	—
Dressmakers	13,290	24.0	4.4	—	—
Singers	147	23.8	4.7	—	—
Bakers	161	23.0	4.8	−10.9	0
Paper mill operatives	3,556	21.3	3.7	− 6.1	0.1
Music teachers	1,784	19.6	4.2	—	—
Carpet factory operatives	1,516	18.5	3.3	3.9	0.3
Clerks (in offices)	233	16.7	5.9	—	—
Chair makers	236	16.5	4.7	3.3	−1.2
Compositors and printers	960	16.4	4.5	− 6.5	−0.3
Other occupations	12,514	15.5	4.7	− 1.9	−0.2
Restaurant employees	1,507	12.0	4.2	0.6	0.7
Saleswomen	3,829	11.7	4.7	− 4.7	−0.1
City and town government service	451	11.5	4.1	− 4.9	0.1
Boarding house employees	1,475	10.8	4.0	—	—

Table A.9. *(cont.)*

Occupation	Number employed	Unemployment frequency (%)	Mean duration (mo.)	Difference between male and female:[a] UF (%)	MD (mo.)
State government service	625	10.2	5.6	—	—
Bookkeepers and clerks	5,374	9.2	4.6	− 1.9	0.3
Servants (in families)	48,687	6.8	4.6	3.3	0.3
Hotel employees	1,865	6.0	4.6	4.0	0.1
Housekeepers	5,069	3.7	4.8	—	—
Merchants and dealers	1,358	3.6	5.5	0.5	−0.7

[a]Figure for females subtracted from figure for males belonging to the same (or analogous) occupation.
Source: MBSL, *18 AR*, pp. 280–4.

Table A.10. *Unemployment levels by occupation, females, 1890*

Occupation	Number employed	Unemployment frequency (%)	Mean duration (mo.)[a]	Difference between male and female:[b] UF (%)	MD (mo.)
Straw workers	1,585	61.3	3.7	—	—
Boot- and shoemakers and repairers	16,566	49.8	3.0	−1.4	0
Gold and silver workers	936	49.0	2.3	−8.4	0
Rubber factory operatives	2,994	47.1	2.5	0.6	−0.4
Professors and teachers	11,883	30.0	2.9	—	—
Nurses and midwives	3,745	26.8	4.1	—	—
Box makers (paper)	2,292	26.2	3.1	—	—
Rope and cordage makers	1,006	24.8	3.1	—	—
Messengers, packers, and porters	1,181	22.4	3.6	−7.5	0.6
Tailoresses	4,691	20.2	3.5	−6.5	0
Dressmakers, milliners, seamstresses	31,715	17.6	3.7	—	—
Cotton, woolen, and other textile operatives	56,903	16.2	3.1	−1.6	0
Printers, engravers, and bookbinders	3,023	15.0	3.6	−5.1	−0.2
Launderers	5,535	14.5	3.7	—	—
Paper mill operatives	3,911	14.3	3.1	−2.9	0.2

Table A.10. *(cont.)*

Occupation	Number employed	Unemployment frequency (%)	Mean duration (mo.)[a]	Difference between male and female:[b] UF (%)	MD (mo.)
Musicians and teachers of music	2,401	10.7	3.4	—	—
Stenographers and typists	1,480	10.2	3.8	—	—
Saleswomen	5,898	8.7	3.7	−3.0	0.1
Bookkeepers and accountants	5,526	7.2	3.7	−2.3	−0.1
Clerks and copyists	5,200	6.9	3.6	−2.0	− 0
Servants	65,630	5.9	3.5	3.4	−0.2
Clock- and watchmakers and repairers	1,324	5.1	3.3	—	—
Housekeepers and stewardesses	6,647	3.9	3.9	—	—
Merchants, dealers, and peddlers	1,554	3.7	3.5	0	0.2
Hotel and boardinghouse keepers	2,982	1.1	4.9	—	—

[a]See note *a* to Table A.2.
[b]Figure for females subtracted from figure for males belonging to the same (or analogous) occupation.
Source: Eleventh U. S. Census, Population, part II, pp. 568–9.

Table A.11. *Unemployment levels in selected occupations, females, 1895*

Occupation	Number employed	Unemployment frequency (%)	Mean duration (mo.)	Difference between male and female:[a] UF (%)	MD (mo.)
Boot and shoe workers					
Lynn:					
Total	3,121	34.0	4.9	4.7	0.2
Foremen	85	15.3	4.7	− 2.4	1.1
Packers	58	43.1	5.3	−12.4	0.9
Stitchers	1,035	37.2	4.9	4.0	0.5
Trimmers	97	34.0	4.9	2.6	1.2
Brockton:					
Total	1,472	39.4	3.9	3.2	−0.1

Table A.11. *(cont.)*

Occupation	Number employed	Unemployment frequency (%)	Mean duration (mo.)	Difference between male and female:[a]	
				UF (%)	MD (mo.)
Haverhill:					
Total	1,862	50.2	4.6	− 2.0	0
Packers	170	59.4	4.8	−13.1	0.4
Stitchers	934	45.4	4.7	− 4.3	0.9
Cotton mill operatives					
Fall River:					
Total	11,380	89.4	3.0	− 3.9	0
Card room operatives	115	89.6	3.1	4.2	0.1
Doffers	224	91.1	3.3	− 0.6	−0.3
Drawers-in	491	90.8	2.9	− 1.8	0.1
Spinners	1,444	89.8	3.2	2.0	−0.1
Weavers	4,961	90.3	3.0	0.7	0.3
Yarn room hands	108	66.7	2.8	24.0	−0.8
Woolen and worsted mill operatives					
Lawrence:					
Total	2,957	14.1	5.1	3.5	0.5
Combers	60	6.3	5.3	22.6	0.3
Spinners	500	12.0	4.9	5.8	0.2
Weavers	154	14.9	4.5	− 0.3	1.5
Lowell:					
Total	1,071	26.9	3.4	− 0.6	1.0
Spinners	92	39.1	3.2	− 8.8	1.2
Weavers	510	21.0	3.1	− 0.1	1.4
Paperworkers					
Holyoke:					
Total	1,596	18.8	5.1	2.2	0.6
Calenderers	175	14.3	4.7	8.4	0.6
Cutters	92	14.1	5.7	7.3	0.6
Finishers	160	8.1	4.6	9.2	0.2

[a]Figure for females subtracted from figure for males belonging to same (or analogous) occupation.
Sources: MBSL, *Bulletin 13*, pp. 16–24; *Bulletin 14*, pp. 54–67. See Table A.3.

Table A.12. *Unemployment levels by occupation: females, 1900*

Occupation	Number employed	Unemployment frequency (%)	Mean duration (mo.)	Difference between male and female:[a]		% of occupation members who were:		
				UF (%)	MD (mo.)	Female[b]	Single[c]	Foreign-born[c]
Straw workers	1,581	79.3	4.3	−28.8	−1.4	82.9	73.6	6.5
Boot- and shoemakers and repairers	17,012	56.0	3.3	− 0.4	0	25.9	77.5	18.7
Rubber factory operatives	2,866	43.7	2.9	− 9.0	0.4	40.8	87.5	40.4
Teachers and professors in colleges, etc.	15,868	43.6	3.0	−14.4	0.1	84.2	94.2	7.5
Hat and cap makers	664	39.3	3.6	4.8	−0.2	40.1	79.4	41.4
Actresses and professional show-women	356	39.0	3.3	− 9.5	0.7	21.9	66.9	15.4
Gold and silver workers	1,909	38.9	2.6	− 2.8	−0.1	30.5	88.4	26.1
Corsetmakers	791	38.3	2.9	—	—	100.0	91.9	21.4
Leather curriers and tanners	186	33.9	3.1	2.2	0.7	2.5	84.9	29.0
Packers and shippers	2,485	33.7	3.7	−18.7	−0.1	33.2	91.1	20.8
Unspecified laborers	931	32.4	3.8	9.4	0.3	1.2	48.3	47.0
Nurses and midwives	9,035	30.9	4.5	−11.4	0	90.3	63.3	41.2
Milliners	4,929	30.8	4.6	—	—	100.0	82.2	18.5
Tailoresses	3,524	30.6	3.8	− 6.0	0	33.0	75.0	57.5
Seamstresses	6,277	30.5	4.0	− 7.7	0.1	96.8	73.7	33.1
Carpet factory operatives	1,275	28.2	3.2	− 5.0	0.3	55.2	87.2	35.8

Iron- and steelworkers	421	27.6	3.6	− 8.1	−0.1	2.6	90.3	18.1
Shirt, collar, and cuff makers	1,355	26.7	3.0	−11.4	−0.5	86.6	79.4	28.9
Silk mill operatives	1,584	26.6	2.8	−11.4	0.3	65.5	93.5	31.8
Confectioners	991	25.8	3.5	−11.9	0.5	44.7	93.5	37.2
Agricultural laborers	214	25.7	4.7	− 5.1	−0.5	0.7	59.3	43.9
Sewing machine operators	282	25.5	4.2	—	—	100.0	87.2	36.5
Box makers (paper)	2,872	24.8	3.4	− 3.3	−0.3	86.7	91.7	16.0
Messengers and office errand girls	727	24.6	5.3	− 3.4	−0.3	14.4	99.6	17.6
Paper and pulp mill operatives	3,890	24.6	3.3	− 6.3	−0.1	44.9	80.0	36.5
Woolen mill operatives	10,383	23.0	3.3	− 0.9	0.1	42.0	81.5	46.7
Dressmakers	19,658	22.9	3.9	—	—	100.0	67.4	34.0
Upholsterers	241	22.0	4.4	− 1.4	−0.5	10.3	78.4	29.0
Hucksters and peddlers	221	21.7	5.2	− 6.6	−1.1	3.7	25.3	87.3
Laundresses	8,883	21.1	4.3	−18.0	−0.4	69.1	42.0	52.3
Broom and brush makers	422	20.4	3.7	− 9.2	1.1	47.6	95.0	22.5
Photographers	245	20.0	3.9	− 9.8	0.8	18.5	80.8	21.6
Tobacco and cigar factory operatives	552	19.9	3.5	− 2.4	−0.2	19.9	76.3	43.1
Trunk and leather case makers	256	19.9	3.9	2.1	−0.1	49.7	84.8	10.2
Worsted mill operatives	1,135	19.6	3.4	0.5	−0.1	51.4	85.3	49.7
Wire workers	433	19.4	3.9	− 4.6	0	10.2	91.9	25.2
Hosiery and knitting mill operatives	3,581	19.0	3.6	− 3.7	−0.1	76.9	89.1	48.1
Bleachery and dye works operatives	219	18.7	4.6	− 0.5	−1.3	6.2	83.6	33.3

continued

Table A.12. (cont.)

Occupation	Number employed	Unemployment frequency (%)	Mean duration (mo.)	Difference between male and female:[a]		% of occupation members who were:		
				UF (%)	MD (mo.)	Female[b]	Single[c]	Foreign-born[c]
Musicians and teachers of music	3,483	18.3	4.1	− 4.5	−0.4	57.4	82.3	8.9
Linen mill operatives	503	18.3	3.3	4.0	0.2	59.0	87.5	52.9
Furniture manufactory employees	254	17.7	5.0	− 0.2	−1.5	9.0	78.0	35.0
Textile mill operatives (not otherwise specified)	8,634	17.5	3.7	− 1.4	−0.3	50.7	82.5	34.7
Buttonmakers	427	17.1	3.6	− 1.0	−0.3	60.0	94.4	25.3
Bookbinders	1,724	16.7	3.6	− 2.6	0.3	54.4	94.5	18.4
Artists and art teachers	889	16.5	4.4	− 8.3	0.2	48.2	77.1	10.1
Printers, lithographers, and presswomen	1,973	16.2	4.2	− 3.4	−0.4	18.0	91.4	13.4
Farmers, planters, and overseers	1,595	15.0	5.6	−12.0	−0.7	5.1	14.9	20.7
Agents	818	14.2	4.7	− 8.6	−0.3	6.0	47.9	19.2
Print works operatives	438	14.2	2.9	− 2.6	0.3	20.3	89.7	24.0
Janitors and sextons	268	13.8	3.3	− 1.5	0.5	5.1	23.5	44.8
Cotton mill operatives	37,924	13.3	3.7	− 2.2	−0.1	49.4	73.6	68.1
Rope and cordage factory operatives	697	13.3	4.3	− 2.7	0.1	37.3	89.0	35.2
Stenographers and typists	6,450	12.0	4.9	− 2.4	−0.4	86.5	96.0	9.3
Barbers and hairdressers	350	11.7	4.3	− 4.5	−0.1	5.2	70.0	22.6
Saleswomen	11,985	11.0	4.4	− 3.6	−0.3	27.1	90.4	20.0

Servants and waitresses	70,103	9.9	4.2	— 3.5	−0.4	85.6	85.9	68.2
Clerks and copyists	6,607	9.7	4.5	— 3.1	0	17.7	91.2	12.1
Clock and watchmakers and repairers	1,401	9.0	2.8	— 2.4	0.7	44.7	89.2	29.1
Telegraph and telephone operators	1,386	8.9	5.4	— 2.1	−1.0	50.6	94.2	10.1
Literary and scientific personnel	850	8.9	4.8	— 3.1	0.3	48.7	83.1	3.8
Bookkeepers and accountants	11,357	8.6	4.6	— 1.4	0.2	50.9	92.5	11.4
Bakers	299	8.4	5.2	3.4	−1.1	5.7	60.5	34.1
Journalists	180	7.8	5.9	— 4.0	−0.4	10.7	69.4	10.0
Housekeepers and stewardesses	11,356	7.1	4.6	6.5	0.5	94.6	56.1	38.5
Manufacturers and officials	285	6.3	4.6	— 1.7	−0.4	1.8	52.6	24.6
Restaurant keepers and saloon keepers	224	5.4	5.8	0.1	−1.3	8.5	31.3	42.4
Clergymen	188	5.3	6.7	— 0.8	−0.7	5.0	72.3	21.3
Government officials	282	5.3	4.7	0.3	−0.5	6.9	71.3	9.9
Physicians and surgeons	729	4.5	4.0	— 2.6	1.6	13.3	0	16.2
Hemp and jute mill operators	490	2.9	4.4	0	−1.9	47.0	86.1	73.5
Merchants and dealers	2,125	2.8	4.6	0.9	0.6	5.2	37.5	51.1
Boarding and lodging house keepers	4,221	2.7	5.5	0.3	−4.2	85.8	17.9	45.1

[a]Figure for females subtracted from figure for males belonging to the same (or analogous) occupation.
[b]Based on the total number of males and females belonging to the same occupation or analogous occupations, e.g., tailors and tailoresses.
[c]Percentage of females who were single or foreign-born.
Source: Twelfth U.S. Census, Occupations, pp. 300–7. See also note a to Table A.4.

Table A.13. *Unemployment in manufacturing and mechanical industries, by state, 1900*

State	Both sexes		Males		Females	
	UF (%)[a]	MD (mo.)[b]	UF (%)[a]	MD (mo.)[b]	UF (%)[a]	MD (mo.)[b]
Maine	29.8	3.8	30.7	3.7	26.5	4.0
New Hampshire	19.1	3.6	19.8	3.6	17.3	3.8
Vermont	20.7	3.8	20.2	3.7	23.6	4.0
Massachusetts	25.9	3.6	26.0	3.6	25.6	3.6
Rhode Island	18.9	3.8	18.7	3.8	19.4	3.8
Connecticut	20.4	3.6	20.3	3.6	20.6	3.4
New York	25.2	3.5	25.8	3.5	23.4	3.3
New Jersey	26.7	3.3	27.0	3.3	25.3	3.2
Pennsylvania	27.8	3.6	29.4	3.6	19.7	3.6
Delaware	21.9	3.4	22.1	3.3	20.7	3.8
Maryland	26.9	3.7	29.4	3.7	18.2	3.5
Dist. of Columbia	20.3	4.0	21.2	4.0	17.2	4.1
Virginia	27.5	3.6	27.5	3.5	27.4	3.9
West Virginia	31.3	3.2	32.0	3.1	22.2	3.8
North Carolina	23.6	3.3	24.6	3.3	20.8	3.4
South Carolina	17.3	3.1	18.0	3.1	15.6	3.2
Georgia	21.0	3.3	21.7	3.2	18.3	3.5
Florida	33.1	3.0	33.1	3.0	32.4	3.0
Ohio	28.8	3.6	30.2	3.6	21.7	3.9
Indiana	34.2	3.7	35.8	3.7	24.6	4.2
Illinois	31.3	3.7	32.9	3.7	22.8	3.9
Michigan	27.0	3.7	27.6	3.6	23.4	4.0
Wisconsin	26.0	3.6	27.0	3.5	21.1	4.1
Minnesota	27.0	3.8	28.2	3.8	20.4	4.2
Iowa	31.6	3.8	33.3	3.8	23.0	4.3
Missouri	30.6	3.8	32.1	3.8	23.0	3.9
North Dakota	28.3	4.0	30.3	4.0	17.2	4.3
South Dakota	24.0	3.9	25.2	3.9	16.3	4.4
Nebraska	23.6	3.7	24.3	3.6	19.8	4.2
Kansas	28.7	3.9	29.6	3.9	22.7	4.5
Kentucky	30.3	3.9	31.5	3.9	25.2	4.1
Tennessee	30.0	3.4	30.7	3.3	25.6	3.9
Alabama	29.1	3.0	30.1	3.0	22.0	3.4
Mississippi	24.6	3.3	26.0	3.2	17.4	3.9
Louisiana	26.0	3.7	27.7	3.7	17.4	3.7
Texas	25.0	3.8	25.5	3.7	21.6	4.3
Oklahoma	32.1	3.8	33.0	3.8	25.2	4.0
Arkansas	31.0	3.6	31.6	3.6	24.2	4.3
Montana	34.1	3.7	34.6	3.7	21.7	4.5
Wyoming	20.9	3.2	20.9	3.2	21.8	3.1
Colorado	29.9	3.7	30.5	3.7	21.8	4.4

Table A.13. *(cont.)*

State	Both sexes		Males		Females	
	UF (%)[a]	MD (mo.)[b]	UF (%)[a]	MD (mo.)[b]	UF (%)[a]	MD (mo.)[b]
New Mexico	24.2	3.7	26.3	3.6	10.7	4.2
Arizona	24.2	3.5	25.3	3.6	16.4	3.5
Utah	31.2	3.9	32.1	3.8	24.3	4.8
Nevada	33.1	4.7	33.3	4.6	29.0	5.2
Idaho	39.7	4.3	40.4	4.3	24.5	4.8
Washington	30.1	3.4	30.6	3.4	21.9	4.6
Oregon	30.2	4.0	30.8	3.9	25.0	4.8
California	24.5	4.3	24.7	4.2	23.2	4.8
United States	27.2	3.6	28.3	3.6	22.4	3.7

[a]Unemployment frequency. See Chapter 10, note 3.
[b]Estimated mean duration based upon census data indicating the number of persons unemployed for 1–3 months, 4–6 months, and 7–12 months. See Appendix B.
Source: Twelfth U.S. Census, Occupations, pp. lxxxix–xciii, ccxxviii, 219.

Appendix B

About the numbers: unemployment statistics before the Great Depression

Statistics regarding the incidence and distribution of unemployment prior to 1930 are more abundant for the Commonwealth of Massachusetts than they are for any other state in the nation. This treasure trove of evidence must, however, be handled with care and interpreted with more than a little caution. This is so not merely because nineteenth-century social survey methods were, by modern standards, fairly primitive, but also because the phenomenon of unemployment is intrinsically difficult to measure with precision. Although the concept of unemployment is, and long has been, unambiguous in its core meaning (the condition of being out of work and needing, or wanting, to work), it nonetheless contains ambiguities that complicate efforts to count the unemployed. A person's need to work, or desire to work, can be difficult to gauge; there is, moreover, no particular level of need (or desire) that self-evidently distinguishes the unemployed from men and women who simply are not working. The "objective" dimension of unemployment, the condition of being out of work, also loses some of its simplicity when confronted with individual cases: should a person who has lost a full-time job, but is laboring one day a week, be considered employed or unemployed? There is, in effect, no sharp, obvious boundary separating the voluntarily from the involuntarily idle or the jobless from the working. The status of most workers can generally be determined with ease, but counting the unemployed is not – and never has been – as straightforward an enterprise as counting births, deaths, marriages, or many other indicators of the economic and social condition of a population.[1]

This conceptual issue is of particular importance in assessing or interpreting unemployment statistics collected prior to 1940. In that year, the federal government began to measure the unemployment rate by conducting a monthly survey (later called the Current Population Survey) of a sample of American households. Detailed criteria were established to distinguish the unemployed from men and women who were either "employed" or "not in the labor force"; lengthy questionnaires, as well as interviews, began to be utilized to determine whether sample members met those criteria. The Current Population Survey did, and does, draw a clear (if sometimes disputed) boundary around the unemployed. Prior to 1940, however, methods of counting the jobless were less refined, while operative definitions of unemployment (the criteria used to identify the unemployed) were less concrete and specific. As importantly, both the techniques of measuring joblessness and the operative definitions of unemployment tended to change fairly frequently. No two of the five major collections of statistics analyzed in this study, for example, are based upon identical methods and identical definitions of unemployment. This means, of course, that a person who was in identical circumstances in two different years might not have been counted as unemployed on both occasions.[2]

Two general caveats flow from these facts. First: it is essential, in using unemployment statistics, to know how the statistics were collected and exactly what was measured. The technique influences the tally. Second: historical statistics of unemployment must be regarded as less precise than the sheer presence of numbers on a page might suggest. Unemployment data derived from the census and from surveys of trade unionists are of considerable value to historians: they reveal, at the very least, the order of magnitude of the problem of joblessness. But they do not permit reliable conclusions to be drawn from small (and particularly nonrecurring) numerical changes or contrasts.[3]

Throughout this study, efforts have been made to respect both these caveats. The conclusions drawn from the quantitative data are based, almost exclusively, upon large-scale and clearly visible numerical differentials, upon patterns that appear in more than one set of statistics, and upon findings that were corroborated by other types of evidence. In addition, one eye has been kept on the nature of the sources themselves, on the changes that occurred in the definitions of unemployment and the techniques of counting the unemployed. But the reader ought not be obliged to accept these authorial assurances at face value. Thus, this appendix – which contains background information regarding the statistical data, as well as some discussion of the procedures used in this study to gauge the trustworthiness and comparability of the different collections of quantitative evidence. It is hoped that this information will prove to be useful not only to the probing reader but also to the happy few who are interested in the history of social statistics in the United States.

State and federal census data

Questions regarding unemployment were included in every population census conducted by federal or Massachusetts authorities from 1880 to 1910. Not all these surveys, however, produced usable unemployment statistics. The responses to the unemployment questions in the 1880 census were judged by the compilers of the census to be too erratic and incomplete to warrant tabulating the results. (An inspection of the census manuscripts confirms the judgment of these nineteenth-century officials.) The 1905 state census data were never compiled, in part because officials at the Massachusetts Bureau of Statistics of Labor concluded that it was not worth their while to spend several years developing statistics that would be out of date before they were published. Federal officials, similarly, did not tabulate the unemployment data from the 1910 census – although national totals, unaccompanied by any state-by-state breakdowns, were eventually assembled in 1948.[4]

The only available unemployment statistics for the state of Massachusetts prior to 1908 are, therefore, those that emerged from the 1885 and 1895 state censuses and from their federal counterparts in 1890 and 1900. (Manuscript census schedules, which were utilized for some parts of this book, were available only for the 1900 census.) The objective of these surveys was to determine the "frequency" of unemployment in the population, that is, the percentage (and number) of working people who were unemployed at all in the course of the census year. They also attempted to measure the length of time that each unemployed person remained without work during that period. In contrast to later inquiries (such as the Current Population Survey), the census enumerations did not lead to the publication of unemployment "rates" – figures that would indicate the percentage of workers who were idled simultaneously on a particular day or during a given week or month.[5]

These census surveys had several other noteworthy features in common.

The gainful worker concept

All pre-1940 census unemployment statistics are based upon what has come to be called the "gainful worker" concept. Put simply, a man was considered a gainful worker if he reported that he had an occupation and normally performed remunerative productive labor; the same definition applied to women. All gainful workers (and only gainful workers) were eligible to be counted as unemployed: unemployment frequencies developed from the census data indicate the percentage of gainful workers who were jobless in the course of the census year. The gainful worker concept is more broad-gauged, and less exact, than the "labor force" concept that has been in use since 1940. The latter notion relies upon a set of specific criteria, regarding a person's current and recent activities, to determine whether he or she ought to be counted as a member of the labor force. Persons who have neither worked nor actively sought employment for several months, for example, are generally excluded from the labor force totals and consequently from the ranks of the unemployed. (The unemployment rate, in these modern figures, is the percentage of labor force members who are jobless.) Since the gainful worker concept is more inclusive, it gives rise to slightly higher unemployment percentages than does the labor force concept.[6]

Self-reporting

Each individual respondent to the census determined whether or not he or she would be counted as unemployed. No judgments or decisions were made by the government officials who supervised and conducted the enumeration. All gainful workers were asked if they had been unemployed during the census year and for how long. The answers to these questions were recorded directly on the census schedules.

This method of self-reporting raises two issues for users of the census data. The first is that the accuracy of the enumeration depended upon the candor of respondents to the inquiry: if contemporary attitudes toward joblessness led any significant number of persons to misrepresent their experiences, then self-reporting could easily have produced a distortion in the statistics. But there is little reason to believe that biases of this sort seriously influenced the totals. Since a large (and cyclically fluctuating) proportion of the work force did report some unemployment, it appears unlikely that feelings of shame or embarrassment led any sizable number of workers to conceal their spells of joblessness. And there is no reason whatsoever to suspect that the unemployment totals were inflated because working people boasted of imaginary spells of involuntary idleness. Unemployment was a common feature of working-class life, and it is reasonable to infer that workers, on the whole, reported their experiences frankly and honestly.[7]

The second issue is closely tied to the conceptual problems discussed above. The technique of self-reporting meant that no detailed or uniform criteria were utilized to distinguish the voluntarily from the involuntarily idle. Most respondents, certainly, were aware of the distinction between being "idle" and being "unemployed," but it is nonetheless possible that some men and women declared themselves to be unemployed even if their idleness was not "genuine" unemployment. In fact, recorded unemployment frequencies in some occupations, in some years, suggest that the system of self-reporting did lead to inappropriate inclusions in the tabulated ranks of the unemployed. Several thousand Massachusetts farmers reported themselves to be unemployed in 1885 although, presumably, many of these men were self-employed individuals who were not, strictly speaking, involuntarily idle. In 1900 nearly one-third of all teachers claimed that they had been unemployed in the course of the census year – leading one to suspect that summer "vacations" were being counted as spells of unemployment. For these men and women (and others in similar occupations), the census figures do appear to be problematic and potentially misleading. This criticism does not apply, however, to the vast majority of men and women who were counted as unemployed in the census surveys. As the designers of the censuses knew, and, as is discussed in Chapters 3 and 6, virtually all members of blue-collar occupations were employees whose wages were sufficiently low that joblessness was almost invariably accompanied by the need or desire to work. The aggregate unemployment totals were only slightly – very slightly – inflated by the inclusion of persons whose experiences would not conform to any meaningful definition of unemployment. Moreover, state and federal officials were aware of this methodological issue, and efforts were made in the later census surveys (as described below) to exclude persons who had been inappropriately counted in earlier enumerations.[8]

Durations as estimates

All the census surveys attempted to determine how long unemployed men and women had remained without work in the course of the census year. In some years, detailed breakdowns of these data were offered in the census publications; in others, the unemployed were divided into broad durational groupings, for example, 1–3 months, 4–6 months, and 7–12 months. But regardless of the format in which the data were published, the statistics regarding unemployment durations ought to be regarded as estimates. This is so, in part, because respondents to the census tended to round off their answers, usually to the nearest month. In addition, as an internal census bureau memo pointed out in 1917, respondents to a census inquiry were less likely to know exactly how long they (or members of their household) had been idled than whether or not they had been unemployed at all. The caveat noted above, regarding the general imprecision of these statistics, applies with extra force to the data regarding the length of spells of unemployment.[9]

Descriptions of the conceptual and methodological underpinnings of individual census surveys are presented below.

The Massachusetts Census of 1885

This survey, conducted by the Bureau of Statistics of Labor, included two questions concerning unemployment. The first asked each respondent to specify the number of months, during the year ending May 1, 1885, that he or she was "unemployed at that work which constituted the principal trade or calling of each person or that work upon which he depended chiefly for a livelihood." The second question sought to determine "the whole number of months" that each person in the state was "employed at any kind of work." Respondents were directed to count "both the time employed at the principal occupation . . . and the number of months employed at other work, the other work having been done during the whole or a part of the time unemployed at the principal occupation." By asking both these questions, state officials hoped to measure the overall irregularity of employment in the commonwealth as well as the ability of working people to find supplementary jobs when work was unavailable in their "principal occupations." The answers to these questions were cross-tabulated with other census data, producing hundreds of pages of printed tables regarding unemployment in every community and occupation in Massachusetts.[10]

The attempt to simultaneously measure both unemployment at a person's principal occupation and unemployment per se appears to have been something less than a resounding success. Less than 6 percent of all males and only 1 percent of all females who were unemployed at their principal occupations reported that they had found work in other trades. Such figures suggest that supplementary jobs were hard to find, but they are also suspiciously low. Indeed, the bureau concluded that it had probably undercounted the number of persons who had located supplementary employment, and consequently many of the tables that it published did not bother to identify (or screen out) the small number of unemployed workers who had reported finding jobs outside their trades. Except where otherwise noted, thus, the 1885 figures presented in this study treat unemployment at a person's principal occupation. The inclusion of men and women who were known to have worked at other jobs had only a marginal inflationary effect upon the unemployment totals.[11]

The unemployment questions in the 1885 census were addressed to a very broadly defined population of gainful workers, including employers and the self-employed. The survey "comprehended all remunerative occupations of whatever description, and included all persons of any age who were earning their living" in any sector of the economy. The only productive citizens who were excluded were "housewives and those who assisted in the housework at home only and for which they received no stated compensation." As noted earlier, the inclusion of the self-employed (e.g., farmers) in the survey population probably did produce an inappropriate, though slight, augmentation of the *number* of persons who were counted as unemployed. At the same time, it depressed (slightly) the aggregate unemployment *frequency* – since few of the self-employed (or employers) reported that they had, in fact, been out of work. The inclusion of young children in the survey population, although conceptually dubious, had little impact upon the numerical totals.[12]

The Massachusetts Census of 1895
In its second effort to utilize the state census survey to count the unemployed, the MBSL significantly altered and refined its operative definition of unemployment. Once again, the survey encompassed an entire census year (May 1, 1894, to April 30, 1895), but in 1895 the distinction between unemployment per se and unemployment at a person's principal occupation was abandoned. Respondents to the census were counted as unemployed only if they were altogether idle, if they spent some part of the year without performing any remunerative labor at all.[13]

More importantly, the bureau elected, in 1895, to restrict the unemployment count to "persons earning wages or salaries, whose income is directly dependent on active employment." "The question of employment and unemployment," the bureau noted, "is of particular interest to those whose work is of such a nature that their failure to obtain employment means permanent loss of pay." The concept of unemployment was not considered to be relevant or "applicable" to

> professional persons or the proprietary and employing classes, whose active employment is from its nature not continuous, or whose incomes are from profits or emoluments which are either not cut off by the cessation of active employment or can be enlarged during periods of activity so as to offset periods of depression.

To operationalize this conceptual distinction, the bureau developed a list of occupations whose members were excluded from the unemployment survey. The list encompassed virtually all professionals (including historians), employers (ranging from farmers to fishermen to manufacturers to "capitalists"), and men and women who were self-employed (including saloonkeepers, peddlers, and proprietors of street sprinklers). As it had done in 1885, the survey also excluded housewives, students, dependents, and other persons who were not gainful workers at all. (The 1895 unemployment census registered the experiences of 37% of the commonwealth's population; a decade earlier, the figure had been 42%.) In 1895, thus, the bureau sharpened the definitional boundaries of unemployment, eliminated one of the hazards of self-reporting, and excluded from the jobless totals a number of persons who had been idled but not necessarily unemployed. In so doing, it also generated a slight (roughly 2 percentage points) upward bias in the 1895 unemployment frequencies, as compared with the figures developed in 1885, 1890, and 1900.[14]

In addition to changing the operative definition of unemployment, officials at the MBSL also chose to compile and publish tables that were less richly detailed than those that had emerged from the 1885 census. The publications of the bureau did present unemployment data for every city and town in the commonwealth, and they also contained raw numerical totals that permitted monthly unemployment rates, as well as annual unemployment frequencies, to be calculated. But no data regarding the age or place of birth of the unemployed were ever assembled, while figures regarding joblessness within individual occupations were made available for only a handful of trades. Finally, it should be noted that the published data do not permit annual unemployment frequencies (or mean durations) to be developed for men and women separately. Monthly unemployment rates, however, can be calculated for males and females independently: since these monthly rates were higher for men than they were for women (8.4%, on average, compared to 6.4%), it seems likely that men also had higher annual unemployment frequencies.[15]

Federal census data: 1890 and 1900

The eleventh and twelfth U.S. censuses collected and compiled very similar data regarding unemployment. The publications that emerged from each census survey revealed the number of persons who were unemployed in the nation as a whole, in every state and territory, and in every city with a population greater than 50,000. Unemployment data for individual occupations were assembled for each geographic unit, with statistics reported for males and females separately. Both surveys were limited to persons ten years of age and older. In 1890, the period covered by the census inquiry was June 1, 1889, to May 31, 1890; a decade later, the enumeration spanned the year between June 1, 1899, and May 31, 1900.[16]

There was, however, one noteworthy methodological difference between the two surveys. The 1890 census, like the 1885 census of Massachusetts, attempted to obtain information regarding both unemployment at a person's principal occupation and unemployment per se. This double-pronged inquiry again produced considerable confusion and murky results: the Census Bureau eventually concluded that the joblessness totals probably represented an amalgam of complete joblessness and unemployment at principal occupations. Learning from this experience, the designers of the twelfth census abandoned the effort to measure unemployment at a person's principal trade. Census enumerators were given very clear instructions to find out only "the number of months . . . during which a person ordinarily engaged in gainful labor was not employed at all." In effecting this change, federal officials were retracing the path of the 1885 and 1895 Massachusetts surveys.[17]

The Census Bureau also concluded, early in the twentieth century, that the 1900 unemployment measurement was substantially more accurate than its 1890 predecessor had been. There were, according to the bureau, several "reasons . . . for accepting the figures of 1900 as more correctly reflecting actual proportions of nonemployment than did those of 1890." Among these reasons were the utilization of a "simpler and more definite schedule" in 1900, better instructions to enumerators, and the fact that there had been, in 1890, a substantial undercount of young children who worked as agricultural laborers. (This undercount, which occurred primarily in the South, had little or no effect upon the Massachusetts figures.) The bureau concluded that the 1890 totals were, at best, to be regarded as "approximate"; it suggested that the actual frequency of unemployment, in the nation as a whole, was probably 7 percentage points higher than the census reports had indicated. The precise impact of these measurement problems upon the Massachusetts figures cannot be determined, but it appears that the 1890 statistics (the lowest recorded in peacetime in Massachusetts between 1880 and 1923) understated the incidence of involuntary idleness.[18]

One other peculiarity of these two collections of data requires mention. Detailed figures regarding the duration of unemployment were not provided in either the 1890 or the 1900 census reports. Instead, the census tables indicated only the number of unemployed persons who were idled for periods of 1–3 months, 4–6 months, and 7–12 months. Calculating mean durations therefore entailed estimating the average duration of unemployment for workers who were grouped into each of these durational categories. The estimates utilized were 1.5, 4.8, and 8.5 months, respectively. The mean duration figures presented in the 1890 and 1900 tables in this study (except those drawn from the census manuscripts) are weighted averages based upon these estimates.[19]

Federal census data: 1910

The thirteenth U.S. census did include questions regarding unemployment, but, as noted earlier, the results of this inquiry were not fully tabulated until 1948, and, even in that year, only national figures were developed. These belated tabulations (which have never been published but are available from the Bureau of the Census) exist in the form of two lengthy tables. The first indicates the percentage of wage and salary earners who were at least sixteen years old in 1910 and who had been unemployed in 1909. Breakdowns by sex and occupation are provided, and the table further specifies the number of weeks of joblessness experienced by these men and women. The second table indicates, for the same groupings, the proportion who were unemployed on April 15, 1910. The thirteenth census was designed to yield an unemployment *rate* as well as a frequency.

The 1910 survey, like its immediate predecessor, counted as unemployed only those persons who were not working at all – either at some point during the census year or on April 15, 1910. But unlike both the 1890 and 1900 censuses, the 1910 inquiry was restricted to men and women who were employees. The concept of unemployment was judged to be relevant to all wage and salary earners but not to all gainful workers. This definitional shift was a meaningful one, but, as Alba Edwards, the director of the Census Bureau, noted in 1917, it did not "materially" affect the statistics in most occupations.[20]

Technical problems that arose in the course of tabulating the figures leave the reliability of the numerical totals open to question. And an internal Census Bureau study concluded that the data regarding unemployment in agriculture were of "doubtful value." Nonetheless, the 1910 figures are useful as a supplement to earlier census surveys and to the Massachusetts trade union series. Alba Edwards, after examining the returns for a small sample of major occupations, concluded that they did provide an adequate basis for comparisons with earlier surveys. He judged, in particular, that the data regarding unemployment on April 15, 1910, could be viewed as fairly complete and reliable.[21]

The trade union unemployment series

The MBSL began to collect unemployment data from trade unionists toward the end of the "panic" of 1907–8. It continued doing so, quarterly, until 1923. The figures that the MBSL compiled were unemployment rates rather than frequencies: they revealed the number and percentage of unionists who were simultaneously jobless. For state officials, statistics of this type were preferable to census data in two respects: they could be assembled quickly and inexpensively, and they permitted the MBSL to monitor short-run fluctuations in unemployment. The trade union statistics were published every three months by the bureau, with summary and cumulative tables presented in the bureau's annual reports.[22]

Throughout this period, the MBSL utilized "identical methods in the collection and tabulation of the returns in order that the reports for the successive quarters might be strictly comparable in every respect." Four times each year, the bureau mailed printed forms to officials of every local trade union in the commonwealth. The officials were instructed to record, on the form, the name and location of the trade union, the occupation represented by the union, the total membership of the local, and the number of members who were unemployed on a specified date. The quarterly reporting dates were March 31, June 30, September 30, and December 31. The union officer was also asked to account for the causes of unemployment among the local's membership, using five different categories provided by the bureau. Participation in these surveys was voluntary, although agents of the MBSL were occasionally sent out to retrieve unreturned, but completed forms. After the data had been collected, the bureau developed tables that revealed the unemployment rate in the entire sample, in individual occupations, and in the largest cities of the commonwealth. As Table 3.3 indicates, by 1909 the survey was registering the experiences of more than 100,000 unionists; by 1918 the figure had risen above 200,000. After 1909, at least 60 percent, and often more than 70 percent, of all trade union members in the state were covered by the survey. The majority of these unionists were male, but there were sizable contingents of women in the trade union samples for certain industries, including shoes and textiles.[23]

Given this method of enumeration, the figures published by the MBSL must be regarded as informed estimates. Although some union officials may well have meticulously counted their unemployed members on each quar-

terly reporting date, others certainly provided the bureau with more approx-
imated figures. That these estimates were very well informed, however,
seems beyond dispute. Trade union locals were small in size (in 1913, the
average membership of a reporting local was 172 persons), and keeping track
of unemployed members was one of the customary responsibilities of union
officials. There is, moreover, no a priori reason to suspect that these officials
systematically distorted the figures in one direction or another.[24]

The following pages explore, in some detail, several other issues relevant
to the use and interpretation of these statistics.

Definitions: the "causes" of unemployment

As noted above, the trade union survey asked local officials to group their
unemployed workers according to the causes of their unemployment. The
list of causal categories provided by the MBSL reveals that the bureau was
still groping for a conceptually coherent yet usable definition of unemployment. The five categories were: lack of work (including lack of materials),
unfavorable weather, strikes or lockouts, disability, and "other" (which included vacations as well as temporary plant shutdowns for repairs and stock-
taking). These categories indicate that the bureau counted as unemployed
some workers whose idleness was not involuntary, such as strikers and men
who were on vacations. Yet they also signal the MBSL's awareness of the
distinction between voluntary and involuntary idleness, as well as its desire
to operationalize that distinction by measuring the relative importance of different sources of joblessness.[25]

A large majority of all unionists who were counted as unemployed were,
in fact, jobless because of "lack of work or materials." Moreover, for the trade
union sample as a whole, quarterly unemployment rates were generally inflated by less than 2 percentage points as a result of the inclusion of unionists
who would not, according to more modern definitions, be counted as unemployed – those who were idled due to strikes, lockouts, vacations, and
disability. Figures indicating the extent of unemployment due to "lack of
work" are available for the aggregate trade union sample and are presented
in Table 3.3. But, unfortunately, the MBSL published only "all-causes" unemployment rates for individual occupations and cities; those figures (e.g.,
Table A.5) ought therefore to be regarded as inflated by an average of 1.8
percentage points. In the tables in this study where this inflation might significantly influence the import of the statistics (e.g., those that contain estimated unemployment frequencies), the "all-causes" figures have been adjusted downward by 1.8 percentage points.[26]

The reporting sample in individual occupations

Unlike the statistics drawn from the census, the trade union figures are based
upon the experiences of only a sample of the commonwealth's working population. And this sample was not, and was not intended to be, random. In
using and interpreting these data, thus, some attention must be paid to the
size and the composition of the samples whose unemployment was reported
to the MBSL.

Table B.1 presents data indicating the average number of persons and the average number of local unions represented in the unemployment statistics for individual occupations. As is readily apparent from the table, the size of the reporting sample, in most trades, was far from trivial: in a majority of occupations, the recorded unemployment rates registered the experiences of more than a thousand workers who were drawn from at least ten different local unions. In many of these trades, the union sample included at least 30 percent of all occupation members. On the whole, then, the samples were sufficiently large to generate useful quantitative evidence. However, the size of the reporting sample did obviously vary among occupations, and the unemployment figures for those trades that had small reporting samples ought to be examined further before being burdened with the weight of significant conclusions. It should also be noted that the size of the reporting sample, in most occupations, tended to increase over time and to fluctuate slightly from one quarter to the next. An inspection of the quarterly data indicates that these changes in sample size were not echoed in the unemployment figures, but, in light of these changes, the temptation to perceive meaningful trends in small quarter-to-quarter shifts in the recorded unemployment rates must be resisted.[27]

The trade union statistics for individual occupations inescapably raise one additional issue: did these unemployment rates accurately reflect conditions throughout the occupation? Or, to state the question somewhat differently, did unionists and nonunionists who belonged to the same trade encounter roughly the same quantity of unemployment? Hypothetically, trade union members might be expected to have had either higher or lower idleness frequencies than their unorganized colleagues. Union members could have been laid off relatively often because they were more reluctant to work for reduced wages or because employers tried to avoid hiring unionized workers. On the other hand, unions may have been formed more easily in locales with fairly low unemployment rates, and, once in existence, labor organizations had the potential to control jobs and offer relatively steady work to their members. It could also be argued that unions, during this period, were too small and too weak to have made much difference, that in occupations that were, at best, partially organized, labor market conditions would have been very similar for union members and their unorganized fellow tradesmen.

Unfortunately, these hypotheses cannot be tested directly or definitively – since no unemployment data are available for nonunionized workers in Massachusetts between 1908 and 1923. But, as a rough and indirect exploration of these issues, the trade union unemployment rates were compared with the national data collected in the 1910 census. Annual unemployment rates for the census year of 1909 were contrasted with the trade union figures for the same year, while national unemployment rates on April 15, 1910, were compared with the union figures for March 31, 1910. In twenty-seven of the thirty-five occupations for which these comparisons could be made, the unemployment rates were very similar either in 1909 or in the spring of 1910 (or both). This suggests that joining a union, early in the twentieth century, did not have a significant impact upon a man's chances of becoming unem-

Table B.1. *Trade union members covered by the MBSL unemployment survey, by occupation, 1908–1922*

Occupation	Average no. of members reporting[a]	Average no. of local unions reporting[a]
Boot and shoe workers (total)[b]	39,641	87
Boot and shoe workers (mixed)	12,029	27
Cutters	4,648	9
Edgemakers	1,266	5
Lasters	3,214	9
Stitchers	6,344	8
Treers, dressers, packers	3,378	7
Others	14,312	35
Textile operatives (total)[b]	17,784	56
Loomfixers	2,589	11
Mule spinners	1,871	7
Weavers	4,644	7
Others	8,575	27
Building trades and related occupations		
Bricklayers, masons, and plasterers	3,466	38
Carpenters	14,311	105
Hod carriers and building laborers	3,268	15
Painters, decorators, and paperhangers	4,559	51
Plumbers, gas fitters, and steamfitters	2,514	32
Engineers (hoisting and portable)	415	5
Electrical workers	2,299	18
Granite cutters and polishers	1,740	15
Quarry workers	488	7
Iron- and steelworkers, metal workers, machinists		
Boilermakers	844	7
Machinists	6,039	24
Metal polishers, buffers, platers	657	10
Molders and coremakers (iron and brass)	2,750	22
Sheet metal workers	570	11
Blacksmiths and horseshoers	837	9
Printing and related industries		
Bookbinders	641	4
Compositors	2,676	17
Printing pressmen	1,214	11
Stereotypers and electrotypers	372	5
Paper and pulpmakers	1,104	7
Transportation		
Railway clerks	2,017	23
Railway conductors	976	6
Engineers (locomotive)	1,410	7
Firemen and enginemen (locomotive)	1,761	8

Table B.1. *(cont.)*

Occupation	Average no. of members reporting[a]	Average no. of local unions reporting[a]
Station agents and employees	1,602	10
Street and electric railway employees	9,075	21
Railroad telegraphers	1,085	5
Railroad trainmen	4,069	15
Teamsters, chauffeurs, etc.	5,191	25
Food, tobacco, and related industries		
Bakers and confectioners	785	11
Bartenders	3,075	21
Bottlers and drivers	1,059	7
Brewery workmen	1,312	12
Cigarmakers	2,299	14
Cooks and waiters	2,359	8
Other		
Barbers	2,107	27
Clerks (retail and wholesale)	1,352	13
Engineers (stationary)	1,568	16
Firemen (stationary)	2,005	12
Garment workers	5,588	18
Municipal employees	5,174	39
Theatrical stage employees	977	19

[a]Average (mean) based on returns from selected quarterly reporting dates. Figures not available for all trades.
[b]The figures for "total" boot and shoe workers and textile operatives are not identical to the totals of all constituent unions because figures for the latter were not consistently available on each reporting date.
Sources: See Table A.5 source note.

ployed. It also suggests that the trade union statistics for individual occupations constitute a reasonably accurate indicator of employment conditions for all members of that occupation in the commonwealth.[28]

The reporting sample in individual cities
The figures presented in Table B.2 indicate, for every major city, the average number of trade union members and local unions that reported their unemployment experiences to the MBSL between 1908 and 1923. For most of these cities, the unemployment rates were based upon the experiences of more than three thousand workers from more than thirty different locals. The latter figure implies that there was considerable occupational diversity in the returns for most cities, but the MBSL – again, unfortunately – never published data that revealed the occupational composition of the reporting sample for

Table B.2. *Trade union members covered by the MBSL unemployment survey, by city, 1908–22*

| City | Average number of:[a] | |
	Local unions reporting	Members reporting
Boston	223	69,064
Brockton	38	13,525
Fall River	33	7,527
Fitchburg	24	1,723
Haverhill	31	10,066
Holyoke	33	3,239
Lawrence	32	5,706
Lowell	47	6,153
Lynn	46	12,949
New Bedford	33	8,038
Quincy	18	2,668
Salem	27	3,890
Springfield	57	8,641
Worcester	52	6,848
Cambridge	9	1,408
Taunton	25	1,723

[a]Average (mean) based on returns from selected quarterly reporting dates.
Sources: See Table A.5 source note.

each city. It is likely that building tradesmen, coupled with workers in the dominant manufacturing industry (if there was one), constituted a sizable proportion of the sample in each community. But there is, in fact, no way to determine the representativeness of these samples or to detect any changes that may have occurred in the occupational composition of the reporting samples. Consequently, it cannot be assumed that the trade union statistics reflected unemployment conditions for all workers in these cities. Shifts in the unemployment rates may also have resulted from changes in the composition of the sample rather than from changing economic conditions. Finally, it should be noted that many local unions that were included in the Boston returns had members who did not live or work in that city.

The statewide sample and the aggregate statistics
The aggregate trade union unemployment rates were, as indicated above, based upon the experiences of a very large sample of workers, drawn from scores of occupations in dozens of communities. Nonetheless, these statewide trade union figures cannot be utilized or interpreted as an accurate measure of the extent of unemployment in the labor force as a whole. The trade union sample excluded all members of the upper echelons of the Bay State's occupational hierarchy (as well as most clerical employees), and conse-

quently it was biased in the direction of relatively high unemployment rates. In 1909, the estimated unemployment frequency for Massachusetts unionists was, in fact, nearly 10 percentage points greater than a frequency, derived from the 1910 national census statistics, for a sample that structurally resembled the Bay State's labor force. As the MBSL repeatedly claimed, the trade union series did accurately reflect *fluctuations* in employment conditions for the entire work force. But the recorded unemployment rates for trade unionists were almost certainly higher than those that prevailed for all economically active residents of the commonwealth.[29]

The aggregate trade union statistics do, however, offer a reliable guide to the incidence of unemployment among blue-collar employees in manufacturing, trade, and transportation. Although trade union members were not, in all respects, "typical" industrial workers, the occupations to which they belonged were, on the whole, neither particularly steady nor unsteady. A comparison of the composition of the aggregate trade union sample with the composition of the state's *blue-collar* labor force (as revealed in the censuses of 1910 and 1915) indicates that the trade union sample was not biased toward either high- or low-unemployment occupations. The sample did contain a disproportionately large number of skilled workmen, but, as discussed in Chapter 3, there was little connection between unemployment rates and skill levels in Massachusetts during this period.[30]

The 1910 census survey provides supporting evidence for the claim that the trade union series can serve as an indicator of the extent of unemployment among all industrial workers. Both in the spring of 1910 and during the entire census year of 1909, national unemployment rates for wage and salary earners in manufacturing and mechanical industries were very similar to the rates reported by Massachusetts unionists (because of "lack of work"). On April 15, 1910, the national rate was 5.8 percent; two weeks earlier, on March 31, the figure for trade unionists was 5.3 percent. In 1909, the annual unemployment rate in manufacturing was 5.4 percent; for the Bay State's union members, the rate was 5.6 percent. A few years later, a supplementary investigation sponsored by the MBSL also indicated that "the conclusions relative to the unemployment of *organized* workmen at the close of the quarter . . . hold true also of *unorganized* workmen." Facts such as these, of course, cannot prove that the trade union sample was a representative one, but, at the very least, they strongly suggest that the unemployment rates recorded for trade unionists were of the same order of magnitude as those prevailing for the industrial working class as a whole.[31]

The conversion of unemployment rates into unemployment frequencies

One methodological argument of this study is that annual unemployment frequencies provide a more meaningful indicator of the significance of joblessness in the lives of working people than do unemployment rates. For this reason, and to permit comparisons between the trade union statistics and the census data, the unemployment rates reported by trade unionists have, in several places, been converted into annual unemployment frequencies. At other junctures (e.g., Tables 3.1 and A.1–A.4) the operation has been performed in reverse, and unemployment frequencies have been converted into annual unemployment rates (i.e., the average percentage of persons unemployed simultaneously). This has been done, in part, to facilitate comparisons between these historical statistics and the more modern (and familiar) rate figures compiled and published monthly by the U.S. Bureau of Labor Statistics.

The arithmetic basis for these conversions is the following formula:

$$\text{Annual unemployment rate (\%)} \times \frac{12}{\text{Mean duration (mo.)}} = \text{Annual unemployment frequency (\%)}$$

The meaning of the formula, put simply, is that the relationship between the annual unemployment rate and the unemployment frequency was determined by the extent of turnover that occurred among the unemployed in the course of a year. The rate of turnover itself varied inversely with the mean duration of unemployment. For example: in 1909, the unemployment rate (all causes) among Massachusetts unionists was 8.0 percent. If the same persons had remained unemployed during the entire year, then the mean duration of unemployment would have been twelve months, and the unemployment frequency would also have been 8.0 percent. If, however, the average unemployed person had been out of work for only four months, then a threefold turnover in the ranks of the unemployed would have occurred during the year, and the unemployment frequency would have been 24.0 percent.

The following is a more formal statement of these relationships and the derivation of the conversion formula.

1. Let

R = the annual unemployment rate (%)
U = the number of persons unemployed in a given month, for the month
L = the number of persons in the labor force (assumed to be constant for the year)
P = the number of persons unemployed at all in the course of a year
M = the total number of months of unemployment experienced by all workers in the course of the year
F = the annual unemployment frequency (%)
D = the mean duration of unemployment (months per unemployed person)

2.

$$R = \frac{U_1 + U_2 + \ldots + U_{12}}{L \times 12},$$

$$F = P/L, \quad \text{and} \quad D = M/P.$$

Since $M = U_1 + U_2 + \ldots + U_{12}$, then

$$R = \frac{M}{L \times 12} = \frac{D \times P}{L \times 12} = \frac{D \times F}{12} \quad \text{and} \quad F = \frac{R \times 12}{D}.$$

3. This formula cannot yield an unemployment frequency higher than 100% because D can never be less than $R \times 12$. This is so because P cannot be larger than L: the number of persons unemployed cannot be larger than the number of persons in the labor force.

Thus, D can never be less than

$$\frac{M}{L} = \frac{U_1 + U_2 + \ldots + U_{12}}{L} = R \times 12,$$

which (in English) means that $R \times 12$ equals the mean duration of unemployment that would prevail if everyone in the labor force experienced some unemployment. This would necessarily be the lowest possible mean duration for any given R.

Finally, it should be noted that the trade union series does not contain data regarding the mean duration of unemployment – a key ingredient in the use of this conversion formula. Consequently, estimated mean durations were inserted into the formula in order to convert the union unemployment rates into unemployment frequencies. The estimates used were 4.0 months for 1908, 1914, and 1922, 4.5 months for 1920 and 1921, and 3.5 months for all other years for which trade union data were collected. Since these figures are merely estimates (grounded as they may be in the historical record), so too are the unemployment frequencies presented for the commonwealth's trade unionists.

Notes

Sources and organizations frequently cited in the notes are identified by the following abbreviations:

AC-B: Associated Charities of Boston. *First* to *Thirty-eighth Annual Reports* (identified by no., *(1–38*, preceding *AR)* (Boston, 1880–1917).

AC-W: Associated Charities of Worcester. *First to Twenty-fifth Annual Reports* (identified by no., *1–25*, preceding *AR)* (Worcester, 1891–1915).

ALLR: American Labor Legislation Review

AR: Annual Report. Used to identify annual reports of AC-B, AC-W, BSPP, IAS, and MBSL.

BCC: Boston Chamber of Commerce

BISU Hearings: Massachusetts Board to Investigate the Subject of the Unemployed, 1894–5, hearings transcripts and documents. Archives of the Commonwealth of Massachusetts, Boston.

BISU Report: Report of the Massachusetts Board to Investigate the Subject of the Unemployed, House Document 50 (Boston, 1895).

BSPP: Boston Society for the Prevention of Pauperism. *Annual Reports* up to the *Thirtieth* (1865), after which name was changed to Industrial Aid Society (IAS).

IAS: Industrial Aid Society (for the Prevention of Pauperism). *Thirty-first* to *Eighty-second Annual Reports* (identified by no., *31–82*, preceding *AR)* (Boston, 1866–1917).

Mass. AFL, *CP:* Massachusetts State Branch of the American Federation of Labor, annual *Convention Proceedings* from the ninth to the thirty-eighth annual conventions (identified by annual convention no. preceding *CP)* (various Mass. cities, 1894–1923).

MBSL, *AR:* Massachusetts Bureau of Statistics of Labor, *First* through *Fifty-second Annual Reports, Public Document 15* (identified by no., *1–52*, preceding *AR)* (Boston, 1870–1921).

MBSL, *Bulletin:* Massachusetts Bureau of Statistics of Labor, *Labor Bulletin of the Commonwealth of Massachusetts*, nos. *1–140* (Boston, 1897–1923). (In some cases, printed in and pages numbered as part of MBSL, *AR.*)

MBSL, *Quarterly Report:* Massachusetts Bureau of Statistics of Labor, *Quarterly Report on Employment in Massachusetts*, nos. *17–36* (Boston, 1912–16). (See source note to Table A.5 regarding minor changes in the title of this series.)

SWJ: Shoe Workers' Journal (until 1902, called *The Union Boot and Shoe Worker;* published in Boston).

USBLS: Bureau of Labor Statistics, U.S. Department of Labor

1. Introduction

1 *The Carpenter* 33, no. 5 (May 1914): 1.

2 MBSL, *10 AR*, pp. 3–7. The 1878 survey did have two precursors: in 1871 and again in 1877, the bureau had attempted, far less systematically, to gauge the extent of work irregularity in the commonwealth. MBSL, *2 AR*, p. 5; *9 AR*, p. 3. The bureau itself was founded in 1869.

3 MBSL, *10 AR*, pp. 4–12.

4 Ibid., pp. 4–12.

5 Ibid., pp. 3–6, 12–13.

6 Ibid., pp. 12–13; *Mass. Census, 1875*, I (Boston, 1876–7), pp. xlix, 607ff.

7 *Oxford English Dictionary* (London, 1933), XI, p. 174; Raymond Williams, *Keywords: A Vocabulary of Culture and Society* (New York, 1976), pp. 273–5; *BISU Report*, app. A, pp. 5–11. Both Williams and E. P. Thompson report that the modern word "unemployed" did appear with some frequency in England during the first half of the nineteenth century, particularly in Radical or Owenite writings. E. P. Thompson, *The Making of the English Working Class* (New York, 1963), p. 776n. The earliest American usage of which I am aware is in a letter from Thomas Jefferson to James Madison, dated Oct. 28, 1785. As Jefferson used the term, however, it had different implications than it was to acquire in the nineteenth century: Jefferson appears to have viewed "the unemployed" as men who were permanently landless rather than temporarily out of work. Robert A. Rutland and William M. E. Rachal, eds., *The Papers of James Madison*, 14 vols. to date (Chicago, 1962–85), VIII, pp. 385–7. (I am grateful to Jennifer Nedelsky for calling this letter to my attention.) Aside from this letter, I have not encountered the term, in its modern definition, in any American writing published before 1850. Appendix A to the *BISU Report* (cited above), contains excerpts of newspaper articles dealing with the problem of "involuntary idleness" that were written during the major depressions of the nineteenth century. The word "unemployed" did not appear in any of the articles written before 1857. For examples of the word's appearance in the 1850s and 1860s, see Committee Report on the Hours of Labor, Massachusetts House Document 153 (1850), repr. in John R. Commons, et al., eds., *A Documentary History of American Industrial Society*, 10 vols. (New York, 1958; orig. pub. Cleveland, 1910–11), VIII, pp. 174, 185; Boston *Herald*, June 10, 1854; BSPP, *25 AR* (Boston, 1860), p. 16; and *BISU Report*, app. A, pp. 5–11.

8 *Oxford English Dictionary*, XI, p. 174; Williams, *Keywords*, pp. 273–5; *Vindicator* (Lynn, Mass.), Jan. 6, 1877.

9 *Vindicator*, March 23, 1878.

10 MBSL, *18 AR*, pp. 4, 261. This is the earliest usage that I have encountered of the word "unemployment." As John A. Garraty has recently noted, this Massachusetts report was the subject of the article in *Science* that the *Oxford English Dictionary* offers as its first entry under the heading "unemployment." John A. Garraty, *Unemployment in History: Economic Thought and Public Policy* (New York, 1978), pp. 4–5, 108–9n. Once

again, E. P. Thompson reports that the word did appear earlier in England, although less frequently than "unemployed." Thompson, *Making*, p. 776n ; Williams, *Keywords*, pp. 273–5.

11 Regarding the social and economic changes that gave rise to these shifts in language, see Chapter 2.

12 Gareth Stedman Jones, *Outcast London: A Study in the Relationship between Classes in Victorian Society* (Oxford, 1971), p. v. That the term "unemployment" had not entered common parlance in the United States by the 1890s is clearly indicated by the appointment in Massachusetts of a "Board to Investigate the Subject of the Unemployed." Moreover, only occasionally does the word "unemployment" appear in the very lengthy final report of that board (see note 7 above). Regarding twentieth-century definitions, see Appendix B.

13 See Appendix B regarding the history of efforts to count the unemployed.

14 William H. Beveridge, *Unemployment: A Problem of Industry* (London, 1930), p. 1. The recent literature regarding the social consequences of unemployment is extensive and laced with controversy. For examples, see M. Harvey Brenner, *Mental Illness and the Economy* (Cambridge, Mass., 1973); M. Harvey Brenner, "Personal Stability and Economic Security," *Social Policy* 8 (May–June 1977): 1–4; and Marcia Guttentag, "The Relationship of Unemployment to Crime and Delinquency," *Journal of Social Issues* 24 (Jan. 1968): 105–14. See also Chapters 6 and 9.

15 *SWJ* 6, no. 5 (May 1905): 24–5; *American Federationist*, 29, no. 1 (Jan. 1922): 20. In the course of the twentieth century, both union contracts and legislation prohibiting discrimination have, of course, circumscribed the right of employers to decide which individuals shall be laid off. But they nonetheless retain an unbridled right to release as many workers as they choose.

16 Among the works that have appeared are Stanley Lebergott, *Manpower in Economic Growth* (New York, 1964); August C. Bolino, "The Duration of Unemployment: Some Tentative Historical Comparisons," *Quarterly Review of Economics and Business* 6 (1966): 31–49; Garraty, *Unemployment in History*; Daniel Nelson, *Unemployment Insurance: The American Experience, 1915–1935* (Madison, Wis., 1969); Roy Lubove, *The Struggle for Social Security, 1900–1935* (Cambridge, Mass., 1968); and Herbert G. Gutman, "The Failure of the Movement by the Unemployed for Public Works in 1873," *Political Science Quarterly* 80 (June 1965): 254–75.

2. The social origins of unemployment

1 See Douglas L. Jones, "The Strolling Poor: Transiency in Eighteenth-Century Massachusetts," *Journal of Social History* 8 (1975): 28–54; George R. Taylor, *The Transportation Revolution, 1815–60* (New York, 1977, orig. pub. 1951), pp. 334–50; Stanley Lebergott, "Labor Force and Employment, 1800–1960," in National Bureau of Economic Research, *Output, Employment, and Productivity in the United States after 1800* (New York,

1966), pp. 184–5. There is, in fact, no way to develop precise unemployment statistics for the antebellum period. For estimates of national unemployment levels from 1800 to 1960, see Stanley Lebergott, *Manpower in Economic Growth* (New York, 1964), pp. 188–9.

2 See, e.g., Edward Pessen, *Most Uncommon Jacksonians; The Radical Leaders of the Early Labor Movement* (Albany, N.Y., 1967); John R. Commons, et al., eds., *A Documentary History of American Industrial Society*, 10 vols. (New York, 1958; orig. pub. Cleveland, 1910–11), VI, VIII; and Marvin Meyers, *The Jacksonian Persuasion: Politics and Belief* (Stanford, Calif., 1957).

3 Lebergott, *Manpower*, pp. 170–1; Jonathan Prude, *The Coming of Industrial Order: Town and Factory Life in Rural Massachusetts, 1810–1860* (Cambridge, 1983), pp. 15–17; Alfred D. Chandler, Jr., *The Visible Hand: The Managerial Revolution in American Business* (Cambridge, Mass., 1977), p. 35; Samuel G. Goodrich, *Recollections of a Lifetime*, 2 vols. (New York, 1857), I, pp. 87, 332, and II, p. 78; Samuel Eliot Morison, *The Ropemakers of Plymouth: A History of the Plymouth Cordage Company, 1824–1949* (Boston, 1950), pp. 24–5; George S. Gibb, *The Whitesmiths of Taunton: A History of Reed and Barton, 1824–1943* (Cambridge, Mass., 1946), p. 60; Henry Bass Hall, "A Description of Rural Life and Labor in Massachusetts at Four Periods" (Ph.D. diss., Harvard University, 1917), p. 89; and Timothy Dwight, *Travels in New England and New York*, Barbara M. Solomon, ed., 4 vols. (Cambridge, Mass., 1969), II, p. 2. Regarding the rhythms of work in Philadelphia during a slightly later period, see Bruce Laurie, "'Nothing on Compulsion': Life Styles of Philadelphia Artisans, 1820–1850," *Labor History* 15 (1974): 337–66. See also Keith Thomas, "Work and Leisure in Pre-Industrial Society," *Past and Present*, no. 29 (Dec. 1964): 50–62, and E. P. Thompson, "Time, Work-Discipline, and Industrial Capitalism," *Past and Present*, no. 38 (Dec. 1967): 56–97.

4 Alexander James Field, "Sectoral Shift in Antebellum Massachusetts: A Reconsideration," *Explorations in Economic History* 15 (1978): 153; Alan Dawley, *Class and Community: The Industrial Revolution in Lynn* (Cambridge, Mass., 1976), p. 46.

5 Dwight, *Travels*, II, pp. 184–6, 232, and IV, 239; Percy W. Bidwell, "The Agricultural Revolution in New England," *American Historical Review* 26 (1921): 684. For definitions of underemployment, see Louis J. Ducoff and Margaret J. Hagood, "The Meaning and Measurement of Partial and Disguised Unemployment," in National Bureau of Economic Research, *The Measurement and Behavior of Unemployment* (Princeton, N.J., 1957), pp. 155–66; and David Gordon, *Theories of Poverty and Underemployment* (Lexington, Mass., 1972).

6 Victor S. Clark, *History of Manufactures in the United States, 1607–1860*, 3 vols. (New York, 1929), I, pp. 129–32; Walter B. Smith and Arthur H. Cole, *Fluctuations in American Business 1790–1860* (Cambridge, Mass., 1935), pp. 12–17, 31; Rolla M. Tryon, *Household Manufactures in the United States, 1640–1860* (Chicago, 1917; repr. New York, 1966), pp. 86–7.

7 Tryon, *Household Manufactures*, pp. 1, 2, 131, 146, 183, 207, 221, 223, 228;

Goodrich, *Recollections*, I, pp. 64, 71; Clark, *Manufactures*, I, pp. 186, 579–80; Hall, "Rural Life and Labor," pp. 8, 52–3; Clarence H. Danhof, *Change in Agriculture: The Northern United States, 1820–1870* (Cambridge, Mass., 1969), pp. 3, 16, 147; and Richard L. Bushman, "Family Security in the Transition from Farm to City, 1750–1850," in Eleutherian Mills–Hagley Foundation, *Working Papers from the Regional Economic History Research Center* (Wilmington, Del., 1980), p. 38.

8   Oscar Handlin and Mary F. Handlin, *Commonwealth*, rev. ed. (Cambridge, Mass., 1969), pp. 60, 66, 123; Danhof, *Agriculture*, pp. 3, 15, 25, 81; Tryon, *Household Manufactures*, pp. 145, 239–40, 280; Bidwell, "Agricultural Revolution," p. 697; Goodrich, *Recollections*, I, pp. 60, 77; Hall, "Rural Life and Labor," p. 56; Chandler, *Visible Hand*, p. 53; Clark, *Manufactures*, I, pp. 159, 441; Dawley, *Class and Community*, pp. 46–8; Blanche E. Hazard, *The Organization of the Boot and Shoe Industry in Massachusetts Before 1875* (Cambridge, Mass., 1921), pp. 138–9, 183, 210ff.

9   See Hall, "Rural Life and Labor," p. 54; Bushman, "Family Security," pp. 32, 38.

10   Dawley, *Class and Community*, pp. 25, 46; Paul G. Faler, "Workingmen, Mechanics, and Social Change: Lynn, Massachusetts 1800–1860" (Ph.D. diss., University of Wisconsin, 1971), pp. 111, 122; Bushman, "Family Security," pp. 32–40.

11   Field, "Sectoral Shift," pp. 150–3; Goodrich, *Recollections*, II, p. 78.

12   Robert W. Kelso, *The History of Public Poor Relief in Massachusetts, 1629–1920* (Boston, 1922; repr. Montclair, N.J., 1969), pp. 62, 93, 97; Louis J. Picarello, "Poor Relief in Nineteenth Century Danvers," unpubl. research paper, Brandeis University; David J. Rothman, *The Discovery of the Asylum* (Boston, 1971), pp. 30, 32, 155–60.

13   Tryon, *Household Manufactures*, p. 144.

14   Robert F. Dalzell, Jr., "The Rise of the Waltham-Lowell System and Some Thoughts on the Political Economy of Modernization in Ante-Bellum Massachusetts," *Perspectives in American History* 9 (1975): 229. Between 1820 and 1870, the population of Massachusetts increased from 523,287 to 1,457,351. *A Compendium of the Census of Massachusetts: 1875*, prepared by Carroll D. Wright (Boston, 1877), p. 31.

15   Field, "Sectoral Shift," p. 153; Bidwell, "Agricultural Revolution," pp. 688–93; Danhof, *Agriculture*, pp. 4, 18, 73–4n. Precise statistics regarding the number of persons in agriculture and in manufactures from 1820 to 1870 cannot be developed from available census data. But it appears that the number of persons engaged in farming in Massachusetts remained roughly constant while the number in manufactures rose dramatically. See *Digest of Accounts of Manufacturing Establishments in the United States*, Book II of the Fourth Census, made under the direction of the Secretary of State (Washington, 1823), unpaged; U.S. Department of State, *Compendium of the Enumeration of the Inhabitants and Statistics of the United States from the Returns of the Sixth Census* (Washington, 1841), p. 11; J. D. B. Debow, Superintendent of the U.S. Census, *Compendium of the Seventh*

Census (Washington, 1854), pp. 128–9; *Mass. Census, 1875,* I (Boston, 1876–7), pp. 476–7.

16 Figures regarding the proportion of working people who were employees are based on a detailed analysis of the 1875 census of Massachusetts. For a tabular presentation of the data and an explanation of the methods used, see Alexander Keyssar, "Men Out of Work" (Ph.D. diss., Harvard University, 1977), pp. 30, 468–9. Cf. David Montgomery, *Beyond Equality: Labor and the Radical Republicans, 1862–1872* (New York, 1972; orig. pub. New York, 1967), pp. 25–30, and Stanley Lebergott, "The Pattern of Employment Since 1800," in Seymour Harris, ed., *American Economic History* (New York, 1961), pp. 290–2.

17 Norman Ware, *The Industrial Worker 1840–1860* (Chicago, 1964; orig. pub. Boston, 1924), p. 13; Tryon, *Household Manufactures,* pp. 242, 290, 293, 303, 306, 308, 314, 370; Bidwell, "Agricultural Revolution," pp. 693–4; Chandler, *Visible Hand,* p. 51.

18 MBSL, *3 AR,* pp. 429–30.

19 By 1875, cotton mills in Massachusetts had an average of 300 employees, while those producing woolens employed slightly more than 100. In almost all other industries, however, plants were much smaller. *Mass. Census, 1875,* II (Boston, 1876–7) pp. xxix–xxxvi, 226–8. See also Montgomery, *Beyond Equality,* pp. 25–6; and Arthur B. Darling, "The Workingmen's Party in Massachusetts, 1833–1834," *American Historical Review* 29 (1923): 83. For an example of personalized management in a small firm, see Gibb, *Whitesmiths,* p. 135.

20 *Third Grand Rally of the Workingmen of Charlestown, Massachusetts, Held October 23, 1840,* Kress Library of Business and Economics, Harvard Business School, p. 10.

21 Chandler, *Visible Hand,* p. 245; Handlin and Handlin, *Commonwealth,* pp. 186–8; Vera Shlakman, *Economic History of a Factory Town: A Study of Chicopee, Massachusetts,* Smith College Studies in History, 20 (Northampton, Mass., 1934–35), pp. 139–40; Donald B. Cole, *Immigrant City: Lawrence, Massachusetts, 1845–1921* (Chapel Hill, N.C., 1963), p. 34.

22 Peter R. Knights, *The Plain People of Boston, 1830–1860* (New York, 1971), p. 20; *Mass. Census, 1875,* I, pp. xxvi–xxx; Michael H. Frisch, *Town into City: Springfield, Massachusetts, and the Meaning of Community, 1840–1880* (Cambridge, Mass., 1972), pp. 14, 15, 24, 123–4. Many of the state's rural towns had declining populations during these years. MBSL, *11 AR,* p. 239.

23 Morison, *Ropemakers,* pp. 23–4; David N. Johnson, *Sketches of Lynn* (Lynn, Mass., 1880), pp. 157–62. Paul Faler persuasively argues that Johnson's portrait of the self-sufficiency of Lynn's shoemakers is overdrawn. According to Faler, only the most established of the town's shoemakers owned livestock or land. Faler, "Workingmen," pp. 163–4, 168–74, 184–9, 479.

24 Oscar Handlin, *Boston's Immigrants* (New York, 1976; orig. pub. Cambridge, Mass., 1941), pp. 47–69, 86, 118, 242; *Compendium of 1875 Mass. Census* p. 45.

25 See Peter Temin, "Labor Scarcity in America," *Journal of Interdisciplinary History* 1 (1971): 251–64; Paul J. Uselding, "An Early Chapter in the Evolution of American Industrial Management," in Uselding and Louis P. Cain, eds., *Business Enterprise and Economic Change* (Kent, Ohio, 1973), p. 77.

26 *Atlantic Monthly*, 42 (Dec. 1878): 723. Cf. Richard D. Brown, *Modernization: The Transformation of American Life, 1600–1865* (New York, 1976), pp. 112–16.

27 Cf. Thompson, "Time, Work-Discipline, and Industrial Capitalism." This change of expectations underscores the importance of the "subjective" component of the definition of unemployment: an unemployed person is one who is not merely out of work but also in need of work or wanting to work. The difficulties that this subjective element introduces into efforts to count the unemployed are discussed in Appendix B.

28 MBSL, *10 AR*, p. 122.

29 Circular, orig. pub. in *The Man*, May 13, 1835, reprinted in Commons, et al., *Documentary History*, VI, p. 95. Although Boston's craftsmen were arguing for shorter hours, they were not claiming (as workers would in subsequent decades) that shorter hours would spread the work and thus eliminate or reduce unemployment.

30 Lebergott, *Manpower*, 143–4, 172, 188.

31 Gibb, *Whitesmiths*, p. 47; George S. Gibb, *The Saco-Lowell Shops; Textile Machinery Building in New England 1813–1949* (Cambridge, Mass., 1950), pp. 47, 146; Daniel Nelson, *Managers and Workers: Origins of the New Factory System in the United States, 1880–1920* (Madison, Wis., 1975), pp. 88–90; BSPP, *22 AR*, (Boston, 1857), p. 6; Thomas R. Navin, *The Whitin Machine Works Since 1831* (Cambridge, Mass., 1950), pp. 44, 54, 62, 75.

32 James D. Burn, *Three Years Among the Working-Classes in the United States during the War* (London, 1865), p. 189; "The Merrimack River Group and the Lawrence Manufacturing Company, 1811–65" (manuscript, Merrimack papers, Baker Library, Harvard University), p. 16.

33 Constance M. Green, *Holyoke, Massachusetts: A Case History of the Industrial Revolution in America* (New Haven, Conn., 1939), pp. 60, 76, 77–9; Gibb, *Whitesmiths*, pp. 79, 147; Gibb, *Saco-Lowell Shops*, p. 53; Navin, *Whitin Machine Works*, p. 53.

34 Lance E. Davis and H. Louis Stettler III, "The New England Textile Industry, 1825–60: Trends and Fluctuations," in National Bureau of Economic Research, *Output, Employment, and Productivity*, p. 221; John M. Cudd, *The Chicopee Manufacturing Company, 1823–1915* (Wilmington, Del., 1974), pp. 258–9; Thomas Dublin, *Women at Work: The Transformation of Work and Community in Lowell, Massachusetts, 1826–1860* (New York, 1979), pp. 9, 21, 133; Chandler, *Visible Hand*, pp. 57, 60; Clark, *Manufactures*, I, p. 449; Arthur H. Cole, *The American Wool Manufacture*, 2 vols. (Cambridge, Mass., 1926), I, pp. 267–9; Paul F. McGouldrick, *New England Textiles in the Nineteenth Century* (Cambridge, Mass., 1968), p. 18; *Mass. Census, 1875*, I, pp. 575–611, and II, pp. xxix–xxxvi.

35 Cole, *Wool Manufacture*, I, pp. 13–14, 19, 59; Prude, *Industrial Order*, pp. 3–33, 183–216.

36 Clark, *Manufactures*, I, p. 441; Dublin, *Women*, pp. 14, 16, 59; Cole, *Wool Manufacture*, I, pp. 223–34, 293; Cudd, *Chicopee*, pp. 5, 10; McGouldrick, *Textiles*, p. 18; Prude, *Industrial Order*, pp. 36–49, 70–8, 107, 123, 188, 200–1.

37 Barbara M. Tucker, "The Family and Industrial Discipline in Ante-Bellum New England," *Labor History* 21 (1979–80): 67–8; Dublin, *Women*, pp. 24, 26–38, 60, 99.

38 Prude, *Industrial Order*, pp. 78–99, 100–32; Ware, *Industrial Worker*, pp. 73–4; Cole, *Wool Manufacture*, I, p. 368; McGouldrick, *Textiles*, p. 35; Caroline F. Ware, *The Early New England Cotton Manufacture* (Boston and New York, 1931), p. 13.

39 Dublin, *Women*, pp. 141, 161, 188–90; Cudd, *Chicopee*, p. 156; Prude, *Industrial Order*, pp. 183–228; Cole, *Wool Manufacture*, I, pp. 240–371.

40 Dublin, *Women*, pp. 138–40, 147; Prude, *Industrial Order*, pp. 183–237; Clark, *Manufactures*, I, p. 398; Cudd, *Chicopee*, pp. 88–90.

41 Dublin, *Women*, pp. 140–1, 171–2, 177, 181, 189, 198–9; Prude, *Industrial Order*, pp. 207–37; Tucker, "Family," p. 74; Handlin, *Boston's Immigrants*, pp. 54–87.

42 McGouldrick, *Textiles*, pp. 13, 104; Cudd, *Chicopee*, pp. 79–81, 126.

43 The conclusions regarding employment stability in the textile industry are based, in part, on a detailed analysis of quarterly payroll records from several of the mills in the Slater complex in Oxford, Dudley, and Webster, Mass. The payroll records themselves are in the Baker Library, Harvard University, and preliminary tabulations were generously given to me by Jonathan Prude. These conclusions were supported by an examination of monthly employment fluctuations in the Thorndike Mills (the records for which are also in Baker) presented in an unpublished paper at Brandeis University by Mindy Berman. See also Prude, *Industrial Order*, pp. 92–6, 208–16; Dublin, *Women*, pp. 59, 140, 156, 175; Cudd, *Chicopee*, pp. 90–2, 99–100; Clark, *Manufactures*, I, p. 556; and Massachusetts House Document 50, March 1845, repr. in Commons, et al., *Documentary History*, VIII, p. 142.

44 Dublin, *Women*, pp. 18, 108; Prude, *Industrial Order*, pp. 84–5; Joshua Aubin, "Woolen Manufacturing in Amesbury, 1821–1857," manuscript diary, Baker Library, Harvard University, p. 3; Cudd, *Chicopee*, pp. 8–9; Clark, *Manufactures*, I, p. 556; Montgomery, *Beyond Equality*, p. 13; Ware, *Industrial Worker*, p. 12; Green, *Holyoke*, p. 76; *BISU Report*, app. A, pp. 2–9.

45 *Compendium of 1875 Mass. Census*, p. 129; Dawley, *Class and Community*, p. 47; Faler, "Workingmen," pp. 7, 46–7, 124; *Mass. Census, 1875*, I, pp. 575–611, and II, pp. xxix–xxxvi.

46 Dawley, *Class and Community*, pp. 46, 47, 51, 14–16; Faler, "Workingmen," pp. 33, 169; Hazard, *Boot and Shoe*, pp. 12, 19, 23, 24.

47 Hazard, *Boot and Shoe*, pp. 42, 44, 52, 58, 86–90, 94–5; Faler, "Workingmen," pp. 41, 54, 55; Dawley, *Class and Community*, pp. 29–30, 53.

48 Dawley, *Class and Community*, pp. 52–3, 85; Faler, "Workingmen," pp. 168–74.
49 Dawley, *Class and Community*, pp. 48–50, 52, 140; Faler, "Workingmen," pp. 160, 452; Hazard, *Boot and Shoe*, p. 137.
50 Faler, "Workingmen," pp. 122, 124, 164–5, 332, 450; Hazard, *Boot and Shoe*, pp. 97–100, 109, 124; Ware, *Industrial Worker*, pp. 46–8.
51 MBSL, *4 AR*, p. 305; see also *2 AR*, p. 242.
52 Dawley, *Class and Community*, pp. 115, 139, 140, 142; T. J. Pinkham, *Farming As It Is* (Boston, 1860), p. 23; Augusta E. Galster, *The Labor Movement in the Shoe Industry* (New York, 1924), p. 37.
53 Faler, "Workingmen," pp. 129, 137, 159–63, 179, 181–8, 192–6, 202, 292–5, 457; Hazard, *Boot and Shoe*, pp. 45, 64–5, 117–19, 229–30; Dawley, *Class and Community*, pp. 168–9; Picarello, "Poor Relief," pp. 31–2.
54 Green, *Holyoke*, pp. 90–101; Frank T. Stockton, *The International Molders Union of North America* (Baltimore, 1921), pp. 12–14; George E. McNeill, ed., *The Labor Movement: The Problem of Today* (Milwaukee, 1891), pp. 88, 308–9, 340–1; Gibb, *Whitesmiths*, pp. 110–11; Gibb, *Saco-Lowell Shops*, pp. 89, 100, 170, 172, 216; Handlin and Handlin, *Commonwealth*, p. 188; Ware, *Industrial Worker*, pp. 48, 55, 66–7; *Seventh Census of the United States: 1850* (Washington, 1853), p. 57; *Mass. Census, 1875*, I, p. 586.
55 Gibb, *Saco-Lowell Shops*, p. 88; Gibb, *Whitesmiths*, p. 135.
56 Massachusetts Commission on the Hours of Labor, Hearings, Nov. 22, 1865, box 1, Archives of the Commonwealth, Boston.
57 Letter dated July 1829, cited in Prude, *Industrial Order*, p. 95.
58 Taylor, *Transportation Revolution*, pp. 334–8; Gibb, *Whitesmiths*, pp. 25, 47; Clark, *Manufactures*, I, pp. 378–80; Gibb, *Saco-Lowell Shops*, p. 26; Smith and Cole, *Fluctuations*, p. 20; Faler, "Workingmen," pp. 224ff.; Ware, *Cotton Manufacture*, p. 269; Lebergott, *Manpower*, pp. 173–4; Lebergott, "Pattern of Employment," pp. 293–4; Samuel Rezneck, "The Depression of 1819–1822: A Social History," *American Historical Review* 39 (1933): 30–3.
59 *A Portrait of the Character and Conduct of Aaron Dow and Nathaniel Magoon* (Boston, 1837), Kress Library, Harvard Business School; McNeill, *Labor Movement*, p. 340; David J. Rothman, *The Discovery of the Asylum* (Boston, 1971), p. 177; Pessen, *Jacksonians*, p. 113; Nathan I. Huggins, *Protestants against Poverty: Boston's Charities, 1870–1900* (Westport, Conn., 1971), p. 26; BSPP, *25 AR*, pp. 7–12.
60 *BISU Report*, app. A, pp. 1–2; Johnson, *Sketches*, p. 156; Faler, "Workingmen," pp. 163–4, 184–6, 326; Gibb, *Whitesmiths*, pp. 94–5; Clark, *Manufactures*, I, p. 381; Shlakman, *Economic History*, pp. 99, 141–2, 157; Cole, *Immigrant City*, p. 34; Lebergott, "Pattern of Employment," p. 295; Samuel Rezneck, "The Social History of an American Depression, 1837–1843," *American Historical Review* 40 (1935): 665.
61 Johnson, *Sketches*, pp. 156–62; Faler, "Workingmen," pp. 168–74, 184–6, 233, 425–6, 479; Dawley, *Class and Community*, pp. 52–3, 61; Ware, *Industrial Worker*, pp. 39–40, 74, 149; *BISU Report*, app. A, p. 2.
62 MBSL, *8 AR*, p. 65; McNeill, *Labor Movement*, pp. 77–80, 99; Ware, *Industrial Worker*, pp. 27, 30; Picarello, "Poor Relief," pp. 10, 33; Rothman,

Asylum, pp. 172–3; Faler, "Workingmen," pp. 224ff.; Rezneck, "American Depression, 1837–1843," p. 667; BSPP, *25 AR*, p. 12. See also Thomas Thwing, "An Address Delivered Before the Association of Delegates from the Benevolent Societies of Boston," Oct. 10, 1843, Kress Library, Harvard Business School; Theodore Parker, *Sermon of the Perishing Classes in Boston* (Boston, 1846); and R. C. Waterston, *An Address on Pauperism* (Boston, 1844).

63 Committee Report on the Hours of Labor, House Document 153, 1850, reprinted in Commons, et al., eds., *Documentary History*, VIII, p. 174; BSPP, unnumbered *AR* (Boston, 1852), pp. 11–12; Stephan Thernstrom, *Poverty and Progress: Social Mobility in a Nineteenth-Century City* (New York, 1972; orig. pub. New York, 1964), pp. 18–25; Handlin, *Boston's Immigrants*, pp. 60–1, 86, 118; Knights, *Plain People*, p. 78.

64 Boston *Herald*, June 10, 1854.

65 Boston *Herald*, Jan. 8, 1855.

66 BSPP, *23 AR*, (Boston, 1858), pp. 6–7.

67 BSPP, *25 AR*, pp. 2, 16; see also BSPP, *24 AR*, (Boston, 1859), p. 5, and *20 AR* (Boston, 1855), pp. 6–8; IAS, *58 AR*, p. 13; Shlakman, *Economic History*, pp. 141–2; Thernstrom, *Poverty and Progress*, pp. 20, 43–4, 87, 90, 134; Faler, "Workingmen," pp. 191–2, 457; *BISU Report*, app. A, pp. 3–4; Dawley, *Class and Community*, p. 85.

68 Gibb, *Whitesmiths*, p. 101; Thernstrom, *Poverty and Progress*, pp. 20–1, 87; Leah H. Feder, *Unemployment Relief in Periods of Depression* (New York, 1936), pp. 21, 26–8, 32; Faler, "Workingmen," pp. 233–4, 427–8, 457; Hazard, *Boot and Shoe*, pp. 103–9; Clark, *Manufactures*, I, p. 382; Green, *Holyoke*, pp. 59–63; Shlakman, *Economic History*, pp. 139–40, 143; Ware, *Industrial Worker*, p. 7; *BISU Report*, app. A, pp. 11–12; Fall River *News*, Sept. 24, Oct. 22, Nov. 19, Dec. 3 and 17, 1857; March 18, April 8, May 22, 1858.

69 IAS, *31 AR*; *32 AR*, pp. 7–9; *59 AR*, p. 13. The number of applicants for jobs to the Industrial Aid Society remained low throughout the 1860s. See also Hazard, *Boot and Shoe*, pp. 117–119; Gibb, *Saco-Lowell Shops*, pp. 195–6; Burn, *Three Years*, pp. 188–9; Howard M. Gitelman, *Workingmen of Waltham: Mobility in American Urban Industrial Development 1850–1890* (Baltimore, 1974), p. 52; Gibb, *Whitesmiths*, pp. 181–93; Cudd, *Chicopee*, pp. 125–6, 156; Cole, *Wool Manufactures*, I, pp. 376–85; Frisch, *Town*, pp. 53, 63, 65, 72–81, 118–19; Lebergott, "Pattern of Employment," p. 295; Montgomery, *Beyond Equality*, pp. 5, 262–4; Green, *Holyoke*, pp. 71–3; BSPP, *27 AR* (Boston, 1862), pp. 8–9; *30 AR*, (Boston, 1865), p. 15; and *26 AR*, (Boston, 1861), p. 8.

70 Massachusetts House Document 153, 1850, repr. in Commons, et al., eds., *Documentary History*, VIII, p. 185; *Vindicator* (Lynn, Mass.), Jan. 13, 1877.

71 MBSL, *2 AR*, p. 552.

72 Marx, of course, in his well-known discussion of labor reserves, argues that the "relative surplus-population" always has three different forms:

"the floating, the latent, the stagnant," *Capital*, 3 vols. (New York, 1967), I, pp. 628–41.

73 Regarding the abundance or scarcity of labor in general, see Field, "Sectoral Shift"; Temin, "Labor Scarcity"; and Uselding, "An Early Chapter."

3. The era of uncertainty

1 MBSL, *2 AR*, p. 147; *10 AR*, p. 137; *Labor Leader*, Oct. 1, 1887; BISU Hearings, p. 120; Boston *Evening Transcript*, Dec. 23, 1910; Whiting Williams, *What's on the Worker's Mind* (New York, 1921), p. 39.

2 See Chapter 1.

3 *Mass. Census, 1915* (Boston, 1918), pp. iv, 290–6, 324–5; Joseph J. Huthmacher, *Massachusetts People and Politics, 1919–1933* (Cambridge, Mass., 1959), p. 5.

4 *Mass. Census, 1915*, pp. 34–8, 79–81.

5 *Fourteenth Census of the United States*, IX, *Manufactures* (Washington, 1923), pp. 588–9, 602–3; Massachusetts Bureau of Statistics, *Thirty-Second Annual Report on the Statistics of Manufactures, 1917, Public Document 36* (Boston, 1919), pp. x–xi, and *Thirty-third Annual Report on the Statistics of Manufactures, 1918*, (Boston, 1920), pp. vii, xxiii. See also MBSL, *20 AR*, p. 289; *21 AR*, pp. 165ff., 179, 220, 226, 251ff.; Edward C. Kirkland, *Men, Cities, and Transportation*, 2 vols. (Cambridge, Mass., 1948), I, p. 524; Henry B. Hall, "A Description of Rural Life and Labor in Massachusetts at Four Periods" (Ph.D. diss. Harvard University, 1917), pp. 148, 174–5; Richard Abrams, *Conservatism in a Progressive Era; Massachusetts Politics, 1900–1912* (Cambridge, Mass., 1964), p. 75; George S. Gibb, *The Whitesmiths of Taunton: A History of Reed and Barton, 1824–1943* (Cambridge, Mass., 1946), p. 208; and Huthmacher, *People*, pp. 1–2.

6 *Mass. Census, 1915*, p. 507; *Fourteenth U.S. Census*, IX, pp. 589, 617–18; Mass., *Thirty-third Annual Report on Manufactures*, p. xxiii; MBSL, *Bulletin 2*, pp. 28ff.; *Bulletin 5*, pp. 1ff; *Bulletin 48*, pp. 191ff., 197ff.; MBSL, *20 AR*, p. 289; *21 AR*, p. 220; *36 AR*, p. 80; John W. Hammond, "Twentieth Century Manufactures," in Albert B. Hart, ed., *Commonwealth History of Massachusetts*, 5 vols. (New York, 1927–1930), V, pp. 372–90; Abrams, *Conservatism*, pp. 73–4; Seymour L. Wolfbein, *The Decline of a Cotton Textile City* (New York, 1944), pp. 9ff., 84–6; John M. Cudd, *The Chicopee Manufacturing Company, 1823–1915* (Wilmington, Del., 1974), p. 173.

7 *Fourteenth U.S. Census*, IX, p. 602; Hammond, "Manufactures," pp. 399–400; Gibb, *Whitesmiths*, p. 195; MBSL, *36 AR*, p. 79; see also Alfred D. Chandler, *The Visible Hand: The Managerial Revolution in American Business* (Cambridge, Mass., 1977), pp. 114, 194, 207–9, 229, 238, 241–5, 316–17, 332, 365.

8 MBSL, *36 AR*, pp. 79, 92; Massachusetts Bureau of Statistics, *Thirty-first Annual Report on the Statistics of Manufactures, 1916, Public Document 36* (Boston, 1918), pp. 2–4ff.; *Fourteenth U.S. Census*, IX, p. 602; Daniel Nelson, *Managers and Workers: Origins of the New Factory System in the United States 1880–1920* (Madison, Wis., 1915), pp. 5–10; Vera Shlakman, *Eco-*

nomic History of a Factory Town: A Study of Chicopee, Massachusetts, Smith College Studies in History 20 (Northampton, Mass., 1934–5), p. 227; Hammond, "Manufactures," pp. 382, 384; Constance M. Green, *Holyoke, Massachusetts: A Case History of the Industrial Revolution in America* (New Haven, Conn., 1939), pp. 174–95; Gibb, *Whitesmiths,* pp. 284, 299, 305, 367; George S. Gibb, *The Saco-Lowell Shops; Textile Machinery Building in New England, 1813–1949,* p. 445; Thomas R. Navin, *The Whitin Machine Machine Works Since 1831* (Cambridge, Mass., 1950), pp. 140–8; David Montgomery, *Workers' Control in America* (Cambridge, 1979), p. 101.

9 There were, of course, exceptions to these patterns. Many immigrants did return to their country of origin when confronted with a scarcity of industrial jobs, but, as a rule, the distances and the costs were too great for such trips to be made routinely and repeatedly. The one group of workers who did maintain effective ties (resembling those of the antebellum period) with the worlds of both agriculture and industry were the "floaters" from northern New England and Canada mentioned later in this chapter. These floaters constituted a significant presence in some trades, in some communities, but they comprised only a small – and shrinking – proportion of the labor force as a whole.

10 Changes in the sectoral and occupational categories utilized in the census prohibit a precise grasp of the shifts in the distribution of the labor force, but a comparison of Tables 2.1 and 3.1 suggests that the broad contours of the sectoral distribution remained intact from 1875 to 1915. The most marked changes in the occupational structure appear to have been a decline in the proportion of men engaged in agriculture, a decline in the proportion of women performing domestic work, and an increase in the percentage of women belonging to clerical occupations. The number of self-employed persons did increase during this period, but the proportion dropped steadily. A conservative estimate of the percentage of employees in the labor force in 1915, based on an analysis of very detailed occupational listings, indicates that 79% of all males and virtually all females were employees. Alexander Keyssar, "Men Out of Work," (Ph.D. diss., Harvard University, 1977), pp. 60, 474. The MBSL estimated that 86% of the productive residents of the state were either wage earners or employees with small salaries at the turn of the century. MBSL, *29 AR*, p. 628. See also *Fourteenth U.S. Census,* IX, p. 588. Cf. Stanley Lebergott, "The Pattern of Employment Since 1800," in Seymour Harris, ed., *American Economic History* (New York, 1961), p. 292.

11 Only 17.2% of all male employees performed white-collar work in 1915. Keyssar, "Men Out of Work," pp. 60, 474. The ratio of salaried employees to wage earners rose during this period, but it was still 1:10 in 1914 and 1:8 after World War I. *Fourteenth U.S. Census,* IX, p. 588. Regarding the growth of semiskilled work, see Nelson, *Managers and Workers,* p. 96; Montgomery, *Workers' Control,* p. 101; and Chandler, *Visible Hand,* pp. 243–5.

12 Statements regarding the spectrum of wage levels in the late nineteenth century are based upon the following sources: MBSL *3 AR,* pp. 339, 341,

343; *4 AR*, p. 402; *7 AR*, pp. 193ff., 214; *13 AR*, pp. 421ff.; *20 AR*, p. 430; *28 AR*, pp. 3–4, 12ff.; *Mass. Census, 1875*, II (Boston, 1876–7), pp. xlvi–xlvii; and USBLS, *Bulletin 499: History of Wages in the United States from Colonial Times to 1928* (Washington, 1929), pp. 153–218, 228–31, 256–60, 261–72, 277–80, 312–18, 363–421, 450–4. That significant wage differentials persisted into the twentieth century is indicated both by the data presented in USBLS, *Bulletin 499*, and by the following state sources: MBSL, *41 AR*, pp. 199, 283–4, 301, 323; MBSL, *Bulletin 17*, pp. 18–20; Massachusetts Bureau of Statistics, *Thirteenth Annual Report on Manufactures, 1898, Public Document 36* (Boston, 1899) pp. xxxviii, 80–119; and *Report of the Commission on the Cost of Living, Massachusetts House Document 1750* (Boston, 1910), pp. 84–5. Wage rates, of course, varied within occupations as well as among occupations, partly due to geographic variations and partly because workers with the same generic occupational label (e.g., "shoe worker") often performed very different kinds of work.

13   BISU Hearings, p. 61; for additional evidence, see pp. 6, 17, 77, 203, 823, 887, 1016.

14   Data regarding the cost of living, household budgets, and the tight fit between incomes and the cost of necessities in the latter decades of the nineteenth century can be found in MBSL, *3 AR*, pp. 251, 532; *4 AR*, p. 115; *6 AR*, p. 380; *28 AR*, pp. 37–41; *Report on the Cost of Living*, pp. 573–4; and Frank H. Streightoff, *The Standard of Living among the Industrial People of America* (Boston and New York, 1911), pp. 13, 159. Despite the existence of numerous surveys indicating that working-class households often had more than one wage earner or source of income, it is difficult to gauge the proportion of households that did not rely totally on the earnings of the household head – since the surveys produced very disparate figures. Nonetheless, it seems clear that children and married women entered the labor force out of economic need: their labor force participation rates varied inversely with the earnings of the adult, male household head. It also should be noted that the ability of a family to generate more than one income changed in the course of its own life cycle. A married couple with four teenage children was in a very different position than it had been ten years earlier. See also Chapters 4 and 6. Regarding multiple wage earners and household incomes and their effect on the standard of living from 1870 to 1920, see MBSL, *6 AR*, pp. 357–84; *7 AR*, pp. 71, 28–9; *32 AR*, p. 276; *43 AR*, p. 31; *Report of the Special Commission on Social Insurance, Massachusetts House Document 1850* (Boston, 1917), p. 14; U.S. Commissioner of Labor, *Eighteenth Annual Report* (Washington, 1904), pp. 362–7; Clarence D. Long, *The Labor Force Under Changing Income and Employment* (Princeton, N.J., 1958), pp. 7, 88; Maurice Parmelee, *Poverty and Social Progress* (New York, 1920), pp. 97–8, 105; Mary K. Simkhovitch, *The City Worker's World in America* (New York, 1917), pp. 84–5, 166; W. Jett Lauck and Edgar Sydenstricker, *Conditions of Labor in American Industries* (New York, 1917), pp. 357–76; Paul H. Douglas and Aaron Director, *The Problem of Unemployment* (New York, 1931), p. 484; Donald B. Cole, *Immigrant City: Lawrence, Massachusetts,*

1845–1921 (Chapel Hill, N.C., 1963), p. 118; and Howard M. Gitelman, *Workingmen of Waltham: Mobility in American Urban Industrial Development 1850–1890* (Baltimore, 1974), p. 85.

15 Whether or not real wages and real annual earnings improved significantly between the 1870s and the 1920s has been a matter of some debate, but the debate does not, in the end, affect the argument put forward in this study. The most recent and authoritative national studies of wage levels, those of Long, Lebergott, and Rees, do offer convincing evidence of an increase in real wages and earnings, but none of these studies suggests that the increases were great enough to vitiate the need for steady work. Clarence D. Long, *Wages and Earnings in the United States, 1860–1890* (Princeton, N.J., 1960), pp. vii, 109–118; Stanley Lebergott, *Manpower in Economic Growth* (New York, 1964), p. 524; Albert Rees, *Real Wages in Manufacturing, 1890–1914* (Princeton, N.J., 1961), esp. pp. 5, 33, 44–53, 120, 121–6; Paul H. Douglas, *Real Wages in the United States 1890–1926* (Boston, 1930), pp. 476ff., 572; Parmelee, *Poverty*, pp. 68–71, 362–3; Streightoff, *Standard of Living*, p. 50. Regarding the cost of living in Massachusetts and the living conditions and budgets of the state's working people during the first decades of the twentieth century, see *Report on the Cost of Living*, pp. 72, 75, 79, 84–5, 88, table opposite p. 88; MBSL, *28 AR*, pp. 35–7; *32 AR*, pp. 294–5, 306; U.S. Commissioner of Labor, *Eighteenth Annual Report*, pp. 15ff., 580; MBSL, *Quarterly Report 36*, p. 1; Parmelee, *Poverty*, pp. 86–92; MBSL, *Bulletin 44*, p. 435; *Report of the Commission on Social Insurance*, p. 14; Thomas L. Norton, *Trade-Union Policies in the Massachusetts Shoe Industry 1919–1929* (New York, 1932), pp. 48–60; AC-B, *11 AR*, p. 22; and Cudd, *Chicopee*, p. 20. Norton, in his study of the shoe industry (p. 60), concluded that even in 1919, after the wartime boom, "it is probable that if the average male shoe worker had received full-time yearly earnings it would not have enabled him to maintain his family in much more than a minimum of comfort."

16 *Labor Leader*, March 5, 1887.

17 Want ads placed in newspapers reveal that employers were well aware of the desirability of steady employment. For example, an ad placed in the Boston *Globe* by the Washington Mills of Lawrence carried the headline "Steady Work for Weavers." *Globe*, April 16 and 20, 1894.

18 Asher Achinstein, "Economic Fluctuations," in Harris, ed., *American Economic History*, pp. 162–3; Willard L. Thorp and Wesley C. Mitchell, *Business Annals* (New York, 1926), pp. 31–7; Robert A. Gordon, *Business Fluctuations*, 2d ed. (New York, 1961), pp. 339ff.

19 Achinstein, "Economic Fluctuations," pp. 165–8; Thorpe and Mitchell, *Annals*, pp. 130–45; a narrative of the cycles is presented in Maurice W. Lee, *Economic Fluctuations* (Homewood, Ill., 1955), pp. 130–76. See also Wesley C. Mitchell, "Business Cycles," in National Bureau of Economic Research, *Business Cycles and Unemployment* (New York, 1923); Edwin Frickey, *Production in the United States, 1860–1914* (Cambridge, Mass., 1947); and Rendig Fels, *American Business Cycles 1865–1897* (Chapel Hill, N.C., 1959). These studies are national in scope, but there can be little

doubt that a state as industrialized as Massachusetts participated more
or less fully in the fluctuations of the national economy.

20 Achinstein, "Economic Fluctuations," pp. 164–9; Thorpe and Mitchell,
Annals, pp. 37–8; Gordon, Fluctuations, pp. 253–88; Charles Hoffmann,
The Depression of the Nineties (Westport, Conn., 1970), pp. 15–24, 271–83;
Samuel Rezneck, "Patterns of Thought and Action in an American
Depression, 1882–1886," American Historical Review 61 (1956): 285; BISU
Hearings, pp. 205–6.

21 Cudd, Chicopee, p. 173; Green, Holyoke, pp. 77, 137–9; 179–82; Wolfbein,
Cotton Textile City, pp. 21–2; Navin, Whitin Machine Works, pp. 236–7;
Abrams, Conservatism, pp. 229–30. David Brody has observed that in the
twentieth century, at least, steel manufacturers often sought to hold
prices steady while reducing output during depressions. David Brody,
Steelworkers in America: The Nonunion Era (New York, 1969; orig. pub.
Cambridge, Mass., 1960), pp. 153–4. The quotation from the Emerson
Piano Company official is from a form that was distributed to Massachusetts firms by the Boston Chamber of Commerce in the course of an
investigation of the problem of seasonal unemployment in Sept. 1914.
This form, entitled "Questions on Seasonal Employment," posed a variety of detailed questions regarding business practices and the opinions
of employers. The scores of forms (and accompanying letters) that were
returned to the chamber constitute an invaluable source for understanding the dynamics of unemployment from the viewpoint of employers.
The collection is located in files 332–53 and 311–77 of the Boston Chamber of Commerce papers, at Baker Library, Harvard Business School,
Boston, Mass. These documents will hereafter be referred to as BCC,
"Questions on Seasonal Employment."

22 Petition, dated Dec. 21, 1886, to the Massachusetts Board of Arbitration
and Conciliation, Archives of the Commonwealth (Boston). See also
Chapter 7, and BISU Hearings, pp. 407, 722. The example of Francis
Breed's employees raises a conceptual issue that can be (and has been)
debated with great passion and little reward: should workers who are
jobless because they have refused to accept pay cuts be counted as unemployed? Breed's employees were not, strictly speaking, "involuntarily" idled. But the concept of unemployment would lose much of its utility if workers were required to accept any job, at any wage rate, in order
to be counted among the unemployed. Fortunately, this particular Pan-
dora's box – just how big a pay cut would it be reasonable for a worker
to refuse and still be considered unemployed? – need not be opened here
because there is no evidence to suggest that choices such as those made
by Breed's employees accounted for anything other than a small proportion of the recorded unemployment in the commonwealth. A few additional instances are mentioned in the BISU Hearings, pp. 344, 786–7.

23 BISU Hearings, pp. 407, 722; Gibb, Whitesmiths, pp. 276, 345, 352; Norton, Trade-Union Policies, pp. 88–90; Gibb, Saco-Lowell Shops, p. 200; Labor
Leader, Aug. 19, 1893, and March 31, 1894; Navin, Whitin Machine Works,
pp. 4, 102–5, 242, 367; MBSL, 18 AR, pp. 252–4; 35 AR, p. 243; 46 AR,

part IX, p. 43; and part II, p. 43; *47 AR,* part VI, p. 38; *49 AR,* part IV, p. 35; MBSL, *Quarterly Report 25,* p. 3; MBSL, *Bulletin 77,* p. 136. Among workers who were paid by the piece, rather than by the day, short time was often less formalized: men and women reported to work but simply had less work to perform. As the Martin Manufacturing Company of West Newton noted in 1914, piece-rate employees "are simply not on high speed at slack times." BCC, "Questions on Seasonal Employment." There is also some evidence to suggest that manufacturers tended to shift from time rates to piece rates during depressions. AC-B, *29 AR,* p. 44; BISU Hearings, p. 126; D. P. Smelser, *Unemployment and American Trade Unions* (Baltimore, 1919), pp. 43–5.

24 Memo from RAB to Mr. Holmes, March 25, 1921, Plymouth Cordage Company papers, Baker Library, Harvard Business School, Boston, Mass. See also Smelser, *Unemployment,* pp. 125ff.; Green, *Holyoke,* pp. 77–8; Navin, *Whitin Machine Works,* p. 367. In some industries, there were technological impediments to the use of short time, but for many firms layoffs and short time were not mutually exclusive strategies and often accompanied one another.

25 William H. Beveridge, *Unemployment: A Problem of Industry* (London, 1930), p. 114; see Smelser, *Unemployment,* p. 126.

26 See Chapter 1 regarding the failure of Carroll Wright's initial efforts to count the unemployed in 1878. The methods that Wright utilized to conduct his survey almost certainly yielded an undercount of the unemployed, and the survey happened to be carried out as the economic downturn was coming to an end – so it would not, in any case, have captured joblessness levels during the heart of the depression. The Massachusetts state censuses of 1885 and 1895 produced the only direct and comprehensive data that exist regarding unemployment levels during nineteenth-century depressions. They possess the virtue of being based not upon samples but upon surveys of the entire population, and, in certain respects, they constitute the richest collections of unemployment data assembled anywhere in the United States prior to the 1930s. See Appendix B for a brief history of efforts to count the unemployed, as well as for a discussion of those features of the surveys that affect interpretations of the statistics. It should be noted that the phrase "labor force" is used in this study as a general referent to the working population; it does not carry the technical definition (discussed in Appendix B) that has been utilized by the USBLS since 1940. Regarding the location of the 1885 and 1895 surveys in the business cycle and the claim that neither of these censuses measured the worst unemployment of the era, see MBSL, *18 AR,* p. 3; *23 AR,* pp. 398–404; *24 AR,* pp. 114–16; Fels, *Business Cycles,* pp. 128, 193–4; and Frickey, *Production,* pp. 60, 128. The Boston *Evening Transcript* (Dec. 31, 1884) observed that "the year 1884 has been one of curtailment in production and industry but yet has not been a year of great depression."

27 At first glance, it may seem surprising that the unemployment frequency recorded during the well-known depression year of 1894–5 was no

greater than that recorded in 1885. And the mean duration of unemployment was actually lower in 1895 than it was 10 years earlier. But the temporary upswing in trade that occurred during the 1895 census year effectively served to limit both the incidence of unemployment and the length of spells of joblessness. As discussed in Appendix B, comparisons of the figures for the 2 years must also take into account several changes that occurred in the methods of measurement.

It is important to note that the census surveys do not specify whether the annual duration of unemployment for a worker occurred in one spell or several spells in the course of the year. In some occupations (as indicated later in this chapter), workers were often idle more than once in the course of a year, and the durational figures consequently must be regarded as composites. There is, unfortunately, no way to break the data down further, to determine whether the "average" worker who was jobless for 4 months was out of work continuously for a third of the year or was repeatedly laid off for shorter spells. The distinction between single and multiple spells of joblessness probably had little bearing upon the material consequences of unemployment, but it may well have affected the psychological impact of the experience, as discussed in Chapter 6.

The distinction between unemployment rates and unemployment frequencies is a critical one. Unemployment rates are, obviously, of great use in gauging changes in the incidence of joblessness, but unemployment frequencies constitute a more valuable indicator of the role that joblessness played in the lives of working people. Unemployment rates can be converted into unemployment frequencies (and vice-versa) if the mean duration of unemployment is known. The formula for performing this conversion is presented in Appendix B. As a rough rule of thumb, one can assume that the unemployment frequency was 3 times greater than the unemployment rate during the depressions that occurred between 1870 and 1920.

28   MBSL, 7 AR, pp. 20, 84, 193ff.; 10 AR, pp. 62, 108, 118, 144–6; 24 AR, pp. 124–9; 37 AR, p. 292; MBSL, Bulletin 5, p. 19; BISU Report, part IV, p. 16. The estimate that more than 40% of the working class was unemployed in the course of the bleakest years of the period is a relatively conservative one. (See Appendix A, Tables A.1, A.2, A.3, and A.4.) In 1885 the overall unemployment frequency for blue-collar employees was nearly 40%, and 1885, as has been noted, was not one of the most depressed years of the period. Unfortunately, no reliable data exist regarding the duration of unemployment during the troughs of depressions. For impressionistic evidence that idleness levels were well above 30% for workers during depressions, see BISU Hearings, pp. 30–1, 214, 375, 491, 820. For estimates of national unemployment rates during these years, see Lebergott, Manpower, pp. 187–9; Douglas, Real Wages, pp. 440–6; and Leah H. Feder, Unemployment Relief in Periods of Depression (New York, 1936), p. 79.

29   See Appendix B regarding the trade union series, its limits, and its util-

ity. Regarding the origin of the series, see MBSL, *Bulletin 46*, p. 61; MBSL, *47 AR*, part VI, p. 31.

30 Since the trade union series does not contain any data regarding the duration of unemployment, mean durations had to be estimated in order to convert the rates into frequencies. If the estimated means are too high, then the estimated frequencies are correspondingly low. E.g., if the actual mean unemployment duration was less than the estimated 4.0 months in 1914, then more than 32% of all unionists were idled at some point during the year. The rough accuracy of the trade union statistics during this period is affirmed by their close fit with several local surveys that were conducted simultaneously. The trade union statistics are also comparable to the national figures for nonagricultural employees developed and utilized by other scholars. MBSL, *Quarterly Report 28*, pp. 2, 11; Douglas, *Real Wages*, pp. 413, 440; Royal Meeker, "The Dependability and Meaning of Unemployment and Employment Statistics in the United States," *Harvard Business Review* 3 (1930): 388; Lebergott, *Manpower*, p. 512; Hornell Hart, *Fluctuations in Unemployment in Cities of the United States, 1902–1917* (Cincinnati, 1918), p. 48. The estimate that 450,000 persons were jobless in 1914 assumes that the unemployment frequency for the labor force as a whole was roughly 28% and that there were 1.6 million persons in the labor force.

31 Unfortunately, the compilers of the 1895 census chose not to assemble statewide data by occupation. Table A.3 contains the only available statistics regarding unemployment levels within individual occupations during that year.

32 A detailed table, indicating the proportion of the male labor force exposed to occupational unemployment frequencies of different magnitudes, in 1885 and in 1900, is presented in Keyssar, "Men Out of Work," p. 88.

33 Teachers appear as an obvious exception to these generalizations regarding low white-collar unemployment rates, but the figures for teachers are clearly anomalous: many teachers apparently declared themselves to be unemployed because they did not work during the summer months. That they did so certainly reveals some of the ambiguity latent in the concept of unemployment (as discussed in Appendix B), and it may also tell something about the economic history of teaching in the late nineteenth century.

34 BISU Hearings, p. 2 and W. B. Llewelling to W. M. Cole, July 15, 1894.

35 In 1885 (the only depression year for which sectoral data are available), the unemployment frequency for males was 41.4% in "manufacturing and mechanical industries," 39.0% in domestic and personal service (a grouping that included laborers), and 10.6% in trade and transportation. MBSL, *18 AR*, pp. 166–225, 280–7, 291; Keyssar, "Men Out of Work," p. 290. Sectoral breakdowns for more prosperous years followed similar lines (see Tables A.2 and A.4), and Table A.5 suggests that there was far more unemployment in manufacturing than in trade or transportation during the downturns of 1908, 1914, and 1921. According to unpublished

data from the 1910 census, the national unemployment frequency in manufacturing and mechanical industries was 23.1%, while in transportation it was 14.9%, and in trade, 8.0%. See Appendix B regarding the 1910 census data, which are available from (and were provided to me by) the Bureau of the Census, Washington.

36 Within any given year, there appears to have been relatively little variation in the mean duration of unemployment from one occupation to another. E.g., in 1885 the mean duration was between 3.7 and 4.7 months in virtually all major occupations. This consistency was in part an artifact of the statistics themselves: mean duration figures are less exact than unemployment frequencies (for reasons explained in Appendix B), and respondents to the census survey seem to have "rounded off" their answers to the nearest month. But the consistency of mean durations was also rooted in the needs of working people: unusually long spells of idleness would likely have led workers to change occupations or, perhaps, to leave the state altogether and thus disappear from the census. The variations that did occur display a few patterns worthy of note. Factory operatives in some industries (such as rubber or textiles) were idled for relatively short stints; outdoor workers (such as laborers, masons, and fishermen) had fairly lengthy stretches of joblessness; and many low-frequency occupations had relatively long mean durations. This last pattern (which might reflect either a low vacancy rate in steady jobs or the ability of workers in such trades to be selective in choosing jobs) underscores the fact that the amount of time that a person spent unemployed was not necessarily dependent upon the number of his colleagues who were also idled. (See Appendix A, Tables A.1–A.4 and A.9–A.12 for abundant evidence of this phenomenon.) Indeed, the amount of time that a person spent without a job seems to have depended largely upon the overall health of the economy and upon the seasonal rhythms of work in his or her trade. MBSL, *18 AR*, p. 264. For a long-run and national view, see August C. Bolino, "The Duration of Unemployment: Some Tentative Historical Comparisons," *Quarterly Review of Economics and Business* 6 (1966): 31–49.

37 The best available data regarding the linkage between skill levels and unemployment during a depression are in MBSL, *Bulletin 13*, pp. 16–24; *Bulletin 14*, pp. 54–67; and *Bulletin 17*, pp. 14–5. These bulletins present unemployment data, from the 1895 census, for workers in the textile, shoe, paper, and construction industries. The unusual virtue of these figures is that they are broken down into extremely detailed occupational categories. The data reveal that the *most* skilled workers in these industries were often kept on when operatives or laborers were laid off. At the same time, they make clear that very few people possessed this type of security and that there was no overall relationship between skill level and unemployment. Skill-level categories, of course, are always problematic (particularly when applied historically), and the categories utilized here are admittedly rough. One helpful guide to skill levels in the early twentieth century is William J. Harris, director, U.S. Bureau of the

Census, *Index to Occupations at the Thirteenth Census* (Washington, 1915), pp. 324–30, 332ff. See also MBSL, *Bulletin 46*, pp. 66, 71; Brody, *Steelworkers*, p. 90; Beveridge, *Unemployment*, pp. 20–1; and Bruce Laurie, Theodore Hershberg, and George Alter, "Immigrants and Industry," in Hershberg, ed., *Philadelphia: Work, Space, Family, and Group Experience in the Nineteenth Century* (New York, 1981), pp. 93–6.

38 Springfield *Union*, Feb. 15, 1915; AC-B, *36 AR*, p. 16; BISU Hearings, pp. 61, 491. The absence of a close relationship between skill levels and unemployment does not imply that employers were reluctant to distinguish among their employees based on competence. Indeed, there is every reason to believe that employers did try to keep their most able and productive workers when they were making layoff decisions. But these, of course, were distinctions within skill or job categories. See Smelser, *Unemployment*, p. 125.

39 BISU Hearings, p. 372; Green, *Holyoke*, p. 180; see Table A.3.

40 These changes in the distribution of unemployment during depressions displayed no discernible secular trends.

41 This estimate is based upon the assumption (grounded in the statistics) that there was considerable turnover in the unemployed population. If the annual unemployment frequency was in the vicinity of 35% for 2 years, and if half the persons unemployed in one year labored steadily in the other, then roughly 50% of all workers would have been unemployed at some point during the 2-year period. Here and elsewhere, an annual loss of 4 months' work is considered to be "prolonged" unemployment.

42 For workers, the consequences of depressions were, of course, shaped by short time as well as by outright unemployment. Although there are no reliable data indicating the number of persons who were obliged to work on short time during business downturns, in some industries the practice was extremely common. E.g., Norton claims that in Feb. 1914 61% of the employees in a sample of shoe factories were working less than full time. *Trade-Union Policies*, pp. 88–90.

43 *Final Report of the Commission on Industrial Relations*, Frank P. Walsh, Chairman (Washington, 1915) p. 169; BISU Hearings, pp. 94–5; Brody, *Steelworkers*, p. 39; Gibb, *Saco-Lowell Shops*, pp. 200, 237–8, 496; Samuel E. Morison, *The Ropemakers of Plymouth: A History of the Plymouth Cordage Company 1824–1949* (Boston, 1950), p. 72; Green, *Holyoke*, pp. 77, 179, 181–2; Wolfbein, *Cotton Textile City*, pp. 23–5; AC-B, *29 AR*, pp. 34–5; Blanche E. Hazard, *The Organization of the Boot and Shoe Industry in Massachusetts Before 1875* (Cambridge, Mass., 1921), p. 125; Navin, *Whitin Machine Works*, pp. 102–3; Norton, *Trade-Union Policies*, pp. 41–2.

44 For examples of references to previous depressions, see MBSL, *46 AR*, part IX, pp. 32–3; AC-W, *25 AR*, pp. 18–19; Boston Provident Association, *Annual Report for 1875–6* (Boston, 1876), p. 7; IAS, *80 AR*, pp. 6–7; Green, *Holyoke*, pp. 138–9; Navin, *Whitin Machine Works*, p. 308; and *Vindicator* (Lynn, Mass.), Dec. 30, 1876.

45 BISU Hearings, p. 1031.

46   The estimated unemployment frequencies in Table 3.3 are conservative
     because they are based upon an estimated mean duration of 3.5 months
     during nondepression years. (See the conversion formula in Appendix
     B.) This figure was selected based upon the 1890 and 1900 census data,
     but it may be slightly high for nondepression years in the twentieth cen-
     tury. National data from the 1910 census suggest that the mean duration
     was closer to three months. If so, then the frequency of unemployment
     for trade unionists was proportionally higher than the figures presented
     in Table 3.3. Regarding the location of the 1890 and 1900 census surveys
     in the business cycle, see Fels, *Business Cycles*, p. 159; and Frickey, *Pro-
     duction*, p. 60. As explained in Appendix B, the Census Bureau regarded
     the 1900 statistics as more reliable than those collected in 1890, but the
     problems that the bureau detected in the 1890 figures dealt primarily
     with agricultural populations and have little bearing upon Massachu-
     setts.

47   MBSL, *Bulletin 46*, p. 66. See, for supporting data, the figures collected
     from employers regarding the annual range in employment levels in
     manufacturing from the late 1880s to the early 1900s. *BISU Report*, part
     IV, p. 16; MBSL, *24 AR*, pp. 124–8; *36 AR*, p. 350; *37 AR*, pp. 292–4; *38
     AR*, p. 356. Similarly, a study of 2,570 Bay State households in 1901,
     conducted by the U.S. Commissioner of Labor, found that 24.1% of all
     household heads had been unemployed during the previous year. U.S.
     Commissioner of Labor, *Eighteenth Annual Report*, pp. 42–3, 262–3. Al-
     though contemporaries were unaware of the fact, the 1910 census survey
     also confirmed the rough accuracy of the trade union statistics. The an-
     nual unemployment frequency for all workers (male and female) in the
     mechanical and manufacturing industries of the nation in 1909 was
     22.1%; the estimate for 1909 in Table 3.3 is 22.3%. The national unem-
     ployment *rate* for these same workers on April 15, 1910, was 5.6%; the
     rate for trade unionists in Massachusetts on March 30, 1910 (adjusted for
     causes of idleness that would not conform to the census definition of
     unemployment), was 5.3%. See Appendix B. Cf. also Lebergott, *Man-
     power*, pp. 187–9, 512; Douglas, *Real Wages*, pp. 411, 440–6; and Hart,
     Fluctuations, p. 48.

48   The mean duration of unemployment was certainly lower in prosperous
     years than it was during depressions. The 1895 figure, which would
     seem to contradict this conclusion, is misleading as an indicator of the
     length of spells of joblessness during the depression of the 1890s. (See
     note 27 and Appendix B.) And the 1890 and 1900 figures are, of course,
     estimates. Cf. also BISU Hearings, p. 359. Unemployment levels during
     the relatively prosperous years that preceded the panic of 1873 seem,
     according to contemporary testimony and rough quantitative indicators,
     to have been much like those recorded in 1890, 1900, and during the
     Progressive era. MBSL, *2 AR*, pp. 118, 133, 147, 177, 242–3, 290, 303, 308,
     324, 348, 417, 552; *3 AR*, pp. 33, 56; *4 AR*, pp. 93, 290–1, 303ff., 403; and
     10 AR, pp. 147–56, 162.

49   As mentioned earlier in this chapter, the occupational distribution of un-

employment among women is discussed in Chapter 4. But – to anticipate
– many of the patterns described here appeared among female workers
as well. It is in light of those similarities (and the data presented in Chapter 4 and in Appendix A, Tables A.9–A.12) that many of the conclusions
offered in this chapter refer to all workers or to the entire working class.

50   In 1900, more than a third of the male labor force belonged to occupations in which the frequency of unemployment was greater than 20%;
one-fourth of all gainfully employed males had to contend with frequencies that exceeded 30%. In both 1890 and 1900, roughly one-quarter of
all males in "manufacturing and mechanical industries" were jobless.
The frequency was slightly higher in "domestic and personal service," a
category that included laborers, while it was less than 10% in trade and
transportation. Keyssar, "Men Out of Work," pp. 88–90; *Eleventh Census
of the United States, Population,* part II (Washington, 1897), pp. 448–53,
568–9; *Twelfth Census of the United States, Occupations* (Washington, 1904),
pp. 300–7.

51   During prosperous as well as depressed years, the mean duration of unemployment appears to have varied less, from one occupation to another, than did the frequency of unemployment. In 1900, most occupations had mean durations that were within 2 weeks of the mean for the
entire labor force; the 1890 figures for Massachusetts, as well as the national figures collected in 1910, are similar. Some of the reasons for this
consistency are indicated in note 36. That there were not more occupations with relatively low mean durations in 1890 and 1900 (a phenomenon that one might expect during prosperous years) may be the result of
the format in which the census data were published. As indicated in
Appendix B, compilers of the census grouped all spells of joblessness
that lasted from 1 to 3 months into one category. This broad grouping
(as well as the groupings of workers who were jobless for 4–6 months
and 7–12 months) could easily have obscured variations that did exist
from one trade to the next. The method used in this study to derive mean
durations from the census data also – if unavoidably – reinforced this
potentially inaccurate flattening out of differences. It should also be
noted that there is evidence to suggest that spells of joblessness lasting
less than 1 month were underreported. See Appendix B.

52   Keyssar, "Men Out of Work," pp. 88–90. Among the blue-collar workers
who had secure jobs during prosperous years were railroad employees,
printers, and machinists.

53   The conclusion that unemployment affected skilled, semiskilled, and unskilled employees even during prosperous years is based largely on the
data presented in Tables A.2, A.4, A.5, and A.6. The occupational categories in these tables are far from ideal for the purpose of assessing the
links between skill and joblessness, but unfortunately no data comparable to the detailed 1895 statistics exist for prosperous years. A study of
a sample of more than 400 Brockton shoe workers in 1900 did, however,
reveal patterns similar to those known to have occurred during depressions: highly skilled and quasi-managerial employees, such as foremen

and machinists, tended to work quite steadily, but other employees were laid off without regard to the degree of skill demanded by their jobs. Regarding the Brockton sample, see Chapter 4. For additional evidence, see MBSL, *3 AR*, p. 56; and MBSL, *Bulletin 46*, pp. 66–71.

54 Note also that unemployment levels for masons, tailors, plumbers, and rubber factory operatives were quite different in 1900 than they had been in 1890. See also MBSL, *44 AR*, p. 364; BISU Hearings, p. 72; and Thomas F. Gallagher to the Commission on Unemployment, Aug. 4, 1894, in the BISU Hearings files.

55 *BISU Report*, part IV, p. iii. The collision between the belief that under "normal" conditions everyone who wanted to work could find a job and the mounting evidence to the contrary produced some remarkable locutions. At the end of the Progressive era, for example, charity officials in Boston referred to statistics "which show indisputably not only that there was an abnormal amount of unemployment last winter but also that there is an abnormal amount of unemployment during certain periods of every year." AC-B, *36 AR*, p. 16. It should be noted that the USBLS does currently assemble data regarding the frequency or incidence of unemployment in the labor force. Such data are usually referred to as "work experience" statistics. See, e.g., USBLS, *Work Experience of the Population in 1970*, Special Labor Force Report 141 (Washington, 1972). That such statistics rarely appear in public discussions of unemployment in the United States in the late twentieth century is an intriguing fact, the explanation of which lies outside the scope of this study.

56 Solomon B. Griffin, *People and Politics Observed by a Massachusetts Editor* (Boston, 1923), pp. 117ff.; *SWJ* 6, no. 4 (April 1905): 3; *Labor Leader*, Jan. 15, 1887; IAS, *38 AR*, pp. 4–6; AC-B, *35 AR*, p. 21; Morison, *Ropemakers*, p. 75; BCC, "Questions on Seasonal Employment," forms from Boston Ice Company and Groton Leatherboard Company, and memo from J. A. and W. Bird and Co. to BCC, Sept. 30, 1914; "The Portuguese in Boston," *North End Mission Magazine* 2, no. 3 (July 1873); *BISU Report*, part IV, p. lx; MBSL, *2 AR*, p. 290; *11 AR*, p. 285.

57 Shlakman, *Economic History*, p. 202; Robert A. Woods and Albert J. Kennedy, *The Zone of Emergence* (Cambridge, Mass., 1962), p. 137.

58 *Labor Leader*, Jan. 8, 1887; BISU Hearings, pp. 10–11, 68–70, 85, 139, 141–2, 170–2, 178, 363–4, 561–2, 578–9, 672; newspaper clipping, dated March 8, 1911, in Springfield Scrapbooks, vol. 12, Springfield Public Library, Springfield, Mass.

59 The entire collection of documents in BCC, "Questions on Seasonal Employment," is valuable to an understanding of business rhythms and practices, but see, especially, the questionnaires from Lever Brothers, Otis Elevator, the Bunker Hill Brewery, the George Close Company, W. D. Quimbly and Company, and the George A. Daniels Company. See also, in the same collection, A. G. Van Nostrand to Nathan Heard, Oct. 6, 1914, and R. W. Scott to N. Heard, Oct. 8, 1914. In addition, see BISU Hearings, pp. 69, 125, 131, 144, 165, 173, 200, 317, 567, 1523ff., and a memo from F. W. Jacques to the Board, July 24, 1894; Norton, *Trade-*

Union Policies, pp. 34–6, 84–5, 109–11; MBSL, *2 AR*, p. 348; *3 AR*, p. 33; *4 AR*, p. 303; *10 AR*, pp. 53, 55, 149–54; *24 AR*, pp. 121–3, 227, 238; *46 AR*, part IX, p. 42, and part II, p. 43; MBSL, *Bulletin 7*, pp. 12–13; MBSL, *Quarterly Report 33*, pp. 7–8; *BISU Report*, part IV, pp. vii–xl; and J. Parker Bursk, *Seasonal Variations in Employment in Manufacturing Industries* (Philadelphia, 1931), pp. 5, 20–3ff., 176–81.

60 In few industries and occupations were there insurmountable environmental obstacles to continuous activity. By the 1920s, it was even acknowledged that climate was not the critical or decisive impediment to year-round work in most segments of the construction industry. Bursk, *Seasonal Variations*, p. 111; William Haber, *Industrial Relations in the Building Industry* (Cambridge, Mass., 1930), p. 111.

61 *BISU Report*, part IV, pp. viff., xiv, xl, lx; BISU Hearings, p. 913; Juliet S. Poyntz, "Report to the Committee on Industrial Relations of the Boston Chamber of Commerce on Seasonal Irregularity in Industry in Boston, Massachusetts," pp. 4–5, BCC papers, file 332–53. See also, in the same BCC collection, Stetson Shoe Company to Nathan Heard, Oct. 9, 1914, and Faunce and Spinney to N. Heard, Sept. 29, 1914; Douglas and Director, *Unemployment*, p. 90.

62 Chandler, *Visible Hand*, pp. 86, 211, 282; *BISU Report*, part IV, pp. xl, xlv, lx; Norton, *Trade-Union Policies*, pp. 25–7, 84–6, 94–5, 109, 175–6; BISU Hearings, pp. 70, 139, 141–3, 374, 913–4, 923; *Labor Leader*, Feb. 5, 1887; BCC, "Questions on Seasonal Employment," e.g., form from Alfred Kimball Shoe Company; Wolfbein, *Cotton Textile City*, p. 23; Lynn *News*, Oct. 3, 1899, clipping in Lynn Public Library scrapbook, vol. 33, no. 19.

63 BCC, "Questions on Seasonal Employment," form from A. J. Bates and Company; see also the reply from Warren Brothers Company. The Brockton quote is from the BISU Hearings, p. 392. See also BISU Hearings, pp. 625, 914; and Smelser, *Unemployment*, pp. 126–7.

64 BISU Hearings, pp. 710, 862, 1155; AC-B, *25 AR*, pp. 44–7; *28 AR*, p. 30; *29 AR*, pp. 32–3; *30 AR*, p. 37; *36 AR*, pp. 18–19; Robert A. Woods, *The City Wilderness* (Boston and New York, 1898), p. 92; Robert A. Christie, *Empire in Wood: A History of the Carpenters' Union* (Ithaca, N.Y., 1956), pp. 14–15.

65 The most systematic data available regarding seasonal rhythms of employment and unemployment are the trade union unemployment statistics, which were collected quarterly. A table presenting average unemployment rates, by occupation, on the last days of March, June, Sept., and Dec., for 1908–16, is presented in Keyssar, "Men Out of Work," pp. 270–2. Similar data, displaying similar patterns, were assembled for 1917–22. For additional evidence regarding the pervasive, yet highly variable, seasonal rhythms of employment, see MBSL, *2 AR*, pp. 118, 133, 147, 177, 242–3, 303, 308, 324, 417, 552; *3 AR*, pp. 33, 56; *4 AR*, pp. 93, 290–1, 303ff., 403; *5 AR*, p. 100; *10 AR*, pp. 147, 149–50, 153–5; *24 AR*, pp. 121–4, 227, 238; *36 AR*, pp. 337–9; *37 AR*, pp. 279–81; *38 AR*, pp. 356, 373, 437–9; *45 AR*, part VII, p. 96; *46 AR*, part II, p. 43; MBSL, *Quarterly Report 33*, pp. 7–8; *BISU Report*, part IV, pp. vii, xii, xxvi ff., xxxiii, xl,

xlvi; BISU Hearings, pp. 67, 69, 73, 125–6, 131, 144, 157, 166, 173, 363–4, 521–3, 590 (quotation in text is from p. 567); BCC, "Questions on Seasonal Employment," entire series, and in the same collection, the memo from Juliet S. Poyntz to J. W. Plaisted, July 30, 1914, as well as "Report of the Committee on Industrial Relations Regarding Seasonal Employment," May 1, 1914; and Norton, *Trade-Union Policies*, pp. 78–83.

Analyses of the 1895 census data for every community in the state indicate that winter increases in unemployment were most pronounced in small towns, particularly those with fewer than 2,000 inhabitants. The Massachusetts Bureau also suggested that seasonal idleness in the building trades was less extreme in the large cities of the Bay State than elsewhere. *Mass. Census, 1895*, VII (Boston, 1900), pp. 5–91; MBSL, *Bulletin 17*, p. 15.

66 BISU Hearings, p. 779.
67 The existence of alternating periods of overwork and idleness was acknowledged by both workers and employers. See BISU Hearings, pp. 56–8; MBSL, *10 AR*, pp. 121–2, 149, 162; and BCC, "Questions on Seasonal Employment," especially returns from Boston Woven Hose and Rubber Company, Bay State Tap and Die Company, Bartlett Company, the St. Louis Rubber Company, as well as the numerous responses from brewers, shoe manufacturers, and contractors. See also James D. Burn, *Three Years Among the Working Classes in the United States During the War* (London, 1865), p. 18.
68 MBSL, *4 AR*, pp. 303ff.; BISU Hearings, pp. 16–18, 50–1, 56–8, 63, 68, 98, 100, 163, 175, 365, 575, 592–3, 596, 728, 965; *Labor Leader*, June 16, 1888; Alan Dawley, *Class and Community: The Industrial Revolution in Lynn* (Cambridge, Mass., 1976), p. 115; Navin, *Whitin Machine Works*, p. 164.
69 Smelser, *Unemployment*, p. 32; Lebergott, *Manpower*, pp. 242–50, 309.
70 MBSL, *10 AR*, p. 122. Data similar to those presented in Table 3.4 were compiled for the period 1917–22; they reveal variations even more extreme. If the worst depression years were excluded from such tables, the variations would still be considerable. For additional evidence of this unpredictability, see Keyssar, "Men Out of Work," p. 278; BISU Hearings, p. 69; *Labor Leader*, July 22, 1893; and Don D. Lescohier, *The Labor Market* (New York, 1919), p. 307.
71 For additional evidence that seasonal workers did try to work year-round, see BISU Hearings, pp. 7–8, 17, 521–3.
72 BISU Hearings, pp. 10–11.
73 Regarding the cadence of technological unemployment, see BISU Hearings, pp. 23–4, 58, 68–70, 72, 81, 83, 85, 86, 107, 139, 141, 156–7, 170–1, 174, 178–80, 185, 207, 211, 216, 309, 313, 363–4, 374, 561–2, 568, 578–9, 773, 829, 913, 917, 922, 1015, 1152; Lynn *News*, Oct. 3, 1899, in Lynn Public Library, Scrapbooks, vol. 33, no. 19; Lynn *Item*, March 13 and 21, 1901, Lynn Public Library, Scrapbooks, vol. 48; *Labor Leader*, Dec. 3, 1887; *SWJ*, Jan. 1906, pp. 12ff.; Christie, *Empire*, pp. 25–8, 79–81; Jacob Loft, *The Printing Trades* (New York, 1944), pp. 43–6; Haber, *Industrial Relations*, pp. 36–7; and Burn, *Three Years*, p. 186.

74   *Final Report of the Commission on Industrial Relations*, pp. 167–8. A similar acknowledgment can be found in MBSL, *46 AR*, part IX, p. 33. Regarding the diversity of unemployment experiences, see Chapter 6.

75   The available statistics are admittedly far from ideal for the purpose of detecting secular trends. As discussed in Appendix B, methods of counting the unemployed changed often during this period, and the differences between the census data and the trade union figures are sufficiently great that comparing the two sets of statistics would not reliably reveal anything other than a very marked shift in the incidence of joblessness.

76   The suggestion that during prosperous years unemployment levels may have been slightly lower in the early twentieth century than they were late in the nineteenth century is based upon a comparison of the trade union statistics with the 1890 and 1900 census data. The aggregate figures are similar, but (as explained in Appendix B) members of the trade union sample were probably subject to more unemployment than was the labor force as a whole. National data from the 1910 census point in the same direction. They also suggest that the duration of unemployment may have declined early in the twentieth century. It is, of course, true that there were proportionally fewer depressed years between 1900 and 1922 than there were between 1870 and 1900, but the depression of the 1930s made clear that this was not a secular trend. On balance, thus, the picture seems to be one of consistency rather than change. Similar conclusions have been reached by other scholars, dealing with national data. See Douglas and Director, *Unemployment*, p. 33; Lebergott, *Manpower*, pp. 188–90; and Bolino, "The Duration of Unemployment," pp. 31, 46.

77   In addition to the problems alluded to in note 75, changes in the occupational labels and categories used by the collectors of unemployment statistics hinder the detection of long-run trends within individual occupations. The data presented in Table 3.5 are derived from Tables A.1 to A.5. The occupational labels and groupings utilized are distillations of the various labels and groupings that appear in the original data; in numerous cases, figures for two or more occupations listed in the appendix tables (and original data) had to be combined for presentation in Table 3.5, in order to maintain (as far as possible) the consistency of the occupational groupings. Unemployment rates (rather than frequencies) were developed here to maximize the comparability of the different statistics: the census figures can be converted into "rates" with some precision, whereas unemployment frequencies can be generated from the trade union rates only by estimating the mean duration. The apparent increase in unemployment levels among textile workers (in Table 3.5) may be the result of changes in the size and composition of the reporting sample for unionists in the industry. See Appendix B.

78   These shifts in the distribution of idle time can be discerned by comparing the 1890 and 1900 census figures (Tables A.2 and A.4) and by comparing the 1895 data presented in Table A.3 with 1885 figures for the

same occupations and communities. The relevant 1885 statistics are presented in Keyssar, "Men Out of Work," p. 452; they are derived from MBSL, *18 AR*, pp. 166–215. Obviously, such evidence is fragmentary. The absence of durational data from the trade union series makes it impossible to determine whether the perceived changes constituted the beginning of a trend (foreshadowing later developments in American labor markets) or mere blips in the numbers.

79 MBSL, *Bulletin 77*, p. 136; *Bulletin 80*, pp. 12–13; *Bulletin 89*, p. 51; *Bulletin 90*, p. 51; MBSL, *Quarterly Report 17*, p. 3; *Quarterly Report 25*, p. 3; MBSL, *46 AR*, part II, p. 43, and part IX, p. 43; *47 AR*, part VI, p. 38; *49 AR*, part IV, p. 35; Norton, *Trade-Union Policies*, p. 111.

80 Strategies and policies developed by management and labor are discussed in Chapters 7 and 9.

81 High-unemployment occupations were not stagnant during these years, but they grew less rapidly than did other types of jobs with more stable employment patterns. Clerks and salesmen constituted a higher proportion of the labor force in 1910 than they had in 1890 or 1900; the reverse was true for shoe workers, carpenters, masons, and painters. *Eleventh U.S. Census, Population*, part II, p. 568; *Thirteenth Census of the United States, Population*, IV (Washington, 1914), pp. 470–4. See also IAS, *80 AR*, pp. 6–7.

82 The quotation is from MBSL, *Bulletin 87*, p. 28. Other uses of the "reserve army" phrase (or variants thereof) can be found in MBSL, *10 AR*, p. 10; *Labor Leader*, Feb. 5, 1887, Oct. 7, 1893, and Dec. 16, 1893. Marx's discussion of the industrial reserve army is in *Capital*, vol. I, chap. 25. The concept of a reserve was also used by Beveridge in his pathbreaking work: he went on to note that "from the beginning to the end of fifty years of unprecedented expansion, unemployment has been recorded continuously." Beveridge, *Unemployment*, p. 15. In the United States, early in the twentieth century, the idea of a reserve was used by Lescohier (*Labor Market*, pp. 13, 17) and Hart (*Fluctuations*, p. 53). The acceptance of the idea in the United States is discussed in detail in William M. Leiserson, "The Problem of Unemployment Today," *Political Science Quarterly* 31 (March 1916): 1–16.

83 MBSL, *48 AR*, part IV, pp. 31–5; MBSL, *Quarterly Report 31*, p. 10; *Quarterly Report 32*, p. 14; *Quarterly Report 33*, pp. 8, 11–12; *Quarterly Report 34*, pp. 6–7, 11; *Quarterly Report 35*, pp. 5–8; *Quarterly Report 36*, pp. 1, 11–12. See Table A.5.

84 See Tables 3.3 and A.5. The claim that trade union unemployment levels during the war were half those that had prevailed during the most prosperous peacetime years is based upon the "lack of work" rather than "all causes" figures collected by the Massachusetts Bureau. The "all causes" figures are particularly inflated for the war years because they included joblessness that resulted from strikes. (See Appendix B.) The wartime statistics also make it possible to estimate the quantity of unemployment that can be attributed to "unemployable" workers. The lowest annual unemployment rate recorded was 2.5%, and if 1.0% can be attributed to

unavoidable friction in the labor markets, then an idleness rate of 1.5% (and a frequency of perhaps 5%) can be attributed to workers who were unemployable rather than to the performance of the economy. For contemporary comments regarding labor market conditions during the war, see: IAS, *81 AR*, p. 6; AC-B, *37 AR*, pp. 13, 29.

85   The idea of a "reserve" or "reserve army" is, in effect, an abstraction that describes the workings of the very concrete "reserves" that existed in the commonwealth and elsewhere.

86   MBSL, *2 AR*, p. 324; *4 AR*, pp. 290–1; BISU Hearings, pp. 2, 15, 16, 18, 50–1, 56, 63, 126, 175, 308, 501, 728, 796–7, 1516, and memo from W. B. Llewelling to W. M. Cole, July 15, 1894; *Labor Leader*, Oct. 25, 1887; June 16, 1888; BCC, "Questions on Seasonal Employment," especially forms from New Hat Frame Company and Martin Manufacturing Company; Lescohier, *Labor Market*; Hearings Before the Special Commission on Unemployment, Unemployment Compensation and the Minimum Wage, Oct. 6, 1922, p. 39, Mass. State Library, Boston, pp. 16–21, 52–3. The durability of a labor reserve was the subject of testimony by a Fall River textile worker in the 1890s: "From 1873 up to the present time," he told a commission, "my experience is, in the city of Fall River, that we always have this surplus class. I don't really know myself that we have more today than we had years ago." BISU Hearings, p. 310.

87   MBSL, *44 AR*, p. 349.

88   Ibid., p. 349; *BISU Report*, part IV, entire.

89   To be sure, the need for a labor reserve was not, in all respects, identical with the need for an unemployed population. As indicated in Chapter 2, there existed in Massachusetts in the early nineteenth century (and later in other parts of the United States), an underemployed agricultural population that constituted a latent reserve of labor. By the late nineteenth century, however, the agricultural population in the Bay State was far too small to provide an adequate reserve for its industries. Whether a latent agricultural reserve, even if large enough, could have answered the needs of industry after 1860 is an issue that this study cannot answer.

90   "The American employer has been able to assume, as a matter of course, that there would be idle men at his gate this morning, tomorrow morning, every morning. He has accepted orders upon the security of that expectation. If the reserve at his place of business or in the immediate locality disappeared, he complained of a labor shortage. In his mind, consciously or unconsciously, was an idea that he was entitled to have available at all times enough labor to man his plant to maximum capacity, even though he did not run at maximum capacity thirty days in the year." Lescohier, *Labor Market*, pp. 13–16. This indictment was echoed by a manufacturer in a memo from the R. P. Hazard Company to the BCC, Sept. 30, 1914, BCC, "Questions on Seasonal Employment." See also *Labor Leader*, Oct. 8, 1887. Many manufacturers, of course, would have preferred to run their businesses steadily. As Alfred Chandler has pointed out, large firms, such as Du Pont, tried not to monopolize the market for their goods but rather to control the more stable and predictable portions

of the market. Controlling 60% rather than 100% of the market permitted them to run steadily. Doing so, obviously, obliged other manufacturers to cope with the irregularity of demand. Chandler, *Visible Hand*, p. 442. Marx's claim (*Capital*, I, chap. 25) that capitalism itself requires a reserve army has – not surprisingly – generated considerable controversy. More surprisingly, it has given rise to little empirical research.

91 BISU Hearings, p. 214. See also the *Final Report of the Commission on Industrial Relations*, pp. 167–8. It should be stressed that this chapter offers a portrait of unemployment in Massachusetts prior to the flight of manufacturing industries from the state, a process that began in the 1920s and continued until after World War II.

92 See Tables A.1 to A.6. A study conducted in 1875 found that wage earners in Massachusetts averaged 250 days of work during the year, while salaried employees averaged 290 days. MBSL, *7 AR*, pp. 210–11. See also Brown and Adams to Nathan Heard, Sept. 29, 1914, BCC, "Questions on Seasonal Employment."

93 *Labor Leader*, May 12, 1888.

94 *Labor Leader*, Nov. 4, 1893.

4.   Sharing the burden

1 IAS, *38 AR*, p. 16. BISU Hearings, p. 1014.

2 MBSL, *43 AR*, pp. 6–7, 86–7; *45 AR*, part III, pp. 5, 8, 264; *Mass. Census, 1915* (Boston, 1918), pp. 290, 295; *Report of the Commission on Immigration on the Problem of Immigration in Massachusetts, House Document 2300* (Boston, 1914), pp. 29–34; MBSL, *Bulletin 38*, p. 328; *Bulletin 81*, pp. 1, 5, 17; *Fourteenth Census of the United States, Population*, vol. IV (Washington, 1923), p. 941.

3 BISU Hearings, pp. 5, 15, 16, 100, 163, 175, 575, 965; Stanley Lebergott, *Manpower in Economic Growth* (New York, 1964), p. 45; AC-B, *16 AR*, p. 11; *29 AR*, p. 39; IAS, *39 AR*, p. 16; MBSL, *Bulletin 57*, pp. 53–62; *Bulletin 75*, p. 8; MBSL, *43 AR*, pp. 14–16; *45 AR*, part III, p. 12; and *46 AR*, part V, pp. 5, 12. For a richly detailed contemporary assembly of information regarding immigration, see Isaac A. Hourwich, *Immigration and Labor* (New York, 1912); for a valuable theoretical treatment, see Michael J. Piore, *Birds of Passage: Migrant Labor and Industrial Societies* (Cambridge, 1979).

4 *Problem of Immigration in Massachusetts*, pp. 37–45; Grace Abbott, *The Immigrant and the Community* (New York, 1917), pp. 26–54; Charlotte Erickson, *American Industry and the Immigrant 1860–1885* (Cambridge, Mass., 1957), p. 67. Data regarding the occupational backgrounds and skills of immigrants were periodically collected and published by the MBSL. See, e.g., *Bulletin 38*, p. 328; and *43 AR*, p. 10.

5 MBSL, *18 AR*, pp. 254–60; and *Mass. Census, 1885*, I, part 2 (Boston, 1888), pp. 612–21. In 1890, the national unemployment frequency was 17.8% for foreign-born whites and 14.7% for native-born whites; in 1900, the figures were 21.0% and 21.2%, respectively. No figures regarding the

duration of unemployment for immigrants and natives in Massachusetts are available, but the national statistics suggest that natives tended to be slightly less vulnerable to very prolonged (more than 6 months) spells of idleness. *Eleventh Census of the United States, Population*, part II (Washington, 1897), pp. 744–9; *Twelfth Census of the United States, Occupations* (Washington, 1904), pp. ccxxvi, ccxxxiv.

6 Quotation from the U.S. Immigration Commission cited in MBSL, *43 AR*, p. 69. See also U.S. Commissioner of Labor, *Eighteenth Annual Report* (Washington, 1904), p. 43. National statistics indicate that the relatively thin margin between native and immigrant unemployment levels cannot be attributed to high unemployment frequencies experienced by the children of immigrants. Both in 1890 and in 1900, native white males with native-born parents were idled virtually as often (and for as long) as natives with foreign-born parents. *Eleventh U.S. Census, Population*, part II, pp. 744–9; *Twelfth U.S. Census, Occupations*, pp. ccxxvi, ccxxxiv.

7 That most low-risk occupations in 1900 were, in fact, white-collar or managerial can be seen by comparing parts A and B of Table 4.2. In the labor force as a whole, there were 270,000 men who were attached to occupations with unemployment frequencies below 10%; among blue-collar workers alone, there were only 55,000. The figures presented in Table 4.2, part B, were derived by subtracting the number of men who worked in unmistakably professional, managerial, and white-collar occupations from the labor force totals assembled in Table 4.2, part A. Supporting evidence that immigrants were underrepresented in these occupations was provided by "concentration index" figures (such as those in Table 4.1) that were developed for all occupations in 1890 and 1900. In both of these years, immigrants were underrepresented in almost all professions (the figure for lawyers, in 1900, was .1) and in commerce. At the same time, they were overrepresented in manufacturing and in "domestic and personal service," a census category that included day laborers. The children of immigrants, not surprisingly, were more likely to be found in white-collar positions than were their parents. *Eleventh U.S. Census, Population*, part II, pp. 348–53, 568–9; *Twelfth U.S. Census, Occupations*, pp. 300–7. See also Alexander Keyssar, "Men Out of Work" (Ph.D. diss., Harvard University, 1977), pp. 166–71.

8 The occupations listed in Table 4.1 are the only occupations for which such statistics could be derived; no comparative data regarding the mean duration of unemployment are available. The figures presented in Table 4.1 are less exact than are other unemployment frequency statistics because the occupational categories used in the 1885 census report (which indicated the number of immigrants employed in each occupation) were not, in all cases, identical to those used in the report on unemployment for the same year.

9 In 12 of the 16 occupations in which the difference between the 2 unemployment frequencies exceeded 5%, immigrants had the higher frequency. In several cases, these differences probably reflected the looseness of the occupational labels utilized in the census reports. E.g.,

among "steam railroad employees," it is likely that natives and immigrants did not hold identical jobs. Many immigrants were likely to have been laborers, while most of the station agents, engineers, and firemen were, in all probability, native-born.

10   The statistics for men in Brockton, utilized here and elsewhere, are based upon the manuscript census schedules of the twelfth census of the United States (1900). The sample was selected through formal random procedures and was not skewed toward any particular neighborhood or area of Brockton. The sample consisted of 406 men who worked in the shoe industry, which dominated the city's economy. The sample contained 60 lasters, 58 cutters, 24 edgemakers, 20 stitchers, 34 finishers, 20 treers, 156 other blue-collar operatives, 12 foremen and overseers, and 22 white-collar and managerial personnel. For some purposes, as in Table 4.3, separate figures have been developed for blue-collar workers alone – by excluding all foremen, as well as white-collar and managerial personnel. Since not all pieces of information were available for all members of the sample, the total (n) may vary slightly among the different tables. The difference between immigrant and native unemployment frequencies was not statistically significant even at a level of .10. Here and below, statistical significance was determined through use of a difference of proportions test. Unless otherwise noted, differences are reported as significant only if they were so at a level of .05. For supplementary evidence regarding the native-immigrant differential, see MBSL, *43 AR*, p. 69; and U.S. Commissioner of Labor, *Eighteenth Annual Report*, p. 43.

11   The sample of Boston's laborers was also a random one, drawn originally from the census manuscripts by Jeffrey Adler, then a student at Brandeis University, for his own study of the laborers of Boston. He generously provided me with the raw data file, which was reprocessed for use in this study. The sample consists of 250 men who lived in Boston and worked as "laborers." Unemployment information was available for 223 members of the sample. Comparing the characteristics of sample members with published data for all of Boston's laborers in 1900 (19,545 men) suggests that the sample is a representative one. The unemployment frequency for sample members was 39.5%; for all laborers, it was 40.6%. Of all sample members, 78.5% were immigrants, while 76.2% of all laborers in the city were immigrants. *Twelfth U.S. Census, Occupations*, p. 494. The difference between native and immigrant unemployment frequencies in this sample, presented in Table 4.3, was significant only at a .10 level. The statement that newly arrived immigrant laborers tended to encounter the most severe unemployment is based upon an analysis of the experiences of 121 foreign-born laborers, in the Boston sample, who were between the ages of 21 and 50. (The age spectrum was restricted in order to limit the effects of age, as a variable, upon comparisons of the experiences of men who had been in the United States for different lengths of time.) Laborers who had been in the United States for 1–3 years ($n = 12$) had an unemployment frequency of 58.3%; the figure dropped to 41.4% ($n = 29$) for those who had been in the country 4–10

years and to 27.5% (n = 80) for those who had resided in the U.S. for at least 11 years. No comparable pattern emerged from the data for Brockton's shoe factory operatives.

12   National statistics for 1890 and 1900 display the same pattern. *Eleventh U.S. Census, Population*, part II, pp. 457–65, 354–9; *Twelfth U.S. Census, Occupations*, pp. cxiv–cxv, ccxxvi, 78–83. See also Keyssar, "Men Out of Work," pp. 161–5.

13   The absence of a close relationship between unemployment levels and the proportion of immigrants in an occupation was also apparent in the concentration indices developed for 1890 and 1900. (See note 7.) In addition, rank-order correlation coefficients (Pearson's r) were calculated for 1885 and 1900; they too indicated that there was no significant link between the unemployment frequency in an occupation and the percentage of occupation members who were either foreign-born or the children of immigrants.

14   Table 4.2, part B, does, of course, indicate both that native-born workers with native-born parents had the best access to the most stable working-class jobs and that the children of immigrants did better than their parents. But the margins were slight, and the similarities more pronounced – and more socially significant – than the differences.

15   The figures presented in Table A.7 are subject to the methodological problems mentioned in notes 8 and 9 above. Those problems may account for some of the extreme figures that appear in the table, e.g., unemployment frequencies of 100%. Close inspection of the table suggests nonetheless that, with certain exceptions, unemployment levels were fairly consistent within individual occupations.

16   *Mass. Census, 1885*, I, part 2, pp. 532–664.

17   The 1900 figures presented in Table 4.5 are based upon census data that assign a worker to a particular nativity group if both of his parents were born in that nation; a man whose parents were born in different countries was assigned to a separate "mixed" group. No data based upon the birthplaces of workers themselves are available for 1900. The figures in the table, for 1900, represent the proportion of gainfully employed members of each ethnic or immigrant group who belonged to the 21 major occupations with the highest unemployment frequencies. The figures for 1915 (which are based upon a worker's actual country of birth) encompass 19 of the same occupations. Changes in both the nativity and occupational categories utilized in the census surveys prohibit the development of more precisely comparable statistics. Regarding ethnic clustering in occupations and ethnic job-search networks, see *Problem of Immigration in Massachusetts*, pp. 37, 74; Erickson, *American Industry*, pp. 88–105, 190–2.

18   This conclusion is, of necessity, conjectural, although it is based upon an extensive analysis of the occupational location of natives and immigrants from 1900 to 1920. Such an analysis was prompted by the absence of direct unemployment data and by the importance of occupational location in determining the unemployment experiences of different groups

in the late nineteenth century. Comparisons were made of the percentage of immigrants, natives with foreign-born parents, and natives with native-born parents who worked in each sector of the economy in 1900, 1910, and 1920. In addition, concentration indices (as in Table 4.1) were developed, for all 3 years, for the 20 occupations that (in 1900) had the highest unemployment frequencies and the 20 with the lowest unemployment frequencies. The results of this large-scale consumption of paper can be briefly summarized. The proportion of native white males of native parentage in the labor force as a whole declined slightly (from 35.7% to 29.5%) while the proportion of immigrants remained constant and the proportion of natives with foreign parents rose slightly. The figures for manufacturing followed suit. And the concentration index figures – allowing for numerous, frustrating changes in occupational labels – changed hardly at all (and not at all systematically) in both the steadiest and least steady occupations in the state. Immigrants were not increasingly confined to high-unemployment occupations; nor were those occupations becoming more exclusively the domain of immigrants. Unless there was a significant shift in the extent of discrimination within occupations, thus, the relationship between native and immigrant unemployment levels did not change appreciably between 1900 and 1920. *Twelfth U.S. Census, Occupations*, pp. 300–7; *Thirteenth Census of the United States, Population*, IV (Washington, 1914), pp. 470–4; *Fourteenth U.S. Census*, IV, pp. 941–6.

19 See also *Problem of Immigration in Massachusetts*, pp. 38–9, 49–50.
20 *Eleventh U.S. Census, Population*, part II, pp. 568–9; *Fourteenth U.S. Census*, IV, pp. 941–6.
21 AC–B, *15 AR*, pp. 31–2; *19 AR*, p. 38; *20 AR*, pp. 69–70; *South End House Reports* (Boston, 1905), p. 33; Robert A. Woods, *The City Wilderness* (Boston and New York, 1898), p. 45; *Eleventh U.S. Census, Population*, part II, pp. 568–9; *Twelfth U.S. Census, Occupations*, pp. 300–7; *Thirteenth U.S. Census*, IV, 470–4; *Fourteenth U.S. Census*, IV, 941–6. National unemployment frequencies for blacks were tabulated in both 1890 and 1900 (pp. 744–9 of the 1890 volume cited above and pp. cxiv–cxvi, 86–7 in the 1900 volume), and they indicate that blacks who did work in manufacturing encountered unemployment levels that were well above average.
22 MBSL, *24 AR*, pp. 84ff.; *43 AR*, pp. 72ff.; MBSL, *Bulletin 21*, p. 24; *Bulletin 46*, pp. 70–1; *Bulletin 48*, p. 231; *Problem of Immigration in Massachusetts*, p. 88; Springfield *Union*, Feb. 5, 1915.
23 Some skilled trades with relatively high wage levels were, in fact, less steady than many of the low-wage, semiskilled factory jobs that were commonly filled by immigrants. As Michael Piore has noted (*Birds of Passage*, pp. 3, 35–40), steady demand for a product often encouraged the routinization of production and the de-skilling of work, while firms faced with erratic demand or a demand for diverse products often needed a relatively skilled labor force.
24 Albert Rees, *Real Wages in Manufacturing 1890–1914* (Princeton, N.J., 1961), p. 126; Hourwich, *Immigration*, pp. 4–7; 23, 34, 49, 125–39, 176,

511–13; *Twelfth U.S. Census, Occupations,* pp. ccxxv–ccxxvi; *BISU Report,* part IV, pp. vff.; and part V, pp. xlvii, 101–3; BISU Hearings, pp. 215, 492, 964; *Problem of Immigration in Massachusetts,* p. 80; MBSL, *Bulletin 33,* p. 256; regarding unemployment levels in manufacturing in other states, see Appendix A, Table A.13.

25 See Chapter 3, as well as Don D. Lescohier, *The Labor Market* (New York, 1919), pp. 14–15; *Problem of Immigration in Massachusetts,* pp. 76–80; and David Montgomery, *Workers' Control in America* (Cambridge, 1979), p. 38.

26 Here and below, statements regarding the age composition of the male labor force and individual occupations are (except where otherwise noted) based upon the following sources: *Statistics of the Population of the United States at the Ninth Census,* I, (Washington, 1872), p. 739; *Statistics of the Population of the United States at the Tenth Census,* (Washington, 1883), p. 828; *Eleventh U.S. Census, Population,* part II, pp. 568–9; *Twelfth U.S. Census, Occupations,* pp. 300–7; *Thirteenth U.S. Census,* IV, pp. 470–4; and *Fourteenth U.S. Census,* IV, pp. 941–6. The age categories utilized in these census reports were too broad and too changeable to permit a precise grasp of shifts in the age structure of the labor force, but there does seem to have been a slight increase in the average age of male workers. See also John D. Durand, *The Labor Force in the United States, 1890–1960* (New York, 1948), pp. 28–41.

27 USBLS, *Employment and Unemployment in 1974, Special Labor Force Report no. 178* (Washington, 1975), p. A-4.

28 The incidence of unemployment in different cities and towns is examined in detail in Chapter 5. No data regarding age-specific unemployment levels by occupation are available.

29 No statewide data, other than those collected in 1885, are available, but national statistics for 1890 display the same general patterns. In the nation's labor force as a whole, the incidence of unemployment declined slightly as men aged, but this did not occur among workers in manufacturing or in "domestic and personal service." The duration of spells of unemployment was also relatively consistent for men of different ages although the youngest and oldest workers in the nation were idled for longer periods than were men in midlife. *Eleventh U.S. Census, Population,* part II, pp. 744ff. Unemployment frequencies and mean durations based on these data are presented in Keyssar, "Men Out of Work," pp. 135–40.

30 As noted in Chapter 3, for at least some workers, figures regarding the duration of unemployment represent the total amount of working time that they lost during the year from two or more stints of joblessness. There is, unfortunately, no way to determine how many unemployed workers were laid off more than once in the course of the year. (See note 27, Chapter 3.) The unusually low unemployment frequency reported for boys aged 10 to 13 is an obviously suspect figure. The number of boys whose experiences were recorded by the census was very small, and the attachment of 12-year-olds to the labor force was certainly weak at best.

31 The unemployment frequencies for workers under age 21, presented in

Tables 4.7 and 4.8, were not significantly higher, statistically, than the frequencies for men who were in their 20s and 30s. But the presence of this pattern in both samples, coupled with its appearance in the 1885 survey of the entire population, strongly suggests that younger workers were indeed idled more often than their older colleagues. The statement that young workers were not, on the whole, disproportionately concentrated in high-risk occupations is based upon an examination of the census data referred to above in note 26. A table outlining the age structure of every major occupation in Massachusetts in 1900 is presented in Keyssar, "Men Out of Work," pp. 453–5. For an example of the grumbling referred to in the text, see BISU Hearings, p. 665.

32 RAB to Mr. Holmes, March 25, 1921, Plymouth Cordage Company Papers, Baker Library, Harvard Business School. See also William H. Pear of the Boston Provident Association to J. Randolph Coolidge, Feb. 6, 1914, in BCC papers, file 332–53, and the form from Carter's Ink Company in BCC, "Questions on Seasonal Employment" (see Chapter 3, note 21), Baker Library, Harvard Business School; Thomas R. Navin, *The Whitin Machine Works Since 1831* (Cambridge, Mass., 1950), p. 104; and AC-W, *19 AR*, p. 1.

33 In 1885, an unemployed man who was in his twenties had an 80% chance of being jobless for less than 5 months; for a man who was in his fifties, the odds were less than 60%. MBSL, *18 AR*, pp. 152–7. National statistics for 1890 also indicate that spells of unemployment became longer as men aged. *Eleventh U.S. Census, Population*, part II, pp. 744ff. The very marked (and statistically significant) increase in unemployment frequencies for older laborers in Boston was also, in all likelihood, a reflection of the difficulties that faced older workers who were job hunting. Since most laborers frequently changed employers, the key to working steadily was rapidly getting a new job.

34 BISU Hearings, p. 673.

35 *Eleventh U.S. Census, Population*, part II, pp. 744 ff.; Keyssar, "Men Out of Work," pp. 137–9. Cf. also the unemployment frequency figures for all shoe industry personnel with the figures for blue-collar workers in Table 4.7.

36 *American Federationist* 18, no. 4 (April 1911): 290. See also BISU Hearings, pp. 766–7, 1403; David Brody, *Steelworkers in America: The Nonunion Era* (New York, 1969; orig. pub. Cambridge, Mass., 1960), pp. 25, 90; Durand, *The Labor Force*, p. 112; MBSL, *Bulletin 45*, p. 43; Jacob Loft, *The Printing Trades* (New York, 1944), p. 48.

37 Based upon an examination of the age structure of the labor force and age-specific unemployment levels in 32 Massachusetts communities that had populations of less than 2,500 in 1885. (The sources of the data are indicated in Table A.8.) In most of these communities teenage unemployment levels were unusually high, and there were comparatively few male labor force members who were in their 20s.

38 See Stephan Thernstrom, *Poverty and Progress: Social Mobility in a Nineteenth-Century City* (Cambridge, Mass., 1964), and *The Other Bostonians:*

Poverty and Progress in the American Metropolis, 1880–1970 (Cambridge, Mass., 1973).

39 There is no evidence to suggest that the age distribution of unemployment was notably different for immigrants than it was for natives. This issue, however, could be tested directly only in the samples drawn from the census manuscripts. Among Brockton's blue-collar shoe workers, unemployment frequencies for natives in different age groups ranged from 69.9% to 78.0%; for immigrants, the range was from 61.3% to 71.8%. Mean durations in both groups followed the aggregate pattern. The figures for Boston's laborers were less consistent, but the cell sizes (particularly for natives) were too small to yield reliable results. It should also be noted that the differences between native and immigrant unemployment frequencies cannot be attributed to differences in the age composition of the two populations – since there were, in fact, proportionately more teenagers among native-born workers than among the foreign-born. Regarding the presence of mature men among the unemployed, see also MBSL, *24 AR*, pp. 153–4; MBSL, *Bulletin 46*, pp. 74, 82.

40 There were, of course, some de facto seniority arrangements in individual plants, but had they been widespread they would presumably have had a discernible impact on age-specific unemployment levels. For an example of one such arrangement, see Navin, *Whitin Machine Works*, p. 104.

41 Between 1900 and 1922, things did begin to change – as unions began to press for seniority agreements and as employers began to fret about turnover – but the changes that occurred affected only a small portion of the labor force. These changes are discussed, at some length, in Chapters 7 and 9.

42 MBSL, *2 AR*, p. 206; *13 AR*, pp. 202–3; BCC, "Questions on Seasonal Employment," form from Carter's Ink Company.

43 The proportion of the labor force that was female rose from 22.1% in 1870 to 29.1% in 1920. Here and in the following pages, except where otherwise noted, references to the number of women in the labor force and in specific occupations (as well as breakdowns by age and by place of birth) are derived from *Ninth U.S. Census*, I, p. 739; *Tenth U.S. Census, Population*, p. 828; *Eleventh U.S. Census, Population*, part II, pp. 568–9; *Twelfth U.S. Census, Occupations*, pp. 300–7; *Thirteenth U.S. Census*, IV, pp. 470–4; *Fourteenth U.S. Census*, IV, pp. 941–6.

44 There was an increase, during this period, in both the number and the proportion of working women who were married. The median age of female labor force members rose as well. But the female labor force remained youthful and dominated by women who were not married. In 1900, 44% of all gainfully employed women were under the age of 25, and only 11.7% were married (78.5% were single and 9.8% were widowed or divorced). In addition to the census sources listed in the previous note, see *Mass. Census, 1915*, pp. 490, 504; MBSL, *20 AR*, p. 570; Valerie K. Oppenheimer, *The Female Labor Force in the United States* (Berkeley, Calif., 1970), pp. 2, 3, 8, 20, 42, 163; Durand, *Labor Force*, pp. 22–4;

Clarence D. Long, *The Labor Force under Changing Income and Employment* (Princeton, N.J., 1958), p. 299; Martha N. Fraundorf, "The Labor Force Participation of Turn-of-the-Century Married Women," *Journal of Economic History* 35 (June 1979): 401–17.

45 This sex-typing is evident in all the census tables referred to in note 43. Table A.12 indicates, for 1900, the percentage of occupation members who were female. It should be noted, moreover, that the broad occupational labels utilized in the census reports obscure (and understate) the degree to which jobs were sex-typed. As the unusually detailed occupational listings presented in Table A.11 reveal, jobs in the textile, shoe, and paper industries were far more sex segregated than figures for broader occupational categories (e.g., shoe workers) suggest. See also Oppenheimer, *Female Labor Force*, pp. 65, 75–6.

46 Such notions appear in popular attitudes (contemporary and historical) toward the employment of women, as well as in a more technical, yet often politicized, literature regarding the economics of unemployment and the interpretation of unemployment statistics. See Robert W. Smuts, *Women and Work in America* (New York, 1971; orig. pub. New York, 1959), pp. 108, 119, 148; Stanley Lebergott, "Annual Estimates of Unemployment in the United States, 1900–1950," in National Bureau of Economic Research, *The Measurement and Behavior of Unemployment* (Princeton, N.J., 1957), p. 214; Ruth Milkman, "Women's Work and the Economic Crisis," in Nancy F. Cott and Elizabeth Pleck, eds., *A Heritage of Her Own* (New York, 1979), pp. 516–20; Linda S. Rosenman, "Unemployment of Women: A Social Policy Issue," *Social Work* 24 (Jan. 1979): 20–5; Nancy S. Barrett and Richard D. Morgenstern, "Why Do Blacks and Women Have High Unemployment Rates?" *Journal of Human Resources* 9 (Fall 1974): 456–8.

47 See Tables A.12 and 4.9. The published census data provide only indirect evidence regarding the household position of female workers – since they reveal a person's marital status but not her relationship to the head of the household. According to one study of 20,000 women in Boston in the 1880s, two-thirds of all working women lived at home with their parents or with other relatives. MBSL, *15 AR*, p. 127.

48 Two separate samples of working women in Brockton were examined for this study; each was randomly drawn from the 1900 manuscript census schedules. The first sample consists of women who worked in the shoe industry; the second consists of women who held jobs in all other occupations and industries. The composition of each sample is indicated in Table 4.9. Analyses of these samples suggest that year-round employment was, indeed, more important to women in certain household situations than it was to others. In the "non–shoe workers" sample, only 26.7% of all female household heads ($n = 30$) belonged to occupations that had unemployment frequencies that were above 25%; for boarders the figure was 39.5% ($n = 43$); for daughters of the head of household, it was 44.2% ($n = 86$); and for wives it was 58.3% ($n = 24$). (The difference between household heads and wives was significant at a level of

.05; the difference between household heads and daughters was significant only at .10). Married women as a group ($n = 46$), moreover, were significantly (.05) less likely to belong to occupations that had below-average unemployment frequencies than were widows and divorced women ($n = 42$). A similar pattern could be detected among shoe workers. Only 6.7% of all female household heads ($n = 30$) worked in the most unsteady jobs in the shoe industry (with unemployment frequencies above 65%), while for daughters of household heads, the figure was 36.3% ($n = 113$). This difference was also significant at .05.

49   MBSL, 2 AR, p. 206; 3 AR, pp. 68–82; Carroll D. Wright, *The Working Girls of Boston*, repr. from MBSL, 15 AR, pp. 98–102, 128–9.

50   MBSL, 2 AR, p. 224; 3 AR, p. 73; 15 AR, p. 57; 20 AR, p. 567; BISU Hearings, pp. 884, 1031–5; *Labor Leader*, Dec. 10, 1887; *SWJ* 6, no. 10 (Oct. 1905): 12; Oppenheimer, *Female Labor Force*, p. 10; Solomon Fabricant, "The Changing Industrial Distribution of Gainful Workers: Comments on the Decennial Statistics, 1820–1940," in National Bureau of Economic Research, *Studies in Income and Wealth*, XI (New York, 1949), pp. 8–13.

51   See Appendix B for a general discussion of the census surveys and the implications of the self-reporting of unemployment.

52   Female unemployment frequencies and durations were compared to the figures for males in all communities and years for which data are available: every city and town in the state in 1885, the 6 largest cities in 1890, and the 10 largest cities in 1900. There was, of course, some variety in the relationship between male and female unemployment levels, but the general pattern that emerged from these comparisons was overwhelmingly one of similarity. MBSL, *18 AR*, pp. 5–294; *Eleventh U.S. Census, Population*, part II, pp. 638–9, 644–5, 668–9, 686–7, 688–9, 742–3; *Twelfth U.S. Census, Occupations*, pp. 494–9, 506–11, 560–3, 588–91, 598–601, 600–3, 624–7, 732–7, 736–9, 760–3. No data regarding the unemployment of Massachusetts women between 1900 and 1922 are available, but thousands of women were included in the trade union statistics presented in Chapter 3. See also Table 5.3.

53   In 1900 the distribution of working women among occupations with unemployment frequencies of different magnitudes was virtually identical to the distribution recorded for men. *Twelfth U.S. Census, Occupations*, pp. 300–7.

54   That the exceptions appear particularly plentiful in 1885 was the result, in part – but only in part – of the occupational categories or labels utilized in the 1885 census. That census listed, as separate occupations, jobs held in a comparatively large number of seasonal manufacturing industries. See also note 64.

55   Based upon comparisons of male and female unemployment frequencies and mean durations in the shoe and textile industries in the 6 largest cities in the state in 1890, the 10 largest in 1900, the cities listed in Table A.11, and more than a dozen cities and towns (for each industry) in 1885. Unemployment levels were also similar for male and female shoe workers in Brockton in 1900. *Eleventh U.S. Census, Population*, part II, pp.

638–9, 644–5, 668–9, 686–9, 742–3; *Twelfth U.S. Census, Occupations*, pp. 494–9, 506–11, 560–3, 588–91, 598–601, 600–3, 624–7, 732–7, 736–9, 760–3; MBSL, *18 AR*, pp. 166–215.

56 BISU Hearings, p. 318.
57 As Table A.11 indicates, unemployment was less evenly distributed among men and women who performed the same tasks in the paper industry. The variations that occurred from industry to industry invite further research, research that would almost certainly have to penetrate beneath the occupational labels utilized in the census reports.
58 See the census reports listed in note 43. See also Margery Davies, "Woman's Place is At the Typewriter: The Feminization of the Clerical Labor Force," *Radical America* 8, no. 4 (July–Aug. 1974): 1–28.
59 MBSL, *2 AR*, p. 206; *15 AR*, pp. 47, 86–92, 98–110.
60 MBSL, *2 AR*, pp. 209–4; *3 AR*, pp. 68–115; *15 AR*, pp. 86–110; *Labor Leader*, March 31, 1888; BCC, "Questions on Seasonal Employment," reply from H. D. Foss and Company. The statement that the proportion of working women who belonged to occupations of this type probably declined is based less on statistical evidence (the occupational categories in the census reports changed too often to permit a reliable grasp of the issue) than on impressionistic accounts. Reports from the 1870s and 1880s (cited at the beginning of this note) consistently described women's work as being chronically and pervasively irregular. Later accounts, however, were less insistent on this issue, and the unemployment statistics themselves indicate that most women did work year-round in 1890 and 1900. There is no evidence to suggest that unsteady occupations became systematically more or less feminized between 1870 and 1920. To explore this issue, calculations were made to determine the percentage of women in 20 of the most unsteady occupations in the state at each federal census from 1870 to 1920; these figures displayed no clear, or even discernible, trends.
61 See Tables 4.9 and A.12. See also MBSL, *3 AR*, pp. 114–5; *SWJ* 6, no. 10 (Oct. 1905): 12.
62 MBSL, *15 AR*, p. 57.
63 That these patterns obtained within individual communities, as well as statewide, suggests that discrimination of this type was a widespread practice rather than a quirk resulting from aggregated statistics. For the census years 1890 and 1900, comparisons were made of male and female unemployment frequencies and durations in all occupations that had members of both sexes in all the cities for which such data were available. In 1890, women were idled more often than men in a majority of occupations in 5 of the 6 listed cities. In 1900, the same pattern prevailed in 8 out of 10 cities; in several of the largest urban centers, including Boston and Somerville, the imbalance was very marked. For the census year of 1885, comparisons were made of unemployment levels for men and women who belonged to the same trades in more than 40 different communities, with very diverse economic structures: men – in most occupations, in most places – tended to work more steadily. MBSL, *18 AR*,

pp. 166–215; *Eleventh U.S. Census, Population*, part II, pp. 638–9, 644–5, 668–9, 686–9, 742–3; *Twelfth U.S. Census, Occupations*, pp. 494–9, 506–11, 560–3, 588–91, 598–603, 624–7, 732–9, 760–3. See also Thomas L. Norton, *Trade-Union Policies in the Massachusetts Shoe Industry 1919–1929* (New York, 1932), pp. 64–77.

64   The suggestion that the margin of discrimination may have diminished during the final decades of the nineteenth century is based largely on the fact that the recorded gaps between male and female unemployment levels were notably greater in 1885 than they were in any subsequent years (see also note 54). That those gaps were relatively narrow during the prosperous years of 1890 and 1900 is, of course, not surprising, but they were also smaller in 1895 than they were in 1885 in the few industries and communities for which such comparisons could be made. The 1895 figures presented in Table A.11 were compared to figures developed for the same industries in the same communities in 1885. The results were striking: in every case, the advantage possessed by males in 1885 either diminished in size or was reversed by 1895. MBSL, *18 AR*, pp. 166–215. The combination of skill dilution, the sex-typing of tasks, and the persistence of male–female wage differentials may, therefore, have eroded the preferential treatment that employers had traditionally accorded to men.

65   For examples, see the quotations at notes 32 and 42 in this chapter. See also Oppenheimer, *Female Labor Force*, pp. 40–41.

66   *Mass. Census, 1895*, VII (Boston, 1900), pp. 5–91. For general discussions of the labor force participation of women during depressions, see Durand, *Labor Force*, pp. 86–7, 101ff.; and Long, *Labor Force*, pp. 14ff., 194ff. See also Chapter 6.

67   Elizabeth H. Pleck, "A Mother's Wages: Income Earning Among Married Italian and Black Women, 1896–1911," in Nancy F. Cott and Elizabeth H. Pleck, *A Heritage of Her Own* (New York, 1979), p. 381; AC–B, *16 AR*, p. 37; Fraundorf, "Labor Force Participation," pp. 408, 413. See also Chapter 6.

68   In 1900, only 11% of the female labor force in Massachusetts was between the ages of 45 and 64, but more than 20% of all women who worked in occupations with unemployment frequencies below 10% were in that age group. *Twelfth U.S. Census, Occupations*, pp. 300–7. That most working women who were over the age of 40 were not married was confirmed by data from the Brockton samples. Among shoe workers, there were 43 women who were at least 40 years old. Only 16 of these women were married; 17 were widowed or divorced, and 10 were single. In the non–shoe workers sample, there were 68 women who had reached the age of 40. Only 13 of these women were married, while 31 were widowed or divorced. As indicated in note 48, widowed and divorced women did tend to work in relatively steady occupations, and they were, in fact, unemployed less often than were married or single workers. Among non–shoe workers, for example, the unemployment frequency for widowed and divorced women ($n = 42$) was 9.5% compared to 37.0% for

married women ($n = 46$), a contrast that was significant at a level of .05. Finally, it should be acknowledged that the unemployment frequencies for women over the age of 40, presented in Table 4.11, were not significantly lower, statistically, than the frequencies for women in their 20s and 30s. Nonetheless, the appearance of similar patterns in both Brockton samples, as well as in the 1885 survey of the entire population, strongly suggests that women did acquire at least a modicum of job security as they aged. An examination of age-specific unemployment levels for women in 20 communities in 1885 supports this conclusion. Those communities (and the sources of the data) are listed in the analogous table for men, Table A.8.

69 This compassion for older women, if indeed it did exist, did not extend to the hiring of new workers. The data presented in Tables 4.10 and 4.11 indicate that women, like men, were idled for relatively long spells once they had reached their 40s and 50s. That fact also suggests that older women did not work relatively steadily because they were more skilled than their younger colleagues.

70 MBSL, *18 AR*, pp. 254–60; *Mass. Census, 1885,* I, part 2, 612–21, 630–1. Among Brockton's non–shoe workers, the native-born unemployment frequency was 29.2% ($n = 202$), and the mean duration was 4.5 months; for immigrant women, the frequency was 13.0% ($n = 100$), and the mean duration was also 4.5 months. The contrast in unemployment frequencies was significant at a .05 level. Among the immigrant women in the sample, 59% were domestics, compared to less than 25% for native-born women. In the state as a whole, in 1900, nearly 50% of all foreign-born working women were in the "domestic and personal service" sector; 35% were listed as "servants and waitresses," a category that embraced only 10% of all native-born white working women. Within occupations, not surprisingly, immigrants did not enjoy any particular advantage over native-born women. In fact, the limited available data suggest that native women, much like native men, tended to work slightly more steadily than their immigrant colleagues. Among Brockton's shoe workers, for example, the idleness frequency for natives was 61.1%, while for immigrants it was 74.1%. (The number of immigrants was too small, however, for the contrast to attain statistical significance.) For 1885 data bearing on this issue, see MBSL, *18 AR*, pp. 254–60; *Mass. Census, 1885,* I, part 2, pp. 612–21.

71 In 1885, the unemployment frequencies for women born in different nations were: Ireland, 19.4; Germany, 18.9; English Canada, 22.0; Sweden, 12.3; French Canada, 37.4; and England, 39.0. MBSL, *18 AR*, pp. 254–7; *Mass. Census, 1885,* I, part 2, pp. 630–1.

72 No unemployment data for black women in Massachusetts are available. In 1900, 56.9% of all black working women were "servants and waitresses." Regarding the occupational distribution of black women, as well as women from different immigrant and ethnic groups, see the census reports listed in note 43.

73 No direct evidence regarding unemployment levels for different immi-

grant and ethnic groups are available for the period after 1900. Figures regarding occupational location were drawn from the census reports cited in note 43 and from *Mass. Census, 1915*, pp. 536–631.

74 Cf. Milkman, "Women's Work and the Economic Crisis." It may be, however, that women did serve as a reserve army during historical periods when the rate of immigration was far lower than it was between 1870 and 1920. The subject requires more research, but it is possible that the role of women as a reserve source of labor has varied, from time to time and from place to place, depending upon the volume of male immigration.

75 See Chapter 3. Cf. Oppenheimer, *Female Labor Force*, p. 70.

76 *Labor Leader*, Oct. 15 and 29, 1887; BISU Hearings, pp. 164, 170–2, 1031–7, 1049–50.

77 See Chapters 7 and 9. Regarding the history of labor market structures, see David M. Gordon, Richard Edwards, and Michael Reich, *Segmented Work: Divided Workers: The Historical Transformation of Labor in the United States* (Cambridge, Engl., 1982).

5. From place to place

1 MBSL, *18 AR*, p. 164; *Mass. Census, 1895*, VII (Boston, 1900), pp. 90–103. The only years for which data by county are available are 1885 and 1895. Suffolk County, which includes Boston, had an unemployment frequency below 20% in 1885 and 1895, as did the island (and county) of Nantucket.

2 The only years for which unemployment statistics for all communities are available are 1885 and 1895. Figures for 1885 were computed for women separately and for men and women together; the patterns displayed by these figures were similar to those presented for men in Table 5.1.

The relatively low unemployment frequency recorded in 1885 for towns with fewer than 2,000 inhabitants demands explanation, as does also the contrast between the 1885 and 1895 figures for these small towns. As discussed in Appendix B, the 1885 census measured unemployment for *all* male and female gainful workers, while the 1895 survey was effectively limited to employees. This limitation appears to have had a significant and revealing effect upon the size and composition of the population surveyed in small towns. In communities with fewer than 2,000 inhabitants, less than 30% of the population was "covered by" the 1895 unemployment survey, while in cities with populations above 30,000, the figure was close to 40%. This suggests that small towns contained a disproportionately large number of self-employed men. The 1885 unemployment frequency, thus, may have been relatively low because of the presence of these men – who tended to work steadily. The 1895 frequency was higher because it registered only the experiences of employees – who were idled as often, or slightly more often, in small towns as they were elsewhere in the state. *Mass. Census, 1895,* VII, pp. 90–103.

3 As the statistics presented in Table 5.3 indicate, unemployment rates for Boston's trade unionists were not always markedly lower than those recorded in other cities. But these figures may well be somewhat misleading. As explained in Appendix B, there is no way to determine the occupations of the trade unionists, from individual cities, whose unemployment was reported to the MBSL. In all likelihood, the Boston sample contained a disproportionately large number of building tradesmen – which would have had the effect of creating an upward bias in the unemployment rates. It should also be noted that many unionists who belonged to Boston-based locals did not live or work in the city. MBSL, *49 AR,* part IV, p. 16.

4 The evidence does suggest that after 1885 unemployment levels were, on the whole, slightly lower in the major cities than they were in smaller communities. In 1890, the aggregate unemployment frequency for all men who lived in the 6 largest cities was 15.7%; in the 5 largest cities outside Boston it was 17.6%; and in the rest of the state, the figure was 20.9%. For women, the frequencies were 13.4%, 15.8%, and 18.5%, respectively. In 1900, men who lived in the 10 largest cities had an overall unemployment frequency of 17.5%, while 22.1% of those who lived elsewhere were jobless; for women, the figures were 16.5% and 23.4%. Among trade union members too, unemployment rates, from 1908 to 1922, were usually marginally lower in the major cities than they were in the rest of the state. (The sources of these figures are listed in Table 5.3 and in note 12.) There are several possible explanations of this phenomenon: urban settings may have been better protected against weather-induced interruptions of work; cities tended to have larger commercial sectors in which the rhythms of employment were relatively stable; and urban firms were probably larger than small-town firms and may consequently have had better access to stable segments of the market. (Cf. Stanley Lebergott, *Manpower in Economic Growth* (New York, 1964), p. 144.) It should be stressed, however, that outside Boston the urban advantage was slight and far from pervasive.

5 Regarding the extent of industrialization in nonurban areas, see MBSL, *21 AR,* pp. 140–67, 179ff.

6 Regarding the restriction of the 1895 survey to employees, see note 2 and Appendix B. That the link between high unemployment levels and low rates of population growth appeared in the data for the 1890s but not in the figures for the 1880s may mean that employment conditions were changing in the stagnant communities. But it is at least as likely that many of these stagnant communities (most of which were small towns) contained relatively large numbers of self-employed individuals who tended to work steadily and whose inclusion in the 1885 survey lowered the reported unemployment frequencies for that year.

7 The data presented in Table 5.2 are, for many reasons, not ideally suited to the task of exploring the potentially complex links between unem-

ployment levels and population growth. But, unfortunately, they do constitute the best data available – since population growth figures can be computed only for 5-year or 10-year periods, and unemployment statistics for all communities can be obtained only for the census years of 1885 and 1895. This issue was investigated further by examining and analyzing other data that are not presented in tabular form. The unemployment breakdowns in Table 5.2 were compared with 5-year growth rates from 1880 to 1900; the 1885, 1890, 1895, and 1900 unemployment figures for major cities were matched against 5- and 10-year population growth rates; and unemployment and growth figures were compared, for the 1880s and 1890s, in communities dominated by the shoe and textile industries. The only clear trend to emerge from this mass congregation of numbers was among shoe manufacturing towns in the 1890s: in those communities, low population growth rates were strongly associated with unusually high unemployment frequencies and mean durations. (The data for these analyses are located in the sources listed in Tables 5.2 and 5.3, as well as *Mass. Census, 1895*, VII, pp. 1–90, 108–13.)

The apparent weakness of the links between recorded unemployment levels and population growth rates can be explained, in part, by the fact (discussed later in this chapter) that local unemployment levels were in a constant state of flux. Unemployment statistics for any one year do not necessarily offer a reliable guide to unemployment levels over a 5-year or 10-year period. It is certainly possible, thus, that average decadal unemployment rates, if known, would display a much stronger relationship with decadal growth rates. But it should be noted that in an economy that relied heavily on a reserve army of labor, the absence of a strong link between growth and unemployment is not altogether surprising. Low population growth rates could have reflected either a saturated labor market or the absence of capitalist industry. And economic expansion created jobs but not necessarily steady or secure jobs. It is notable, in this regard, that in 1885 and 1895 the communities that were growing most rapidly were particularly likely to have had unemployment frequencies between 20% and 40%. (See Table 5.2.) These cities and towns were obviously thriving – attracting industry and attracting workers – but they were nonetheless vulnerable to very considerable unemployment levels during depressions.

8 Average unemployment rates for the years 1908–16, for trade unionists living in different cities, were compared to population growth rates in those cities for the decade 1905–15. (The sources are those listed in note 12 and *Mass. Census, 1915* (Boston, 1918), pp. 54–58.) That there was a strong short-run relationship between unemployment and population growth, that men and women did move from one community to another in response to local labor market conditions, is discussed later in this chapter.

9 The differences between the 1885 and 1895 figures for "all communities," presented in Table 5.2, probably reflect changes in the method of measuring unemployment rather than a shift in the actual distribution of

joblessness. See notes 2 and 6, as well as Appendix B. Mean unemployment durations were also computed (from the sources listed in Table 5.2) for all communities in both 1885 and 1895. These figures did display considerable variety, but the variations were neither as widespread nor as extreme as were the variations in unemployment frequencies. In 1885, for example, the mean duration was between 3 and 5 months in 250 communities; many of the exceptions were extremely small towns in which the mean registered the experiences of a minuscule number of jobless workers. Presumably, high rates of geographical mobility (discussed below) placed a "ceiling" on the mean duration in individual communities. Some additional reasons for the relative uniformity of unemployment durations are discussed in the notes to Chapters 3 and 4.

10   MBSL, *18 AR*, pp. 5–151, 267–9; *Mass. Census, 1895*, VII, pp. 5–103. In 1895, in towns with populations below 2,000, unemployment frequencies ranged from 1.7 to 74.5%. Mean durations were also uneven (the range was from 1 to 6.8 months), but they were more clustered around the statewide average. Sharp contrasts in unemployment frequencies were found among communities in all size categories.

11   In 1885 and in 1900 (but not in 1890 or 1895), there was a tendency, among the major cities, for mean durations of unemployment to be relatively high where idleness frequencies were low, indicating that unemployment rates were somewhat more even than the frequency figures alone suggest.

12   Unemployment data are available only for the 6 largest cities in 1890 and the 10 largest in 1900. Annual unemployment rates for trade unionists in different cities were considerably more varied than the summary figures in Table 5.3 suggest. E.g., in the prosperous year of 1918, the annual unemployment rate for union members was less than 3% in Haverhill and Lowell but greater than 7% in Springfield, Fall River, and Worcester. In 1920, when the economy was in decline, the unemployment rate was in the vicinity of 10% in Boston, Springfield, and Worcester, while it was close to (or above) 30% in Lynn, Lawrence, Fall River, and Haverhill. Most of the data from which the trade union statistics for individual cities have been assembled can be found in MBSL, *47 AR*, part VI, pp. 58–9; *49 AR*, part IV, p. 54; and *52 AR*, part III, p. 44. But these summary tables are not complete, and it was necessary to fill in the gaps with data from the individually published quarterly reports on unemployment. These are located in MBSL, *Labor Bulletin*, nos. 62–4, 66, 69, 72, 74, 77, 79, 80, 82, 85, 89; MBSL, *Quarterly Report*, nos. 17–36; MBSL, *Industrial Review*, no. 7 (March 1922), no. 8 (June 1922), and no. 11 (July 1923). See Appendix B regarding the particular difficulties of interpreting the trade union figures for individual communities.

13   Similarly, the unemployment rate for trade unionists in Worcester in 1919 was much higher than it was for their counterparts in Lawrence. But the tables were turned in 1920, when the postwar depression deepened. MBSL, *52 AR*, part III, p. 44.

404 **Notes to pp. 118–19**

14   MBSL, *18 AR*, pp. 267–9; *Mass. Census, 1895*, VII, pp. 5–103. Mean durations of unemployment also fluctuated with the business cycle and from year to year – and with a comparable lack of system. But the range of the fluctuations was, with some exceptions, relatively narrow.

15   See note 12 for the sources of the trade union figures.

16   MBSL, *Bulletin 12*, pp. 167–8; *Bulletin 15*, p. 133; MBSL, *39 AR*, p. 184; *44 AR*, p. 361; *52 AR*, part III, p. 43.

17   MBSL, *18 AR*, pp. 166–216; *Mass. Census, 1895*, VII, pp. viii–xv, 90–103. Regarding the extent of self-employment in small towns, see note 2.

18   MBSL, *18 AR*, pp. 166–216; *Mass. Census, 1895*, VII, pp. viii–xv, 90–113.

19   BISU Hearings, p., 361. See also MBSL, *18 AR*, pp. 166–216.

20   See Table 5.3, as well as MBSL, *18 AR*, pp. 166–216, and *Mass. Census, 1895*, VII, pp. 90–113. Some dominant industries also produced fairly distinctive unemployment durations: e.g., in 1895, mean durations of unemployment tended to be lower in communities dominated by the textile industry than in communities where the shoe industry was preeminent. For more extensive data bearing on this issue, see Alexander Keyssar, "Men Out of Work" (Ph.D. diss., Harvard University, 1977), pp. 217–21.

21   See the sources listed in Table 5.3. In 1895, unemployment frequencies were also well below average in the Boston-area communities of Medford, Newton, Brookline, and Arlington. The significance of the size of a city's commercial sector was demonstrated by the experiences of Somerville and Lawrence in 1900. The unemployment frequency in manufacturing was very similar in the two cities (20.9% v. 22.9%), but Lawrence had a much higher overall unemployment frequency because its manufacturing sector was much more dominant. For additional evidence of the links between economic diversity and relatively low unemployment levels, see Michael H. Frisch, *Town into City: Springfield, Massachusetts, and the Meaning of Community, 1840–1880* (Cambridge, Mass., 1972), p. 119; MBSL, *41 AR*, p. 235: MBSL, *Quarterly Report 29*, pp. 8–9; Jonathan T. Lincoln, *The City of the Dinner-Pail* (Boston and New York, 1909), p. 3; and Solomon Bulkley Griffin, *People and Politics Observed by a Massachusetts Editor* (Boston, 1923), p. 14.

22   In 1885, among 10 cities that were centers of textile manufacturing, the frequency of unemployment ranged from 14.2% to 62.8%; mean durations ranged from 3.7 months to 5.0 months. The spread was similar in 1895, and those communities that had relatively high (or low) idleness levels in 1885 did not necessarily have the same experience a decade later. Similarly, among 26 communities that specialized in shoe manufacturing in 1885, the frequency of unemployment exceeded 60% in 10 and was under 40% in 6. MBSL, *18 AR*, pp. 166–216, 267–9; *Mass. Census, 1895*, VII, pp. 1–90, 108–13; MBSL, *Industrial Review 8* (1922), p. 28. See also MBSL, *Industrial Review 3* (1920), pp. 25, 29, and Keyssar, "Men Out of Work," pp. 217–21.

23   See Chapter 3. Cf. MBSL, *Industrial Review 2* (1920), p. 23, and *5* (1920), p. 29.

24 BISU Hearings, p. 707.

25 MBSL, *18 AR*, pp. 166–219. For additional evidence and a tabular presentation of the 1885 data, see Keyssar, "Men Out of Work," pp. 217–28.

26 Table 5.4 presents only a portion of the available data for 1890 and 1900. Unemployment frequencies and mean durations of unemployment were also calculated (for men and women separately) for dozens of other occupations in each of the 6 largest cities in the state in 1890 and the 10 largest in 1900. (These are the only communities for which such data are available for any nondepression years.) In nearly all these occupations, unemployment levels varied – sometimes markedly – from place to place.

27 Not surprisingly, in communities that had relatively high (or low) aggregate unemployment frequencies, joblessness levels also tended to be comparatively high (or low) in most occupations. E.g., in Boston in 1890 unemployment frequencies for men were below average in 33 out of 35 major occupations. But, as Table 5.4 indicates, this consistency was not always so marked. Supplementary analyses of the available data for 1885, 1890, and 1900 confirmed that the overall condition of a community's labor market was not necessarily matched by conditions in all occupations.

28 See, e.g., *The Carpenter* 25, no. 5 (May 1905): 22; vol. 28, no. 2 (Feb. 1908): 15. See also *Labor Leader*, Dec. 7, 1887.

29 Changes in the types of data available seriously hamper efforts to detect long-term trends, and there can be little doubt that sizable local variations in unemployment levels persisted well into the 1920s. But the trade union figures (problematic as they may be), coupled with the relatively homogeneous unemployment levels reported for the state's 10 largest cities in 1900, suggest that some long-run diminution of the variations may have been taking place.

30 Boston Provident Association, *Annual Report for 1876–7* (Boston, n.d.), p. 8; BISU Hearings, p. 915.

31 MBSL, *Bulletin 30*, pp. 61–4; *Report of the Commission on Immigration on the Problem of Immigration in Massachusetts*, House Document 2300 (Boston, 1914), p. 50; Stephan Thernstrom, *The Other Bostonians: Poverty and Progress in the American Metropolis, 1880–1970* (Cambridge, Mass., 1976; orig. pub. 1973), pp. 16–20, 39–42, 222, 228–9.

32 E.g., Thernstrom notes that "one wonders whether the exceptional earlier volatility of the American working class, and especially of its least-skilled members, does not point to the existence of a permanent floating proletariat made up of men ever on the move spatially but rarely winning economic gains as a result of spatial mobility. Did these droves of laborers, factory workers, and service employees leave Boston in the 1880s for the same reason that engineers and lawyers leave it today, namely, because they have been offered a better job in Denver? Or was their movement more often drifting than purposeful, initiated by the loss of a job rather than by the offer of a better one? The question is moot . . ." *Other Bostonians*, p. 42.

Historical studies of geographic mobility have generally been restricted to males, and these pages, unfortunately, are no exception – in part because the aim of this foray into the subject is to help explain the findings of other studies. As Thernstrom notes (p. 7), the task of tracing women, to determine the extent of their mobility, is a particularly difficult one both because women changed their names when they married and because city directories often omitted female occupational listings. Obviously, women shared in much of the residential mobility recorded for men, but the links between unemployment and mobility may well have been different for female workers than they were for males – since women played different roles in household economies and were concentrated in different types of occupations (see Chapter 4). It would indeed be of great value to learn whether women constituted a distinctively sedentary reserve of labor, but this subject – like many others in the social history of working-class women – awaits further research.

33   In Boston and elsewhere, persistence rates were lower for both skilled and unskilled manual workers than they were for men who held either "low" or "high" white-collar positions. Thernstrom, *Other Bostonians*, p. 230. For a discussion of transportation costs see Theodore Hershberg, et al., "The 'Journey-to-Work': An Empirical Investigation of Work, Residence, and Transportation, Philadelphia 1850 and 1880," in Hershberg, ed., *Philadelphia: Work, Space, Family, and Group Experience in the Nineteenth Century* (New York, 1981), pp. 128–73.

34   BISU Hearings, p. 813; *BISU Report*, part V, p. xviii. Depressions probably had highly variable effects on the mobility rates of workers in different industries and in different life circumstances. As noted later in this chapter, economic downturns did increase the number of "tramps" on the road, but impressionistic evidence suggests that they reduced the number of seasonal "floaters" in some occupations (BISU Hearings, p. 15). It also seems likely that migration rates changed in the course of a depression (initially high, perhaps, followed by a slowdown as workers realized that the business downturn was widespread, and then increasing as men became more desperate), and these changes may well have occurred at different moments in different communities. That depressions did not have a simple, linear impact upon mobility was confirmed by a research effort designed to detect one. Samples of 100 workers were drawn from the Boston city directories for the years 1880, 1893, 1906, and 1910. These workers were then traced for two successive years to determine whether or not they remained in the city of Boston. The expectation that persistence rates would be notably lower for the 1893 and 1906 cohorts than for the other samples was roundly defeated by the data. Persistence rates were relatively low for the 1893 group, but the difference was not statistically significant, and all the other cohorts seem to have had roughly similar experiences.

35   BISU Hearings, pp. 15, 200, 592–3, 1035, and E. L. Daley to William M. Cole, July 16, 1894; IAS, *82 AR*, p. 5; *The Carpenter* 29, no. 4 (April 1908): 40; *Problem of Immigration in Massachusetts*, pp. 73–5.

36 The sample of male shoe workers whose mobility experiences were investigated is introduced in Chapter 4. The 1900 manuscript census schedules indicated whether or not these men were unemployed at all during the 12-month period from June 1, 1899, to May 31, 1900. Sample members were then traced to the 1901 city directory of Brockton, which was compiled in the spring of that year. Men were counted as persistent if they appeared in the directory at the same address at which they had lived at the time of the census survey or if they could reliably be identified as living at another address in the city of Brockton. All cases of ambiguous or problematic identification were discarded from the sample. Men were included in the mobility totals only if they could be positively identified in the 1901 city directory or if there was literally no trace of them (under any imaginable spelling or at any conceivable occupation) in the directory.

Careful as the procedures were, there are nonetheless some limitations to the method itself. Most importantly, perhaps, the census sample is intrinsically biased against the possibility of detecting a widespread and pervasive connection between spells of unemployment and geographic mobility. This is so because the only unemployed men who appeared in the census schedules for Brockton were those who were still living in the city at the end of the 1-year period covered by the census survey. A man who was laid off in December 1899 and left town immediately simply would not show up in the sample that was drawn from the census manuscripts. An additional shortcoming of the method is that there is no way to ascertain whether the men who were included in the census survey, who were unemployed during the census year, and who subsequently left Brockton were actually jobless at the time that they moved. Tracing the census sample into the city directories, therefore, cannot provide a precise measure of the odds that a shoe worker would leave town in direct response to a layoff. But linking these two sets of data does make it possible to determine whether men who were unemployed during a particular year (and whose idleness may or may not have been ongoing or recurrent) were more likely to leave town in subsequent months than were men who had worked steadily. Obviously this measuring gauge is not finely calibrated, but the combination of the 1900 census manuscripts and the 1901 city directories probably constitutes the best available data for research on this issue. On balance, the limits in the method would seem more likely to have produced an understatement, rather than an exaggeration, of the influence of unemployment upon mobility – which makes the findings reported here that much more striking.

One further problem of method warrants mention. Scholars who have utilized city directories have noted that these documents were not exhaustive in their listing of individuals and that there were some biases in the patterns of omission: blue-collar workers tended to be omitted more often than professionals, blacks than whites, immigrants than natives, and new arrivals – in the middle of the nineteenth century, at least

– were often not included until they had established their membership
in the community by remaining in town for some time, often as long as
two years (Thernstrom, *Other Bostonians*, pp. 283–8). If these biases were
present in the 1901 directory of Brockton (the directories of small cities
like Brockton may have been more inclusive than those for a metropolis
like Boston) and if they coincided with the odds of a man becoming unemployed, then they could have skewed the results of this inquiry. To
state the most obvious case, if men who were unemployed were more
likely to have been inaccurately omitted from the directory than men
who worked year-round, then the relatively high rate of nonappearance
in the city directory, on the part of the unemployed, could have been a
reflection not of geographic mobility but of biases in the directory itself.
Happily, this does not appear to have been the case. The vast majority
of sample members were blue-collar workers, and, for most purposes,
statistics were assembled separately for these men. Immigrants constituted only a minority of the labor force, and immigrants were not idled
any more often than native-born workers. All sample members worked
in Brockton's dominant industry and thus had some claim to membership in its economic community, and they also would have been in
Brockton for at least 9 months (and probably more) by the time that the
city directory was compiled. It should also be noted that the most compelling differences that emerged between the unemployed and the employed were among members of the sample who were quite unlikely to
have been excluded from the directories because of these putative biases
of omission: adult, native-born, heads of households.

37 Significance levels were measured through use of a difference of proportions test. The notations in Tables 5.5–5.7 indicate that the difference
between the two figures referred to was statistically significant at a level
of .05. The difference in the aggregate persistence rates of employed and
unemployed blue-collar operatives was significant only at a level of .19.
The absence of any clear trend in the persistence rates of men who had
been unemployed for different lengths of time may well have been the
result of one of the methodological limitations discussed in the preceding note; i.e., the only unemployed men whose names appeared in the
census were those who were still in Brockton in June 1900. If, as seems
likely, the odds of a man leaving town increased as his spell of unemployment lengthened, then a disproportionately large number of workers who had experienced long-term unemployment during the census
year would have departed from Brockton before the census survey was
conducted.

38 The difference between employed and unemployed household heads
was statistically significant at a level of .07.

39 The comparatively low recorded persistence rates for all immigrants may
have resulted from a bias against the inclusion of immigrants in the city
directory. See note 36.

40 Of all native-born men who were over the age of 30 and who worked
year-round, 97.1% were persistent ($n = 35$), while only 81.6% of those

who had been unemployed were persistent (n = 98). This difference is significant at a level of .05.

41 That unemployment accounted for an annual departure rate of 5–10% of Brockton's shoe workers is, in fact, a conservative estimate. The figures presented in Table 5.7 suggest that unemployment could easily have been directly responsible for the annual out-migration of 10% of all native-born household heads and 7% of all other native-born workers. These figures alone would account for the departure of more than 5% of the city's shoe workers. The percentage would certainly be higher if immigrants, as well as unemployed men who left Brockton before the census survey was conducted, were included. Nor do such figures take into consideration men who left the city as an indirect consequence of unemployment: e.g., those who were not actually unemployed but who migrated because they anticipated being laid off.

42 Seasonal slowdowns, as discussed earlier in this chapter, may well have generated a great deal of temporary transience. But it seems likely that much of this seasonal mobility did not result in "permanent" changes of residence or in a person's disappearance from a city directory.

43 *Problem of Immigration in Massachusetts*, p. 255; Isaac A. Hourwich, *Immigration and Labor* (New York, 1912), p. 274.

44 Robert A. Woods and Albert J. Kennedy, *The Zone of Emergence* (Cambridge, Mass., 1962), pp. 68–9; William H. Beveridge, *Unemployment: A Problem of Industry* (London, 1930), p. 216; BISU Hearings, pp. 592–3; *The Carpenter* 28, no. 4 (April 1908): p. 40.

45 For an example of what proved to be a very unsuccessful migration for a large number of workmen, see AC-B, *21 AR*, p. 27.

46 Thernstrom, *Other Bostonians*, pp. 220–32; Jonathan D. Prude, *The Coming of Industrial Order* (Cambridge, Engl., 1983), pp. 144–8.

47 Thernstrom, *Other Bostonians*, pp. 228–32. Seniority provisions and unemployment insurance are discussed in Chapters 7 and 9.

48 BISU Hearings, pp. 754, 1694–5.

49 Don D. Lescohier, *The Labor Market* (New York, 1919), p. 272; Paul T. Ringenbach, *Tramps and Reformers 1873–1916: The Discovery of Unemployment in New York* (Westport, 1973), pp. xii–xv, 3–10; Robert V. Bruce, *1877: Year of Violence* (Chicago, 1970; orig. pub. Indianapolis, 1959), pp. 20–2; Edwin A. Brown, *"Broke": The Man without the Dime* (Boston, 1920), p. 14; Whiting Williams, *What's on the Worker's Mind* (New York, 1921), p. 225; Louis Picarello, in an unpublished study of poor relief in Danvers, Mass. (Brandeis University, 1978), found that the first use of the word "tramp" in the public records of Danvers was in the 1870s.

50 *BISU Report*, part II, esp. pp. 86–7, 96; BISU Hearings, pp. 327, 608, 716, 1210, 1694. Cf. also Williams, *Worker's Mind*, p. 225; Brown, *"Broke"*, pp. xiv–xv; and Daniel T. Rodgers, *The Work Ethic in Industrial America 1850–1920* (Chicago, 1978), pp. 226–8.

51 MBSL, *3 AR*, p. 116; *8 AR*, pp. 189, 211–14; Frisch, *Town into City*, pp. 223–4; *BISU Report*, part II, entire; BISU Hearings, pp. 448, 646, 681, 746, 844–6, 961, 1361, 1387, 1692, 1694; Ringenbach, *Tramps and Reformers*, p.

24; MBSL, *Bulletin 49*, p. 312; Leah H. Feder, *Unemployment Relief in Periods of Depression* (New York, 1936), pp. 65–6, 269.

52 The data commonly collected by public officials indicated the number of nightly lodgings that were given to homeless wayfarers and tramps in the course of a particular month or year. Such figures constitute a fairly reliable index of fluctuations in the tramp population, but they are less useful as a guide to the actual number of tramps – since there is no way to determine how many different men contributed to the total number of lodgings. Different communities had different rules regarding the number of nights in succession that a man could receive free shelter, and public officials claimed that tramps often used different names at different shelters. The state tried to overcome these problems by conducting formal census surveys of the tramp population on May 1, 1895, and again exactly a decade later. On those dates, the state tabulated the number of men sleeping in almshouses, station houses, wayfarers' lodges, and similar abodes: this procedure yielded a count of 802 tramps in 1895 and 370 in 1905. MBSL, *Bulletin 2*, pp. 32ff.; *Bulletin 36*, p. 62. Public officials conceded that these figures would have been doubled had the surveys been conducted in winter, when men could not sleep outside, but even still the totals seem remarkably low – too low to have warranted the investigations that produced them. The procedures utilized were, in all likelihood, not up to the unusual task of counting people who – technically at least – were in the midst of committing a crime. That the "tramp census" figures understate the number of homeless wayfarers is indicated by all the available data regarding the number of lodgings given to tramps and vagrants. E.g., in the 1890s, hundreds of lodgings were given each month in small cities like Taunton and Holyoke; in 1906 the Salvation Army in Boston gave approximately 50,000 lodgings to homeless men; and during the first months of 1915, lodgings were given to 639 persons per night in Boston alone. (The sources of these statistics are listed in the previous note.)

53 This figure is based on estimates that the average number of tramps on the road between 1870 and 1920 was 1,000 and that the average length of time that a man spent tramping in Massachusetts was 1 year. It is certainly possible that the first figure exaggerates the average number of tramps in the state at any one time, but it is even more possible, indeed likely, that the average amount of time that a man spent tramping was considerably less than one year. If so, the "turnover" rate among tramps was even greater, and the total number of men who had the experience of tramping would be correspondingly higher.

54 Feder, *Unemployment Relief*, p. 65; MBSL, *8 AR*, p. 212; Frisch, *Town into City*, pp. 223–4; Alvan Francis Sanborn, *Moody's Lodging House* (Boston, 1895), pp. 22–3; Brown, *"Broke"*, pp. xv, 161–2, 319; Frances Kellor, *Out of Work* (New York, 1915), pp. 8, 9, 158, 417; Williams, *Worker's Mind*, passim; Walter A. Wyckoff, *The Workers: An Experiment in Reality: The West* (New York, 1898), pp. 54ff.; Samuel Rezneck, "Patterns of Thought and

Action in an American Depression, 1882–1886," *American Historical Review* 61 (1956): 298; BISU Hearings, pp. 1210, 1692, 1694, 1714.

55 *BISU Report*, part II, entire; BISU Hearings, pp. 301, 1363, 1689–90; Brown, *"Broke"*, pp. 82–7; Sanborn, *Moody's Lodging House*, passim; Josiah Flynt, *Tramping with Tramps* (Montclair, N.J., 1972: orig. pub. New York, 1899), pp. 96–7, 317–35; Feder, *Unemployment Relief*, p. 65; Griffin, *People and Politics*, p. 77; Springfield Scrapbooks, Springfield Public Library, vol. 2, newspaper clipping dated Dec. 10, 1907.

56 *BISU Report*, part II, entire; *Acts and Resolves Passed by the General Court of Massachusetts in the Year 1910*, (Boston, 1910), chap. 248, p. 187. (Items in this series will hereafter be cited as *Acts and Resolves of Massachusetts*, with identifying year.)

57 *BISU Report*, part II, pp. ix, 17, 89–90, 96; BISU Hearings, pp. 716, 775, 949. See also Ringenbach, *Tramps*, p. 39; and New York *Times*, May 21, 1879.

58 *Acts and Resolves of Massachusetts, 1866*, chap. 235, pp. 229–30; *1875*, chap. 70, pp. 648–9; *1878*, chap. 160, p. 115; *1880*, chap. 257, pp. 231–2; *1896*, chap. 385, pp. 335–6. See also *The Public Statutes of the Commonwealth of Massachusetts, enacted Nov. 19, 1880, to take effect Feb. 1, 1882* (Boston, 1883), chap. 207, pp. 1169–70. Why the exemption for women was eliminated is unclear – particularly since discussions of the "tramp problem," as well as collections of data regarding the number of tramps, focused exclusively on males.

59 *Acts and Resolves of Massachusetts, 1905*, chap. 344, p. 268. The rationale for passing this law was explained by the Massachusetts Civic League in its pamphlet *The Tramp Problem* (Boston, 1905).

60 BISU Hearings, pp. 448, 451–2, 511, 683, 687, 844–6, 1372, 1387, 1424, 1693; *BISU Report*, part II, pp. ix, 17, 32, 36, 82.

61 BISU Hearings, p. 511.

62 Ibid., p. 1696.

63 *BISU Report*, part II, pp. x, xi, 9; BISU Hearings, p. 1689; MBSL, *Bulletin 36*, p. 61; Brown, *"Broke"*, p. 33.

64 Brown, *"Broke"*, pp. 154–9.

65 *Acts and Resolves of Massachusetts, 1913*, chap. 76, p. 1158; Brown, *"Broke"*, p. 47; Ringenbach, *Tramps*, pp. xv, 60–70. AC–B, *35 AR*, p. 29.

66 Cf. Ringenbach, *Tramps*, pp. xv, 60–70. Evidence that most tramps were jobless migrants rather than shirkers appeared in abundance in the BISU Hearings. The publication of some of this evidence, in part II of the *BISU Report*, may well have influenced public opinion. See the BISU Hearings, especially pp. 327, 646. The first decades of the twentieth century also witnessed some discussion of the possibility that men turned to tramping because they were utterly worn out by years of monotonous, arduous labor begun when they were children. See, e.g., MBSL, *Bulletin 30*, p. 77. Examples of the persistence of deeply suspicious attitudes toward tramps can be found in a pamphlet (the front page of which is Figure 5.2) published by the Massachusetts Civic League, *The Tramp Problem* (Boston, 1905); in the *Twenty-fourth Annual Report of the Union*

Relief Association of Springfield (Springfield, Mass., 1900–1), p. 10; and in a clipping, dated 1912, in the Springfield Scrapbooks, Springfield Public Library, II, p. 94. The evolution of public policy and attitudes toward the unemployed is discussed at length in Chapter 9.

67 Neither the problem of tramping nor the trends in policy toward tramps were unique to Massachusetts. Cf. Ringenbach, *Tramps,* and Morton Keller, *Affairs of State* (Cambridge, Mass., 1977), pp. 490–1. See also Alice Solenberger, *One Thousand Homeless Men* (New York, 1914).

6. Coping

1 MBSL, *10 AR*, p. 138; Robert A. Woods, ed., *Americans in Process* (Boston and New York, 1903), pp. 128–9; BISU Hearings, p. 116.

2 Although there were precursors (some of which are cited later in this chapter), studies of the effects of unemployment and the process of coping with unemployment began to appear only in the wake of the depression of 1913–14 and, more frequently, in the early 1920s. Probably the richest collection of materials to be assembled on these subjects, prior to the Great Depression, emerged from a national survey sponsored by the National Federation of Settlements in 1928–29. Case studies of unemployed families, compiled by settlement house residents who were well acquainted with the families, were collected by the NFS. Summaries of some of the case studies were published in Marion Elderton, ed., *Case Studies of Unemployment* (Philadelphia, 1931), with an introduction by Helen Hall. Clinch Calkins published a deft, popular, and widely read version of these materials in *Some Folks Won't Work* (New York, 1930). The manuscript survey schedules and interviews for many of the case studies have been preserved in the Helen Hall Papers (folders 396–407) at the Social Welfare History Archives at the University of Minnesota, Minneapolis.

3 Whether or not some strategies for coping with unemployment became more (or less) common during these years is an important but still unanswerable question. The paucity of data does, however, lend support to the argument (offered later in this chapter) that most jobless workers coped with their unemployment through private and informal strategies of a type that left few traces on the written historical record.

4 Boston *Globe*, Feb. 25, 1894.

5 *BISU Report*, part V, app. B, p. 81; see also p. 78.

6 Ibid., p. 25.

7 BISU Hearings, p. 417.

8 Detailed breakdowns of unemployment durations in the labor force as a whole are available only for the 1885 census year. Less detailed figures for 1890 and 1900, when the compilers of the census utilized unfortunately spacious durational categories, are presented in Table 3.2. Samples drawn from the census manuscripts for 1900 indicate that in Brockton one-fifth of all unemployed male shoe workers were jobless for only a month, while an almost identical number were out of work for at

least five months. Among Boston's day laborers, 7% returned to work after a month while more than 20% were idled for more than 6 months. (See Chapter 4 regarding these samples.) As noted in Chapters 3 and 4, there is no way to determine from the census data whether jobless workers were idled for more than one stint in the course of the year. See also Appendix B, note 19.

9 As Table 6.1 indicates, workers who belonged to the same occupation were commonly unemployed for widely varying lengths of time. For additional evidence, see the sources listed in Tables A.2 and A.4.

10 See Chapter 3 regarding incomes, the cost of living, and the life cycles of households. For valuable discussions of the links between life-cycle stages and incomes, see John Modell and Tamara K. Hareven, "Urbanization and the Malleable Household: Boarding and Lodging in American Families," *Journal of Marriage and the Family* 35 (1973): 467–79; John Modell, "Patterns of Consumption, Acculturation, and Family Income Strategies in Late Nineteenth-Century America," in Tamara K. Hareven and Maris A. Vinovskis, eds., *Family and Population in Nineteenth-Century America* (Princeton, N.J., 1978), pp. 206–40.

11 There is, unfortunately, no satisfactory way to determine the percentage of unemployed workers whose encounters with joblessness could be characterized as "benign" (or severe or moderate). There were too many variables involved, many of them not recorded in the census – or elsewhere. But an educated guess is that roughly 20% of all unemployed workers, in prosperous years, were relatively unfazed by their idleness. The 1890 and 1900 census figures suggest that roughly 15% of the unemployed returned to work after only a month: if two-thirds of these men and women had "benign" unemployment experiences and if they were joined by a comparable number of teenagers and craftsmen – who were jobless for longer periods but needed their incomes less urgently – then the 20% figure would seem to be in the ballpark. Obviously, during depressions, the percentage would have declined.

12 Perhaps one-quarter of the men and women who were unemployed in average years (and a higher percentage in depressions) experienced severe material hardship. This figure, like its predecessor, is only a rough estimate, based upon the available durational, wage rate, and cost of living data. The quotation is from the Boston *Globe*, Feb. 27, 1894. Evidence regarding the existence of suffering and hardship among the unemployed is presented later in this chapter. See also BISU Hearings, pp. 538, 853, 885; AC-B, *11 AR*, p. 22; IAS, *40 AR*, p. 2; AC–W, *4 AR*, p. 4; MBSL, *3 AR*, p. 246; Robert A. Woods, *The City Wilderness* (Boston and New York, 1898), p. 92; and Philip Klein, *The Burden of Unemployment: A Study of Unemployment Relief Measures in 15 American Cities* (New York, 1923), pp. 32–7. Further evidence on this and other issues can be found in a source that is peculiarly difficult to cite with precision: a box of late-nineteenth-century and early-twentieth-century case records that are currently in the custody of the Family Service Association of Greater Boston. These records are probably from the Boston Provident Associa-

tion, but it was not possible to make a positive identification of the files. Reference to specific cases is further hampered by the understandable unwillingness of the Family Service Association to permit the names of individuals to be published, although the case files themselves are identified only by name. These records will be cited as the Family Service Association archival collection.

13   MBSL, *11 AR*, p. 134; Boston *Globe*, April 18, 1894; BISU Hearings, pp. 5–6, 77, 203, 431, 638–9, 697–9, 823, 887; AC-B, *30 AR*, p. 37.

14   See Chapter 3 regarding household budgets and the cost of living. Regarding the range of unemployment experiences for workers in the early 1920s, see Klein, *Burden of Unemployment*, pp. 32–7; and Stuart A. Rice, "The Effect of Unemployment Upon the Worker and His Family," in *Business Cycles and Unemployment: Report and Recommendations of a Committee of the President's Conference on Unemployment*, foreword by Herbert Hoover (New York, 1923), pp. 99–109.

15   The records of charity and relief organizations, as well as the utterances of public officials and investigators, strongly suggest that unemployment was causing more hardship by the early 1920s than it had in the 1870s. Short depressions, such as those of 1907–8 and 1913–14, produced far more visible signs of acute suffering than had the longer downturns of the 1870s and 1880s, and the postwar depression produced sharper cries of pain and commanded more public attention than did the depression of the 1890s. To be sure, the documentary record is colored by changes in middle-class perceptions of the problem (see Chapter 9), but there also seems to have been a shift in the underlying social reality. See BISU Hearings, pp. 442, 1193–4; IAS, *60 AR*, pp. 2–6; *61 AR*, pp. 3–7; *80 AR*, pp. 6–7; and Donald B. Cole, *Immigrant City: Lawrence, Massachusetts 1845–1921* (Chapel Hill, N.C., 1963), p. 65. Regarding urbanization and the needs of the unemployed, see also Chapters 3 and 5.

16   "A Study of a Portuguese Family," dated "circa 1922" in the Plymouth Cordage Company papers, file H3, Baker Library, Harvard Business School.

17   BISU Hearings, p. 362; AC-B, *29 AR*, p. 46.

18   *BISU Report*, part I. Regarding institutional relief before and after the depression of the 1890s, see the sources listed in notes 19–24.

19   MBSL, *8 AR*, p. 38; *39 AR*, p. 201; *40 AR*, p. 296; MBSL, *Bulletin 87*, pp. 364–5; *BISU Report*, part I, pp. xxxvi–xxxvii, 35; Boston *Globe*, March 13, 1909; Leah H. Feder, *Unemployment Relief in Periods of Depression* (New York, 1936), pp. 151–4; Bryce M. Stewart, *Unemployment Benefits in the United States* (New York, 1930), p. 88. See also Chapter 7.

20   The evolution of relief policy is discussed in Chapter 9. Regarding the number of different institutions that provided aid to the unemployed and the types of aid proffered, see BISU Hearings, pp. 396, 501, 621, 713, 717–18, 763, 962–3, 1019, 1080, 1124, 1196, 1220, 1355–9, 1389–95, 1405, 1467–70; *BISU Report*, part I; Boston Provident Association, *Annual Report 1875–6* (Boston, 1876), p. 7; AC-B, *15 AR*, pp. 26–7; *19 AR*, pp. 34–5; *20 AR*, pp. 28–9; *29 AR*, pp. 8–15, 32–54; *35 AR*, pp. 24–31; *36 AR*, pp. 13–

32; IAS, *40 AR*, p. 9; *53 AR*, pp. 12–13; *59 AR*, pp. 12–13; *63 AR*, pp. 10–13; *73 AR*, pp. 8–9; *77 AR*, pp. 8–9; *82 AR*, p. 8; MBSL, *24 AR*, pp. 86–104, 208–15; Society of St. Vincent de Paul, *First Annual Report of the Metropolitan Central Council of Boston* (Boston, 1914), pp. 4–15; *Report of the Bureau of Employment and Relief of the Worcester Chamber of Commerce, November 1914–April 1915* (Worcester, 1915), pp. 4–8; *Annual Report of the Board of Overseers of the Poor, Worcester, Mass.* (1920), p. 6, and (1922), p. 7; New York *Times*, April 25, 1919; Springfield *Union*, Feb. 5, 1915; AS-W, *24 AR*, p. 11; *25 AR*, pp. 18–19; Andover House Association, *Third Yearly Report, circular number 11* (Cambridge, Mass., 1894), pp. 6–7; Klein, *Burden of Unemployment*, pp. 77, 81, 133–8, 223–4, 237; National Civic Federation: New England Section, *Report on Unemployment among Boston Women in 1915*, prepared by Eleanor A. Woods, assisted by Sue Ainslee Clark (n.p., n.d.), unpaged; Family Service Association, archival collection; Feder, *Relief*, pp. 80, 124, 147–8, 180–1; and Edith P. Estes, "Boston's Unemployed," *Harper's Weekly* 38 (March 3, 1894): 197.

21 BISU Hearings, pp. 396, 621, 718, 760, 808, 962–3, 1109–10, 1141–2, 1196, 1201–2, 1358, 1370, 1380, 1475; *BISU Report*, part I; AC-B, *4 AR*, p. 54; *19 AR*, pp. 34–5; *23 AR*, pp. 24–34; *29 AR*, pp. 44–5; *35 AR*, pp. 24–5, 30–1; Boston Provident Association, *Annual Report 1884–5* (Boston, 1885), p. 7; IAS, *38 AR*, pp. 4–6; MBSL, *24 AR*, pp. 86–104; Feder, *Relief*, pp. 60ff., 80ff.; AC-W, *24 AR*, p. 11; Society of St. Vincent de Paul, *Eighteenth Annual Report of the Central Council of Boston* (Boston, 1907), p. 11; *Nineteenth Annual Report of the Central Council of Boston* (Boston, 1908), pp. 6–9; *Seventh Annual Report of the Metropolitan Central Council of Boston* (Boston, 1920), pp. 5–45. See Chapter 9 regarding changes in relief policy and administration.

22 *BISU Report*, part I, especially pp. xxvii, 26–8, and part V, p. ix; MBSL, *24 AR*, pp. 86–104, 169; Estes, "Boston's Unemployed," p. 197; Feder, *Relief*, pp. 80, 124, 147–8, 180–1; Springfield *Union*, Feb. 5 and 11, 1915; Family Welfare Society of Boston, "The Faith that Is in Us," *Forty-third Annual Report* (Boston, 1922); AC-B, *20 AR*, pp. 26–7; *Lend a Hand, A Record of Progress* 12, no. 2 (Feb. 1894): 128–33; *The American City* 25, no. 6 (Dec. 1921): 501–2; BISU Hearings, pp. 396, 1141–2.

23 "How to Relieve Distress among the Poor This Winter," signed by 19 separate charitable organizations and published in AC-B, *13 AR*, unpaged; BISU Hearings, pp. 396, 437–9, 1359, 1370, 1380, 1452, 1467; AC-B, *29 AR*, p. 14; AC-W, *25 AR*, pp. 18–19; *BISU Report*, part V, app. B; "What I Went Through in Trying to Get a Position," *Ladies Home Journal*, March 15, 1911, pp. 15–6, 49; *Lend a Hand* 12, no. 2 (Feb. 1894): 128. Public works projects that were started during depressions constituted something of an exception to these policies. Men who were hired to work on such projects were generally not obliged to prove their need or their moral worth. See Chapter 9.

24 Boston *Globe*, Feb. 20, 1894; *BISU Report*, part I, pp. xlv–xlvi, lvi, 18, 28, 151, and part V, app. B; BISU Hearings, pp. 340, 464, 505, 540, 657, 713, 763, 871–2, 1198, 1264, 1469; MBSL, *24 AR*, pp. 84–5, 202–13; IAS, *47 AR*,

p. 9; *53 AR*, pp. 12–13; *78 AR*, p. 8; AC-B, *15 AR*, pp. 26–7; *36 AR*, pp. 16–19; Springfield *Union*, Feb. 5, 1915; Edwin Brown, *"Broke": The Man without the Dime* (Boston, 1920), p. 299; Boston Provident Association, *Report 70–2* (1920–3), pp. 6–7; Rice, "The Effect of Unemployment," p. 106; Emma O. Lundberg, *Unemployment and Child Welfare: A Study Made in a Middle Western and an Eastern City during the Industrial Depression of 1921 and 1922*, U.S. Department of Labor, Children's Bureau publication no. 125 (Washington, 1923), p. 82.

25   MBSL, *Bulletin 46*, pp. 68–9; MBSL, *38 AR*, pp. 420ff.; IAS, *37 AR*, pp. 3–4; *BISU Report*, part V, app. B. For examples of the reports on the activities of the Free Employment Offices, see MBSL, *Quarterly Reports*, nos. 17–36.

26   AC-B, *18 AR*, p. 23; MBSL, *Bulletin 48*, pp. 230–40; *Bulletin 54*, pp. 294–6.

27   Letter from G. G. (full name withheld at request of Schlesinger Library) to Mr. Greener, Oct. 20, 1921, in papers of North Bennet Street Industrial School (file MC 269 II A ix, 43), Schlesinger Library, Radcliffe College, Cambridge, Mass.

28   MBSL, *24 AR*, pp. 166–7; *BISU Report*, part I, p. 27; Lundberg, *Child Welfare*, pp. 30, 82–3.

29   *BISU Report*, part V, app. B, pp. 17, 78.

30   The strategies that workers used to cope with unemployment between 1870 and 1922 appear to have been much the same as those used by jobless men and women later in the 1920s and during the Great Depression. Regarding the 1920s, see note 2. The literature on the 1930s is abundant and well-known. Perhaps the most valuable studies, for comparative purposes, are E. Wight Bakke, *The Unemployed Worker* (New Haven, Conn., 1940) and *Citizens without Work* (New Haven, Conn., 1940); Marie Jahoda, Paul Lazarsfeld, and Hans Zeisel, *Marienthal: The Sociography of an Unemployed Community* (Chicago, 1971); Mirra Komarovsky, *The Unemployed Man and His Family* (New York, 1940); and Robert C. Angell, *The Family Encounters the Depression* (New York, 1936).

31   *Lend a Hand* 12, no. 2 (Feb. 1894): 126–7. See also Nathan I. Huggins, *Protestants against Poverty: Boston's Charities, 1870–1900* (Westport, Conn., 1971), pp. 39–42.

32   *Report of the Commission on the Cost of Living, Massachusetts House Document 1750* (Boston, 1910), p. 741; *BISU Report*, part V, app. B; MBSL, *24 AR*, p. 161; Klein, *Burden of Unemployment*, pp. 24–5; Rice, "Effect of Unemployment," p. 103; BISU Hearings, pp. 538, 698, 903, 910, 1426; AC-B, *29 AR*, pp. 11, 14, 32, 39.

33   MBSL, *3 AR*, p. 293; *10 AR*, p. 122; *24 AR*, pp. 160–1; AC-B, *11 AR*, p. 22; *29 AR*, p. 49; *30 AR*, p. 37; *BISU Report*, part I, p. 27; Lundberg, *Child Welfare*, pp. 34–5, 52–5, 60–1, 82–3.

34   Boston *Globe*, Dec. 19, 1893; "Unemployment Survey, 1914–15," *ALLR* 5 (Nov. 1915): 489; BISU Hearings, pp. 538–40, 638–9, 697; AC-W, *4 AR*, p. 4.

35   Only 197 of the 406 members of the Brockton male shoe workers sample

were the sole wage earners in their household; 109 belonged to households in which there were boarders. Of the 239 male household heads, 175 were the sole wage earners in their households; in 33 households, there were children at work, and in 32 there was at least one boarder. The case records of charity organizations also suggest that a sizable number of nonnuclear households contained two or more relatives (e.g., siblings), both of whom worked. *BISU Report*, part V, app. B; MBSL, *6 AR*, pp. 212, 357–75. Klein, "Burden of Unemployment," pp. 22, 28–9; *Report of the Commission on Immigration on the Problem of Immigration in Massachusetts, House Document 2300* (Boston, 1914), pp. 61, 243.

The recent literature on the importance of the household economy in the nineteenth and early twentieth centuries is richly detailed and valuable. See Modell, "Patterns of Consumption"; Modell and Hareven, "Urbanization and the Malleable Household"; Modell, Frank F. Furstenberg, Jr., and Theodore Hershberg, "Social Change and Transitions to Adulthood in Historical Perspective," in Michael Gordon, ed., *The American Family in Social-Historical Perspective*, 2d ed. (New York, 1978), pp. 192–219; Hareven and Maris A. Vinovskis, "Patterns of Childbearing in Late Nineteenth-Century America: The Determinants of Marital Fertility in Five Massachusetts Towns in 1880," in Hareven and Vinovskis, eds., *Family and Population*, pp. 85–125; Claudia Goldin, "Household and Market Production of Families in a Late Nineteenth Century American City," *Explorations in Economic History* 16 (1979): 111–31; Goldin, "Family Strategies and the Family Economy in the Late Nineteenth Century: The Role of Secondary Workers," in Theodore Hershberg, ed., *Philadelphia: Work, Space, Family, and Group Experience in the Nineteenth Century* (New York, 1981), pp. 277–310; and Michael R. Haines, "Poverty, Economic Stress, and the Family in a Late Nineteenth-Century American City: Whites in Philadelphia, 1880," in Hershberg, ed., *Philadelphia*, pp. 240–76.

36 "Report on a Study of the Italian Quarter in Boston," by Miss Skinner, dated June 20, 1910, in North Bennet Street papers, box X, folder 31, p. 6; "Report of Special Inquiry in the North End," by Lila Verplanck North, dated Jan. 1914, in North Bennet Street papers, box XII, folders 10 and 10a, pp. 31, 44–6. See also Woods, *Americans in Process*, p. 125. Cf. Goldin, "Family Strategies."

37 "Study of the Industrial Future of North End Children," in North, "Report of Special Inquiry," pp. 1–8 (see also pp. 14, 27); AC-B, *25 AR*, pp. 35–7; *29 AR*, pp. 30, 46; Lundberg, *Child Welfare*, pp. 34, 65, 83; AC-W, *19 AR*, p. 1; BISU Hearings, p. 885; *BISU Report*, part V, app. B.

38 Cf. Elderton, ed., *Case Studies*; Calkins, *Some Folks*; Bakke, *Unemployed Worker*.

39 MBSL, *2 AR*, p. 134; *4 AR*, pp. 290–1; BISU Hearings, pp. 796–7.

40 Boston *Globe*, Feb. 13 and 27, 1894; *BISU Report*, part V, app. B, esp. pp. 61, 64, 70, 71, 75; MBSL, *2 AR*, p. 417; *3 AR*, p. 33; *24 AR*, p. 161; MBSL, *Bulletin 57*, pp. 53–62; *Bulletin 75*, p. 1; Woods, *City Wilderness*, pp. 42–3; IAS, *42 AR*, p. 5; *43 AR*, p. 4; *44 AR*, p. 15; *68 AR*, p. 7; Lundberg, *Child Welfare*, pp. 27–33, 83; AC-B, *19 AR*, p. 35; *20 AR*, p. 50; *29 AR*, pp. 33,

40–1, 45, 50; Springfield *Union*, Dec. 22, 1914; *Labor News* (Worcester), Feb. 25, 1921.

41 BISU Hearings, p. 361; AC-B, *10 AR*, p. 28; *17 AR*, p. 38; *22 AR*, p. 32; *29 AR*, p. 47; *36 AR*, p. 18; Springfield *Union*, Dec. 12, 1914; Lundberg, *Child Welfare*, pp. 28, 48–53; NFS survey files for the Daly family (Jamaica Plain) and the Moran family (Roxbury) in the Helen Hall papers, folders 396–407 (all names in these case study files were changed by the settlement house workers themselves); Family Service Association archival collection. In the sample of Boston's day laborers, drawn from the 1900 manuscript census schedules (see Chapter 4), 11.9% of all unemployed household heads ($n = 59$) had boarders, while only 4.9% of household heads who worked year-round ($n = 81$) had boarders.

42 See Chapter 4; National Civic Federation, *Report on Unemployment among Boston Women in 1915*, unpaged. The figures for married women presented in Table 6.2 are derived from two separate random samples drawn from the 1900 manuscript census schedules. The sample of married women in the paid labor force is a subgroup of the sample of working women in Brockton presented in Chapter 4 (see Table 4.9). It consists of all married women, working in either the shoe or other industries, who were in the labor force and who lived with their husbands. (A notable by-product of this breakdown was the discovery that 44 of the 100 women in that sample who identified themselves as "married" were, in fact, not living with their husbands.) The sample of "married women at home" was drawn separately from the census schedules. (This sampling strategy was necessary in order to produce a sufficiently large number of married working women.) Differences between the two groups were reported as significant if, using a difference of proportions test, they were statistically significant at a level of at least .05.

Since the census schedules do not reveal the date of a person's entry into the labor force, there is no way to be certain that these women began to work only after their husbands lost their jobs. It is, in fact, likely that some of these married women were working for pay prior to the unemployment of their husbands, that their participation in the labor force was more a matter of self-insurance than an emergency response to joblessness. But given the unpredictability of unemployment, it is very unlikely that the observed difference between the two samples was entirely the result of decisions made before the male household head was laid off. The most plausible interpretation of the figures is that both strategies (self-insurance and emergency income production) were operating among sample members and that some of these married women did, in fact, enter the paid labor force because their husbands were laid off.

43 Lundberg, *Child Welfare*, pp. 28–30, 129–32; AC-B, *29 AR*, p. 49. See Chapter 4 regarding teenage unemployment levels.

44 Of all male household head shoe workers who were unemployed for three months or longer ($n = 177$), 22.1% had children who were at work; only 9.9% ($n = 162$) of those who worked steadily or were jobless for one or two months had children in the labor force. In the sample of

Boston's day laborers, 52.5% ($n = 59$) of all unemployed household heads had other wage earners in the family, while the percentage was only 38.3 ($n = 81$) for those who worked year-round. (See Chapter 4 regarding these samples.) That similar patterns occurred in other occupations (and among laborers and shoe workers who lived elsewhere) is suggested by data presented in MBSL, *32 AR*, pp. 268–85.

45 The figures dealing with children in Table 6.2 are based upon a random sample of 14- to 16-year-old children drawn from the 1900 census manuscripts for Brockton. (An attempt was made to hold the occupation of the father constant by looking only at the children of members of the shoe worker sample, but this method produced groupings far too small for any analytic purposes.) As with the samples of married women, there is no way of determining precisely when these working children entered the labor force, and consequently the caveats mentioned in note 42 apply to the statistics for children as well. Significance was noted when the difference between two figures was significant at a level of at least .05, using a difference of proportions test. Why girls appear to have been more affected than boys by the unemployment of their fathers is unclear. Since Goldin finds the opposite pattern in Philadelphia in 1880, the explanation may reside in the type of employment opportunities available in local labor markets. Goldin, "Household and Market Production," p. 124; "Family Strategies and the Family Economy," p. 291.

46 Regarding the legal working age of children, see Forest Chester Ensign, *Compulsory School Attendance and Child Labor* (Iowa City, 1921), pp. 46–86.

47 Boston *Globe*, Feb. 25, 1894; *BISU Report*, part I, app. B, pp. 65–86; BISU Hearings, p. 464; AC-B, *29 AR*, pp. 50–2; Woods, *Americans in Process*, pp. 128–9; Klein, *Burden of Unemployment*, pp. 32–6; *Labor News*, Feb. 27, 1915; Paul H. Douglas and Aaron Director, *The Problem of Unemployment* (New York, 1931), pp. 64–6; Lundberg, *Child Welfare*, pp. 48–51, 72–3; "What I Went Through in Trying to Get a Position," pp. 15–16, 45. As Ruth Milkman has noted, many of the methods utilized to reduce expenses involved additional labor on the part of women. Ruth Milkman, "Women's Work and the Economic Crisis," *Review of Radical Political Economics* 8 (Spring 1976): 73–97.

48 MBSL, *10 AR*, p. 138; Lundberg, *Child Welfare*, pp. 26–7; AC-B, *29 AR*, p. 49; Klein, *Burden of Unemployment*, pp. 29, 31; *BISU Report*, part V, app. B. There were changes of address, within Brockton, in 10.2% of all households headed by unemployed male shoe workers ($n = 127$). See Chapter 5 regarding tracing methods.

49 In households that contained only one wage earner (the head of household), the rate of mobility within Brockton was 13.2% ($n = 91$); in households that contained more than one wage earner, the figure was 2.8% ($n = 36$). One-third of the twelve unemployed household heads who had boarders ended up leaving Brockton altogether by 1901; the figure for household heads without boarders was 18.3% ($n = 115$). See Chapter 5.

50 Lundberg, *Child Welfare*, pp. 66–79, 112–3; AC–B, *17 AR*, pp. 38–9; *29 AR*, pp. 32, 34, 38–9, 42–4; *30 AR*, p. 37; MBSL, *10 AR*, p. 138; IAS, *39*

AR, pp. 14–15; *42 AR,* p. 19; *43 AR,* p. 14; *BISU Report,* part V, app. B, esp. pp. 61, 63, 64, 65, 67–72, 77, 78, 82, 83; BISU Hearings, pp. 466, 691.

51 "Unemployment Survey, 1914–1915," p. 489; Boston *Globe,* Feb. 27, 1894; Woods, *City Wilderness,* pp. 92–3; Feder, *Relief,* p. 140; MBSL, *24 AR,* p. 160; Lundberg, *Child Welfare,* pp. 29–31, 34–5, 62, 66–79, 83, 112–13; *BISU Report,* part V, app. B; AC-B, *29 AR,* pp. 11, 39–44; *30 AR,* p. 37.

52 Lundberg, *Child Welfare,* pp. 68–9. The family described here lived either in Springfield, Mass., or in Racine, Wis., the two cities that Lundberg studied.

53 Klein, *Burden of Unemployment,* pp. 26–8; Lundberg, *Child Welfare,* pp. 66–75. The proportion of loans that were purely commercial transactions may have increased during this period.

54 AC-B, *19 AR,* p. 27; *29 AR,* pp. 12, 14, 43–9; *37 AR,* p. 13; MBSL, *24 AR,* pp. 160–1; Lundberg, *Child Welfare,* pp. 29, 31, 82; "Example Eleven," in North, "Report of Special Inquiry," p. 36; Klein, *Burden of Unemployment,* pp. 26–8; *BISU Report,* part V, app. A; BISU Hearings, p. 537; regarding the rate of return migration, see note 73.

55 AC-B, *29 AR,* pp. 12, 14, 46, 49; *30 AR,* p. 37; *37 AR,* p. 13; Society of St. Vincent de Paul, *18 AR,* p. 19; Woods, *City Wilderness,* pp. 92–3, BISU Hearings, pp. 537, 924; MBSL, *24 AR,* p. 161; Brown, *"Broke",* pp. 161–2; "The Portuguese in Boston," *North End Mission Magazine* 2, no. 3 (July 1873): 59; *BISU Report,* part V, app. B.

56 AC-B, *29 AR,* p. 41; *36 AR,* p. 17; Klein, *Burden of Unemployment,* p. 145. For a detailed account of trade union efforts to aid the unemployed, see Chapter 7.

57 Boston *Globe,* Dec. 9 and 18, 1893, Feb. 1 and 23, 1894; Walter A. Wyckoff, *A Day with a Tramp* (New York, 1901), p. 32; BISU Hearings, pp. 341, 510, 749; Maurice Parmelee, *Poverty and Social Progress* (New York, 1920), p. 289.

58 William D. Howells, *A Traveler from Alturia* (New York, 1957; orig. pub. New York, 1894), pp. 105–6.

59 Cf. Woods, *City Wilderness,* p. 93.

60 The best descriptive materials regarding the psychological effects of unemployment in the late 1920s are contained in Elderton, ed., *Case Studies.* For the 1930s, see Bakke, *Unemployed Workers* and *Citizens without Work;* Komarovsky, *Unemployed Man and His Family;* Philip Eisenberg and Paul F. Lazarsfeld, "The Psychological Effects of Unemployment," *Psychological Bulletin* 35 (1938): 358–90; Bohan Zawadski and Paul Lazarsfeld, "The Psychological Consequences of Unemployment," *Journal of Social Psychology* 6 (1935): 224–51. Studies conducted in more recent years are less impressionistic and more quantitative but not necessarily more penetrating; see, e.g., Donald W. Tiffany, James R. Cowan, and Phyllis M. Tiffany, *The Unemployed: A Social-Psychological Portrait* (Englewood Cliffs, N.J., 1970); Stanislav V. Kasl, Susan Gore, and Sidney Cobb, "The Experience of Losing a Job: Reported Changes in Health, Symptoms and Illness Behavior," *Psychosomatic Medicine* 37 (March–April 1975): 106–21.

61 Robert H. Bremner, *From the Depths* (New York, 1956), pp. 14–15; Bakke, *Unemployed Worker*, p. 25; AC-B, *28 AR*, pp. 30–3.

62 MBSL, *10 AR*, p. 118; IAS, *44 AR*, p. 14; Rice, "Effect of Unemployment," pp. 107–9; NFS survey file for the Taber family (Roxbury) in Helen Hall Papers, folders 396–407; Walter A. Wyckoff, *The Workers: An Experiment in Reality: The West* (New York, 1898), pp. 49–50, 76, 120ff., 130; Whiting Williams, *What's on the Worker's Mind* (New York, 1921), pp. 6, 39, 154, 206–7; MBSL, *Bulletin 32*, p. 225.

63 NFS survey file for Sciarro family (Cambridge) and Moran family (Roxbury) in Helen Hall Papers, folders 396–407; Williams, *Worker's Mind*, pp. 6, 76, 154, 256, 259–60; Wyckoff, *The Workers: The West*, pp. 2, 46–50; *The Survey* 45 (Feb. 19, 1921): 735–6; *American Federationist* 5, no. 12 (Feb. 1899): 239; Rice, "Effect of Unemployment," pp. 107ff.; Stuart Rice, "Psychological Effects of Unemployment on the Jobless Man," *ALLR* 15 (March 1925): 45–9; David Montgomery, *Workers' Control in America* (Cambridge, 1979), pp. 35–6; Klein, *Burden of Unemployment*, p. 37.

64 NFS survey files for Sciarro family (Cambridge), Murphy family (Boston), and Daly family (Jamaica Plain) in Helen Hall papers, folders 396–407; Rice, "Effect of Unemployment," pp. 107ff.; Klein, *Burden of Unemployment*, p. 37; Elderton, *Case Studies*, p. 382; National Civic Federation, *Report on Unemployment among Boston Women in 1915*, unpaged.

65 BISU *Report*, part V, app. B; "Three Typical Workingmen," *Atlantic Monthly* 42 (Dec. 1878): 717; *The Carpenter* 38, no. 4 (April 1918): 16; Rice, "Effect of Unemployment," pp. 100–7. Cf. Bakke, *Unemployed Worker*, and Angell, *The Family.*

66 The Taber family history was compiled by the Roxbury Neighborhood House; the Murphy family history was assembled by Lincoln House in Boston. (The names were changed on the survey schedules themselves in order to protect the privacy of the families.) Both these family histories were compiled in the winter of 1928–9. Helen Hall Papers, folders 396–407.

67 Boston *Globe*, April 7, 1894; *Labor News*, Feb. 25, 1921. See also Terence Powderly, "The Army of Unemployed," in George McNeill, ed., *The Labor Movement: The Problem of Today* (Milwaukee, 1891), p. 577; IAS, *40 AR*, p. 11; *The Carpenter* 28, no. 10 (Oct. 1908): 3; M. Harvey Brenner, *Mental Illness and the Economy* (Cambridge, Mass., 1973), pp. 35–73, 190–2, 230.

68 Records of the Medical Examiners, 1895/Executive Office of Public Safety/ Medical Examiners' Records (Archives of the Commonwealth, Boston), pp. 818–19, 1026–7; 1896, pp. 728–9, 786–7, 894–5, 924–5. Initials (and, in some cases, other personal identifiers) have been altered in compliance with archival regulations. Slightly more than a dozen cases of unemployment-related suicide were discovered in an examination of all suicide records in the medical examiners' files for the years 1895 and 1896.

69 MBSL, *Bulletin 57*, p. 60.

70 Rice, "Effect of Unemployment," pp. 105–9; Vera Shlakman, *Economic History of a Factory Town: A Study of Chicopee, Massachusetts*, Smith College

Studies in History 20 (Northampton, Mass., 1934–5), pp. 193–4; Don D. Lescohier, *The Labor Market* (New York, 1919), p. 307; *The Family*, I (Jan. 1921): 4–9.

71 Frances Kellor, *Out of Work* (New York, 1915), pp. 30–1; Lescohier, *Labor Market*, pp. 107, 263ff.; Parmelee, *Poverty*, p. 127; *BISU Report*, part I, p. 39; Wyckoff, *The Workers: The West*, p. 249; Helen Hall Papers, folders 396–407. Cf. Stephan Thernstrom, *The Other Bostonians: Poverty and Progress in the American Metropolis, 1880–1970* (Cambridge, Mass., 1976; orig. pub. 1973), pp. 64–70.

72 BISU Hearings, p. 780; North, "Report of Special Inquiry," pp. 53–6; AC-B, *27 AR*, pp. 9–10; *SWJ* 22, no. 5 (May 1921): 6; Kellor, *Out of Work*, p. 30; MBSL, *Bulletin 30*, p. 75; *Bulletin 46*, p. 67; MBSL, *44 AR*, p. 350.

73 Philip S. Foner, *American Labor Songs of the Nineteenth Century* (Urbana, 1975), pp. 286–7; Shlakman, *Economic History*, pp. 137, 215; David Brody, *Steelworkers in America: The Nonunion Era* (New York, 1969; orig. pub. Cambridge, Mass., 1960), p. 105; Feder, *Relief*, p. 191; IAS, *40 AR*, p. 9. For statistics regarding return migration to Europe from the United States and from Massachusetts, see MBSL, *39 AR*, p. 16; *44 AR*, part III, p. 12; and MBSL, *Bulletin 75*, p. 92; *Bulletin 81*, pp. 8, 24; *Bulletin 90*, pp. 59, 62. Immigrants seem to have been less likely to return to their country of origin during the cyclical downturn of 1920–2 than they had been during earlier depressions. See Klein, *Burden of Unemployment*, pp. 29–31.

74 Cited in Lescohier, *Labor Market*, p. 108. See also Kellor, *Out of Work*, pp. 30–1; *SWJ* 22, no. 5 (May 1921): 6; *The Family*, I (Jan. 1921): 4–9.

75 See Chapters 3 and 5. Cf. Woods, *City Wilderness*, p. 3, and Robert A. Woods and Albert J. Kennedy, *Zone of Emergence* (Cambridge, Mass., 1962), pp. 68–85. The proportion of unemployed workers who had access to informal support networks may also have been lessened by the postwar increase (see note 73) in the percentage of immigrants who remained in the United States when they were jobless.

7. Organizing labor

1 BISU Hearings, pp. 376, 587, 822.

2 MBSL, *Bulletin 10*, pp. 48–55; George E. McNeill, ed., *The Labor Movement: The Problem of To-day* (Milwaukee, 1891), pp. 137–54, 220, 276, 278, 371; David Montgomery, *Beyond Equality: Labor and the Radical Republicans, 1862–1872* (New York, 1972; orig. pub. 1967), pp. 124, 136–41; Constance M. Green, *Holyoke, Massachusetts: A Case History of the Industrial Revolution in America* (New Haven, Conn., 1939), p. 196. Alan Dawley, *Class and Community: The Industrial Revolution in Lynn* (Cambridge, Mass., 1976), pp. 175–89; MBSL, *8 AR*, p. 42; Augusta E. Galster, *The Labor Movement in the Shoe Industry* (New York, 1924), p. 43; Don D. Lescohier, *The Knights of Saint Crispin 1867–74* (Madison, Wis., 1910), pp. 5–55.

3 Philip S. Foner, *History of the Labor Movement in the United States*, 6 vols.

(New York, 1947–82), I, pp. 167–70, 219–23; MBSL, *Bulletin 10*, p. 55; McNeill, *Labor Movement*, pp. 89, 122.

4   McNeill, *Labor Movement*, pp. 170, 423; *Labor Leader*, Aug. 27, 1887.

5   MBSL, *39 AR*, pp. 158, 185; *41 AR*, p. 237; *44 AR*, p. 330; *47 AR*, part IV, p. 9, and part VI, pp. 7, 22; *52 AR*, part III, pp. 8–26; Vera Shlakman, *Economic History of a Factory Town: A Study of Chicopee, Massachusetts*, Smith College Studies in History 20 (Northampton, Mass., 1934–5), p. 213; Lloyd Ulman, *The Rise of the National Trade Union* (Cambridge, Mass., 1966), pp. 4–6.

6   MBSL, *47 AR*, part VI, p. 22; *52 AR*, part III, pp. 8–26.

7   MBSL, *39 AR*, pp. 156–7; *42 AR*, p. 80; *46 AR*, part IX, p. 7; *49 AR*, part IV, p. 19; *52 AR*, pp. 21–6. The estimate that less than one-quarter of the labor force was organized is based on a comparison of the trade union membership figures reported to the MBSL with the labor force figures, for men and women, reported in: *Mass. Census, 1915* (Boston, 1918), pp. 490–1, and *Fourteenth Census of the United States, Population*, IV (Washington, 1923), pp. 941–6.

8   MBSL, *10 AR*, p. 133; *38 AR*, p. 15; *39 AR*, pp. 26–30, 38; *40 AR*, p. 126; *47 AR*, part IX, p. 9; MBSL, *Quarterly Report 32*, p. 3; *Quarterly Report 35*, p. 1; MBSL, *Bulletin 25*, pp. 40–3; BISU Hearings, p. 373; *Labor Leader*, Oct. 8, 1887; *SWJ* 6, no. 6 (June 1905): 10. Cf. David Montgomery, *Workers' Control in America* (Cambridge, 1979), pp. 93–6.

9   MBSL, *25 AR*, pp. 309ff.; MBSL, *Bulletin 7*, pp. 12–13; Boston *Globe*, Feb. 8, 9, 10, and 13, 1894; McNeill, *Labor Movement*, pp. 226–8, 237–9; BISU Hearings, p. 495; *Labor News* (Worcester), Sept. 19, Dec. 3, 1920; *Labor Leader*, Aug. 25, 1888; March 31, 1894.

10   MBSL, *12 AR*, pp. 63–4; *38 AR*, pp. 9, 15; *39 AR*, pp. 38, 40–6, 63ff.; MBSL, *Bulletin 25*, pp. 40–3; MBSL, *Quarterly Report 35*, p. 1. See also McNeill, *Labor Movement*, p. 602; Montgomery, *Workers' Control*, p. 94; Shlakman, *Economic History*, p. 214; Ulman, *Rise*, pp. 426–41; and Gerald Grob, *Workers and Utopia* (Chicago, 1969; orig. pub. Evanston, Ill., 1961), pp. 37, 147. For a valuable assembly of strike statistics, in general and for Massachusetts, see John I. Griffin, *Strikes* (New York, 1939), esp. chap. 7.

11   MBSL, *Bulletin 34*, pp. 320–2; Boston *Evening Transcript*, Dec. 23, 1910; MBSL, *38 AR*, p. 493; Ulman, *Rise*, p. 447; Thomas L. Norton, *Trade-Union Policies in the Massachusetts Shoe Industry, 1919–1929* (New York, 1932), p. 133.

12   BISU Hearings, p. 524; see also pp. 114, 178–80. For further evidence of the complexity and difficulty of the problem as perceived in labor circles, see *Labor Leader*, May 7, Aug. 13, 1887; Nov. 17, 1888; Dec. 23, 1893; Jan. 6, 13, and 20, 1894; *The Carpenter* 29, no. 4 (April 1909): 44, 70; vol. 31, no. 11 (Nov. 1911): 7–8; and *SWJ* 22, no. 9 (Sept. 1921): 15.

13   MBSL, *26 AR*, p. 718. Suspicions that employers were laying more men off than was necessary seem to have been voiced most frequently in the early 1920s. See, e.g., *Labor News*, Nov. 19, Dec. 3, 1920, March 4, 1921; and *SWJ* 22, no. 3 (March 1921): 15.

14 MBSL, *10 AR*, p. 118; Montgomery, *Beyond Equality*, pp. 249–60; Joseph Dorfman, *The Economic Mind in American Civilization*, 5 vols. (New York, 1946–59), III, parts 2, 3, 4. BISU Hearings, p. 512; Ulman, *Rise*, p. 442; D. P. Smelser, *Unemployment and American Trade Unions* (Baltimore, 1919), p. 34. As discussed later in this chapter, trade unionists did begin to place some emphasis on the possibilities of public sector job creation, through public works programs, toward the end of the period.

15 McNeill, *Labor Movement*, pp. 411, 515–23; *Labor Leader*, Jan. 8, 1887; Dec. 10, 1887; Aug. 4, 1888; MBSL, *17 AR*, pp. 195–229.

16 BISU Hearings, pp. 180, 893, 929; Samuel Gompers, *Seventy Years of Life and Labor: An Autobiography*, 2 vols. (New York, 1925), II, 4–11; *Labor Leader*, Sept. 3, 1887.

17 Henry F. Bedford, *Socialism and the Workers in Massachusetts, 1886–1912* (Amherst, Mass., 1966), pp. 2, 5, 50, 88–96, 128, 181, 212, 233–8, 277; *Labor Leader*, Dec. 23, 1893; *BISU Report*, part V, app. H, p. 130; *The Carpenter* 32, no. 8 (Aug. 1912): 24–5. For an expression of the socialist view, see Morris Hillquit, "Unemployment" in *World Tomorrow* 4 (Feb. 1921): 38–41.

18 There were, of course, other systemic diagnoses of the problem of unemployment in addition to the socialist and cooperative ones. For examples of the single tax and Bellamyite views, see *Labor Leader*, Dec. 23, 1893; J. H. Schonfarber to G. F. Morland, Oct. 8, 1894, in BISU Hearings; *BISU Report*, part III, pp. 109–17; *Labor News*, March 20, 1915.

19 Cf. Smelser, *Unemployment*, pp. 29ff.

20 McNeill, *Labor Movement*, p. 607; BISU Hearings, p. 144.

21 BISU Hearings, pp. 86, 201, and J. Goldberg to William M. Cole, July 17, 1894, and Mr. Reilly of Local 216 of the United Brotherhood of Carpenters and Joiners to the Board, July 31, 1894; *BISU Report*, part V, app. F, pp. 112–22; MBSL, *Bulletin 28*, p. 207; Boston *Globe*, April 15, 1894; *Labor Leader*, Nov. 19, Dec. 10, 1887; *The Carpenter* 32, no. 2 (Feb. 1912): 36; Smelser, *Unemployment*, pp. 55ff., 64–7, 81–90.

22 Bryce M. Stewart, *Unemployment Benefits in the United States* (New York, 1930), pp. 80–3, 206, 256; Smelser, *Unemployment*, pp. 130–46; *SWJ* 6, no. 12 (Dec. 1905): 7–8; *The Carpenter* 35, no. 3 (March 1915): 4–5; also vol. 38, no. 4 (April 1918): 15–16.

23 See Chapter 6 regarding the limited availability of trade union benefit programs. See also *Labor Leader*, Oct. 1, 1887; BISU Hearings, pp. 80, 86, 127, 138, 144, 561, 659, 671, 743, 1006; MBSL, *26 AR*, p. 718; Smelser, *Unemployment*, pp. 130–47; John B. Andrews, "Out-of-Work Benefits," in *Business Cycles and Unemployment: Report and Recommendations of a Committee of the President's Conference on Unemployment* (New York, 1923), pp. 294–5.

24 BISU Hearings, pp. 34, 51, 132, 142, 155, 165, 176, 193, 385, 726, 915, as well as Thomas F. Gallagher of the Clothing Cutters' and Trimmers' Union to the Board, Aug. 4, 1894, and undated letter from Local 151, Waltham, of the Cigarmakers' Union; Boston *Globe*, March 13, 1909; *SWJ* 6, no. 4 (April 1905): 26; Frank Stockton, *The International Molders' Union*

of North America (Baltimore, 1921), pp. 23, 67–8; Andrews, "Out-of-Work Benefits," p. 299; Smelser, *Unemployment*, pp. 99–102, 145, 148.

25 John Griffin, recording secretary, to William Cole, in BISU Hearings.

26 MBSL, *26 AR*, p. 711; *30 AR*, pp. 79, 140–1; *34 AR*, p. 417; *36 AR*, p. 553; *42 AR*, pp. 128–37; Smelser, *Unemployment*, pp. 54–6.

27 *Labor Leader*, Oct. 27, 1894; MBSL, *25 AR*, p. 308; *American Federationist* 1, no. 1 (March 1894): 13; *Labor News*, Nov. 4, 1921; Ulman, *Rise*, p. 546; Smelser, *Unemployment*, pp. 110, 117, 120–3.

28 MBSL, *Bulletin 33*, p. 252; *Bulletin 34*, p. 365; MBSL, *24 AR*, p. 281; *42 AR*, pp. 230–1; Smelser, *Unemployment*, pp. 113–29; Norton, *Trade-Union Policies*, pp. 135–8, 216, 223, 239; Hermann Schluter, *The Brewery Industry and the Brewery Workers' Movement in America* (Cincinnati, 1910), p. 219. The brewery workers appear to have had a "rotation of lay-off" clause in their contract as early as 1893. For an employer's attitude toward such contracts, see the form filed by the Roeggle Brewery Company with the Boston Chamber of Commerce, in BCC, "Questions on Seasonal Employment," Baker Library, Harvard Business School (see Chapter 3, note 21).

29 Smelser, *Unemployment*, pp. 45–9; Ulman, *Rise*, pp. 540–61; David Brody, *Steelworkers in America: The Nonunion Era* (New York, 1969; orig. pub. Cambridge, Mass., 1960), p. 70; Montgomery, *Workers' Control*, pp. 12–15, 115, 125, 143; Jacob H. Hollander and George E. Barnett, eds., *Studies in American Trade Unionism* (London, 1906), pp. 295ff., 305–8; Pearce Davis, *The Development of the American Glass Industry* (Cambridge, Mass., 1949), pp. 128–9, 144; Stanley Mathewson, *The Restriction of Output Among Unorganized Workers* (New York, 1931), pp. 6, 15, 86–102, 161–2. See also U.S. Commissioner of Labor, *Regulation and Restriction of Output, Eleventh Special Report* (Washington, 1904).

30 Smelser, *Unemployment*, pp. 112, 120–9; Ulman, *Rise*, pp. 546–7; Norton, *Trade-Union Policies*, pp. 216–41.

31 BISU Hearings, pp. 148, 320, 794, 838, 972, 1244–9, 1275, 1517; *Labor Leader*, Feb. 5, 1887, Aug. 11 and 18, 1888; *BISU Report*, part III, pp. 104–18; Samuel Rezneck, "Patterns of Thought and Action in an American Depression, 1882–1886," *American Historical Review* 61 (1956): 301–2; see also note 18.

32 McNeill, *Labor Movement*, pp. 77–87, 139–44; Montgomery, *Beyond Equality*, pp. 124–6, 234–7; *Labor Leader*, July 14, 1888. Cf. Daniel T. Rodgers, *The Work Ethic in Industrial America 1850–1920* (Chicago, 1978), pp. 156–65.

33 MBSL, *10 AR*, pp. 118, 121; *Labor Leader*, Feb. 5, 1887; BISU Hearings, pp. 564, 578–9. Many workers, it should be noted, believed that shorter hours were necessary as a response to new machinery – which permitted a fixed quantity of goods to be produced in a shorter span of time.

34 MBSL, *10 AR*, pp. 118, 121.

35 *Labor Leader*, March 12, 1887; March 17 and 24, Oct. 27, 1888; Feb. 9 and 23, July 19, 1889; BISU Hearings, pp. 433, 891; McNeill, *Labor Movement*, pp. 463, 470–1, 582–3, 596 e, f, g, m, 607; Boston *Globe*, March 12, 1894;

BISU Report, part V, app. H, pp. 127–30; Stockton, *Molders*, pp. 168–9; Robert A. Christie, *Empire in Wood: A History of the Carpenters' Union* (Ithaca, N.Y., 1956), p. 47.

36   BISU Hearings, pp. 379, 565, 801. Cf. Christie, *Empire*, p. 47, and Stockton, *Molders*, p. 169.

37   BISU Hearings, pp. 379, 565; Christie, *Empire*, p. 47; Stockton, *Molders*, p. 169; Smelser, *Unemployment*, pp. 50–1.

38   BISU Hearings, p. 800; *Labor Leader*, April 2, 1887.

39   *Labor Leader*, Jan. 25, 1890; also Feb. 5, May 7, 1887; Sept. 1, 1888; and Jan. 18, 1890.

40   George Gunton, *The Economic and Social Importance of the Eight-Hour Movement*, American Federation of Labor, Eight-Hour Series, no. 2 (Washington, 1889), pp. 11–14; Montgomery, *Beyond Equality*, pp. 249–51; see also Terence V. Powderly, *Thirty Years of Labor 1859–1889* (Philadelphia, 1890), pp. 240–70.

41   See MBSL, *10 AR*, pp. 99–137; BISU Hearings, passim.

42   BISU Hearings, pp. 433, 800; *Labor Leader*, Oct. 27, 1888; Feb. 23, 1889; MBSL, *30 AR*, p. 135. For further evidence that such sentiments were widespread by the mid-1890s, see BISU Hearings, pp. 113, 186, 319, 379, 433, 498, 564, 585, 596, 798, 800–2, 838–9, 891, 926, 1305–6.

43   *Labor Leader*, April 30, 1887; April 1, May 27, Nov. 4, 1893; March 3, Aug. 11, 1894; Jan. 12 and 19, Feb. 2, 1895.

44   McNeill, *Labor Movement*, pp. 596 e, f; Foner, *Labor Movement*, II, pp. 103, 178–83, 243; *Labor Leader*, Dec. 12 and 24, 1887; Feb. 4, March 31, June 2 and 23, Oct. 27, 1888; Feb. 1, 1890; Christie, *Empire*, pp. 48–60.

45   MBSL, *24 AR*, pp. 271ff.; *25 AR*, pp. 307ff.; *Labor Leader*, Feb. 18 and 25, April 1, July 22, Aug. 5, 1893.

46   MBSL, *26 AR*, pp. 711–14; *27 AR*, pp. 309ff.; *28 AR*, pp. 313–15ff.; *Labor Leader*, Oct. 28, 1893; March 16, Nov. 24, 1894.

47   Mass. AFL, *17 CP*, p. 25; *21 CP*, pp. 28–9; *25 CP*, p. 12; Springfield *Union*, Nov. 16, 1914; *SWJ* 22, no. 5 (May 1921): 50; *Labor News*, March 13, 1915; May 31, Nov. 15, 1918.

48   MBSL, *Bulletin 29*, p. 8; MBSL, *25 AR*, p. 308; *27 AR*, pp. 309ff.; *39 AR*, pp. 175–6; Paul H. Douglas, *Real Wages in the United States, 1890–1926* (Boston, 1930), pp. 112–16, 136, 180, 208–9; Mass. AFL, *21 CP*, pp. 28–9; *26 CP*, p. 39; Norton, *Trade-Union Policies*, pp. 199–213; *SWJ* 22, no. 6 (June 1921): 13; *Labor News*, Nov. 8, 1917; Dec. 10, 1920; Daniel Nelson, *Managers and Workers: Origins of the New Factory System in the United States, 1880–1920* (Madison, Wis., 1975), p. 126.

49   *SWJ* 16, no. 12 (Dec. 1915): 13–15, and no. 7 (July 1915): 50–1; *Labor News*, March 4, 1916; April 5, 1917; *Proceedings of the Forty-first Convention of the American Federation of Labor 1921* (Washington, 1921), p. 376.

50   *The Carpenter* 39, no. 2 (Feb. 1919): 21; *Labor News*, Dec. 10, 1910. See also *The Carpenter* 33, no. 12 (Dec. 1914): 28; vol. 36, no. 5 (May 1916): 8; vol. 42, no. 12 (Dec. 1922): 13; *Labor News*, March 13, 1915; testimony of Joseph Poitras at the "Public Hearings Upon the Subject of Unemployment Before the Special Commission on Social Insurance," 1916 (State Library,

Boston), p. 4; Smelser, *Unemployment*, pp. 50–3; *SWJ* 23, no. 2 (Feb. 1922): 7–8.

51 *Labor Leader*, Sept. 24, 1887; BISU Hearings, p. 586; Henry Lloyd, "The Unemployed and the Short Workday," *American Federationist* 4, no. 7 (Sept. 1897): 187; Smelser, *Unemployment*, p. 52; *The Carpenter* 42, no. 12 (Dec. 1922): 13; *SWJ* 23, no. 2 (Feb. 1922): 7–8. Regarding unemployment levels themselves, see Chapters 3 and 4.

52 Cf. Robert Christie's conclusion that for carpenters "the eight-hour movement was a practical and actual, as well as a philosophical, half-way station between the past and the future. The eight-hour day movement translated past hatred for the middleman into the craft unionism of the future. It may be likened to a cocoon into which utopian unionism disappeared, to emerge four years later as job-conscious unionism." *Empire*, p. 60.

53 MBSL, *37 AR*, p. 51. Quotation preceding this paragraph is from *SWJ* 16, no. 12 (Dec. 1915): 18.

54 MBSL, *10 AR*, p. 136; *Labor Leader*, May 7 and July 10, 1887; Sept. 22, 1888; BISU Hearings, pp. 66, 98, 154, 163, 492–3, 575, 928, 964–5, 772, 895, 970; McNeill, *Labor Movement*, pp. 310–11; John Higham, *Strangers in the Land* (New York, 1974; orig. pub. New Brunswick, N.J., 1955), pp. 48–9, 55, 70–3, 112, 163–4.

55 BISU Hearings, pp. 75, 83–4, 98, 104, 150, 163, 896, 928, 1017, 1306, 1480–2; *Labor Leader*, Nov. 11, 1893; April 21, 1894; *American Federationist* 1, no. 10 (Dec. 1894): 216–18; Higham, *Strangers*, pp. 70–3, 112, 163–4; A. T. Lane, "American Trade Unions, Mass Immigration, and the Literacy Test: 1900–1917," *Labor History* 25 (1984): 5–25.

56 *SWJ* 4, no. 6 (June 1903): 24, and no. 7 (July 1903): 9–10; *American Federationist* 22, no. 1 (Jan. 1915) 31–3; *The Carpenter* 33, no. 10 (Oct. 1913): 10–11; Marc Karson, *American Labor Unions and Politics 1900–1918* (Carbondale, Ill., 1958), pp. 136–7; Mass. AFL, *31 CP*, p. 11; Lane, "American Trade Unions," pp. 5–25.

57 *Labor News*, June 1, 1923; *SWJ* 25, no. 3 (March 1924): 1. See also *Labor News*, May 30, July 18, July 25, Aug. 29, 1919; Jan. 21, 1921; March 17, 1922; Jan. 19, May 4, 1923; *American Federationist* 26, no. 8 (Aug. 1919): 692. The *SWJ* in the early 1920s hammered away at the question of immigration restriction in virtually every issue.

58 Cf. the views of Eugene Debs, in 1910, as cited in Karson, *American Labor Unions*, p. 189.

59 Reply from Georgetown Boot and Shoe Company to inquiry from Massachusetts Board to Investigate the Subject of the Unemployed, BISU Hearings; see also the reply from Francis Batcheller, Dec. 12, 1894; *Labor Leader*, March 5, June 18, July 30, 1887; March 24, June 9, 1894; BISU Hearings, p. 187; and *SWJ* 6, no. 12 (Dec. 1905), 16.

60 Alice Kessler-Harris, *Out to Work: A History of Wage-Earning Women in the United States* (New York, 1982), pp. 152–9, and "Where Are the Organized Women Workers," in Nancy F. Cott and Elizabeth H. Pleck, *A Heritage of Her Own* (New York, 1979), pp. 343–66.

61 Montgomery, *Beyond Equality*, p. 147; McNeill, *Labor Movement*, pp. 135, 183, 200; MBSL, *8 AR*, p. 19; *25 AR*, p. 315; *37 AR*, pp. 9, 36–8, 51; MBSL, *Bulletin 41* pp. 201–6; Galster, *Labor Movement*, pp. 75, 102; William Haber, *Industrial Relations in the Building Trades* (Cambridge, Mass., 1930), pp. 132–7, 277; Green, *Holyoke*, pp. 219–22; Stockton, *Molders*, pp. 170–3; Jacob Loft, *The Printing Trades* (New York, 1944), p. 216; Mark Perlman, *The Machinists; A New Study in American Trade Unionism*, (Cambridge, Mass., 1961), p. 247; *Labor Leader*, April 21, 1888; Norton, *Trade-Union Policies*, p. 190; BISU Hearings, pp. 25, 209; IAS, *37 AR*, p. 9. See also a broadside from the National Loom Fixers Association of America, in Fall River, dated April 19, 1899, in the Lyman papers, Baker Library, Harvard Business School.

62 Smelser, *Unemployment*, pp. 35–7; Boot and Shoe Workers' Union, Local 357, Bridgewater, Mass., Minute books, 1903–16, vol. 2, entry dated Dec. 10, 1912, Baker Library, Harvard Business School.

63 Smelser, *Unemployment*, pp. 37–41, 82–3, 90–2, 108; BISU Hearings, p. 590; Norton, *Trade-Union Policies*, pp. 213–4. For examples of locals repeatedly warning fellow tradesmen away from their communities, see *The Carpenter* for any stretch of years between 1905 and 1912.

64 BISU Hearings, pp. 90–1, 141–2, 198, 377–8, 597, 928, 1327–8; Boston *Globe*, April 2 and 6, 1894; Mass. AFL, *18 CP*, pp. 46–7; *30 CP*, p. 120.

65 Boston *Globe*, Dec. 28, 1893; April 2 and 6, 1894; Mass. AFL, *18 CP*, pp. 46–7; *23 CP*, pp. 12–13; BISU Hearings, pp. 202, 594; Thomas Stone, of the Boston branch of the Granite Cutters' National Union to Board to Investigate the Subject of the Unemployed, Aug. 10, 1894, BISU Hearings.

66 Christie, *Empire*, pp. 106–11, 171–82; Mass. AFL, *17 CP*, pp. 37–8; *18 CP*, pp. 64ff.; Smelser, *Unemployment*, pp. 41–2. Regarding the prevalence and intensity of jurisdictional disputes, see also Haber, *Industrial Relations*, pp. 36–41, 151–7, 536n; Stockton, *Molders*, pp. 45ff.; Garth L. Mangum, *The Operating Engineers* (Cambridge, Mass., 1964), p. 52; Perlman, *Machinists*, pp. 231–4; Hollander and Barnett, *Studies*, pp. 305–12; Ulman, *Rise*, p. 315; Harold S. Roberts, *The Rubber Workers* (New York, 1944), p. 26. The attitudes expressed in turn-of-the-century jurisdictional conflicts contrast sharply with an earlier ethos (still evident in the 1870s) that skilled workmen did not take jobs or perform work in any trades other than their own. MBSL, *2 AR*, p. 134; *4 AR*, pp. 290–2.

67 MBSL, *Bulletin 35*, p. 52; *Bulletin 43*, p. 371; MBSL, *42 AR*, pp. 212, 268; Smelser, *Unemployment*, pp. 43–6, 58–68, 124–5; Montgomery, *Workers' Control*, pp. 140–3; Loft, *Printing Trades*, p. 116; Perlman, *Machinists*, p. 248; Harry Henig, *The Brotherhood of Railway Clerks* (New York, 1937), p. 273; Sumner H. Slichter, *Union Policies and Industrial Management* (Washington, 1941), pp. 103–10, 115–22.

68 See Smelser, *Unemployment*, pp. 43–4, 107; Slichter, *Union Policies*, pp. 112, 139–57.

69 Mass. AFL, *29 CP*, p. 76; *30 CP*, pp. 63, 70; *32 CP*, p. 51; *33 CP*, pp. 1–18; testimony of J. Poitras, Commission on Social Insurance, 1916, pp. 2–3.

70 Michael H. Frisch, *Town into City: Springfield, Massachusetts, and the Mean-ing of Community, 1840–1880* (Cambridge, Mass., 1972), p. 199; Green, *Holyoke*, p. 150; *Vindicator* (Lynn, Mass.), Dec. 30, 1876; Herbert G. Gut-man, "The Failure of the Movement by the Unemployed for Public Works in 1873," *Political Science Quarterly* 80, no. 2 (June 1965): 254–76; *Labor Leader*, Aug. 27, 1887; Nov. 25, 1893; BISU Hearings, pp. 357, 567, 668, 827, 1007, 1305; *American Federationist* 4, no. 3 (May 1897): 56; vol. 16, no. 1 (Jan. 1909): 58–9; vol. 28, no. 11 (Nov. 1921): 960; *Labor News*, Jan. 17, Feb. 28, 1919; July 29, Aug. 19, Dec. 6 and 20, 1921.

71 BISU Hearings, pp. 680, 777, 1476, 1515; *Labor Leader*, Nov. 25, 1893; cf. Gutman, "Failure," p. 258.

72 Mass. AFL, *35 CP*, p. 77; *Labor News*, Oct. 12, 1923; Feb. 28, 1914; July 29, 1921; *American Federationist* 23, no. 1 (Jan. 1916): 1; *The Carpenter* 43, no. 6 (June 1923): 16.

73 Mass. AFL, *30 CP*, pp. 94–5; *Labor News*, Jan. 13, 1922; *American Federa-tionist* 29, no. 1 (Jan. 1922): 13–23; *Proceedings of the Forty-second Annual Convention of the American Federation of Labor, 1922* (Washington, 1922), pp. 72–7.

74 *Labor Leader*, July 21, 1894; *The Carpenter* 41, no. 11 (Nov. 1921): 41; *Amer-ican Federationist* 28, no. 11 (Nov. 1921): 954–60, and no. 12 (Dec. 1921): 1012–15.

75 Mass. AFL *29 CP*, p. 101; *30 CP*, p. 112; *SWJ* 17, no. 7 (July 1916): 19; *American Federationist* 21, no. 4 (April 1914): 310–12; *The Carpenter* 35, no. 1 (Jan. 1915): 31; testimony of William Haskins of the Central Labor Union of Worcester, Commission on Social Insurance, Nov. 16, 1916; Smelser, *Unemployment*, p. 147.

76 *Proceedings of the A.F. of L., Forty-first Convention*, pp. 375–8; *Labor News*, Oct. 12, 1923; *SWJ* 22, no. 7 (July 1921): 4; vol. 22, no. 8 (Aug. 1921): 15–16; vol. 17, no. 3 (March 1916): 15; *American Federationist* 29, no. 1 (Jan. 1922): 13–28; Joseph J. Huthmacher, *Massachusetts People and Politics* (Cambridge, Mass., 1959), pp. 59–60; Daniel Nelson, *Unemployment In-surance: The American Experience, 1915–35* (Madison, Wis., 1969), pp. 67–8, 72–6, 79–80, 93–8, 174; Roy Lubove, *The Struggle for Social Security, 1900–1935* (Cambridge, Mass., 1968), pp. 15–24; Mass. AFL, *36 CP*, pp. 53, 62; *38 CP*. Unfortunately, an extensive search for the proceedings of the thirty-seventh annual convention (1922) of the Massachusetts state branch of the AFL has failed to turn up a copy of that perhaps pivotal document. For an example of a left-wing program for unemployment, presumably from the late Progressive era, see the undated "Manifesto on the Unemployed," from the Right to Work Committee of Greater Bos-ton, an organization affiliated with the Socialist Party. A copy of this manifesto has survived, interestingly enough, in BCC papers, file 332–53.

77 Nelson, *Insurance*, pp. 70–7, 151–61, 174–5; *The Carpenter* 43, no. 6 (June 1923): 16; Philip Taft, *The A.F. of L. in the Time of Gompers* (New York, 1957), p. 366. See also Chapter 9.

78 *Labor News,* Aug. 30, 1913; *American Federationist* 21, no. 4 (April 1914): 310–12.
79 Smelser, *Unemployment,* pp. 148–50. Another feature of this process of rationalization was the signing of contracts that would expire on relatively "neutral" dates in seasonal industries, i.e., dates that did not fall in either the busiest or slowest seasons of the year. Such contracts were designed to prevent the chaos that resulted when both workers and employers repeatedly tried to take advantage of labor market conditions to press for their own advantage. E.g., see Norton, *Trade-Union Policies,* p. 133. For valuable general discussions of the rationalization of labor markets, see Michael J. Piore, *Birds of Passage: Migrant Labor and Industrial Societies* (Cambridge, 1979), and David M. Gordon, Richard Edwards, and Michael Reich, *Segmented Work: Divided Workers: The Historical Transformation of Labor in the United States* (Cambridge, 1982).
80 Mass. AFL, *29 CP,* p. 101; Smelser, *Unemployment,* p. 35; *SWJ* 22, no. 10 (Oct. 1921): 6.
81 Foner, *Labor Movement,* II, 346; Christie, *Empire,* pp. 30, 37.
82 Cf. Green, *Holyoke,* p. 369; Isaac A. Hourwich, *Immigration and Labor* (New York, 1912), p. 347.
83 Bedford, *Socialism,* pp. 223–5; Christie, *Empire,* pp. 11–15, 62, 64–77, 152, 230, 249, 322–3; *The Carpenter* 28, no. 12 (Dec. 1908): 17–18; BISU Hearings, p. 19; Smelser, *Unemployment,* pp. 58–68.
84 See Slichter, *Union Policies,* pp. 154–6.
85 Selig Perlman, *A Theory of the Labor Movement* (New York, 1928), pp. 182–219, 237–53, 272–9. Cf. his discussion of cyclical influences on labor in *A History of Trade Unionism in the United States* (New York, 1950; orig. pub. 1922), pp. 275–7.
86 *American Federationist* 27, no. 2 (Feb. 1920): 173; vol. 28, no. 11 (Nov. 1921): 954–60; vol. 29, no. 1 (Jan. 1922): 13–25; *SWJ* 24, no. 7 (July 1923): 24; no. 11 (Nov. 1923): 5–6; no. 12 (Dec. 1923): 4; *Labor News,* Sept. 9, 1921.
87 For a more extensive discussion of this new political economy, see Chapter 9.

8. From the Common to the State House

1 See Chapter 3 and Appendix B regarding turnover rates within the unemployed population.
2 Bohan Zawadski and Paul Lazarsfeld, "The Psychological Consequences of Unemployment," *Journal of Social Psychology* 6 (1935): 245.
3 See Chapter 7.
4 See Chapter 6. Cf. E. Wight Bakke, *Citizens without Work* (New Haven, Conn., 1940), pp. 7, 82–3, and Kenneth D. Brown, *Labour and Unemployment* (Newton Abbot, England, 1971), pp. 166–7.
5 *Vindicator* (Lynn, Mass.), Dec. 30, 1876; Boston *Globe,* Feb. 16, April 6, 1894; Boston *Herald,* Jan. 30, 1915; Springfield *Union,* Feb. 5, 1915; *Labor News* (Worcester), Feb. 14, 1919; Michael Frisch, *Town into City: Spring-*

field, Massachusetts, and the Meaning of Community, 1840–1880 (Cambridge, Mass., 1972), p. 199; Constance M. Green, *Holyoke, Massachusetts: A Case History of the Industrial Revolution in America* (New Haven, Conn., 1939), p. 150.

6   Cf. Herbert G. Gutman, "The Failure of the Movement by the Unemployed for Public Works in 1873," *Political Science Quarterly* 80 (June 1965): 254–75.

7   *Capitalists Are the Cause of the Unemployed* was the title of a pamphlet published by Swift in Boston in 1894.

8   Lawrence Stone, "The Anatomy of an American Radical; Morrison Isaac Swift – A Biography" (senior thesis, Brandeis University, 1980), pp. 1–7. I am indebted to Lawrence Stone for permission to use some of the biographical material that he uncovered in the course of his research. Since Stone's paper is unpublished, and since some confusion seems to exist regarding details of Swift's life, the sources that Stone utilized will, where relevant, be indicated in brackets. Regarding the first 31 years of Swift's life, e.g., see [Williams College Alumni Report, 1946; Statistics of the Class of 1879, Williams College; Transcript of Morrison Swift, Johns Hopkins University; James T. Bacon to Alumni Office of Williams College, June 12, 1946; George Swift, *William Swift and Some of His Descendants, 1635–1888* (Millbrook, N.Y., 1900), p. 53.]

9   Stone, "Swift," pp. 7–11; [Supplement to the biographical records of the Kappa Alpha Society, Williams College, June 1882–Oct. 1890; Alumni records, Western Reserve University, 1920; Morrison Swift to the Faculty and Trustees of the Johns Hopkins University, April 8, 1891; Morrison Swift to President Griffin of the Johns Hopkins University, May 15, 1891]; Howard H. Quint, *The Forging of American Socialism* (Columbia, S.C., 1953), pp. 255–6, 271.

10   Boston *Globe*, Feb. 7 and 21, 1894. It is notable that the newspaper coverage of these (and subsequent) demonstrations contains no references to women among the protestors. Whether this reflects a bias in the coverage or reveals an interesting political fact is unclear. Following the sources, I have generally referred to the demonstrators as "men."

11   Boston *Globe*, Feb. 20 and 21, 1894.

12   Boston *Globe*, Feb. 21, 1894.

13   Ibid.

14   Ibid.

15   Boston *Globe*, Feb. 27 and 28, March 5, 21, and 26, 1894.

16   Boston *Globe*, Feb. 28, March 5, 20, and 23, 1894. The results of the board's investigation were published as the *BISU Report*.

17   Boston *Globe*, March 12 and 21, 1894; *Labor Leader* (Lynn, Mass.), Feb. 24, March 3, 1894; Leah H. Feder, *Unemployment Relief in Periods of Depression* (New York, 1936), pp. 94–5.

18   Boston *Globe*, April 18 and 20, 1894; Donald L. McMurry, *Coxey's Army: A Study of the Industrial Army Movement of 1894* (Boston, 1929), pp. 21–34, 227–9, 255.

19   Boston *Globe*, April 23, 1894.

20   Boston *Globe*, April 23, 24, 25, 26, and 27, 1894.

21   Boston *Globe*, April 30, 1894; McMurry, *Coxey's Army*, pp. 104–26, 224–59.

22   Boston *Globe*, Jan. 20, 1908; Quint, *Forging of American Socialism*, pp. 271, 282–5; Stone, "Swift," pp. 19–22.

23   MBSL, *Bulletin 57*, pp. 58–9.

24   Ibid., pp. 59–62; Boston *Globe*, Jan. 22, 1908.

25   Boston *Globe*, Jan. 20, 1908; Boston *Herald*, Jan. 20, 1908.

26   Boston *Globe*, Jan. 20, 1908; Boston *Herald*, Jan. 20, 1908; MBSL, *Bulletin 57*, pp. 57–62.

27   MBSL, *Bulletin 57*, pp. 57–62; Boston *Globe*, Jan. 20, 1908; Boston *Herald*, Jan. 20, 1908.

28   Stone, "Swift," pp. 28–9; *Labor News*, May 8, 1909.

29   Springfield *Union*, March 22, 1914; New York *Times*, March 13, 1914.

30   Boston *Globe*, March 24, 1914; Springfield *Union*, March 24, 1914.

31   Boston *Globe*, May 8, 1914; Springfield *Union*, May 8, 1914.

32   Boston *Herald*, June 12, 1946; New York *Times*, May 12, July 12, 1915; Stone, "Swift," pp. 32–9; [Newton *Graphic*, June 20, 1946].

33   New York *Times*, April 10, 1941.

34   William L. Chenery, "Mr. Zero," *The Survey*, 47 (Oct. 1, 1921): 15–16; New York *Times*, April 10, 1941; *Newsweek* 17 (April 21, 1941): 19.

35   Chenery, "Mr. Zero," pp. 15–16; *The Nation* 113 (Oct. 5, 1921): 364–5; Boston *Herald*, Sept. 10 and 14, 1921.

36   Boston *Herald*, Aug. 30, 1921; New York *Times*, Aug. 30, 1921.

37   Boston *Herald*, Sept. 5, 1921; New York *Times*, Sept. 5, 1921.

38   Boston *Herald*, Sept. 6, 1921; New York *Times*, Sept. 6, 1921.

39   Boston *Herald*, Sept. 8, 1921; Boston *Globe*, Sept. 8, 1921.

40   Boston *Globe*, Sept. 9, 1921.

41   Ibid.

42   Ibid.; Boston *Herald*, Sept. 9, 1921; New York *Times*, Sept. 9, 1921.

43   Boston *Globe*, Sept. 10, 11, and 17, 1921; Boston *Herald*, Sept. 10 and 11, 1921; New York *Times*, Sept. 10 and 11, 1921.

44   Boston *Globe*, Sept. 12, 1921; New York *Times*, Sept. 12 and 19, 1921.

45   Boston *Globe*, Sept. 9, 12, 13, and 22, 1921; Boston *Herald*, Sept. 13–15, 1921.

46   Boston *Globe*, Sept. 16, 17, and 19, 1921; Boston *Herald*, Sept. 16 and 17, 1921. Brice, the son of a former senator from Ohio, gave modest sums of money to Ledoux to subsidize his work in behalf of the unemployed.

47   Boston *Globe*, Sept. 17 and 19, 1921; Boston *Herald*, Sept. 17, 1921; New York *Times*, Sept. 19, 1921.

48   Boston *Globe*, Sept. 13, 15, 23, and 24, 1921; Boston *Herald*, Sept. 16 and 23, 1921.

49   Boston *Herald*, Sept. 14, 18–22, and 26, 1921; New York *Times*, Sept. 15, 17, 19, 21, 23–4, and 26, 1921; Boston *Globe*, Sept. 13 and 15, 1921.

50   New York *Times*, Sept. 25–7, 1921; Boston *Herald*, Sept. 27, 1921.

51   New York *Times*, Sept. 25–8, 1921; Boston *Herald*, Sept. 27, 1921; Boston

Globe, Sept. 28, 1921. See Chapter 9 regarding the President's Conference.

52 Boston *Globe,* Nov. 3, 1921; New York *Times,* Oct. 10, and 19, Nov. 3, 1921.

53 New York *Times,* Dec. 15, 18, and 28, 1921.

54 *Newsweek* 17 (April 21, 1941): 19; New York *Times,* April 10, 1941; Boston *Globe,* April 10, 1941.

55 Regarding traditional ideological sources of working-class protest, secular and religious, see Alan Dawley, *Class and Community: The Industrial Revolution in Lynn* (Cambridge, Mass., 1976); David Montgomery, *Beyond Equality: Labor and the Radical Republicans, 1862–72* (New York, 1967); Herbert Gutman, "Protestantism and the American Labor Movement," in *Work, Culture, and Society in Industrializing America* (New York, 1976), pp. 79–117; James Lazerow, "A Good Time Coming: Religion and the Emergence of Labor Activism in Ante-bellum New England" (Ph.D. diss., Brandeis University, 1982).

56 Fragments of evidence suggesting who the participants in these protests were can be found in Boston *Globe,* Feb. 21, April 18, 1894; MBSL, *Bulletin 57,* pp. 57–62; Boston *Globe,* Jan. 20, 1908; Boston *Herald,* Jan. 20, 1908; Boston *Globe,* Sept. 9–12, 1921; Boston *Herald,* Sept. 9–12, 1921.

57 See Chapter 9.

9. "The greatest evil of our competitive industrial system"

1 Massachusetts state legislature, committee on relations between employer and employee, hearings, Aug. 18 to Nov. 7, 1903, State Library (Boston), p. 116; MBSL, *46 AR,* part II, pp. 24–6.

2 *The Journal of the House of Representatives of the Commonwealth of Massachusetts, 1865–1894* (Boston, 1865–94); *The Journal of the Senate of the Commonwealth of Massachusetts, 1868–1894* (Boston, 1868–94). (These publications will hereafter be cited as *Journal of the House* and *Journal of the Senate,* with identifying years.) The problem of unemployment was rarely mentioned, during nondepression years, in the *Annual Report of the Board of State Charities* (Boston, 1865–90) or in the annual reports of the Boston Provident Association, which were examined for all years between 1852 and 1890. Comments regarding newspaper coverage are based upon a search for newspaper articles regarding unemployment in the Boston *Globe,* the Boston *Transcript,* and the Springfield *Republican:* this search began as a systematic one, but, given its futility, it devolved into spot checking.

3 AC-B, *4 AR,* p. 64; Alexander Keyssar, "Social Change in Gilded Age Massachusetts," in Jack Tager, ed., *Massachusetts in the Gilded Age* (Amherst, Mass., forthcoming); Nathan I. Huggins, *Protestants against Poverty: Boston's Charities, 1870–1900* (Westport, Conn., 1971), pp. 135–59. Regarding Carroll Wright, see Chapter 1.

4 John A. Garraty, *Unemployment in History: Economic Thought and Public Policy* (New York, 1978), pp. 73, 92, 104ff.; Frederick C. Mills, *Contempo-*

rary Theories of Unemployment and Unemployment Relief, Columbia University Studies in History, Economics and Public Law, vol. 79, no. 1 (New York, 1917), pp. 13–21, 124–7; IAS, *49 AR*, pp. 13–14; *56 AR*, p. 6; William M. Leiserson, "The Problem of Unemployment Today," *Political Science Quarterly* 31, no. 1 (March 1916): 5–7. As Leiserson points out (pp. 7–9), the most significant nineteenth-century challenge to these views came from Marx.

5   AC-B, *9 AR*, pp. 10–11; Robert Kelso, *The History of Public Poor Relief in Massachusetts, 1629–1920* (Montclair, N.J., 1969; orig. pub. Boston, 1922), pp. 91–164; Morton Keller, *Affairs of State* (Cambridge, Mass., 1977), pp. 289–342. Regarding antebellum patterns, see Paul Faler, "Cultural Aspects of the Industrial Revolution: Lynn, Massachusetts, Shoemakers and Industrial Morality, 1826–60," *Labor History* 15 (1974): 367–94.

6   See Chapter 2 regarding relief during antebellum depressions.

7   AC-B, *Report of the Ward VI Work Room for the Summer of 1875* (Boston, n.d.), p. 4; AC-B, *1 AR*, p. 42; *2 AR*, pp. 6–17, 29; *3 AR*, p. 13; *6 AR*, p. 45; *25 AR*, p. 8; *First Annual Report of the Union Relief Association of Springfield, Massachusetts* (Springfield, Mass., 1877), pp. 4–5; IAS, *40 AR*, pp. 3–4; *44 AR*, pp. 3–6, 14–17; *45 AR*, pp. 3–4; *48 AR*, pp. 18–19; Springfield *Republican*, Nov. 18, 1877; *Vindicator* (Lynn, Mass.), Feb. 15, 1879; MBSL, *8 AR*, pp. 211, 214; Leah H. Feder, *Unemployment Relief in Periods of Depression* (New York, 1936), pp. 40, 48–9, 63–8, 328, 348; Huggins, *Protestants*, pp. 139–44; Michael Frisch, *Town into City: Springfield, Massachusetts, and the Meaning of Community, 1840–1880* (Cambridge, Mass., 1972), pp. 223–41.

8   "Rules and Suggestions for Visitors of the Associated Charities," in AC-B, *Annual Report for 1879*, p. 2; AC-B, *2 AR*, p. 45; *4 AR*, p. 64; *9 AR*, pp. 10–11; MBSL, *8 AR*, p. 215; IAS, *39 AR*, p. 3; Feder, *Relief*, pp. 41, 68–9; Kelso, *Public Poor Relief*, p. 97; Huggins, *Protestants*, pp. 139–59; *First Annual Report of Union Relief Association*, pp. 4–5.

9   Boston *Globe*, Dec. 18 and 19, 1893; Feb. 1 and 2, March 20, 1894; BISU Hearings, esp. pp. 396, 501, 621, 993, 1080, 1110, 1141–2, 1366, 1369, 1411, 1443; *BISU Report*, part I entire, esp. pp. xi–lviii; *Documents of the House of Representatives of the Commonwealth of Massachusetts, 1894* (Boston, 1894), nos. 607, 608 (items in this series will hereafter be cited as *House Documents*, with identifying years); IAS, *60 AR*, pp. 6–7; *61 AR*, pp. 2–3, 6–7; Andover House Association, *Third Yearly Report* (Cambridge, Mass., 1894), pp. 6–7; AC-B, *15 AR*, pp. 26–8; Feder, *Relief*, pp. 63–8, 75–6, 92–3, 126–37, 160, 331–6, 349–51; MBSL *24 AR*, pp. 97–104. See also Chapter 6.

10 "How to Relieve Distress among the Poor this Winter," unpaged insert, dated Nov. 1893, in AC-B, *14 AR*; *15 AR*, p. 40; *20 AR*, p. 17; BISU Hearings, pp. 295–7, 396, 439, 714, 945, 962, 1051–2, 1080, 1110, 1141–3, 1367; Boston *Globe*, Dec. 19, 1893, March 12, 1894; Edith P. Estes, "Boston's Unemployed," *Harper's Weekly* 38 (March 3, 1894): 197–8; *Twenty-fourth Annual Report of the Union Relief Association of Springfield* (Springfield, Mass., 1901), p. 10; *BISU Report*, part II, pp. ix, 84.

11 BISU Hearings, pp. 296, 437–40, 621, 858, 945, 1069, 1126, 1183–4, 1412,
    1449, 1467–70; IAS, *58 AR*, p. 8; *60 AR*, p. 6; Boston *Globe*, Feb. 1, 22, and
    24, March 23, 1894; Feder, *Relief*, pp. 31n, 67–9, 75–6, 89, 170, 180, 352.
    For a contemporary indictment of relief practices, see John R. Commons,
    "A Comparison of Day Labor and Contract System on Municipal Works,"
    American Federationist 3, no. 11 (Jan. 1897): 229–33.
12 See *BISU Report*, and BISU Hearings, entire.
13 BISU Hearings, esp. pp. 480–90, 782, 842, 989, 1176, 1182–5, 1257, 1355–
    6; *BISU Report*, part III.
14 *BISU Report*, part V, pp. xxi–xxxix; cf. also Irwin Yellowitz, "The Origins
    of Unemployment Reform in the United States," *Labor History* 9 (1968):
    338–60.
15 BISU Hearings, pp. 403–6, 555, 632–3, 786–90, 946, 1294, 1375–7, 1490;
    AC-B, *15 AR*, p. 46; *BISU Report*, part II, p. 100.
16 E.g., see Boston *Globe*, Feb. 16, March 23, April 16, 1894.
17 *BISU Report*, part I, p. xxv; Feder, *Relief*, p. 347; *Acts and Resolves of the
    Commonwealth of Massachusetts, 1893–98* (Boston, 1893–8). (Items in this
    series will hereafter be cited as *Acts and Resolves*, with identifying years.)
18 MBSL, *Bulletin 46*, p. 61.
19 Richard Abrams, *Conservatism in a Progressive Era; Massachusetts Politics,
    1900–1912* (Cambridge, Mass., 1964), pp. 11–12, 29–46, 58–116, 162–8,
    182; Michael E. Hennessy, *Four Decades of Massachusetts Politics 1890–1935*
    (Norwood, Mass., 1935), pp. 60–111; *House Documents, 1903*, nos. 128,
    129, 547; *Journal of the House, 1903*, pp. 69, 733, 755, 764; *Journal of the
    Senate, 1903*, pp. 73, 153, 550; *Journal of the Senate, 1904*, p. 232; Henry F.
    Bedford, *Socialism and the Workers in Massachusetts 1886–1912* (Amherst,
    Mass., 1966), p. 220; MBSL, *Bulletin 27*, p. 141; see also the hearings of
    the committee on relations between employer and employee, 1903.
20 The number of persons who obtained positions through the Free Em-
    ployment Offices tended to peak during periods of labor scarcity (e.g.,
    1916) and to dip during depressed years (e.g., 1914, 1921). For annual
    statistics regarding the activities of the Free Employment Offices for the
    years from 1906 through 1922, see *Report of the Special Commission on Un-
    employment, Unemployment Compensation, and the Minimum Wage, Massa-
    chusetts House Document 1325* (Boston, 1923), pp. 72–5. See also MBSL,
    Bulletin 25, p. 50; *Bulletin 35*, p. 4; *Bulletin 46*, pp. 68–9; *Bulletin 49*, pp.
    330–5; MBSL, *24 AR*, pp. 81ff., 107–9, 111; *38 AR*, pp. 416–17, 420ff.; *44
    AR*, p. 75; *Report of the Commission on Immigration on the Problem of Immi-
    gration in Massachusetts, House Document 2300* (Boston, 1914) pp. 41–5;
    Massachusetts Committee on Unemployment, Bulletin 1, *Why Labor Ex-
    changes?* (Boston, 1915), p. 12.
21 Leslie G. Ainley, *Boston Mahatma* (Boston, 1949), pp. 45, 48; Joseph F.
    Dineen, *The Purple Shamrock: The Honorable James Michael Curley of Boston*
    (New York, 1949), pp. 21–2, 46–7; Abrams, *Conservatism*, p. 68; *Labor
    Leader*, Dec. 8, 1888; Donald B. Cole, *Immigrant City: Lawrence, Massachu-
    setts, 1845–1921* (Chapel Hill, N.C., 1963), p. 52; John D. Buenker, "The

Mahatma and Progressive Reform," *New England Quarterly* 44 (Sept. 1971): 397–419.

22 It is worthy of note that the economic downturn of 1907–8 led to a sharp increase in the number of Boston-area residents who sought to enlist in the army and navy; similarly, a very slight economic decline in 1910 produced a surge in registrations for Civil Service positions. Ainley, *Mahatma*, pp. 48–51; Dineen, *Shamrock*, pp. 48, 53, 57–64; Abrams, *Conservatism*, pp. 143–9; Robert A. Woods, *The City Wilderness* (Boston, 1898), p. 88; William Haber, *Industrial Relations in the Building Industry* (Cambridge, Mass., 1930), p. 117; *BISU Report*, part III, pp. 12ff.; *Boston Transcript*, Dec. 17, 1910; MBSL, *Bulletin 57*, p. 57.

23 Cole, *Immigrant City*, pp. 52, 151; Woods, *City Wilderness*, p. 135; Robert A. Woods, ed., *Americans in Process* (Boston, 1903), pp. 147ff.; BISU Hearings, pp. 1017, 1068, 1157–8; Ainley, *Mahatma*, pp. 48–51; Dineen, *Shamrock*, pp. 46–57, 64; Abrams, *Conservatism*, p. 68.

24 MBSL, *46 AR*, part II, p. 26; "Public Hearings upon the Subject of Unemployment before the Special Commission on Social Insurance," Sept. 1916, State Library (Boston), p. 3; Letter from Boston Chamber of Commerce to Boston-area manufacturers, dated Nov. 25, 1914, in BCC papers, file 332-53, Baker Library, Harvard Business School.

25 *Report of the Special Commission on Social Insurance, House Document 1850* (Boston, 1917), p. 110. For similar statements regarding the gravity of unemployment, see *Final Report of the Commission on Industrial Relations*, Frank P. Walsh, chairman (Washington, 1915), pp. 167–8; MBSL, *46 AR*, part II, pp. 26–8; *The Survey* 33 (Feb. 6, 1915): 516–17. For a sampling of periodical articles published during this period, see Julia E. Johnsen, ed., *Unemployment* (New York, 1915) and Arthur O. Taylor, ed., *Persistent Public Problems* (Boston, 1916).

26 See Chapters 3 and 6.

27 Wesley C. Mitchell, *Business Cycles* (Berkeley, Calif., 1913); Mills, *Contemporary Theories*, pp. 42–117, 138–62; William H. Beveridge, *Unemployment: A Problem of Industry* (London, 1930), pp. 68–110, 192–218, 235–7. John Garraty's *Unemployment in History* (see esp. pp. 129–45) offers a valuable overview of the place of unemployment in both European and American economic thought. See also Leiserson, "Problem of Unemployment," pp. 1–16. Leiserson, although not a Marxist, viewed Marx as the economic thinker who had "really established the modern scientific theory of employment, the details of which have been worked out by Beveridge, the Webbs, and other scholars."

28 Robert H. Bremner, *From the Depths: The Discovery of Poverty in the United States* (New York, 1956), p. 88; Leiserson, "Problem of Unemployment," pp. 1–24. For a general account of social progressivism, see Arthur S. Link and Richard McCormick, *Progressivism* (Arlington Heights, Ill., 1983), pp. 67–104.

29 William C. Ewing to James A. McKibben, May 19, 1915, BCC papers, file 332-53; *ALLR* 5 (June and Nov., 1915), entire; Don D. Lescohier, *The Labor Market* (New York, 1919), p. 170. For detailed accounts of the role of

reformers, nationally, in the campaign for unemployment reform, see Yellowitz, "Origins"; Roy Lubove, "Economic Security and Social Conflict in America: The Early Twentieth Century," *Journal of Social History* 1 (1967): 61–87, 325–50; Daniel Nelson, *Unemployment Insurance: The American Experience 1915–1935* (Madison, Wis., 1969).

30 *The Survey* 33 (Feb. 6, 1915): 516–17; Commission on Social Insurance, Hearings, Sept. 1916, p. 2; "The Unemployment Crisis of 1914–15," *ALLR* 5 (Nov. 1915): 476–94; Bremner, *From the Depths*, pp. 125, 134; Paul H. Douglas and Aaron Director, *The Problem of Unemployment* (New York, 1931), p. xi; Maurice Parmelee, *Poverty and Social Progress* (New York, 1920), p. 92; Charles B. Spahr, *America's Working People* (New York, 1900), p. 25.

31 Commission on Social Insurance, Hearings, Sept. 1916, p. 2; Woods, *Americans in Process*, pp. 147ff.; Frances Kellor, *Out of Work* (New York, 1915), pp. 30–1; *The Survey* 45 (Dec. 18, 1920): 430; Springfield *Union*, Jan. 10, 1915; MBSL, *11 AR*, pp. 170–1; *Report of the Commission on Social Insurance*, pp. 11, 107, 108, 113, 294; "Unemployment Crisis of 1914–15," pp. 491–2; Woods, *City Wilderness*, p. 135; James Leiby, *Carroll Wright and Labor Reform* (Cambridge, Mass., 1960), p. 200.

32 Robert G. Valentine, "What the Awakened Employer is Thinking about Unemployment," *ALLR* 5 (June 1915): 423; unpaged "Comments from Prominent Men" on the Program of the AALL's National Conference on Unemployment, New York, Feb. 27–9, 1914, a copy of which is in the BCC papers. For other comments of this type, see Bedford, *Socialism*, p. 218; *Final Report of the Commission on Industrial Relations*, p. 254; Leiserson, "Problem of Unemployment," p. 3; Paul Ringenbach, *Tramps and Reformers 1873–1916: The Discovery of Unemployment in New York* (Westport, Conn., 1973), pp. 165ff.; Kellor, *Out of Work*, p. 392; and *SWJ* 16, no. 11 (Nov. 1915): 4.

33 John B. Andrews, *A Practical Program for the Prevention of Unemployment in America* (New York, 1914). The text of the "program," slightly revised, was also printed in *ALLR* 5 (June 1915): 171–94. See also Leiserson, "Problem of Unemployment," pp. 18–20; Roy Lubove, *The Struggle for Social Security, 1900–1935* (Cambridge, Mass., 1968), pp. 147–9.

34 Henry S. Dennison, "Irregular Employment of the Masses," *Journal of the American Society of Mechanical Engineers* 37 (May 1915): 280–1; "Methods of Reducing the Labor Turnover," *Proceedings of the Conference of Employment Managers' Association of Boston, Mass.: May 10, 1916*, United States Bureau of Labor Statistics, Bulletin 202 (Washington, 1916), pp. 56–9; "Plan in Use by an American Industry for Combatting Unemployment," by the Personnel Division, Dennison Manufacturing Company, *ALLR* 11 (March 1921): 53–8; Hearings, Special Commission on Unemployment, Unemployment Compensation, and the Minimum Wage, Nov. 29, 1922, State Library (Boston), p. 2; Nelson, *Insurance*, pp. 41, 50–3.

35 Magnus Alexander, "Hiring and Firing: Its Economic Waste and How to Avoid it," *Annals of the American Academy of Political and Social Science* 65 (May 1916): 128–44; Henry Eilbert, "The Development of Personnel

Management in the United States," *Business History Review* 33 (1959): 345–64; David Montgomery, *Workers' Control in America* (Cambridge, 1979), pp. 32–3, 41, 119; Lescohier, *Labor Market*, pp. 111–17, 124–9, 167; Nelson, *Insurance*, pp. 40–2; Daniel Nelson, *Managers and Workers: Origins of the New Factory System in the United States, 1880–1920* (Madison, Wis., 1975), pp. 85–6, 150–1; Douglas and Director, *Unemployment*, pp. 91, 110–12; Sumner H. Slichter, *The Turnover of Factory Labor* (New York, 1921), pp. vii, 3, 17–26, 32, 43, 85–6, 107–41.

36 Meyer Bloomfield, "Steady Work: The First Step in Sound Industrial Relations," *ALLR* 11 (March 1921): 38–40; Eilbert, "Personnel," pp. 352–60; Ordway Tead to August P. Loring, Aug. 12, 1916, with enclosure ("The Personnel Department") and C. P. Marshall to Mr. Holmes, Feb. 2, 1922, both in Plymouth Cordage Company papers, file H-3, Baker Library, Harvard Business School; Nelson, *Managers and Workers*, pp. 79–82, 143–8; cf. Morris L. Cooke, "Unemployment Within Employment," *American Federationist* 26, no. 11 (Nov. 1919): 1034–6.

37 BCC papers, files 332-13 and 332-53. See especially the following: "Report of the Committee on Industrial Relations Regarding Seasonal Employment," May 1, 1914; Cover letter from the chairman of the Committee on Industrial Relations, accompanying the "Questions on Seasonal Employment," Sept. 28, 1914; "file copy: seasonal employment, newspaper story, Dec. 17, 1914"; John B. Andrews to John W. Plaisted, April 11, 1914; "Report to the Committee on Industrial Relations of the BCC on Seasonal Irregularity in Industry in Boston, Massachusetts," Nov. 1914, unsigned but written by Juliet Poyntz; "Questions on Seasonal Employment," forms returned from Commonwealth Shoe and Leather Company, Priscilla Publishing Company, Breslin and Campbell, Gray and Davis, Appley Rubber Company, H. L. Frost and Company, E. T. Wright and Company (see Chapter 3, note 21).

38 BCC papers, file 311-77. See esp. "Memo for the Executive Committee by the Executive Committee," June 8, 1915; "Report of the Special Committee on Irregular Employment," May 1, 1916; "Report of the Committee on Irregular Employment," Nov. 1, 1915; printed report from the Special Committee on Irregular Employment, dated 1916–17, pp. 29–30; letter from office of BCC president to Magnus Alexander, June 19, 1917.

39 "Report to the Committee on Industrial Relations," Nov. 1914, BCC papers, file 332-53; Montgomery, *Workers' Control*, pp. 32–3; Nelson, *Insurance*, pp. 28–30; Nelson, *Managers and Workers*, pp. 35–42, 143–8, 79–82, 84; Committee on Elimination of Waste in Industry of the Federated Amerian Engineering Societies, *Waste in Industry* (New York, 1921), pp. 13–20.

40 "File copy: seasonal employment, news story," BCC papers, file 332-53; G. McCaffrey to Ordway Tead, Jan. 19, 1916, BCC papers, file 311-77; Nelson, *Insurance*, pp. 28–30, 42; Whiting Williams, "The Job and Utopia," *ALLR* 11 (March 1921): 19–20; Valentine, "Awakened Employer," p. 423. Regarding Swift's demonstration, see Chapter 8; regarding organized labor, see Chapter 7.

41   Abrams, *Conservatism,* pp. 189, 222–3, 226, 231–4, 245, 249, 257, 267, 273–85, 250; Hennessey, *Four Decades,* pp. 22–7, 143, 160–2, 202–5, 218, 244.

42   Joseph J. Huthmacher, *Massachusetts People and Politics 1919–1933* (Cambridge, Mass., 1959), pp. 45–7, 59, 60–5, 72–3; Dorothy G. Wayman, *David I. Walsh: Citizen-Patriot* (Milwaukee, 1952), pp. 26–48, 51, 59, 67, 83–4, 128–9; David I. Walsh, "Labor in Politics," *The Forum* 62 (Aug. 1919): 215–18; Hennessey, *Four Decades,* pp. 307–8; Abrams, *Conservatism,* pp. 259–60.

43   Springfield *Union,* Dec. 2 and 12, 1914, Jan. 30, 1915; *Thirty-fifth Annual Report of the Union Relief Association of Springfield* (April 1915), p. 19; AC-B, *36 AR,* pp. 14–5, 20–1.

44   Springfield *Union,* Nov. 28, Dec. 2 and 14, 1914; Jan. 15, Feb. 11, 1915; AC-B, *36 AR,* p. 23; *Report of the Bureau of Employment and Relief of the Worcester Chamber of Commerce, November, 1914–April, 1915* (Worcester, 1915); "Recommendations from the Committee on Relief of the Massachusetts Committee on Unemployment" (Feb. 26, 1915), Daniel J. McDonald to BCC (Feb. 17, 1915), Memorandum from Executive Committee to Board of Directors (Jan. 16, 1915), and James M. Curley to Elmer J. Bliss (Jan. 11, 1915), all in BCC papers, file 332-53; Dineen, *Shamrock,* pp. 109–11.

45   New York *Times,* Jan. 8 and 31, 1915; Springfield *Union,* Feb. 28, 1914; *Labor News* (Worcester), Oct. 31, 1914; MBSL, *46 AR,* part VII, pp. 10–11, 92–5; *The Survey* 34 (June 19, 1915): 265; AC-B, *36 AR,* p. 15; *Journal of the House, 1915,* pp. 112, 468, 177, 157, 565, 1067; *Journal of the Senate, 1915,* pp. 4–5; *Acts and Resolves, 1915,* pp. 4, 5, 6, 87–8, 240, 393–4, 401, 440.

46   William C. Ewing to James A. McKibben, May 19, 1915, BCC papers, file 332-53; *Report of Bureau of Employment and Relief, Worcester Chamber of Commerce,* p. 10; Hennessey, *Four Decades,* pp. 224–8; *Report of the Commission on Social Insurance,* p. 107; "Unemployment Insurance," *ALLR* 5 (Nov. 1915): 591.

47   Yellowitz, "Origins," p. 344; Andrews, "Practical Program," pp. 182–92; MBSL, *46 AR,* part II, pp. 29–30; see also note 40.

48   Andrews, "Practical Program," pp. 182–92; Committee on Unemployment, *Why Labor Exchanges?;* Commission on Social Insurance, Hearings, Sept. 1916, pp. 1–13, 25; Federated Engineering Societies, *Waste in Industry,* pp. 277–8ff.; Lescohier, *Labor Market,* pp. 111–16, 130, 145, 231; Leiserson, "Problem of Unemployment," pp. 17–18; Magnus Alexander to G. H. McCaffrey, June 21, 1916, BCC papers, file 311-77; speech of Walter L. Sears to the New England Association of Commercial Engineers, April 11, 1914, BCC papers, file 332-53; Springfield *Union,* Jan. 10, 1915; AC-B, *36 AR,* p. 21; regarding organized labor's program, see Chapter 7.

49   Commission on Social Insurance, Hearings, Sept. 1916, pp. 1–13, 25.

50   Andrews, "Practical Program," pp. 171–92; Douglas and Director, *Unemployment,* pp. 368–71ff.; Nelson, *Insurance,* pp. 6–11; MBSL, *Bulletin 46,* pp. 83–7; *Report of the Commission on Social Insurance,* pp. 306–11; Gar-

raty, *Unemployment in History*, pp. 131–9, 147–9; Leiserson, "Problem of Unemployment," pp. 20–2; Lubove, *Struggle*, pp. 144–74.

51 Massachusetts Committee on Unemployment, Bulletin 2, *Unemployment Insurance for Massachusetts* (Boston, 1916); *Report of the Commission on Social Insurance*, p. 107; Joseph L. Cohen, *Insurance against Unemployment* (London, 1921), pp. 477–92; Bloomfield, "Steady Work," pp. 38–40; *Report of the Bureau of Employment of Worcester Chamber of Commerce*, p. 10; AC-B, *36 AR*, p. 21; *37 AR*, p. 14; MBSL, *Bulletin 46*, pp. 83ff.; "Report of the Committee regarding Unemployment Insurance," BCC papers, file 332-48; A. E. Lunt to Commission on Social Welfare, Massachusetts legislature, March 9, 1916, BCC papers, file 332-48c; *Documents of the Senate of the Commonwealth of Massachusetts, 1916* (Boston, 1916), no. 1 (items in this series will hereafter be cited as *Senate Documents*, with identifying year); Nelson, *Insurance*, pp. 17–19.

52 *House Documents, 1916*, no. 825; Douglas and Director, *Unemployment*, p. 480; Nelson, *Insurance*, pp. 17–19; Bryce M. Stewart, *Unemployment Benefits in the United States* (New York, 1930), p. 97.

53 *House Documents, 1916*, no. 825; Committee on Unemployment, *Unemployment Insurance*, pp. 3–26.

54 *Report of the Commission on Social Insurance*, p. 7; MBSL, *47 AR*, part IV, p. 37; Correspondence of the Special Commission on Social Insurance, 1916–17, microfilm box no. 1, State Library Annex (Boston).

55 *Report of the Commission on Social Insurance*, pp. 16, 107, 108, 113, 125; MBSL, *47 AR*, part IV, p. 37; Commission on Social Insurance, Hearings, Sept. and Oct. 1916; A. E. Lunt to Committee on Social Welfare, March 9, 1916, and A. E. Lunt to James A. McKibben, March 14, 1916, BCC papers, file 332-48c. Two members of the special commission indicated that they favored the immediate establishment of an unemployment insurance system.

56 Commission on Social Insurance, Hearings, Sept. 1916; Nelson, *Insurance*, p. 18.

57 New York *Times*, April 25, 1919; Jan. 7 and 30, Aug. 20, Oct. 7 and 11, 1921; Boston *Herald*, April 25, 1919; Jan. 19, 1920; March 13, Oct. 7, 11, 27, and 29, 1921; *Labor News*, Dec. 6 and 20, 1918; Feb. 7, March 14, June 10, Oct. 14, 1919; Sept. 2, 1921; Boston *Transcript*, Oct. 6, 1921; *Senate Documents, 1922*, no. 1; "How Gardner Met the Unemployment Problem," *American City* 25 (Dec. 1921): 501–3; "Governors' Messages," *ALLR* 11 (March 1921): 108; "Distributing the Load," *The Family* 1 (Jan. 1921): 4–9; Philip Klein, *The Burden of Unemployment: A Study of Unemployment Relief Measures in Fifteen American Cities* (New York, 1923), pp. 55, 61, 70, 76, 84, 105, 120, 137–8, 158, 223–5, 237; Memorandum to Director, from Mr. McKibben, Oct. 14, 1921, BCC papers, file 332-53.

58 Huthmacher, *Massachusetts People and Politics*, pp. 45–73; "Unemployment Survey – 1920–21," *ALLR* 11 (Sept. 1921): 191–220; Mass. AFL, *36 CP*, pp. 30–5, 42, 46, 53, 63. Most trade unions in the early 1920s were preoccupied with protecting the gains they had achieved between 1908

and 1918, gains that were being strenuously attacked by business. See also Chapter 7.

59 Huthmacher, *Massachusetts People and Politics,* pp. 45–7, 58–75; Hennessey, *Four Decades,* pp. 281, 294, 307–8; *Labor News,* Oct. 14, 1921.

60 John B. Andrews, "Report of Work, 1919," *ALLR* 10 (March 1920): 76–7; John B. Andrews, "Report of Work, 1920," *ALLR* 11 (March 1921): 115; Federated Engineering Societies, *Waste in Industry,* pp. 277–8; "Unemployment Survey – 1920–21," pp. 205–6; Don D. Lescohier, "The Unemployment Program of the International Labor Conference and its Application to the United States," *ALLR* 10 (March 1920): 51–68; Lescohier, *Labor Market,* p. 231; *House Documents, 1920,* no. 854; Lubove, *Struggle,* pp. 156–7.

61 *House Documents, 1922,* no. 278; Henry L. Shattuck, "Unemployment Insurance Legislation in Massachusetts," *ALLR* 12 (March 1922): 45–9. Shattuck's bill was technically the third insurance bill to be introduced into the legislature. In 1920, Wendell Phillips Thore (who had been a member of the Commission on Social Insurance) introduced an old-age insurance bill (*House Documents, 1920,* no. 466) that contained a provision calling for unemployment insurance; this bill was, however, ignored by the legislature. For additional background regarding Shattuck's bill and similar efforts in Wisconsin, see Nelson, *Insurance,* pp. 109–19.

62 Boston *Transcript,* Feb. 2, 1922; Hearings, Special Commission on Unemployment, Unemployment Compensation, and the Minimum Wage, Nov. 9, Dec. 14 and 19, 1922, State Library (Boston); *The Carpenter* 42, no. 5 (May 1922): 23; Nelson, *Insurance,* p. 175.

63 *Report of the Special Commission on Unemployment, Unemployment Compensation, and the Minimum Wage,* pp. 39–46; Hearings, Special Commission on Unemployment, Unemployment Compensation, and the Minimum Wage, Dec. 19, 1922.

64 *Report of the Special Commission on Unemployment, Unemployment Compensation, and the Minimum Wage,* pp. 22–37, 45.

65 Ibid., pp. 22–37; Henry S. Dennison, "Management," *Recent Economic Changes: Report of the Committee on Recent Economic Changes of the President's Conference on Unemployment,* 2 vols. (New York, 1929), II, 508, 517, 518, 522, 524, 531, 544–6; Eilbert, "Personnel," pp. 350–3, 358–64; MBSL, *46 AR,* part II, p. 30; Federated Engineering Societies, *Waste in Industry,* pp. 67, 149, 157–8; Nelson, *Insurance,* pp. 32–4, 47, 56–8, 60ff.; Thomas L. Norton, *Trade-Union Policies in the Massachusetts Shoe Industry, 1919–1929,* (New York, 1932), p. 85; Herman Feldman, *The Regularization of Employment* (New York, 1925), pp. 31, 61, 64–5, 80–3, 238, 375.

66 Feldman, *Regularization,* pp. 62–5. Feldman's study, sponsored by the American Management Association, argues throughout that little had been done to regularize employment by 1925. See also Federated Engineering Societies, *Waste in Industry,* pp. 24–6, 60, 67, 96, 133, 149, 157–62; Norton, *Trade-Union Policies,* pp. 84–6, 338; "Unemployment Survey – 1920–21," p. 211. Regarding the perceived difficulty of regularizing, see

the questionnaire from Hirsh and Ginzburg, dated Sept. 28, 1914, in "Questions on Seasonal Employment," BCC papers, file 332-53.

67   "Unemployment Survey – 1920–21," pp. 191, 210–11.

68   C. P. Marshall to Mr. Holmes, Feb. 2 and 4, 1922, Plymouth Cordage papers, file H-3; Feldman, *Regularization*, pp. 253–4; Eilbert, "Personnel," p. 353. An interesting variant of this pattern emerged in the shoe industry in the early 1920s after a formal work-sharing system had been established through a union contract. The contract specified that jobs had to be shared or rotated among all workers who had been employed by a firm for at least five weeks. A number of firms responded by repeatedly laying off workers just before they reached the 5-week mark. Norton, *Trade-Union Policies*, p. 289. Regarding the deliberate employment of women for seasonal jobs, see also the questionnaire from H. O. Foss and Co. in "Questions on Seasonal Employment," BCC papers, file 332-53.

69   See Chapter 7 regarding seniority systems. See also Montgomery, *Workers' Control*, p. 160. C. P. Marshall of Plymouth Cordage noted in his memo of Feb. 4 (cited in note 68) that "another way to meet this question of the security of the job would be to give some form of recognition for length of service." Seniority rules, of course, could be – and were – installed even in the absence of unions.

70   *Labor News*, Sept. 30, 1921; New York *Times*, Sept. 26, 1921; *American Federationist* 29, no. 1 (Jan. 1922): 21.

71   *American Federationist* 29, no. 1 (Jan. 1922): 13–25; Boston *Herald*, Sept. 11, 1921. Among the publications to emerge from the conference were *Business Cycles and Unemployment: Report and Recommendations of a Committee of the President's Conference on Unemployment* (Washington, 1923) and *Seasonal Operation in the Construction Industries: The Facts and Remedies*, foreword by Herbert Hoover (New York, 1924).

72   New York *Times*, Jan. 28, 1922; *American Federationist* 28, no. 11 (Nov. 1921): 954–60; vol. 28, no. 12 (Dec. 1921): 1012–17; vol. 29, no. 1 (Jan. 1922): 17–18. See also *Proceedings of the Forty-second Annual Convention of the American Federation of Labor, 1922* (Washington, 1922), pp. 72–7.

73   The only workers who could not be laid off at a moment's notice were those protected by union contracts that regulated layoffs. Even these men and women, of course, were subject to sudden job loss under certain conditions, such as a plant closing.

74   Montgomery, *Workers' Control*, pp. 160–1; Norton, *Trade-Union Policies*, pp. 90–1, 181–2; W. J. Donald and Edith K. Donald, "Trends in Personnel Administration," *Harvard Business Review* 7 (Jan. 1929): 143–55. For an account of the declining interest in unemployment insurance in Massachusetts and the persistence of reform efforts in several other states, notably Wisconsin, see Nelson, *Insurance*, pp. 36–46, 79–118.

75   Huthmacher, *Massachusetts People and Politics*, pp. 126–30, 146, 157–61, 191, 209; Norton, *Trade-Union Policies*, pp. 64–71, 90–1, 95, 178, 185–6; Thomas R. Navin, *The Whitin Machine Works since 1831* (Cambridge, Mass., 1950), pp. 336–9; George S. Gibb, *The Saco-Lowell Shops: Textile*

Machinery Building in New England 1813–1949 (Cambridge, Mass., 1950), p. 446; *SWJ* 24, no. 12 (Dec. 1923): 9–10; Seymour Wolfbein, *The Decline of a Cotton Textile City* (New York, 1944), pp. 30–5, 104–11; Charles H. Trout, *Boston, the Great Depression, and the New Deal* (New York, 1977), pp. 3, 4, 9, 18. No reliable unemployment statistics for the state are available for the years between 1923 and 1930.

76 Donald H. Davenport and John J. Croston, "Unemployment and Prospects for Reemployment in Massachusetts," Graduate School of Business Administration, Harvard University, Business Research Studies 22, no. 6 (Aug. 1936), pp. 1–28; *Fifteenth Census of the United States: Unemployment,* I (Washington, 1931), pp. 453–96; Massachusetts Department of Labor and Industries, "Report on the Census of Unemployment in Massachusetts as of January 2, 1934," typescript, Boston Public Library; Stanley Lebergott, *Manpower in Economic Growth* (New York, 1964), p. 512; Wolfbein, *Decline*, p. 39; Trout, *Boston*, pp. 81, 173–7; Lester V. Chandler, *America's Greatest Depression, 1929–41* (New York, 1970), p. 5.

77 Huthmacher, *Massachusetts People and Politics*, pp. 192, 196, 210–11, 219–24; Trout, *Boston*, pp. 32–3, 40, 45–9, 51, 54, 71–2, 75–6, 85, 88, 93, 100, 178; Chandler, *Depression*, pp. 47–50; Harriet Ropes, "Summary of the Effects Since 1929 of Unemployment in 119 Families Known to Members of the Greater Boston Federation of Neighborhood Houses," Jan. 1932, North Bennet Street Industrial School Papers, Schlesinger Library, Radcliffe College, Cambridge, Mass.

78 Davenport and Croston, "Unemployment," p. 12; Mass. Dept. of Labor and Industries, "Report on the Census of Unemployment," especially pp. 18, 21, 106; Chandler, *Depression*, p. 42; Boston *Globe*, Feb. 10, 1931; Wolfbein, *Decline*, pp. 43–8; Trout, *Boston*, pp. 175, 177–81, 258, 263; *Fifteenth Census: Unemployment*, I, 457.

79 Huthmacher, *Massachusetts People and Politics*, pp. 222–5; Trout, *Boston*, pp. 59–60, 68, 88, 100; Chandler, *Depression*, pp. 47–50.

80 Trout, *Boston*, pp. 54–6, 83, 213–14, 297, 307; Huthmacher, *Massachusetts People and Politics*, p. 192.

81 Trout, *Boston*, pp. 57–9, 92, 100, 208, 282; Huthmacher, *Massachusetts People and Politics*, pp. 222–5, 247, 255–60, 267; Chandler, *Depression*, pp. 48–50.

82 Trout, *Boston*, pp. 149, 173–4, 179, 181–3, 210, 223–4; Chandler, *Depression*, pp. 189–207; see Chapter 7. For a summary of the programs launched by the New Deal, see William E. Leuchtenberg, *Franklin D. Roosevelt and the New Deal* (New York, 1963).

83 Nelson, *Insurance*, pp. 155–6, 175–9, 190; Trout, *Boston*, pp. 59–60, 77; Hennessey, *Four Decades*, p. 459; *Report of the Interstate Commission on Unemployment Insurance, Appointed by the Governors of Connecticut, Massachusetts, New Jersey, New York, Ohio, Pennsylvania, and Rhode Island* (n.p., 1932).

84 Nelson, *Insurance*, pp. 127–37, 145, 151–8, 190–3, 211–21; Leuchtenberg, *FDR*, pp. 130–7; Edwin E. Witte, *The Development of the Social Security Act* (Madison, Wis., 1962), pp. 3–21, 49–52, 201–2.

85 Trout, *Boston*, pp. 199, 216–17; Navin, *Whitin Machine Works*, pp. 540–1; Gibb, *Saco-Lowell Shops*, p. 720; Sumner H. Slichter, *Union Policies and Industrial Management* (Washington, 1941), pp. 98–163; Walter Galenson, *The CIO Challenge to the AFL* (Cambridge, Mass., 1960), pp. 122, 183, 191, 274, 276; Montgomery, *Workers' Control*, pp. 139–52, 161–4.

86 Lebergott, *Manpower*, pp. 188–9, 512; Robert W. Eisenmenger, *The Dynamics of Growth in New England's Economy, 1870–1964* (Middletown, Conn., 1967), pp. 68–9; Richard Du Boff, "Unemployment in the United States: A Historical Summary," *Monthly Review* 29 (Nov. 1977): 10–25; Joseph Zeisel, "A Profile of Unemployment," in Stanley Lebergott, ed., *Men without Work* (Englewood Cliffs, N.J., 1964), p. 120; U.S. Department of Commerce, *Historical Statistics of the United States: Colonial Times to 1970* (Washington, 1975), part I, p. 136. From the vantage point of the mid-1980s, it could well be argued that, over the long run, unemployment levels have increased since the New Deal.

87 Robert Stein, "Work History, Attitudes and Incomes of the Unemployed," in Lebergott, ed., *Men without Work*, pp. 133–7. For journalistic accounts of the hardships of the unemployed, see Boston *Globe*, June 7, 1980; Nov. 9, 1981; Dec. 29, Aug. 19, 1982; July 12, 1983; New York *Times*, July 9, 1980; Dec. 5, 1981; Jan. 20, 1982; April 2, 1983.

88 Cf. Michael J. Piore, *Birds of Passage: Migrant Labor and Industrial Societies* (Cambridge, 1980; orig. pub. 1979), pp. 15–49, 146–7; David M. Gordon, Richard Edwards, and Michael Reich, *Segmented Work, Divided Workers: The Historical Transformation of Labor in the United States* (Cambridge, 1982), pp. 193–8. Unemployment levels still vary considerably by industry, of course, and within some industries the employees of large (often unionized) firms, with dominant positions in the market, tend to work more steadily than do the employees of smaller, less advantaged (and often nonunionized) companies.

89 As David Montgomery and Ronald Schatz point out in an important essay, the inequalities that could and did result from the installation of seniority systems were recognized by unionists in the 1930s – who debated the merits of seniority provisions and experimented with other methods of regulating layoffs. Montgomery, *Workers' Control*, pp. 139–51. See also Slichter, *Union Policies and Industrial Management*, pp. 98–163; Trout, *Boston*, p. 263; Philip M. Hauser, "Differential Unemployment and Characteristics of the Unemployed in the United States: 1940–54," in National Bureau of Economic Research, *Measurement and Behavior of Unemployment* (Princeton, N.J., 1957), pp. 246–53, 274–6; Zeisel, "Profile," pp. 115–19. Between 1971 and 1974, the national unemployment rate for teenagers (aged 16–19) was roughly 3 times as great as it was for men and women over the age of 20. During these same years, the unemployment rate for whites was only half the rate recorded for "blacks and other races." A decade later, during the economic downturn of the early 1980s, the pattern was similar. In July 1982, the unemployment rate was 8.8% for all adult males, while it was 24.1% for teenagers and 18.5% for blacks. USBLS, *Employment and Unemployment in 1974, Special Labor Force Report*

no. 178 (Washington, 1975), p. 6; Boston *Globe,* Aug. 6, 1982. For more comprehensive data regarding the distribution of unemployment from the late 1940s through the late 1970s, see USBLS, Bulletin 2070, *Handbook of Labor Statistics* (Washington, Dec. 1980), pp. 61–79.

10. Epilogue: the Bay State and the nation

1 Valuable studies of antebellum industrialization have been proliferating in recent years, and some of these studies even focus on communities outside Massachusetts. See, among others, Bruce Laurie, *Working People of Philadelphia: 1800–1850* (Philadelphia, 1980); Anthony Wallace, *Rockdale: The Growth of an American Village in the Early Industrial Revolution* (New York, 1978); Susan E. Hirsch, *Roots of the American Working Class: The Industrialization of Crafts in Newark 1800–1860* (Philadelphia, 1978); Sean Wilentz, *Chants Democratic: New York City and the Rise of the American Working Class, 1788–1850* (New York, 1984). A richly detailed source for understanding the rhythms of work in the agricultural South in the late nineteenth and early twentieth centuries is Theodore Rosengarten's *All God's Dangers: The Life of Nate Shaw* (New York, 1974).

2 Herbert G. Gutman, "The Failure of the Movement by the Unemployed for Public Works in 1873," *Political Science Quarterly* 80 (June 1965): 254–76; Alexander Keyssar, "Men Out of Work" (Ph.D. diss., Harvard University, 1977), pp. 397–8. Statistics indicating unemployment levels in "manufacturing and mechanical industries" for all states and for the U.S. in 1900 are presented in Appendix A, Table A.13. Similar figures for 1890 were also developed, although they are not presented here in tabular form; such figures can be derived from data in the *Eleventh Census of the United States, Population,* part II (Washington, 1897), pp. 303, 453. Regarding the 1880 census, see Appendix B.

3 Several caveats must accompany the statistics presented in Tables 10.1, 10.2, and A.13. First: the differences between the 1890 and 1900 figures, which are quite pronounced for some states, may reflect changes in the enumeration procedures rather than changes in actual unemployment levels. (See Appendix B.) Moreover, as discussed in Appendix B, the Census Bureau itself concluded that the 1900 statistics were more accurate than those collected in 1890. Conclusions based on contrasts between the 1890 and 1900 figures must, therefore, be regarded as tentative at best. Second: the Census Bureau in 1900 warned that the accuracy of the enumeration may have varied from region to region. Expressing surprise that the 1900 census registered slightly less unemployment in the Northeast than in many other areas, officials of the bureau also suggested that there may have been a relative undercount of the unemployed in the North Atlantic states. If so, unemployment levels in Massachusetts in 1900 may actually have been slightly higher than the national average. This alleged undercount does not, of course, affect the argument (put forward in this chapter) that unemployment rates in most other states were of the same order of magnitude as those recorded in

Massachusetts and discussed in Chapters 3, 4, and 5 of this study. (*Twelfth Census of the United States, Occupations* (Washington, 1904), p. ccxxxvi.) Finally, it should be stressed that, without further investigation, it is difficult to interpret the unemployment figures for predominantly rural states and, in many areas, for women. As is often the case with quantitative evidence, Tables 10.1 and 10.2 raise as many questions as they answer. Were farmers in states like Alabama and Kansas reporting themselves to be unemployed? Did the relatively high unemployment frequencies reported for women in Kansas, Nebraska, South Dakota, and Iowa in 1900 reflect faulty census procedures, or did women play a different role in the economies of those states than they did in Massachusetts? Table A.13 is of some help in answering such questions, since it reveals the extent of unemployment among workers in manufacturing in each state. (See also *Eleventh U.S. Census, Population*, part II, pp. 303, 453.) Nonetheless, trustworthy interpretations of the figures for the less industrial states must await further, and much more detailed, scrutiny of the census data, as well as other sources. See also David Montgomery, *Beyond Equality: Labor and the Radical Republicans, 1862–72* (New York, 1972; orig. pub. New York, 1967), pp. 448–52; Keyssar, "Men Out of Work," pp. 397–8.

4 Keyssar, "Men Out of Work," pp. 399–400, 460–1, 536; *Eleventh U.S. Census, Population*, part II, pp. cxxxviii, 568–9; *Twelfth U.S. Census, Occupations*, pp. ccxxviii ff., 300–7.

5 "The Unemployment Crisis of 1914–15," *ALLR* 5, (Nov. 1915): 482; John R. Commons et al., *History of Labor in the United States*, 4 vols. (New York, 1918–35), III, p. 130; MBSL, *46 AR*, part II, pp. 34–5; Frances Kellor, *Out of Work* (New York, 1915), pp. 20–3; Hornell Hart, *Fluctuations in Unemployment in Cities of the United States, 1902–1917* (Cincinnati, 1918), pp. 47–59; Scott Nearing, "The Extent of Unemployment in the United States," *Journal of the American Statistical Association*, no. 87 (Sept. 1909): 525–42; Alice W. Solenberger, *One Thousand Homeless Men* (New York, 1911); Carleton Parker, *The Casual Laborer and Other Essays* (New York, 1920). The national unemployment data from the 1910 census have been tabulated but remain unpublished. On April 15, 1910, the national unemployment rate for workers in manufacturing and mechanical industries was 5.8%; in Massachusetts, at almost exactly the same time, the figure for trade union members was 5.3%. For the census year of 1909, the national unemployment rate for workers in manufacturing was 5.4%; among Massachusetts unionists, the rate was 5.6%. See Appendix B regarding these figures and the 1910 census data in general.

6 William M. Leiserson, "The Problem of Unemployment Today," *Political Science Quarterly* 31, no. 1 (March 1916): 15; "Unemployment Survey – 1920–21," *ALLR* 11 (Sept. 1921): 191–217.

7 "Unemployment Crisis of 1914–15," p. 482; "Unemployment Survey – 1920–21," pp. 191–217; Marion Elderton, ed., *Case Studies of Unemployment* (Philadelphia, 1931), entire; Philip Klein, *The Burden of Unemployment: A Study of Unemployment Relief Measures in Fifteen American Cities*

(New York, 1923), esp. pp. 22–37; Stephan Thernstrom, *The Other Bostonians: Poverty and Progress in the American Metropolis, 1880–1970* (Cambridge, Mass., 1976; orig. pub. 1973), pp. 220–32; Morton Keller, *Affairs of State* (Cambridge, Mass., 1977), pp. 490–1; Paul T. Ringenbach, *Tramps and Reformers 1873–1916: The Discovery of Unemployment in New York* (Westport, Conn., 1973); Walter A. Wyckoff, *A Day with a Tramp* (New York, 1901), and *The Workers: An Experiment in Reality: The West* (New York, 1898). Regarding the labor movement nationally, see David Montgomery, *Workers' Control in America* (Cambridge, 1979), pp. 139–52; and Sumner H. Slichter, *Union Policies and Industrial Management* (Washington, 1941), pp. 98–163. See also the periodicals from national trade unions, as well as the studies of individual national unions, cited in Chapter 7.

8   Leah H. Feder, *Unemployment Relief in Periods of Depression* (New York, 1936), pp. 37–353; "Unemployment Crisis of 1914–15," pp. 475–94; "Unemployment Survey – 1920–21," pp. 191–220; *American Federationist* 22, no. 2 (Feb. 1915): 125; MBSL, *46 AR*, part II, pp. 31–2, and part IX, p. 34; Ringenbach, *Tramps and Reformers*, p. 139; Don D. Lescohier, *The Labor Market* (New York, 1919), p. 169; Leiserson, "Problem of Unemployment," pp. 2–4, 9–11, 17–24; Commons, *History of Labor*, III, pp. 130–2; "Report of the Mayor's Committee on Unemployment, New York City," USBLS, *Monthly Review of the Bureau of Labor Statistics* (May 1916): 16–26; Daniel Nelson, *Unemployment Insurance: The American Experience, 1915–1935* (Madison, Wis., 1969), pp. 13–15, 72, 107–118.

9   Regarding the fluidity, variety, and unpredictability of unemployment levels in different locales and industries, see Chapters 3 and 5. As indicated in note 3, any definitive assessment of the typicality of the Massachusetts experience must await – at the very least – more detailed scrutiny of the existing quantitative evidence for other states.

10   One other comparative question inescapably arises: were unemployment levels in the United States higher or lower than they were in Europe? The question is of obvious significance, but the task of comparing American and European unemployment rates is hindered – indeed, crippled – by the fact that the statistics collected in different nations were based upon different samples of workers and widely varying operative definitions of unemployment. (In some countries, for example, unemployment statistics were and are based exclusively on the experiences of the insured unemployed.) It is nonetheless worthy of note that most analyses of the available international data, conducted during the Progressive era and the 1920s, have suggested that there was more unemployment in the United States than in the majority of western European nations. The Massachusetts Bureau of Labor Statistics frequently published figures indicating that idleness levels were higher in Massachusetts and New York than they were in England. Paul Douglas and Aaron Director, after examining all the existing evidence, concluded that the United States almost certainly had more unemployment than did Denmark, Belgium, Sweden, Germany, the United Kingdom, Canada, and

Australia. Similarly, a study conducted by the National Industrial Conference Board in the early 1920s judged that the incidence of unemployment "is probably higher in the United States than it is in the European
industrial countries." The accuracy of these conclusions is uncertain, but
they suggest, at the very least, that the comparatively late adoption of
unemployment insurance in the United States cannot be attributed to the
existence of relatively low idleness levels on this side of the Atlantic.
MBSL, *41 AR*, p. 227; *42 AR*, p. 94; *44 AR*, p. 353; *46 AR*, part II, p. 33,
and part IX, p. 34; Paul H. Douglas and Aaron Director, *The Problem of
Unemployment* (New York, 1931), pp. 35–55; National Industrial Conference Board, *Unemployment Insurance in Theory and Practice*, Research Report 51 (New York, 1922), pp. 69, 71; British Board of Trade, *The Cost of
Living in American Towns*, Command Paper 5609 (London, 1911), p. 498.
See also Walter Galenson and Arnold Zeller, "International Comparison
of Unemployment Rates," in National Bureau of Economic Research, *The
Measurement and Behavior of Unemployment* (Princeton, N.J., 1957), pp.
439–582.

Appendix B. About the numbers: unemployment statistics before the Great Depression

1 See William H. Beveridge, *Unemployment: A Problem of Industry* (London,
   1930), p. 27; National Bureau of Economic Research, *The Measurement and
   Behavior of Unemployment* (Princeton, N.J., 1957), part I; John E. Bregger,
   "Unemployment Statistics and What They Mean," *Monthly Labor Review*
   94 (Nov. 1971): 22–9.
2 Louis J. Ducoff and Margaret J. Hagood, *Labor Force Definition and Measurement* (New York, 1947), pp. 9ff.; Clarence D. Long, *The Labor Force
   under Changing Income and Employment* (Princeton, N.J., 1958), pp. 388ff.;
   National Bureau of Economic Research, *Measurement and Behavior*, pp. 18,
   63, 326 ff.; Bregger, "Unemployment Statistics," pp. 22–9; USBLS, *How
   the Government Measures Unemployment*, Report 505 (Washington, 1977);
   USBLS, *Workers, Jobs, and Statistics*, Report 698 (Washington, Sept. 1983);
   USBLS, *Concepts and Methods Used in Labor Force Statistics Derived from the
   Current Population Survey*, Report 463 (Washington, Oct. 1976); USBLS,
   BLS Handbook of Methods, I (Washington, 1976), chap. 1.
3 Unemployment statistics collected after 1940, through the Current Population Survey, are not necessarily more meaningful than their predecessors (indeed, the reverse may be true), but they are more precise – both
   because measurement techniques have improved and because there is
   less uncertainty about what is being measured. The CPS figures also
   have the advantage of being directly and easily comparable with one
   another over a lengthy span of time. The monthly survey is, in fact,
   designed largely to permit the government to monitor short-term fluctuations in unemployment levels, a goal that, in certain respects, inhibits
   measurement of other dimensions of the problem. See Bregger, "Unemployment Statistics," pp. 25–9.

4 MBSL, *Bulletin 46* p. 61; *Twelfth Census of the United States, Occupations* (Washington, 1904), pp. ccxxv–ccxxvii.

5 The 1890 census manuscripts were destroyed by fire, while those from the 1885 and 1895 state censuses were apparently discarded. The manuscripts from the 1910 census were opened to the public after research for this study had been completed.

6 Useful discussions of the differences between the "gainful worker" and "labor force" concepts are presented in Ducoff and Hagood, *Labor Force;* Long, *Labor Force;* Gertrude Bancroft, *The American Labor Force: Its Growth and Changing Composition* (New York, 1958). See also Stanley Lebergott, *Manpower in Economic Growth* (New York, 1964), p. 398; Bregger, "Unemployment Statistics," pp. 25–9; USBLS, *Concepts and Methods,* pp. 3–5. Whether one judges the "gainful worker" or the "labor force" statistics to be more "accurate" would, of course, depend upon the details of one's preferred definition of unemployment. See note 3.

7 If lack of candor did influence the statistics, it seems more likely that it led to underreporting, rather than overreporting, of unemployment. If joblessness levels were, in fact, higher than reported, the central quantitative arguments of this study would, of course, be strengthened.

8 *Twelfth U.S. Census, Occupations,* pp. ccxxv, ccxxxiii; cf. Lebergott, *Manpower,* pp. 403–5. See Tables A.1 and A.4.

9 Memorandum from Alba M. Edwards to Mr. Hunt, Oct. 31, 1917, entitled "The Thirteenth Census Returns on Unemployment and Their Accuracy," available from the U.S. Department of Commerce, Bureau of the Census; MBSL, *18 AR,* p. 264.

10 MBSL, *18 AR,* p. 261.

11 Ibid., pp. 227–51, 288–90.

12 Ibid., pp. 4, 216–19. Regarding the small number of young children who were counted as unemployed, see Chapter 4.

13 *Mass. Census, 1895,* VII (Boston, 1900), pp. 2, 90–1. The 1895 census did, however, distinguish between persons who were employed at their "regular" occupations and persons who were employed at "other" occupations. Each month, roughly 3% of all employed men and women were working at "other" occupations.

14 Ibid., pp. 2–3, 104–5. Regarding the estimate that the upward bias was in the vicinity of 2 percentage points, see Alexander Keyssar, "Men Out of Work" (Ph.D. diss., Harvard University 1977), p. 416. In comparison with the 1885 (and perhaps 1890) figures, this upward bias was partially offset by the 1895 survey's avoidance of the miscounting (described above) that resulted from the effort to measure unemployment at a person's principal occupation in addition to unemployment per se.

15 *Mass. Census, 1895,* VII, pp. 90–1, 102–3.

16 *Eleventh Census of the United States, Population,* part II (Washington, 1897), p. cxxxvi; *Twelfth U.S. Census, Occupations,* pp. cclii, 427.

17 *Eleventh U.S. Census, Population,* part II, p. cxxxvi; *Twelfth U.S. Census, Occupations,* pp. 91, ccxxv–ccxxvii, cclii; Ernest S. Bradford, "Industrial Unemployment," USBLS, *Bulletin 310* (Washington, 1922), pp. 6–7.

18 *Twelfth U.S. Census, Occupations,* pp. lxv–lxxi, ccxxv–viii, ccxxxii–ccxxxiii.

19 Cf. Paul H. Douglas, *Real Wages in the United States, 1890–1926* (Boston, 1930), pp. 409–11; and August C. Bolino, "The Duration of Unemployment: Some Tentative Historical Comparisons," *Quarterly Review of Economics and Business* 6 (1966): 37, 46. Several analysts have claimed that the 1900 census survey did not count as unemployed many persons who were jobless for less than one month. If so, then the census figures understate the overall incidence of unemployment while overstating the actual mean duration (but not the mean duration for those who were counted). Royal Meeker, "The Dependability and Meaning of Unemployment and Employment Statistics in the United States," *Harvard Business Review* 8 (1930): 386; Frank D. Sargent, "Statistics of Unemployment," USBLS, *Bulletin 109* (Washington, 1912), p. 11.

20 Memo from Edwards to Hunt, Oct. 31, 1917; U.S. Bureau of the Census, "Instructions to Enumerators at the Thirteenth Census," p. 38, available from the U.S. Department of Commerce, Bureau of the Census, Washington. These materials, along with the tables themselves and the memo referred to in the following note, were kindly provided to me by the Bureau of the Census, thanks in part to the energetic efforts of Paula Schneider. My efforts to obtain copies of the 1910 data were also aided by Stanley Lebergott and Clarence D. Long.

21 Memo from Edwards to Hunt, Oct. 31, 1917; J. C. Capt to Clarence D. Long, Sept. 17, 1948, available from U.S. Department of Commerce, Bureau of the Census. See also Lebergott, *Manpower,* pp. 384–7, 405–6.

22 MBSL, *47 AR,* part VI, p. 31. Trade union unemployment statistics were first collected in New York. The publications containing the detailed quarterly reports are listed in Table A.5 source note.

23 MBSL, *42 AR,* pp. 95, 116; *46 AR,* part II, pp. 8–9, 16, and part IX, p. 38; *49 AR,* part IV, pp. 14, 28, 48–9; MBSL, *Bulletin 87,* p. 362.

24 MBSL, *46 AR,* part II, p. 33; MBSL, *Bulletin 87,* p. 349; Walter Galenson and Arnold Zeller, "International Comparison of Unemployment Rates," National Bureau of Economic Research, *Measurement and Behavior,* pp. 450–1; Hearings before the Special Commission on Unemployment, Unemployment Compensation and the Minimum Wage, Dec. 6, 1922, State Library (Boston).

25 MBSL, *49 AR,* part IV, p. 30.

26 Ibid. For additional details, see Keyssar, "Men Out of Work," pp. 429–30.

27 Efforts to determine the percentage of all occupation members who belonged to the reporting samples were hindered by a lack of congruence between the census and trade union occupational labels. For additional details, see Keyssar, "Men Out of Work," pp. 436–8.

28 Once again, the lack of congruence between the occupational labels utilized in the census and those used in the trade union series hindered the comparisons. A study of 3 leading industries in Massachusetts in 1921 also concluded that unionized and nonunionized employees who worked in the same industry encountered very similar unemployment

rates. Bradford, "Industrial Unemployment," p. 11. For further details regarding the comparisons to the 1910 census data, see Keyssar, "Men Out of Work," pp. 439–40.

29 MBSL, *49 AR*, part IV, pp. 26–7. The sample that structurally resembled the Massachusetts labor force consisted of members of more than 70 occupations listed both in the 1910 unemployment tables and in the 1910 census report on occupations in Massachusetts. Occupations that were prominent nationally but not in Massachusetts (e.g., coal miners and agricultural laborers) were excluded from the sample. An aggregate unemployment frequency was developed for this sample using a weighted average, based upon the national unemployment frequencies in these occupations and the number of workers belonging to the occupations in Massachusetts. The latter figures were drawn from the *Thirteenth Census of the United States, Population,* IV (Washington, 1914), pp. 470–4.

30 Some early-twentieth-century analysts maintained that trade union unemployment rates exaggerated the incidence of joblessness among blue-collar workers because the samples on which they were based included a disproportionately large number of workers from the building trades and other highly irregular occupations. Others made precisely the opposite claim – that union figures understated the quantity of unemployment because unionists tended to be more skilled and, therefore, less often unemployed than unorganized workers. See Douglas, *Real Wages,* p. 407; British Board of Trade, *The Cost of Living in American Towns,* Command paper 5609 (London, 1911), p. 497; Bradford, "Industrial Unemployment," pp. 10–11; as well as Galenson and Zeller, "International Comparison," pp. 448–50. The sources used to compare the composition of the trade union sample with the composition of the blue-collar labor force were those listed in Table A.5 source note; *Thirteenth U.S. Census,* IV, 470–4; and *Mass. Census, 1915* (Boston, 1918), pp. 409–505. The trade union data were also examined to determine whether changes in the occupational composition of the statewide sample had a discernible impact upon reported unemployment rates. This did not appear to be the case. See also Keyssar, "Men Out of Work," pp. 441–4, 542.

31 MBSL, *Quarterly Report 28,* pp. 1–2; MBSL, *49 AR,* part IV, pp. 26–7; Hearings, Special Commission on Unemployment, Unemployment Compensation, and the Minimum Wage, Dec. 6, 1922. To obtain an unemployment rate for the 1909 census year, the national unemployment frequency (taken from the unpublished tables) was converted into a rate, using the formula discussed in the last section of Appendix B and the durational data provided in the tables.

Index